Eels at the Edge
Science, Status, and Conservation Concerns

Funding for the symposium and these proceedings was provided by:

 **MINISTRY OF NATURAL RESOURCES**
MINISTÈRE DES RICHESSES NATURELLES

Eels at the Edge
Science, Status, and Conservation Concerns

Edited by

John M. Casselman
Queen's University, Department of Biology
2406 Biosciences Complex, 116 Barrie Street
Kingston, Ontario K7L 3N6 Canada

and

David K. Cairns
Department of Fisheries and Oceans
P. O. Box 1236
Charlottetown, Prince Edward Island C1A 7M8 Canada

American Fisheries Society Symposium 58

Proceedings of the
International Eel Symposium

Held in Québec City, Québec, Canada
11–13 August 2003

American Fisheries Society
Bethesda, Maryland
2009

A suggested citation format for this book follows

Entire Book

Casselman, J. M., and D. K. Cairns, editors. 2009. Eels at the edge: science, status, and conservation concerns. American Fisheries Society, Symposium 58, Bethesda, Maryland.

Chapter within the Book

Miller, M. J., J. Aoyama, and K. Tsukamoto. 2009. New perspectives on the early life history of tropical anguillid eels: implications for resource management. Pages 71–84 *in* J. M. Casselman and D. K. Cairns, editors. Eels at the edge: science, status, and conservation concerns. American Fisheries Society, Symposium 58, Bethesda, Maryland.

Cover art © Peter Buerschaper 2009

© Copyright 2009 by the American Fisheries Society

All rights reserved. Photocopying for internal or personal use, or for the internal or personal use of specific clients, is permitted by AFS provided that the appropriate fee is paid directly to Copyright Clearance Center (CCC), 222 Rosewood Drive, Danvers, Massachusetts 01923, USA; phone 978-750-8400. Request authorization to make multiple copies for classroom use from CCC. These permissions do not extend to electronic distribution or long-term storage of articles or to copying for resale, promotion, advertising, general distribution, or creation of new collective works. For such uses, permission or license must be obtained from AFS.

Printed in the United States of America on acid-free paper.

Library of Congress Control Number 2008940158
ISBN 978-1-888569-96-4
ISSN 0892-2284

American Fisheries Society Web site: *www.fisheries.org*

American Fisheries Society
5410 Grosvenor Lane, Suite 110
Bethesda, Maryland 20814
USA

The Editors

John Casselman was born in eastern Ontario, Canada, and grew up along the shores of the St. Lawrence River, acting as a summer fishing guide. He received a BSA from Ontario Agricultural College, University of Toronto; completed his MSc from the University of Guelph while studying northern pike in the upper St. Lawrence River; and a PhD from the University of Toronto, working with Drs. Fry, Crossman, Harvey, and Scott on environmental physiology, studying calcified structures of fish. He immediately commenced his career in the Research Branch of the Ontario Ministry of Natural Resources, stationed at Maple and working across Ontario and internationally, specializing in fish age, growth, production, ecology, and population and community dynamics, publishing his first paper on eels in the 1980 North American Eel Conference. In 1987, John transferred to the Glenora Fisheries Station as Senior Scientist, supervising research on Lake Ontario for the Ontario government. He has been cross-appointed as an adjunct professor and assisted at numerous universities, advising and sitting on graduate-student committees and supervising students at Guelph, Trent, and Queen's universities. He has been actively involved in many aspects of the American Fisheries Society, including president of the Canadian Aquatic Resources Section. Having seen the abundance of eels in the St. Lawrence River in the 1950s and 1960s, he became alarmed about the decline of the species in the late 1990s.

David Cairns was born and raised on Prince Edward Island, Canada, where he completed his BSc (UPEI). He then studied the ecology of seabirds in eastern and Arctic Canada at Laval (MSc), Carleton (PhD), and Memorial University of Newfoundland (post-doctoral). In 1987 he joined the Department of Fisheries and Oceans in Moncton, New Brunswick, to do population assessments of herring. After a two-year teaching assignment at the Université de Moncton, he made the philopatric migration back to Prince Edward Island, where he continues his work as a DFO Research Scientist, dealing primarily with American eels. The long-term theme of David's work in eels is to generate the capability to produce robust species-wide population assessments. David has Adjunct or Research Associate appointments at the University of New Brunswick, Acadia University, and the University of Prince Edward Island. In 2003, David Cairns and John Casselman were the founding co-chairs of the Canadian Eel Science Working Group.

Table of Contents

Preface..xi
Symposium Participants Group Photograph..xv
Symposium Program...xvii
Reviewer Acknowledgments...xxiii
Symbols and Abbreviations...xxv

Part I: Overviews

A Conceptual Management Framework for the Restoration of the
    Declining European Eel Stock...3
    Willem Dekker

Present Status of the Japanese Eel: Resources and Recent Research..................21
    Katsumi Tsukamoto, Jun Aoyama, and Michael J. Miller

Forty Years On—the Impact of Commercial Fishing on Stocks of
    New Zealand Freshwater Eels..37
    Don J. Jellyman

Part II: Science, Ecology, and Life History

Genetic Differentiation of the Japanese Eel..59
    Mei-Chen Tseng, Wann-Nian Tzeng, and Sin-Che Lee

New Perspectives on the Early Life History of Tropical Anguillid Eels:
    Implications for Resource Management..71
    Michael J. Miller, Jun Aoyama, and Katsumi Tsukamoto

Reproductive Strategy of Female American Eels Among Five Subpopulations
    in the St. Lawrence River Watershed...85
    Valérie Tremblay

Morphological Discrimination of the Silvering Stages of the European Eel..........103
    Caroline Durif, Aymeric Guibert, and Pierre Elie

Age, Growth, Mortality, and Sex Ratio of American Eels in Maryland's
    Chesapeake Bay..113
    Julie A. Weeder and Stephen D. Hammond

American Eel Movements, Growth, and Sex Ratio Following Translocation........129
    Guy Verreault, Willy Dargere, and Rémi Tardif

Growth and Habitat Residence History of Migrating Silver American Eels
Transplanted to Taiwan 137
    Wann-Nian Tzeng, Yu-San Han, and Brian M. Jessop

Does Stocking of Danish Lowland Streams with Elvers Increase
European Eel Populations? 149
    Michael I. Pedersen

Differential Production and Condition Indices of Premigrant Eels in Two
Small Atlantic Coastal Catchments of France 157
    Anthony Acou, Gaelle Gabriel, Pascal Laffaille,
    and Eric Feunteun

The Metazoan Parasites of Eels in Ireland: Zoogeographical, Ecological
and Fishery Management Perspectives 175
    T. Kieran McCarthy, Karen Creed, Oisin Naughton,
    Paula Cullen, and Lorraine Copley

Part III: Status and Dynamics

Long-Term Trends in Size and Abundance of Juvenile American Eels
Ascending the Upper St. Lawrence River 191
    Lucian A. Marcogliese and John M. Casselman

Decline of the American Eel in the St. Lawrence River: Effects of
Local Hydroclimatic Conditions on CPUE Indices 207
    Yves de Lafontaine, Michel Lagacé, Fernand Gingras,
    Denis Labonté, François Marchand, and Edith Lacroix

The American Eel Fishery in Delaware: Recent Landings Trends and
Characteristics of the Exploited Eel Population 229
    John H. Clark

Long-Term Changes in Recruitment, Population Dynamics, and Status of
the European Eel in Two English River Systems 241
    Anthony Bark, Beth Williams, and Brian Knights

Abundance Trends of Glass Eels between 1978 and 1999 from Fisheries
Data in the Gironde Basin, France 257
    Laurent Beaulaton and Gérard Castelnaud

Part IV: Movement, Migration, and Barriers

Three-Dimensional Movement of Silver-Phase American Eels in the Forebay
of a Small Hydroelectric Facility 277
    Leah Brown, Alex Haro, and Theodore Castro-Santos

Determining Exit Locations for Eel Ladders at Hydroelectric Power Dams
on the St. Lawrence River..293
    Kevin J. McGrath, Richard Verdon, Denis Desrochers,
    Carole Fleury, Scott Ault, and John Skalski

Seasonal Movements of Large Yellow American Eels Downstream of
a Hydroelectric Dam, Shenandoah River, West Virginia................................309
    Stephen D. Hammond and Stuart A. Welsh

Part V: Stock Assessment and Management

Eel Population Modeling and its Application to Conservation Management......327
    Giulio A. De Leo, Paco Melià, Marino Gatto,
    and Alain J. Crivelli

Are American Eel Harvests in Maryland's Chesapeake Bay Sustainable?..........347
    Julie A. Weeder and James H. Uphoff, Jr.

Management of American Eels in Lake Ontario and the Upper
St. Lawrence River...359
    Alastair Mathers and Thomas J. Stewart

Management of European Eel Populations in England and in Wales:
a Critical Review and Pragmatic Considerations..367
    Brian Knights, Anthony Bark, and Beth Williams

Managing Human Impact on Downstream Migrating European Eel
in the River Meuse...381
    Maarten C. M. Bruijs, R. H. Hadderingh, U. Schwevers,
    B. Adam, U. Dumont, and H. V. Winter

Management, Research, and Stock Assessment of Anguillids in
New Zealand..391
    Peter R. Todd

Part VI: Panel: Status, Assessment, and Conservation Concerns

International Eel Symposium Panel Presentations and Discussions.................407

Part VII: Closing

Traditional Haudenosaunee Closing and Blessing..429
    Henry Lickers

Part VIII: Posters—Titles, Authors, and Abstracts

Posters of the International Eel Symposium...435

Part IX: Québec Declaration of Concern
(Reprinted from American Fisheries Society *Fisheries* Magazine)

Québec Declaration of Concern 447
    Dekker, W., J. M. Casselman, D. K. Cairns, K. Tsukamoto,
    D. Jellyman, and H. Lickers. 2003. Worldwide decline of
    eel resources necessitates immediate action. Quebec
    Declaration of Concern. Fisheries 28(12):28–30.

Index 451

Preface

In the public and scientific imagination, eels of the worldwide genus *Anguilla* are no ordinary fish. They are shrouded in mystery and easily stir passion and fascination. Eels are neither sleek and spectacular like swordfish, nor do they count monarchs and millionaires among their fans as do salmon. The eel's cachet flows from diversity and ability, not beauty. This polyvalent animal has found ways to reach, survive, and often flourish in nearly every type of aquatic habitat on the planet. For example, the two Atlantic *Anguilla* species occupy (or occupied) a historic range stretching from the American Great Plains to the Russian Steppes, from Arctic Norway to tropical South America, and most of the oceanic, coastal, and inland waters in between. Eels are often prominent, and indeed can be dominant, in many of the habitats they occupy (Helfman et al. 1987). As generalists, anguillid eels are jacks of all trades, but no other fish are masters of so many. And most importantly, they are universal integrators and valuable indicators.

We now have ample historic evidence that large populations and broad ranges do not preclude population collapse or even species extinction (e.g., American bison, passenger pigeon, Atlantic cod). To turn around the negative trends found in many eel populations will require broad acceptance and public policy guided by sound science. Anguillid eels, collectively and internationally, are at an edge. We hope hindsight shows that this book and the ongoing, integrated conservation efforts of the contributors and symposium participants are playing a part in placing anguillid eels at the edge of recovery rather than at the edge of oblivion. *Eels at the Edge*! Only time will tell.

The International Eel Symposium at the American Fisheries Society 2003 Annual Meeting in Quebec City was motivated not only by the usual desire to share and disseminate science but also by growing apprehension about the state of *Anguilla* stocks (stocks meaning management units). Evidence presented at the meeting crystallized into the consensus that *Anguilla* species around the world are at substantial risk or even in crisis.

Some might wonder why, after two other excellent recent eel symposia (Aida et al. 2003; Dixon 2003), there was a need for "another eel symposium." The dramatic and unprecedented declines in recruitment and abundance in some locales had become an increasing concern, and very importantly, valuable fisheries were disappearing. As mentioned at the beginning of the symposium, there was a sense of frustration bordering on urgency that, after years of workshops, conferences, and symposia, no major concerted action had been taken to reverse these declines. And, quite importantly, in spite of the concern and the status of eel resources, scientifically defendable conservation advice was wanting. Biological data were generally poorly understood and even limited or lacking. Not the least of these was that spawning remained undescribed and spawning grounds were virtually unknown. Standard fish population models were inadequate because of the unique life cycle and complex mix of generation times. Up-to-date insights on resource status and new approaches to stock assessment and management were needed.

Our call for presentations and participation was received so enthusiastically that it was somewhat overwhelming. We were fortunate to assemble so much worldwide expertise on catadromous eels and hoped that the outcome would move the issue of declining eel resources to a new level of universal and joint action. It seemed appropriate to convene the symposium at this AFS annual meeting, because the overall conference theme was "Worldwide Decline of Native Fish Populations" and because Quebec City, on the St. Lawrence River, had special historical and current eel significance. This was a place of well-documented change in eel abundance, for in 1633, Samuel de Champlain had reported that the Montagnais and Algonkian assembled at the "narrows," Quebec, to "catch the phenomenal quantities of eels that were smoked and stocked up for the winter," and now this once truly enormous stock of American eels was in dramatic and precipitous decline (Casselman 2003).

In many ways, the present symposium paralleled and updated an earlier eel conference held in Toronto, Ontario, and published in 1982 (Loftus 1982). This earlier conference was also convened because of "a significant concern over the recent substantial increase in harvest of American eels from Lake Ontario" and "declining abundance of the European eel." For the latter, opinions differed strongly, but conditions and perceptions have now changed. The key to change is in increasing awareness, fostered by new insights and knowledge.

These proceedings are set against the backdrop of the urgent international conservation situation, and many papers deal with it specifically. Contributions to the symposium came from North America, Europe, and the Asia-Pacific region and consider several anguillid species, especially the well-known ones found in fresh water (European eel, *A. anguilla*; American eel, *A. rostrata*; Japanese eel, *A. japonica*. The peer-reviewed papers published here flowed from 37 oral and 17 poster symposium presentations. It is impossible for us to single out individual contributions; however, the lively and to-the-point panel discussion is particularly noteworthy. It focused on the issues and demonstrated just how passionate people can be about eels, the issues around them, and the desire that these be resolved and declining trends reversed. Indeed, many saw the issue as urgent, and some felt that little time was left to reverse the disturbing trends.

The group outing at the end of the symposium to visit an eel weir in the St. Lawrence River was particularly important. This get-together gave an opportunity for symposium participants to have informal discussions, which resulted in one of the major contributions of the symposium—the creation of a declaration of concern. The symposium and panel discussion had emphasized that a concerted effort was urgently needed to conserve the species and their resources and called for international conservation action that was broadly based, vigorous, and immediate. It was decided that this declaration would be drafted, circulated among the symposium participants for their supporting signatures, and then immediately submitted for high-profile publication. This resulted in the "Quebec Declaration of Concern" (Dekker et al. 2003), published in AFS *Fisheries* magazine. In retrospect, we believe that this declaration was a major contribution, because it stimulated a new level of worldwide concern for the science, status, and conservation of all species of anguillid eels. Indeed, many of the more recent accomplishments in addressing conservation concerns can be traced to this communiqué (reprinted at the end of these proceedings).

The "Quebec Declaration of Concern" was a pivotal contribution of the symposium, which was unanimously endorsed by symposium participants. The declaration emphasized the unprecedented decline in recruitment and abundance of major eel resources, indicating that some were collapsing. It urged concerted action, unilateral if necessary, and included a supporting annotated bibliography. The declaration triggered a series of articles, many in the popular press, that initiated a broad call to action. Species declines are now better documented, with some seeing them as extreme. The future for recovery may appear bleak; however, we are generally optimistic, because now there is broad acceptance of declining abundance and virtually unanimous support and effort to do something about it. Only time will tell whether the responses are appropriate enough and quick enough to make the necessary difference.

The symposium, most specifically the panel discussion and, to some extent, the informal discussions at the eel-trap outing, resulted in recommendations that 1) the problem be communicated more widely; 2) the science be transferred at all levels; 3) there be cooperative and joint action by scientists, managers, and agencies (federal, provincial, and state), power and water utilities and commissions, and First Nations; 4) innovative approaches be used to reduce human-induced mortality, increase spawner escapement and thereby enhance recruitment; 5) assessment programs be maintained and possibly expanded and more thorough commercial catch statistics be acquired; 6) depleted and extirpated stocks and habitats be restored and inaccessible and vacant habitats be opened up and stocked if for no less an important reason than to keep the species and its resource value in our consciousness and to encourage restoration; 7) we review science needs and initiate needed research, but not to the detriment of immediate action to protect the species and the resource; 8) where appropriate, the species be listed as one at risk and the status re-evaluated regularly. All this emphasizes a need to respond to conserve the species and its resource value with immediate action, preferably coordinated, but unilateral if necessary.

We gratefully acknowledge funding provided for the symposium and its publication. The bulk of the funds to support publication came through a Coordination Activities Program (CAP) grant from the Great Lakes Fishery Commission (GLFC). We especially thank executive chair Chris Goddard, his staff, and the GLFC for this and their ongoing encouragement and assistance with all aspects of the symposium. Additional funds for publication were provided by the Aquatic Research Section of the Ontario Ministry of Natural Resources (OMNR) through the assistance of the section manager, Cheryl Lewis. Funds for commissioning the cover illustration were generously provided by the Lake Ontario Management Unit, OMNR, with the assistance of the lake manager, Rob MacGregor. Funds to support travel and accommodations for some symposium participants from abroad were very generously provided by the Electric Power Research Institute (EPRI) with the assistance of senior project manager Doug Dixon. Similar support was also provided by the Ontario Commercial Fisheries' Association (OCFA) with the assistance of the late Rob Graham, executive director.

We are very pleased that Peter Buerschaper accepted the challenge of illustrating the cover of the proceedings. His depiction of a silver eel leaving toward the edge on the front cover and leptocephali returning on the back cover symbolically captures our theme. Peter was ably assisted by his son, Mark Buerschaper, who laid out the graphics. Peter has long experience as an illustrator, probably best known for his many published fish illustrations, in particular the distinctive multi-coloured and green cover of the original edition of *Freshwater Fishes of Canada*.

The group photograph of symposium participants was taken quite spontaneously at the end of the panel discussion and includes those assembled at the time. We specially thank Michael Miller, University of Tokyo, Japan, for having a camera ready for the occasion and Suzanne Gouveia for very ably assisting in the difficult task of herding the eelers, who, unlike their fishy associates, seemed remarkably cooperative.

Special thanks to Yves de Lafontaine, Environnement Canada, Montreal, who made it possible for the group to visit the Quebec City eel box trap. The GLFC very generously provided the necessary funds for the event and arranged bus transportation for this outing, which was an exciting experience for many. A picnic lunch and fish fry was also laid on. Special thanks to Nancy Leonard, GLFC, for arranging the transportation and lunch, and to Suzanne Gouveia, OMNR.

The International Eel Symposium and these proceedings were a cooperative effort that drew on the dedication, hard work, and assistance of many people. Very importantly, we were encouraged by AFS meeting program chair Martin Castonguay and the local Arrangements Committee, who facilitated the symposium and ably assisted in many ways. We especially thank the session moderators; oral and poster contributors (Symposium Program, page xvii); and the panel: facilitator Mike Jones, Michigan State University, Lansing, Michigan; and members Martin Castonguay, Fisheries and Oceans, Mont-Joli, Quebec; Willem Dekker, Netherlands Institute for Fisheries Research, IJmuiden, The Netherlands; Henry Lickers, Mohawk Council of Akwesasne, Cornwall, Ontario; Roy Stein, Ohio State University, Columbus, Ohio; and Gail Wipplehauser, Department of Marine Resources, Augusta, Maine. We especially thank Henry Lickers for First Nations support and encouragement and for his moving and inspirational traditional Haudenosaunee opening and closing of the meeting. We thank the authors and referees (acknowledged, page xxiii) and particularly appreciate the careful and capable copy editing of Lois Casselman and the assistance, professionalism, and patience of AFS publication staff Aaron Lerner and Kurt West in bringing this volume to its final form.

We have come to realize that when concerned about the state of the environment, and specifically the well-being of eels and our association with this ancient and unique fish, our job is never done.

John M. Casselman
Queen's University, Kingston, ON
(casselmj@queensu.ca)

David K. Cairns
Fisheries and Oceans, Charlottetown, PE
(david.cairns@dfo-mpo.gc.ca)

References

Aida, K., K. Tsukamoto, and K. Yamauchi (editors) 2003. Eel biology. Springer-Verlag, Tokyo. 497 p.

Casselman, J.M. 2003. Dynamics of resources of the American eel, Anguilla rostrata: declining abundance in the 1990s. Pages 255-274, chapter 18, in K. Aida, K. Tsukamoto, and K. Yamauchi (editors), Eel biology, Springer-Verlag, Tokyo.

Dekker, W., J.M. Casselman, D.K. Cairns, K. Tsukamoto, D. Jellyman, and H. Lickers. 2003. Worldwide decline of eel resources necessitates immediate action. Quebec Declaration of Concern. Fisheries 28(12):28-30.

Dixon, D. (editor) 2003. Biology, management and protection of catadromous eels: 1st International Catadromous Eel Symposium, August 2000. American Fisheries Society Symposium 33. Bethesda, Maryland. 388 p.

Helfman, G.S., D.E. Facey, L.S. Hales, and E.L. Bozeman Jr. 1987. Reproductive ecology of the American eel. Pages 42-56 in M.J. Dadswell, R.J. Klauda, C.M. Moffitt, R.L. Saunders, R.A. Rulifson, and J.E. Cooper (editors). Common strategies of anadromous and catadromous fishes. American Fisheries Society Symposium 1, Bethesda, Maryland.

Loftus, K.H. (editor) 1982. Proceedings of the 1980 North American Eel Conference. Ontario Fisheries Technical Report Series No. 4. 97 p.

Symposium Participants

1 Dave Meerburg	13 Unidentified	25 Patrick Lambert	37 John Casselman
2 Willem Dekker	14 Katsumi Tsukamoto	26 Laurent Beaulaton	38 Lucian Marcogliese
3 Håkan Wickström	15 Paula Cullen	27 Henry Lickers	39 Caroline Durif
4 Jan Breine	16 Beth Williams	28 Gail Wippelhauser	40 Brian Knights
5 Mike Miller	17 Heidi El-Hosaini	29 Kevin Reid	41 Tony Bark
6 Giulio De Leo	18 Uli Dumont	30 Claude Belpaire	42 Peter Todd
7 Eric Feunteun	19 Kenichi Tatsukawa	31 Tony Robinet	43 Valérie Tremblay
8 Laura Lee	20 Don Jellyman	32 Julie Weeder	44 Wann-Nian Tzeng
9 Gregory Maes	21 Keiran McCarthy	33 Brian Jessop	45 Alastair Mathers
10 Alex Hoar	22 Jun Aoyama	34 Michael Pedersen	
11 Jacques Boubée	23 Unidentified	35 Guy Verreault	
12 Maarten Bruijs	24 Jim McCleave	36 David Cairns	

Group photograph taken after panel discussion

Symposium Program

AMERICAN FISHERIES SOCIETY 2003 ANNUAL MEETING
QUEBEC

GENERAL MEETING THEME:

WORLDWIDE DECLINE OF NATIVE FISH POPULATIONS

INTERNATIONAL EEL SYMPOSIUM, 11–13 August 2003

WELCOME AND INTRODUCTION

Monday 1:30 p.m.	John Casselman David Cairns	Welcome and introduction
	Henry Lickers	A traditional Haudenosaunee opening and blessing

OVERVIEWS
Moderator: Chris Goddard

Monday 2:00 p.m.	Willem Dekker	A conceptual framework for management and restoration of the declining European eel stock
Monday 2:20 p.m.	Katsumi Tsukamoto* Jun Aoyama Michael J. Miller	Research or resources: The present status of the Japanese eel
Monday 2:40 p.m.	Don J. Jellyman	The status of freshwater eels in New Zealand
Monday 3:00 p.m.	John Casselman	American eel dynamics and abundance: A fish resource in unprecedented decline
Monday 3:20 p.m.		Coffee break

Theme: STATUS AND DYNAMICS
Moderator: Doug Dixon

Monday 3:40 p.m.	Yves de Lafontaine* Michel Lagacé Fernand Gingras Denis Labonté François Marchand Edith Lacroix	The American eel in the St. Lawrence River: Prelude to the loss of a resource

Monday 4:00 p.m.	Lucian A. Marcogliese* John M. Casselman	Size of juvenile American eels ascending the upper St. Lawrence River—trends and declining recruitment
Monday 4:20 p.m.	Claude Belpaire	Eel fisheries and management in Flanders, Belgium: Status and trends
Monday 4:40 p.m.	L. Beaulaton G. Castelnaud*	Glass eel abundance trend in the Gironde Basin for the period 1978-1999 and speed migration
Monday 5:00 p.m.	Anthony Bark* Brian Knights Beth Williams	Long-term changes in recruitment, population dynamics and stock status of the European eel in a river and coastal lagoon system in southern England

Theme: MOVEMENT, MIGRATION, AND BARRIERS
Moderator: Don Jellyman

Tuesday 8:40 a.m.	Leah Brown* Alex Haro Theodore Castro-Santos	Movements and behaviors of silver-phase migrant American eels at a small hydroelectric facility characterized by three-dimensional acoustic telemetry
Tuesday 9:00 a.m.	Kevin McGrath* Scott Ault John Skalski Carole Fleury Alan Fairbanks	Avoidance of artificial light by downstream migrating American eel (*Anguilla rostrata*) in the St. Lawrence River
Tuesday 9:20 a.m.	Uli Dumont B. Adam	Protection of downstream migrating silver eels with the early warning system MIGROMAT
Tuesday 9:40 a.m.	Kevin McGrath* Richard Verdon Denis Desrochers Carole Fleury Scott Ault John Skalski	Determining release location for upstream migrating juvenile American eels (*Anguilla rostrata*) exiting an eel ladder
Tuesday 10:00 a.m.	Doug Dixon	Review of current and future EPRI sponsored research for American eel protection at hydroelectric projects
Tuesday 10:20 a.m.		Coffee break

Theme: SCIENCE, ECOLOGY, AND LIFE HISTORY (I)
Moderator: Guy Verreault

Tuesday 10:40 a.m.	James D. McCleave* Don J. Jellyman	Sex ratio of longfin eels in New Zealand rivers: Effects of commercial fishing
Tuesday 11:00 a.m.	Caroline Durif* Pierre Elie	The silvering process of the European eel: Characterization of intermediate stages for identification of downstream migrants
Tuesday 11:20 a.m.	Christine Séchet* Pierre Elie	Analysis of the morpho-anatomical changes occurring during artificially-induced sexual maturation for European eel from Loire River in experimental conditions
Tuesday 11:40 a.m.	T. Kieran McCarthy* Karen Creed Oisin Naughton Paula Cullen Lorraine Copley	The metazoan parasites of eels (*Anguilla anguilla*) in Ireland: Zoogeographical, ecological and fishery management perspectives
Tuesday 12:00	T. W. Lee* H. T. Moon W. S. Kim T. J. Stewart	Inter-annual variation in glass eel catch of *Anguilla japonica* in Korean estuaries
Tuesday 12:20 p.m.		Lunch

Theme: SCIENCE, ECOLOGY, AND LIFE HISTORY (II)
Moderator: Katsumi Tsukamoto

Tuesday 1:40 p.m.	Brian Knights	Speculations on the adaptive strategies and survival to recruitment of anguillid leptocephali in relation to long-term trends in ocean-climate change
Tuesday 2:00 p.m.	Michael J. Miller* Jun Aoyama Katsumi Tsukamoto	New perspectives on the early life history of tropical eels: Implications for resource management
Tuesday 2:20 p.m.	Eric Edeline* S. Dufour Pierre Elie	Triggers and phenomenon of watershed colonization by European glass eels: State of the art and new approaches

Tuesday 2:40 p.m.		Michael I. Pedersen	The effect of stock enhancement by elvers *Anguilla anguilla* in some Danish fresh and brackish waters—two case stories
Tuesday 3:00 p.m.		Guy Verreault* Willy Dargere Rémi Tardif	American eel (*Anguilla rostrata*) movements, growth, and sex ratio following glass eel introduction
Tuesday 3:20 p.m.			Coffee break

Theme: SCIENCE, ECOLOGY, AND LIFE HISTORY (III)
Moderator: Eric Feunteun

Tuesday 3:40 p.m.		Wann-Nian Tzeng* Yu-San Han Brian M. Jessop	Variability of growth rate and age at maturity of American eels, *Anguilla rostrata*, transplanted from North America to tropical Taiwan

Theme: STOCK ASSESSMENT AND MANAGEMENT (I)

Tuesday 4:00 p.m.		Alastair Mathers* Thomas J. Stewart	Management of American eel, *Anguilla rostrata*, in Lake Ontario and the upper St. Lawrence River
Tuesday 4:20 p.m.		Kevin B. Reid* P. J. R. Meisenheimer S. S. Crawford	Using decision analysis and adaptive management to determine research and management priorities for American eel in the Lake Ontario-St. Lawrence River ecosystem
Tuesday 4:40 p.m.		Julie A. Weeder* James H. Uphoff, Jr.	Are American eel harvests in Maryland's Chesapeake Bay sustainable?

POSTER PREVIEWS—RAPID PRESENTATIONS

Tuesday 5:00 p.m.		John Casselman David Cairns	Introduction of posters and contributors

Theme: STOCK ASSESSMENT AND MANAGEMENT (II)
Moderator: Jim McCleave

Wednesday 8:40 a.m.		Giulio A. De Leo* Paco Melià Alain J. Crivelli Marino Gatto	Eel population modeling and its application to conservation management
Wednesday 9:00 a.m.		David Cairns	Development of conservation reference points for the American eel from a stochastic life table model

Wednesday 9:20 a.m.	Patrick Lambert Eric Feunteun E. Rochard	A matrix model for the inland part of the European eel population dynamics
Wednesday 9:40 a.m.	Anthony Acou Gabriel Gaelle Pascal Laffaille Eric Feunteun*	Typology of silver eel (*Anguilla anguilla*) production in small coastal catchments: from methodological reflections towards a theoretical approach
Wednesday 10:00 a.m.	Peter Todd	Management, research and stock assessment of *Anguilla* spp. in New Zealand
Wednesday 10:20 a.m.		Coffee break
Wednesday 10:40 a.m. to 12:20 p.m.		AFS general poster session
Wednesday 12:20 p.m.		Lunch

Theme: STOCK ASSESSMENT AND MANAGEMENT (III)
Moderator: Martin Castonguay

Wednesday 1:40 p.m.	Laura M. Lee* Julie Weeder	Interstate resource management and assessment of American eel in the U.S.
Wednesday 2:00 p.m.	Eric Feunteun	Management and restoration of the European eel (*Anguilla anguilla*): an impossible mission? A conceptual thinking

PANEL: STATUS, ASSESSMENT, AND CONSERVATION CONCERNS (panelists and audience)

Facilitator/Moderator: Mike Jones
Panel Participants: Willem Dekker, Martin Castonguay, Roy Stein, Gail Wippelhauser
       With audience participation

Wednesday 2:20 to 3:20 p.m.	Panel presentation and discussion: Status, assessment, and conservation concerns
	Closing remarks

CLOSING:

Henry Lickers	A traditional Haudenosaunee closing and blessing

OUTING:
Thursday   Visit to St. Lawrence River Saint-Nicolas experimental eel weir fishery and box trap organized by Yves de Lafontaine, shore lunch provided by Great Lakes Fishery Commission, and discussions concerning preparation of a ***Quebec Declaration of Concern***

*author giving oral presentation

Reviewer Acknowledgments

The following individuals assisted with reviewing manuscripts. Their efforts are greatly appreciated.

Eric Acou
Jun Aoyama
Miran Aprahamian
Anthony Bark
Laurent Beaulaton
Jacques Boubée
Rod Bradford
Leah Brown
Maarten Bruijs
Anna Cairns
Martin Castonguay
John Clark
Willem Dekker
Yves de Lafontaine
Giulio De Leo
Dawn Dittman
Doug Dixon
Pierre Dumont
Caroline Durif
Jean-Denis Dutil
Pierre Elie
Eric Feunteun
Merry Gallagher
Marino Gatto
Chris Goddard
Alex Haro
Don Jellyman
Brian Jessop
Ruth Kirk
Brian Knights
Richard Kraus
Bill Krueger
Pascal Laffaille
Patrick Lambert
Heather Lamson

Laura Lee
Tae Won Lee
Karin Limburg
Gregory Maes
Yves Mailhot
Alastair Mathers
T. K. McCarthy
Jim McCleave
Kevin McGrath
Jason Melendy
Mike Miller
Chris Moriarty
Wendy Morrison
Ken Oliveira
Mike Pawson
Bruce Pease
Michael Pedersen
Tom Pratt
Ian Russell
Jen-Chieh Shiao
Roy Stein
Peter Todd
Valérie Tremblay
Wann-Nian Tzeng
James Uphoff
Vic Vecchio
Richard Verdon
Guy Verreault
Leif Asbjørn Vøllestad
Chris Walsh
Julie Weeder
Stuart Welsh
Håkan Wickström
Thierry Wirth

Symbols and Abbreviations

The following symbols and abbreviations may be found in this book without definition. Also undefined are standard mathematical and statistical symbols given in most dictionaries.

A	ampere	G	giga (10^9, as a prefix)
AC	alternating current	gal	gallon (3.79 L)
Bq	becquerel	Gy	gray
C	coulomb	h	hour
°C	degrees Celsius	ha	hectare (2.47 acres)
cal	calorie	hp	horsepower (746 W)
cd	candela	Hz	hertz
cm	centimeter	in	inch (2.54 cm)
Co.	Company	Inc.	Incorporated
Corp.	Corporation	i.e.	(id est) that is
cov	covariance	IU	international unit
DC	direct current; District of Columbia	J	joule
D	dextro (as a prefix)	K	Kelvin (degrees above absolute zero)
d	day	k	kilo (10^3, as a prefix)
d	dextrorotatory	kg	kilogram
df	degrees of freedom	km	kilometer
dL	deciliter	l	levorotatory
E	east	L	levo (as a prefix)
E	expected value	L	liter (0.264 gal, 1.06 qt)
e	base of natural logarithm (2.71828…)	lb	pound (0.454 kg, 454g)
		lm	lumen
e.g.	(exempli gratia) for example	log	logarithm
eq	equivalent	Ltd.	Limited
et al.	(et alii) and others	M	mega (10^6, as a prefix); molar (as a suffix or by itself)
etc.	et cetera		
eV	electron volt	m	meter (as a suffix or by itself); milli (10^{-3}, as a prefix)
F	filial generation; Farad		
°F	degrees Fahrenheit	mi	mile (1.61 km)
fc	footcandle (0.0929 lx)	min	minute
ft	foot (30.5 cm)	mol	mole
ft³/s	cubic feet per second (0.0283 m³/s)	N	normal (for chemistry); north (for geography); newton
g	gram	N	sample size

NS	not significant	tris	tris(hydroxymethyl)-aminomethane (a buffer)
n	ploidy; nanno (10^{-9}, as a prefix)		
o	ortho (as a chemical prefix)	UK	United Kingdom
oz	ounce (28.4 g)	U.S.	United States (adjective)
P	probability	USA	United States of America (noun)
p	para (as a chemical prefix)	V	volt
p	pico (10^{-12}, as a prefix)	V, Var	variance (population)
Pa	pascal	var	variance (sample)
pH	negative log of hydrogen ion activity	W	watt (for power); west (for geography)
ppm	parts per million	Wb	weber
qt	quart (0.946 L)	yd	yard (0.914 m, 91.4 cm)
R	multiple correlation or regression coefficient	α	probability of type I error (false rejection of null hypothesis)
r	simple correlation or regression coefficient	β	probability of type II error (false acceptance of null hypothesis)
rad	radian	Ω	ohm
S	siemens (for electrical conductance); south (for geography)	μ	micro (10^{-6}, as a prefix)
		′	minute (angular)
		″	second (angular)
SD	standard deviation	°	degree (temperature as a prefix, angular as a suffix)
SE	standard error		
s	second	%	per cent (per hundred)
T	tesla	‰	(per thousand)

Part I

Overviews

A Conceptual Management Framework for the Restoration of the Declining European Eel Stock

WILLEM DEKKER[1]
Netherlands Institute for Fisheries Research
Post Office Box 68, 1970 AB IJmuiden, The Netherlands

Abstract.—The stock of the European eel *Anguilla anguilla* is in a critical state. A prolonged downward trend in landings since 1960 suggests a steady decline of the continental stock, while incoming recruitment fell to record low levels in the 1980s over almost all of Europe. Although the effect of oceanic factors cannot be ruled out, continental processes that have depleted the spawning stock are the most likely cause of the decline. Management strategies that are successful with other fish stocks may not work well for eels. An innovative management scheme that preserves adequate spawner production is urgently required. This paper examines the specific problems of the eel and proposes a solution from existing concepts in fish-stock management. It covers the problem of the wide and scattered distribution, the inability to set targets for the oceanic life stages, the distribution of responsibilities among management levels, the need to adapt management measures to local and time-varying (environmental) conditions, and the short time left to develop and implement a complex management system that achieves a sustainable regime. A conceptual framework for restoration of the declining European eel stock being outlined, progress in management and restoration of the eel is now a matter of political decisions.

Introduction

The stock of the European eel *Anguilla anguilla* (L.) has shown a marked decline over past decades. Recruitment to (Moriarty 1986; Dekker 2000a), and harvest from continental waters (Dekker 2003a) have been well below the long-term average for two or more decades. Several authors have speculated on possible causes of the decline (Castonguay et al. 1994a; Moriarty and Dekker 1997; ICES 2002a), but none of the available hypotheses adequately explains the observed decline (Dekker 2004a). A stock protection and recovery plan is urgently needed (ICES 1999), but no substantial progress in managing the stock has been achieved, and the decline continues (ICES 2004). Scientific advice to restrict fisheries to prevailing levels (ICES 1997a), to redistribute recruitment of glass eels towards the outskirts of the distribution area (Moriarty and Dekker 1997), or to reduce all human impacts on the stock to as close to zero as possible (ICES 2002b) has not yet been followed.

In past decades, substantial effort has been invested in formulating a precautionary approach to exploitation of fish resources (United Nations 1983; FAO 1995) and to deriving quantitative reference points for fisheries management (Caddy and Mahon

[1] E-mail: Willem.Dekker@wur.nl

1995; ICES 1997b). This framework is now routinely applied in scientific advice on the exploitation of marine fish stocks in Europe (ICES 1997b) and has been the basis for advice on eels (ICES 1999, 2002b). However, despite the alarming state of the eel stock, few factual management measures have been imposed (ICES 2004).

This paper summarizes existing evidence on the decline of the stock, reviews potential causes, and proposes a conceptual framework for stock management. I use the word *eel* (without qualification) to indicate the European eel, although the presented ideas also have broad application in other *Anguilla* species, especially those in temperate waters.

Managing the Eel Stock: An Impossible Bargain?

Management strategies that are readily applied to other fish stocks may not work well for eels (Feunteun 2002). Complications arise from the eel's biology, fisheries, and management.

The eel in Europe, northern Africa, and Mediterranean Asia (Dekker 2003b) constitutes an (almost) panmictic population (Wirth and Bernatchez 2001; Avise 2003; Dekker 2004a). Spawning has not been observed in the wild, but all evidence supports the view of semelparous reproduction in or near the Sargasso Sea 3000–7000 km from European coastlines. The fisheries, in contrast, are scattered over the continental distribution area in water bodies estimated to number more than 10,000 (Dekker 2000a). Fisheries are prosecuted in over 30 countries, of which 10 are regularly involved in the international advisory process on stock management (author's unpublished data). Commercial fisheries organizations rarely have a strong influence on eel management, and national or regional authorities generally have minimized involvement. Fisheries legislation is generally designed to deal with management of typical marine and freshwater species, sometimes with specific reference to salmonids, but does not accommodate the peculiarities of the eel.

The continental life stage lasts for 5–15+ years, during which fisheries occur on migratory (glass eel and silver eel) and resident (yellow eel) forms. Concentrated in space during migration or vulnerable to exploitation over many years, the eel is a preferred target for exploitation, fetching more than twice the price per kilogram of any other finfish (except sturgeon) (FAO 2000). The long migrations require open routes from the sea to inland waters. Additionally, the occurrence in systems up to the highest headwaters maximizes vulnerability to anthropogenic impacts, including pollution, habitat loss, and poaching. Highest densities are found in downstream stretches, around which human populations reach peak densities. Managing the eel comes down to managing anthropogenic impacts that often affect the eel only indirectly.

Typical fisheries management relies heavily upon scientific information on the status of the stock and on the impact of exploitation, as well as upon opportunities to steer exploitation pressures. For the eel, neither present knowledge nor available management options satisfy current needs, while conflicting anthropogenic interests complicate the matter. Rather than giving in to this seemingly impossible bargain, I will analyze the problem and assemble a solution from existing concepts in fish-stock management.

Status of the stock

The overall status of the eel stock is poorly known (Moriarty and Dekker 1997). Neither the absolute size nor the overall impact of exploitation and other anthropogenic factors have been reliably assessed (Dekker 2000b, 2004a). Local monitoring schemes have been set up to meet local needs, and posterior meta-analyses of these data sets have shown

Figure 1. Indices of European glass eel recruitment during the 20th century. Individual data series given in thin gray; common trend (geometric mean of the four longest data series) in thick black (data from Dekker 2002).

common downward trends in large parts of the distribution area, in recruitment (Dekker 2000a), and fishing harvest (Dekker 2003a).

Recruitment from the Ocean

Along the southwestern shores of Europe, commercial fisheries target freshly recruited glass eels in estuaries and river mouths (Moriarty and Dekker 1997; Dekker 2003b). Landing statistics have been recorded in a number of systems for periods up to several decades. Although variation in fishing effort may have occurred, the trend in landings will also reflect trends in incoming recruitment. North of 50°N, glass eels are mostly fished to restock inland waters, making fishing effort more or less independent of fishing success (an exception is the fully commercial glass eel fishery in the Bristol Channel on the British west coast at 51°36'N). North of 55°N, the pigmentation process of glass eels has started before they enter fresh waters and are trapped for restocking. Statistics have been recorded for a period of decades up to a century. Finally, scientific glass eel monitoring has been ongoing in the Netherlands since 1938.

These data were recorded because of their relevance to local management. In the mid-1980s it was realized that several of the data series showed a common, downward trend (Figure 1; EIFAC 1985; Moriarty 1986). Subsequent analysis (Dekker 2000a) indicated high correlations between all stations, with exceptions in the Baltic (where the decline might have started earlier) and the British Isles (where the decline was less severe). Apparently, local monitoring programs were tracking a global development throughout most of the distribution area.

Fishing Harvest from Continental Waters

Fisheries for yellow eel and silver eel are found throughout the distribution area of the species (Dekker 2003a, 2003b). Statistics on total landings are notoriously incomplete. ICES (1988) and Moriarty (1997) have shown that official statistics often capture only about half the true harvest. However, reported data series display a common trend through most of the 20th century (Figure 2; Dekker 2003a). A reconstruction of total landings shows a peak in the 1960s at 47,000 mt, then a slow

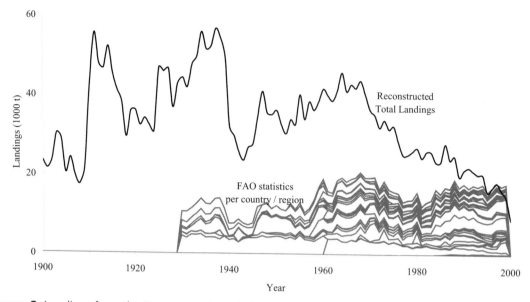

Figure 2. Landings from the European eel stock during the 20th century by country, and the reconstructed trend in the total landings (Dekker 2004a). The number of countries with data increases with time, making the sum of reported landings an inadequate indicator of the overall trend.

decline to a historic low of under 15,000 mt in 2000.

This trend in harvest parallels the trend in the stock detected in various sources of circumstantial (Moriarty and Dekker 1997) and direct (Dekker 2004b) evidence. Thus, harvest trends apparently reflect stock abundance rather than variation in fishing pressure.

Causes of the Decline

The decline in glass eel recruitment was first noticed in 1985 (EIFAC 1985). The prolonged decline in landings was mentioned as early as 1975 (ICES 1976) but has received much less attention than that of recruitment. Several hypotheses for the recruitment decline have been suggested (Castonguay et al. 1994a; Moriarty and Dekker 1997; ICES 2002a), but without firm evidence, no definite causes can be assigned, and a parallel effect of several of the proposed factors is most plausible (Dekker 2004b).

The suggested hypotheses fall into two groups. First, some process in the ocean may have reduced larval survival, growth, or both (Castonguay et al. 1994b; Desaunay and Guerault 1997; Dekker 1998). Such a process could be related to the North Atlantic Oscillation (ICES 2001a; Knights 2003). This process is unlikely to be anthropogenic (unless indirectly) and would not be related to the size of the spawning stock. If the cause is oceanic, recovery of the original climate conditions should lead to a rapid restoration of abundant recruitment. Given the observed spatial correlation in the decline in recruitment and the near-panmictic reproductive system, any oceanic processes that affect eels can be expected to affect the stock as a whole.

Second, a range of continental factors has been suggested, including pollution; habitat loss due to barrages and dams; overexploitation of glass, yellow, and silver stages; and artificial transfers of parasites and diseases (Castonguay et al. 1994a; Mo-

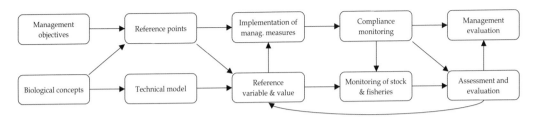

Figure 3. A framework of conceptual and technical steps in the implementation of a management scheme for fisheries (After Caddy and Mahon 1995; strongly modified). Arrows indicate the flow of concepts, information and data.

riarty and Dekker 1997; ICES 2002a; Robinet and Feunteun 2002). All of these factors are anthropogenic, operate primarily in the continental life stages, and affect recruitment abundance through their effect on the size or quality of the spawning stock. When a fatal reduction in the size or quality of the spawning stock occurs, an abrupt drop in recruitment is expected. This will be hard to reverse, since lower recruitment in turn will further reduce the spawning stock. Each of the processes affects a local sub-stock on the continent, but it is their combined effect on the shared spawning stock that has caused the recruitment decline.

Although tentative analyses indicate that the group of hypotheses based on continental factors fits available data better (Dekker 2004a, 2004b), no convincing proof exists. A stock restoration plan must be developed in the absence of fully adequate scientific information (FAO 1995). Restoration measures cannot realistically target oceanic life stages. Protective measures are therefore restricted to the continental phases, while it is unclear whether they will address the cause of the decline. However, excessive anthropogenic impacts on the stock must be curtailed irrespective of the ultimate cause of the decline. Whether these impacts are the cause of the global decline does not affect the need to take conservation measures.

A Framework for the Management Process

In the past decades, a precautionary approach to exploitation of fisheries resources has been developed (United Nations 1983; FAO, 1995). This framework is routinely applied in scientific advice on fisheries (ICES 1997b), including advice on the European eel stock (ICES 1999, 2002b). Caddy and Mahon (1995) outline the conceptual steps in the development of quantified reference points for fisheries management. The current discussion will extend their ideas, distinguishing between the management process proper (Figure 3, top row) and the development of scientific advice (bottom row) and elaborating on the special case of European eel fisheries.

Recent scientific advice and the current discussion were triggered by the decline in recruitment observed since 1980. In the preceding decades, management focused on the development of stocks and fisheries, as witnessed by the implementation of large-scale restocking programs (Dekker 2003c). This focus has recently been replaced by an emphasis on stock protection. The coincidence of the decline in recruitment during the 1980s and 1990s with the upsurge in discussions on stock protection implies that the current abundance of the stock is below acceptable management limits. If possible, the stock should be sustained at levels higher than those that are current.

The biology of the eel has been described as incompletely and poorly known, providing only a weak basis for management and restoration (ICES 1976, 1999; Moriarty and Dekker 1997; Tesch 2003). This claim embraces two aspects: qualitatively speaking, processes operating on the stock might be unidentified; on the quantitative side, parameters of the processes and the state of the stock might be inadequately known. In the 1970s and early 1980s, attention was focused on quantification, with the compilation of an international database on stocks and fisheries, but in the 1990s, focus shifted to identification of the causes of the recruitment decline. All suggested hypotheses fit the general framework of fish population dynamics (i.e., if more data had been available, a selection-and-elimination procedure could easily have shown which process caused the observed decline). But neither the data nor a common analysis exists. Twenty years after the onset of the recruitment decline, the scientific community working on eels still lacks a comprehensive technical model for the dynamics of the population. Analysis of the (potential) processes causing the current stock decline is still in a primordial phase, tracing correlations without knowing if they are causative or spurious. Therefore, the derivation of preliminary reference variables and values for stock management (ICES 2001b) hinges on the assumed parallel to fish species with very different life histories and does not relate to existing management practices for the eel.

There is a long tradition of regulating local exploitation of eels, but there are marked regional variations in approach. Local monitoring has been shown to provide reliable information on the overall status of glass eel recruitment (Dekker 2000a, 2002), but assessment of fisheries and escapement has only recently been attempted. Management measures have been listed (Moriarty and Dekker 1997; ICES 2001a, 2001b) but have not been quantitatively linked to objectives or stock status. Clearly, there is an intention to protect and restore the declining stock and there is a list of available tools, but the connection between detailed scientific advice and implementation of management measures is still lacking.

Temporal and Spatial Scales of Stock Dynamics

Management, monitoring, and fundamental research on eels have been carried out at the national level, with limited coordination among countries. The spatial distribution of the stock exhibits fractal characteristics, showing large-scale, as well as small-scale, variation (Dekker 2000b). The temporal structure shows comparable fractal patterns. In setting up a management system for the stock and fisheries, these patterns should be considered, and an appropriate spatial and temporal scale for management actions must be selected. In this section, the major processes in the dynamics of the stock will be characterized in time and space (Figure 4), setting the scene for a corresponding management scheme, developed later.

The European eel is distributed in almost all continental waters of Europe and along the coasts of northern Africa and Mediterranean Asia. That makes it probably the most widely distributed exploited single fish stock, but individuals in inland waters are confined to single rivers or lakes averaging less than 10 km^2 (Dekker 2000a). In comparison to many other exploited fish species, the eel shows extreme longevity, which is related to its slow growth and late maturation. Age at maturation for females ranges from 5 years in the Mediterranean to over 15 in the Baltic (Vøllestad 1992). In contrast to the small-scale and long-duration character of the continental part of the life cycle, the oceanic phases cross thousands of kilometres (van Ginneken and van den Thillart 2000) in a time frame that is most likely about two years (McCleave et al. 1998).

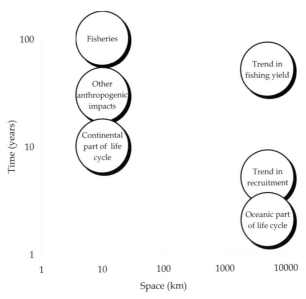

Figure 4. Temporal and spatial scale of observed trends, major processes and anthropogenic impacts on the stock.

In this life phase, individuals from across the continental range contribute to a common and almost panmictic spawning stock (Avise 2003; Dekker 2004a). The ocean phase is thus a short-duration and large-scale phenomenon.

Anthropogenic impacts on the stock range from instantaneous (e.g., pollution spills, glass and silver eel fisheries) to long-term (e.g., gradual land reclamation, yellow eel fisheries). However, most anthropogenic impacts directly affect only a minor part of the population. Spatially significant effects occur only where local impacts are driven by a common force, such as the worldwide demand for glass eels, or continent-wide industrialization. The introduction of the swim bladder parasite *Anguillicola*, rapidly spreading over almost the entire distribution area, is probably the only anthropogenic impact at a wide spatial scale. Incidents such as pollution spills seldom cover more than an isolated area and hardly influence the stock. Significant anthropogenic impacts operate on small spatial, but prolonged temporal, scales. Most stock-wide effects only occur because of external synchronization between impacts on small and isolated waters.

The glass eel decline has been described as a gradual, slow, and prolonged recruitment failure (Dekker 2000a). But as early as 1985 (EIFAC 1985), it was realized that recruitment of the European eel was in decline in the major part of the distribution area (i.e., within 5 years, a widespread regime shift was noted). In contrast, the gradual decline in fishing harvest began in the mid-1960s and has continued consistently (i.e., it has a prolonged temporal scale). Like the recruitment failure, it occurred throughout the distribution area.

There is a sharp contrast in temporal and spatial scales between the oceanic (widespread, short time frame) and continental (localized, long-lived) life stages. Anthropogenic impacts are consistent with the patterns of the continental phase, but the gradual and widespread decline in fishing harvest suggests a causatory process of a different temporal and spatial scale: widespread and gradually developing.

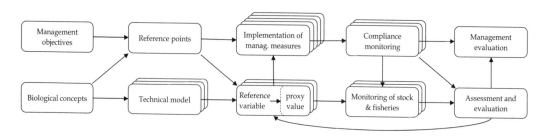

Figure 5. A revised framework for management of eel fisheries, taking into account the spatial differentiation of the eel stock and fisheries. For the sake of readability, items with a limited number of instances are shown in triplicate, while the thousands of waters in which management measures must be implemented is shown as just five.

Cracking the Management Problem

The contrast in spatial and temporal scales in major processes and anthropogenic impacts, sketched above, poses a serious challenge for managing the stock. Long-term global objectives must be achieved by small-scale and immediate actions in rural areas all over the continental range. Neither central managers without direct influence on small-scale fisheries all over Europe nor national and regional managers bereft of opportunities to influence the overall stock will be able to solve the problem unless a dedicated framework is developed. In this section, I propose elements of a management scheme (Figure 5) that might achieve this goal.

Objective and Target

Implicit in developing a precautionary approach is the assumption that there is a relationship between spawning stock and recruitment. The precautionary approach dictates that, unless proven otherwise, such a relationship should also be assumed to exist for the eel; available evidence seems to corroborate the relation (Dekker 2003a, 2004a). Current scientific knowledge is inadequate to derive spawning stock size targets specific for the eel. Under data-poor conditions, exploitation securing 30% of the virgin spawning stock biomass is generally considered a reasonable provisional reference target. This rule is conventionally labeled as %SPR, for percentage spawner production per recruit, which presupposes that spawner production is proportional to recruitment. In southwestern Europe, with overabundant recruitment (Dekker 2003b), silver eel production is more likely to be proportional to (accessible) habitat, disabling the per recruit basis. However, the notion of a targeted spawning stock size relative to pristine conditions stands. Considering the many uncertainties in eel management and biology and the uniqueness of the eel (single stock, spawning only once per lifetime), a precautionary reference point for eels must be stricter than the universal target of 30%. A value of 50% has been suggested (ICES 2001b).

Reference Points and Proxies

For the eel, protection of the spawning stock remains a theoretical concept: spawning has never been observed in the wild. The escapement of spawners from the continental stock, however, is thought to be a good indicator of the supposed spawning stock size, for which management targets can be derived (ICES 2001a). Measurements of silver eel escapement are rare (Ask and Erichsen 1976; Westin 1990; Sers et al. 1993; Pedersen and

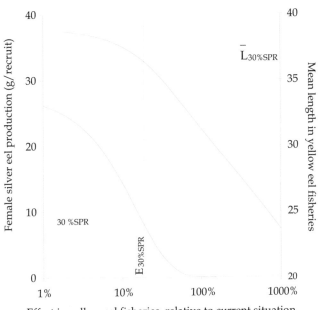

Figure 6. Mean length (upper curved line) in yellow eel fishery in Lake IJsselmeer (the Netherlands) provides a proximate indicator for the level of female silver eel production (lower curved line) under varying fishing effort. Dashed reference lines indicate 30%SPR, the corresponding effort $E_{30\%SPR}$ and mean length $L_{30\%SPR}$, based on current gear selectivity and the minimum legal size of 28 cm. (Unpublished results from the author; see also Dekker 2000c).

Dieperink 2000) and not likely to be extended considerably because of the research effort required. Cascading one step further, an assessment of the stock in continental waters producing the silver eel run (Dekker 2000c) suffers from the same high research requirements.

Less demanding approaches based on the yellow eel stock, such as mean size in the catch, are not adequate for year-to-year management (Francis and Jellyman 1999) but might be suitable for long-term purposes (Figure 6). In my view, there is considerable scope for development of further low-demanding approximations to escapement targets, such as mean size in the catch, percentage of the catch above a certain size, or slope of the length-frequency distribution. Management schemes for local situations can be built upon easy-to-grasp local targets if these proxy targets correspond to their ultimate counterparts theoretically and if monitoring corroborates the net effect. For glass eel fisheries, the concepts of stock abundance, habitat availability, and carrying capacity still need to be worked out (ICES 2002a), but for this case, too, a simplification in proxies will be required for implementation in any practical management situation.

Subsidiarity and Orchestration

At what spatial level can an adequate recovery plan be executed? The (unknown) spawning stock receives contributions from many (if not all) countries, while the continental stock is fragmented over local waters. Can the implementation of restoration measures more effectively be handed over to lower management levels (subsidiarity), and what role remains, in that case, for the international management level?

Management of local fisheries interacts with the common (oceanic) stock only through immigration of glass eels and escapement of silver eels. Intervention of international management in local fisheries need only concern the inputs (glass eel) and outputs (silver eel) of national systems. Global evaluation of local management considers the (relative) impact of local actions on spawner escapement and need not concern local means and local consequences. Whether a sustainable management regime is achieved by means of habitat restoration; by restrictions on glass, yellow, or silver eel fishing; or by any adequate combination of measures is irrelevant for protection of the overall stock. Spatial variation in management measures is allowable and might even be advantageous. In particular, there is no basis for a continent-wide ban on either glass eel or silver eel fisheries, as is sometimes proposed by rival stakeholders.

Taking subsidiary one step further, the responsibility for management of national fisheries might be shared by governments and fisheries organizations, opening up the whole suite of co-management opportunities and tools (e.g., Pinkerton 1994). In particular, this might avert the need to monitor and manage a multitude of water bodies if monitoring samples a small but representative fraction of waters (random or stratified, but not fixed) and if results are used to manage the fishery in the whole population of waters.

While implementation (and monitoring) can be executed only at the lowest management level, objectives, reference points, and evaluation necessarily refer to the whole stock at the international level. Local managers have virtually no ability to influence the overall status of the stock and have no natural incentive for implementing sustainable management. International managers, in contrast, cannot influence the stock directly but have the option to enforce common objectives through lower management levels and to evaluate global effects on the basis of widespread local monitoring. Subsidiarity and orchestration of lower management levels constitute the global managers' tools to achieve the overall objectives.

Adaptive Management

At the national and regional level, global objectives and targets must be translated into actual and quantified management measures. Fishing effort, fishing season, mesh size, closed area, etc., must be set to produce the required escapement levels, mortality rates, or stock abundances. The quantitative effect of specific measures is generally poorly known, and local experiments do not extrapolate well to other water bodies because of variations in size, morphology, physical and chemical characteristics, exploitation patterns, and ecosystem characteristics. Assuming the net effect of a specific set of measures on the stock and fishery is adequately monitored, an adaptive management scheme may help quantify the appropriate measures (i.e., monitoring results can be used to tune management measures, establishing a short-term feedback in the management system: Figure 3, leftward pointing arrow).

In its initial definition (Walters and Hilborn 1976), adaptive management was introduced as active experimentation, with alternative (extreme) management regimes, to gain insight into biological processes. For management of eel stocks in scattered waters all over Europe, only a self-regulating feedback in establishing local management measures is required. Since the overall dynamics of the stock will not respond to local actions, local experimentation will not produce insights into global processes. Local adaptive management requires, apart from correct implementation and monitoring, that measures are strengthened or weakened over short time horizons when monitoring so indicates. Changes must be moderate, since big steps may overshoot the target, creating oscillations, or jitter, but steps that are too small or delayed may jeopardize a convincing effect. Applying a stricter rule for weakening restrictive measures rather than for strengthening them creates a reference zone rather than a reference point, ensuring greater stability in the feedback system and allowing for somewhat more severe initial measures.

Tit-for-Tat

A major advantage of a continuous feedback system is its ability to correct for external perturbations. Adverse (e.g., influx of cormorants) or favorable (e.g., habitat restoration) conditions automatically translate into appropriate management measures that suit the prevailing conditions, avoiding the need to assess subpopulations in each and every water body. If, in a comanagement arrangement, adaptive management uses a single measure that is easy to implement and to enforce (e.g., season closure times), while other potential measures (e.g., fishing effort, closed areas, etc.) are left to the fishery as voluntary options to improve their business, a conceptually very simple management model results. For an adaptive management scheme, voluntary options constitute external perturbations, to which the feedback will respond appropriately. For example, an overexploited state might trigger a shorter open season, while a voluntary reduction in fishing effort will result in a longer season after the stock has recovered to a sustainable level. This arrangement between government and fisheries is similar to the set-up known as tit-for-tat in game theory (Axelrod and Hamilton 1981), in which voluntary cooperation has been shown to be an optimal and stable strategy for both players.

Targets and Tools

Eels are fished in three well-separated *metiers*, which harvest glass, yellow, and silver eels, typically at high, medium, and low densities, respectively (Dekker 2003b). Eel populations are also affected by habitat losses due to dams and other causes. Rather than developing and establishing separate management schemes for each system in all countries (ICES 1997a), a small set of reference situations might be studied, that cover the major processes and concepts in typical settings. In my opinion, a half-dozen model systems would suffice to demonstrate management approaches for almost all eel fisheries in Europe, while the use of such a small set of common methodologies will greatly enhance the opportunities for evaluation at the global level.

Habitat Loss

Loss of habitat may have significantly contributed to the decline of the stock, but its restoration is probably not the most urgent issue in most of the distribution area. Although loss of (accessible) habitat might ultimately have contributed to the collapse in recruitment (through a stock–recruitment relation), cause and effect are definitely not in proportion: recruitment has switched to a much lower state, while habitat has only gradually declined. Recruitment has declined to 1–10% of former levels and requires only 1–10% of the former habitat until the stock–recruitment relation switches back to its abundant state. Restocking and (local) trap and transport programs have been shown to contribute to fishing yield. Where increased recruitment benefits production, available habitat cannot be the limiting factor.

In contrast to the rest of Europe, southwestern France and the Atlantic coasts of the Iberian Peninsula receive abundant recruitment (Dekker 2000b, 2003b), and here, the amount of accessible habitat is of paramount significance. Since the greatest loss of habitat (Moriarty and Dekker 1997) has occurred exactly in the areas of highest recruitment (Dekker 2003b), local restoration projects in the Bay of Biscay and the Iberian Peninsula might have significance for the global stock. However, unlike management of fisheries, in which long-term gains are balanced against short-term profits for a single stakeholder group, setting targets for habitat restoration requires Solomonian judgments among numerous users. In these cases, reference points cannot be objectively derived, and agreed targets express political willingness to invest in sustainable management. A pragmatic ranking of management options on the basis of their feasibility, as ICES (2002a) proposed (i.e., full use of existing habitat; restore habitat where easily done; full use of existing recruitment; restore historical habitat; restore pristine conditions), aids the Solomonian decision process but in no way relates to sustainable management targets or stock status.

Glass Eel Fisheries

It is generally assumed that glass eel fisheries exploit surplus recruitment that would have experienced intense density-dependent mortality if not harvested (Moriarty and Dekker 1997; ICES 2000). This assumes a limited carrying capacity of inland habitats. Management targets must relate to the abundance of the yellow eel rather than to mortality rates exerted by the fishery on the immigrating glass eel. The %SPR rule allows for a reduction of the stock below carrying capacity, but managing a glass eel fishery at 30% of the carrying capacity will yield only slightly more than managing at full carrying capacity. Restricting glass eel exploitation progressively, until no further rise in the abundance of the yellow eel occurs in the hinterland, would constitute a realistic target for an adaptive management scheme. Management of glass eel fisheries thus requires monitoring of yellow eels.

None of the conventional regulatory tools (effort restrictions, closed areas or seasons, gear controls) establish a constant fulfilment of the carrying capacity under time-varying glass eel immigration. After a substantial decline in recruitment, considerably lower fishing effort in the glass eel fishery will be required to keep yellow eel abundance at target level.

Yellow Eel Fisheries

Yellow eel fisheries in inland waters typically yield between 1.6 and 80 (max. 400) kg·ha^{-1}·yr^{-1} of water surface (Dekker 2003b). Since restocking generally has a positive effect on yield (Wickström 2001), the wide range in density and yield is primarily related to variation in abundance, and not to carrying capacity and production potential. Management targets related to potential abundance (in terms of biomass states) differ considerably from those related to the mortality exerted on the actual stock (in terms of mortality rates). Because of the very unequal distribution of recruitment among countries (Dekker 2003b), the choice between these two options requires political backup. However, the approach based on (potential) biomass may be impractical, since it requires disproportionate protection of the outskirts of the distribution area and time-varying restrictions on fisheries under temporal recruitment fluctuation. In particular, there is substantial evidence that current stock abundance is less than 30% of the historical level in most of the distribution area (Dekker 2003a). Application of the biomass approach dictates that all fisheries should now completely close until the stock recovers to at least 30% of the historical abundance level. In a mortality-based approach, however, fishing mortality should not exceed the 30% SPR level and might therefore need restrictions, but full and prolonged closures are not obligatory. Additionally, applying a mortality-rate approach brings the major part of eel fisheries management in line with that of most other exploited fish species.

Unlike glass eel fisheries, all conventional fisheries measures may apply, including restrictions on number of nets; closed areas or seasons; gear controls, including minimum mesh size; and minimum legal sizes. However, variations in minimum size preclude the use of mean length of the catch as a management target.

Silver Eel Fisheries and Hydropower Plants

During the descent of silver eels from inland waters to the sea, mortality occurs due to fisheries and to turbines in hydro dams. Control of these impacts is essential to sustaining adequate spawner escapement. Absolute numbers of silver eels killed by fisheries and by turbines are fairly easily determined, but the relative impact on the silver eel run is hard to assess because of the absence of direct information on survivors. Estimation of the total number of migrating silver eels, based on yellow eel production estimates or mark–recapture programs, is generally too laborious or too inaccurate for routine application of adaptive management. Therefore, anthropogenic silver eel mortality is probably best treated as a fixed mortality, which is severely restricted to protect the eel but which is not affected by an adaptive feedback process when monitoring indicates the stock is off target. Management measures (closed areas, closed season or periods, restricted number of nets—for fisheries as well as for hydropower generation) will be required to establish and maintain an acceptable mortality level.

Temporal and Spatial Scales of the Management Process

The stock and fisheries of the European eel have shown a prolonged and widespread decline for which the development of a stock-wide restoration plan has been advised, requiring 5–20 years to become effective because of the longevity of the species. In the foregoing, stock-wide management objectives have been discussed, essential concepts for a management strategy have been presented, and targets and tools for implementation at local levels have been proposed. The question arises whether these together constitute a viable management scheme (Figure 7).

Management of eel stocks and fisheries has been carried out for centuries at national and regional scales, aiming at various local objectives. Since the continent-wide decline in stock and recruitment, most fishermen and managers are painfully aware of the alarming state of the stock. Although views on causes and consequences vary, many stakeholders have expressed a willingness to cooperate in a stock-wide management network aiming at restoring the stock.

To implement the proposed framework, further development is required of proxy targets and of global monitoring and assessment programs. After a prolonged period of bottom-up data collection and status and trend assessment (ICES 1988–2004), the first priority is to strengthen the central level and impose objective-driven, top-down management. The development of (proxy) targets is a long-term process requiring strict coordination to acquire spatial consistency. As an alternative to stringent emergency measures (closure of fisheries), as proposed by ICES (2002b), one might consider initiating local management aiming at the final objective, using provisional (somewhat over-restrictive) proxy targets (i.e., initiate the local short-term management process immediately rather than installing an intermediate pan-European regime). This would also produce a start for a stock-wide monitoring and assessment program based on coordinated (but not necessarily standardized) local data series (c.f. Dekker 2002).

Sustainable management is a long-term aim that must be accomplished by time-varying local actions. The substitution of proxy

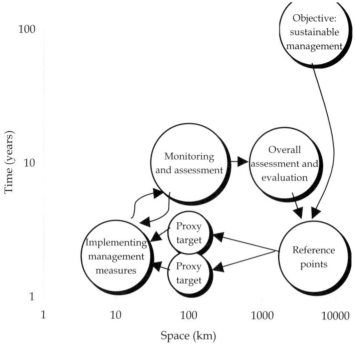

Figure 7. Temporal and spatial scale of the proposed framework for management of the stock and fisheries. Implementation of local management of eel stocks, together with the global development of reference points (and their proxies) related to global evaluation, constitute an overall framework establishing a sustainable management of the stock and fisheries. Arrows indicate the flow of concepts, information and data.

targets allows managers to implement local management schemes, including monitoring and adaptive feedback. Because of the need for adaptive feedback, the objectives will not be adequately met for several years, Additionally, the proxy targets might turn out to be poor representations of the ultimate goals, which would necessitate intensified initial monitoring and assessment. However, because of the longevity and widespread distribution of the eel, local management can be off target for a considerable period as long as local situations collectively add up to a global pattern that meets the global target at a temporal scale of an eel's lifetime. If systematic bias is avoided, considerable scattering in management achievements will not jeopardize the global management objective.

The decline in harvest began four decades ago. Subsequently, in the early 1980s, a failure in recruitment developed over a few years. But it was only in 1993 (EIFAC 1993) that the effect upon stock and fisheries was first considered and only in 1998 (ICES 1999) that adequate management advice was formulated. No substantial action has yet been undertaken to restore the stock (ICES 2004). In my view (Dekker 2004a), the recruitment failure was a consequence of the (spawning) stock decline. In turn, reduced recruitment now induces a further decline of the stock and thereby establishes negative feedback in the dynamics of the stock. Restoration measures will have to compensate for the ultimate causes of the decline and find an escape route out of the negative-feedback loop. The longer we wait, the smaller the remaining stock and the lower the odds for reversing the downward trends. Current harvest is about half that of 1980, when the recruitment failure began.

Reckoning the trend in spawning stock developed in parallel with the decline in harvest, management measures that fall short of doubling silver eel escapement will likely be in vain. Establishing a management scheme that might be sustainable in normal circumstances may not help the current depleted situation. Immediate and widespread restoration measures are required—the sooner the better.

From Plan to Action

In sum, the urgently required protection of the European eel can be achieved from a selection of existing fish stock management techniques. The following requirements flow from the conceptual framework presented in this paper:

- The establishment of national and international management systems in which the targets and tools are developed and then evaluated centrally while measures are implemented locally. This requires political decisions to establish national and international management structures (legal structure, implementation and control structures, and monitoring structures) and to develop an adequate communication structure between levels. Comanagement by local governments and fisheries organizations might improve the quality and speed of implementation at the lowest management level.
- The acceptance of an overall required protection level (e.g., the 30%SPR [or 50%SPR] norm). Because of the occurrence of strong density dependence in the central parts of the continental distribution area, the general %SPR concept needs to be augmented with an eel-specific, density-dependent equivalent.
- The translation of theoretical concepts into practical targets (i.e., selection of suitable proxy indicators and reference values corresponding to sustainable protection levels). Development of a universal technical (simulation) model might greatly assist this development.
- The implementation of protective measures, preferably based on technical advice (c.f. the bullet above), but, in any case, implemented several years before the most recent recruitment decline (in 2000) translates into a further decline of spawner production (i.e., before 2010).
- The development of a stock-wide monitoring and evaluation program in which local targets, protective measures, the actual state of the stock, and the match between targets, tools and attainment are recorded at local management levels and reported to higher management levels, culminating in an up-to-date assessment of the state of the whole stock and the protection achieved.

The available time for the development and implementation of an eel management framework might be in the order of only a few years (Dekker 2004a). Swift and parallel elaboration of each of these topics is therefore recommended.

A conceptual framework for restoring the declining European eel outlined above, achieving progress in management and restoration of the eel is not an impossible bargain (Feunteun 2002) but a matter of political decision.

Acknowledgments

In this article, I compiled many concepts; taken together, these constitute a coherent framework for protection of the eel, I hope. Most of the ideas are not brand new, but derived from recurrent discussions with many colleagues and fishermen. I am thankful for this stimulating and cooperative working environment. Wim van Densen and Charlotte Deerenberg gave valuable comments on the first draft of this text, while Don Jellyman and Håkan Wickström contributed considerably to the comprehensiveness and readability of the final text.

References

Ask, L., and L. Erichsen. 1976. Blankålsmärkningar vid svenska Östersjökusten 1941–1968. Meddn Havsfiskelaboratoriet Lysekil 199:1–117. (In Swedish).

Avise, J. C. 2003. Catadromous eels of the North Atlantic: a review of molecular genetic findings relevant to natural history, population structure, speciation and phylogeny. Pages 31–50 *in* K. Aida, K. Tsukamoto, and K. Yamauchi, editors. Eel biology. Springer-Verlag, Tokyo.

Axelrod, R., and W. D. Hamilton. 1981. The evolution of cooperation. Science 211:1390–1396.

Caddy, J. F., and R. Mahon. 1995. Reference points for fisheries management. FAO Fisheries Technical Paper N. 347.

Castonguay, M., P. V. Hodson, C. M. Couillard, M. J. Eckersley, J. D. Dutil, and G. Verreault. 1994a. Why is recruitment of the American eel, *Anguilla rostrata*, declining in the St. Lawrence River and Gulf? Canadian Journal of Fisheries and Aquatic Sciences 51:479–488.

Castonguay, M., P. V. Hodson, C. Moriarty, K. F. Drinkwater, and B. M. Jessop. 1994b. Is there a role of ocean environment in American and European eel decline? Fisheries Oceanography 3:197–203.

Dekker, W. 1998. Long-term trends in the glass eels immigrating at Den Oever, The Netherlands. Bulletin Français de la Pêche et de Pisciculture. Conseil Superieur de la Pêche, Paris (France) 349:199–214.

Dekker, W. 2000a. The fractal geometry of the European eel stock. ICES Journal of Marine Science 57:109–121.

Dekker, W. 2000b. A Procrustean assessment of the European eel stock. ICES Journal of Marine Science 57:938–947.

Dekker, W. 2000c. Impact of yellow eel exploitation on spawner production in Lake IJsselmeer, the Netherlands. Dana 12:17–32.

Dekker, W., editor. 2002. Monitoring of glass eel recruitment. Report C007/02-WD, Netherlands Institute of Fisheries Research, IJmuiden.

Dekker, W. 2003a. Did lack of spawners cause the collapse of the European eel, *Anguilla anguilla*? Fisheries Management and Ecology 10:365–376.

Dekker, W. 2003b. On the distribution of the European eel and its fisheries. Canadian Journal of Fisheries and Aquatic Sciences 60:787–799.

Dekker, W. 2003c. Status of the European eel stock and fisheries. Pages 237–254 *in* K. Aida, K. Tsukamoto, and K. Yamauchi, editors. Eel biology. Springer-Verlag, Tokyo.

Dekker, W. 2004a. Slipping through our hands-population dynamics of the European eel. Doctoral dissertation. University of Amsterdam, Amsterdam.

Dekker, W. 2004b. What caused the decline of Lake IJsselmeer eel stock since 1960? ICES Journal of Marine Science 61:394–404.

Desaunay, Y., and D. Guerault. 1997. Seasonal and long-term changes in biometrics of eel larvae: a possible relationship between recruitment variation and North Atlantic ecosystem productivity. Journal of Fish Biology 51:317–339.

EIFAC. 1985. Report of the 1985 meeting of the working party on eel and of the workshop on eel aquaculture. European Inland Fisheries Advisory Commission of the Food and Agriculture Organization of the United Nations, Rome, EIFAC/XIV/86/3.

EIFAC. 1993. Report of the 8th session of the Working Party on eel. EIFAC occasional paper 27. Food and Agriculture Organization of the United Nations, Rome.

FAO. 1995. Precautionary Approach to Fisheries. FAO Fisheries Technical Paper No. 350 part 1. FAO, Rome.

FAO. 2000. Food and Agriculture Organization. FAO yearbook. Fishery Statistics. Capture Production. Food and Agriculture Organization of the United Nations, Rome.

Feunteun, E. 2002. Management and restoration of European eel population (*Anguilla anguilla*): an impossible bargain. Ecological Engineering 18:575–591.

Francis, R., and D. J. Jellyman. 1999. Are mean size data adequate to monitor freshwater eel fisheries? Marine and Freshwater Research 50:355–366.

ICES (International Council for the Exploration of the Sea). 1976. First report of the working group on stocks of the European eel. ICES C.M. 1976/M:2.

ICES (International Council for the Exploration of the Sea). 1988. European Eel Assessment Working Group report, Nantes France, 22–24 September 1987. ICES C.M. 1988/Assess:7.

ICES (International Council for the Exploration of the Sea). 1997a. Report of the Tenth Session of the Joint Working Group on Eels. ICES C.M. 1997/M:1.

ICES (International Council for the Exploration of the Sea). 1997b. Report of the Study Group on the precautionary approach to fisheries management. ICES C.M. 1997/Assess:7.

ICES (International Council for the Exploration of the Sea). 1999. ICES cooperative research report N° 229, Report of the ICES Advisory Committee on Fisheries Management 1998:393–405.

ICES. 2000. International Council for the Exploration

of the Sea. Report of the EIFAC/ICES Working Group on Eels. ICES C.M. 2000/ACFM:6.

ICES. 2001a. International Council for the Exploration of the Sea. Report of the ICES/EIFAC Working Group on Eels. ICES C.M. 2001/ACFM:03.

ICES. 2001b. International Council for the Exploration of the Sea. ICES cooperative research report N° 246, Report of the ICES Advisory Committee on Fishery Management, 2001:357–366.

ICES. 2002a. International Council for the Exploration of the Sea. Report of the ICES/EIFAC Working Group on Eels. ICES C.M. 2002/ACFM:03.

ICES. 2002b. International Council for the Exploration of the Sea. ICES cooperative research report N° 255, Report of the ICES Advisory Committee on Fishery Management, 2002: 940–948.

ICES. 2004. International Council for the Exploration of the Sea. Report of the ICES/EIFAC Working Group on Eels. ICES C.M. 2004/ACFM:09.

Knights, B. 2003. A review of the possible impacts of long-term oceanic and climate changes and fishing mortality on recruitment of anguillid eels of the Northern Hemisphere. The Science of the Total Environment 310:237–244.

McCleave, J. D., P. J. Brickley, K. M. O'Brien, D. A. Kistner, M. W. Wong, M. Gallagher, and S. M. Watson. 1998. Do leptocephali of the European eel swim to reach continental waters? Status of the question. Journal of the Marine Biological Association of the United Kingdom 78:285–306.

Moriarty, C. 1986. Riverine migration of young eels *Anguilla anguilla* (L.). Fisheries Research 4:43–58.

Moriarty, C. 1997. The European eel fishery in 1993 and 1994: first Report of a working group funded by the European Union Concerted Action AIR A94–1939. Fisheries Bulletin (Dublin) 14.

Moriarty, C., and W. Dekker, editors 1997. Management of the European eel. Fisheries Bulletin (Dublin) 15.

Pedersen, M. I., and C. Dieperink. 2000. Fishing mortality on silver eels (*Anguilla anguilla* (L.)), in Denmark. Dana 12:77–82.

Pinkerton, E. W. 1994. Local fisheries co-management: a review of international experiences and their implications for salmon management in British Columbia. Canadian Journal of Fisheries and Aquatic Sciences 51:2363–2378.

Robinet, T., and E. Feunteun. 2002. Sublethal effects of exposure to chemical compounds: a cause for the decline in Atlantic eels? Ecotoxicology 11:265–277.

Sers B., E. Meyer, and O. Enderlein. 1993 Sammanställning av fiskmärkningar utförda under åren 1980–85. Swedish Board of Fisheries, Institute of Freshwater Research, Drottningholm, Sweden.

Tesch, F. W. 2003. The eel, 3rd edition. Blackwell Scientific Publications, Oxford, UK.

United Nations. 1983. The law of the sea. Official text of the United Nations Convention on the Law of the Sea with Annexes and Tables. United Nations, New York.

van Ginneken, V., and G. van den Thillart. 2000. Eel fat stores are enough to reach the Sargasso. Nature (London) 403:156–157.

Vøllestad, L. A. 1992. Geographic variation in age and length at metamorphosis of maturing European eel: environmental effects and phenotypic plasticity. Journal of Animal Ecology 61:41–48.

Walters, C. J., and R. Hilborn. 1976. Adaptive control of fishing systems. Journal of the Fisheries Research Board of Canada 33:145–159.

Westin, L. 1990. Orientation mechanisms in migrating European silver eel (*Anguilla anguilla*): temperature and olfaction. Marine Biology 106:175–179.

Wickström, H. 2001. Stocking as a sustainable measure to enhance eel populations. Stockholm University, Stockholm, Sweden.

Wirth, T., and L. Bernatchez. 2001. Genetic evidence against panmixia in the European eel. Nature (London) 409:1037–1040.

Present Status of the Japanese Eel: Resources and Recent Research

Katsumi Tsukamoto[1], Jun Aoyama, and Michael J. Miller

Ocean Research Institute, The University of Tokyo
1-15-1 Minamidai, Nakano, Tokyo, 164-8639 Japan

Abstract.—The Japanese eel, *Anguilla japonica*, is an important food fish in East Asia, and catches of glass eels and of eels in freshwater appear to have declined dramatically in recent decades, causing increasing concern for the health of wild stocks. During that time, research efforts to understand its biology have progressed considerably. The spawning area was successfully outlined to the west of the Mariana Islands in 1991, and other research suggests that their recruitment success may be related to El Niño events, which appear to affect the transfer of leptocephali from the north equatorial current into the Kuroshio Current. Otolith microstructure and microchemistry studies have revealed various aspects of their early life history that relate to their oceanic larval migration. The discovery of sea eels that live in marine habitats without entering freshwater may change the common understanding of freshwater eel ecology and affect management plans. Most genetic studies suggest that the Japanese eel is composed of a single panmictic population throughout East Asia. Therefore, international management is needed among the countries of China, Taiwan, Korea, and Japan, where glass eels recruit from a common stock and are used extensively for aquaculture.

Introduction

In recent years, there has been growing concern about declining stocks of various species of anguillid eels around the world, including the commercially important Japanese eel, *Anguilla japonica* (Dekker et al. 2003). The Japanese eel is an extremely important food fish in Japan and is also eaten in other East Asian countries. This species is reared extensively from wild-caught glass eels by an aquaculture industry in four different countries, and after some bad recruitment seasons in recent years, such as in 1997 and 2005, concern for the health of the species' resources has increased considerably. Although recruitment has been better in subsequent years, the extent of the decline is not well known, because there are relatively few reports on this subject (Tatsukawa 2003).

One problem with quantifying the health of stocks of this species is that there has been little research on its freshwater phase even though it is extensively harvested as a food fish and as stock for aquaculture when it enters freshwater rivers upon recruitment. To help address this problem, some recent research projects have been carried out in Japan to provide basic knowledge about sex ratio, size, age, and growth. These studies have found that growth rates of eels using both freshwater and estuarine or coastal habitats are higher than those observed in other

[1] Corresponding author: ktpc@ori.u-tokyo.ac.jp

temperate anguillid species (Tzeng et al. 2003; Anonymous 2004; Kotake et al. 2005, in press; Yokouchi 2005). Other studies on Japanese eels have examined their homing behavior (Aoyama et al. 2002), morphology of their burrows in soft mud sediments (Aoyama et al. 2005) and habitat use (Shiao et al. 2003), and various aspects of silver eel ecology including their gonadal morphology (Han et al. 2003a; Utoh et al. 2004), silvering stages (Okamura et al. 2007), salinity preference (Han et al. 2003a), and spawning behavior in captivity (Dou et al. 2007).

However, until recently most researchers have worked on ecological or physiological subjects instead of focusing on the freshwater ecology of the Japanese eel, with many studies related to artificial spawning and production of glass eels (see Aida et al. 2003), which has recently succeeded (Tanaka 2003; Kagawa et al. 2005). Ecological researchers have focused more on other subjects, such as understanding the various aspects of migration and marine life history.

As a result, knowledge of the ecology of the Japanese eel has increased remarkably in the past 15 years because of a considerable number of studies, including some on the much less studied species of tropical eels. Studies have dealt with anguillid taxonomy (Watanabe 2003, 2004, 2005), phylogeny (e.g., Tsukamoto and Aoyama 1998; Aoyama et al. 2001; Lin et al. 2001), and population structure (e.g., Sang et al. 1994; Chan et al. 1997; Ishikawa 1998; Ishikawa et al. 2001a; Tseng et al. 2006). Other studies have focused on early life history (e.g., Tsukamoto 1990; Tsukamoto and Umezawa 1990; Otake et al. 1994; Cheng and Tzeng 1996; Arai et al. 1997, 2001a, 2001b, 2002; Sugeha et al. 2001; Dou et al. 2003; Kuroki et al. 2005, 2006a,b, 2007; Sasai et al. 2007), adult migration (Kuo et al. 1996; Aoyama et al. 1999a, 2002; Sasai et al. 2001; Okamura et al. 2002), larval distribution (e.g., Tsukamoto 1992; Aoyama et al. 1999b, 2003, In press; Ishikawa et al. 2001b; Miller et al. 2002), larval transportation (Kimura et al. 1994, 1999), and oceanic glass eels (Otake et al. 2006).

Much recent research is reviewed in the book *Eel Biology*, which covers all major areas of basic eel biology but focuses on the biology of the Japanese eel and other anguillid species rather than resource management (Aida et al. 2003).

However, despite all the ecologically related research, compared with the two Atlantic species—the European eel *A. anguilla*, and the American eel *A. rostrata*—basic knowledge of the resources and the freshwater phase of the Japanese eel is still lacking. Furthermore, wild freshwater eel fisheries for this species provide less than 1% of total eel consumption, with the remainder coming from aquaculture (Tatsukawa 2003). However, to restore healthy wild populations of the Japanese eel and to maintain stable use of the eel resource, ecological research on the freshwater phase, as well as the marine phase, will be indispensable.

In this paper, we describe the general status of research on the Japanese eel and its resources in east Asia and review the research on some of the factors affecting population fluctuations in order to help build a better understanding of the causes of the declines of this important commercial species.

Resources of the Japanese eel

Eel Industry in East Asia

One of the unique characteristics of the Japanese eel resource is that glass eels recruit to the four widely separated East Asian countries of Taiwan, Japan, China, and Korea, where they are used for aquaculture. These glass eels are extensively fished and reared in aquaculture facilities in each country, but in recent years, a much greater proportion of annual aquaculture production is occurring in China (Figure 1). China still imports Euro-

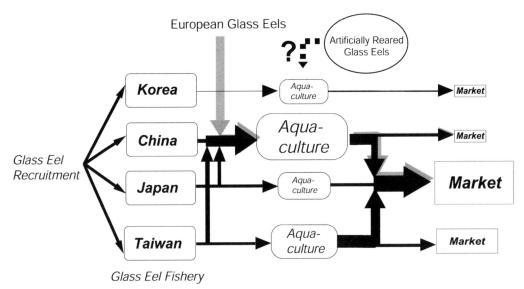

Figure 1. A diagrammatic representation of the use and international trade of the Japanese eel, *A. japonica*, in East Asia, showing the countries where glass eels recruit, their various general pathways into the aquaculture industry, and the pathways of the products to the market. Import and use of the European eel, *A. anguilla*, in some countries is shown with shaded arrows. Relative thickness of the arrows and sizes of the components reflect the general proportions of the quantity of glass eels or eel products in the industry.

pean glass eels to supplement their eel production, most of which is sold in Japan. However, American glass eels have been found to be less successful for aquaculture production than the Japanese and European eels, and are not used to any great extent in recent years in China or Japan.

Once eels reach marketable size, they are sold to eel traders and distributed to commercial outlets. Although production of eels in Japan has been decreasing, Japan is still the biggest consumer of cultured eels, now up to about 130,000 metric tons (mt) per year. Grilled eel, or *kabayaki*, is popular in restaurants and is also sold in supermarkets year-round in Japan. However, the less expensive *kabayaki* is imported from other East Asian countries, and mtDNA analysis has shown that about 70% of this is European eel (T. Wakao, unpublished data). Introduced European eels also have been found living in the wild in Japan after they escaped or were released (Miyai et al. 2004; Okamura et al., In press).

Research efforts have been underway for years to artificially spawn and rear eel larvae so that the aquaculture industry will not have to rely on wild-caught glass eels. Because of the unusual physiology and feeding biology of leptocephalus larvae, progress has been quite slow and difficult. However, leptocephali have recently been reared through metamorphosis into glass eels and even into yellow eels in small numbers (Tanaka 2003; Kagawa et al. 2005), so there is still hope for revolutionizing the eel industry through artificial production.

Decline in Catches

Statistics about the resources of the Japanese eel are not widely available for many parts of its range, but catches appear to be decreasing in Japan. Catches of yellow and silver

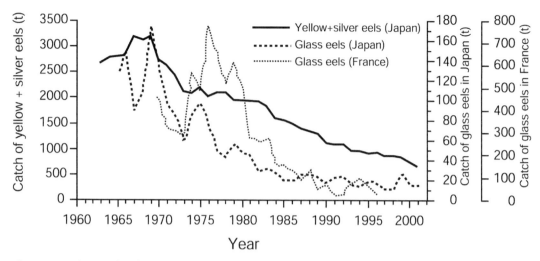

Figure 2. Historical eel catches in Japan and France, showing the catches of yellow and silver eels and glass eels of the Japanese eel in Japan, and catches of glass eels of the European eel at the estuary of the Loire River in France. Data for the Japanese eel were obtained from the Japan Fisheries Agency (Anonymous 2004).

eels in Japanese freshwater habitats decreased continuously from 1969 (3,194 mt) through 2001 (ca 677 mt) (Figure 2). Catches of glass eels in Japanese estuaries also decreased from a peak of 174 mt in 1969 to 14 mt in 2001. Other evidence, such as microsatellite analysis of temporal genetic variation of the Japanese eel, suggests that effective population size appears to be declining (Tseng et al. 2003a).

A similar decreasing trend has been seen for the glass eel fishery in France, which peaked in 1976 (770 mt) and then decreased to only 1% of that at present (Figure 2). This appears to reflect a general decrease in recruitment of the European eel since about 1976 (Dekker 2003), and similar declines have been observed for the American eel (Casselman 2003). The exact timing of the decrease of the Japanese eel in the Pacific seems to have been different from that of the European eel in the Atlantic. In addition, the magnitude of the resources was different: catches of European glass eels in France were approximately six times larger than those of Japanese eels. This suggests that mechanisms for population fluctuation between these species may be different or may be the same but over different time periods; thus, we need to determine the fluctuation mechanisms for each species.

Population Estimates

An important aspect to better understanding the population fluctuations of a heavily exploited species such as the Japanese eel is to begin to build a model for estimating overall population size. This is very difficult to do for the Japanese eel because there is relatively little quantitative data on regional stocks or on mortality of the various life history stages. However, to illustrate the types of data needed to build such a model, the tentative population model of Tsukamoto and Otake (1994) can be useful. This model shows the connectivity of the different stages of the total life history of the species, so if changes at one stage are thought to occur, the effects on the other stages can be predicted.

Based on an estimated 72 mt of glass eel catches by all East Asian countries in the 1994 fishing season, we roughly estimated the number of silver eels that successfully leave

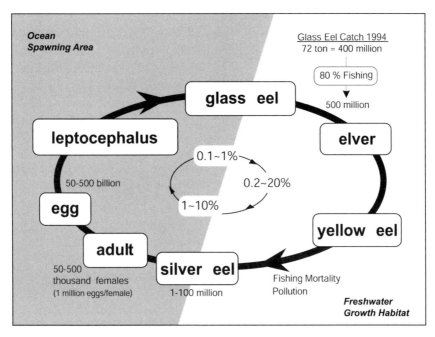

Figure 3. Population estimates for some developmental stages in the catadromous life history of the Japanese eel and estimates of mortality rates. Values in the center of the plot are possible survival rates during larval migration and the yellow and silver eel stages.

their growth habitats in East Asia (spawner escapement) and begin their migration to the spawning area (Figure 3, Tsukamoto and Otake 1994). Seventy-two mt is equivalent to about 400 million glass eels (5,500 fish/kg), so at least 500 million glass eels should have recruited to the estuaries of East Asia because of heavy exploitation of glass eels at estuaries. More than 80% of glass eel recruitment may be caught at estuaries in Japan (Tsukamoto and Otake 1994), and a similar estimate of 85% has been made for exploitation of glass eels in Europe (Dekker 2003). Assuming a 0.1% to 1.0% survival rate during larval migration from the spawning area to estuaries, 50 to 500 billion eggs should have been spawned; this number is equivalent to about 50,000 to 500,000 females (at 1 million eggs per female). Thus, silver eels that escape from growth habitats in East Asia were estimated to be 1 million to 100 million by assuming a roughly 1:1 sex ratio and a 1% to 10% survival rate during the spawning migration. This estimation may be useful as a starting point for further detailed population estimates and a quantitative ecological approach to mortality rates during each developmental stage, which have so far only been hypothesized.

Possible Reasons for Decline

When discussing population fluctuations, it is helpful to separate resource trends into three different time scales: short-, mid-, and long-term. Short-term changes are annual to several-year variations in recruitment caused by changes of climate or ocean-atmosphere events such as El Niño, while mid-term changes occur over 10 to hundreds of years and include events such as regime shifts or global warming. Long-term changes refer to an extremely long fluctuation, including extinction caused by long geological events such as glacial cycles or continental drift.

Fluctuations shown in most data sets (Figure 2) are likely a mixture of the first two time-scale changes due to the relatively short time periods for which data are available.

Three major factors are possible causes for the population decrease of the Japanese eel: (1) overfishing, (2) environmental destruction in freshwater habitats, and (3) environmental fluctuations in oceanic habitats. The first and second factors are derived from anthropogenic effects. Overfishing is obviously a major factor for population decrease, since most of the glass eels each year that have recruited to estuaries in East Asia (60–80% or more) have been caught before growing into yellow eels (e.g., Tzeng 1984). Human impacts such as pollution and construction of river channelization structures and dams have drastically decreased freshwater habitat for eels (Tatsukawa 2003), as well as reducing prey in the affected river communities. These human impacts may cause short- or mid-term fluctuations in eel resources. The third type of possible causes are short- or mid-term environmental fluctuations in the ocean, which could include changes in food available to the leptocephali or changes in oceanographic conditions affecting the transport of leptocephali to their recruitment areas (Kimura et al. 2001; Knights 2003; Friedland 2007), as is discussed later.

Factors Affecting Population Fluctuation

Spawning Area

The offshore spawning area of freshwater eels is both the end and the beginning of their life cycle, and thus the location and number of spawning areas of a species has a significant influence on their recruitment success, population fluctuations, and population structure. Recently, the spawning area of the Japanese eel has been identified as a relatively small area in the North Equatorial Current to the west of Guam (Figure 4; Tsukamoto 1992, 2006; Tsukamoto et al. 2003; Ishikawa et al. 2001b). This is in contrast to the vast region previously estimated for the spawning area of Atlantic eels in the Sargasso Sea, which spreads over more than one million square km (about 20 to 30°N, 48 to 79°W; McCleave et al. 1987), and is also in contrast to the local spawning areas of some tropical anguillids in the Indonesian Seas region (Aoyama et al. 2003).

The spawning area of the Japanese eel in the North Equatorial Current appears to be south of a salinity front in the region, but it is also near three seamounts in the West Mariana Ridge (15°N, 142 to 143°E), which, based on the distribution of leptocephali, have been hypothesized to be associated with the spawning area (Figure 4, seamount hypothesis; Tsukamoto et al. 2003). These seamounts are located about 200 km northwest of the Mariana Islands (Guam) along the northern margin of the unbroken westward flow of the north equatorial current and may serve as landmarks by providing olfactory or geomagnetic cues to migrating eels that help define the spawning area.

Although tiny preleptocephali 4–6 mm TL have been collected recently (Tsukamoto 2006), for a more precise determination of the spawning site, we need to collect eggs or observe adults spawning. This challenge will be helped by the new moon hypothesis, which resulted from otolith analyses of leptocephali (Tsukamoto 1996; Tsukamoto et al. 2003). These data indicate that the Japanese eel does not spawn continuously throughout the long spawning season from April to November (Tsukamoto 1990), but may spawn periodically once a month during the new moon. This knowledge will allow sampling for eggs and spawning eels to be more concentrated during new moon periods.

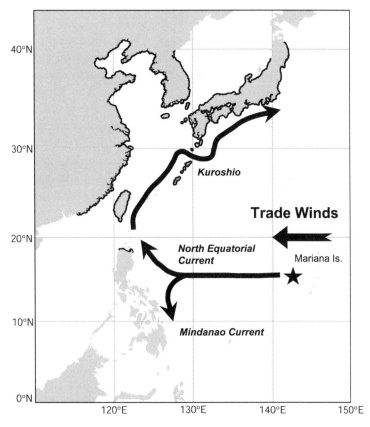

Figure 4. Estimated spawning area of the Japanese eel (closed star), and the major current systems affecting larval transport. Thick black lines on the coastlines of East Asia show the range of the Japanese eel.

Oceanographic Conditions

The success of the larval migration of Japanese eel leptocephali from their offshore spawning area to their growth habitats in East Asia may be one of the key factors affecting yearly recruitment. They must move westward and metamorphose into glass eels in the Kuroshio Current system before recruiting to coastal waters and estuaries (Figure 4). In typical years, many leptocephali may be found within a strong current zone on the southern side of an east-to-west salinity front (34.6 psu) that is normally present at the northern margin of the North Equatorial Current at about 16°N (Kimura et al. 1994, 2001), because in 1991, the largest catches of leptocephali were made just south of this front (Tsukamoto 1992).

This transport of leptocephali along the northern margin of the North Equatorial Current may be important in the recruitment success of leptocephali, because they must avoid southward transport into the Mindanao Current, which would cause recruitment failure (Kimura et al. 1994). At the end of their larval migration, the leptocephali must become entrained into the northward-flowing branch that flows into the Kuroshio Current in the bifurcation zone of the North Equatorial Current (Figure 4), around 127°E (Toole et al. 1990). This is particularly important because the North Equatorial Current also has a southward-flowing branch that becomes the Mindanao Current (Lukas et al. 1991).

One mechanism that has been proposed to help ensure that leptocephali entrain into the northward flow is that when they reach a certain large size as they approach the bifurcation zone, they develop a diel vertical migration into the Ekman layer. This increased northward Ekman transport is driven by the trade winds and has been proposed to be a key factor facilitating the transfer of leptocephali from the North Equatorial Current into the Kuroshio for successful recruitment to East Asia (Kimura et al. 1994). Therefore, disruptions in the trade winds could result in southward transport, or excessive northward Ekman transport might result in entrainment into the eddy of the Kuroshio countercurrent at about 20 to 24°N, which could also result in unsuccessful transport to East Asia.

Other environmental factors such as ENSO events (El Niño) have also been proposed as affecting the transport of Japanese eel leptocephali. The latitude of the westward flow south of the salinity front appears to shift among years and be influenced by El Niño, which may also affect recruitment of glass eels to East Asia (Kimura et al. 2001; Kimura 2003; Kimura and Tsukamoto 2006). This type of disruption would be caused by a southward shift of the salinity front, which could cause a greater proportion of leptocephali to be entrained into the southward flow of the Mindanao Current. This hypothesis has been supported by a correlation between years with poor glass eel recruitment and El Niño years as expressed by the Southern Oscillation Index (Kimura et al. 2001). Recently the first direct evidence that some leptocephali are transported southward by the Mindanao Current has been obtained as a result of the collection of a 42.8 mm Japanese eel leptocephalus in the Celebes Sea, which has an inflow of water from the Mindanao current (Miller et al., unpublished manuscript).

Sea Eels

New information about habitat use by species such as the Japanese eel has indicated that the freshwater environment may not be the only growth habitat that is important for the health of eel populations. Although freshwater eels have been generally believed to migrate upstream after recruitment to estuaries, recent studies based on otolith strontium and calcium ratios have shown that in some areas, many individuals remain in estuaries or even in marine coastal areas. This discovery of non-catadromous individuals (residents), termed "sea eels," which spend all their life in marine habitat without entering freshwater (Tsukamoto et al. 1998; Tsukamoto and Arai 2001), in addition to the normal catadromous individuals ("river eels"), has shown that there is considerable plasticity in the migratory behavior of freshwater eels (Daverat et al. 2006). An intermediate type of migratory pattern used by eels that inhabit estuaries or move between estuarine and freshwater habitats also has been found, and individuals exhibiting this pattern were termed "estuarine eels" (Tsukamoto and Arai 2001).

Factors affecting the occurrence of eels that don't move into freshwater are not known, but the phenomenon appears to be quite widespread among temperate eels in some areas. The occurrence of sea eels and estuarine eels in temperate areas has been reported in the Japanese eel (Tsukamoto et al. 1998; Tsukamoto and Arai 2001; Tzeng et al. 2002, 2003; Kotake et al. 2003, 2005), European eel (Tsukamoto et al. 1998; Tzeng et al. 2000; Daverat et al. 2006), the American eel (Jessop et al. 2002, 2004), and New Zealand eels (Arai et al. 2004). However, the distribution of the three types of migratory patterns may vary among localities and species, because a latitudinal cline has been suggested in the occurrence of sea eels along the Japanese coast (Figure 5, Kotake 2003). Tsukamoto and Arai (2001) hypothesized that more sea eels would occur in species that are distributed at higher latitudes, where food is more available in the marine environment than in the nutrient-poor stream and small river freshwater habitats, and proposed that sea eels may be an eco-phenotype that uses an ancient type of behavior of anguillid eels. As a mirror image to sea eels of the catadromous freshwater eels, anadromous salmonids have river residents or land-locked populations (Tsukamoto et al. 2002).

These new findings on the presence of sea eels may be important enough for species such as the Japanese eel that the common understanding of their life histories may change and stock management plans would be affected. Some indication of this was found recently when the proportion of river eels among 500 silver eels collected around the Japanese coast as they were migrating back to their spawning area was estimated as only 16% (Kotake 2003). This proportion was unexpectedly small, suggesting that the contribution to the next generation by river eels may be smaller than by other migratory types in some areas of Japan. It is unclear whether this is a typical historical proportion for some areas of Japan or if recent human impacts in

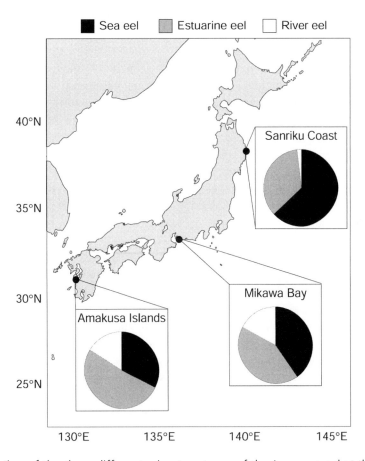

Figure 5. Proportion of the three different migratory types of the Japanese eel at three sampling sites along the Japanese coast. Each type of eel was categorized as being either a sea eel, an estuarine eel, or a river eel, based on otolith Sr:Ca ratios (sample sizes: Amakusa Islands, 37; Mikawa Bay, 199; and Sanriku Coast, 47).

freshwater and estuarine habitats have caused the low number of river eels in these samples. Similar detailed studies are urgently needed in other East Asian coastal waters around Taiwan, China, and Korea to estimate the overall proportion of migratory types in the Japanese eel.

Population Structure

Knowledge about the population structure of anguillid eels is also important for better management of eel resources. The exact nature of the population structure of temperate species such as Japanese and Atlantic eels has been the subject of considerable debate because of their long-distance spawning migrations and unique catadromous life histories (see Avise 2003). For the Japanese eel, mtDNA analysis showed no geographic difference in genetic composition of individuals from all over their range in East Asia, suggesting that it has a panmictic population structure (Sang et al. 1994; Ishikawa et al. 2001a). However, Chan et al. (1997) reported that an allozyme analysis indicated a geographic cline in allele frequency at some loci in glass eels and suggested some genetic heterogeneity among populations. A similar discrepancy was observed in the American eel when an mtDNA analysis suggested a single population (Avise et al. 1986), while a geographic cline was found at a few allozyme loci (Williams et al. 1973; Koehn and Williams 1978). It was assumed that these geographic clines detected by allozyme analysis might be derived from natural selection within the single generation after hatching (Nishida 2001).

New techniques using nuclear DNA markers of microsatellite loci have also found variable results in population studies of anguillid eels. For example, the Wirth and Bernatchez (2001) study on the European eel and a study using microsatellite loci suggested the presence of genetic heterogeneity over the range of the Japanese eel (Tseng et al. 2003b, 2006, 2009, this volume). However, a more extensive study of the European eel that used the same techniques found no evidence of population structure (Dannewitz et al. 2005), and no evidence of population structure was found recently using microsatellite loci in the American eel (Wirth and Bernatchez 2003). These recent microsatellite studies may need to be interpreted with caution, however, because other research on Atlantic eels has suggested that the molecular evolutionary nature of these microsatellite loci may not always be easy to interpret (Mank and Avise 2003).

Regardless of the significance of various studies on population structure of anguillid eels, all found remarkably low levels of genetic variation compared with studies of other marine species (Avise 2003). This may be due in part to the influence of other factors such as single spawning areas, ocean current variability, or the effect of variable growth rates during the leptocephalus stage on regulating the timing of metamorphosis (Kuroki et al. 2006a), which, in the case of the Japanese eel, could determine the timing of detrainment from the Kuroshio and therefore the region of recruitment in East Asia (Tsukamoto and Umezawa 1990).

Future Perspectives

It is likely that overfishing and habitat loss have had a major role in the overall decline of stocks of the Japanese eel, but recent research is beginning to suggest that the important factors that affect short-term population fluctuations may be hidden in the ocean. In fact, this may be more so for the Japanese eel than for most other anguillid species because of the precarious position of its spawning area, which is within a current that bifurcates into two completely different directions. Of course, we cannot manipulate events that occur far offshore or longer-term ocean-atmosphere changes, but building a greater understanding of the mechanisms of population fluctuation is important for the conservation of this species even if they are beyond our control. In contrast, human impacts such as overfishing of glass and silver eels and destruction of river environments can be reduced to conserve eel resources, and the potential influence of these factors urgently needs to be evaluated in East Asia.

For conservation of Japanese eels, attention also must be focused on international trade of the species (Figure 1), and international management plans need to be developed in cooperation with all four East Asian countries. Five years ago, we established a nongovernmental organization called the East Asia Eel Consortium (EASEC), in which scientists and eel traders of the four East Asian countries discuss issues related to the Japanese eel and work toward the conservation and sustainable use of this shared resource. These and other recent efforts indicate the beginning of what we hope will be a new era of research on the resources of the Japanese eel that can bring together knowledge from both science and industry to ensure the survival of this remarkable fish.

References

Aida, K., K. Tsukamoto, and K. Yamauchi, editors. 2003. Eel biology. Springer Verlag, Tokyo.

Anonymous. 2004. Five year research summary for the eel resource conservation project. Japan Fisheries Agency, Tokyo.

Aoyama, J., K. Hissmann, T. Yoshinaga, S. Sasai, T. Uto, and H. Ueda. 1999a. Swimming depth of migrating silver eels *Anguilla japonica* released at seamounts of the West Mariana Ridge, their estimated spawning sites. Marine Ecology Progress Series 186:265–269.

Aoyama, J., N. Mochioka, T. Otake, S. Ishikawa, Y. Kawakami, P. H. J. Castle, M. Nishida, and K. Tsukamoto. 1999b. Distribution and dispersal of anguillid leptocephali in the western Pacific Ocean revealed by molecular analysis. Marine Ecology Progress Series 188:193–200.

Aoyama, J., M. Nishida, and K. Tsukamoto 2001 Molecular phylogeny and evolution of the freshwater eel, genus *Anguilla*. Molecular Phylogeny and Evolution 20:450–459.

Aoyama, J., S. Sasai, M. J. Miller, A. Shinoda, A. Nakamura, K. Kawazu, and K. Tsukamoto. 2002. A preliminary study of the movements of yellow and silver eels, *Anguilla japonica*, in the estuary of the Fukui River, Japan, as revealed by acoustic tracking. Hydrobiologia 470:31–36.

Aoyama, J., A. Shinoda, S. Sasai, M. J. Miller, and K. Tsukamoto. 2005. First observations of the burrows of the Japanese eel, *Anguilla japonica*. Journal of Fish Biology 67:1534–1543.

Aoyama, J., S. Wouthuyzen, M. J. Miller, T. Inagaki, and K. Tsukamoto. 2003. Short-distance spawning migration of tropical freshwater eels. Biological Bulletin 204: 104–108.

Aoyama J., S. Wouthuyzen, M. J. Miller, Y. Minegishi, G. Minagawa, M. Kuroki, S. R. Suharti, T. Kawakami, T. Inagaki, K. O. Sumardiharga, and K. Tsukamoto. In press. Distribution of leptocephali of the freshwater eels, genus *Anguilla*, in the waters off west Sumatra in the Indian Ocean. Environmental Biology of Fishes.

Arai, T., J. Aoyama, S. Ishikawa, M. J. Miller, T. Otake, T. Inagaki, and K. Tsukamoto. 2001b. Early life history of tropical *Anguilla* leptocephali in the western Pacific Ocean. Marine Biology 138:887–895.

Arai, T., A. Kotake, P.M. Lokman, M.J. Miller, and K. Tsukamoto. 2004. Evidence of different habitat use by New Zealand freshwater eels *Anguilla australis* and *A. dieffenbachii*, as revealed by otolith microchemistry. Marine Ecology Progress Series 266:213–225.

Arai, T., D. Limbong, T. Otake, and K. Tsukamoto. 2001a. Recruitment mechanisms of tropical eels *Anguilla* spp. and implications for the evolution of oceanic migration in the genus *Anguilla*. Marine Ecology Progress Series 216:253–264.

Arai, T., M. Marui, M. J. Miller, and K. Tsukamoto. 2002. Growth history and inshore migration of the tropical eel, *Anguilla marmorata*, in the Pacific. Marine Biology 140:309–316.

Arai, T., T. Otake, and K. Tsukamoto. 1997. Drastic changes in otolith microstructure and microchemistry accompanying the onset of metamorphosis in the Japanese eel *Anguilla japonica*. Marine Ecology Progress Series 161:17–22.

Avise, J. C. 2003. Catadromous eels of the North Atlantic: a review of molecular genetic finding relevant to natural history, population structure, speciation, and phylogeny. Pages 31–48 *in* K. Aida, K. Tsukamoto, and K. Yamauchi, editors. Eel biology. Springer Verlag, Tokyo.

Avise, J. C., G. S. Helfman, N. C. Saunders, and L. S. Hales. 1986. Mitochondrial DNA differentiation in North Atlantic eels: population genetic consequences of an unusual life history pattern. Proceedings of the National Academy of Science USA 83:4350–4354.

Casselman, J. M. 2003. Dynamics of resources of the American eel, *Anguilla rostrata*: declining abundance in the 1990s. Paged 255–274 *in* K. Aida, K. Tsukamoto, K. Yamauchi, editors. Eel biology. Springer-Verlag, Tokyo.

Chan, I. K. K., D. K. O. Chan, S. C. Lee, and K. Tsukamoto. 1997. Genetic variability of the Japanese eel *Anguilla japonica* (Temminck & Schlegel) related to latitude. Ecology of Freshwater Fish 6:45–49.

Cheng, P. A., and W. N. Tzeng. 1996. Timing of metamorphosis and estuarine arrival across the dispersal range of the Japanese eel *Anguilla japonica*. Marine Ecology Progress Series 131:87–96.

Dannewitz, J., G. E. Maes, L. Johansson, H. Wickström, F. A. M. Volckaert, and T. Järvi. 2005. Panmixia in the European eel: a matter of time. Proceedings of the Royal Society of London B 272:1129–1137.

Daverat F, K. E. Limburg, I. Thibault, J. C. Shiao, J. J. Dodson, F. Caron, W. N. Tzeng, Y. Iizuka, and H. Wickström. 2006. Phenotypic plasticity of habitat use by three temperate eel species, *Anguilla anguilla*, *A. japonica* and *A. rostrata*. Marine Ecology Progress Series 308:231–241.

Dekker, W. 2003. Status of the European eel stock and fisheries. Pages 237–254 *in* K. Aida, K. Tsukamoto, and K. Yamauchi, editors. Eel biology. Springer Verlag, Tokyo.

Dekker, W., J. M. Casselman, D. K. Cairns, K. Tsukamoto, D. Jellyman, and H. Lickers. 2003. Worldwide decline of eel resources necessitates immediate action. Quebec Declaration of Concern. Fisheries 28(12):28–30.

Dou, S., M. J. Miller, and K. Tsukamoto. 2003. Growth, pigmentation and activity of juvenile Japanese eels in relation to temperature and fish size. Journal of Fish Biology 63:1–14.

Dou S. Z., Y. Yamada, A. Okamura, S. Tanaka, A. Shinoda, and K. Tsukamoto. 2007. Observations on the spawning behavior of artificially matured Japanese eels *Anguilla japonica* in captivity. Aquaculture 266:117–129.

Friedland, K. D., M. J. Miller, and B. Knights. 2007. Oceanic changes in the Sargasso Sea and declines in recruitment of the European eel. ICES Journal of Marine Science 64:519–530.

Han Y. S., I. C. Liao, Y. S. Huang, J. T. He, C. W. Chang, and W. N. Tzeng. 2003a. Synchronous changes of morphology and gonadal development of silvering Japanese eel *Anguilla japonica*. Aquaculture 219:783–796

Han, Y. S., J. Y. L Yu, I. C. Liao, and W. N. Tzeng. 2003b. Salinity preference of silvering Japanese eel *Anguilla japonica*: evidence from pituitary prolactin mRNA levels and otolith Sr:Ca ratios. Marine Ecology Progress Series 259:253–261.

Ishikawa, S. 1998. Molecular study on the population structure of *Anguilla marmorata*. Doctoral dissertation. University of Tokyo, Tokyo.

Ishikawa, S., J. Aoyama, K. Tsukamoto, and M. Nishida. 2001a. Population structure of the Japanese eel *Anguilla japonica* as examined by mitochondrial DNA sequencing. Fisheries Science 67:246–253.

Ishikawa, S., K. Suzuki, T. Inagaki, S. Watanabe, Y. Kimura, A. Okamura, T. Otake, N. Mochioka, Y. Suzuki, H. Hasumoto, M. Oya, M. J. Miller, T. W. Lee, H. Fricke, and K. Tsukamoto. 2001b. Spawning time and place of the Japanese eel, *Anguilla japonica*, in the North Equatorial Current of the western North Pacific Ocean Fisheries Science 67:1097–1103.

Jessop, B. M., J. C. Shiao, Y. Iizuka, and W. N. Tzeng. 2002. Migratory behaviour and habitat use by American eels *Anguilla rostrata* as revealed by otolith microchemistry. Marine Ecology Progress Series 233:217–229.

Jessop, B. M., J. C. Shiao, Y. Iizuka, and W. N. Tzeng. 2004. Variation in the annual growth, by sex and migration history, of silver American eels *Anguilla rostrata*. Marine Ecology Progress Series 272:231–244.

Kagawa, H., H. Tanaka, H. Ohta, T. Unuma, and K. Nomura. 2005. The first success of glass eel production in the world: basic biology on fish reproduction advances new applied technology in aquaculture. Fish Physiology and Biochemistry 31:193–199.

Kimura, S. 2003. Larval transport of the Japanese eel. Pages 169–179 *in* K. Aida, K. Tsukamoto, and K. Yamauchi, editors, Eel biology. Springer Verlag, Tokyo.

Kimura, S., and K. Tsukamoto. 2006. The salinity front in the North Equatorial Current: A landmark for the spawning migration of the Japanese eel (*Anguilla japonica*) related to the stock recruitment. Deep-Sea Research II 53:315–325.

Kimura, S., K. Doos, and A. C. Coward. 1999. Numerical simulation to resolve the issue of downstream migration of the Japanese eel. Marine Ecology Progress Series 186:303–306.

Kimura, S., T. Inoue, and T. Sugimoto. 2001. Fluctuation in the distribution of low-salinity water in the north equatorial current and its effect on the larval transport of the Japanese eel. Fisheries Oceanography 10:51–60.

Kimura, S., K. Tsukamoto, and T. Sugimoto. 1994. A model for the larval migration of the Japanese eel: roles of the trade winds and salinity front. Marine Biology 119:185–190.

Knights, B. 2003. A review of the possible impacts of long-term oceanic and climate changes and fishing mortality on recruitment of anguillid eels of the Northern Hemisphere. The Science of the Total Environment 310:237–244.

Koehn, R. K., and G. C. Williams. 1978. Genetic differentiation without isolation in the American eel, *Anguilla rostrata*. II. Temporal stability of geographic patterns. Evolution 32:624–637.

Kotake, A. 2003. Ecological study on the migratory history of the Japanese eel, *Anguilla japonica*, inferred from otolith Sr/Ca ratios. Master's thesis. University of Tokyo, Tokyo.

Kotake, A., T. Arai, T. Ozawa, S. Nojima, M. J. Miller, and K. Tsukamoto. 2003. Variation in migratory history of Japanese eels, *Anguilla japonica*, collected in coastal waters of the Amakusa Islands, Japan, inferred from otolith Ca/Sr ratios. Marine Biology 142:849–854.

Kotake, A., T. Arai, A.Okamura, Y. Yamada, T. Utoh, H. P. Oka, M. J. Miller, and K. Tsukamoto. In press. Ecological aspects of Japanese eels, *Anguilla japonica*, collected from coastal areas of Japan. Zoological Science.

Kotake, A., A. Okamura, Y. Yamada, T. Utoh, T. Arai, M. J. Miller, H. P. Oka, and K. Tsukamoto. 2005. Seasonal variation in migratory history of the Japanese eel, *Anguilla japonica*, in Mikawa Bay, Japan. Marine Ecology Progress Series 293:213–221.

Kuo, C. L., A. Nakamura, K. Tsukamoto, K. Suzuki, and I. C. Liao. 1996. Tracking of Japanese eel *Anguilla japonica* by ultrasonic transmitter in the southwestern waters of Taiwan. Journal of the Fisheries Society Taiwan 23:279–287.

Kuroki, M., J. Aoyama, M. J. Miller, T. Arai, H. Y. Sugeha, G. Minagawa, S. Wouthuyzen, and K. Tsukamoto. 2005. Correspondence between otolith microstructural changes and early life history events in *Anguilla marmorata* leptocephali and glass eels. Coastal Marine Science 29:154–161.

Kuroki, M., J. Aoyama, M. J. Miller, S. Wouthuyzen, T. Arai, and K. Tsukamoto. 2006a. Contrasting patterns of growth and migration of tropical anguillid leptocephali in the western Pacific and Indonesian Seas. Marine Ecology Progress Series 309:233–246.

Kuroki, M., J. Aoyama, S. Wouthuyzen, K. O. Sumardhiarga, M. J. Miller, G. Minagawa, and K. Tsukamoto. 2006b. Age and growth of *Anguilla interioris* leptocephali collected in Indonesian waters. Coastal Marine Science 30:264–268.

Kuroki, M., J. Aoyama, S. Wouthuyzen, K. Sumardiharga, M. J. Miller, and K. Tsukamoto. 2007. Age and growth of *Anguilla bicolor bicolor* leptocephali in the eastern Indian Ocean. Journal of Fish Biology 70:538–550.

Lin, Y. S., Y. P. Poh, and C. S. Tzeng. 2001. A phylogeny of freshwater eels inferred from mitochondrial genes. Molecular Phylogeny and Evolution 20:252–261.

Lukas, R., E. R. Firing, P. Hacker, P. L. Richardson, C. A. Collins, R. Fine, and R. Gammon. 1991. Observations of the Mindanao current during the western Equatorial Pacific Ocean Circulation Study. Journal of Geophysical Research 96:7089–7104.

Mank, J. E., and J. C. Avise. 2003. Microsatellite variation and differentiation in North Atlantic eels. Journal of Heredity 94:310–314.

McCleave, J. D., R. C. Kleckner, and M. Castonguay. 1987. Reproductive sympatry of American and European eels and implications for migration and taxonomy. Pages 286–297 *in* M. J. Dadswell, R. J. Klauda, C. M. Moffitt, R. L. Saunders, R. A. Rulifson, and J. E. Cooper, editors. American Fisheries Society, Symposium 1, Bethesda, Maryland.

Miller, M. J., N. Mochioka, T. Otake, and K. Tsukamoto. 2002. Evidence of a spawning area of *Anguilla marmorata* in the western North Pacific. Marine Biology 140:809–814.

Miyai, T., J. Aoyama, S. Sasai, M. J. Miller, and K. Tsukamoto. 2004. Ecological aspects of the downstream migration of introduced European eels in the Uono River, Japan. Environmental Biology of Fishes 71:105–114.

Nishida, M. 2001. Population structure of the Japanese eel. Pages 7–9 *in* K. Aida, K. Tsukamoto, and K. Yamauchi, editors, Proceedings of the International Symposium Advances in Eel biology. The University of Tokyo, Tokyo.

Okamura, A., Y. Yamada, S. Tanaka, N. Horie, T. Utoh, N. Mikawa, A. Akazawa, and H. P. Oka. 2002. Atmospheric depression as the final trigger for the seaward migration of the Japanese eel *Anguilla japonica*. Marine Ecology Progress Series 234:281–288.

Okamura, A., Y. Yamada, K. Yokouchi, N. Horie, N. Mikawa, T. Utoh, S. Tanaka, and K. Tsukamoto. 2007. A silvering index for the Japanese eel *Anguilla japonica*. Environmental Biology of Fishes 80:77-89.

Okamura, A., H. Zhang, N. Mikawa, A. Kotake, Y. Yamada, T. Utoh, N. Horie, S. Tanaka, H. P. Oka, K. Tsukamoto. In press. Decline in non-native freshwater eels in Japan: ecology and future perspectives. Environmental Biology of Fishes.

Otake, T., T. Ishii, M. Nakahara, and R. Nakamura. 1994. Drastic changes in otolith strontium:calcium ratios in leptocephali and glass eels of Japanese eel *Anguilla japonica*. Marine Ecology Progress Series 112:189–193.

Otake, T., M. J. Miller, T. Inagaki, G. Minagawa, A. Shinoda, Y. Kimura, S. Sasai, M. Oya, S. Tasumi, Y. Suzuki, M. Uchida, and K. Tsukamoto. 2006. Evidence for migration of metamorphosing larvae of *Anguilla japonica* in the Kuroshio. Coastal Marine Science 30:453–458.

Sang, T. K., H. Y. Chang, C. T. Chen, and C. F. Hui. 1994. Population structure of the Japanese eel, *Anguilla japonica*. Molecular Biology and Evolution 11:250–260.

Sasai, S., J. Aoyama, S. Watanabe, T. Kaneko, M. J. Miller, and K. Tsukamoto. 2001. Occurrence of migrating silver eels *Anguilla japonica* in the East China Sea. Marine Ecology Progress Series 212:305–310.

Sasai, S., F. Katoh, T. Kaneko, and K. Tsukamoto. 2007. Ontogenic change of gill chloride cells in leptocephalus and glass eel stages of the Japanese eel, *Anguilla japonica*. Marine Biology 150:487–496.

Shiao J. C, Y. Iizuka, C. W. Chang, and W. N. Tzeng. 2003. Disparities in habitat use and migratory behavior between tropical eel *Anguilla marmorata* and temperate eel *A. japonica* in four Taiwanese rivers. Marine Ecology Progress Series 261:233–242.

Sugeha, H. Y., T. Arai, M. J. Miller, D. Limbong, and K. Tsukamoto. 2001. Inshore migration of the tropical eels, *Anguilla* spp., recruiting to the Poigar River estuary on Sulawesi Island. Marine Ecology Progress Series 221:233–243.

Tanaka, H. 2003. Techniques for larval rearing. Pages 427–434 *in* K. Aida, K. Tsukamoto, and K. Yamauchi, editors. Eel biology. Springer Verlag, Tokyo.

Tatsukawa, T. 2003. Eel resources in East Asia. Pages 293–298 *in* K. Aida, K. Tsukamoto, and K. Yamauchi, editors. Eel biology. Springer Verlag, Tokyo.

Toole, J. M., R. C. Millard, Z. Wang, and S. Pu. 1990. Observations of the Pacific North Equatorial Current bifurcation at the Philippine coast. Journal Physical Oceanography 20:307–318.

Tseng, M. C., W. N. Tzeng, and S. C. Lee. 2003a. Historical decline in the Japanese eel *Anguilla japonica* in northern Taiwan inferred from temporal genetic variations. Zoological Studies 42:556–563.

Tseng, M. C., W. N. Tzeng, and S. C. Lee. 2006. Population genetic structure of the Japanese eel *Anguilla japonica* in the northwest Pacific Ocean: evidence of non-panmictic populations. Marine Ecology Progress Series 308:221–230.

Tseng, M. C., W. N. Tzeng, and S. C. Lee. 2009. Genetic differentiation of the Japanese eel. Pages 59–69 *in* J. M. Casselman and D. K. Cairns, editors. Eels at the edge: science, status, and conservation concerns. American Fisheries Society, Symposium 58, Bethesda, Maryland.

Tsukamoto, K. 1990. Recruitment mechanism of the eel, *Anguilla japonica*, to the Japanese coast. Journal of Fish Biology 36:659–671.

Tsukamoto, K. 1992. Discovery of the spawning area for the Japanese eel. Nature (London) 356:789–791.

Tsukamoto, K. 1996. Breeding places of freshwater eels. Pages 11–21 *in* O. Tabeta, editor. Early life history and prospects of seed production of the Japanese eel *Anguilla japonica*. Kouseisya-Kouseikaku, Tokyo. (In Japanese)

Tsukamoto, K. 2006. Spawning of eels near a seamount. Nature 439:929.

Tsukamoto, K., and J. Aoyama. 1998. Evolution of freshwater eels of the genus *Anguilla*: a probable scenario. Environmental Biology of Fishes 52:139–148.

Tsukamoto, K., J. Aoyama, and M. J. Miller. 2002. Migration, speciation and the evolution of diadromy in anguillid eels. Canadian Journal Fisheries and Aquatic Science 59:1989–1998.

Tsukamoto, K., and T. Arai. 2001. Facultative catadromy of the eel *Anguilla japonica* between freshwater and seawater habitats. Marine Ecology Progress Series 220:265–276.

Tsukamoto, K., I. Nakai, and F. W. Tesch. 1998. Do all freshwater eels migrate? Nature 396:635–636.

Tsukamoto, K., and T. Otake. 1994. Japanese eel population and human impact on the resources. Pages 85–89 *in* Proceedings of the Fourth LIPI-JSPS Joint Seminar on Marine Science, Jakarta.

Tsukamoto, K., T. Otake, N. Mochioka, T. W. Lee, H. Fricke, T. Inagaki, J. Aoyama, S. Ishikawa, S. Kimura, M. J. Miller, H. Hasumoto, M. Oya, and Y. Suzuki. 2003. Seamounts, new moon and eel spawning: the search for the spawning site of the Japanese eel. Environmental Biology of Fishes 66:221–229.

Tsukamoto, K., and A. Umezawa. 1990. Early life history and oceanic migration of the eel, *Anguilla japonica*. La Mer 28:188–198.

Tzeng, W. N. 1984. An estimate of the exploitation rate of *Anguilla japonica* elvers immigrating into the coastal waters off Shuang-Chi River, Taiwan. Bulletin of the Institute of Zoology, Academic Sinica 23: 173–180.

Tzeng W. N., Y. Iizuka, J. C. Shiao, Y. Yamada, and H. P. Oka. 2003. Identification and growth rates comparison of divergent migratory contingents of Japanese eel (*Anguilla japonica*). Aquaculture 216:77–86.

Tzeng, W. N., C. H. Wang, H. Wickström, and M. Reizenstein. 2000. Occurrence of the semi-catadromous European eel *Anguilla anguilla* in the Baltic Sea. Marine Biology 137:93–98.

Tzeng, W. N., J. C. Shiao, and Y. Iizuka. 2002. Use of otolith Sr:Ca ratios to study the riverine migratory behaviors of Japanese eel *Anguilla japonica*. Marine Ecology Progress Series 245:213–221.

Utoh, T., N. Mikawa, A. Okamura, Y. Yamada, S. Tanaka, N. Horie, A. Akazawa, and H. P. Oka. 2004. Ovarian morphology of the Japanese eel in Mikawa Bay. Journal of Fish Biology 64:502–513.

Watanabe, S. 2003. Taxonomy of the freshwater eels, genus *Anguilla* Schrank, 1798. Pages 3–18 *in* K. Aida, K. Tsukamoto, and K. Yamauchi, editors. Eel biology, Springer Verlag, Tokyo.

Watanabe, S., J. Aoyama, and K. Tsukamoto. 2004. Reexamination of Ege's (1939) use of taxonomic characters of the genus *Anguilla*. Bulletin of Marine Science 74:337–351.

Watanabe, S., J. Aoyama, M. Nishida, and K. Tsukamoto. 2005. A Molecular genetic evaluation of the taxonomy of eels of the genus *Anguilla* (Pisces:Anguilliformes). Bulletin of Marine Science. 76:675–690.

Williams, G. C., R. K. Koehn, and J. B. Mittonne. 1973. Genetic differentiation without isolation in the American eel, *Anguilla rostrata*. Evolution 27:194–204.

Wirth, T., and Bernatchez, L. 2001. Genetic evidence against panmixia in the European eel. Nature (London) 409:1037–1040.

Wirth, T., and L. Bernatchez. 2003. Decline of North Atlantic eels: a fatal synergy? Proceedings of the Royal Society of London Ser. B 270:681–688.

Yokouchi, K. 2005. Ecological study of the Japanese eel in the Hamana Lake system. Master's thesis. University of Tokyo, Tokyo.

Forty Years On—The Impact of Commercial Fishing on Stocks of New Zealand Freshwater Eels

Don J. Jellyman[1]
National Institute of Water and Atmospheric Research Ltd.
P. O. Box 8602, Riccarton, Christchurch, New Zealand

Abstract.—The two main species of freshwater eels in New Zealand, the shortfin *Anguilla australis* and the endemic longfinned eel *A. dieffenbachii*, are extensively commercially exploited and also support important customary fisheries. Since there are no commercial glass eel fisheries in New Zealand, other indices must be used to indicate changes in recruitment over time. While there is some anecdotal evidence of reductions in glass eel recruitment, there is evidence of poorly represented cohorts of longfins within some populations, and modeling of these data indicate a substantial reduction in recruitment over the past two decades. Growth of both species is typically slow at 2–3 cm per year, meaning that both species are susceptible to commercial capture for many years until spawning escapement. Extensive commercial fishing has resulted in more substantial changes in length-frequency distributions of longfins than in shortfins; likewise, regional reductions in catch per unit effort are more significant for longfins. Theoretical models of silver eel escapement indicate that longfin females are especially susceptible to overexploitation. Shortfins would have been more impacted than longfins by loss of wetlands, but the impact of hydro stations on upstream access for juvenile eels and downstream access for silver eels would have been more severe for longfins. Overall, there is no clear evidence that the status of shortfin eel stocks has been seriously compromised by the extensive commercial eel fishery, but there is increasing evidence that longfins are unable to sustain present levels of exploitation.

Introduction

The New Zealand native freshwater fish community is relatively sparse, comprising 35 species (McDowall 2000) of which half are under 10 cm in adult length. Eels are the largest native species and frequently comprise more than 90% of total fish biomass (Hopkins 1970; Hicks and McCaughan 1997). New Zealand has three species of freshwater eels—the endemic longfin *Anguilla dieffenbachii*, the Australasian shortfin *A. australis*, and the recently discovered speckled longfin *A. reinhardtii*. The latter species was first recorded in 1996 (Jellyman et al. 1996) and, having a primarily tropical range in Australia, is confined to the top half of the North Island of New Zealand. Although there is evidence of regular recruitment, the species has restricted distribution and is a minor component of freshwater fish stocks and commercial eel landings. The other species, hereafter referred to as longfin and shortfin, are widely distributed throughout mainland New Zealand and offshore islands, with the longfin being the most common and ubiquitous native fish species in lotic environ-

---

[1]E-mail: d.jellyman@niwa.co.nz

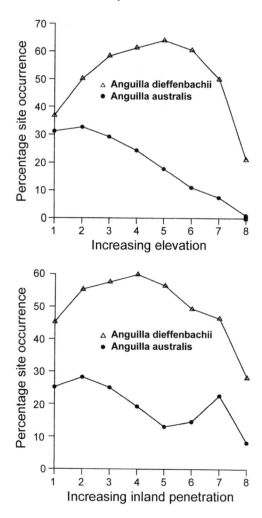

Figure 1. Distribution of shortfin (closed circles) and longfin (open triangles) eels by elevation and distance inland. Elevation octiles are (m), 0–5, 6–20, 21–40, 41–79, 80–119, 120–209, 210–389, 390–1460; inland penetration octiles are (km), 0–1, 2–4, 5–9, 10–26, 27–69, 70–115, 116–187, 188–430 (from McDowall and Taylor 2000).

ments and the shortfin the fourth most common (Minns 1990). The shortfin also occurs in southeast Australia and Tasmania, as well as Norfolk and Lord Howe Islands (McDowall 1990).

Trajectories of the occurrence of both species by increasing elevation and distance inland (Figure 1) show that the likelihood of occurrence of shortfins declines regularly with both elevation and distance inland, highlighting the more coastal and lowland distribution of this species. This contrasts with the distribution of longfins, which are more frequently encountered than shortfins, and show higher occurrence at greater elevations and distances inland than shortfins. From present-day distributions of longfins, it might be concluded that they avoid coastal and lowland lakes, but historical data indicate that they also frequented such habitats in large numbers (Cairns 1941; Hobbs 1947), thus their comparative absence today is likely to be a consequence of harvest.

It is also likely that the present-day riverine distribution of both species has been affected by commercial harvest. Earlier descriptions of the distribution of both species (Cairns 1941) state that extensive sampling in nonestuarine waters of South Island rivers produced exclusively longfins, whereas today, shortfins typically comprise between 5% and 10% of these populations (Beentjes and Chisnall 1997, 1998). Given that the local distribution of shortfins can increase in the absence of larger longfins (Chisnall et al. 2003), it is possible that shortfins have become more widely distributed as a result of the harvest of longfins by commercial fishers.

The genetic structure of both species has been investigated, and in common with other temperate species of *Anguilla*, results indicate single panmictic populations (Smith et al. 2001); there is some evidence of small differences between adult populations that could result from different selective pressures within the adult environment. Although Australian and New Zealand stocks of the shortfin were previously designated as separate subspecies (Schmidt 1928; Griffin 1936), lack of genetic differences has led to a taxonomic revision as a single species (Dijkstra and Jellyman 1999), with the recommendation that management of the species needs to be carried out cooperatively between both countries.

Shortfin and longfin eels sustain very important customary and commercial fisheries in New Zealand. This paper reviews information on the biology and exploitation relevant to assessing the status of stocks of both species.

Biology

Spawning

Spawning areas of both species are unknown but are almost certainly in the tropics. Castle (1963) and Arai et al. (1999) suggested that the spawning area of the shortfin might lie between Fiji and Tahiti, although Jellyman (1987) considered the area would be farther north. Differences in ages of glass eels recruiting to Australia and New Zealand led Shiao et al. (2001) to conclude that different current systems would be needed to transport leptocephali to both land masses. Larvae of all South Pacific eel species have been collected, with the exception of the longfin eel (Jellyman 2003). Jellyman (1987) suggested that the spawning area for this species might lie east of Tonga, and research using pop-up tags is underway to try to further delimit the possible area (Jellyman and Tsukamoto 2002).

Recruitment

For northern hemisphere species (*A. anguilla*, *A. rostrata*, *A. japonica*), extensive fisheries for glass eels have resulted in substantial time series of recruitment (e.g., Moriarty 1986; Moriarty and Dekker 1997; Richkus and Whalen 1999). Apart from some experimental capture in the early 1970s (Jellyman 1979), no fisheries for glass eels have been permitted in New Zealand. As a result, there are no long-term data on recruitment from commercial catch data. In the absence of these, other indices have been investigated to see whether there are indications of changes in recruitment over time.

There is anecdotal evidence that the extensive migrations of glass eels that characterized recruitment into the Waikato River in the 1930s (Cairns 1941) seldom occur these days (Jellyman et al. 2000). However, electrofishing samples of glass eels at 14-d intervals from up to six North Island and seven South Island streams from 1995 to 1999 showed no evidence of a decline in either species over this period (Jellyman et al. 2002). When more recent data are included (Figure 2), the effect of year is still not significant (analysis of variance [ANOVA], $P > 0.05$; i.e., shortfins, $F = 0.07$, 6 df; longfins, $F = 1.67$, 6 df). Both species showed similar trends in density, indicating that the same processes influence their

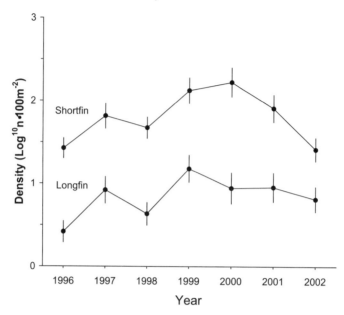

Figure 2. Mean densities (±1 SE) of shortfin and longfin glass eels, 1995–2002, from six sites around New Zealand.

recruitment. While there was no evidence that the overall strength of recruitment was associated with the El Niño Southern Oscillation phenomenon (ENSO), it is possible that ENSO may influence the direction of recruitment to New Zealand (Chisnall et al. 2002). However, results from population simulations indicate that data sets of 10–20 years would be required to reliably detect historical trends in recruitment because of natural variation and autocorrelations in glass eel runs (Francis and Jellyman 1999).

Each summer large numbers of juvenile eels of both species (length range 60–300 mm) migrate upstream, sometimes as far as 130 km (Jellyman 1977). Such migrations tend to be associated with increased water levels and water temperatures (Jellyman and Ryan 1983) and enable eels to populate upstream areas progressively. At a number of hydro dams where these juvenile eels accumulate downstream in large numbers, eel ladders have been installed (Beentjes et al. 1997) or the juvenile eels are trapped and liberated upstream. The quantities of juvenile eels caught are being evaluated as a measure of recruitment strength of both species. Since these migrations are mixtures of several age classes, extensive aging studies will be needed to identify strengths of specific cohorts. There are also concerns that annual variations in catch are partly due to changed capture techniques rather than simply abundance of eels (Jellyman et al. 2000). Assuming that inter-annual variations in the Karapiro catches (Figure 3) indicate absolute abundance, there is no evidence of decreased abundance of longfins over this nine-year period, although the variation in longfin abundance (CV = 0.83) exceeds that of shortfins (CV = 0.45).

Similar to northern hemisphere species of *Anguilla*, variability in annual recruitment of New Zealand species can be high. For example, glass eel catches over four years in the Waikato River varied by a factor of 9 (Jellyman 1979), while recruitment of juvenile eels into a small North Island lake varied by a factor of 28 over four consecutive years (Jellyman and Ryan 1983). Cohort analysis has been carried out to determine changes in

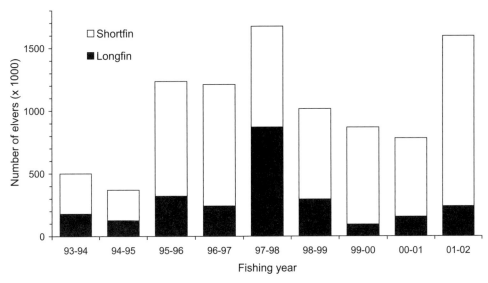

Figure 3. Estimated annual catches of juvenile shortfin and longfin eels at Karapiro Dam, Waikato River, 1993/94–2001/02 fishing years.

the relative numbers of eels of different ages. Maximum likelihood analysis showed that recruitment of longfins had declined significantly in two of three study streams (Jellyman et al. 2000) at about 7% per annum, with recruitment in 2000 averaging only 23% of 1980 levels.

The comparative absence of small longfins has been reported from a number of New Zealand waterways. Thus, length-frequency data from systematic electrofishing (from lower to upper reaches) of five waterways (Table 1) shows that the smallest size-class (<100 mm) dominated shortfin catches in three of the five waterways but in none of the waterways for longfins. From the proportion of larger eels recorded in the Ashley River and the species composition from a previous study (n = 939 eels, longfins = 81%; Glova 1988), this river would be classified as principally a longfin habitat; however, glass eel records do not confirm this, since only 4% of glass eels recorded from the Ashley River over three years were longfins (Jellyman et al. 1999).

Age-frequency histograms have been reviewed for evidence of stronger-than-average cohorts that might indicate the commercial fishery is maintained by periodic strong recruitment. Although the modal age in adjacent catchments varied by up to eight years, large confidence intervals meant it was not possible to make inferences about long-term trends in recruitment from these age frequencies (Jellyman et al. 2000).

Age and Growth

From a review of the variability in growth rates of New Zealand eels, Jellyman (1997) concluded that length at a given age was characterized by high intra- and interpopulation variability. Compared with other temperate eel species, growth rates for eels longer than 30 cm were typically slow (2–3 cm per year) and linear. For example, using annual length-increment data (weighted by sample number) for South Island riverine eels collected during an extensive market-sampling program (Beentjes 1999), the mean annual increment for longfins is 2.3 cm per year (range 1.5–3.5; n = 424) and for shortfin, 3.3

Table 1. Numbers of shortfin and longfin eels per 100 mm size groups sampled from various New Zealand waterways, arranged north to south. Te Maari Stream, Firewood Creek and Horokiwi Stream are in the North Island, Ashley River and Pigeon Bay Stream are in the South Island. Data from Glova et al. 1998, Jellyman et al. 2003.

Eel size group (mm)	Shortfin						Longfin				
	Te Maari Stream	Firewood Creek	Horokiwi Stream	Ashley River	Pigeon Bay Stream	Total	Te Maari Stream	Firewood Creek	Horokiwi Stream	Ashley River	Pigeon Bay Stream	Total
<100	160	34	112	150	576	1032	120	-	9	-	21	150
100–199	97	134	480	97	264	1072	371	29	61	59	101	621
200–299	13	81	107	8	43	252	134	23	71	58	159	445
300–399	4	61	46	6	6	123	52	24	78	70	122	346
400–499		28	20	6	2	56	34	46	70	85	42	277
500–599		13	2	1		16	22	42	27	18	24	133
600–699	1	3		-	1	5	11	12	3	2	7	35
700–799		1	2	1		4	10	3	1	1	2	17
800–899	1	-	1	-		2	3	3		-	4	10
>900	1	-		-	1	1	7	1	2	1	5	16
Total	277	355	770	269	892	2563	764	183	322	294	487	2050

cm per year (range 1.3–5.1; $n = 159$). Similar data for North Island rivers (calculated from data in Chisnall and Kemp 2000) are 3.4 cm per year for longfins (range 2.3–4.0; $n = 148$) and 4.1 cm per year for shortfins (range 2.6–7.5; $n = 321$). More rapid growth of both species in the North Island is a consequence of the longer growing season (Jellyman 1995). Eels at the minimum commercial size (220 g) average 13 years and 17.5 years for shortfins and longfins, respectively, in the South Island (Beentjes 1999) and 12 years and 14 years for North Island shortfins and longfins (Chisnall and Kemp 2000).

Densities of unfished New Zealand eel stocks can be particularly high, with densities in streams with abundant cover averaging 145 g/m² (Burnet 1952). However, subsequent studies have indicated that annual production can be quite low (e.g., 10–59 g/m²/y, Hopkins 1971; 8.0 g/m²y, Hicks and McCaughan 1997), reflecting the fact that growth is usually limited by food (Graynoth and Taylor 2000). Thus, high biomass has been achieved by low productivity over long periods. Not surprisingly, natural mortality rates are low (typically 0.04, Annala et al. 2002) and survival rates high (e.g., 0.80 for juvenile shortfins in a large coastal lake, Graynoth and Jellyman 2002).

While growth rates include the slowest recorded for any species of eel (Jellyman 1997), both species have the potential for rapid growth, achieving 40–45 cm during a year in captivity (Jellyman and Coates 1976; Jones et al. 1983) and within two years in the wild where densities are low (e.g., Lake Karapiro, a North Island hydro lake, Beentjes et al. 1997). There is evidence of increased growth rates resulting from extensive commercial harvest (Chisnall and Hayes 1991). Further, small eels (30–50 cm) transferred to waters where recruitment has been limited but harvest has been extensive grow at faster rates than resident preharvest eels (e.g., Lake Hawea, a South Island high-country lake affected by a hydro weir, Beentjes et al. 1997; Beentjes and Jellyman 2003). Accelerated growth rates have also been associated with changes in diet from invertebrates to fish (Jellyman 2001).

Sex Ratios

The national minimum legal size of 220 g corresponds to lengths of 48 and 45 cm for shortfins and longfins, respectively. Given that the mean length of shortfin male silver eels is about 43 cm, then the shortfin fishery is based principally on immature females. In contrast, silver male longfins range from 48 to 74 cm (Table 2), meaning that both immature males and females are potentially available to the fishery. Sizes at sexual differentiation (review by Davey and Jellyman (2005) are 27–48 cm and 32–49 cm for shortfin males and females, respectively, and 33–65 and 42–64 cm for longfin males and females.

The predominance of female shortfins in commercial catches is apparent from catch sampling programs; for example, Beentjes (1999) recorded a sex composition of 78% females and 22% males ($n = 3,050$) from South Island catchments. The sex ratios of longfins (Table 3) show a slight predominance of females in the North Island and upper South Island regions, but there is a tendency for reduced proportions of females in the lower half of the South Island. In a more detailed study of sex composition in a Southland river, McCleave and Jellyman (2004) recorded only five female longfins from a sample of 471 eels whose sex could be determined. Historically, such areas were dominated by females (Cairns 1942; Burnet 1952). McCleave and Jellyman (2004) suggested that changes in sex ratios could be partly attributed to selective harvest of females but also to changes in the structure of the population resulting from commercial fishing that favored differentiation of males. Given that the Southland region supports the largest longfin eel fishery in

Table 2. Lengths, ages and migration seasons of New Zealand silver eels. M = male, F = female.

	Sex	Length (cm) Mean	Range	Number	Age (years) Mean	Range	Number	Season	Reference
Shortfin	M	43	38–60	12205	14	6–24	1377	Feb-Mar	Todd 1980
	M	42	35–53	109	22	14–33	49	Dec-Apr	Author's unpublished data
	F	62	48–102	859	22	10–35	242	Mar	Todd 1980
	F	109	54–135	32	13	7–30	32	Feb-May	Boubée et al. 2001
	F	89	65–111	116	19	9-25	50	Mar	Jellyman 2001
	F	74	57–109	177	41	26-60	78	Dec-Apr	Author's unpublished data
Longfin	M	62	48–74	374	23	12-35	158	Apr	Todd 1980
	F	115	74–156	198	38	25-60	20	Apr-May	Todd 1980
	F	134	95–158	18	42	27-61	18	Feb-May	Boubée et al. 2001

Table 3. The proportions of immature male and female longfin eels recorded from fishery dependant surveys. Regions are arranged by increasing latitude. Data from Beentjes and Chisnall 1998, Beentjes 1999, Chisnall and Kemp 2000, Speed et al. 2000. N = sample number

Region	Male (%)	Female (%)	N	Region	Male (%)	Female (%)	N
North Island				**South Island (cont.)**			
Waikato 33	67	67		N. Canterbury	37	63	257
Wellington	48	52	150	S. Canterbury	53	47	158
				Waitaki	52	48	619
South Island				Otago	65	35	1833
Nelson	56	44	153	Southland	83	17	4368
Marlborough	49	51	115				
West Coast	48	52	412				

the country, the lack of females in this region is of particular concern.

Silver Eel Escapement

A consequence of slow growth is that silver eels are relatively old at migration (Table 2): for one population in a cool oligotrophic lake, the average generation time for female longfins was 93 years (Jellyman 1995). Given the variability in growth rates and hence age at migration (Table 2), it is difficult to talk of average generation times. An approximation can be obtained by assuming the mean growth increments listed previously and an average length of silver female eels of 120 cm for longfins and 75 cm for shortfins. Corresponding average ages are 52 years for longfin females and 23 years for shortfin females in the South Island and 35 and 18 years for longfin and shortfin females in the North Island. Thus the substantial development of the commercial fishery (1968 to present) has taken place in a period equivalent to the average generation time of longfin females in the North Island but less than a generation of South Island females, and the full expression of any reduction in recruitment may be yet to come.

In a study of silver eels at Lake Ellesmere, Hobbs (1947) estimated that 500 metric tons (mt) (= 508 t) of shortfin females were migrating, compared with only 2–3 mt over recent years (Jellyman and Todd 1998). Hobbs also estimated that 3,850 longfin females were migrating, although numbers over recent years would probably range from only 50–100 (Jellyman, personal observation). The selective removal of larger eels of both species by commercial fishing has been a major factor in the change from female-dominated stocks of both species (Hobbs 1947) to the present fishery, which is dominated by shortfin males (Jellyman and Todd 1998).

Hoyle and Jellyman (2002) modeled the effect of the commercial eel fishery on escapement of migratory longfin and shortfin eels. Their model predicted that, compared with unexploited levels, an exploitation rate of 10% per annum would reduce the spawning per recruit by 48% for shortfin females but 97% for longfin females (Figure 4). Further, the model predicted that the current upper size limit of 4 kg for longfin females is likely to be ineffectual, since there is a high probability of capture before eels achieve this size. For example, assuming linear growth of 3 cm a year, a female longfin eel would spend an average of 21 years within the fishery before reaching the 4-kg upper size limit. Although actual exploitation rates are unknown, based on these results, these authors suggested that current levels of fishing could seriously affect sustainability of the longfin fishery, and they advocated an increase in the areas of unfished waters.

Fisheries

Customary and Recreational Fisheries

Being both nutritious and widely distributed, eels were of particular importance as a food to Maori, New Zealand's indigenous people, who developed an extensive knowledge of the seasonality of life history events (McDowall 1990). Maori had more than 100 names for eels (Best 1929), based on species, sexes, color variations, and life history stages, and developed sophisticated fishing techniques that included weirs with wings up to 400 m in length (Best 1929). A few waters have been set aside for exclusive customary eel fishing, and an allocation for customary catch is included in any regional management quotas. Customary allocations are not based on actual catches because the extent of the customary catch is undocumented, but it is substantially less than the commercial catch.

There is a small (unrecorded) but growing recreational fishery for eels in New Zealand. The daily catch is limited to six eels per person per day, and there is increasing interest by European anglers in catch-and-release fishing for large longfin eels.

Commercial Fishery

The commercial fishery commenced in earnest in the 1960s and rapidly rose to peak production by 1972; present catches average about 1,200 mt per annum (Figure 5). The quantity of both species has remained relatively constant over the past 10 years, with catches averaging 1,248 mt (SE 46 mt). Catch data are recorded by 12 North Island and 9 South Island regions, with fishers giving estimates of the weight and species composition of catches, while the more accurate figure of annual harvest comes from the weights of eels processed by Licenced Fish Receivers.

Fishers do not always record the species of eels, and for the period 1990–1999, 30% of the total weight of eels caught was unspecified (data from Beentjes and Bull 2002). Therefore, to observe any trends in species proportions, records where the species was unrecorded have been allocated to either shortfin or longfin on a *pro rata* basis, according to the recorded proportions of either species. On this basis, over the past 10 years, longfins averaged 42% of the total catch and showed less variation in annual catches than shortfins (CV longfins = 0.08, versus CV shortfins = 0.13).

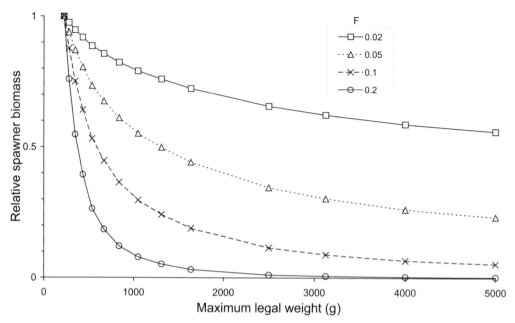

Figure 4. Relative spawning per recruit for female longfin silver eels for various exploitation rates, F (from Hoyle and Jellyman 2002).

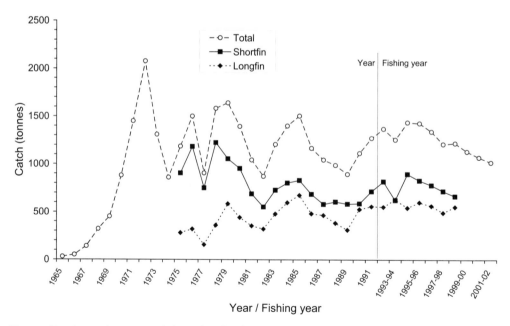

Figure 5. Annual commercial catch of eels, by species, in New Zealand, 1965–1991 (calendar year), 1993–1994 to 2001–2002 (fishing year).

With the exception of Lake Ellesmere, there are no targeted fisheries for silver eels in New Zealand. Given the high flow variability of New Zealand rivers (Jowett and Duncan 1990) and the tendency of silver eels to migrate during times of high flow (Todd 1981; Boubée et al. 2001), capture of riverine silver eels would be difficult. The Lake Ellesmere silver eel fishery is based on shortfin males, and within a gazetted area and time, fishers are able to take eels less than the minimum legal size; up to 100 t of shortfin males are caught annually.

Changes in CPUE

While the estimated total catch of both species does not appear to have changed very much over the past decade, a more sensitive measure of stock well-being is catch per unit effort. Comparison of historic CPUE data (1984–1989; Jellyman 1993) with more recent data (1991–1999, Beentjes and Bull 2002) shows that unstandardized CPUE (kg/net/night) has declined over most areas of New Zealand by one to several kilograms per lift (from a historic mean of 6.5 kg/lift). Standardized CPUE analysis provides a more accurate representation of trends in CPUE since it takes into account factors that can affect catch rates, such as experience of fishers, season, and region. Results of this analysis (Beentjes and Bull 2002) showed that for the ten regions examined (encompassing the whole of New Zealand), standardized CPUE showed no significant changes for shortfins except in one area that had a significant decline (that fishers claim was an effect of recent droughts). However, for longfins, of the eight areas where there were sufficient data, four showed no significant change, while the other four showed significant decreases. The most marked decline occurred in Southland (Figure 7), the largest longfin area in the South Island.

Changes in Size Distributions

As would be expected, commercial harvesting of eels has substantially altered size distributions. For example, samples of longfin eels collected from Lake Wakatipu almost 50 years apart showed a reduction in modal length from 91 to 64 cm and a reduction in the percentage of eels exceeding 70 cm (the minimum size of silver female eels) from 69% to 27% (NIWA unpublished data). Impacts are also evident over much shorter time intervals; for example, Figure 6 shows the length distribution of shortfin eels at the same location three years apart. When the 1974 sample was taken, there had been virtually no fishing at this location, but extensive fishing commenced shortly afterwards; in contrast, the 1977 data showed a virtual absence of eels under 43 cm, which equated to the minimum commercial size of eels at that time.

A further index of changes in size distributions comes from processing-factory records of the proportion of eels of various size classes processed over time. While the size-class data are subject to short-term changes in market demand, they integrate eel size data over 30+ years. Comparison of the size grades from the largest South Island processor, representing about 1/3 of the total New Zealand production (Figure 8), shows a marked change in the proportion of eels of both species larger than 454 g processed between the 1970s and 1990s, with an associated decrease in the proportion of larger eels. Collectively, these data show a substantial shift toward smaller eels over time.

Longfin eels are considered more vulnerable to overfishing than shortfin eels and females more vulnerable than males (Chisnall et al. 2003). This vulnerability of females may be due to their being an apex predator, since their presence affects the activity and habitat use of smaller eels of both species (Glova 2001; Chisnall et al. 2003). Although longfins grow to a larger size than do shortfins (e.g.,

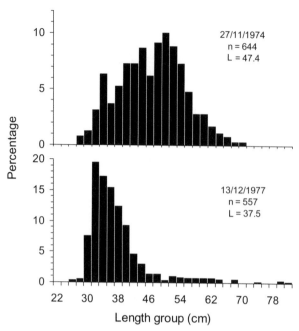

Figure 6. Length frequency of shortfin eels from the same location in Lake Ellesmere, New Zealand, 3 years apart. L = mean length (cm).

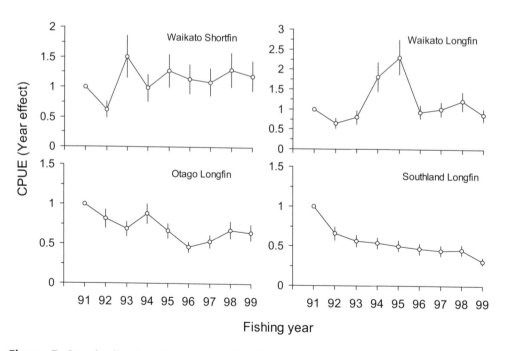

Figure 7. Standardized catch-per-unit-effort for shortfins and longfins from the Waikato, and longfins from Otago and Southland. Error bars are 95% confidence intervals (from Beentjes and Bull 2002).

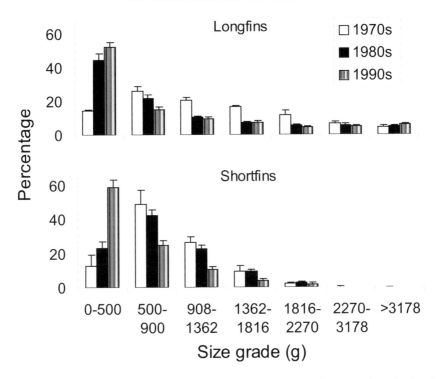

Figure 8. Comparison of size grades of both species of eel processed over 3 decades by the main South Island eel processor. Bars are standard errors (from Beentjes and Chisnall 1997).

>15 kg versus 3 kg), the average size of longfins in commercial catches is almost always less than the average size of shortfins (e.g., Beentjes and Chisnall 1997, 1998; Beentjes 1999), indicating that fishing pressure has not affected shortfin populations to the same extent as longfin populations (Beentjes 1999). Further, in accessible waters (site 1 in Figure 9), the length-frequency distributions of longfins are typically strongly unimodal slightly above the minimum commercial size with relatively few large eels, whereas catches of shortfins are more evenly spread over a wider size range (Figure 9). In contrast, length-frequency distributions of longfins from less accessible areas (site 2, Figure 9) have a much higher proportion of large females (Beentjes and Chisnall 1997, 1998; Broad et al. 2002).

Results from a simulation model developed to see whether changes in the mean size of eels could be used to monitor eel fisheries showed that size data by themselves were useful for detecting long-term changes in stock status but were not good indicators for use in year-to-year management (Francis and Jellyman 1999). Even when fishing pressure was constant, natural variations in eel recruitment caused substantial year-to-year variations in the mean size of eels, making detection of changes in size difficult. Assuming no sampling errors, then biomass would have to drop by 40% or more before such changes could be reliably detected.

Habitat Loss

Being a somewhat lowland species, shortfins have been particularly affected by drainage of wetlands and channelization of rivers. It is estimated that wetlands that covered at least 670,000 ha before European settlement have now been reduced to about 100,000 ha

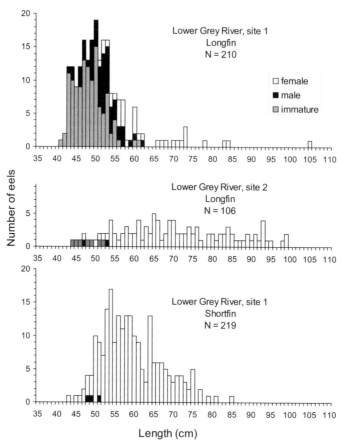

Figure 9. Length frequency of longfin and shortfin eels from the lower Grey River, New Zealand; site 2 is upstream of site 1 and less accessible (from Beentjes 1999).

(Ministry for the Environment 1997). Within the Waikato Catchment, the most productive eel-fishing region, the loss of wetlands was estimated to be 84% between 1840 and 1976 (McDowall 1990). Much of this drainage predated the commencement of commercial eel fishing but nonetheless resulted in a huge loss of habitat for shortfins. Shortfins are also the species that responds most to flooding and feeds extensively in newly inundated areas (Jellyman 1989; Chisnall and Hayes 1991), and channelization of waterways has reduced such feeding opportunities (Chisnall 1989). The biomass of larger eels has been directly related to the amount of suitable cover (Burnet 1952), so the loss of cover by such practices as macrophyte removal and channelization of waterways, together with siltation, reduces the quality of habitat available to both species.

There has also been a substantial loss of forest both pre- and post-European settlement; for example, over the past 200 years, forests have been reduced from 53% of land area to 23%, with a corresponding increase in grassland from 30 to 50% (Ministry for the Environment 1997). Ironically, conversion to pasture may have benefited eels, especially shortfins, since higher densities occur in pastoral streams than in either native or exotic forest streams (Hicks and McCaughan 1997).

Table 4. Summary – indicators of the status of shortfin and longfin eels. ? = not known; O = OK or no apparent change; x = significant (local) negative change; X = substantial (national) negative change.

	Shortfin	Longfin
Recruitment issues		
Glass eels	?	?
Juvenile eel age/size abundance	O	X
Cohort analysis	?	X
Fishery impacts		
Sex ratio	O	x
Size changes (commercial fishery)	x	X
CPUE	x	X
Silver eel escapement (modelling)	O	X
Habitat impacts		
Wetland loss	X	O
Access – upstream at hydro stations	x	X
– downstream at hydro stations	x	X

Since longfins are the species that penetrate farthest inland, the installation of hydro dams has often compromised their upstream access. Thus almost 10% and 22% of the total area of North and South Island catchments, respectively, are affected by hydro, with attendant problems for recruitment of juvenile eels and escapement of silver eels.

Management Initiatives

Current management practices include restrictions on gear and licences, as well as size limits (220 g, national minimum size, 4 kg maximum size in South Island only). The South Island fishery entered the Quota Management System in October 2000 and is now controlled by a total allowable catch of 539 t for both species combined. Based on their catch history, individual fishers have been allocated an annual quota, although this is not allocated by species. The North Island fishery entered the Quota Management System in October 2004, and quota is allocated by species, with the objective of reducing catches of longfins (regarded as the more vulnerable of the two species). The export of glass eels is not allowed, and future capture of glass eels for use within New Zealand as farming seed stock will probably involve a reciprocal reduction in quota of yellow eels.

A major focus of eel management in New Zealand has been the retention of closed areas to provide escapement of silver eels. A previous survey of these areas (Jellyman 1993) highlighted the extent to which they were often compromised by hydro impacts; for instance, while on paper, National Parks seemed to provide a reasonable level of protection for longfins (almost 30% of the total lake area of New Zealand), over 80% of the area is affected by hydro dams. As a precursor to evaluating the adequacy of silver eel escapement from these areas, a GIS-based survey is underway to estimate the extent of protected areas and potentially protected areas and the stock of eels contained in such areas,. A number of initiatives are ongoing to facilitate recruitment into such areas and also provide opportunities of escapement of silver eels by such techniques as time-specific spillway releases of water (Watene and Boubée 2005), installation of subsurface outfalls, or trapping and downstream transfer.

The eel industry, government, and Maori have undertaken enhancement of areas where hydro dams have affected upstream recruitment. Currently there are transfer programs into 18 rivers and lakes, and between 2 and 3 t (approximately 2–3 million juvenile eels) are transferred annually. Growth rates of transplanted eels can be rapid, achieving the 220-g minimum size within 2 years (Beentjes et al. 1997; Jellyman and Beentjes 1998). Trial transfers of larger eels (30–50 cm) of both species have also been carried out from areas of high to low density; recaptures of coded-wire tagged eels have indicated the likelihood that low densities have favored differentiation into females (Jellyman and Beentjes 1998; Beentjes and Jellyman 2003), a process of potential benefit to management of longfin eels.

Summary

There is no clear evidence that stocks of shortfin eels have been seriously compromised by the extensive commercial eel fishery. While there is some anecdotal evidence of reduced glass eel recruitment in the Waikato River, this will be partly offset by the increased survival of juvenile eels in this major catchment as a result of manual transfer above hydro stations. However, such augmented stocks will contribute few silver eels, because downstream migration is impeded by the hydro stations. Although the wild eel fishery selectively harvests female shortfins, this species tends to grow more rapidly than longfins and matures at a smaller size and younger age. There is little evidence of a decline in CPUE, while theoretical models predict that an annual exploitation rate of 10% would reduce escapement of female eels by only about 50%. Perhaps of greatest concern for this species is the extensive loss of lowland habitat as a result of wetland drainage and river channelization (Table 4). Because Australian and New Zealand shortfins appear genetically identical (Smith et al. 2001), this geographic range and assumed panmixia may afford a degree of buffering of New Zealand stocks to local overexploitation.

In contrast, longfins are slower-growing, have longer generation times, and have been more affected by reduced upstream access; as well, there is some evidence of reduced recruitment and CPUE. Whereas it might be expected that high fecundity in species like eels confers high resilience to overfishing with a consequent low likelihood of extinction, this is not supported by either fishery theory (Sadovy 2001) or studies (Sadovy and Cheung 2003). When reviewing criteria that describe fish most at risk to overexploitation, Sadovy (2001) noted that such species are usually relatively large, long-lived, and slow-growing, with late sexual maturation and often with a limited geographic range. Longfin eels exhibit all these criteria and, in addition, are semelparous, which accentuates their vulnerability.

The vulnerability of longfins to even relatively light fishing pressure led Hoyle and Jellyman (2002) to recommend conservative management based on the precautionary principle. In response to increasing concern about the status of longfins, a number of recent management initiatives have been designed to provide a greater measure of protection to this species, including catch-and-carry programs to transport juvenile eels above hydro dams, continuing research on silver eel bypass options, reduced quota for North Island longfins, increased reserve areas, and voluntary bans by commercial fishers on catching silver eels. Continuation of monitoring recruitment at index sites is of obvious importance in assessing whether there is evidence of changes in recruitment. Of course, given the long generation time for female eels in New Zealand, the full impact of changes in recruitment may not yet be evident in the wild eel fishery.

Acknowledgments

I thank my NIWA colleague Eric Graynoth for helpful comments on the text. Research was partly funded by the New Zealand Foundation for Research, Science and Technology Contract CO1X0211. Thanks also to the American Fisheries Society and the Great Lakes Fisheries Commission for financial assistance in attending the Eel Symposium at the 2003 AFS conference, and to helpful comments from two anonymous referees, and final editing by John Casselman.

References

Annala, J. H., K. J. Sullivan, C. J. O'Brien, N. W. McL. Smith, and S. J. A. Varian. 2002. Report from the Fishery Assessment Plenary, May 2002: stock assessments and yield estimates. Part 1: albacore to ling. Unpublished report held in NIWA library. Wellington.

Arai, T., T. Otake, D. J. Jellyman, and K. Tsukamoto. 1999. Differences in the early life history of the Australasian shortfinned eel *Anguilla australis* from Australia and New Zealand, as revealed by otolith microstructure and microchemistry. Marine Biology 135:381–389.

Beentjes, M. P. 1999. Size, age, and species composition of commercial eel catches from South Island market sampling, 1997–98. National Institute of Water and Atmospheric Research, New Zealand. Technical Report 51.

Beentjes, M. P., and B. Bull. 2002. CPUE analysis of the commercial freshwater eel fishery. New Zealand Fisheries Assessment Report 2002/18.

Beentjes, M. P., and B. L. Chisnall. 1997. Trends in size and species composition and distribution of commercial eel catches. New Zealand Fisheries Data Report 89.

Beentjes, M. P., and B. L. Chisnall. 1998. Size, age, and species composition of commercial eel catches from market sampling, 1996–97. National Institute of Water and Atmosphere, New Zealand. Technical Report 29.

Beentjes, M. P., B. L. Chisnall, J. A. T. Boubée, and D. J. Jellyman. 1997. Enhancement of the New Zealand eel fishery by elver transfers. New Zealand Fisheries Technical Report 45.

Beentjes, M. P., and D. J. Jellyman. 2003. Enhanced growth of longfin eels *Anguilla dieffenbachii* transplanted into Lake Hawea, a high country lake in South Island, New Zealand. New Zealand Journal of Marine and Freshwater Research 37:1–11.

Best, E. 1929. Fishing methods and devices of the Maori. Dominion Museum Bulletin 12:1–230.

Boubée, J. A. T., C. P. Mitchell, B. L. Chisnall, D. W. West, E. J. Bowman, and A. Haro. 2001. Factors regulating the downstream migration of mature eels (*Anguilla* spp,) at Aniwhenua Dam, Bay of Plenty, New Zealand. New Zealand Journal of Marine and Freshwater Research 35:121–134.

Watene, E. M., and J. A. T. Boubée. 2005. Selective opening of hydroelectric dam spillway gates for downstream migrant eels in New Zealand. Fisheries Management and Ecology 12:69–75.

Broad, T., C. R. Townsend, G. P. Closs, and D. J. Jellyman. 2002. Riparian land use and accessibility to fishers influence size class composition and habitat use by longfin eels in a New Zealand river. Journal of Fish Biology 61:1489–1503.

Burnet, A. M. R. 1952. Studies on the ecology of the New Zealand longfinned eel, *Anguilla dieffenbachii* Gray. Australian Journal of Marine and Freshwater Research 3:32–63.

Cairns, D. 1941. Life-history of the two species of New Zealand freshwater eel. Part I. Taxonomy, age, growth, migration, and distribution. New Zealand Journal of Science 23:53–72.

Cairns, D. 1942. Life-history of the two species of freshwater eel in New Zealand. II. Food and inter-relationships with trout. New Zealand Journal of Science 23:132–148.

Castle, P. H. J. 1963. Anguillid leptocephali in the southwest Pacific. Zoology Publication 33. Victoria University of Wellington, New Zealand.

Chisnall, B. L. 1989. Age, growth, and condition of freshwater eels (*Anguilla* sp.) in backwaters of the lower Waikato River, New Zealand. New Zealand Journal of Marine and Freshwater Research 23:459–465.

Chisnall, B. L., and J. W. Hayes. 1991. Age and growth of shortfinned eels (*Anguilla australis*) in the lower Waikato basin, North Island, New Zealand. New Zealand Journal of Marine and Freshwater Research 25:71–80.

Chisnall, B. L., B. J. Hicks, and M. L. Martin 2003. Effect of harvest on size, abundance, and production of freshwater eels *Anguilla australis* and *A. dieffenbachii* in a New Zealand stream. P. 177–189 *in* D. A. Dixon, editor. Biology, management, and protection of catadromous eels. American Fisheries Society, Symposium 33, Bethesda, Maryland.

Chisnall, B. L., D. J. Jellyman, M. L. Bonnett, and J. R. E. Sykes. 2002. Spatial and temporal variability in size of glass eels (*Anguilla* spp.) in New Zealand. New Zealand Journal of Marine and Freshwater Research 36:89–104.

Chisnall, B. L., and C. Kemp. 2000. Size, age, and species composition of commercial eel catches from market sampling in the North Island, 1997–98. Technical Report 87. National Institute of Water and Atmosphere, New Zealand.

Davey, A. J. H., and D. J. Jellyman. 2005. Sex determination in freshwater eels and management options for manipulation of sex. Reviews in Fish Biology and Fisheries 15:37–52.

Dijkstra, L. H., and D. J. Jellyman. 1999. Is the subspecies classification of the freshwater eels *Anguilla australis australis* Richardson and *A. a schmidtii* Phillipps still valid? Marine and Freshwater Research 50:261–263.

Francis, R. I. C. C., and D. J. Jellyman. 1999. Are mean size data adequate to monitor freshwater eel fisheries? Marine and Freshwater Research 50:355–366.

Glova, G. J. 1988. Fish density variations in the braided Ashley River, Canterbury, New Zealand. New Zealand Journal of Marine and Freshwater Research 22:9–15.

Glova, G. J. 2001. Effects of the presence of subadult longfinned eels (*Anguilla dieffenbachii*) on cover preferences of juvenile eels (*Anguilla* spp.) in replicate channels. New Zealand Journal of Marine and Freshwater Research 35:221–233.

Glova, G. J., D. J. Jellyman, and M. L. Bonnett, M. L. 1998: Factors associated with the distribution and habitat of eels (*Anguilla* spp.) in three New Zealand streams. New Zealand Journal of Marine and Freshwater Research : 32:283–297.

Graynoth, E., and D. J. Jellyman. 2002. Growth, survival, and recruitment of juvenile shortfinned eels (*Anguilla australis*) in a large New Zealand coastal lake. New Zealand Journal of Marine and Freshwater Research 36:25–37.

Graynoth, E., and M. J. Taylor. 2000. Influence of different rations and water temperatures on the growth rates of shortfinned eels and longfinned eels. Journal of Fish Biology 57:681–699.

Griffin, L. T. 1936. Revision of the eels of New Zealand. Transactions and Proceedings of the Royal Society of New Zealand 66:12–26.

Hicks, B. J., and H. M. C. McCaughan. 1997. Land use, associated eel production, and abundance of fish and crayfish in streams in Waikato, New Zealand. New Zealand Journal of Marine and Freshwater Research 31:635–650.

Hobbs, D. F. 1947. Migrating eels in Lake Ellesmere. Transactions and Proceedings of the Royal Society of New Zealand 77:228–232.

Hopkins, C. L. 1970. Some aspects of the bionomics of fish in a brown trout nursery stream. New Zealand Marine Department, Fisheries Research Bulletin 4.

Hopkins, C. L. 1971. Production of fish in two small streams in the North Island of New Zealand. New Zealand Journal of Marine and Freshwater Research 5:280–290.

Hoyle, S. D., and D. J. Jellyman. 2002. Longfin eels need reserves: modelling the impacts of commercial harvest on stocks of New Zealand eels. Marine and Freshwater Research 53:887–895.

Jellyman, D. J. 1977. Summer upstream migration of juvenile freshwater eels in New Zealand. New Zealand Journal of Marine and Freshwater Research 11:61–71.

Jellyman, D. J. 1979. Upstream migration of glasseels (*Anguilla* spp.) in the Waikato River. New Zealand Journal of Marine and Freshwater Research 13:13–22.

Jellyman, D. J. 1987. Review of the marine life history of Australasian temperate species of *Anguilla*. Pages 276–285 in M. J. Dadswell, R. J. Klauda, C. M. Moffitt, R. L. Saunders, R. A. Rulifson, and J. E. Cooper, editors. Common strategies of anadromous and catadromous fishes. American Fisheries Society, Symposium 1, Bethesda, Maryland.

Jellyman, D. J. 1989. Diet of two species of freshwater eel (*Anguilla* spp.) in Lake Pounui, New Zealand. New Zealand Journal of Marine and Freshwater Research 23:1–10.

Jellyman, D. J. 1993. A review of the fishery for freshwater eels in New Zealand. New Zealand Freshwater Research Report 10.

Jellyman, D. J. 1995. Longevity of longfinned eels *Anguilla dieffenbachii* in a New Zealand high country lake. Ecology of Freshwater Fish 4:106–112.

Jellyman, D. J. 1997. Variability in growth rates of freshwater eels (*Anguilla* spp.) in New Zealand. Ecology of Freshwater Fish 6:108–115.

Jellyman, D. J. 2001. The influence of growth rates on the size of migrating female eels (*Anguilla australis*) in Lake Ellesmere, New Zealand. Journal of Fish Biology 58:725–736.

Jellyman, D. J. 2003. The distribution and biology of the South Pacific species of *Anguilla*. P. 275–292 in K. Aida, K. Tsukamoto, and K. Yamauchi, editors. Eel biology. Springer, Tokyo.

Jellyman, D. J., and M. P. Beentjes. 1998. Enhancement of the eel stocks of Coopers Lagoon, Canterbury, by transfer of juvenile eels. Technical Report 22. National Institute of Water and Atmosphere, New Zealand.

Jellyman, D. J., M. L. Bonnett, J. R. E. Sykes, and P. Johnstone. 2003. Contrasting use of daytime habitat by two species of freshwater eel (*Anguilla* spp.) in New Zealand rivers. P. 63–78 *in* D. A. Dixon, editor. Biology, management and protection of catadromous eels. American Fisheries Society, Symposium 33, Bethesda, Maryland.

Jellyman, D. J., B. L. Chisnall, M. L. Bonnett, and J. R. E. Sykes. 1999. Seasonal arrival patterns of juvenile freshwater eels (*Anguilla* spp.) in New Zealand. New Zealand Journal of Marine and Freshwater Research 33:249–262.

Jellyman, D. J., B. L. Chisnall, L. H. Dijkstra, and J. A. T. Boubée. 1996. First record of the Australian longfinned eel, *Anguilla reinhardtii*, in New Zealand Marine and Freshwater Research 47:1037–1040.

Jellyman, D. J., B. L. Chisnall, J. R. E. Sykes, and M. L. Bonnett. 2002. Variability in spatial and temporal abundance of glass eels (*Anguilla* spp.) in New Zealand waterways. New Zealand Journal of Marine and Freshwater Research 36:511–517.

Jellyman, D. J., and G. D. Coates. 1976. The farming of freshwater eels in New Zealand. Indo-Pacific Fisheries Council 17th Session, Symposium on the Development and Utilisation of Inland Fisheries Resources, panel II (c). Indo-Pacific Fisheries Council, Colombo, Sri Lanka.

Jellyman, D. J., E. Graynoth, R. I. C. C. Francis, B. L. Chisnall, and M. P. Beentjes. 2000. A review of the evidence for a decline in the abundance of longfinned eels (*Anguilla dieffenbachii*) in New Zealand. Final research report for Ministry of Fisheries Research Project EEL9802 73. National Institute of Water and Atmospheric Research, Christchurch, New Zealand.

Jellyman, D. J., and C. M. Ryan. 1983. Seasonal migration of elvers (*Anguilla* spp.) into Lake Pounui, New Zealand, 1974–1978. New Zealand Journal of Marine and Freshwater Research 17:1–15.

Jellyman, D. J., and P. R. Todd. 1998. Why are migrating male shortfinned eels (*Anguilla australis*) in Lake Ellesmere, New Zealand, getting smaller but not younger? Bulletin Francais de la Peche et Pisciculture 349:141–152.

Jellyman, D. J., and K. Tsukamoto. 2002. First use of archival transmitters to track migrating freshwater eels *Anguilla dieffenbachii* at sea. Marine Ecology Progress Series 233:207–215.

Jones, J. B., M. Astill, and E. Kerei. 1983. The pond culture of *Anguilla australis* in New Zealand–with special reference to techniques and management of the experimental farm at Te Kaha, Bay of Plenty. Estratto dalla Rivista Italiana di Piscicoltura e Ittiopatologia Anno 18:85–117.

Jowett, I. G., and M. J. Duncan. 1990. Flow variability in New Zealand rivers and its relationship to in-stream habitat and biota. New Zealand Journal of Marine and Freshwater Research 24:305–317.

McCleave, J. D., and D. J. Jellyman. 2004. Male dominance in the New Zealand longfin eel population of a New Zealand river: probable causes and implications for management. North American Journal of Fisheries Management 24:90–505.

McDowall, R. M. 1990. New Zealand freshwater fishes: a natural history and guide. Heinemann-Reed, Auckland.

McDowall, R. M. 2000. The Reed field guide to New Zealand freshwater fishes. Reed Books, Auckland.

McDowall, R. M., and M. J. Taylor. 2000. Environmental indicators of habitat quality in a migratory freshwater fish fauna. Environmental Management 25:357–374.

Ministry for the Environment. 1997. The state of New Zealand's Environment 1997. The Ministry for the Environment, Wellington.

Minns, C. K. 1990. Patterns of distribution and association of freshwater fish in New Zealand. New Zealand Journal of Marine and Freshwater Research 24:31–44.

Moriarty, C. 1986. Variations in elver abundance at European catching stations from 1938 to 1985. Vie Milieu 36:233–235.

Moriarty, C., and W. Dekker. 1997. Management of the European eel. Fisheries Bulletin (Dublin) 15.

Richkus, W., and K. Whalen. 1999. American eel (*Anguilla rostrata*) scoping study. A literature and data review of life history, stock status, population dynamics and hydroelectric impacts. EPRI, Palo Alto, California.

Sadovy, Y. 2001. The threat of fishing to highly fecund fishes. Journal of Fish Biology 59 (Supplement A):90–108.

Sadovy, Y., and W. L. Cheung. 2003. Near extinction of a highly fecund fish: the one that nearly got away. Fish and Fisheries 4:86–99.

Schmidt, J. 1928. The fresh-water eels of Australia with some remarks on the shortfinned species of *Anguilla*. Records of the Australian Museum 16:179–201.

Shiao, J. C., W. N. Tzeng, A. Collins, and D. J. Jellyman. 2001. Dispersal pattern of glass eel stage of *Anguilla australis* revealed by otolith growth increments. Marine Ecology Progress Series 219:241–250.

Smith, P. J., P. G. Benson, C. Stanger, B. L. Chisnall, and D. J. Jellyman. 2001. Genetic structure of New Zealand eels *Anguilla dieffenbachii* and *A. australis* with allozyme markers. Ecology of Freshwater Fish 10:132–137.

Speed, S. R., G. N. Browne, and R. O. Boyd. 2000. Assessment and monitoring of commercial eel fisheries. Final report to the New Zealand Ministry of Fisheries.

Todd, P. R. 1980. Size and age of migrating New Zealand freshwater eels (*Anguilla* spp.). New Zealand Journal of Marine and Freshwater Research 14:283–293.

Todd, P. R. 1981. Timing and periodicity of migrating New Zealand freshwater eels (*Anguilla* spp.). New Zealand Journal of Marine and Freshwater Research 15:225–235.

Part II

Science, Ecology, and Life History

Genetic Differentiation of the Japanese Eel

MEI-CHEN TSENG*
Institute of Zoology, National Taiwan University, Taipei 10764, Taiwan

WANN-NIAN TZENG
Institute of Fishery Science, National Taiwan University, Taipei 10764, Taiwan

SIN-CHE LEE[1]
Institute of Zoology, Academia Sinica, Taipei 11529, Taiwan

Abstract.—Polymorphic microsatellite loci as genetic markers were used to reject the null hypothesis of panmixia for the Japanese eel, *Anguilla japonica*. Observed heterozygosity showed slight heterozygote deficiencies over all loci. One of the eight loci (MS-4) in one sample showed departure from Hardy-Weinberg equilibrium. Unbiased Nei's genetic distances ranged from approximately 0.058 to 0.134. A slight genetic differentiation was determined by F_{ST} and R_{ST} statistics when adjusted with Bonferroni correction. Although isolation by distance is often observed in marine species, its use as a null hypothesis seems questionable. Although the freshwater eel is categorized as a catadromous fish, the value of genetic diversity obtained fell within that of marine fishes. A higher correlation ($P < 0.001$) resulting from AMOVA supports the separation of Japanese eels into two management units: a low-latitude group (Shantou, Tanshui, and Fangliao) and a high-latitude group (Daecheon-myon, Yalu River, Hangzhou, and Mikawa Bay). Such a population subdivision will be useful for further applications of fisheries conservation and management in the northwestern Pacific Ocean.

Introduction

Although population structures of European eel *Anguilla anguilla*, Japanese eel *A. japonica*, and American eel *A. rostrata* have been studied intensively, controversy still exists as to whether these species are made up of single panmixia or multiple geographically based populations (Table 1). For European eel alone, protein electrophoresis and sequences of the mitochondrial DNA (mtDNA) control region support the hypothesis that eels from European and North African rivers belong to a panmictic population (De Ligny and Pantelouris 1973; Comparini et al. 1977; Lintas et al. 1998). Similar conclusions have been reached for American eel (Williams et al. 1973; Koehn and Williams 1978; Avise et al. 1986). Although results derived from both nuclear and cytoplasmic markers support the panmixia hypothesis for the genetic structure of Atlantic freshwater eels, Wirth and Bernatchez (2001) challenged existing opinion concerning genetic structure. Slight genetic dif-

---

[1] Corresponding author: sinchelee@yahoo.com.tw
*Current address: Department of Aquaculture, National Pingtung University of Science and Technology, Pingtung 912, Taiwan

Table 1. Studies of population genetics of freshwater eels (1973 to 2004).

Species	Molecular tool	Sampling locations	Result	Reference
American eel, *Anguilla rostrata*	isozyme	Northeastern America	panmictic population	Williams et al. (1973)
	mtDNA	Northeastern America coastline	panmictic population	Avise et al. (1986)
	microsatellite loci	Northeastern American	Population decline	Wirth and Bernatchez (2003)
European eel, *A. anguilla*	allozyme	Spain, Greece, Holland and Poland	panmictic population	De Ligny and Pantelouris (1973)
	isozyme	Mediterranean Sea and Welsh Atlantic coasts	panmictic population	Comparini et al. (1977)
	mtDNA	Northwestern Atlantic and Mediterranean coastal regions	panmictic population	Lintas et al. (1998)
	microsatellite loci	North Atlantic, Baltic Sea and Mediterranean Sea basins	differentiation	Wirth and Bernatchez (2001)
	mtDNA and microsatellite loci	Italy, Ireland, Morocco, Sweden, and U.K.	differentiation	Daemen et al. (2001)
	microsatellite loci	European	isolation by distance	Maes and Volckaert (2002)
Marble eel, *A. marmorata*	mtDNA	Indo-Pacific Ocean	differentiation	Ishikawa et al. (2004)
Japanese eel, *A. japonica*	isozyme	Taiwan and China	geographic clines	Chen et al. (1997)
	mtDNA	Taiwan, China and Japan	panmictic population	Sang et al. (1994)
		Taiwan, China and Japan	panmictic population	Ishikawa et al. (2001)
	microsatellite loci	Taiwan	historical decline	Tseng et al. (2003)
	microsatellite loci	Taiwan, China, Japan and Korea	differentiation	This study

ferentiation among 13 samples of European eels from the North Atlantic, the Baltic Sea, and the Mediterranean Sea basins refutes the panmictic population hypothesis (Wirth and Bernatchez 2001).

The Japanese eel is a temperate freshwater fish that is distributed in rivers of northeastern Asian countries, including Taiwan, Japan, China, and Korea (Tesch 1977). As a catadromous fish, it spawns in the sea and grows and matures in freshwater rivers. The spawning grounds are thought to be to the west of the Mariana Islands, at 15°N 140°E (Tsukamoto 1992), evidenced by the occurrence of newly hatched leptocephali in the area. Taking 4 to 6 months to drift passively to the coasts of northeast Asia by the Kuroshio Current, the leptocephali undergo metamorphosis on the way to their freshwater destinations. The metamorphosis into translucent elvers is complete before upstream migration. Eels live in rivers for 5 to 20 years, until they mature. Maturity occurs in late autumn, when they emigrate downstream to the ocean and return to the spawning grounds (Tesch 1977).

The Japanese eel is an important aquaculture species in northeastern Asian countries. Eel farmers in these countries catch large numbers of juveniles in estuaries from November to March during their upstream migration (Tzeng 1985). In these populations, the mitochondrial DNA sequences in the D-loop regions (Sang et al. 1994; Ishikawa et al. 2001) do not show interpopulation genetic differentiation, suggesting panmixia with low levels of genetic structuring due to high levels of gene flow. However, Japanese eels on the western Pacific fringe exhibit clear geographic clines when the IDHP and PGDH allozyme loci are used as genetic markers (Chan et al. 1997). A migration time lag from different parts of continents to the spawning grounds west of the Mariana Islands is hypothesized as a possible reason for the formation of this cline. However, the above results remain somewhat uncertain and controversial.

Previous studies of life cycles and population structures of aquatic animals have been limited due to the lack of proper markers. A possible solution to the question in the Japanese eel is the use of microsatellite DNA markers, which are characterized by high variability. The consistencies of microsatellite sequences include unique DNA sequences and tandem repeats of 1 to 5 bases in length (Beckmann and Weber 1992).

Because of a tendency for higher variability to be inherited in a Mendelian fashion and only the least amounts of tissue are required for PCR assay, microsatellites have been regarded as the most adequate genetic markers for solving many questions of biology (Wright and Bentzen 1994). The purpose of this study was to use eight polymorphic microsatellite loci to test genetic differentiation of Japanese eels in the northwestern Pacific Ocean.

Methods

Sampling

In total, 328 Japanese eel elvers were caught alive from seven distant locations throughout the species' range in northeastern Asia in the winter and spring of 1999 to 2000. The collections came from Tanshui and Fangliao in Taiwan; the Yalu River, Hangzhou, and Shantou in China; Mikawa Bay in Japan; and Daecheon-myon in Korea (Figure 1). All specimens were preserved in 95% ethanol prior to DNA extraction.

DNA Extraction

Genomic DNA was isolated and purified from muscular tissue. Five hundred micrograms of tissue with 1 mL lysis buffer was digested with 55 µL proteinase K solution (10 mM tris-HCl, pH 8.0, 2 mM ethylene diamine tetra-acetic acid (EDTA), 10 mM NaCl, 1% sodium dodecyl sulfate (SDS), 10

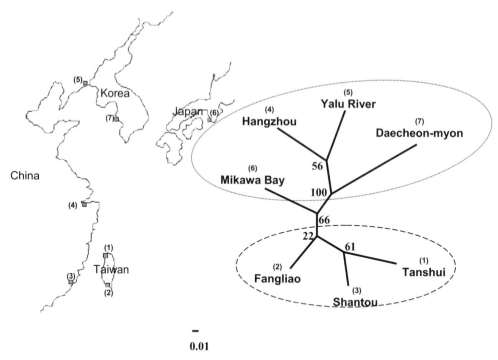

Figure 1. Sampling localities and topological tree for *Anguilla japonica*. The UPGMA tree is drawn using Nei's genetic distance measured for seven samples of Japanese eels.

mg/mL dithiothreitol (DTT), 0.5 mg/mL proteinase K). DNA extraction was carried out twice with phenol, twice with phenol/chloroform/isoamyl alcohol (25:24:1), and once with chloroform/isoamyl (24:1) as described by Kocher et al. (1989). DNA was precipitated once with 95% ethanol and once with 70% ethanol and then dissolved in TE buffer (10 mM tris-HCl, pH 8.0, 1 mM EDTA) following a standard procedure outlined by Sambrook et al. 1989.

Screening and Analysis of Microsatellite Loci

We screened eight microsatellite loci from the Japanese eel genome. The sequences submitted to EMBL under the accession numbers AJ297599-AJ297603, AJ297605, and AM062761-AM062762 (Tseng et al. 2001; Tseng et al. 2006) are listed in Table 2. Microsatellites were amplified via the polymerase chain reaction (PCR) and electrophoreses. Forward primers were labeled with FAM, TAMRA, or HEX flu, and then PCR was performed in a volume of 25 µL, including 1 ng genomic DNA, 2 pmol reverse primer, 2 pmol labeled forward primer, 25 mM dNTP, 0.05 to 0.1 mM $MgCl_2$, 10X buffer, and 0.5 U *Taq* polymerase (supplied by Takara, Shuzo Co., Shiga, Japan 2003). Amplification was performed in a PC-960G Microplate Thermal Cycler (Corbett Research) programmed with the following schedule: initial denaturing at 95°C for 4 min; and 38 cycles of 30 s each at successive thermal regimes of 94°C, 56–58°C, and 72°C. Eight microliters of product was precipitated with 95% alcohol. Semiautomated genotyping was performed by a capillary MEGABACE-500 Analysis system. Data were scored by Genetic profiler Software 1.5 (Amersham Biosciences).

Table 2. Locus name, repeat motifs, primer sequence, and PCR conditions of Japanese eel microsatellite loci detected by PCR amplification.

Locus	Repeat motifs	Primer sequence (5'–3')	Annealing temp (°C)(mM)	MgCl$_2$	Range of allele sizes (bp)
MS-1	(GT)$_{16}$	F:TCGAGACACCAGATAGTCAC R:ACATCCTAGGCTCACACC	58	0.5	188–230
MS-2	(GA)$_{15}$	F:ATTTCACGTCATCGGACCTGC R:GCTGGGAGCGACGCTTTATC	56	0.5	103–143
MS-3	(GT)$_{10}$	F:GGTATGAATGCAGGCGTTTATG R:GCAACCGATTTGATCTCCAG	56	0.5	79–97
MS-4	(GT)$_{15}$	F:CCTTCAGATTGCTAGCAC R:CGGAGTCTAATTGTCTCCTC	58	0.5	117–155
MS-5	(GT)$_{19}$	F:ACAGAGCCAGACAAACAGAC R:GGTCAGCAAGCAAAACGAAC	56	1.0	83–115
MS-6	(GA)$_{17}$	F:TGTCTAACACTAAGAAAAGGAGAGG R:GGCTGCCAGTATCTTCTCAAAG	58	1.0	133–181
MS-7	(GT)$_9$	F:AGTAAAGAGTCCCACGCATTC R:AAGGTGGATTTTTGCTGGCTC	54	0.5	76–90
MS-8	(GT)$_{12}$	F:AGGCTGAAGTGAGTATGCTCAG R:AGATATGGAAGCAGGATGGAG	56	0.5	100–120

Data Analysis

The observed (H_O) and expected (H_E) heterozygosities were independently calculated for each locus (Yang and Yeh 1993). Expected genotypic frequencies under random mating were calculated using the algorithm by Levene (1949), and likelihood ratio (G^2) tests for Hardy-Weinberg equilibrium were performed for each locus. To examine the relationship among populations, Nei's unbiased genetic distances (Nei 1978) were computed between all pairs of populations. The original topology of the phylogenetic tree was inferred from the neighbor-joining method based on Nei's unbiased genetic distances. One thousand bootstrap resamplings were used for evaluating support of the data set for the relationships.

F_{ST} and R_{ST} were used to examine population subdivisions (Weir and Cockerham 1984; Raymond and Rousset 1995). R_{ST} is an analog of F_{ST} that assumes a stepwise mutation model of repeat DNA (Raymond and Rousset 1995). The significance level was adjusted by sequential Bonferroni correction (Holm 1979; Rice 1989; Sankoh et al. 1997).

We tested isolation by distance (IBD) as an indicator of an emerging population structure by a typical regression of geographic distance on Nei's genetic distance. We used Mantel tests for correlation of two parameters to examine the significance of IBD relationships (Mantel 1967; Smouse et al. 1986). The hierarchical genetic structure was investigated by analysis of molecular variance (AMOVA; Excoffier et al. 1992) based on an analysis of the variance of genetic distances.

Results

Primer sequences and PCR conditions, including different concentrations of MgCl$_2$ and annealing temperatures of the eight polymorphic microsatellite loci that were correctly amplified, are given in Table 2. All eight loci were highly variable, with the number of alleles ranging from 10 in MS-3 to 25 in MS-6, with an average of 19.25. The sizes of the

Table 3. Levels of genetic variation observed at eight microsatellite loci within seven Japanese eel samples: sample size (n), number of alleles detected at each locus, observed (H_o) and expected (H_E) heterozygosity within samples, number of unique alleles (U) in each sample, number of solitary missing alleles (S) in each locus, observed number of alleles (na), and effective number of alleles (ne). *Indicates a significant Hardy-Weinberg disequilibrium level at 5%.

Locus	Location	Tanshui $n = 49$	Fangliao $n = 50$	Shantou $n = 46$	Hangzhou $n = 47$	Yalu River $n = 44$	Mikawa Bay $n = 47$	Daecheon-myon $n = 45$	Mean	na	ne
MS-1	No. alleles (U/S)	12 (0/0)	14 (2/0)	14 (0/1)	14 (2/1)	15 (0/0)	11 (0/1)	16 (0/0)	13.71	21	9.82
	H_o	0.774	0.759	0.758	0.767	0.778	0.731	0.800	0767		
	H_E	0.868	0.899	0.880	0.871	0.897	0.866	0.927	0.887		
MS-2	No. alleles (U/S)	15 (0/0)	16 (0/1)	18 (0/0)	15 (0/0)	15 (0/1)	17 (0/0)	15 (0/0)	15.86	22	13.55
	H_o	0.742	0.828	0.818	0.833	0.833	0.846	0.829	0.818		
	H_E	0.909	0.936	0.925	0.906	0.921	0.929	0.913	0.920		
MS-3	No. alleles (U/S)	5 (1/0)	5 (0/0)	7 (1/0)	6 (0/0)	6 (0/0)	7 (1/0)	4 (0/0)	5.714	10	2.99
	H_o	0.516	0.586	0.667	0.567	0.528	0.654	0.514	0.576		
	H_E	0.619	0.693	0.698	0.672	0.635	0.706	0.628	0.664		
MS-4	No. alleles (U/S)	11 (0/0)	12 (0/0)	12 (0/0)	11 (1/0)	10 (0/0)	11 (0/0)	10 (0/0)	11	17	9.49
	H_o	0.742	0.759	0.788*	0.767	0.778	0.769	0.743	0.764		
	H_E	0.881	0.883	0.898	0.898	0.857	0.903	0.880	0.886		
MS-5	No. alleles (U/S)	12 (0/0)	11 (1/0)	12 (0/0)	9 (0/1)	9 (0/0)	11 (0/0)	14 (1/0)	11.14	17	6.72
	H_o	0.774	0.724	0.758	0.667	0.667	0.731	0.800	0.731		
	H_E	0.868	0.838	0.841	0.793	0.791	0.864	0.905	0.843		
MS-6	No. alleles (U/S)	17 (0/0)	19 (0/0)	21 (0/0)	16 (0/1)	19 (1/0)	15 (0/0)	18 (1/1)	17.86	25	17.10
	H_o	0.871	0.828	0.848	0.833	0.833	0.846	0.829	0.841		
	H_E	0.936	0.947	0.947	0.936	0.946	0.939	0.938	0.941		
MS-7	No. alleles (U/S)	13 (0/0)	12 (1/0)	12 (0/1)	13 (0/1)	11 (1/0)	9 (0/1)	13 (0/1)	11.86	22	7.95
	H_o	0.742	0.793	0.758	0.767	0.750	0.808	0.771	0.770		
	H_E	0.879	0.863	0.878	0.895	0.847	0.871	0.889	0.875		
MS-8	No. alleles (U/S)	16 (1/1)	13 (0/0)	16 (1/0)	18 (1/0)	16 (1/0)	12 (0/2)	15 (0/1)	15.14	20	12.83
	H_o	0.839	0.759	0.849	0.800	0.694	0.769	0.771	0.783		
	H_E	0.918	0.893	0.915	0.933	0.768	0.876	0.915	0.888		
Mean	No. alleles	12.62	12.75	14	12.75	12.62	11.62	13.12	12.78	19.25	10.06
	H_o	0.750	0.754	0.780	0.75	0.733	0.769	0.757	0.756		
	H_E	0.860	0.869	0.873	0.863	0.833	0.869	0.874	0.863		
Total	U/S	2/1	4/1	2/2	4/4	3/1	1/4	2/3			

Table 4. Nei's unbiased genetic distance for Japanese eel samples from seven locations.

Location	Daecheon-myon	Mikawa Bay	Yalu River	Hangzhou	Shantou	Tanshui	Fangliao
Daecheon-myon	0						
Mikawa Bay	0.072	0					
Yalu River	0.066	0.091	0				
Hangzhou	0.060	0.086	0.058	0			
Shantou	0.086	0.083	0.081	0.131	0		
Tanshui	0.096	0.105	0.0894	0.116	0.078	0	
Fangliao	0.092	0.069	0.134	0.103	0.088	0.101	0

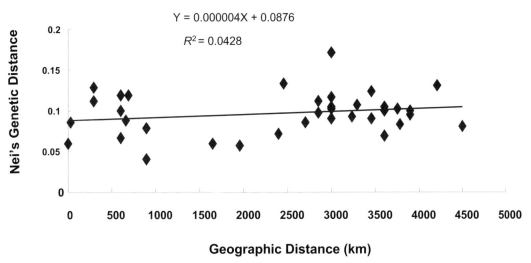

Figure 2. Relationships between Nei's genetic distance and geographic distance (km). Pearson correlation coefficients (r) and significance of the correlations (P) are given in text.

alleles over the eight loci ranged from 79 bp in MS-3 to 230 bp in MS-1. Among them, locus MS-3 was the shortest (<100 bp, Table 2). The observed heterozygosity (H_O) over all loci ranged from 0.514 ± 0.068 (MS-3) to 0.871 ± 0.031(MS-6), with an average of 0.756 ± 0.075. The expected heterozygosity (H_E) ranged from 0.619 (MS-3) to 0.947 (MS-6), with an average of 0.863 (Table 2). The result showed slight heterozygote deficiencies when tested with Hardy-Weinberg equilibrium.

For studying evolutionary relationships among seven spatial samples, unbiased Nei's genetic distances were examined and shown to range from approximately 0.058 (Yalu River/Hangzhou) to 0.134 (Yalu River/Fangliao), with an average of 0.09 ± 0.021 (Table 3). For further determination of population subdivisions, F_{ST} and R_{ST} were used to obtain respective values of 0.002 to 0.015 (mean, 0.008) and –0.009 to 0.05 (mean, 0.016) (Table 4).

Nei's unbiased genetic distance versus coastal geographical distances for all possible paired combinations of seven Japanese eel samples showed no significant correlation (Figure 2). The Mantel test for correlation of param-

Table 5. Pair-wise F_{ST} estimates between samples above the diagonal and R_{ST} estimates below the diagonal. The significance level was adjusted by Bonferroni's correction.

Location	Daecheon-myon	Mikawa Bay	Yalu River	Hangzhou	Shantou	Tanshui	Fangliao
Daecheon-myon	-----	0.006*	0.005	0.002	0.006**	0.009**	0.007*
Mikawa Bay	0.011	-----	0.008**	0.007*	0.006*	0.015**a	0.004
Yalu River	0.007	0.048**a	-----	0.003	0.007**a	0.009**	0.015**a
Hangzhou	0.010	0.050**a	0.019*	-----	0.013**a	0.012**a	0.009*
Shantou	–0.002	0.016	0.023**	0.005	-----	0.005	0.006
Tanshui	0.005	0.036**a	0.028**	0.011**	–0.009	-----	0.009**
Fungliao	0.017	0.022*	0.030**	0.024	–0.008	–0.003	-----

* $p < 0.05$; ** $p < 0.01$; a $p < 0.0014$.

eters excludes a possible isolation-by-distance principle in Japanese eel samples ($r = 0.123$, $P = 0.258$). When Nei's genetic distances were substituted by F_{ST} and R_{ST} values, results were similar. The neighbor-joining tree constructed on the basis of the genetic distance data set can be grouped into two clades.

When Japanese eels were grouped into two clades including high-latitude groups (Daecheon-myon, Yalu River, Hangzhou, and Mikawa Bay) and low-latitude groups (Shantou, Tanshui, and Fangliao), the hierarchical genetic structure tested by AMOVA indicated that 1.95% of the total genetic variation partitioned in the among-groups category ($P < 0.05$), 95.73% was within populations ($P < 0.001$), and 2.32% was among populations within a group. Nei's genetic distance ranged from 0.058 to 0.091 in the high-latitude group, 0.078 to 0.101 in the low-latitude group, and 0.069 to 0.134 between high- and low-latitude populations. The tree topology suggested that dispersion of Japanese eel elvers to the coast does not occur randomly.

Discussion

As a catadromous fish, the Japanese eel has more alleles per unit of microsatellite locus (mean 19.25) than do anadromous (mean 10.8) and freshwater fishes (mean 9.1) but slightly fewer than marine fishes (mean 19.9) (DeWoody and Avise 2000). The mean number of alleles per locus per sample varied between 11.62 and 14.00 in Japanese eels and between 9.6 and 12.4 (Daemen et al. 2001) or 12.9 and 21.2 (Wirth and Bernatchez 2001) in European eels, all of which are within the range for teleosts. These results imply a progressive change in genetic variability among freshwater, anadromous, catadromous, and marine fishes. In addition, the significantly low mean heterozygosity of 0.54 assayed in freshwater fishes and the high value of 0.77 in marine fishes (DeWoody and Avise 2000) reveal that Japanese eels (0.75) are intermediate with respect to mean levels of microsatellite variation. Although the freshwater eel is categorized as a catadromous fish, its genetic diversity is close to that of marine fishes.

One of eight loci showed a slight departure from expected heterozygosity (H_E) in one sample (Table 2). This may be associated with the Wahlund (1928) effect, where the decrease in heterozygosity is caused by a mixing of differentiated subsamples, and to the null allele effect, where the increase in homozygosity is caused by failure of amplification of an allele mutated in the primer region.

Genetic differentiation indices (F_{ST}, R_{ST}) estimated at the time when glass eels approach the estuaries indicate a weak but significant spatial divergence among samples. Recent studies have argued for a random mating system in anguillid eels, but Wirth and Bernatchez (2001) viewed the European eel differently. However, we support the nonpanmictic hypothesis in Japanese eels because of the significant genetic differentiation index. The magnitude of spatial differentiation in Japanese eels (F_{ST} = 0.002 to 0.015, mean 0.008) is higher than that of the European eel (0.0017 in Daemen et al. 2001; 0.004 in Wirth and Bernatchez 2001). Each species consists of different genetic structures found in the Pacific and Atlantic habitats due to their own particularly hydrographic systems.

We can reject the isolation-by-distance hypothesis for the eels analyzed in the present study; however, when examining the Mantel relation test, the European eel otherwise conforms to this model (Wirth and Bernatchez 2001). Interspecific differences in genetic structure result from various current systems and evolutionary histories. The inconsistency with the isolation-by-distance model is evidenced by the greater divergence between some closely spaced sites. For example, the genetic distance between Mikawa Bay and Fangliao is smaller than the genetic distance between Mikawa Bay and Daecheon-myon. The different groups of elvers passively drifting to destinations depend on complicated subcurrent systems of the northwestern Pacific Ocean.

The Φ-statistic of AMOVA (hierarchical analysis of molecular variance) shows the genetic variance between two groups (Φ_{CT} = 0.009, $P < 0.05$). Thus, Japanese eel populations can be clearly distinguished into a two-groups model, whose general profile is clearly shown in the relevant tree topology (Figure 1). The older metamorphosis age was determined in the high-latitude group compared with that in the lower-latitude group (Cheng and Tzeng 1996).

Current world fisheries have been threatened by overfishing and habitat destruction through dam construction and industrial pollution. Management efforts are extremely important for commercial fisheries, which, through overharvesting, can become economically extinct well before the exploited species becomes threatened with biological extinction (Botsford et al. 1997). In this case, eel populations in the northwestern Pacific Ocean can be classified into two groups based on significant divergence in nuclear allele frequencies. Furthermore, the major roles that ecology, behavior, and environmental conditions of fish populations play in fisheries management need to be recognized.

Acknowledgments

The authors wish to express their gratitude to H. Y. Teng and C. W. Chang for collecting specimens from Taiwan. Special thanks are due to Profs. Y. H. Xie and H. P. Oka for providing us with the samples from China and Japan. We thank two anonymous reviewers for their constructive comments on the manuscript.

References

Avise, J. C., G. S. Helfman, N. C. Saunders, and L. S. Hales. 1986. Mitochondrial DNA differentiation in North Atlantic eels: population genetic consequences of an unusual life history pattern. Proceedings of the National Academy of Sciences of the USA 83:4350–4353.

Beckmann, J. S., and J. L. Weber. 1992. Survey of human and rat micosatellites. Genomics 12:627–631.

Botsford, L. W., J. C. Castilla, and C. H. Peterson. 1997. The management of fisheries and marine ecosystems. Science 277:509–515.

Chan, I. K. K., D. K. O. Chan, S. C. Lee, and K. Tsukamoto. 1997. Genetic variability of the Japanese eel *Anguilla japonica* (Temminck and Schlegel) related to latitude. Ecology of Freshwater Fish 6:45–49.

Cheng, P. W., and W. N. Tzeng. 1996. Timing of metamorphosis and estuarine arrival across the dispersal range of the Japanese eel *Anguilla japonica*. Marine Ecology Progress Series 131:87–96.

Comparini, A., M. Rizzotti, and E. Rodino. 1977. Genetic control and variability of phosphoglucose isomerase (PGI) in eels from the Atlantic Ocean and the Mediterranean Sea. Marine Biology 43:109–116.

Daemen, E., T. Cross, F. Ollevier, and F. A. M. Volckaert. 2001. Analysis of the genetic structure of European eel (*Anguilla anguilla*) using microsatellite DNA and mtDNA markers. Marine Biology 139:755–764.

De Ligny, W., and E. M. Pantelouris. 1973. Origin of the European eel. Nature (London) 246:518–519.

DeWoody, J. A., and J. C. Avise. 2000. Microsatellite variation in marine, freshwater and anadromous fishes compared with other animals. Journal of Fish Biology 56:461–473.

Excoffier, L., P. E. Smouse, and J. M. Quattro. 1992. Analysis of molecular variance inferred from metric distances among DNA haplotypes: application to human mitochondrial DNA restriction data. Genetics 131:479–491.

Holm, S. 1979. A simple sequentially rejective multiple test procedure. Scandinavian Journal of Statistics 6:65–70.

Ishikawa, S., J. Aoyama, K. Tsukamoto, and M. Nishida. 2001. Population structure of the Japanese eel *Anguilla japonica* as examined by mitochondrial DNA sequencing. Fisheries Science 67:246–253.

Ishkawa, S., K. Tsukamoto, and M. Nishida. 2004. Genetic evidence for multiple geographic populations of the giant mottled *Anguilla marmorata* in the Pacific and Indian oceans. Ichthyological Research 51:343–353.

Kocher, T. D., W. K. Thomas, A. Meyer, S. V. Edwards, S. Pabo, F. X. Villablabca, and A. C. Wilson. 1989. Dynamics of mitochondrial DNA evolution in animals: amplification and sequencing with conserved primers. Proceedings of the National Academy of Sciences of the USA 86:6196–6200.

Koehn, R. K., and G. C. Williams. 1978. Genetic differentiation without isolation in the American eel *Anguilla rostrata*. II: Temporal stability of geographic variation. Evolution 32:624–637.

Levene, H. 1949. On a matching problem in genetics. The annals of mathematical statistics 20:91–94.

Lintas, C., J. Hirano, and S. Archer. 1998. Genetic variation of the European eel *Anguilla anguilla*. Molecular Marine Biology and Biotechnology 7:263–269.

Maes, G. E., and F. A. M. Volckaert. 2002. Clinal genetic variation and isolation by distance in the European eel *Anguilla anguilla* (L.). Biological Journal of the Linnean Society 77:509–521.

Mantel, N. 1967. The detection of disease clustering and a generalized regression approach. Cancer Research 27:209–220.

Nei, M. 1978. Estimation of average heterozygosity and genetic distance from a small number of individuals. Genetics 89:583–590.

Raymond, M., and F. Rousset. 1995. An exact test for population differentiation. Evolution 49:1280–1283.

Rice, W. R. 1989. Analyzing tables of statistical tests. Evolution 43:223–225.

Sambrook, J., E. F. Fritsch, and T. Maniatis. 1989. Molecular cloning, a laboratory manual, 2nd edition. Cold Spring Harbor Laboratory Press, New York.

Sang, T. K., H. Y. Chang, C. T. Chen, and C. F. Hui. 1994. Population structure of the Japanese eel *Anguilla japonica*. Molecular Biology and Evolution 11:250–260.

Sankoh, A. J., M. F. Huque, and S. D. Dubey. 1997. Some comments on frequently used multiple endpoint adjustments methods in clinical trials. Statistics in Medicine 16:2529–2542.

Smouse, P. E., J. C. Long, and R. R. Sokal. 1986. Multiple regression and correlation extensions of the Mantel test of matrix correspondence. Systematic Zoology 35:627–632.

Tesch, F. W. 1977. The eel: biology and management of anguillid eels. Chapman and Hall, London.

Tseng, M. C., C. A. Chen, H. W. Kao, W. N. Tzeng, and S. C. Lee. 2001. Polymorphisms of GA/GT microsatellite loci from *Anguilla japonica*. Marine Biotechnology 3:75–280.

Tseng, M. C., W. N. Tzeng, and S. C. Lee. 2003. Historical decline in the Japanese eel *Anguilla japonica* in northern Taiwan inferred from genetic variations. Zoological Studies 42:556–563.

Tseng, M. C., W. N. Tzeng, and S. C. Lee. 2006. Population genetic structure of the Japanese eel, *Anguilla japonica*, in the northwestern Pacific Ocean: evidence of non-panmictic populations. Marine Ecology Progress Series 308:221–230.

Tsukamoto, K. 1992. Discovery of the spawning area for Japanese eel. Nature (London) 356:789–791.

Tzeng, W. N. 1985. Immigration timing and activity rhythms of the eel, *Anguilla japonica*, elvers in the estuary of northern Taiwan, with emphasis on environmental influences. Bulletin of Japanese Society of Fisheries Oceanography 47/48:11–28.

Wahlund, S. 1928. The combination of populations and the appearance of correlation examined from the standpoint of the study of heredity. Hereditas 11:65–106.

Weir, B. S., and C. C. Cockerham. 1984. Estimating F-statistics for the analysis of population structure. Evolution 38:1358–1370.

Williams, G. C., R. K. Koehn, and J. B. Mitton. 1973. Genetic differentiation without isolation in the American eel, *Anguilla rostrata*. Evolution 27:192–204.

Wirth, T., and L. Bernatchez. 2001. Genetic evidence against panmixia in the European eel. Nature (London) 409:1037–1040.

Wirth, T., and L. Bernatchez. 2003. Decline of North Atlantic eels: a fatal synergy? Proceedings of the Royal Society of London, Series B 270:681–688.

Wright, J. M., and P. Bentzen. 1994. Microsatellites: genetic markers for the future. Reviews in Fish Biology and Fisheries 4:384–388.

Yang, R. C., and F. C. Yeh. 1993. Multilocus structure in *Pinus contoria* Dougl. Theoretical and Applied Genetics 87:568–576.

New Perspectives on the Early Life History of Tropical Anguillid Eels: Implications for Resource Management

MICHAEL J. MILLER[1], JUN AOYAMA, AND KATSUMI TSUKAMOTO

Ocean Research Institute, The University of Tokyo
1-15-1 Minamidai, Nakano, Tokyo 164-8639 Japan

Abstract.—Recent studies on leptocephali and glass eels of anguillid species in the western North Pacific and Indonesian Seas suggest that tropical eels have very different life history characteristics than temperate species, which may have important implications for their conservation and management. Some species in the Indonesian Seas region, such as the Indonesian mottled eel *Anguilla celebesensis* and the Indonesian longfinned eel *A. borneensis*, appear to have short spawning migrations and larval durations compared with temperate species. Species such as the Indonesian mottled eel *A. celebesensis* likely have multiple populations that spawn locally and recruit back to the same area. However, the giant mottled eel *A. marmorata* appears to have several separate populations in various regions of the Indian Ocean and western North and South Pacific oceans. The northern population of this species probably spawns in the North Equatorial Current region of the western North Pacific and has a long spawning migration more characteristic of temperate species. These findings suggest that the population structures of various tropical and temperate eel species may be quite different. Therefore some tropical anguillid species may require management at regional levels rather than as single panmictic species, as generally has been the case for temperate species.

Introduction

Eels of the genus *Anguilla* are well known for their long migrations from freshwater or coastal growth habitats to spawning areas far out in the open ocean. Because of this type of offshore spawning and the apparently random return of their larvae throughout their ranges, anguillid eel species in temperate regions such as North America, Europe, East Asia, and Australia and New Zealand have been historically viewed as probably having large single panmictic spawning populations. Each of these species has been considered to have one spawning area where all adults throughout their range return to spawn and then die. Their larvae, called leptocephali, are then transported by currents back toward their juvenile growth habitats.

The question about whether spawning and recruitment patterns shown by northern temperate anguillid eels have resulted in single panmictic populations has been the focus of considerable research using various genetic methods. Although most initial studies of the two species of Atlantic eels found no spatial heterogeneity within either species (see Avise 2003), some recent studies using allozymes (Maes and Volckaert 2002) and the newly developed genetic markers of microsatellite DNA

---

[1] Corresponding author: miller@ori.u-tokyo.ac.jp

(Daemen et al. 2001; Wirth and Bernatchez 2001) have detected some genetic structure in the European eel, *Anguilla anguilla*. In contrast, more recent microsatellite studies have found no evidence of genetic structure in the European eel or the American eel, *A. rostrata* (Wirth and Bernatchez 2003; Dannewitz et al. 2005). Similar studies on the Japanese eel, *A. japonica*, in East Asia have produced evidence both for and against the presence of genetic structure (Sang et al. 1994; Chan et al. 1997; Ishikawa et al. 2001; Tseng et al. 2009, this volume).

However, even if there is some spatial heterogeneity within these species, the level of genetic divergence is very small compared with that found within most species of widely distributed marine organisms (Avise 2000) and may represent only minor levels of reproductive segregation or differential recruitment patterns throughout the species' range. Whether or not catadromous eels have panmictic population structures has important management implications, because if a species is largely or entirely panmictic, then it can be managed as one population throughout its range. This means that the effects of continental habitat loss or overfishing in one part of the range of a species should not significantly affect future recruitment back to that particular area if the population is stable in other areas. For example, even if a particular region of the species' range has very low survival and spawner escapement, recruitment back to that region may remain constant if there is still enough spawner escapement from other regions.

This model for catadromous eels may not be useful for all species, because new information suggests that panmixia may not be typical of tropical anguillids. Recent studies on the distribution of leptocephali of tropical anguillids have found evidence of short spawning migrations and the presence of more than one spawning area for the same species (Aoyama et al. 1999, 2003; Arai et al. 2001a; Kuroki et al. 2006a). Data on larval durations of glass eels from various areas also have suggested that different spawning areas exist for tropical eels in the Indonesia and Philippines region (Arai et al. 2001a, 2003). In addition, the most widespread anguillid, the giant mottled eel has been found to have at least five genetically distinct populations in various regions of the Indian and western Pacific oceans (Ishikawa et al. 2004). Therefore, if some tropical anguillid species have multiple spawning areas or genetically isolated populations, they cannot be viewed by fisheries managers in the same way as temperate eels. Any eel species that is nonpanmictic will require a site-specific, rather than a species-wide, management approach.

This paper examines recent findings on the early life history of tropical eels and discusses their implications for population structure. Improved understanding of the population structure of tropical eels is urgently needed to guide effective conservation efforts for these species that are found in many parts of the world.

Species Ranges of Tropical Anguillids

Tropical eels are widely distributed on both sides of the equator in the Indian and Pacific oceans and in the Indonesian Seas region, with about four species or subspecies found in the Indian Ocean, five in the Indonesian Seas region, five or six in the New Guinea and Solomon Islands region, and four across the south Pacific from eastern Australia to Tahiti (Table 1; Ege 1939; Watanabe 2003). The giant mottled eel, African longfin eel *A. mossambica*, and African mottled eel *A. bengalensis labiata* (*A. nebulosa labiata*) are present in east Africa along the western Indian Ocean, and the Indian mottled eel *A. bengalensis bengalensis* (*A. nebulosa nebulosa*) is present along the Bay of Bengal in the northern Indian Ocean. The ranges of the latter two species also extend southward to the Indian Ocean side of Sumatra and Java Islands of southern Indonesia where the giant mottled eel is also present. In the Indonesian Seas region (Figure 1), the giant mottled

Table 1. Tropical species and subspecies of anguillid eels of the western Pacific and Indian oceans, listing the relative sizes of their ranges and early life history (ELH) studies on their leptocephali and on the inshore migration or otolith microstructure of their glass eels. See Figure 1 for the ranges of the species in the Indonesia region and Watanabe et al. (2003) for the ranges of all species.

Region/Species	Size of species range	ELH studies	Region/Species	Size of species range	ELH studies
Indonesia region			Western South Pacific		
A. borneensis	Very small	3,17	A. reinhardtii	Medium	2
A. interioris	Small	3,18	A. bicolor pacifica	Large	2,7
A celebesensis	Small	3,4,5,8,10,11,12,17	A. megastoma	Large	2
A. bicolor pacifica	Large	1*,3,2,4,5,7,8,11,12,17	A. obscura	Large	2
A. marmorata	Very large	1*,3,4,5,7,8,9,11,12,14,16,17	A. marmorata	Very large	2,7
N. Eastern Indian Ocean			Western Indian Ocean		
A. bengalensis bengalensis	Medium		A. bengalensis labiata	Medium	
A. bicolor bicolor	Large	1,6,13,19	A. mosambica	Medium	1,15
A. marmorata	Very large	1*	A. bicolor bicolor	Large	1,15
			A. marmorata	Very large	1,15

Jespersen 1942[1], Aoyama et al. 1999[2], 2003[3], Arai et al. 1999a[4],b[5],c[6], 2001a[7], b[8], 2002[9], 2003[10], and Marui et al. 2001[11], Sugeha et al. 2001a[12], Setiawan et al. 2001[13], Miller et al. 2002[14], Robinet et al. 2003[15], Kuroki et al. 2005[16], 2006a[17]b[18]*, 2007[19]; *Leptocephali could not be clearly identified, but may have included these species.

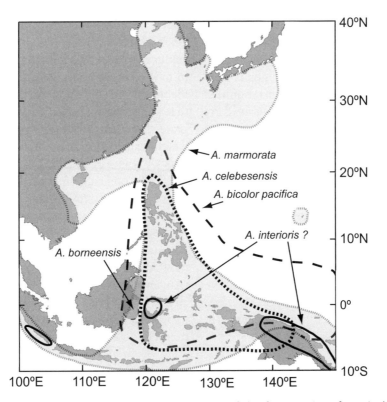

Figure 1. Map showing the estimated species ranges of the five species of tropical anguillid eels that inhabit the western North Pacific and Indonesian Seas regions, according to Ege (1939) and other recent reports or observations of various life history stages of these species.

eel is widely distributed and the Indonesian shortfin eel *A. bicolor pacifica* reaches as far as Taiwan, with a few glass eels being found as far north as southern Japan (Yamamoto et al. 2001). The Indian shortfin eel *A. bicolor bicolor* is also widely distributed and is found on both sides of the Indian Ocean. In contrast, the Indonesian mottled eel *A. celebesensis* is more restricted to Indonesia and the Philippines. The Indonesian longfinned eel *A. borneensis* (*A. malgumora* in Smith 1999) has the smallest range of any anguillid and is found only in eastern Borneo (Kalimantan) Island. The New Guinea eel *A. interioris* has been found only on western New Guinea. but it also appears to live in east-central Sulawesi Island and along western Sumatra based on the collection of genetically identified leptocephali there (Kuroki et al. 2006b).

In the South Pacific Ocean, the giant mottled eel is widely distributed across the tropical islands from New Guinea to New Caledonia and eastward to Tahiti (Ege 1939; Watanabe 2003). This species has also been reported as far east as the Galapagos Islands (McCosker et al. 2003). Polynesian longfin eel *A. megastoma* and the Pacific shortfinned eel *A. obscura* overlap with the giant mottled eel in the tropical South Pacific. The Australian longfinned eel *A. reinhardtii* is found along the east coast of Australia and in New Caledonia. It also has been reported from northern New Zealand but is not very abundant there (Jellyman et al. 1996). Interestingly, there are no tropical anguillids in the Atlantic Ocean, which may be due to factors associated with the historical entry of anguillids into the North Atlantic and the difficulty in their becoming established in a different ocean gyre system (see Tsukamoto et al. 2002).

Recent Advances in Early Life History Studies

Studies on Tropical Eel Leptocephali

The discovery of small anguillid leptocephali in the Indian Ocean off the west coast of Sumatra in 1929 (Jespersen 1942; see Miller 2003) suggested that tropical eels may not migrate as far to spawn as do temperate species. However, the overlapping meristic characters of tropical anguillid leptocephali posed formidable obstacles to species identification, which complicated the interpretation of Jespersen's (1942) survey results. This problem has been solved by the recent development of genetic techniques that definitively identify eels and leptocephali (Aoyama et al. 1999, 2000, 2001). These techniques were used recently to identify the leptocephali of both tropical and temperate anguillid species during a major sampling survey in the western Pacific (Aoyama et al. 1999). The leptocephali collected during other recent surveys in the Indonesian Seas also were genetically identified and have provided clear evidence that some species of tropical anguillids migrate short distances to spawn over the deepwater basins adjacent to their freshwater habitats (Aoyama et al. 2003).

This confirmation of the short spawning migrations of some species of tropical eels was obtained during two sampling surveys in the northern Indonesian Seas that collected small leptocephali of both the Indonesian mottled eel and the Indonesian longfinned eel (Aoyama et al. 2003). The first cruise collected a few small Indonesian mottled eel (12–20 mm TL) and Indonesian longfinned eel (8–13 mm TL) leptocephali in the Celebes Sea in

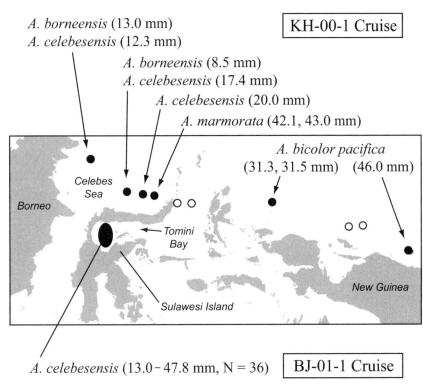

Figure 2. Map showing the locations of collection and sizes of the small tropical anguillid leptocephali in the Celebes Sea and in Tomini Bay during the sampling surveys of KH-00–1 in 2000 and BJ-01–1 in 2001 (data from Aoyama et al. 2003). The stations where anguillid leptocephali were collected during the KH-00–1 cruise are shown as black circles and the negative stations are shown as open circles. During the BJ-01–1 cruise, the leptocephali were collected at locations within or near the black oval in Tomini Bay, but the other stations where sampling occurred around Sulawesi Island and the other anguillid leptocephali that were collected are not shown.

February 2000 (Figure 2). The second cruise collected a larger number of leptocephali of two size classes of the Indonesian mottled eel in Tomini Bay of northern Sulawesi Island (Figure 2). The presence of small (13–23 mm TL) and large (30–48 mm TL) leptocephali in the central part of the semi-enclosed Tomini Bay provided strong evidence that eels from the freshwater rivers surrounding the bay had been spawning in the preceding months after making a short spawning migration. The water depth is greater than 1000 m throughout most of the bay, and there is some suggestion that water exchange due to tidal action may be relatively limited (Hatayama et al. 1996).

Therefore, it is likely that the majority of the leptocephali of the Indonesian mottled eel that are spawned in Tomini Bay may also recruit back to the areas surrounding the bay.

Compared to those in Tomini Bay, tropical eel leptocephali that are spawned in other areas such as the Celebes Sea may become more widely distributed. For example, in the Celebes Sea there is inflow from the western North Pacific (WNP), and some of this water continues southward through Makassar Strait into the Indian Ocean (termed the Indonesian Throughflow, Godfrey 1996; Gordon 2005). Although there may often be one or more large eddies in the Celebes Sea (Kashino et

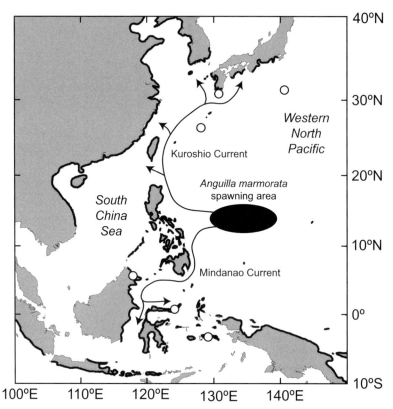

Figure 3. Map of the western Pacific Ocean and Indonesian Seas showing the estimated spawning area of the giant mottled eel *Anguilla marmorata* in the North Equatorial Current region based on the distribution of their leptocephali (Miller et al. 2002). The arrows indicate the likely path of transport of their leptocephali from the spawning area by the Kuroshio and Mindanao Current systems that both originate from the North Equatorial Current (see Fig. 5). The black lines on the coastlines show the estimated range of *A. marmorata*, and the open circles show the sampling locations of Ishikawa et al. (2004) in the region.

al. 2001) that could retain leptocephali, some leptocephali of the Indonesian mottled eel and Indonesian longfinned eel may be transported farther south through Makassar Strait by the consistent southward flow that appears to be present there (Wyrtki 1961; Miyama et al. 1995; Vranes et al. 2002; Gordon 2005). Some water from the Celebes Sea also appears to flow back out into the offshore areas of the WNP (Wyrtki 1961; Miyama et al. 1995).

Although tropical species such as Indonesian mottled eel and Indonesian longfinned eel may depend on some level of retention of their leptocephali near their local growth habitats, available evidence suggests that the giant mot-

tled eel may use more of a dispersal strategy. Leptocephali that resemble the giant mottled eel have been collected in the NEC region during several sampling surveys since 1991, and in recent years they have been confirmed genetically to be the giant mottled eel (Aoyama et al. 1999; Miller et al. 2002; Kuroki et al. 2006a). The consistent collection of giant mottled eel leptocephali in the NEC region indicates that it is a typical spawning area of this species. These leptocephali appear to be spawned by eels from the northern population of the giant mottled eel, which was identified by Ishikawa et al. (2004; see Figure 3 for their sampling locations), and this population appears to include eels from northern Indonesia to southern Japan. A single spawning area for this population in the NEC (Figure 3) could supply larvae to the entire region where the northern population appears to be found because the NEC bifurcates into north and south branches (Toole et al. 1990; Qu and Lukas 2003). This would result in the transport of their leptocephali both northward into the Kuroshio Current system and towards East Asia (Nitani 1972) and southward into the Mindanao Current (Lukas et al. 1991; Wijffels et al. 1995), which flows along the east coast of the southern Philippines before entering the Celebes Sea (Figure 3).

Studies on Tropical Glass Eels

Species Composition and Timing of Recruitment—Temporal patterns of tropical glass eel recruitment have been studied throughout the year near the mouth of the Poigar River estuary on the Celebes Sea side of northern Sulawesi Island, Indonesia. These collections were made with handheld dip nets that were fished in short transects sampled in the same way each month. Arai et al. (1999a) first reported that glass eels of the Indonesian mottled eel and the giant mottled eel were caught in large numbers during several months scattered throughout much of the year, with smaller numbers being collected in other months. The third species of glass eel that was collected at the Poigar River site was the Indonesian shortfin eel, but they were much less abundant than the other two species. However, to the south on the Indian Ocean side of Java Island of Indonesia, the Indian shortfinned eel *A. bicolor bicolor* is the dominant species, and their glass eels have been collected year-round in 1998 and 1999 near the mouth of the Cimandiri River (Setiawan et al. 2001).

These patterns of apparently year-round recruitment of tropical species of glass eels have been confirmed by a 3-year study at the Poigar River site using the same monthly sampling methodology (Sugeha et al. 2001a). This study found that the same three species were identified during all years of sampling. However, the 3-year dataset showed that although there were some generally consistent patterns, such as big catches of Indonesian mottled eels during June and low catches from January to April of all three years, there also was some variability in the recruitment patterns among years. This was especially evident in 1998, which was a strong El Niño year (McPhaden 1999) when catches of both Indonesian mottled eels and giant mottled eels were lower than in 1997 and 1999. Glass eel catches at this site were also large in 2000, with at least a few Indonesian mottled eels and giant mottled eels collected throughout the year (Bataragoa et al. 2001). These studies suggest that the seasonal recruitment pattern of tropical glass eels to the Poigar River estuary in non-El Niño years appears to have been fairly consistent in recent years despite apparent fluctuations in overall abundances. Although these data on glass eel recruitment suggest a prolonged spawning season for tropical anguillids, additional research is needed on the timing of downstream migration of tropical silver eels to determine the seasonality of their spawning migrations.

Age at Metamorphosis and Recruitment—Recent studies on otolith microstructure and microchemistry of glass eels of tropical anguillids have provided valuable new information on their larval durations. The daily deposition of otolith increments of the Indonesian mottled eel (Arai et al. 2000) and the giant mottled eel (Sugeha et al. 2001b) has been validated for glass eels that recruited to coastal areas. For Atlantic anguillids, it is unclear whether there is a period during the leptocephalus or, more likely, the marine glass eel phase when otolith increments are not consistently deposited every day (McCleave et al. 1998; Cieri and McCleave 2000). However, recent research suggests that daily depositions occur consistently

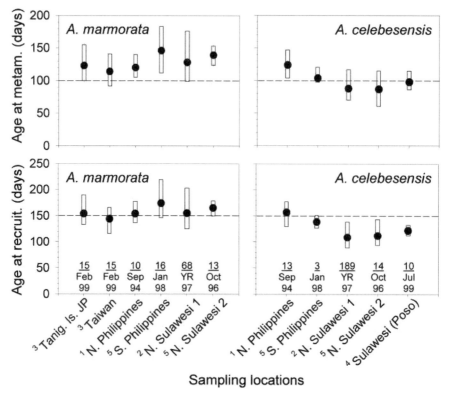

Figure 4. Plots of the estimated ages of tropical anguillid glass eels of the giant mottled eel *Anguilla marmorata* and the Indonesian mottled eel *A. celebesensis* at metamorphosis and at recruitment to the estuaries of Tanegashima Island, just south of mainland Japan, the Tung-Kang River of southern Taiwan, the Cagayan River of the northern Philippines, along the southern coast of Mindanao Island of the southern Philippines, the Poigar River of northern Sulawesi Island, and the Poso River of central Sulawesi Island (see Fig. 5 for locations). The black dots are the means and the narrow rectangles are the ranges. The sample sizes and dates on which the glass eels were collected are shown in the bottom two panels. Data are from Arai et al. 1999b[1], 2001b[2], 2002[3], 2003[4], and Marui et al. 2001[5].

during metamorphosis in the leptocephali of the ophichthid speckled worm eel *Myrophis punctatus* (Powles et al. 2006) and of the tarpon *Megalops atlanticus* (Shiao and Hwang 2004). Tropical glass eels differ from those of temperate Atlantic eels in that they never experience cold water at shallow depths and there are typically no large areas of continental shelf that they must cross. Therefore, they might not experience the same physiological conditions that may affect otolith deposition patterns of temperate glass eels. Nevertheless, distinct differences in larval durations between glass eels of tropical and temperate species and within and among tropical species have been observed. This suggests that these differences reflect significant differences in larval durations even if the question of continuous daily deposition in their otoliths cannot yet be resolved.

Otolith analyses of various samples of Indonesian mottled glass eels from the Indonesian Seas region have suggested that the duration of the leptocephalus stage of this species may vary considerably depending on the location of recruitment (Figures 4 and 5). Duration

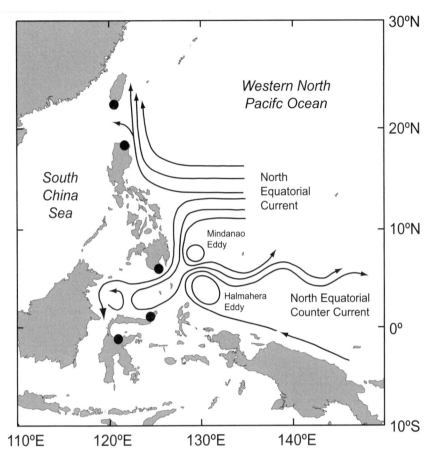

Figure 5. Map showing the typical patterns of surface currents in the western North Pacific and Celebes Sea region (adapted from Toole et al. 1990; Lukas et al. 1991, Wijffels et al. 1995; and Kashino et al. 2001) and the sampling locations for tropical anguillid glass eels used in the studies of their otolith microstructure in Figure 4 (except for Tanegashima Island of southern Japan).

of the leptocephalus stage (age at metamorphosis) and age at recruitment of Indonesian mottled glass eels collected at the mouth of the Poigar River on northern Sulawesi Island appear to be shorter than for those collected at the northern and southern margins of the Philippines. Glass eel ages at the Poigar River site were very stable at around 90 d for the leptocephalus stage and around 120 d at recruitment during each month in 1997 (Arai et al. 2001b). These ages are considerably younger than most of those measured for temperate anguillid glass eels (see Arai et al. 2001b; Marui et al. 2001), and they are also much younger than those of giant mottled eels from the Poigar River and other locations in the western Pacific region (Figures 4 and 5).

Indonesian shortfin and Indian shortfin glass eels collected at the Poigar River and at other locations in the Indonesia region were also much older than Indonesian mottled glass eels. This was clearly the case in the year-round samples of Indonesian shortfin eels at the Poigar River and other individual samples in the region (Arai et al. 1999c, 2001b, Marui et al. 2001) and for Indian shortfin glass eels collected at the Cimandiri River on the Indian Ocean side of Java Island (Arai et al. 1999b). The Indian shortfin glass eels collected each month at the Cimandiri River had mean ages ranging from 144 to 196 d, showing that glass eels at that location were consistently relatively old (Setiawan et al. 2001). However, a sample of the glass eels of this species from Réunion Island to the east of Madagascar Island in the Indian Ocean showed a much younger average age at recruitment, about 80 d (Robinet et al. 2003).

These data on glass eel ages suggest that the same species may have very different larval durations at different locations and also that different species that recruit to the same location can have very different ages. The contrasting ages of samples from different locations of both Indian shortfin and Indonesian mottled eels suggest either that spawning locations are at different distances from their respective recruitment areas or that the circulation patterns that affect how their larvae return to their recruitment areas differ among areas. The differing ages of giant mottled eels, Indonesian shortfin eels, and Indonesian mottled glass eels that recruit to the Poigar River (Arai et al. 2001b) and the distribution of their small leptocephali indicate that Indonesian mottled eels from the Poigar River probably spawn in the adjacent waters of the Celebes Sea. However, data for the other two species indicate that they spawn outside of the Celebes Sea, such as in the NEC, as appears to be the case for the northern population of giant mottled eels (Miller et al. 2002).

Management Implications of Tropical Eel Life History

Separate Spawning and Recruitment Areas

The findings of recent research on both leptocephali and glass eels of tropical anguillid eels clearly indicate that some tropical species of anguillid eels have multiple spawning areas. This new information will be very important for the development of effective management plans for tropical eels. The apparently short spawning migrations of the Indonesian mottled eel and the Indonesian longfinned eel in the Indonesian Seas (Aoyama et al. 2003) contrast with the long spawning migrations of the Japanese eel in the western North Pacific (Tsukamoto 1992) and American and European eels in the North Atlantic (McCleave 1993). Species ranges, distribution of leptocephali, and ages of glass eels also clearly indicate that some species of tropical eels such as the Indonesian mottled eels have multiple spawning areas and possibly different populations. The Indonesian mottled eel appears to spawn in at least three different areas in the vicinity of Indonesia and the Philippines (Aoyama et al. 2003; Arai et al. 2003). The geography of the region and the patterns of ocean currents in the western Pacific (Figure 5) are consistent with the view that this species spawns in multiple areas with limited mixing of leptocephali. This type of multiple spawning areas and recruitment patterns contrasts with the single spawning areas and recruitment patterns of temperate anguillids. Because of this, the eels of Indonesian mottled in each particular area need to be managed as separate stocks that may spawn and recruit back to the same general areas.

The other widespread tropical eel species, such as the two *A. bicolor* subspecies and the giant mottled eel, also have multiple spawning areas based on their geographic ranges and the findings of recent research. Remarkably, the northern population of the most widespread anguillid eel species, the giant mottled eel, which was suggested by Ishikawa et al. (2004) to be distributed from northern Indonesia to southern Japan, appears to spawn in the NEC region (Miller et al. 2002) and may represent a single population with a long spawning migration similar to temperate species. There must also be different spawning areas for each of the other populations of the giant mottled eel that are distributed from the western Indian Ocean, across southern Indonesia, and eastward through the tropical South Pacific, (Ishikawa et al. 2004). No information is available at present on whether the other populations of the giant mottled eel in the Indian Ocean and the South Pacific use a local spawning strategy like the Indonesian mottled eel or a longer spawning migration strategy like the giant mottled eel in the WNP region. More research is needed to clarify this interesting situation of two sympatric tropical eels in northern Indonesia apparently having two completely different spawning migrations and larval recruitment strategies, as appears to be the case for the Indonesian mottled eel and the giant mottled eel.

Management Strategies for Tropical Anguillids

The understanding of tropical eel population structures that is emerging from early life history studies suggests that species in each area should be considered as potentially different populations, at least until this is found not to be the case. The separate populations of giant mottled eels that have been identified in Madagascar, Sumatra, the marginal areas of the WNP (Indonesia to Japan), Fiji, and in Tahiti need to be managed as separate stocks. The complex geography of the islands and ocean currents in the Indonesia and Philippines region (Figure 5) and the early life history data reviewed here also suggest that Indonesian mottled eels inhabiting areas such as the northern Philippines, Celebes Sea, and Tomini Bay are likely separate stocks. The more widespread Indonesian shortfin eel may or may not have separate populations, and the same applies to the relatively widespread Pacific shortfinned eel and Polynesian longfin eel in the equatorial Pacific to the east. However, the Indonesian longfinned eel apparently has a very limited range (Figure 1) and may spawn only in the Celebes Sea or possibly the Sulu Sea, which suggests that it can likely be managed as a single panmictic population.

The apparent multi-population structures of at least some of these tropical species means that they may be more vulnerable to overfishing or localized effects of habitat loss than the more panmictic temperate species. If an efficient fishery for yellow and silver eels develops throughout a region such as Tomini Bay, it is possible that the spawning population could rapidly decline after several years of fishing pressure. There is an extensive system of weirs at the outlet of Poso Lake of central Sulawesi Island (Sugeha 2003), which is one of the largest drainages of Tomini Bay. This fishing pressure could have a major impact on the local stock of Indonesian mottled eels. Although some temperate species are recently showing signs of serious decline, they have been generally considered immune to the threat of local overfishing because the glass eels that recruit back to a particular area are the offspring of silver eels that may have originated from anywhere in the species' range. But in cases like that of the Indonesian mottled eel in Tomini Bay, there may be little or no recruitment from other areas of the species range, so the eels in each particular area need to be conserved to avoid a potential population decline.

There is at present little or no management protection of anguillid eels in Indonesia or the Philippines, and this is probably the case in most areas where tropical eels occur. However, as the human population rises in many of these areas and overfishing, habitat loss, and pollution increase, the need for effective conservation-based management intensifies. In some parts of Indonesia such as at Poso Lake, silver eels now sell at a high price. If these types of commercial activities increase in other areas, some eel populations may be at risk. Population genetics studies need to be done on each species throughout its range to provide a scientific basis for conservation and management efforts. Management plans need to be prepared and implemented sooner rather than later if the drastic population declines that have been recently observed in the northern temperate eels are to be prevented in their tropical counterparts.

Acknowledgments

We thank Sam Wouthuyzen of the Indonesian Institute of Sciences for his continuing collaboration and for his efforts in organizing and carrying out recent cooperative sampling surveys for tropical anguillid leptocephali in the Indonesian Seas. We acknowledge the efforts of S. Ishikawa in studying the population structure of the giant mottled eel *A. marmorata*, T. Arai, M. Marui, and H. Y. Sugeha in studying the recruitment patterns and otolith microstructure of tropical eels, M. Kuroki in studying the age and growth of tropical anguillid leptocephali, and we thank D. Limbong and all the people in Indonesia who helped with the sampling program at the Poigar River over the years. Jim McCleave and Jay Shiao provided useful suggestions for improving the manuscript.

References

Aoyama, J., S. Ishikawa, T. Otake, N. Mochioka, U. Suzuki, S. Watanabe, A. Shinoda, J. Inoue, P. Lockman, T. Inagaki, M. Oya, H. Hasumoto, K. Kubokawa, T. W. Lee, H. Fricke, and K. Tsukamoto. 2001. Molecular approach to species identification of eggs with respect to determination of the spawning site of the Japanese eel *Anguilla japonica*. Fisheries Science 67:761–763.

Aoyama, J., N. Mochioka, T. Otake, S. Ishikawa, Y. Kawakami, P. H. J. Castle, M. Nishida, and K. Tsukamoto. 1999. Distribution and dispersal of anguillid leptocephali in the western Pacific Ocean revealed by molecular analysis. Marine Ecology Progress Series 188:193–200.

Aoyama, J., S. Watanabe, M. Nishida, and K. Tsukamoto. 2000. Discrimination of catadromous eel species, genus *Anguilla*, using PCR-RFLP analysis of the mitochondrial 16SrRNA domain. Transactions of the American Fisheries Society 129:873–878.

Aoyama, J., S. Wouthuyzen, M. J. Miller, T. Inagaki, and K. Tsukamoto. 2003. Short-distance spawning migration of tropical freshwater eels. Biological Bulletin 204:104–108.

Arai, T., J. Aoyama, S. Ishikawa, M. J. Miller, T. Otake, T. Inagaki, and K. Tsukamoto. 2001a. Early life history of tropical *Anguilla* leptocephali in the western Pacific Ocean. Marine Biology 138:887–895.

Arai, T., J. Aoyama, D. Limbong, and K. Tsukamoto. 1999a. Species composition and inshore migration of the tropical eels *Anguilla* spp. recruiting to the estuary of the Poigar River, Sulawesi Island. Marine Ecology Progress Series 188:299–303.

Arai, T., D. Limbong, T. Otake, and K. Tsukamoto. 1999b. Metamorphosis and inshore migration of tropical eels *Anguilla* spp. in the Indo-Pacific. Marine Ecology Progress Series 182:283–293.

Arai, T., D. Limbong, T. Otake, and K. Tsukamoto. 2001b. Recruitment mechanisms of tropical eels, *Anguilla* spp. and implications for the evolution of oceanic migration in the genus *Anguilla*. Marine Ecology Progress Series 216:253–264.

Arai, T., D. Limbong, and K. Tsukamoto. 2000. Validation of otolith daily increments in the tropical eel *Anguilla celebesensis*. Canadian Journal of Zoology 78:1078–1084.

Arai, T., M. Marui, M. J. Miller, and Tsukamoto, K. 2002. Growth history and inshore migration of the tropical eel, *Anguilla marmorata* in the Pacific Marine Biology 140:309–316.

Arai, T., M. J. Miller, and K. Tsukamoto. 2003. Larval duration of the tropical eel, *Anguilla celebesensis*, from Indonesian and Philippines coasts Marine Ecology Progress Series 251:255–261.

Arai, T., T. Otake, D. Limbong, and K. Tsukamoto. 1999c. Early life history and recruitment of the tropical eel *Anguilla bicolor pacifica*, as revealed by otolith microstructure and microchemistry. Marine Biology 133:319–326.

Avise, J. C. 2000. Phylogeography: the history and formation of species. Harvard University Press, Cambridge, Massachusetts.

Avise, J. C. 2003. Catadromous eels of the North Atlantic: a review of molecular genetic finding relevant to natural history, population structure, speciation, and phylogeny. Pages 31–48 *in* K. Aida, K. Tsukamoto, and K. Yamauchi, editors, Eel biology, Springer Verlag, Tokyo.

Bataragoa, N. E., C. Onibala, H. Y. Sugeha, J. Aoyama, and K. Tsukamoto. 2001. Inter-annual variation of the inshore migration of tropical glass eels at the mouth of the Poigar River, Sulawesi Island, Indonesia. Pages 128–130 *in* K. Aida, K. Tsukamoto, and K. Yamauchi, editors. Proceedings of the In-

ternational Symposium: Advances in Eel Biology. The University of Tokyo, Tokyo.
Chan, I. K. K., D. K. O. Chan, S. C. Lee, and K. Tsukamoto. 1997. Genetic variability of the Japanese eel *Anguilla japonica* (Temminck and Schlegel) related to latitude. Ecology of Freshwater Fish 6:45–49.
Cieri, M. D., and J. D. McCleave. 2000. Discrepancies between otoliths of larvae and juveniles of the American eel: is something fishy happening at metamorphosis? Journal of Fish Biology 57:1189–1198.
Daemen, E., T. Cross, F. Ollevier, and F. A. M. Volckaert. 2001. Analysis of the genetic structure of European eel (*Anguilla anguilla*) using microsatellite DNA and mtDNA markers. Marine Biology 139:755–764.
Dannewitz, J., G. E. Maes, L. Johansson, H. Wickström, F. A. M. Volckaert, and T. Jarvi. 2005. Panmixia in the European eel: a matter of time. Proceedings of the Royal Society of London B Biological Science 272:1129–1137.
Ege, V. 1939. A revision of the Genus *Anguilla* Shaw. Dana Report 16:8–256.
Godfrey, J. S. 1996. The effect of the Indonesian throughflow on ocean circulation and heat exchange with the atmosphere: a review. Journal of Geophysical Research 101:12,217–12:237.
Gordon, A. L. 2005. Oceanography of the Indonesian Seas and their throughflow. Oceanography 18:14–27.
Hatayama, T., T. Awaji, and K. Akitomo. 1996. Tidal currents in the Indonesian seas and their effect on transport and mixing. Journal of Geophysical Research 101:12,353–12:373.
Ishikawa, S., J. Aoyama, K. Tsukamoto, and M. Nishida. 2001. Population structure of the Japanese eel *Anguilla japonica* as examined by mitochondrial DNA sequencing. Fisheries Science 67:246–253.
Ishikawa, S., K. Tsukamoto, and M. Nishida. 2004. Genetic evidence for multiple geographic populations of the giant mottled eel *Anguilla marmorata* in the Pacific and Indian oceans. Ichthyological Research 51:343–353.
Jellyman, D. J., B. L. Chisnall, L. H. Dijkstra, and J. A. T. Boubée. 1996. First record of the Australian longfinned eel, *Anguilla reinhardtii*, in New Zealand Journal of Marine and Freshwater Research 47:1037–1040.
Jespersen, P. 1942. Indopacific leptocephalids of the genus *Anguilla*: systematic and biological studies. Dana Report No. 22.
Kashino, Y., T. Firing, P. Hacker, A. Sulaiman, and Lukiyanto. 2001. Currents in the Celebes and Maluku seas, February 1999. Geophysical Research Letters 28:1263–1266.
Kuroki, M., J. Aoyama, M. J. Miller, T. Arai, H. Y. Sugeha, G. Minagawa, S. Wouthuyzen, and K. Tsukamoto. 2005. Correspondence between otolith microstructural changes and early life history events in *Anguilla marmorata* leptocephali and glass eels. Coastal Marine Science 29:154–161.
Kuroki, M., J. Aoyama, M. J. Miller, S. Wouthuyzen, T. Arai, and K. Tsukamoto. 2006a. Contrasting patterns of growth and migration of tropical anguillid leptocephali in the western Pacific and Indonesian Seas. Marine Ecology Progress Series 309:233–246.
Kuroki, M., J. Aoyama, S. Wouthuyzen, K. O. Sumardhiharga, M. J. Miller, G. Minagawa, and K. Tsukamoto. 2006b. Age and growth of *Anguilla interioris* leptocephali collected in Indonesian waters. Coastal Marine Science 30:264–268.
Kuroki, M., J. Aoyama, S. Wouthuyzen, K. Sumardhiharga, M. J. Miller, and K. Tsukamoto. 2007. Age and growth of *Anguilla bicolor bicolor* leptocephali in the eastern Indian Ocean. Journal of Fish Biology 70:538-550.
Lukas, R., E. R. Firing, P. Hacker, P. L. Richardson, C. A. Collins, R. Fine, and R. Gammon. 1991. Observations of the Mindanao Current during the western Equatorial Pacific Ocean Circulation Study. Journal of Geophysical Research 96:7089–7104.
Maes, G. E., and F. A. M. Volckaert. 2002. Clinal genetic variation and isolation by distance in the European eel *Anguilla anguilla* (L.). Biological Journal of the Linnaean Society 77:509–521.
Marui, M., T. Arai, M. J. Miller, D. J. Jellyman, and K. Tsukamoto. 2001. Comparison of early life history between New Zealand temperate eels and Pacific tropical eels revealed by otolith microstructure and microchemistry. Marine Ecology Progress Series 213:273–284.
McCleave, J. D. 1993. Physical and behavioural controls on the oceanic distribution and migration of leptocephali. Journal of Fish Biology 43(Supplement A):243–273.
McCleave, J. D., P. J. Brickley, K. M. O'Brien, D. A. Kistner-Morris, M. W. Wong, M. Gallagher, and S. M. Watson. 1998. Do leptocephali of the European eel swim to reach continental waters? Status of the question. Journal of the Marine Biological Association of the UK 78:285–306.
McCosker, J. E., R. H. Bustamante, and G. M. Wellington. 2003. The freshwater eel, *Anguilla marmorata*, discovered at Galapagos Noticias de Galapagos 62:2–6.
McPhaden, M. J. 1999. Genesis and evolution of the 1997–98 El Niño. Science 283:950–954.

Miller, M. J. 2003. The worldwide distribution of anguillid leptocephali. Pages 157–168 *in* K. Aida, K. Tsukamoto, and K. Yamauchi, editors, Eel biology. Springer Verlag, Tokyo.

Miller, M. J., N. Mochioka, T. Otake, and K. Tsukamoto. 2002. Evidence of a spawning area of *Anguilla marmorata* in the western North Pacific. Marine Biology 140:809–814.

Miyama, T., T. Awaji, K. Akitomo, and N. Imasato. 1995. Study of seasonal transport variations in the Indonesian seas. Journal of Geophysical Research 100:20,517- 20:541.

Nitani, H. 1972. Beginning of the Kuroshio. Pages 129–163 *in* H. Stommel, K. Yoshida, editors, Kuroshio: its physical aspects. University of Tokyo Press, Tokyo.

Powles, P. M., J. A. Hare, E. H. Laban, and S. M. Warlen. 2006. Does eel metamorphosis cause a breakdown in the tenets of otolith applications? A case study using the speckled worm eel (*Myrophis punctatus*, Ophichthidae) Canadian Journal of Fisheries and Aquatic Sciences 63:1460–1468.

Qu, T., and R. Lukas. 2003. The bifurcation of the North Equatorial Current in the Pacific. Journal of Geophysical Research 33:5–18.

Robinet, T., R Lecomte-Finiger, K. Escoubeyrou, and E. Feunteun. 2003. Tropical eels *Anguilla* spp. recruiting to Réunion Island in the Indian Ocean: taxonomy, patterns of recruitment and early life histories. Marine Ecology Progress Series 259:263–272.

Sang, T. K., H. Y. Chang, C. T. Chen, C. F. Hui. 1994. Population structure of the Japanese eel, *Anguilla japonica*. Molecular Biology and Evolution 11:250–260.

Setiawan, I. E., N. Mochioka, H. Amarullah, and A. Nakazono. 2001. Inshore migration and spawning season of the tropical eel *Anguilla bicolor bicolor* recruiting to the Cimandiri River estuary, Java Island, Indian Ocean. Pages 125–127 *in* K. Aida, K. Tsukamoto, and K. Yamauchi, editors. Proceedings of the International Symposium: Advances in Eel Biology. The University of Tokyo, Tokyo.

Shiao, J. C., and P. P. Hwang. 2004. Thyroid hormones are necessary for teleostean otolith growth. Marine Ecology Progress Series 278:271–278.

Smith, D. G. 1999. Anguillidae: freshwater eels. Pages 1630–1636 *in* Carpenter K. E., Niem V. H., editors. FAO species identification guide for fishery purposes: the living marine resources of the western central Pacific 3.

Sugeha, H. Y. 2003. Life history of tropical eel *Anguilla marmorata* in the Indonesian waters. Doctoral dissertation. University of Tokyo, Tokyo.

Sugeha, H. Y., T. Arai, M. J. Miller, D. Limbong, and K. Tsukamoto. 2001a. Inshore migration of the tropical eels, *Anguilla* spp., recruiting to the Poigar River estuary on Sulawesi Island. Marine Ecology Progress Series 221:233–243.

Sugeha, H. Y., A. Shinoda, M. Marui, T. Arai, and K. Tsukamoto. 2001b. Validation of otolith daily increments in the tropical eel *Anguilla marmorata*. Marine Ecology Progress Series 220:291–294.

Toole, J. M., R. C. Millard, Z. Wang, and S. Pu. 1990. Observations of the Pacific North Equatorial Current bifurcation at the Philippine coast. Journal Physical Oceanography 20:307–318.

Tseng, M. C., W. N. Tzeng, and S. C. Lee. 2006. Population genetic structure of the Japanese eel *Anguilla japonica* in the northwest Pacific Ocean: evidence of non-panmictic populations. Marine Ecology Progress Series 308:221-230.

Tseng, M. C., W. N. Tzeng, and S. C. Lee. 2009. Genetic differentiation of Japanese eel A*nguilla japonica*. Pages 59–69 *in* J. M. Casselman, and D. K. Cairns, editors. Eels at the edge. American Fisheries Society, Symposium 58, Bethesda, Maryland.

Tsukamoto, K. 1992. Discovery of the spawning area for the Japanese eel. Nature (London) 356:789–791.

Tsukamoto, K., J. Aoyama, and M. J. Miller. 2002. Migration, speciation and the evolution of diadromy in anguillid eels. Canadian Journal Fisheries and Aquatic Science 59:1,989–1,998.

Vranes, K., A. L. Gordon, and A. Field. 2002. The heat transport of the Indonesian throughflow and implications for the Indian Ocean heat budget. Deep-Sea Research II 49:1391–1410.

Watanabe, S. 2003. Taxonomy of the freshwater eels, Genus *Anguilla* Schrank, 1798. Pages 3–18 *in* K. Aida, K. Tsukamoto, and K. Yamauchi, editors. Eel biology. Springer-Verlag, Tokyo.

Wijffels, S., E. Firing, and J. Toole. 1995. The mean current structure and variability of the Mindanao Current at 8 N. Journal of Geophysical Research 100:18,421–18,435.

Wirth, T., and L. Bernatchez. 2001. Genetic evidence against panmixia in the European eel. Nature (London) 409:1037–1040.

Wirth, T., and L. Bernatchez. 2003. Decline of North Atlantic eels: a fatal synergy? Proceedings of the Royal Society of London Series B 270:681–688.

Wyrtki, K. 1961. Physical oceanography of the Southeast Asian waters. NAGA Report 2. Scripps Institution of Oceanography, La Jolla, California.

Yamamoto, T., N. Mochioka, and A. Nakazono. 2001. Seasonal occurrence of anguillid glass eels at Yakushima Island, Japan. Fisheries Science 67:530–532.

Reproductive Strategy of Female American Eels Among Five Subpopulations in the St. Lawrence River Watershed

VALÉRIE TREMBLAY[1,*]

Département de Biologie, Université du Québec à Rimouski
300 Allée des Ursulines, Rimouski, Québec G5L 3A1 Canada

Abstract.—The American eel *Anguilla rostrata* is declining in the St. Lawrence River watershed, where sex ratio is highly unbalanced in favor of females. Since the American eel is a panmictic species, this demographic dominance is implicated in reproductive potential of the species. The major objective of this study was to evaluate the reproductive strategies of five subpopulations of female eels. It was assumed that fecundity varies among subpopulations according to their migration distance because of the trade-off between energy allocated to gonads and to somatic tissues. Thirty female silver eels were collected from each of five locations in the St. Lawrence watershed 2,850–4,300 km from the spawning area. Among subpopulations, mean length ranged from 67.9 to 104.3 cm, weight from 595 to 2,366 g, fecundity from 6.5 to 14.5 million oocytes, age from 20 to 23 years, gonadosomatic index from 2.9 to 4.1%, and somatic lipid content from 17.5 to 21.7%. Because of panmixia, no genetic influence on intersite variability is expected. Environmental differences in growth habitats and individual fitness might determine acquisition and allocation of resources, as well as subsequent variability in traits that would affect reproduction. In contrast to previous hypotheses, variations in such traits were attributed to eel size rather than migration distance. The number of oocytes per silver eel was positively correlated with length rather than negatively correlated with migration distance. In the St. Lawrence watershed, large eels are highly fecund regardless of their distance from the spawning ground.

Introduction

The American eel *Anguilla rostrata* is showing sharp declines across its distribution range, particularly in the St. Lawrence River watershed (Castonguay et al. 1994; Casselman 2003; Dekker et al. 2003). Although eels within this watershed are a primary source of eggs (Couillard et al. 1997; Barbin and McCleave 1997; Verreault 2002), data are still insufficient to guide fisheries managers toward identification of escapement targets.

The American eel is considered a panmictic species (Avise et al. 1986; Wirth and Bernatchez 2003) and is therefore a unique population. In this study, the term subpopulation is applied to eels coming from the same growth location or watershed (Adam 1997; Verreault 2002).

Trends can be detected between northern and southern subpopulations of female American eels. Eels from northern subpopulations are slower-growing and longer, heavier, and older at migration (Hurley 1972; Facey and

---
[1] E-mail: valerie.tremblay@tecsult.aecom.com.
[*] Current address: Tecsult Inc., 2 Fusey, Trois-Rivières, Québec G8T 2T1 Canada

LaBar 1981; Helfman et al. 1987). Barbin and McCleave (1997) evaluated fecundity of female eels in Maine, but there is no such information for Canada at a watershed level. Nevertheless, studies (Barbin and McCleave 1997; Verreault 2002) have reported that fecundity might be correlated to migration distance between the spawning grounds—the Sargasso Sea (Schmidt 1922)—and growth habitats.

Relying on published data from 38 locations in Europe and North Africa within a range of 2,850 km, Vøllestad (1992) found a positive correlation ($r = 0.458$; $P < 0.01$) between body length at migration and migration distance of European female silver eels *Anguilla anguilla* and a negative correlation ($r = -0.653$; $P < 0.001$) between mean age and migration distance. However, it was not determined whether migration distance from the Sargasso Sea was related to fecundity.

Besides Vøllestad's study (1992) on the genus *Anguilla*, studies on other nonpanmictic diadromous species have also provided evidence that migration distance contributed to variability in reproductive traits. Schaffer and Elson (1975) related variations in life history traits among populations of Atlantic salmon *Salmo salar* across North America to migration distance traveled to reach the spawning grounds. In contrast to Vøllestad's (1992) study on European eels, their results showed that the mean age at first spawning in salmon increases with migration distance ($r = 0.83$; $P < 0.01$). Beacham and Murray (1993) examined fecundity and egg weight for five species of Pacific salmon *Oncorhynchus*. One of their main conclusions was that distance of freshwater migration to the spawning grounds usually had a strongly negative effect on fecundity and egg weight.

Traits such as length, age, and fecundity characterize reproductive strategy (Wootton 1984). However, reproductive traits can show modifications, called tactics, depending on plasticity of the fish (Iguchi and Tsukamoto 2001). Reproductive traits of eels show high phenotypic plasticity (Tesch 1977; Vøllestad 1992; Nilo and Fortin 2001). Indeed, fecundity of females is maximized by an increase in length at migration (Wenner and Musick 1974; Barbin and McCleave 1997; Verreault 2002), and this optimal length varies among habitats and individuals.

Differences in allocation between somatic and reproductive growth (Jobling 1994) can also lead to substantial variations in eel fecundity. In fact, the long prereproductive migration involves high energy costs for locomotion. Moreover, since this migration is considered to be completed without feeding (Pankhurst and Sorensen 1984), somatic energy attributed to migration costs (e.g., locomotion, basal metabolism, maintenance) has to be a priori accumulated. Such resource allocation into somatic energy reserves results in reduced energy for gonadal growth. Because of important migration costs and energy trade-offs, migration distance should be positively correlated with somatic lipid content and negatively correlated with fecundity. Thus, a broader understanding of the importance of energetics as a trade-off between somatic and gonadal growth might help explain differences in reproductive traits among subpopulations.

Few studies have investigated bioenergetics of eels. Larsson et al. (1990) considered fat content of European eels to be a factor inducing migration at a minimal level of 28% of body weight. Svedäng and Wickström (1997) found no correlation between maturity stage (yellow or silver phase) and muscle fat content. Limburg et al. (2003) established fat content on female silver eels within two geographic areas of the Baltic Sea. According to their results, eels exiting the Baltic Sea were significantly fatter (21.1%) than those collected near Denmark in the Danish Baltic Islands (18.6%).

The objective of this study was to determine reproductive strategies of five subpopulations of American eels within the St. Lawrence River watershed. This study is the first research to give insights into the physiological bases of different reproductive tactics of the American eel and considers available energy at migration. The hypothesis is that fecundity varies among subpopulations according to their migration distance. The subpopulation farthest from the Sargasso Sea is expected to show the lowest fecundity at a comparable length and the greatest somatic lipid content. It is expected that a reproductive strategy of eels would be to maintain a somatic condition that allows migration to the Sargasso at the expense of reproductive investment and lower fecundity.

Methods

Study Area and Sampling

Silver-phase females were sampled at time of emigration. All samples were collected during the peak of the spawning run in their respective locations and therefore were representative of subpopulation characteristics. Many peaks were detected in the upper part of the St. Lawrence watershed (McGrath et al. 2003). Samples were collected during one of these. All specimens ($N = 150$, 30 at each site) were obtained from five locations within the St. Lawrence River watershed (Figure 1), where migration distance to the Sargasso Sea varies by 1,450 km. The location of the Sargasso Sea was set at 25°N, 60°W according to McCleave et al. (1987). The shortest distance of each site from the Sargasso Sea was then measured with Softmap© software (topo 250 Canada, scale 1:250 000, 50 km precision). The nearest location is the Gulf of St. Lawrence, with a migration distance of 2,850 km, whereas the farthest is the Upper St. Lawrence River, at 4,300 km.

Sampling was done in 2001 on the North Shore at the Petite Trinité River (a north shore estuary tributary; 49°32'N, 67°14'W; October), on the South Shore at the Sud-Ouest River: (a south shore estuary tributary; 48°22'N, 68°43'W; September–October), and in the Middle Estuary at Kamouraska (47°27'N, 70°03'W; October). In 2002, sampling was conducted in the Gulf of St. Lawrence at Long Pond (a barachois pond connected to the gulf; 46°25'N, 63°05'W; September) and in the Upper St. Lawrence River in the vicinity of the Iroquois Dam (44°49'N, 75°18'W; August). Traps were different at each location, depending upon the capture site: Alaska trap nets, eel counting fences, fixed traps (commercial fishery), fyke nets, and fixed trawls. The commercial eel fishery in the Middle Estuary consisted of out-migrating adults from locations upstream in the watershed, whereas the other sites had resident yellow eels throughout the year but served as migratory corridors for maturing silver eels. Although traps were specific to a site, size selectivity is not suspected. Eels were collected during peaks of downstream migration and corresponded to the size range of female silver eels that have been reported for each site. To verify maturation stage (silver eel), external morphological parameters were measured according to Pankhurst's maturation index established for the European eel (Pankhurst 1982) and used by McGrath et al. (2003) for the American eel; these were ocular index, pectoral fin index, and girth to length.

Treatment of Fresh Eels

Eels were kept alive in an oxygenated holding tank, anesthetized by immersion in a 90 ppm solution of clove oil and ethanol in water. This concentration is about twice the anesthetic dose used by Anderson et al. (1997) and Peake (1998) on rainbow trout and nonsalmonid fishes. Eels were then sacrificed with a higher concentration of 360 ppm. Total body length (±0.5 mm) and total

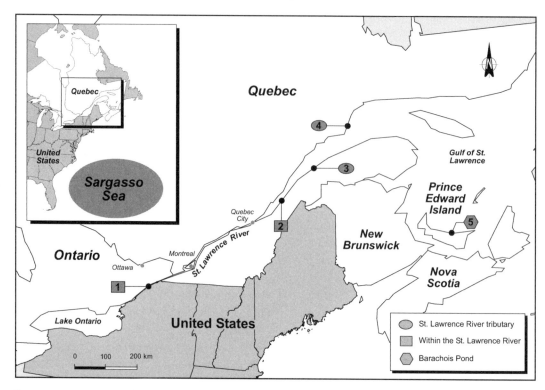

Figure 1. American eel sampling locations within the St. Lawrence River watershed: 1) Upper St. Lawrence River; 2) Middle Estuary; 3) South Shore; 4) North Shore; 5) Gulf of St. Lawrence.

body weight (±0.1 g) were measured for each eel. Both sagittal otoliths were extracted and stored in a solution of ethyl alcohol and glycerin (1:1) until age estimation. Eels were frozen at –2°C until further analysis.

Treatment of Gonads and Fecundity Estimation

Eels were thawed and gonads were removed and weighed to estimate the gonadosomatic index, based on the formula GSI = (gonad weight/total weight) × 100. Prior to counting, gonads were prepared according to Barbin and McCleave (1997) and modified by Verreault (2002). Gonads were submerged in a solution of 2% acetic acid for at least one week and agitated every day. Just prior to counting the oocytes, the solution was diluted with 15% sodium chloride (NaCl) to maintain the oocytes in a single plane. The solution was agitated for 20 min until it became a homogenized oocyte solution. For each eel, five subsamples of 0.1 mL were taken from the previous solution and placed in a Palmer-Maloney chamber (0.1 mL volume). Images were captured under a stereomicroscope Leica MZ9.5 with a CCD camera and viewed with Leica IM1000 system (4× magnification). Oocytes were counted with ImageJ© software, and the mean value of the five subsamples was noted as number of oocytes in 0.1 mL. Once total volume and final dilution were known, overall absolute fecundity (oocyte number) was calculated. Relative fecundity was defined as absolute fecundity of a 1,413-g eel; this weight corresponded to the mean weight of the individuals in the subpopulations sampled (standard individual weight). To ensure a maximal mean coefficient of variation of

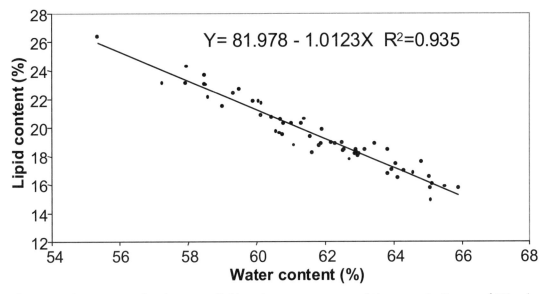

Figure 2. Linear regression between lipid and water contents of the somatic tissues of 56 eels. Regression equation and coefficient of determination are presented.

15%, five subsamples were used because Verreault (2002) reported such values with manual counts on eight subsamples using a McMaster chamber (0.15 mL).

Treatment of Somatic Tissues and Lipid Content

Somatic tissues were homogenized with a commercial meat grinder (U.S. Beckel), 10-g subsamples were dried for 24 h at 101 ± 3°C to estimate water content. Fifty-six randomly chosen dry samples were placed in Soxhlet cells for lipid extraction. Lipid content in the somatic tissues was obtained by gravimetry. The linear regression (Figure 2) between water and lipid contents was applied to the remaining samples. Duplicate analyses of water and lipid content were performed on six homogenates to calculate the variability of the homogenate. Variability was minor (average coefficient of variation <1%). The somatic tissues included all parts of the body posterior to the insertion of the pectoral fins.

Age Estimation

One of each pair of otoliths was prepared for age estimation according to Verreault (2002), a method composed of cleaning, embedding, polishing, etching, and staining. The final step was to observe the otolith under a binocular microscope at 60× magnification equipped with an image grabber that allowed digitization of the otoliths and estimation of ages on the computer. Three people independently performed the aging. If there was any divergence among the readings, the three readers performed an additional reading on the electronic images. Reading of otolith images was facilitated because each reader specifically marked each annulus.

Statistical Analyses

Systat 9.0 (SPSS 1999) and Statview (SAS) softwares were used for statistical analyses. Log_{10} transformed data normality was evaluated visually for each subpopulation. Homogeneity of variance was tested by

Table 1. Overall mean (± SD), range, and coefficient of variation (CV, `%) for each parameter taken from female silver eels captured in five subpopulations (N = 30 at each location) with different migration distances. Relative fecundity (in millions) was established as absolute fecundity for specimens with weight equal to 1,413 g; this weight corresponds to the mean weight of the five subpopulations.

Parameter	Upper St. Lawrence River	Middle Estuary	South Shore	North Shore	Gulf of St. Lawrence	Combined (N = 150)
Migration distance	4300	3500	3400	3200	2850	
Length (cm)	100.1 ± 6.6	83.7 ± 6.9	104.3 ± 6.7	67.9 ± 11.9	69.3 ± 4.7	85.1 ± 17.0
Min–max	89–112.3	71–98.5	90.6–115.9	53.2–91.0	60.1–82.3	53.2–115.9
CV (%)	6.6	8.2	6.5	17.56.8		19.9
Weight (g)	2290 ± 468	1183 ± 315	2366 ± 440	629 ± 364	595 ± 127	1413 ± 858
Min–max	1534–3340	709–1967	1447–3146	260–1407	358–1068	260–3340
CV (%)	20.4	26.6	18.6	57.8	21.3	60.7
Age	21 ± 4	20 ± 4	23 ± 5	20 ± 4	20 ± 3	21 ± 4
Min–max	14–30	14–29	11–32	14–27	15–30	1–32
CV (%)	18.7	19.0	21.0	17.9	14.8	19.1
GSI	2.9 ± 0.6	4.0 ± 0.5	4.0 ± 0.7	4.1 ± 0.5	3.9 ± 0.5	3.8 ± 0.7
Min–max	2.0–4.3	3.1–5.4	2.6–5.6	3.1–5.4	3.1–5.4	2.0–5.6
CV (%)	21.5	13.7	17.4	13.1	13.0	19.0
Fecundity (million)	14.5 ± 2.3	12.2 ± 3.2	13.3 ± 3.2	6.9 ± 3.1	6.5 ± 1.5	10.7 ± 4.3
Min–max	9.3–18.1	6.4–18.8	8.1–22.0	3.4–13.9	4.0–11.0	3.4–22.0
CV (%)	15.6	26.5	23.7	45.2	23.3	40.2
Relative fecundity (million)	9.2 ± 1.9	15.0 ± 4.0	8.0 ± 1.4	16.8 ± 4.3	15.8 ± 3.4	13.0 ± 4.8
Min–max	5.3–12.4	8.3–23.0	4.9–11.0	11.1–28.8	10.5–24.5	4.9–28.8
CV (%)	20.4	26.5	7.8	25.4	21.3	36.9
Somatic lipid (%)	21.7 ± 2.7	18.9 ± 1.7	21.1 ± 2.4	17.9 ± 2.5	17.5 ± 1.7	19.4 ± 2.8
Min–max	17.2–27.3	15.8–22.4	16.7–26.4	13.5–23.9	14.9–21.7	13.5–27.3
CV (%)	12.6	8.8	11.3	13.8	9.5	14.3

the F-max test. Since the variances were heterogeneous, nonparametric tests were used on the data. For each subpopulation, Spearman correlation matrix coefficients were determined for traits that could influence reproduction. Kruskal-Wallis One-Way Analysis of Variance was then used. Each individual comparison was performed by Tukey's test on rank data to identify differences in traits among subpopulations. Linear regressions of fecundity on length and weight followed the form $\log Y = \log a + b \log X$. Analysis of variance (ANOVA) was used on pooled data (by groups). Finally, a discriminant analysis on two canonical axes was performed to establish the main traits that influenced segregation into groups. Weight was combined with fecundity to create a new variable, relative fecundity (absolute fecundity of a 1,413-g eel), because of the variability of weight within subpopulations and to avoid co-linearity between length and weight in the discriminant analysis.

Results

Subpopulation Characteristics

Eels ($N = 30$ at each location) were analyzed, initially combined and then by subpopulation (Table 1; Figure 3). Within the St. Lawrence River watershed, age of eels was 21 ± 4 years at migration, gonad weight (GSI) was $3.8 \pm 0.7\%$, and somatic lipid content was $19.4 \pm 2.8\%$. Among subpopulations, mean length ranged from 67.9 to 104.3 cm, weight from 595 to 2,366 g, and fecundity from 6.5 to 14.5 million oocytes. According to the traits that could affect reproduction (Table 1; Figure 3) of each subpopulation, the Upper St. Lawrence River and South Shore (referred to as group 1) showed similar characteristics, as did the North Shore and Gulf of St. Lawrence (referred to as group 2). Similarities were emphasized by pooling the subpopulations into two groups. Kruskal-Wallis results showed that there was no significant difference in length (group 1: $P = 0.179$; group 2: $P = 0.921$), weight (group 1: $P = 0.964$; group 2: $P = 0.964$), fecundity (Group1: $P = 0.300$; group 2: $P = 0.999$), lipid content (group 1: $P = 0.969$, group 2: $P = 0.691$), and relative fecundity (group 1: $P = 0.162$; group 2: $P = 0.963$) between the Upper St. Lawrence River and South Shore and between the North Shore and Gulf of St. Lawrence. Group 1 was composed of female silver eels having a greater length, weight, and fecundity than eels of group 2. Although fecundity (oocyte number) was greater in eels from group 1, relative fecundity (oocyte number/mean weight) in group 1 was significantly lower than in group 2 (ANOVA, $F_{1,118} = 247,807$, $P < 0.001$): 8.5 million oocytes compared to 15.9 million oocytes, respectively. Pooled data demonstrated that eels from group 1 were significantly fatter (somatic lipid content) than those from group 2 (ANOVA, $F_{1,118} = 76.631$, $P < 0.001$): $21.4\% \pm 2.6\%$ and $17.7\% \pm 2.1\%$.

Variability of GSI was not significant among subpopulations except between the upper St. Lawrence (GSI = 2.9 ± 0.6) and the four other subpopulations (3.9–4.1). This significant difference ($P < 0.001$) occurred even if GSI was based on gonad-free body mass (i.e., gonad mass/(total weight – gonad mass) × 100) to avoid bias from autocorrelation and the effects of possible variability in the degree of maturity among fish (Couillard et al. 1997). There was no significant difference in age among subpopulations except for the Gulf of St. Lawrence and South Shore, which showed the lowest and highest mean ages: 20 ± 3 and 25 ± 5 years, respectively ($P = 0.010$).

At each location, there was a highly significant correlation between length and weight ($P < 0.001$; Table 2). For all subpopulations except the Upper St. Lawrence River, fecundity was positively correlated with length and weight (Table 2). Even though group 1 showed lower relative fecundity and higher lipid content than group 2 (Table 1; Figure 3), there was no significant correlation between relative fecundity and lipid content among subpopulations except for the Upper St. Lawrence River.

Size-Related Fecundity

Eel fecundity data were plotted against total body length and body weight (Figure 4) for each subpopulation. Absolute fecundity varied among subpopulations but increased with length and weight (Figure 4). However, all logarithmic relationships were different, and it was impossible to group the five subpopulations. All results (regressions equations and coefficients of determination) are presented by subpopulation (Table 3). Absolute fecundity of eels ranged between 3.4 million and 22.0 million oocytes for body length ranging from 53.2 to 115.9 cm and body weight ranging from 260 to 3,340 g. When the number of eggs per kilogram of individual is considered, large-bodied eels av-

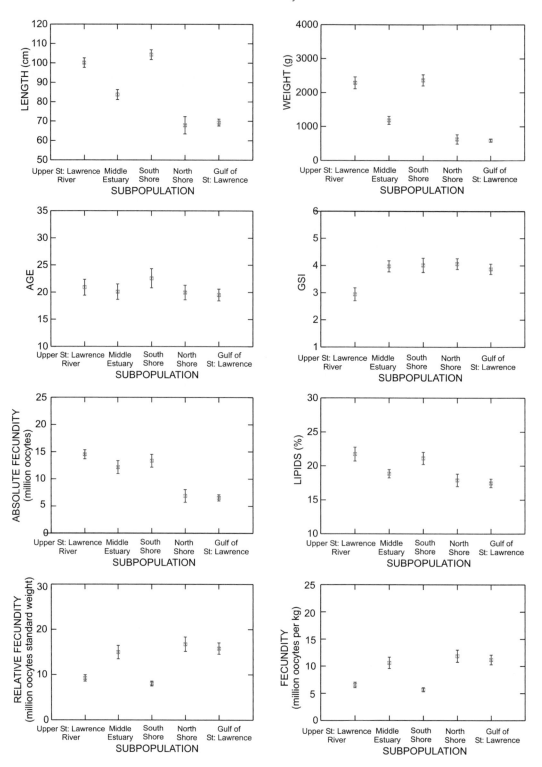

Figure 3. Mean values and 95% confidence intervals for traits associated with reproduction studied in female silver eels collected from five subpopulations in the St. Lawrence River watershed.

Table 2. Spearman correlation coefficients on seven parameters describing female silver eels in the St. Lawrence River watershed. Asterisk (*) indicates coefficients for which probability is significant (*: $0.05 \geq P > 0.01$; **: $0.01 \geq P > 0.001$; ***: $P \leq 0.001$).

A) Upper St. Lawrence River						
Variable	Length	Weight	Age	GSI	Fecundity	Lipid
Weight	0.886***					
Age	0.150	−0.021				
GSI	0.182	0.276	−0.133			
Fecundity	0.334	0.265	0.194	−0.320		
Lipid	0.394*	0.426**	−0.362	0.431*	−0.157	
Relative fecundity	−0.544**	0.721***	0.162	−0.329	0.385*	−0.398*

B) Middle Estuary						
Variable	Length	Weight	Age	GSI	Fecundity	Lipid
Weight	0.904***					
Age	−0.083	−0.160				
GSI	0.341	0.472*	−0.092			
Fecundity	0.400*	0.427*	−0.069	0.277		
Lipid	−0.115	0.012	−0.535**	0.196	0.128	
Relative fecundity	−0.442*	−0.439*	−0.060	−0.173	0.545**	0.223

C) South Shore						
Variable	Length	Weight	Age	GSI	Fecundity	Lipid
Weight	0.837***					
Age	0.351	0.343				
GSI	−0.083	0.098	−0.241			
Fecundity	0.586**	0.668**	0.371*	0.107		
Lipid	−0.163	−0.269	−0.261	−0.071	−0.309	
Relative fecundity	−0.032	−0.112	0.180	−0.002	0.583**	−0.184

D) North Shore						
Variable	Length	Weight	Age	GSI	Fecundity	Lipid
Weight	0.970***					
Age	0.148	0.060				
GSI	0.336	0.215	0.048			
Fecundity	0.874***	0.843***	−0.071	0.314		
Lipid	0.353	0.346	−0.202	0.174	0.435*	
Relative fecundity	−0.532**	−0.601**	−0.230	−0.010	−0.143	0.022

E) Gulf of St. Lawrence						
Variable	Length	Weight	Age	GSI	Fecundity	Lipid
Weight	0.930***					
Age	0.043	0.082				
GSI	0.123	0.152	−0.120			
Fecundity	0.581**	0.574**	0.072*	−0.150		
Lipids	−0.002	0.026	0.159	−0.204	0.249	
Relative fecundity	−0.256	−0.299	−0.096	−0.289	0.551**	0.294

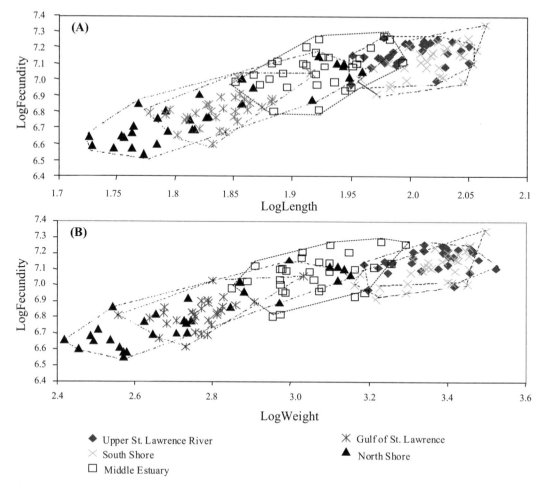

Figure 4. Linear regression among the five subpopulations sampled in the St. Lawrence River watershed of absolute fecundity (millions) on (A) body length (cm) and (B) body weight (g). Variables were log_{10} transformed. Dotted lines indicate maximum convex polygon of each location.

Table 3. Regression equations and coefficients of determination (R^2) derived from the linear regression between absolute fecundity and body length (L) as well as absolute fecundity (F) and body weight (W) for the five subpopulations sampled (N = 30 at each site). Variables were log10 transformed.

Subpopulation	Fecundity–Length	R^2	Fecundity–Weight	R^2
Upper St. Lawrence River	logF = 5.533 + 0.812logL	0.103	logF = 6.372 + 0.234logW	0.086
Middle Estuary	logF = 4.251 + 1.467logL	0.195	logF = 5.592 + 0.483logW	0.204
South Shore	logF = 2.489 + 2.293logL	0.405	logF = 4.547 + 0.762logW	0.425
North Shore	logF = 2.656 + 2.270logL	0.805	logF = 4.831 + 0.719logW	0.792
Gulf of St. Lawrence	logF = 3.565 + 1.761logL	0.289	logF = 5.168 + 0.592logW	0.280

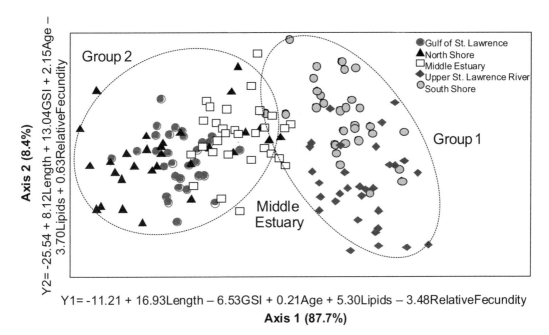

Figure 5. Canonical scores plot for the two major axes of variation (95% confidence ellipse) and associated canonical discriminant functions (all variables were *log*-transformed).

erage about 6.5 million oocytes/kg, whereas small-bodied eels have more than 10 million oocytes/kg.

Overall Significance

A discriminant analysis was performed to evaluate parameters with greater effects on the subpopulations' segregation according to such traits as body length, GSI, relative fecundity, lipid content, and age. The overall significance of the discriminant analysis was highly significant ($F_{(5,20)} = 24.2525; P < 0.001$ (Wilks' lambda)). North Shore and Gulf of St. Lawrence subpopulations were most similar ($F = 1.003$; group 2) whereas the Upper St. Lawrence River and North Shore were quite different ($F = 83.085$). Even though the Middle Estuary is in part composed of eels from the Upper St. Lawrence River, the F-value between these subpopulations was quite high ($F = 38.645$).

Because of high levels of tolerance (0.776–0.931), co-linearity among the five variables included in the discriminant analysis was avoided. Length ($F = 27.93$) and GSI ($F = 23.89$) were the most discriminant variables. Age and lipid content were not useful in discriminating the groups. Relative fecundity showed an intermediate effect ($F = 9.97$).

Only the first two canonical axes were considered for the discriminant analysis, based on their influence on the explanation of the total variance in the model (96.1%) and their eigenvalues. Two distinct groups are found within these two axes (Figure 5): Group 1 (Upper St. Lawrence River and South Shore) and group 2 (North Shore and Gulf of St. Lawrence). The Middle Estuary subpopulation, composed of out-migrating adults from distinct locations upstream in the watershed, is mainly included in group 2 but extends into group 1. Since length was the major discriminant variable and because body weight was included in relative fecundity (intermediate effect), the variability of the

Table 4. Comparison of total length of female silver eels among the five subpopulations (other research and this study).

Subpopulation	N	Total length range (cm)	Source	N	Total length range (cm)
Upper St. Lawrence River	30	89.0–112.3	McGrath et al. (2000)	27	90.0–105.0
Middle Estuary	30	71.0–98.5	Couillard et al. (1997)	473	77.0–92.0
Middle Estuary			McGrath et al. (2003)	60	75.0–92.5
South Shore	30	90.6–115.9	Verreault (2002)	349	71.7–121.9
North Shore	30	53.2–91.0	Fournier & Caron (2001)	852	47.5–95.7
Gulf of St. Lawrence	30	60.1–82.3	Tremblay (2004)	188	52.6–87.8

model was mostly due to eel size. GSI was an important parameter for discriminating subpopulations, mainly between the Upper St. Lawrence River and the other four subpopulations. Female silver eels from the Upper St. Lawrence River showed lower values of GSI (Table 1; Figure 3) and have a lower position in axis 2 (Figure 5).

Discussion

Effect of Phenotypic Plasticity on Reproductive Strategy

The reproductive strategy retained by a species should be the one allowing its survival (Wootton 1984). However, reproductive traits can show modifications, called tactics, depending on fish plasticity (Iguchi and Tsukamoto 2001). This study showed that there is high phenotypic plasticity in reproductive traits of American eels within the St. Lawrence River watershed and to a lesser extent within subpopulations. Overall, body length presents the least variation among subpopulations (Table 1; Figure 3) but is also the main discriminant reproductive trait among subpopulations in the model ($F = 27.93$). Thus, each subpopulation reaches a particular optimal length before migration.

Length at migration has been widely accepted as a stimulus or primary factor inducing migration in the American eel (Helfman et al. 1987; Oliveira 1999). Substantial variability in length of female silver eels is observed within the St. Lawrence River watershed (from 53.2 to 115.9 cm; Table 4). However, comparison with previous investigations of the same subpopulations (Table 4) showed that for each subpopulation, body length of eels caught at migration are quite similar over time, whereas age is much more variable (Table 1; Figure 3). These observations strongly support the hypothesis that length is the factor that triggers migration of female silver eels. Nevertheless, female silver eels in each subpopulation are characterized by a specific optimal length.

Age is not a discriminant trait of reproductive status ($F = 0.85$). Variation of age over time was studied to determine if it is a factor stimulation migration of silver eels. Unfortunately, age data are scarce for most of the subpopulations. Female silver eels in the South Shore were between 15 and 31 years old (Verreault 2002), and Fournier and Caron (2001) estimated age at migration between 13 and 24 years old in the North Shore. These results are comparable to age data obtained herein (11–32 years and 14–27 years, respectively). Previous authors (Vøllestad 1992; Svedäng and Wickström 1997; Verreault 2002) suggested that age at migration might represent the number of years needed for an individual to reach its optimal length. A wide age range was noticed for similar lengths at migration (optimal length). For example, in the North Shore, an eel of 53.5 cm at migration was 14 years old, and another of 53.2 cm was 26 years. In the South Shore, an eel of 103.4 cm was 11 years old compared with another eel of 105.6 cm at 32 years old. Different habitats associated with subpopulations may explain the variance in growth, but individual growth and fitness during the long yellow-eel growth phase might explain the substantial variability seen within a subpopulation. Within a group of fish, some individuals will always grow faster than others, and through time, these differences will be amplified (Jobling 1994). Such individuals may be able to acquire more or better resources and more efficiently, leading to greater energetic investments for gonads and somas (Glazier 1999).

GSI was the reproductive characteristic that discriminated subpopulations on axis 2 ($F = 23.89$; Figure 5). The segregation on axis 2 was between the Upper St. Lawrence River and the other four subpopulations and involves the silvering process. At the onset of their prereproductive migration, female silver eels are partially mature; their gonadal development would probably not be complete until they reach the Sargasso Sea (Durif et al. 2000; Durif 2003). The low GSI values (2.9 ± 0.6; Table 1) obtained on eels from the Upper St. Lawrence River were similar to the values (GSI = ovary weight/(total weight – ovary weight – stomach content weight) × 100) reported by McGrath et al. (2003) as representative of mature eels for Upper St. Lawrence River sites (Lake St. Francis; Lake St. Lawrence; Moses-Saunders vicinity): 3.0 ± 0.7 ($N = 53$). Artificial maturation experiments on female silver European eels (Boëtius and Boëtius 1980) demonstrated that ovary weight can represent up to 58.6% of total eel weight.

Influence of Migration Distance on Size, Lipid, and Fecundity

Female silver eels from group 1 (Upper St. Lawrence River and South Shore) are (1) larger, (2) significantly fatter (ANOVA, $F_{1,118} = 76.631$, $P < 0.001$), and (3) less fecund (ANOVA, $F_{1,118} = 247,807$, $P < 0.001$) than those from group 2 (North Shore and Gulf of St. Lawrence). These results could follow the hypothesis that fecundity varies among subpopulations according to migration distance. Since no geographic parameter was found to determine specific trends in reproductive traits, the reproductive strategy of the American eel does not appear to be related to a trade-off between energetic allocation to gonads and somatic tissues. Indeed, group 1 and group 2 combine subpopulations at different latitudes and migration distances (Figure 1; Table 1).

An eel of greater body length (the main discriminant factor) should show greater absolute fecundity, regardless of the proximity of its growth habitat to the Sargasso Sea. In contrast to other studies (Barbin and McCleave 1997; Verreault 2002) that reported a possible relation between fecundity and migration distance, within the St. Lawrence watershed, variation in reproductive traits was not attributed to migration distance but to eel size. Fecundity of female silver eels is

Table 5. Regression equations and coefficients of determination (R^2) derived from the linear regression between absolute fecundity (F) and body length (L) as well as absolute fecundity (F) and body weight (W) from other studies. Variables were log_{10} transformed.

Subpopulation	Source	Fecundity–Length	R^2	Fecundity–Weight	R^2
Chesapeake Bay	Wenner & Musick (1974)	logF= –0.551 + 3.744logL	0.782	logF= 3.230 + 1.116logW	0.921
Maine	Barbin & McCleave (1997)	logF= 1.260 + 2.964logL	0.90	logF= 4.165 + 0.915logW	0.92
South Shore	Verreault (2002)	logF= –1.795 + 4.377logL	0.935	logF= 2.654 + 1.288logW	0.929

maximized by an increase in length at migration (Wenner and Musick 1974; Barbin and McCleave 1997; Verreault 2002). Within a certain habitat modulated by environmental conditions, length at migration indicates the optimal size and timing for immediate reproductive success against additional growth, depending upon prereproductive mortality rate.

Relationships between reproductive traits (age, length at migration) and migration distance are different from those found in European eels (Vøllestad 1992). Mean age was not negatively correlated to migration distance. Eels from the Gulf of St. Lawrence, the closest subpopulation to the Sargasso Sea, were the youngest, with an average age at migration of 20 ± 3 years (Table 1). Moreover, since no significant difference (P = 0.179) was found between the length of eels from the Upper St. Lawrence and South Shore (group 1), subpopulations separated by 900 km, no relationships existed between mean length and migration distance. This similarity in terms of reproductive traits for these two subpopulations might be explained by the precariousness of both subpopulations. These subpopulations are in decline (Castonguay et al. 1994; Casselman et al. 1997; Verreault 2002; Casselman 2003); therefore, their population structure could be affected and be composed of fewer, older, larger eels.

Linear regressions of absolute fecundity on body length and on body weight were performed on each subpopulation (Figure 4). Nevertheless, compared with other studies (Wenner and Musick 1974; Barbin and McCleave 1997; Verreault 2002; Table 5), all regressions except for the North Shore explained a low percentage of the relation between these reproductive traits (Table 3). The intensity of the relation for the south shore was different from Verreault's (2002) results for the same subpopulation. Estimates of fecundity were greater than those of Verreault's study (2002), even when 95% confidence intervals are included. Fecundity of a 104.3-cm eel in the South Shore was 10.9 (9.8–11.5) million oocytes, based on Verreault's (2002) regression equation, and 13.1 (11.9–14.3) million oocytes based on the present study. Following the weight equations, a 2,366-g eel (mean weight) had 10.0 (9.5–10.9) million oocytes based on Verreault (2002) and 13.1 (12.0–15.1) million oocytes based on the present study. Differences in fecundity estimates of the same subpopulation might be explained by the methods used: manual counts (Verreault 2002) in comparison to the digital analysis used here. However, annual differences might exist based on the fact that the Sud-Ouest River subpopulation is sharply in decline.

Fecundity estimates of female silver eels from the Upper St. Lawrence River and South Shore (group 1), subpopulations of the upper portion of the watershed, were greater than those established for eels from Maine by Barbin and McCleave (1997). The contribution of these two subpopulations to the reproductive potential of the species is major in terms of female gametes in terms of egg production.

Lipid Content as a Triggering Factor?

Previous investigations on eel bioenergetics were specific to the European eel. Svedäng and Wickström (1997) found no correlation between maturity stage (yellow or silver eels) of European eels and their muscle lipid content. Extremely low fat reserves (<10%) were found in silver eels from freshwater sites. Larsson et al. (1990) showed that fat content triggered migration among female European eels and concluded that a lipid content of 28% was needed to initiate prereproductive migration. In the subpopulations studied herein, lipid content was the second least variable trait, after length (Table 1); this suggests a threshold for fat content at migration. Indeed, lipid-content values obtained herein provide measures of the minimum content that may be required for eels of the St. Lawrence watershed to reach the Sargasso. A minimum average lipid content of $17.5 \pm 1.7\%$ was found for Gulf of St. Lawrence female silver eels. The level of somatic fat reserves in this study is similar, particularly for the Upper St. Lawrence River subpopulation (21.7%), to those established by Limburg et al. (2003) for European eels exiting the Baltic Sea (21.1%), at a greater distance from the Sargasso Sea (6,000 km).

Because the minimum lipid content evaluated in the present study (13.5%) was greater than the level of fat stores required (13%) for a migration distance of 6,000 km (Van den Ginneken and Van den Thillart 2000, Van den Thillart et al. 2004), the lipid content of silver American eels is not considered to be a critical factor limiting reproductive success of the species.

Representation of Lake Ontario Eels at the Middle Estuary

The Middle Estuary is a subpopulation composed of eels out-migrating from locations upstream in the St. Lawrence River watershed, including the Upper St. Lawrence River. However, the proportion of eels caught in the Middle Estuary coming from the Upper St. Lawrence River can be questioned. On the basis of mirex concentrations in 1982, the percentage of eels from Lake Ontario caught in the Middle Estuary was evaluated at 74% (Dutil et al. 1985) and decreased by 71% in 1990 (Couillard et al. 1997). More recently Casselman et al. (1997) and Casselman (2003) reported trends of significant declines in abundance of juvenile eels ascending the fish ladder in Cornwall. Their annual recruitment index suggested an obvious decrease since the mid-1980s and corroborated the actual low contribution of female silver eels of Lake Ontario and the Upper St. Lawrence River into the St. Lawrence commercial fishery at the Middle Estuary. According to the discriminant analysis, the eels of these two subpopulations showed different reproductive traits. Representation of eels of the Upper St. Lawrence River in the commercial fishery in Kamouraska (Middle Estuary) must be decreasing over the years.

Conclusions

Reproductive traits of the American eel are highly plastic. Nevertheless, variability within a subpopulation was lower than among subpopulations. Because of panmixia (Avise et al. 1986; Wirth and Bernatchez 2003), variation in reproductive traits of eels must be attributed to the diversity of conditions in growth habitats (Hansen and Eversole 1984; Helfman et al. 1987; Oliveira 1999) among subpopulations and to individual fitness within a subpopulation. In fact, the five subpopulations are associated with different types of habitats (tributary rivers, estuary, barachois pond), and it is not possible to compare their productivity. Svedäng et al. (1996) hypothesized that variations in female size were related to the opportunity for nutrient accumulation among habitats. Indeed, eels, because they are opportunistic feeders (Tesch 1977), may vary substantially in traits associated with reproduction even though they are feeding and growing in the same habitat prior to silvering.

In spite of what was expected, the American eel does not follow a strategy of energetic allocation that reduces the reproductive investment by a lower fecundity to maintain a somatic condition permitting migration to the Sargasso Sea. Substantial migration distance to the spawning area did not show a clear effect on fecundity within these subpopulations. Allocation of a greater proportion of energy reserves to migration was not related to a lower energetic allocation to gonad development. The retained reproductive strategy drives the eels to invest energy in their size, indirectly allocating energy to their absolute fecundity.

Nevertheless, since female silver eels continue to mature during their prereproductive migration, such correlation between distance migration and fecundity could be more obvious at the end of the maturation (i.e., at the spawning grounds). In fact, clearly demonstrated negative relations between migration distance and fecundity for five Pacific salmon species (Beacham and Murray 1993) were for mature salmons, not maturing ones.

Since eels in the St. Lawrence River watershed are mainly large females, it is clear that this watershed contributes a high proportion of the reproductive potential of the species. The biggest and most highly fecund eels were sampled in the upper portion of the watershed, where the greatest decline is observed (Casselman 2003). To preserve the highest female eel contribution to the reproductive potential, these upstream subpopulations must be protected.

Acknowledgments

I would like to thank G. Verreault and R. Cloutier for their supervision during the project. Special thanks to G. Verreault for constant constructive comments and ideas on the project and this paper. I am also grateful to R. Tardif and F. Gagnon for their technical assistance in the laboratory. I want to acknowledge D. Cairns, G. H. Lizotte, J. Dembeck, and K. McGrath for providing the samples. I also thank M. E. Carbonneau for the use of equipment for lipid analysis. Finally, I am grateful to A. Caron for his statistical help and to C. Durif, P. U. Blier, H. Lamson, P. Dumont, J. Casselman, and an anonymus reviewer for comments on an early version of this manuscript. This project was in part funded by La Société de la faune et des parcs du Québec and an NSERC research grant to R. Cloutier.

References

Adam, G. 1997. L'anguille européenne (*Anguilla anguilla* L. 1758): dynamique de la sous-population du lac de Grand-Lieu en relation avec les facteurs environnementaux et anthropiques. Thèse de doctorat. Université Paul Sabatier, Toulouse, France.

Anderson, W. G., R. S. McKinley, and M. Colavecchia. 1997. The use of clove oil as an anesthetic for rainbow trout and its effects on swimming performance. North American Journal of Fisheries Management 17:301–307.

Avise, J. C., G. S. Helfman, N. C. Saunders, and L. S. Hales. 1986. Mitochondrial DNA differentiation and life history pattern in the North Atlantic eels.

Proceedings of the National Academy of Sciences of the USA 83:4350–4354.

Barbin, G. P., and J. D. McCleave. 1997. Fecundity of the American eel *Anguilla rostrata* at 45°N in Maine, U.S.A. Journal of Fish Biology 51:840–847.

Beacham, T. D., and C. B. Murray. 1993. Fecundity and egg size variation in North American Pacific salmon (*Oncorhynchus*). Journal of Fish Biology 42:485–508.

Boëtius, I., and J. Boëtius. 1980. Experimental maturation of female silver eels, *Anguilla anguilla*. Estimates of fecundity and energy reserves for migration and spawning. Dana 1:1–28.

Casselman, J. M., L. A. Marcogliese, and P. V. Hodson. 1997. Recruitment index for the upper St. Lawrence River and Lake Ontario eel stock: a re-examination of eel passage at the R. H. Saunders hydroelectric generating station at Cornwall, Ontario, 1974–1995. Pages 161–169 in R. H. Peterson, editor. The American eel in eastern Canada: stock status and management strategies. Proceedings of Eel Management Workshop, January 13–14, 1997, Québec City, QC. Canadian Technical Report of Fisheries and Aquatic Sciences No. 1296.

Casselman, J. M. 2003. Dynamics of resources of the American eel, *Anguilla rostrata*: declining abundance in the 1990s. Pages 255–274 in K. Aida, K. Tsukamoto, and K. Yamauchi, editors. Eel Biology. Springer-Verlag Tokyo, Japan.

Castonguay, M., P. V. Hodson, C. M. Couillard, M. J. Eckersley, J. D. Dutil, and G. Verreault. 1994. Why is recruitment of the American eel, *Anguilla rostrata*, declining in the St Lawrence River and Gulf? Canadian Journal of Fisheries and Aquatic Sciences 51:479–488.

Couillard, C. M., P. V. Hodson, and M. Castonguay. 1997. Correlations between pathological changes and chemical contamination in American eels, *Anguilla rostrata*, from the St. Lawrence River. Canadian Journal of Fisheries and Aquatic Sciences 54:1916–1927.

Dekker, W., J. M. Casselman, D. K. Cairns, K. Tsukamoto, D. Jellyman, and H. Lickers. 2003. Worldwide decline of eel resources necessitates immediate action. Quebec Declaration of Concern. Fisheries 28(12):28–30.

Durif, C. 2003. La migration d'avalaison de l'anguille européenne *Anguilla anguilla*: Caractérisation des fractions dévalantes, phénomène de migration et franchissement d'obstacles. Thèse de doctorat. Université Paul Sabatier, Toulouse, France.

Durif, C., P. Élie, S. Dufour, J. Marchelidon, and B. Vidal. 2000. Analyse des paramètres morphologiques et physiologiques lors de la préparation à la migration de dévalaison chez l'anguille européenne (*Anguilla anguilla*) du lac de Grand-Lieu (Loire-Atlantique). Cybium 24(3):63–74.

Dutil, J. D., B. Legaré, and C. Desjardins. 1985. Discrimination of a fish stock, the eel (*Anguilla rostrata*), based on the presence of a synthetic chemical, mirex. Canadian Journal of Fisheries and Aquatic Sciences 42(3):455–458.

Facey, D. E., and G. W. LaBar. 1981. Biology of American eels in Lake Champlain, Vermont. Transactions of the American Fisheries Society 110:396–402.

Fournier, D., and F. Caron. 2001. Travaux de recherche sur l'anguille d'Americanérique (*Anguilla rostrata*) de la Petite rivière de la Trinité en 1999 et 2000. Société de la faune et des parcs du Québec, Direction de la recherche sur la faune, Québec.

Glazier, D. S. 1999. Trade-offs between reproductive and somatic (storage) investments in animals: a comparative test of the Van Noordwijk and De Jong model. Evolutionary Ecology 13:539–555.

Hansen, R. A., and A. G. Eversole. 1984. Age, growth, and sex ratio of American eels in brackish-water portions of a South Carolina River. Transactions of the American Fisheries Society 113:744–749.

Helfman, G. S., D. E. Facey, L. S. Hales, Jr., and E. L Bozeman, Jr. 1987. Reproductive ecology of the American eel. Pages 42–56 in M. J. Dadswell, R. L. Klauda, C. M. Moffitt, R. L. Saunders, R. A. Rulifson, and J. E. Cooper, editors. Common strategies of anadromous and catadromous fishes. American Fisheries Society, Symposium 1, Bethesda, Maryland.

Hurley, D. A. 1972. The American eel (*Anguilla rostrata*) in eastern Lake Ontario. Journal of the Fisheries Research Board of Canada 29:535–543.

Iguchi, K., and Y. Tsukamoto. 2001. Semelparous or iteroparous: resource allocation tactics in the ayu, an osmeroid fish. Journal of Fish Biology 58:520–528.

Jobling, M. 1994. Fish bioenergetics. Chapman and Hall, London.

Larsson, P., S. Hamrin, and L. Okla. 1990. Fat content as a factor inducing migratory behaviour in the eel (*Anguilla anguilla* L.) to the Sargasso Sea. Naturwissenschaften 77:488–490.

Limburg, K. E., H. Wickström, H. Svedäng, M. Elfman, and P. Kristiansson. 2003. Do stocked freshwater eels migrate? Evidence from the Baltic suggests "yes". Pages 275–284 in D. A. Dixon, editor. Biology, management, and protection of catadromous eels. American Fisheries Society, Symposium 33, Bethesda, Maryland.

McCleave, J. D., R. C. Kleckner, and M. Castonguay. 1987. Reproductive sympatry of American and European eels and implications for migration and taxonomy. Pages 286–297 *in* M. J. Dadswell, R. L. Klauda, C. M. Moffitt, R. L. Saunders, R. A. Rulifson, and J. E. Cooper, editors. Common strategies of anadromous and catadromous fishes. American Fisheries Society, Symposium 1, Bethesda, Maryland.

McGrath, K. J., J. Bernier, S. Ault, J. D. Dutil, and K. Reid. 2003. Differentiating downstream migrating American eels *Anguilla rostrata* from resident eels in the St. Lawrence River. Pages 315–327 *in* D. A. Dixon, editor. Biology, management, and protection of catadromous eels. American Fisheries Society, Symposium 33, Bethesda, Maryland.

Nilo, P., and R. Fortin. 2001. Synthèse des connaissances et établissement d'une programmation de recherche sur l'anguille d'Americanérique (*Anguilla rostrata*). Société de la faune et des parcs du Québec, Direction de la recherche sur la faune. Université du Québec à Montréal.

Oliveira, K. 1999. Life history characteristics and strategies of the American eel, *Anguilla rostrata*. Canadian Journal of Fish and Aquatic Sciences 56:795–802.

Pankhurst, N. W. 1982. Changes in body musculature with sexual maturation in the European eel, *Anguilla anguilla* (L.). Journal of Fish Biology 21:417–428.

Pankhurst, N. W., and P. W. Sorensen. 1984. Degeneration of the alimentary tract in sexually maturing European *Anguilla anguilla* (L.) and American eels *Anguilla rostrata* (LeSueur). Canadian Journal of Zoology 62:1143–1149.

Peake, S. 1998. Sodium bicarbonate and clove oil as potential anesthetics for non salmonid fishes. North American Journal of Fisheries Management 18:919–924.

Schaffer, W. M., and P. F. Elson. 1975. The adaptative significance of variations in life history among local populations of Atlantic salmon in North America. Ecology 56:577–590.

Schmidt, J. 1922. The breeding places of the eel. Philosophical Transactions of the Royal Society of London, Series B 211:179–208.

SPSS, Inc. 1999. SYSTAT 9.0. SPSS Inc., Chicago.

Svedäng, H., E. Neuman, and H. Wickström. 1996. Maturation patterns in female European eel: age and size at the silver eel stage. Journal of Fish Biology 48:342–351.

Svedäng, H., and H. Wickström. 1997. Low fat contents in female silver eels: indications of insufficient energetic stores for migration and gonadal development. Journal of Fish Biology 50:575–586.

Tesch, F. W. 1977. The eel: biology and management of anguillids eels. Chapman and Hall, London.

Tremblay, V. 2004. A review of the American eel (*Anguilla rostrata*) projects on the system of Long Pond (Dalvay) in Prince Edward Island National Park, prepared for Parks Canada, Québec.

Van den Thillart, V. Van Ginneken, F. Körner, R. Heijmans, R. Van der Linden, and A. Gluvers. 2004. Endurance swimming of European eel. Journal of Fish Biology 65:312–318.

Van Ginneken, V. J. T., and G. E. E. J. M. Van den Thillart. 2000. Eel fat stores are enough to reach the Sargasso. Nature (London) 403(6766):156–157.

Verreault, G. 2002. Dynamique de la sous-population d'anguilles d'Americanérique (*Anguilla rostrata*) du bassin versant de la rivière du Sud-Ouest. Mémoire de Maîtrise en gestion de la faune et ses habitats. Société de la faune et des parcs du Québec, Direction de l'aménagement de la faune de la région du Bas St-Laurent. Université du Québec à Rimouski.

Vøllestad, L. A. 1992. Geographic variation in age and length at metamorphosis of maturing European eel: environmental effects and phenotypic plasticity. Journal of Animal Ecology 61:41–48.

Wenner, C. A., and J. A. Musick. 1974. Fecundity and gonad observations of the American eel, *Anguilla rostrata*, migrating from Chesapeake Bay, Virginia. Journal of the Fisheries Research Board of Canada 31:1387–1391.

Wirth, T., and L. Bernatchez. 2003. Decline of North Atlantic eels: a fatal synergy? Proceedings of the Royal Society of London, Series B, Biological Sciences 270(1516):681–688.

Wootton, R. J. 1984. Introduction: Tactics and strategies in fish reproduction. Pages 1–12 *in* G. W. Potts and R. J. Wootton, editors. Fish reproduction: strategies and tactics. Academic Press, London.

Morphological Discrimination of the Silvering Stages of the European Eel

CAROLINE DURIF[1,*], AYMERIC GUIBERT, AND PIERRE ELIE

*Cemagref, Unité Ressources Aquatiques Continentales,
50 avenue de Verdun, 33612, Cestas cedex, France*

Abstract.—A lack of knowledge on the transition from the resident to the migratory phase has led to a series of studies on the silvering process. Silvering marks the end of the sedentary growth phase and the beginning of the migratory phase. A six-stage classification was developed to describe the physiological and morphological events that occur during this metamorphosis and the subsequent migration. Stages corresponded to a growth phase (I to FII), a premigrant stage for females (FIII), and migrating stages for both sexes (FIV, FV, and MII). Here, the objective was to develop a "silver index" using only external measurements to assess the degree of metamorphosis of eels, based on the same data set that was used in the former study. It consisted of a large number of both resident and migratory eels that were sampled at different times of the year with different types of fishing gear and at several locations representing various types of habitats. Discriminant Analysis was applied on external measurements only: (body length, body weight, pectoral fin length, and eye diameters). Total percentage of correct reclassification into the six silvering stages was 82%. The silver index (classification functions) was able to identify 91% of the migratory eels. This method, associated with proper sampling, could be utilized for the quantification of potential spawners given that they all reach their spawning grounds in the Sargasso Sea.

Introduction

The scientific community agrees that the European eel *Anguilla anguilla* is seriously threatened and that urgent measures should be taken to monitor the remaining population. Indeed, the International Council for the Exploration of the Sea (ICES) considers that eels are outside safe biological limits and that fisheries in recent years have not been sustainable (ICES 1999). In a recent communication, the European Commission has stated that escapement targets need to be established and that the highest initial priority is placed on assuring the survival and escapement of silver eels. Whatever actions are taken, current conditions have to be measured, and this can be realized only through a better knowledge of the biological mechanisms that control the population dynamics (i.e., metamorphosis from the resident to the migratory stage). As catadromous fishes, European eels spend most of their life in freshwater until they head back to the spawning grounds in the Sargasso Sea. Only the freshwater phase

[1] Corresponding author: caroline.durif@imr.no
*Current address: Department of Biology, University of Oslo, P. O. Box 1066 Blindern 0316 Oslo and Institute of Marine Research-Austevoll, 5392, Storebø, Norway.

of the eel is accessible to human observation, since no mature adults have ever been found in the open ocean. Therefore, the only way to evaluate the reproductive potential in a given year is to assess the proportion of potentially emigrating eels for that year. Although the eel's life cycle is well known and major traits of migratory individuals have been described (Bertin 1951; Tesch 2003), tools to identify which eels are physiologically ready to start their spawning migration are lacking.

Before individuals begin to swim downstream, they undergo a series of internal and external changes. These modifications prepare them for the 6,000-km journey back to their spawning grounds in the Sargasso Sea. This metamorphosis referred to as silvering, marks the end of the relatively sedentary growth phase (yellow stage) and the beginning of the migratory phase (silver stage).

Skin color is generally used to differentiate the two stages, as "migratory" eels most often display a white-silver belly and a black dorsal back. However, this counter-shading is not always present, and most migratory eels (especially large ones) often exhibit intermediate features, such as a bronze color on the belly and on the sides. Since the color criterion was found to be subjective and unreliable, Pankhurst (1982) proposed another method for distinguishing yellow and silver stages of female eels. The author developed an index based on eye surface area, which increases at the migratory stage, and set a threshold of 6.5 for sexually maturing European eels.

Physiologically, the differences between the so-called yellow and silver stages are important, since many complex mechanisms are involved in silvering. Migratory individuals stop feeding, and their alimentary tract regresses (Pankhurst and Sorensen 1984; Fontaine 1994; Marchelidon et al. 1999). Osmoregulatory mechanisms, which allow life in seawater, are already active before the eel leaves freshwater (Fontaine 1975; Dutil et al. 1987). Fat stores increase from 8% to 28% (Bergersen and Klemetsen 1988; Larsson et al. 1990). But one of the most important changes at the silver stage is the initiation of the gonadotropic axis and the very beginning of gonad development (see review, Dufour et al. 2003).

As silvering involves many elaborate changes, a simple classification into two groups, namely yellow and silver stages, was not satisfactory. Therefore, we propose here and in Durif et al. (2005) a more detailed classification based on several internal and external parameters: gonad development, regression of digestive tract, gonadotropin and growth hormone levels, eye diameters, pectoral fin length, and condition factor. Five stages were defined for female eels: a growth phase (stages I and FII), during which eels feed and become sexually differentiated; and a premigrating stage (FIII), characterized by high levels of GH (growth hormone) and by the beginning of gonad development in females. Truly migratory individuals were divided into two groups: stage FIV, marked by the beginning of gonadotropin production and cessation of feeding; and stage FV, characterized by a significantly regressed digestive tract, higher gonadotropin levels, and elongated pectoral fins. Variability was found to be much less important in male eels, and results suggested that silvering and sex differentiation in males were simultaneous. Thus two stages were identified for males: the resident sexually undifferentiated stage (I) and the migratory stage (MII).

The purpose of the present study was to develop a noninvasive method for classifying developmental life stages and silvering of eels based on morphological characteristics. Discriminant analysis was used, first, to determine which morphological parameters best discriminated among all six stages, and second, to develop a silvering index based on these parameters. This data set was also used to compare between this silvering index and Pankhurst's criterion.

Methods

Description of the Data Set

The data set consisted of 1,188 eels collected at six different locations in France. Different types of fishing gear were used (electrofishing, eel pots, fyke nets, weir, stow net) in order to obtain resident eels as well as individuals at the migrating silver stage and all other possible intermediate stages. Sampling was carried out between 1994 and 2002. Four morphological measurements were performed (see below) on the eels. Gonads, liver, digestive tract (emptied), and the pituitary (for growth hormone and gonadotropin assays) were then sampled on sacrificed individuals. Based on these parameters, all the eels in the sample were classified into one of six stages: one for undifferentiated resident male and female (I), four for female eels (FII to FV), and one for silver migrating males (MII). The characteristics of each stage are described in Table 1, with the various characteristics summarized for each stage. The procedures used to determine the degree of silvering of eels, as well as the full description of each stage, can be found in Durif et al. (2005).

Morphological Measurements

Four external measurements were made on eels, related to the morphological changes that are most apparent during silvering. Total body length (BL) and wet body weight (W) were measured to reflect condition of the eels. Length of the pectoral fin (FL) was measured from the insertion to the tip of the fin and corresponded to the greatest possible length (Figure 1). Both vertical (Dv) and horizontal (Dh) eye diameters were measured on the left eye, along the visible part of the cornea (Figure captions)

Figure 1). Mean eye diameter (MD) was calculated as MD = (Dh + Dv)/2.

For comparison with Pankhurst's method for silver stage determination, eye index was calculated as EI = $(MD/2)^2 \cdot \pi/L$ (Pankhurst 1982).

Data Analysis

Discriminant analysis was conducted on morphological variables L, W, FL, and MD. Groups corresponded to the six silvering stages described in Durif et al. (2005): stages I, FII, FIII, FIV, FV, and MII. A backward stepwise analysis was carried out on the data using a cross-validation procedure: a model was developed from a model sample, and its predictive accuracy was evaluated with a test sample. Classification functions were derived from the model and were used to determine to which stage each individual most likely belonged. Classification scores for each case were computed for each stage according to the formula

$$S_i = c_i + w_{i1} \times x_1 + w_{i2} \times x_2 + \ldots + w_{in} \times x_n$$

where i denotes the respective stage, n denotes the n variables, c is a constant, w_{in} is the weight for the nth variable in the computation of the classification score for the ith group, and x_n is the observed value for the respective case for the nth variable. S_i is the resultant classification score. An eel was assigned to the stage for which it had the highest S_i. The efficiency of the analysis was evaluated through a classification matrix, which indicated the number of eels that were correctly classified and those that were misclassified.

Results

Silvering Index

The various characteristics were quite different among the stages and provided the basis for developing a silvering index (Table 1). The sample of 1,156 individuals for

Table 1. Mean and standard deviation of morpho-anatomical parameters of undifferentiated and female eels according to life stage and silvering (Durif et al. 2005). BL (body length), K (Fulton's condition factor), EI (eye index), FI (fin index) = pectoral fin length/body length X 100, GSI (gonadosomatic index)=gonad weight/body weight X 100; HSI (hepatosomatic index) = liver weight/body weight X 100; DTI (digestive tract index) = digestive tract weight/body weight X 100; GTH (pituitary gonadotropin hormone or LH-like); GH (pituitary growth hormone).

Silvering stages	I	FII	FIII	FIV	FV	MII
	Undifferentiated males and females resident	Females resident	Females pre-migrant	Females Migrant		Males migrant
N	381	400	72	32	186	85
BL (mm)	399 ±655	526 ±662	658 ±682	746 ±6110	644 ±6122	393 ±623
K	0.172 ±0.026	0.186 ±0.030	0.197 ±0.025	0.218 ±0.022	0.182 ±0.026	0.177 ±0.022
EI	4.5 ±0.9	5.6 ±1.1	7.6 ±1.3	10.8 ±1.7	9.9 ±1.6	9.5 ±1.6
FI	3.7 ±0.5	3.9 ±0.6	4.3 ±0.6	4.3 ±0.4	5.0 ±0.7	4.7 ±0.6
GSI	0.21 ±0.14	0.54 ±0.19	0.82 ±0.24	1.47 ±0.15	1.71 ±0.31	0.16 ±0.11
HSI	1.72 ±0.59	1.41 ±0.44	1.26 ±0.37	1.40 ±0.17	1.24 ±0.30	1.41 ±0.26
DTI	4.75 ±1.90	4.64 ±1.60	3.76 ±1.30	1.84 ±0.61	1.18 ±0.55	1.59 ±0.48
GTH-II (ng.g^{-1})	0.03 ±0.06	0.02 ±0.06	0.06 ±0.15	0.24 ±0.25	0.49 ±0.36	1.08 ±0.95
GH (µg.g^{-1})	0.20 ±0.14	0.18 ±0.15	0.25 ±0.21	0.14 ±0.10	0.15 ±0.16	0.07 ±0.6

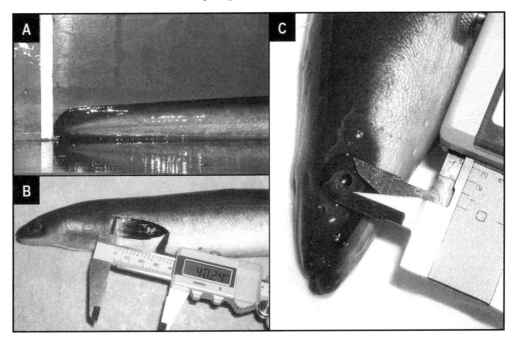

Figure 1. A) Measurement of body length; B) Measurement of pectoral fin length; C) Measurement of horizontal eye diameter.

which pectoral fin length was available was randomly split into a sample to develop the model and a test sample representing 66% (768 individuals) and 34% (388 individuals), respectively. A significant discriminant model was obtained when using all four variables: body length, body weight, mean eye diameter, and pectoral fin length. The first canonical variable accounted for more than 77% of the total dispersion of the groups. Standardized canonical discriminant function coefficients indicated the relative contribution of each variable to the overall discrimination. Mean eye diameter was the major contributor, followed by fin length and body weight (respectively, −1.034, −0.770, and 0.634); the contribution of body length was the lowest (0.183).

Classification functions, using the values in Table 2, were used to compute classification scores for new observations (test sample). The percentage of correct classification was equal to 83% for the model sample, 77% for the test sample, and 82% for the total jackknifed value (Table 3). The analysis usually assigned misclassified individuals to adjoining groups. Resident eels, stages I and FII, showed high percentages of correct classification: respectively, 84% and 86%. Errors were higher for the classification of premigrant eels (stage FIII), of which 30% were classified into FII, FIV, and FV stages. Misclassification was greatest for stage FIV eels, since only 55% of eels were correctly classified; however, none of those eels were assigned as resident. This group also comprised the smallest number of individuals. Twenty-six percent of the FV eels were misclassified, and 1.5% were assigned to the FII stage (2 individuals). Two were considered males (MII), but they could be manually reclassified since they were longer than is usual for European male eels (35–40 cm). The classification of migrant males was 98% accurate, and only one eel was misclassified into stage FV. Likewise, this individual was easily reclassified

Table 2. Classification functions for stage determination (I to FV and MII) of eels. Values correspond to the weights to be assigned to each variable. BL (body length in mm), W (body weight in g), MD (mean eye diameter in mm), FL (fin length in mm).

	I	FII	FIII	FIV	FV	MII
Constant	−61.276	−87.995	−109.014	−113.556	−128.204	−84.672
BL	0.242	0.286	0.280	0.218	0.242	0.176
W	−0.108	−0.125	−0.127	−0.103	−0.136	−0.116
MD	5.546	6.627	9.108	12.187	12.504	12.218
FL	0.614	0.838	1.182	1.230	1.821	1.295

Table 3. Jackknifed classification matrix for the test sample after step-wise discriminant analysis using length, weight, pectoral fin length, and mean eye diameter. Wilks' lambda = 0.057; $p < 0.0001$.

Initial group		Predicted group membership						% correct classification	
		I	FII	FIII	FIV	FV	MII		
I	Resident	206	30	0	0	0	4	86	95
FII		21	221	18	0	0	3	84	
FIII	Pre-migrant	0	6	32	2	6	0	70	70
FIV	Migrant	0	0	5	12	5	0	55	91
FV		0	2	13	19	100	2	74	
MII		0	0	0	0	1	60	98	
Total		227	259	67	35	111	69	82	92

into its correct stage by using body length, since males rarely exceed 45 cm.

Classification efficiency, when grouping stages into resident, premigrant, and migrant (male and female) groups, was 95%, 70%, and 91%, respectively (Table 3), with an overall mean of 92%

Comparison with Pankhurst's Eye Index

Using the classification functions, or silver index, based on body length, body weight, mean eye diameter, and fin length gave an accuracy of 91% for the estimation of migrants (stages FIV and FV). In comparison, when using Pankhurst's threshold, almost all migratory eels (FIV, FV, and MII) were correctly classified (Figure 2). Two individuals had an eye index under 6.5 and would have been considered yellow eels. These were the same two eels that were misclassified by the silver index. However, a large proportion of the resident eels (I and FII), as they were initially defined by their physio-anatomical characteristics, had an eye index above this limit although they did not display any sign of silvering: 3% of stage I and 25% of FII eels would have been considered silver (Figure 2). This percentage increased in FIII eels, since 81% had an eye index over 6.5. In total, applying Pankhurst's limit to our sample would have overestimated the number of migratory eels by 20%.

Application: Seasonal Variation in Silvering Stages

The seasonal variation of silvering stages in our sample was analyzed to illustrate a possible use for this classification method. Samples from the different years were pooled and monthly proportions were calculated (Figure 3). Stages I and FII represented more than 50%

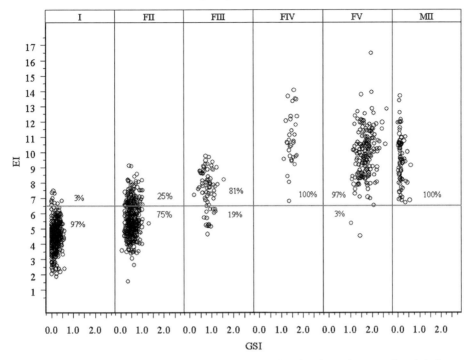

Figure 2. Relationship between gonadosomatic index (GSI) and eye index (EI) for each of the various stages associated with silvering. The horizontal (light) line is set at Pankhurst's 6.5 limit. Percentages indicate the proportions of eels that would have been defined as silver eels (above the limit) and yellow eels (below the limit).

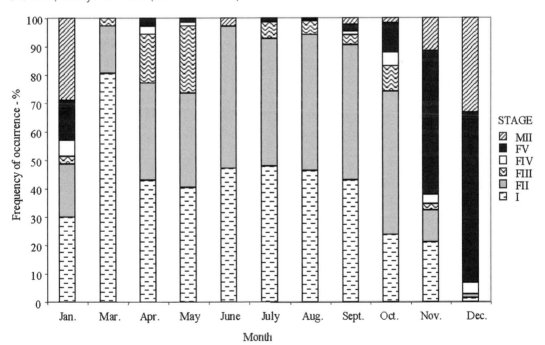

Figure 3. Proportions of the various stages associated with silvering (I, FII, FIII, FIV, FV, and MII) by month.

of the sample every month except from November to January, the period of downstream migration. These two stages totaled 97% of the eels caught during March, with a high proportion of stage I eels (81%). It is very likely that these small undifferentiated individuals were eels that had just been recruited in the months prior to sampling; in France, glass eels migrate upstream from December to April. Stage FIII eels were most abundant in spring (17% in April, 24% in May), when growth conditions are optimal. They were also found from July to October, but in smaller proportions, between 4% and 9%. Migratory eels (FIV, FV, and MII) were present from October to January and comprised up to 97% of the individuals caught in December. Percentages decreased to 49% in January, when most of the eels would have emigrated.

Discussion

The silvering process of eels from Lake Grand-Lieu in France was first described by Durif et al. 2000. This work was then extended to different types of habitats in France (brackish-water marsh, large rivers, small coastal river, and estuary) with different environmental characteristics, to look for variability in physio-anatomical characteristics of migratory eels. A broad classification was defined based on this varied sample of eels from different locations. It consisted of six stages, which represented a growth phase (stages I and FII), a premigrant stage (FIII), and migrating stages (FIV, FV, MII) for male and female eels (Durif et al. 2005). This classification gives a more precise and ecologically appropriate description than do the limited terms yellow and silver phases. It reflects the continuous nature of the silvering process and the fact that although silvering may have started, some individuals may not be ready for active migration nor have started to mature. Since the duration of this process is currently unknown, this description of several silvering stages represents a first step towards understanding the dynamics of silvering and migration.

Reliable criteria were needed to determine whether an eel was physiologically ready to start migration and sexual maturation. Up to now, identification of female silver eels and assumed emigration has generally been based on Pankhurst's eye index. Very importantly, if we had applied only Pankhurst's 6.5 limit on our sample, we would have overestimated emigrants by 20%. Eye index does reflect increasing GSI; however, it is also strongly correlated to body length in the resident stage. Thus, a large yellow eel (such as some stage FII eels) may have a high eye index without necessarily being silver. This partly explains why Pankhurst's criterion of 6.5 overestimated the number of potential female emigrants.

This study complements the description of silvering stages by providing a noninvasive method of determining whether an eel is sedentary, maturing, or physiologically ready to migrate. We found it reasonably accurate (82%) to use only external measurements to assign a developmental stage (I to FV and MII). The use of additional parameters, such as body weight and fin length, was necessary to differentiate some stages more specifically (mainly FIII, FIV, and FV). Misclassification occurred. Errors related to the sex of individuals were easily corrected by using body length, since males are much shorter than females. Other misclassified individuals were assigned to adjoining groups. Misclassification for stages that are closely related would be expected, since the attributes would naturally overlap for certain borderline individuals, but these stages were selected primarily to provide a practical description.

It is not always clear in literature what authors mean when they mention "silver eels," since they can refer to color, eye size, or behavior (actively emigrating eels caught with specific fishing gear). The silver index method for determining stages also represents a way of standardizing observations between different observers and watersheds and periods. To obtain these data, eel populations need to be closely monitored and data must be collected carefully and consistently. Measurements used here are relatively simple and can easily be done on a large scale. Surveys could be carried out over different seasons within the same year: the evolution of the proportion of the different stages would help in understanding the dynamics of the silvering process (time and duration of the metamorphosis); these may vary according to location. Practically, and with an appropriate sampling method, the proportion of eels (stages FIV, FV, and MII) that will start their downstream migration can be evaluated if they are triggered by the appropriate environmental factors. Under the hypothesis that all eels will reach the Sargasso Sea, they will constitute the minimal estimation of progenitors for a given year. Analysis of year-to-year variations in the proportion of these migratory stages could also help to explain quantitative variation in the run of emigrant eels.

Acknowledgments

This study benefited from a grant from the European Union (project Q5RS-2001–01836). Financial support was also given by the French Ministry of Environment and Research, the Conseil Supérieur de la Pêche, the GRISAM, and the Cemagref. We also would like to thank the anonymous reviewers for their helpful comments on improving this manuscript.

References

Bergersen, R., and A. Klemetsen. 1988. Freshwater eel *Anguilla anguilla* L. from North Norway with emphasis on occurrence, food, age and downstream migration. Nordic Journal of Freshwater Research 64:54–66.

Bertin, L. 1951. Les anguilles. Variation, croissance, euryhalinité, toxicité, hermaphrodisme juvénile et sexualité, migrations, métamorphoses. Payot, Paris, France.

Dufour, S., E. Burzawa-Gerard, N. Le Belle, M. Sbaihi, and B. Vidal. 2003. Reproductive endocrinology of the European eel, *Anguilla anguilla*. Pages 373–383 *in* K. Aida, K. Tsukamoto, and K. Yamauchi, editors. Eel biology. Springer-Verlag, Tokyo.

Durif, C., S. Dufour, and P. Elie. 2005. The silvering process of *Anguilla anguilla*: a new classification from the yellow resident to the silver migrating stage. Journal of Fish Biology 66:1025–1043.

Durif, C., P. Elie, S. Dufour, J. Marchelidon, and B. Vidal. 2000. Analysis of morphological and physiological parameters during the silvering process of the European eel (*Anguilla anguilla*) in the lake of Grand-Lieu (France). Cybium 24:63–74.

Dutil, J. D., M. Besner, M., and S. D. McCormick. 1987. Osmoregulatory and ionoregulatory changes and associated mortalities during the transition of maturing American eels to a marine environment. Pages 175–190 *in* M. J. Dadswell, R. J. Klauda, C. M. Moffitt, R. L. Saunders, R. A. Rulifson, and J. E. Cooper, editors. Common strategies of anadromous and catadromous fishes. American Fisheries Society, Symposium 1, Bethesda, Maryland.

Fontaine, M. 1975. Physiological mechanisms in the migration of marine and amphihaline fish. Advances in Marine Biology 13:241–355.

Fontaine, Y. A. 1994. L'argenture de l'anguille: métamorphose, anticipation, adaptation. Bulletin Français de la Pêche et de la Pisciculture 355:171–185.

ICES (International Council for Exploration of the Sea). 1999. ICES cooperative research report no. 229. Report of the ICES Advisory Committee on Fishery Management, Copenhagen.

Larsson, P., S. Hamrin, and A. Okla. 1990. Fat content as a factor inducing migratory behaviour in the eel (*Anguilla anguilla* L.) to the Sargasso Sea. Naturwissenschaften 77:488–490.

Marchelidon, J., N. Le Belle, A. Hardy, B. Vidal, M. Sbaihi, E. Burzawa-Gérard, M. Schmitz, and S. Dufour. 1999. Etude des variations de paramètres anatomiques et endocriniens chez l'anguille européenne (*Anguilla anguilla*) femelle, sédentaire et d'avalaison: application à la caractérisation du stade argenté. Bulletin Français de la Pêche et de la Pisciculture 355:349–368.

Pankhurst, N. W. 1982. Relation of visual changes to the onset of sexual maturation in the European eel *Anguilla anguilla* L. Journal of Fish Biology 21:127–140.

Pankhurst, N. W., and P. W. Sorensen. 1984. Degeneration of the alimentary tract in sexually maturing European *Anguilla anguilla* (L.) and American eels *Anguilla rostrata* (LeSueur). Canadian Journal of Zoology 62:1143–1148.

Tesch, F. W. 2003. The eel, 5th edition. Blackwell Scientific Publications Publishing, Oxford, England.

Age, Growth, Mortality, and Sex Ratio of American Eels in Maryland's Chesapeake Bay

JULIE A. WEEDER[1,*] AND STEPHEN D. HAMMOND

Maryland Department of Natural Resources
Matapeake Work Center
301 Marine Academy Drive
Stevensville, Maryland 21666, USA

Abstract.—We examined the demography of American eels *Anguilla rostrata* at seven Maryland sites, including six Chesapeake Bay estuaries and one bay adjacent to the Atlantic Ocean. Eels caught by baited pots in estuaries tended to be young and small with rapid growth rates. Large eels were a higher proportion of catch in the Atlantic bay, where exploitation started only recently, than in heavily fished Chesapeake estuaries. Histological examinations indicated that all eels longer than 40 cm were female, but smaller eels were female, male, or undifferentiated in roughly equal proportions. Some eels were captured in commercial fishing gear after only one year in continental waters. Total mortality (Z), including postspawning mortality of emigrants, was estimated from catch curve analysis, giving a range of 0.62 to 1.44. Instantaneous natural mortality (M) was calculated as 0.25, from 3/maximum age (12). Instantaneous fishing mortality, $Z-M$, ranged from 0.37 to 1.19 and, in one case, only five age classes were observed. We considered the impact of latitude, habitat productivity, density, sex ratio, and fishing on eel populations. We postulate that heavy fishing pressure reduced the density and modal size of eels in surveyed estuaries. Changes in management policy to reduce fishing mortality and increase spawning emigration are recommended.

Introduction

The American eel *Anguilla rostrata* is native to freshwater and tidal areas of the Chesapeake Bay watershed. This species has played an important role in the ecological and economic history of the region. Eels have been used as bait for blue crabs since colonial times, and during the last 30 to 40 years, an overseas export market has developed (Foster 1981; Weeder and Uphoff 1999). While large eels are in most demand and fetch the highest prices, all sizes caught in commercial eel pot and pound net fisheries are retained and sold. We evaluated the demographics of eels captured in tributaries to Maryland's portion of Chesapeake Bay from 1997 to 2002 to better understand stock status, trends, and management needs.

Methods

Sample Collection

We sampled eels from seven commercially fished locations in Maryland (Figure

---

[1] Corresponding author: jweeder@verizon.net.
*Current address: 3629 S. Renellie Drive, Tampa, Florida 33629, USA

1). Six sites were estuaries of Chesapeake Bay, and one (Assawoman Bay) was a bay adjacent to the Atlantic Ocean. Sample sites ranged over a wide area to maximize spatial coverage, and many sites were sampled in multiple years and seasons (Figure 1). Only one site was nearly fresh (Nanticoke; ≈ 1 ppt). We either purchased eels from commercial watermen or caught them ourselves. All eels were collected with baited pots, except at Pocomoke River, where pound nets were used. Eelers combined catches from numerous days in live boxes. Sampling from these aggregated catches minimized day-to-day variation in sizes of eels caught. For each river, 45 to 90 kg of eels were randomly dipped from the box on each sampled date. Eel pots are cylindrical passive traps constructed of fabric funnels and wire mesh of varying mesh sizes (from 6.4 × 6.4 mm to 12.7 × 25.4 mm). Weeder and Uphoff (2003) found that mesh size differences had little effect on yield per recruit of Maryland eels because they retained similar sizes of eels. Sampled eels were measured to the nearest mm and weighed to the nearest g. For some rivers, we purchased a sub-sample of the largest eels to supplement the number of older eels in our age-length key. These nonrandomly sampled eels were not included in length analyses. No length analysis was performed for Pocomoke River samples because of the large mesh used to capture eels there. We used Sassafras River length data collected in 1981 and 1997–2000 to examine temporal changes in length distributions.

We included Assawoman Bay as a collection site because the broad size distribution of eels there (Weeder and Uphoff 2001), as well as anecdotal reports, suggested that fishing pressure was comparatively low.

In October–November 1999 and 2000, we purchased eels caught in pound nets in the Pocomoke River. We considered these to be silver eels because of the method and timing of their capture and their large size.

Attempts to use morphological characteristics as described by Todd (1981) and Beullens et al. (1997) to categorize maturity level were not successful, perhaps because of the distance of capture sites from the ocean and therefore the possible short length of time that eels had been silver. Even the most southerly Chesapeake sample sites were located well north of the open Atlantic. Hurley (1972) also found external characteristics of limited value in determining sexual maturity. Estuarine eels have small home ranges for most of their lives (Helfman et al. 1987). Only when eels are sexually maturing do they typically leave their home range during fall to travel down the bay toward the ocean to spawn. Nonmigratory eels do not usually encounter pound nets, which operate by leading traveling animals into a maze of mesh chambers. Pound nets are usually constructed with 51-mm stretch mesh and retain only very large eels. Hence, our Pocomoke samples are not representative of smaller sizes of eels in the area. Growth and age of these eels relative to yellow eels was of primary interest.

Sexual Determination and Maturity

Gross morphological examination of anguillid eel gonads has been widely used for sex determination (e.g., Vladykov 1967; Boëtius and Boëtius 1980; Krueger and Oliveira 1997). However, comparisons with histologically prepared tissue have shown this method to be unreliable for yellow American eels (Chisnall and Kalish 1993). We also found that collection and visual sexing of gonadal tissue was problematic in immature specimens (Weeder and Uphoff 1999). The aceto-carmine "squash" method of gonad preparation (Guerrero and Shelton 1974) was ineffective for determining sex of yellow eels in Chesapeake Bay (Weeder and Uphoff 1999). Therefore, in 2000 and 2001, we sexed eels by examining histologically prepared tissue (Chisnall and Kalish 1993).

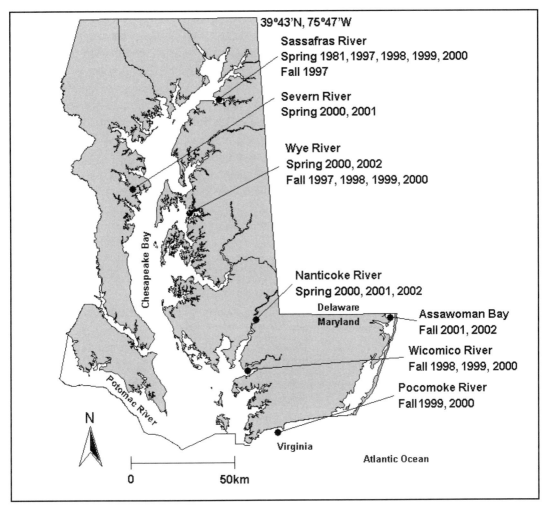

Figure 1. American eel sampling locations in Maryland, 1981 and 1997–2002.

We determined sexual maturity of female eels captured in 2000 and 2001 by using a modified form of the criteria described by Columbo et al. (1984) and Beullens et al. (1997). The absence of any visible nucleoli indicated Stage 1. If some cells had nucleoli, we called it Stage 1.5. If most cells had nucleoli, we called it Stage 2. Some oocytes in Stage 2 also had a few lipid vesicles present. Our Stage 2.5 oocytes had numerous lipid vesicles but they were mostly in the periphery of the cytoplasm. This stage corresponded to Stage 4 in Columbo et al. (1984) and Stage 3 in Beullens et al. (1997). Our Stage 3 had abundant lipid vesicles filling the cytoplasm and corresponded to Stage 4 in Beullens et al. (1997). We assumed that eels in Stages 2.5 and 3 were imminent spawners based on the advanced development of their gonads. We calculated binomial confidence intervals around the state of sexual maturity for each age with Stages 2.5 and 3 pooled. Those ages with confidence intervals that were different from 0 (excluding age 1, because none were mature) were considered sufficiently reliable for use in a regression of proportion mature versus age. The eels used for sexual maturity came from several rivers. We assumed that there were no meaningful differences in sexual maturity of eels from different rivers.

Age Determination

We counted the number of opaque and translucent zones on otoliths, prepared using the grinding and polishing method described by Secor et al. (1996), to determine the number of years each specimen had spent in continental waters. We ignored the core mark to exclude ocean residence. Ages presented in this paper are considered to be the number of years spent in continental waters; hence, eels in their year of arrival in continental waters were considered to be age 0. Translucent zones form during winter when growth is slow, and opaque zones form during periods of faster growth in summer (Vladykov 1967; Gray and Andrews 1971; Harrell and Loyacano 1982; Helfman et al. 1987). One year in continental waters equaled one opaque zone and one translucent zone (Hansen and Eversole 1984). Two biologists read each otolith independently. If readings of a particular otolith did not agree, it was read independently again, at least one day later. If readings still did not agree, the readers discussed the specimen. If the correct age of the eel was still unclear, it was excluded from age analysis.

When more than one growth ring occurs per year, this ring is denoted a "supernumary zone" (Deelder 1976). These zones can occur when growth rate changes because of high water temperatures, low food supplies, low oxygen, or other stressors. Fish may be over-aged if supernumary zones are mistaken for true annuli. We used published criteria (Deelder 1976; Berg 1985; Oliveira 1996) to exclude otoliths with suspected supernumary zones from analysis.

Growth Comparisons

We pooled data based on similarities in slopes of the length at age of eels from the same river in different years, as detected by analysis of covariance (ANCOVA). Only ages common to all rivers in a particular comparison were considered. We evaluated growth for the Wye, Wicomico, Severn, and Nanticoke rivers and Assawoman Bay by using the von Bertalanffy growth function (von Bertalanffy 1938; solved using the Solver tool in Microsoft Excel) and linear regression. We evaluated the fit of these models to the data using the sums of squared deviations between observed and expected values, and the R^2 (for linear regression only).

Mortality

Total instantaneous rate of disappearance (loss) from a stock (Z) was calculated for five sites by using a catch curve based on numbers at age derived from an age-length key (Ricker 1975; Allen 1997). Ages on the descending limb of the catch curve (those subject to fishing pressure) with sample sizes greater than one were used to estimate Z. Eels collected over multiple years from the same river were combined to calculate Z based on statistically similar growth rates. Instantaneous natural mortality rate (M) was assumed to be $3/T_{max}$ (Hoenig 1983), where T_{max} was the oldest age observed at the sites (12, because only one 13-year-old eel was found). We considered natural mortality to include mortality that occurred within Chesapeake Bay and on the spawning ground.

We estimated instantaneous fishing mortality rate (F) by subtracting M from Z. Average size at age of Maryland eels, based on the actual number of fish aged, was used for examining the age ranges observed. When the number at age for a particular group was examined, predicted numbers based on the age-length key were used.

Results

Sexual Determination and Maturity

On average, female eels were longer than male and sexually undifferentiated

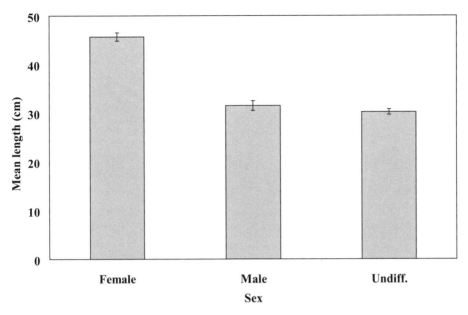

Figure 2. Mean length (±95% confidence interval) of American eels randomly sampled from baited pot catches in Maryland, by sex. 40 cm is the published length above which only females were found.

eels (Figure 2). All sexed eels longer than 40 cm were female. Below this size, examined eels were nearly equally likely to be female (40%), male (31%) or undifferentiated (29%). Sexual maturity of female eels taken in baited pots was described by the equation (proportion mature = 0.094 · age − 0.104, R^2 = 0.99; Figure 3). The logistic relationship, which is often used to model age and maturity, includes an upper asymptotic limit not found in our data. If older eels were available, a logistic equation might have had a better fit. None of the six age 1 female eels examined were sexually mature. The proportion of female eels that were mature was 0.07 at age 2 (n = 41), 0.17 at age 3 (n = 46), 0.29 at age 4 (n = 24), and 0.36 at age 5 (n = 22) (Figure 3). Sample sizes for ages 6 to 10 were too low (n = 1–3) to determine the proportion mature. The linear regression predicted that 100% would be sexually mature by age 12 (Figure 3).

Length Distributions

At all sites except Assawoman Bay, modal length was less than 40 cm, and abundance declined sharply above this size (Figure 4). Eels from Assawoman Bay were most abundant at approximately 40 to 50 cm, and abundance only gradually declined at greater lengths. Industry sources indicated that exploitation in this bay only began in 2000. In the Nanticoke River and Assawoman Bay, length distributions within one site were similar in consecutive years. However, in the Severn River, where commercial fishing is officially prohibited but violations have been reported, large eels decreased in relative abundance from 2000 to 2001. Similarly, in the Wicomico River, the relative abudance of eels larger than 40 cm decreased from 1998/1999 to 2000. Eels longer than 40 cm were abundant in the Sassafras River in 1981, when fishing pressure is believed to have been lower, and in 1997, when they were sampled in fall (Weeder and Uphoff 1999; Figure 4), but in 1998, 1999,

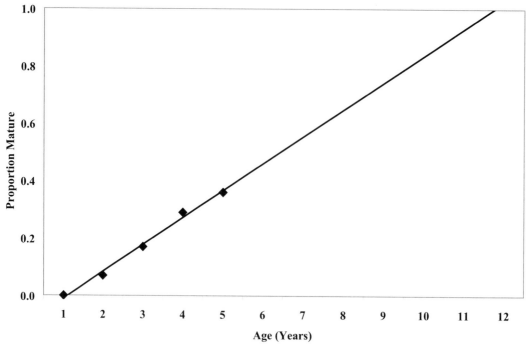

Figure 3. Proportion of female eels, sampled from baited pots, which were found to be sexually mature (stages 2.5 and 3 pooled) at ages 1 through 5, with projected maturity past age 5.

and 2000, lengths were truncated at approximately 35 cm (Figure 4). The modal size of eels in the Sassafras River in 2000 was 29 cm, but 19 years earlier it was 36 cm. The silver eels we purchased from the Pocomoke River were considerably larger than the yellow eels sampled elsewhere and were consistent with the size of sexually mature female eels found off the coast of Virginia (Wenner and Music 1974) and elsewhere on the Atlantic seaboard (Helfman et al. 1987).

Size and Age

At all sites except the Pocomoke River (where large-mesh pound nets were used), eels were first captured in the fishery one year after transformation from elvers to yellow eels (Table 1). In the nearly fresh Nanticoke River, we documented eels aged 1 to 13 years old, and the modal age was 3 (Table 1). In Assawoman Bay, 3-year-olds were the most abundant year-class, and we found eels up to age 8. Eels from the Pocomoke River were up to 9 years old (Table 2).

Because we had no specimens of independently verified age, it was not possible to determine directly whether supernumary zones existed, and undetected zones could have biased our samples. If so, then the true ages of some specimens would be lower than we estimated. Young ages, but large sizes, of most specimens are not consistent with inflated ages. Most otoliths were straightforward to read, since annuli were well defined and wide translucent zones separated opaque zones.

Growth

There were no significant differences in growth among different years from the same river based on ANCOVA ($P > 0.05$), so years were pooled for each area. Comparison of von

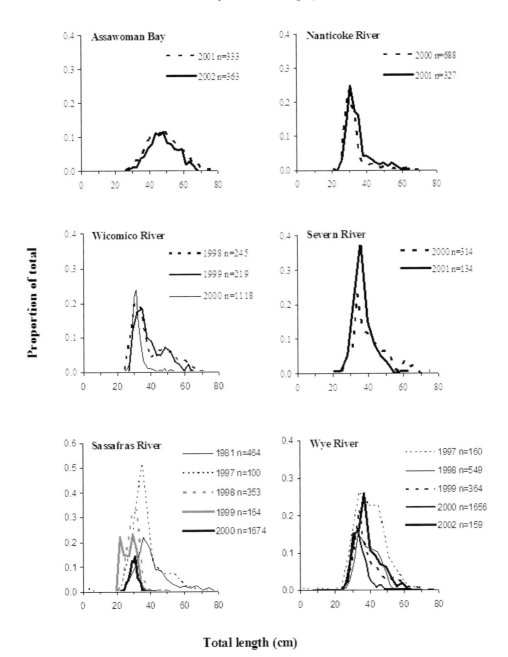

Figure 4. Length distributions of eels randomly sampled from baited pots at six Maryland locations, 1981 and 1997–2002.

Table 1. Instantaneous disappearance rate (Z), number of eels aged (N), and predicted age distribution for five Maryland sites. Instantaneous natural mortality rate $M = 0.25$.

	Location				
	Nanticoke River	Severn River	Wye River	Wicomico River	Assawoman Bay
Year	2000–2001	2000–2001	2000–2002	1998–2000	2001–2002
Z	0.62	0.99	1.44	0.97	0.89
F	0.37	0.74	1.19	0.72	0.64
N in age-length key	320	124	129	187	267
1	22	33	444	75	18
2	89	228	697	1043	137
3	302	99	235	310	237
4	268	48	53	74	227
5	178	8	9	44	49
6	54	0			13
7	51	5			8
8	22				4
9	19				
10	5				
11	2				
12	4				
13	1				

Bertalanffy and linear regression results showed that growth was best described as a linear function of age, consistent with numerous studies of American and European *A. anguilla* eels (e.g., Frost 1945; Hansen and Eversole 1984; Figure 5).

Mortality

Table 1 shows the disappearance rate (Z) as estimated bycatch curve analysis of randomly sampled eels aged 1–12 (age 13 was not used because only one eel of that age was found). Fishing mortality rate, estimated as Z–M, was highest in the Wye River (1.19), where only five year classes were observed, and lowest in the Nanticoke River (0.37) where 13 year classes were found. Some estimated fishing mortality rates were four or more times higher than estimated M (0.25). A fishing mortality rate equivalent to M is the maximum recommended level in situations when the stock is poorly understood (ICES 2001).

Discussion

Sexual Determination and Maturity

The size by which all eels in our study were sexually differentiated (40 cm) was consistent with that of other studies. In the Potomac River estuary of Chesapeake Bay, 29% of eels less than 40 cm long were male (Goodwin and Angermeier 2003), compared to 31% in our study.

Table 2. Mean and median length and weight at age of American eels collected from four Maryland sites 1997–2002. Data from multiple dates within a river are pooled. S.D. = standard deviation of the mean.

Continental Age	Length at age (cm)				Weight at age (g)			
	N	Mean	S.D.	Median	N	Mean	S.D.	Median
Nanticoke River – spring 2000, 2001, 2002								
1	4	25.8	1.7	25.5	4	30.5	5.3	30.0
2	15	29.9	5.3	28.8	15	48.8	26.0	38.0
3	44	31.1	5.3	30.0	44	58.2	30.7	49.5
4	55	36.5	7.9	34.7	55	99.8	66.5	78.0
5	66	43.9	10.2	45.2	66	183.3	128.5	167.0
6	32	48.4	9.6	48.2	32	232.3	158.7	196.5
7	31	50.1	12.5	49.0	31	262.5	178.0	222.0
8	31	54.1	7.8	53.9	32	318.3	145.0	295.0
9	23	55.7	10.5	55.5	23	384.7	188.5	345.0
10	8	56.1	7.3	54.5	8	357.4	133.6	337.0
11	2	57.5	0.7	57.5	2	340.5	0.7	340.5
12	7	61.3	7.5	57.0	7	455.7	182.8	392.0
13	1	59.7	.	59.7	1	344.0	.	344.0
Wye River – fall 1997, 1998, 1999, spring and fall 2000, spring 2002								
1	53	30.0	5.0	29.0	53	50.7	33.0	40.0
2	173	39.7	6.9	39.0	173	111.0	66.5	96.0
3	70	46.4	10.6	44.0	71	207.0	170.7	136.0
4	29	52.4	8.5	52.0	29	290.0	176.0	248.0
5	8	59.1	7.6	58.5	8	446.3	203.9	407.5
6	1	75.0	.	75.0	1	800.0	.	800.0
Assawoman Bay – fall 2001, 2002								
1	11	32.0	3.4	32.0	11	60.4	18.0	59.0
2	52	38.1	6.4	37.6	52	100.9	62.6	83.0
3	83	46.6	8.9	46.0	83	194.6	119.7	152.0
4	92	52.3	9.8	53.8	92	287.9	151.6	278.5
5	25	55.7	8.9	57.0	25	352.2	150.3	339.0
6	7	58.3	1.1	58.2	7	448.4	26.3	42.0
7	3	53.9	3.0	54.1	3	267.0	44.4	267.0
Pocomoke River – fall 1999, 2000								
2	2	48.5	3.5	48.5	2	217.0	46.7	217.0
3	5	57.2	8.3	59.0	5	361.8	161.5	376.0
4	12	63.8	6.6	63.5	12	537.4	183.0	538.5
5	12	64.3	7.3	66.5	12	597.5	202.9	635.0
6	12	64.7	6.1	66.5	12	587.8	205.7	619.0
7	5	65.0	5.5	62.0	5	592.0	133.6	540.0
8	2	68.0	1.41	68.0	2	700.0	62.2	700.0
9	1	67.0	.	67.0	1	600.0	.	600.0

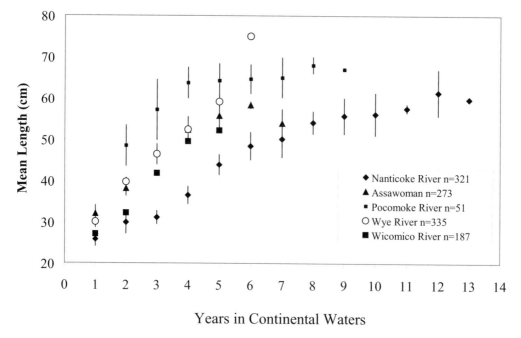

Figure 5. Mean length at continental age of eels from four locations in Maryland's Chesapeake Bay and one off the Atlantic Ocean, with 95% confidence intervals.

We found that 17% of 3-year-old female eels were sexually mature (Figure 3). Three-year-old eels that measured at least 49 cm were found in every sampled river. In Chesapeake Bay in 1982, females matured at ages 10 to 12, while in New Jersey, they matured at 11 to 13 years (Helfman et al. 1987). Our prediction of 100% maturity by age 12 is consistent with the age of many silver eels reported by Helfman et al. (1987) and with the maximum age we observed.

Most of the eels we ranked as Stage 3 were silver eels from the Pocomoke River. Because of limited sampling during fall, the reduced likelihood of capturing silver eels in eel pots (anecdotal evidence) and the potentially narrow window of time between the end of the period of residence and emigration, eel pot sampling probably missed many of the actively migrating, most sexually mature male and female animals (Helfman et al. 1987).

Factors Influencing our Findings

We observed rapid growth rates, small eels, and more females than males. Several factors likely contribute to this pattern and their relative impacts cannot be isolated. Environmental factors, including the inherent productivity of the system and length of the growing season, are likely to influence growth rates. Density can influence growth rates, sex ratios, and age and size at maturity. Fishing pressure can reduce density and selectively remove larger eels from the population.

Environment

Abiotic factors can influence growth, size, and sex ratio. As latitude increases, the length of the growing season and mean water temperatures decrease, causing a negative correlation between growth rates and latitude (Oliveira 1999). Growth in both freshwater (Harrell and Loyacano 1982) and tidal

(Hansen and Eversole 1984) areas of a South Carolina river was faster than that observed in more northern locations (Helfman et al. 1987; Newfoundland—Gray and Andrews 1971; Lake Ontario and Ottawa River—Hurley 1972). As latitude increases, age and size at maturity of American eels increase (Helfman et al. 1987). Maryland is located at the southern end of the U.S. mid-Atlantic region, which is near the middle of the U.S. range of the species.

Estuaries such as Chesapeake Bay are more productive than freshwater areas (Campbell et al. 1999). Eel growth was significantly faster in brackish than freshwater sites in the Hudson River (Morrison and Secor 2003). Higher salinity is associated with increased growth rates, and American eels from marine or brackish areas are generally larger at age than their freshwater counterparts (Helfman et al. 1987; e.g. Altamaha River, Georgia–Helfman et al. 1984; tidal Potomac and freshwater Shenandoah River, Virginia–Goodwin and Angermeier 2003). The slowest growing eels in our study were taken from tidal but nearly freshwater (Nanticoke River), while the other, faster growing populations were taken from higher salinity areas. These growth differences may be due to differing food availability. Yellow-phase American eels living in estuarine environments in Virginia (lower Chesapeake Bay) consumed worms, snails, crustaceans, bivalves, polychaetes, insects, and occasionally fishes (Wenner and Musick 1975). Insects (Wenner and Musick 1975) and crayfish (Wilson and Turner 1982) were major components of freshwater diets.

The sex ratio of American eels may be associated with habitat differences. Oliveira et al. (2001) evaluated sex ratios of silver eels caught at the mouths of five Maine rivers. Males were negatively associated with amount of upstream lacustrine habitat, while females were positively associated with this feature. We did not attribute differences among eel sex ratios in different Chesapeake Bay rivers to differences in habitat, because all rivers had similar muddy bottoms and temperatures. We believe that the eels we sampled likely lived close to where they were caught, because most eels were sexually immature and likely remained in a relatively small home range. In addition, the width of translucent zones between opaque zones, which is indirectly indicative of growth rate, appeared to be consistently broad or narrow within one otolith. If an eel were moving between areas with different growth rate potentials, we would expect to see periods of rapid growth interspersed with periods of slow growth. This observation supports the idea that the specimen stayed in the same environment until it was captured.

Density

Density-dependent processes affect sex, growth, and survival of anguillid eels. Survival of European eels in an Italian lagoon, as well as the proportion of females, female body size, and age and length of both sexes at sexual maturity, increased as density declined (De Leo and Gatto 1996). Increased density was associated with decreased growth rates and an increase in the frequency of males in Ireland's Lough Neagh (Parsons et al. 1977). The proportion of American eel males in a South Carolina river increased as density increased (Harrell and Loyacano 1982); similarly, the frequency of European eel males increased with density in controlled experiments (Roncarati et al. 1997). Bertin (1957) suggested that European eel elvers reaching the coast are asexual and distribute randomly. Later overcrowding and poor feeding would result in males, and low populations and rich feeding would produce females (Bertin 1957). Harrell and Loyacano (1982) postulated that American eel females may leave crowded conditions where only males can survive.

We were not able to determine density of eels in the rivers we sampled. However, the lower frequency of males than females in our samples and the rapid growth and large size at age of females in the highly productive estuaries we studied are consistent with low population densities.

Sex Differences and Sex Ratio

Male anguillid eels are generally thought to grow more slowly than females (but see Helfman et al. 1987). European males in an aquaculture facility grew about 12 cm/year, while females grew about 17 cm/year (Deelder 1981). Yellow American eels greater than 40 cm (likely female) grew more than twice as fast as those less than 40 cm in length (likely male) in a Rhode Island stream (Oliveira 1997). European males grew more slowly than females in a controlled study (Roncarati et al. 1997). Oliveira (1997) determined that growth rates of American eels were more closely related to sex ratio than density. However, as discussed above, density and sex ratio are related. Silver males are nearly always shorter than silver females (e.g., Columbo and Rossi 1978; Vøllestad and Jonsson 1986; De Leo and Gatto 1996; Oliveira 1999; Oliveira and McCleave 2000; Goodwin and Angermeier 2003). Because male gametes are far smaller than female ones, males are expected to be reproductively successful at smaller sizes than females. In addition, in areas where fishing removes larger eels, the small size of these males would enhance their survival.

The female-dominated sex ratios reported by most researchers (e.g., Hansen and Eversole 1984; Harrell and Loyacano 1982; Helfman et al. 1984) and in our study could be due to the late maturation of males. Oliveira and McCleave (2000), Columbo and Rossi (1978), and P. Todd in Helfman et al. (1987) hypothesized that eels destined to be male may differentiate definitively only when they reach the silver stage, while females develop from intersexes when yellow. This would allow a fairly short period of time when males could be intercepted (as they are maturing but before they migrate) and could explain the low occurrence of yellow males in our samples from tidal Maryland estuaries. Length, not weight or age, induces migration (Frost 1945; Vøllestad and Jonsson 1986; Helfman et al. 1987), and length is also likely related to physiological condition (Frost 1945). Body fat reserves, which are dependent on water temperature and food availability, can influence the likelihood or timing of emigration (Larsson et al. 1990). None of the eels we sexed that were greater than 40 cm long were male or undifferentiated, consistent with maximum size of male yellow eels in Maine (Oliveira and McCleave 2000) and Rhode Island (Oliveira 1997) and male silver eels in Maine (Oliveira and McCleave 2000).

Mortality

We found high rates of nonnatural mortality (Table 1). Strong fishing pressure, which can harvest many hundreds of kg of eels per day from small tidal estuaries, is likely to have caused reduced densities consistent with the demographics we observed. The Chesapeake Bay's Sassafras River is a heavily fished system with truncated size distributions consistent with gear selectivity (Figure 4). Catch per unit effort (CPUE, where unit effort is pot-day) of eels from the Sassafras River was much less in 1998 than in 1981, when anecdotal evidence suggests fishing pressure was less (Weeder and Uphoff 1999). Median CPUE in research fishing dropped from 9 to nearly 0 eels per pot, and median total weight dropped from 2.5 kg/pot to nearly 0 kg/pot between 1981 and 1998 (Weeder and Uphoff 1999).

We could not determine M directly; rather we used the maximum age of eels found in our region (12; only a single eel was age 13) to derive M as 3/maximum age (Hoenig 1983). This equation is based on many other fish species that do not share some aspects of the life cycle of anguillid eels. Our estimate of M (0.25) may be high because eels in other areas (freshwater) have been known to live much longer than 12 years and a larger denominator would cause M to be smaller. However, other authors have found similar M values for anguillid species. For yellow European eels in Norwegian brackish waters, Vøllestad (1986) estimated Z and then subtracted an F derived from tag return data to obtain M and U (U = emigration). Vøllestad (1986) estimated $M + U = 0.203$. ICES (2001) estimated Z as 0.25–0.28 at two unexploited Canadian sites, which is also similar to our estimate of M.

Because F is an instantaneous mortality rate, it can exceed one, as compared to annual mortality (the proportion of fish caught in a particular year), which is a fraction of one (Haddon 2001). Our estimates of F ranged from 0.37 for the Nanticoke River to 1.19 for the Wye River (Table 1). Although F values greater than one are unusual in eel studies, they are not unheard of in heavily exploited stocks of other species. For example, McGovern et al. (2002) used a catch curve analysis to estimate F for black sea bass *Centropristis striata* in the Atlantic Ocean off the southeastern U.S. for the years 1978–2000. F was greater than 1 in 14 of the 23 years studied.

Our method of estimating F has limitations. Variable recruitment and differences in catchability with age are two potential biases associated with the catch curve method (Gulland 1983). Where possible, we pooled multiple years of data from the same river to ameliorate the effect of variable recruitment on catch curves (Ricker 1975). Since F is estimated by subtracting M from Z (Gulland 1983), the accuracy of the estimate of M influences the accuracy of the estimate of F. We believe that our mortality estimate was carried out with the best available data and methods and is consistent with findings in other areas.

Although fecundity is directly related to body size and large females produce more eggs than small ones (Wenner and Musick 1974; Todd 1981), our mature female eels were often smaller than the maximum size they could theoretically attain and therefore were less fecund than they could be. Size selectivity in the fishery may explain this finding. In order to grow larger, eels would need to remain longer in continental waters before emigration. Fishing, which selects for the largest animals, would tend to remove older, larger eels. However, younger, faster growing eels, although they may not reach optimal size, would be in the system for a shorter time than slower growing ones and therefore would be subject to less risk of capture over their lives. Over time, these younger, faster growing animals would dominate the population as older, slower growing animals are removed by fishing. This demographic shift has been demonstrated in many fisheries (e.g., snowy grouper *Epinephelus niveatus* (Wyanski et al. 2000), black sea bass (McGovern et al. 2002), vermilion snapper *Rhomboplites aurorubens* (Zhao et al. 1997), and red porgy *Pagrus pagrus* (Harris and McGovern 1997).

We observed an increase in eel size after fishing ceased in the Wye River (Figure 4). This river was commercially fished in 2000 and for many years before that. However, the eeler we collaborated with fished the Wye River in 2000 and then shifted to Assawoman Bay in 2001. When he fished the Wye River in 2002 at our request using the same gear, the abundance of larger eels had increased (Figure 4). The lack of fishing pressure in 2001 could have caused the change. A strong year-class becoming apparent in the 2002 catch could account for this observation in the Wye River, but no strong year-class was evident in the Assawoman River (Figure 4), the only other river sampled in 2002. Similarly, the steady shift in length distribution toward smaller fish in consecutive years of fishing is well explained by heavy exploitation (e.g., Wicomico, Severn, Wye, Sassafras; Figure 4).

Hedgepeth (1983) determined that fishing pressure was the greatest factor influencing size distribution of eels in Virginia's Chesapeake Bay. The availability of female eels large enough to be silver (≈40 cm; Helfman et al. 1987) in Maryland's tidal estuaries may be restricted, given the efficiency of commercial eel pots at capturing eels above ≈35 cm (Figure 4).

Maryland's fishery allows the harvest of small, young eels before they are able to grow to the large sizes needed for spawning and targets large, older eels that have survived to reach spawning size. Those eels that reach maturity may do so at a younger age and smaller size. The resulting lower fecundity and decreased number of spawning adults may reduce the amount of spawner biomass to unsustainable levels. Methods to decrease fishing mortality and allow for escapement of adults in spawning condition, such as seasonal closures, limitations of fishing effort, and maximum size limits, should be considered.

Acknowledgments

Erik Pertain and Keith Whiteford provided extensive assistance with otolith preparation and aging. Rudolph Lukacovic assisted with fieldwork and determined the stage of sexual maturity of our specimens. John Barnette, Edward Fooks, and Byron Cameron shared socioeconomic information about the eel fishery and provided commercially captured eels over multiple years of the study.

References

Allen, M. S. 1997. Effects of variable recruitment on catch-curve analysis for crappie populations. North American Journal of Fisheries Management 17:202–205.

Berg, R. 1985. Age determination of eels, *Anguilla anguilla* (L): comparison of field data with otolith ring patterns. Journal of Fish Biology 26:537–544.

Bertin, L. 1957. Eels: a biological study. Philosophical Library, New York.

Beullens, K., E. H. Eding, P. Gilson, F. Ollevier, J. Komen, and C. J. Richter. 1997. Gonadal differentiation, intersexuality and sex ratios of European eel (*Anguilla anguilla* L.) maintained in captivity. Aquaculture 153:135–150.

Boëtius, I., and J. Boëtius. 1980. Experimental maturation of female silver eels, *Anguilla anguilla*. Estimates of fecundity and energy reserves for migration and spawning. Dana 1:1–28.

Campbell, N. A., J. B. Reece, and L. G. Mitchell. 1999. Biology, 5th edition. Benjamin/Cummings, Menlo Park, California.

Chisnall, B. L., and J. M. Kalish. 1993. Age validation and movement of freshwater eels (*Anguilla dieffenbachii* and *A. australis*) in a New Zealand pastoral stream. New Zealand Journal of Marine and Freshwater Research 27:333–338.

Columbo, G., G. Grandi, and R. Rossi. 1984. Gonad differentiation and body growth in *Anguilla anguilla* L. Journal of Fish Biology 24:215–228.

Culumbo, G., and R. Rossi. 1978. Environmental influences on growth and sex ratio in different eel populations (*Anguilla anguilla*, L.) of Adriatic coasts. Pages 320–331 *in* D. S. McLusky and A. J. Berry, editors. Physiology and behaviour of marine organisms. Pergamon, Oxford, England.

Deelder, C. L. 1976. The problem of the supernumerary zones in otoliths of the European eel (*Anguilla anguilla* Linnaeus, 1758); a suggestion to cope with it. Aquaculture 9:373–379.

Deelder, C. L. 1981. On the age and growth of cultured eels, *Anguilla anguilla* (Linnaeus, 1758). Aquaculture 26:13–22.

De Leo, G. A., and M. Gatto. 1996. Trends in vital rates of the European eel: evidence for density dependence? Ecological Applications 6:1281–1294.

Foster III, J. W. S. 1981. The American eel in Maryland—a situation paper. Maryland Tidewater Administration, Tidal Fisheries Division: 21, Annapolis, Maryland.

Frost, W. E. 1945. The age and growth of eels (*Anguilla anguilla*) from the Windermere catchment area: Part I. Journal of Animal Ecology 14:26–36.

Goodwin, K. R., and P. L. Angermeier. 2003. Demographic characteristics of American eel in the Potomac River drainage, Virginia. Transactions of the American Fisheries Society 132:524–535.

Gray, R. W., and C. W. Andrews. 1971. Age and growth of the American eel (*Anguilla rostrata* (LeSuer)) in Newfoundland waters. Canadian Journal of Zoology 49:121–128.

Guerrero, L. D., and W. L. Shelton. 1974. An acetocarmine squash method of sexing juvenile fishes. Progressive Fish-Culturist 36:56.

Gulland, J. A. 1983. Fish stock assessment: a manual of basic methods. FAO/Wiley series on food and agriculture, Volume 1. John Wiley, New York.

Haddon, M. 2001. Modelling and quantitative methods in fisheries. Chapman and Hall/CRC, New York.

Hansen, R. A., and A. G. Eversole. 1984. Age, growth, and sex ratio of American eels in brackish-water portions of a South Carolina river. Transactions of the American Fisheries Society 113:744–749.

Harrell, R. M., and H. A. Loyacano, Jr. 1982. Age, growth and sex ratio of the American eel in the Cooper River, South Carolina. Proceedings of the Annual Conference of the Southeast Association of Fish and Wildlife Agencies 34:349–359.

Harris, P. J., and J. M. McGovern. 1997. Changes in the life history of red porgy, *Pagrus pagrus*, from the southeastern United States, 1972–1994. Fishery Bulletin 95:732–747.

Hedgepeth, M. Y. 1983. Age, growth, and reproduction of American eels, *Anguilla rostrata*, (Lesueur), from the Chesapeake Bay area. Master's thesis. College of William and Mary, Williamsburg, Virginia.

Helfman, G. S., E. L. Bozeman, and E. B. Brothers. 1984. Size, age, and sex of American eels in a Georgia river. Transactions of the American Fisheries Society 113:132–141.

Helfman, G. S., D. E. Facey, L. S. Hales, Jr., and E. Bozeman. 1987. Reproductive ecology of the American eel. Pages 42–56 *in* M. J. Dadswell, R. J. Klauda, C. M. Moffitt, R. L. Saunders, R. A. Rulifson, and J. E. Cooper, editors. Common strategies of anadromous and catadromous fishes. American Fisheries Society, Symposium 1, Bethesda, Maryland.

Hoenig, J. M. 1983. Empirical use of longevity data to estimate mortality rates. Fishery Bulletin 82:898–903.

Hurley, D. A. 1972. The American eel in eastern Lake Ontario. Journal of the Fisheries Research Board of Canada 29:535–543.

ICES (International Council for the Exploration of the Sea). 2001. Report of the EIFAC/ICES Working Group on Eels. ICES CM 2000/ ACFM:03/2001.

Krueger, W. H., and K. Oliveira. 1997. Sex, size and gonad morphology of silver American eels *Anguilla rostrata*. Copeia 2:415–420.

Larsson, P., S. Hamrin, and L. Okla. 1990. Fat content as a factor inducing migratory behavior in the eel (*Anguilla anguilla* L.) to the Sargasso Sea. Naturwissenschaften 77:488–490.

McGovern, J. C., M. R. Collins, O. Pashuk, and H. S. Meister. 2002. Temporal and spatial differences in life history parameters of black sea bass in the southeastern United States. North American Journal of Fisheries Management 22:1151–1163.

Morrison, W. E., and D. H. Secor. 2003. Demographic attributes of yellow-phase American eels in the Hudson River Estuary. Canadian Journal of Fisheries and Aquatic Sciences 60:1487–1501.

Oliveira, K. 1996. Field validation of annular growth rings in the American eel, *Anguilla rostrata*, using tetracycline-marked otoliths. Fisheries Bulletin 94:186–189.

Oliveira, K. 1997. Movements and growth rates of yellow-phase American eels in the Annaquatucket River, Rhode Island. Transactions of the American Fisheries Society 126:638–646.

Oliveira, K. 1999. Life history characteristics and strategies of the American eel, *Anguilla rostrata*. Canadian Journal of Fisheries and Aquatic Sciences 56:795–802.

Oliveira, K., and J. D. McCleave. 2000. Variation in population and life history traits of the American eel, *Anguilla rostrata*, in four rivers in Maine. Environmental Biology of Fishes 59:141–151.

Oliveira, K., J. D. McCleave, and G. S. Wipplehauser. 2001. Regional variation and the effect of lake: river area on sex distribution of American eels. Journal of Fish Biology 58:943–952.

Parsons, J., K. U. Vickers, and Y. Warden. 1977. Relationship between elver recruitment and changes in the sex ratio of silver eels *Anguilla anguilla* L. migrating from Lough Neagh, Northern Ireland. Journal of Fish Biology 10:211–229.

Ricker, W. E. 1975. Computation and interpretation of biological statistics of fish populations. Fisheries Research Board of Canada Bulletin no. 191.

Roncarati, A., P. Melotti, O. Mordenti, and L. Gennari. 1997. Influence of stocking density of European eel (*Anguilla anguilla*, L.) elvers on sex differentiation and zootechnical performances. Journal of Applied Ichthyology 13:131–136.

Secor, D. H., J. M. Dean, and E. H. Laban. 1996. Manual for otolith removal and preparation for microstructural examination. Technical Publication No. 1991–01. Electric Power Research Institute and Belle W. Baruch Institute for Marine Biology and Coastal Research, Columbia, South Carolina.

Todd, P. R. 1981. Morphometric changes, gonad histology, and fecundity estimates in migrating New Zealand freshwater eels (*Anguilla* spp.). New Zealand Journal of Marine and Freshwater Research 15:155–170.

Vladykov, V. D. 1967. Age determination and age of American eel from New Brunswick waters. Progress Report No. 3. Canadian Department of Fisheries and Forestry, Quebec.

Vøllestad, L. A. 1986. Growth and production of female yellow eels *Anguilla anguilla* from brackish water in Norway. Vie et Milieu 36:267–271.

Vøllestad, L. A., and B. Jonsson. 1986. Life-history characteristics of the European eel *Anguilla anguilla* in the Imsa River, Norway. Transactions of the American Fisheries Society 115:864–871.

von Bertalanffy, L. 1938. A quantitative theory of organic growth (inquiries into growth laws. II). Human Biology 10:181–213.

Weeder, J. A., and J. H. Uphoff, Jr. 1999. Maryland American eel population study. Completion Report No. 34. Maryland Department of Natural Resources, Annapolis.

Weeder, J. A., and J. H. Uphoff, Jr. 2001. Maryland American eel population study. Completion Report Project 3-ACA-065. Maryland Department of Natural Resources, Annapolis.

Weeder, J. A., and J. H. Uphoff, Jr. 2003. Effect of changes in growth and eel pot mesh size on American eel yield per recruit estimates in upper Chesapeake Bay. Pages 169–176 *in* D. A. Dixon, editor. Biology, management, and protection of catadromous eels. American Fisheries Society, Symposium 33, Bethesda, Maryland.

Wenner, C. A., and J. A. Musick. 1974. Fecundity and gonad observations of the American eel, *Anguilla rostrata*, migrating from Chesapeake Bay, Virginia. Journal of the Fisheries Research Board of Canada 31:1387–1390.

Wenner, C. A., and J. A. Musick. 1975. Food habits and seasonal abundance of the American eel, *Anguilla rostrata*, from the lower Chesapeake Bay. Chesapeake Science 16:61–66.

Wilson, J. L., and D. A. Turner. 1982. Occurrence of the American eel in the Holston River, Tennessee. Journal of the Tennessee Academy of Sciences 57:63–64.

Wyanski, D. M., D. B. White, and C. A. Barans. 2000. Growth, population age structure, and aspects of the reproductive biology of snowy grouper, *Epinephelus niveatus*, off North Carolina and South Carolina. Fishery Bulletin 98:199–218.

Zhao, B., J. C. McGovern, and P. J. Harris. 1997. Age, growth, and temporal change in size at age of the vermilion snapper from the South Atlantic Bight. Transactions of the American Fisheries Society 126:181–193.

American Eel Movements, Growth, and Sex Ratio Following Translocation

GUY VERREAULT[1], WILLY DARGERE, AND RÉMI TARDIF

Ministère des Ressources naturelles et de la faune du Québec
506 rue Lafontaine, Rivière-du-Loup, Québec G5R 3C4 Canada

Abstract.—Forty thousand American eel *Anguilla rostrata* elvers were released in a 400-ha lake in an eel-free watershed in eastern Québec in 1999. Subsequent sampling enabled the measurement of poststocking movements, growth, and sex ratio. Populations showed limited movements, and occupancy extended less than 3 km into inflowing tributaries by 2003. Annual growth increments in the lake (118 mm/year) were the highest reported for the species, but growth increments in rivers (40 mm/year) were typical of those found elsewhere. Four of seven eels whose sex could be determined were females, in contrast to other sites in the St. Lawrence watershed where females are more than 99% of the population. American eel translocation to growth areas that have been blocked by artificial barriers may be a useful means to increase production of silver eels.

Introduction

The American eel *Anguilla rostrata* is present in the St. Lawrence watershed from Lake Ontario to the Gulf and associated tributaries. The species is an important ecological component in aquatic communities throughout its distribution range, and it supported fisheries well before European settlement in Canada (Sagard 1636). Recorded landings of silver eels in the St. Lawrence estuary have declined steeply in the past 30 years, from 300 metric tons in 1970 to 72 metric tons in 2000 (Verreault et al. 2003). The decrease in stocks and landings coincides with recruitment failure in Lake Ontario, the species' major growth location in the St. Lawrence watershed (Casselman et al. 1997). In spite of the decline, few actions have been initiated to restore population abundance to previous levels. Management responses have been oriented towards installation of eel ladders for upstream migration over artificial obstacles, mainly hydro dams (Therrien and Verreault 1998; Verdon et al. 2003). The impact of these actions on population demography and abundance is limited by the number of juveniles below the dams. With low annual recruitment from the ocean, upstream passage facilities may not materially assist eel populations, especially so far from the Atlantic Ocean (Berg and Jørgensen 1994).

Eel translocation, or stocking, may be a useful tool to rapidly increase a local population in a specific growth habitat facing poor natural recruitment from the ocean (Knights et al. 1996). It may also be an option to increase escapement of maturing silver-phase eels. Vladykov and Liew (1982) found that eels captured as elvers in southwest New

---

[1] Corresponding author: guy.verreault@mrnf.gouv.qc.ca

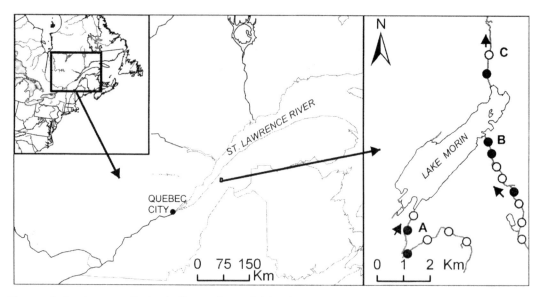

Figure 1. Study area. Circles indicate electrofishing locations. Solid circles = sites with eels, open circles = sites without eels. Arrows indicate direction of water flow.

Brunswick and eastern Québec survived and grew well when stocked in an artificial pond in eastern Ontario. There is a long tradition of stocking European eels *Anguilla anguilla*, but there are relatively few long-term post-stocking studies (Pursiainen and Toivenen 1984; Wickstrøm et al. 1996; Knights and White 1998). Translocation has never been implemented as a management technique for American eels but could be an attractive practice to mitigate current low recruitment in the northern part of the distribution range.

In late 1990s, the Québec Eel Fishermen's Union proposed an experiment to examine the consequences of elver stocking in a small watershed. This paper describes that experiment and reports eel movements, growth, and sex ratio in the 4 years after stocking.

Study Area

The study was performed in Lake Morin on the south shore of the St. Lawrence estuary, 150 km east of Québec City (Figure 1). This mesotrophic lake is located in an eel-free watershed in a forested area. The lake is drained by a 30-km river that is blocked by three hydro dams at sites where natural waterfalls precluded upstream migration. The lake is 400 ha in area, 4.2 m in mean depth, and has a shallow shoreline dominated by common cattail *Typha latifolia*. Two tributaries with natural waterfalls that could be easily overcome by eels feed the lake (A and B in Figure 1). The mean annual discharge at the lake outlet (C in Figure 1) is estimated at 4.57 m^3s^{-1} (Québec Ministry of Environment, unpubl. data). The fish community in the lake is dominated by cyprinids (*Semotilus margarita* and *Phoxinus neogaus*). Brook trout *Salvelinus fontinalis* are dominant in the rivers, while Appalachian brook crayfish *Cambarus bartonii* are abundant and well distributed in both lacustrine and riverine habitats.

Methods

Stocking Material and Procedure

Forty thousand elvers were caught by dip net in early May 1999 in river mouths flowing to the Bay of Fundy (New Brunswick, Canada) and transported seven days later to Lake Morin. At their arrival, mean length (TL) and weight were 60.3 mm (SD = 3.0) and 0.11 g (SD = 0.02), respectively. Elvers were immersed in a hyperosmotic solution (5% sodium chloride) containing 1% tetracycline chlorhydrate (CHTC) for 3.5 min to give a band on the otolith that is readable under fluorescence (Alcobendas et al. 1991). Five hours later, at dusk, the elvers were scattered by boat over the total lake surface for a stocking density of 100 individuals/ha, or 11 g/ha.

Sampling

Sampling was carried out in the lake and rivers during summer. In the lake, in 2001 and 2002, fine-mesh trap nets (3-mm-square mesh) were used in littoral zones at depths of less than 5 m. These trap nets, designed specifically for eels, are nonselective for eels of TL > 180 mm (Adam 1997; Verreault 2002). Effort was 20 trap-net days in 2001 and 90 trap-net days in 2002. In 2003, three longlines, each with 100 hooks, were deployed in the lake for five nights. Longlines are thought to be selective for eels longer than 500 mm as seen in fisheries using the same gear in Lake St. Francis (Dumont 1998). In rivers, electrofishing was performed at a maximum of six sites in tributary A, eight sites in tributary B, and two sites in river C. Electrofishing sites on tributaries were up to 6 km from the lake. Electrofishing was performed in stream sections 10 to 25 m long in water depths less than 1.0 m.

Sampled eels were anesthetized in clove-oil solution, then weighed (±0.1 g) and measured (±1 mm). Sagittal otoliths were removed for aging. Sex identification was performed by morphological examination and histology on a random subsample. Mean growth per year was calculated as $Gi = Lt_{capt} - Lt_{capt-1}$, where Gi is the annual growth increment (mm), Lt_{capt} is mean length at capture, and Lt_{capt-1} is mean length at capture the previous year. Some eels may have been excluded from trap nets in 2001 and longlines in 2003 because of their size. To avoid possible bias caused by gear selectivity, overall mean annual growth in the lake was calculated from samples collected in 2002. Otoliths were processed for age determination according to Verreault (2002), using a five-stage procedure: 1) cleaning with sodium hypochlorite; 2) embedding in epoxy resin; 3) sanding on 800-grit paper and polishing with aluminum oxide powder; 4) etching with EDTA solution, and finally; 5) staining with 0.01% toluidine blue. Otoliths were observed with a binocular microscope (60X) under transmitted light for aging. Tetracycline deposits emit a yellow-green fluorescence (Panfili and Tomás 2001). Tetracycline marks were revealed with an epifluorescent microscope (Leica, 50 W, HBO lamp, 510 nm, H3 filter).

Results

Movements

Eels were captured by trap net in Lake Morin at depths ranging from 1 to 5 m in both 2001 and 2002. Only a single eel was taken with the longlines set in the lake in 2003. Electrofishing in tributaries revealed eels only within 3 km of the lake during each year after translocation. Eels had a limited distribution in the outlet river, primarily within 1 km of the lake. Tetracycline marks were readily observed on all otoliths (n = 70) collected in tributaries and in the lake during the five sampling years.

Growth

We obtained lengths of 88 translocated eels in 2000–2003 (Table 1). Eels from the lake were longer than eels from the rivers when both habitats were sampled in the

Table 1. Length and length increments of translocated eels sampled in Lake Morin and adjoining rivers. T= Trapnet, L= Longline, and E= Electrofishing.

Year	N	Gear[a]	Lake Length (mm)		Length increment (mm/yr)		N	Gear[a]	Rivers Length (mm)		Length increment (mm/yr)	
			Mean	SD	Mean	SD			Mean	SD	Mean	SD
1999	22		60.3	3.0								
2000	0				86.9	12.3	29	E	138.4	20.0	78.1	19.0
2001	2	T	234.0	48.1	86.9	12.3	8	E	150.4	28.2	12.0	8.1
2002	4	T	412.8	66.2	178.8	26.7	42	E	173.4	59.9	23.0	0.2
2003	1	L	512.0	-	99.2	-	2	E	220.0	82.0	46.6	22.4

same year (Kruskal-Wallis, $P < 0.037$ in 2001; $P < 0.0168$ in 2002). Overall mean annual growth increments were 117.5 mm/year for eels sampled in the lake and 39.9 mm/year for eels electrofished in rivers.

Sex ratio

Eleven eels longer than 200 mm (seven from the lake, four from rivers) were sexed by morphological examination of the gonads, then by histological analysis. Four were undifferentiated, three were male, and four were female. Mean lengths of undifferentiated eels (267.0 ± 106.5 mm), male eels (374.3 ± 142.2 mm), and female eels (374.0 ± 116.5 mm) did not differ significantly (Kruskal-Wallis, $P = 0.174$).

Discussion

Juvenile eels normally exhibit upstream migration, and this migratory behavior usually persists during their first years after metamorphosis from glass eel to elver (Wippelhauser and McCleave 1988; Dutil et al. 1989; Verreault 2002). In this study, maximum upstream migration from the lake was less than 3 km over 4 years. This dispersion pattern was seen as early as the first year after the introduction. High downstream densities have been suggested as a trigger for upstream movements of juvenile European eels (Moriarty 1986; Berg and Jørgensen 1994). Eel translocation studies in Europe stocked from 63 (Leopold 1986) to 500 (Quigley and O'Brien 1993) elvers/ha/year. Recommended stocking rates in less productive and coldwater lakes are between 150 and 200 individuals/ha annually (Knights and White 1998). We stocked 100 elvers/ha in a single year. With no subsequent stocking and with populations diminished by natural mortality, our stocking density can be considered low. This low density may have contributed to the limited colonization of rivers.

Published annual growth rates of North American eels typically range from 29 to 83 mm/year (mean 46.4, SD 15.6; Table 2). In the Sud-ouest River 70 km east of the Lake Morin study site, mean annual growth is 44.1 mm/year (Verreault 2002). Eels sampled from Lake Morin showed extraordinarily rapid growth (mean 117.5 mm/year), which is the highest rate reported for the species. Low density of eels in the lake may have contributed to this rapid growth. However, growth in associated rivers (mean 39.9 mm/year), where densities are presumed also to be low, was close to the mean value from published studies. Growth rate in eels is often higher in females than in males (Vøllestad 1992; Oliveira 1997, 1999). The rapid growth found in Lake Morin cannot be attributed to sex ratio because three of seven

Table 2. Mean annual growth for American eel in selected areas

Growth (mm/year)	Location	Reference
54.9	Lake Ontario	Hurley 1972
117.5	Lake Morin	This study
39.9	Lake Morin tributaries	This study
44.1	Sud-ouest River	Verreault 2002
38.2	Topsail Pond (Newfoundland)	Gray and Andrews 1971
55.7	New Brunswick	Vladykov 1970
41.0	La Have & Medway rivers (Nova Scotia)	Jessop 1987
31.7	Maine rivers (male)	Oliveira and McCleave 2002
28.9	Maine rivers (female)	Oliveira and McCleave 2002
29.9	Annaquatucket River (Rhode Island)	Oliveira 1997
82.9	James River (Virginia)	Hedgepeth 1983
53.5	Pinnopolis Dam (South Carolina)	Harrell 1977
49.7	Altamaha River (Georgia)	Helfman et al. 1984

sexed eels were male. We found no significant inter-sex differences in growth rate. In four Maine rivers, Oliveira and McCleave (2002) found no statistically significant differences in growth rates between males and females under age 6. Sex-related differences have been observed for older individuals (Holmgrem and Mosegaard 1996; Adam 1997; Beullens et al. 1997), which could be seen in future years as these translocated eels grow in Lake Morin.

In northern latitudes, especially in the St. Lawrence watershed, sex ratio is heavily biased toward females. Over 99% of eels sampled in the freshwater portion of the St. Lawrence River and tributaries are female (Dutil et al. 1985; Couillard et al. 1997; Verreault 2002). Sex determination for *Anguilla* species is poorly understood, and environmental or demographic features are cited as possible explanations (Roncarati et al. 1997; Pedersen 1998; Krueger and Oliveira 1999). The presence of males in our study cannot be explained by local environmental effects since natural neighboring eel populations in similar habitat are exclusively females (Verreault 2002). We suggest that the origin of these translocated eels may explain the presence of males. The sex of eels in the Bay of Fundy area, where we obtained our elvers, is highly variable. River catchments in Maine, New Brunswick, and Nova Scotia show large variations in male occurrence, from 0 to 98% (Vladykov 1966; Jessop 1987; Oliveira et al. 2001). Although our study is limited to a single location, our data suggest a mechanism for sex determination that acts before eel settlement in freshwater. Vladykov and Liew (1982) raised elvers originating from two different locations in an artificial freshwater pond in Ontario. The first group was trapped as elvers (TL = 56.6 mm) in a tributary of the Bay of Fundy and the second (TL = 60.0 mm) in a tributary of the St. Lawrence estuary, 1,700 km farther from the Sargasso Sea. Kept under the same environmental conditions, sex ratio differed between the groups: the Fundy group was mostly males (71.2%), whereas the St. Lawrence estuary group was mostly females (65.0%). It was postulated that smaller elvers produced males, whereas larger elvers metamorphosed into females. Our findings suggest that duration of marine migration or length at entrance in freshwater, or both, may act as important factors in sex determination.

This study has shown that eels can grow and survive when stocked in a previously eel-free Québec watercourse. This supports the notion that stocking may be a useful tool to offset local population decline. However, decisions on stocking must consider the eel's peculiar life cycle and the continent-wide conservation context. Natural mortality rates for eels in their first year are poorly known but are likely high. Estimated instantaneous daily mortality rates range from 0.0015 to 0.0107–0.0233 for wild European elvers (Berg and Jørgensen 1994). If eel mortality is density-dependent, we could reasonably think that a greater proportion of juvenile eels caught for translocation would have died in their estuaries, where density is greater than in our experimental site with initial density of 100 elvers per ha. Translocation may be seen as a management tool for redistribution from a high-density estuary to a low-density growth habitat. The erection of artificial barriers has caused the loss of 12,140 km^2 of historical freshwater habitat in the St. Lawrence watershed (Verreault et al. 2004). Restocking those habitats might enhance silver eel production. The potential contribution to the species' demography could be especially important in maintaining theoverall abundance of this panmictic species.

Acknowledgments

We gratefully acknowledge G. H. Lizotte, president of the Québec Eel Fisherman's Union, for his collaboration and encouragement during this study. We thank S. Ault, M. I. Pedersen, and A. L. Cairns for constructive comments on a first draft of this paper.

References

Adam, G. 1997. L'anguille européenne (*Anguilla anguilla* L. 1758): dynamique de la sous-population du lac de Grand-Lieu en relation avec les facteurs environnementaux et anthropiques. Doctoral dissertation. Université Paul Sabatier, Toulouse, France.

Alcobendas, M., F. Lecomte, J. Castanet, F.-J. Meunier, P. Maire, and M. Holl. 1991. Technique de marquage en masse de civelles (*Anguilla anguilla* L.) par balnéation rapide dans le fluorochrome. Application au marquage à la tétracycline de 500 kg de civelles. Bulletin Français de la Pêche et de la Pisciculture 321:43–54.

Berg, S., and J. Jørgensen. 1994. Stocking experiments with 0+ eels (*Anguilla anguilla* L.) in Danish streams: post-stocking movements, densities and mortality. Pages 314–325 *in* I. G. Cowx, editor. Rehabilitation of freshwater fisheries. Fishing News Books, Oxford, UK.

Beullens, K., E. H. Eding, F. Ollevier, J. Komen, and C. J. J. Richter. 1997. Sex differentiation, changes in length, weight and eye size before and after metamorphosis of European eel (*Anguilla anguilla* L.) maintained in captivity. Aquaculture 153:151–162.

Casselman, J. M., L. A. Marcogliese, and P. V. Hodson. 1997. Recruitment index for the upper St. Lawrence River and Lake Ontario eel stock: a re-examination of eel passage at the R. H. Saunders Hydroelectric Generating station at Cornwall, Ontario, 1974–1995. Pages 161–169 *in* R. H. Peterson, editor. The American eel in eastern Canada: stock status and management strategies. Canadian Technical Report of Fisheries and Aquatic Sciences no. 2196.

Couillard, C. M., P. V. Hodson, and M. Castonguay. 1997. Correlations between pathological changes and chemical contamination in American eels, *Anguilla rostrata*, from the St Lawrence River. Canadian Journal of Fisheries and Aquatic Sciences 54:1916–1927.

Dumont, P. 1998. Caractérisation des captures d'anguilles d'Americanérique dans des pêcheries commerciales de la rivière Richelieu et du lac Saint-François en 1997. Pages 97–106 *in* M. Bernard and C. Groleau, editors. Compte-rendu du troisième atelier sur les pêches commerciales tenu à Duchesnay du 13 au 15 janvier 1998. Ministère de l'Environnement et de la Faune, Québec.

Dutil, J.-D., B. Légaré, and C. Desjardins. 1985. Discrimination d'un stock de poisson, l'anguille (*Anguilla rostrata*), basé sur la présence d'un produit chimique de synthèse, le mirex. Canadian Journal of Fisheries and Aquatic Sciences 42:455–458.

Dutil, J.-D., M. Michaud, and A. Giroux. 1989. Seasonal and diel patterns of stream invasion by American eels (*Anguilla rostrata*) in the northern Gulf of St. Lawrence. Canadian Journal of Zoology 67:182–188.

Gray, R. W., and C. W. Andrews. 1971. Age and growth of the American eel (*Anguilla rostrata* (LeSueur)) in Newfoundland waters. Canadian Journal of Zoology 49:121–128.

Harrell, R. M. 1977. Age, growth, and sex ratio of the American eel *Anguilla rostrata* (LeSueur) in the Cooper River, South Carolina. Master's thesis, Clemson University, Clemson, South Carolina.

Hedgepeth, M. Y. 1983. Age, growth and reproduction of American eels, *Anguilla rostrata* (LeSueur), from the Chesapeake Bay area. Master's thesis, College of William and Mary, Williamsburg, Virginia.

Helfman, G. S., E. L. Bozeman, and E. B. Brothers. 1984. Comparison of American eel growth rates from tag returns and length-age analyses. Fishery Bulletin 82:519–522.

Holmgrem, K., and H. Mosegaard. 1996. Implications of individual growth status on the future sex of European eel. Journal of Fish Biology 49:910–925.

Hurley, D. 1972. The American eel (*Anguilla rostrata*) in eastern Lake Ontario. Journal of Fisheries Research Board of Canada 29:535–543.

Jessop, B. M. 1987. Migrating American eels in Nova Scotia. Transactions of the American Fisheries Society 116:161–170.

Knights, B., and E. White. 1998. An appraisal of stocking strategies for European eel, *Anguilla anguilla*. Pages 121–140 *in* I. G. Cowx, editor. Stocking and introduction of fish. Fishing News Books, Oxford, UK.

Knights, B., E. White, and I. A. Naismith. 1996. Stock assessment of European eel, *Anguilla anguilla* L. Pages 431–447 *in* I. G. Cowx, editor. Stock assessment in inland fisheries. Fishing News Books, Oxford, UK.

Krueger, W. H., and K. Oliveira. 1999. Evidence for environmental sex determination in the American eel, *Anguilla rostrata*. Environmental Biology of Fishes 55:381–389.

Leopold, M. 1986. Problems in analyzing the effectiveness of eel stocking in interconnected lakes. Vie et Milieu 36:291–293.

Moriarty, C. 1986. Variations in elver abundance at European catching stations from 1938 to 1985. Vie et Milieu 36:233–235.

Oliveira, K. 1997. Movements and growth rates of yellow-phase American eels in the Annaquatucket River, Rhode Island. Transactions of the American Fisheries Society 126:638–646.

Oliveira, K. 1999. Life history characteristics and strategies of the American eel, Anguilla rostrata. Canadian Journal of Fisheries and Aquatic Sciences 56:795–802.

Oliveira, K., and J. D. McCleave. 2002. Sexually different growth histories of the American eel in four rivers in Maine. Transactions of the American Fisheries Society 131:203–211.

Oliveira, K., J. D. McCleave, and G. S. Wippelhauser. 2001. Regional variation and effect of lake:river area on sex distribution of American eels. Journal of Fish Biology 58:943–952.

Panfili, J., and J. Tomás. 2001. Validation of age estimation and back-calculation of fish length based on otolith microstructures in tilapias (Pisces, Cichlidae). Fishery Bulletin 99:139–150.

Pedersen, I. B. 1998. Recapture rate, growth and sex of stocked cultured eels *Anguilla anguilla* (L.). Bulletin Français de la Pêche et de la Pisciculture 349:153–162.

Pursiainen, M., and J. Toivenen. 1984. The enhancement of eel stocks in Finland: a review of introductions and stockings. EIFAC Technical Paper 42(Supplement 1):59–67.

Quigley, D., and T. O'Brien. 1993. The River Shannon eel fishery: a management review. EIFAC Working Party on Eel, Olsztyn, Poland, 1993. FAO, Rome Roncarati, A., P. Melotti, O. Mordenti, and L. Gennari. 1997. Influence of stocking density of European eel (*Anguilla anguilla*, L.) elvers on sex differentiation and zootechnical performances. Journal of Applied Ichthyology 13:131–136.

Sagard, G. 1636. Histoire du Canada et voyages que les frères mineurs Récollets y ont faits pour la conversion des infidèles. Reprint 1866, Edwin Tross, Paris.

Therrien, J., and G. Verreault. 1998. Evaluation d'un dispositif de dévalaison et des populations d'anguilles en migration dans la rivière Rimouski. Ministère de l'environnement et de la faune, Rimouski, Québec.

Verdon, R., D. Desrochers, and P. Dumont. 2003. Recruitment of American eels in the Richelieu River and Lake Champlain: provision of upstream passage as a regional-scale solution to a large-scale problem. Pages 125–138 *in* D.A. Dixon, editor. Biology, management, and protection of catadromous eels. American Fisheries Society, Symposium 33, Bethesda, Maryland.

Verreault, G. 2002. Dynamique de la sous-population d'anguilles d'Americanérique (*Anguilla rostrata*) du bassin versant de la rivière du Sud-ouest. Master's thesis, Université du Québec à Rimouski.

Verreault, G., P. Dumont, and Y. Mailhot. 2004. Habitat losses and anthropogenic barriers as a cause of population decline for American eel (*Anguilla rostrata*) in the St. Lawrence watershed, Canada. ICES Annual Science Conference, CM Document, September 22–25, Vigo, Spain.

Verreault, G., P. Pettigrew, R. Tardif, and G. Pouliot. 2003. The exploitation of the migrating silver American eel in the St. Lawrence River estuary, Québec, Canada. Pages 225–234 *in* D. A. Dixon, editor. Biology, management, and protection of catadromous eels. American Fisheries Society, Symposium 33, Bethesda, Maryland.

Vladykov, V. D. 1966. Remarks on the American eel (*Anguilla rostrata* LeSueur). Sizes of elvers entering streams; the relative abundance of adult males and females; and present economic importance of eels in North America. Verhandlungen der Internationalen Vereinigung für Theoretische und Angewandte Limnologie 16:1007–1017.

Vladykov, V. D. 1970. Progress Reports Nos. 1 to 5 of the American eel (*Anguilla rostrata*) studies in Canada. Department of Fisheries and Forestry, Ottawa.

Vladykov, V. D., and P. K. L. Liew. 1982. Sex of adult American eels (*Anguilla rostrata*) collected as elvers in two different streams along the eastern shore of Canada, and raised in the same freshwater pond in Ontario. Pages 88–93 *in* K. H. Loftus, editor. Proceedings of the 1980 North American Eel Conference. Ontario Fisheries Technical Report 4.

Vøllestad, L. A. 1992. Geographic variation in age and length at metamorphosis of maturing European eel: environmental effects and phenotypic plasticity. Journal of Animal Ecology 61:41–48.

Wickstrøm, H., L. Westin, and P. Clevestam. 1996. The biological and economic yield from a long-term eel-stocking experiment. Ecology of Freshwater Fish 5:140–147.

Wippelhauser, G., and J. D. McCleave. 1988. Rhythmic activity of migrating juvenile American eels *Anguilla rostrata*. Journal of the Marine Biological Association of the United Kingdom 68:81–91.

Growth and Habitat Residence History of Migrating Silver American Eels Transplanted to Taiwan

WANN-NIAN TZENG[1] AND YU-SAN HAN

Institute of Fisheries Science, College of Life Science, National Taiwan University, Taipei, Taiwan 106, ROC

BRIAN M. JESSOP

Department of Fisheries and Oceans, Beddford Institute of Oceanography Post Office Box 1006, Dartmonth, Nova Scotia B2Y 4A2, Canada

Abstract.—In Taiwan, there has been a shortage of local Japanese eel *Anguilla japonica* elvers for culture, so culturists have imported American eel *Anguilla rostrata* (Le Sueur) elvers from North America to meet their needs. From 1999 to 2001, six exotic adult American eels were found in the estuary of the Kaoping River of Taiwan that had escaped from aquaculture ponds as young eels and stayed in the river until silvering. This study compares growth performance and migratory behavior, using otolith strontium (Sr)/calcium (Ca) ratios of those six American eels with cohabitating Japanese eels and American eels in North America. Regardless of sex, mean age at maturity of the exotic American eels was greater and mean annual growth rate was less than that of Japanese eels in Taiwan and similar to that of American eels in the southern United States. Sr/Ca ratios at the otolith edge of the six exotic American eels, which recorded their salinity history, increased significantly. Furthermore, four of the six exotic American eels spent more than one year in the high-salinity estuary. Their extended residence in the estuary may be due to a delayed spawning migration resulting from a failure to orientate and migrate properly to their native spawning site.

Introduction

Anguillid eels are catadromous fish that spawn in the ocean and grow in freshwater (Tesch 1977). Of the 15 described species and 3 subspecies of anguillid eels in the world (Ege 1939; Castle and Williamson 1974), all are distributed in the Indo-Pacific region except for the European eel *Anguilla anguilla* (L.) and the American eel *A. rostrata* (Le Sueur), which occur in the North Atlantic Ocean. In Taiwan, four native anguillid eels exist: Japanese eel *A. japonica* Temminck and Schlegel, marbled eel *A. marmorata* Quoy and Gaimard, *A. bicolor pacifica* Schmidt, and Celebes longfin eel *A. celebesensis* Kaup (Tzeng 1982; Tzeng and Tabeta 1983; Han et al. 2001). Of these species, the Japanese eel is most abundant and is commercially important for aquaculture in Taiwan (Tzeng et al. 1995). The catch of Japanese eel elvers is insufficient to meet the aquaculture demand (Tzeng 1996a), and elvers of exotic eel species, mainly American and European eels, have been imported since 1969 and 1977, respectively (Li 1997).

---
[1] Corresponding author: wnt@ntu.edu.tw

Six exotic American eels—four females (AR1 to AR4) and two males (AR5 and AR6)—were caught in the estuary of the Kaoping River of Taiwan; these were distinguished from Japanese eels (Han et al. 2002) by their different morphology. These eels had thick snouts, round heads, abundant mesenteric fat, and unusually large eyes. Vertebral counts, quantified gonadal histology, and phylogenetic analysis of the mitochondrial cytochrome b gene validated them as American eels in the silver stage (Han et al. 2002). These eels had escaped from culture ponds early in life and had lived in the Kaoping River for years.

Otolith Sr/Ca ratios, in combination with age data, were used to reconstruct the environmental history of these exotic American eels and assist interpretation of their life history. The concentration of strontium (Sr) is approximately 100-fold greater in seawater than in freshwater, and the Sr/Ca ratio in otoliths is positively correlated to ambient salinity (Tzeng 1996b; Campana 1999), making the Sr/Ca ratio a valuable tool for analyzing migration behavior of eels (Tzeng et al. 1997, 2002, 2003). In this study, we (1) compared annual growth rate of the exotic American eels with that of Japanese eels collected at the same time in the Kaoping River and with that of American eels in North America and (2) examined their life history traits (e.g., age at maturity and migration).

Materials and Methods

Specimen Collection

A total of 61 silver Japanese eels and six exotic American eels were collected by plastic eel pots in the Kaoping River estuary of southern Taiwan from 1999 to 2001 (Figure 1) (Han et al. 2002, 2003). The pots were fixed on the bottom along the riverbank. After collection, eels were immobilized with ice and immediately transferred to the laboratory for detailed analysis. Total length (TL ± 0.1 cm) and body weight (BW ± 0.1 g) were measured. Sex of each eel was determined by histological examination of the gonads. Maturation stages were determined, following Han et al. (2002, 2003), by coloration of the pectoral fins and the dorsal region, as well as by silver color on the belly and gonadal development. Growth and age at maturity of the exotic American eels were compared with those of American eels in North America reported in the scientific literature.

Otolith Preparation for Age Determination and Sr/Ca Ratio Analysis

Sagittal otoliths, the largest of the three pairs of otoliths in the inner ear, were used for determining Sr/Ca ratios and ages of the 61 silver Japanese eels and six exotic American eels. An electron probe microanalyzer (EPMA, JEOL JXA-8900R) was used to measure otolith strontium (Sr) and calcium (Ca) concentrations. The procedure for preparing the otoliths for Sr/Ca ratio analysis followed that of previous studies (Tzeng et al. 1997). Sr and Ca concentrations in the otolith were measured from the primordium to the otolith edge at an interval of 20 μm with an electron beam diameter of 5 μm. The accelerating voltage of EPMA was set at 15 kV and probe current at 5 nA. After microchemistry analysis, the otolith was polished to remove the carbon coating and etched 1–2 min with 5% EDTA to reveal the annular marks for age determination (Tzeng et al. 1994, 1997).

Back Calculation of Total Length at Annulus Formation and Growth Rate Measurement

The radii from the primordium to the glass eel mark (r_o), annuli (r_n) and otolith edge (R) were measured to estimate total length at annulus formation (l_n) by the Dahl-Lea formula (Francis 1990):

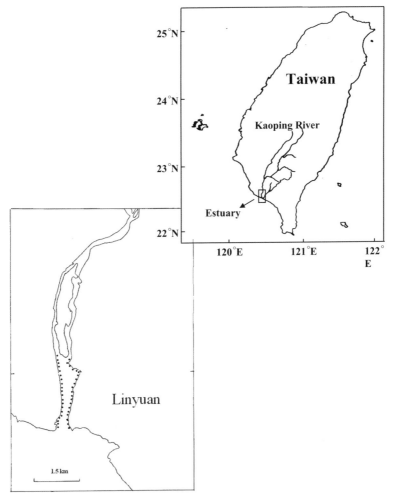

Figure 1. Sampling site of Japanese and exotic American eels in the estuary of the Kaoping River of southern Taiwan. Dots along the shore indicate where eel pots were set.

$$l_n = l_o + (r_n - r_o)(R - r_o)^{-1}(L - l_o)$$

where L is total length of the silver eel at capture. Total length at the glass eel stage (l_o) was defined as 54 mm, based on Tzeng and Tabeta (1983). Mean absolute annual growth rate (G) for individual silver eels was calculated according to the formula:

$$G = (l_n - l_{n-1})$$

where l_n is total length at year n and l_{n-1} is total length at year $n-1$. Mean annual growth rates (G_a) for each geographic and sex group were estimated as G_a = mean TL (mm)/mean age (yr) to enable comparison of data from other sites.

Statistical Analysis

Differences in morphometric indexes among exotic American eels in Taiwan, native American eels in Nova Scotia, Canada, and native Japanese eels in Taiwan were examined by using analysis of variance (ANOVA) followed by Tukey's multiple comparison test, as appropriate. The variable data for each ANOVA were logarithmically (base 10)

Table 1. Morphological characters of the six exotic silver American eels (AR1-AR6) collected in the Kaoping River estuary from 1999 to 2001.

Specimen Characters	AR-1	AR-2	AR-3	AR-4	AR-5	AR-6
Date of collection	Jul. 1999	Jul. 1999	Oct. 2000	Sep. 2000	Feb. 2001	Feb. 2001
Total length (mm)	700	612	635	515	425	415
Body weight (g)	454.6	519.2	591.2	236.3	129.4	125.1
Sex	F	F	F	F	M	M
Age (yr)	10+	9+	10+	8+	8+	9+
G_a (mm/yr)		66.7	64.4	58.8	58.5	52.5	45.6

transformed to reduce their heterogeneity of variance and nonnormality of distribution (differences were considered significant at $\alpha \leq 0.05$).

Results

Comparison of Morphological Indices Among Eel Species and Locations

Length of the female exotic American eels ranged from 515 to 700 mm and the males from 415 to 425 mm, while ages ranged from 8 to 10 years (Table 1). Females were significantly longer ($F = 15.26$, df = 1,4, $P = 0.017$) and heavier ($F = 15.63$, $P = 0.017$) than males and grew faster ($F = 31.18$, $P = 0.005$) but were similar in age at maturity ($F = 0.88$, $P = 0.40$). Mean total length and body weight of the male exotic American eels in the silver stage were larger than those of American eels in Nova Scotia and smaller than those of Japanese eels (male TL: $F = 163.3$, df = 2,53, $P < 0.001$; male BW: $F = 158.1$, df = 2,53, $P < 0.001$) (Table 2a, 2b). Mean TL of the female exotic American eels was similar to that of Japanese eels and larger than that of American eels from Nova Scotia, while body weight was greater than that of American eels from Nova Scotia and less than Japanese eels (female TL: $F = 51.1$, df = 2,69, $P < 0.001$; female BW: $F = 30.6$, df = 2,69, $P < 0.001$). Mean ages of American eels of both sexes in Taiwan were lower than those of eels from Nova Scotia but higher than those of Japanese eels (male: $F = 126.5$, df = 2,53, $P < 0.001$; female: $F = 127.1$, df = 2,69, $P < 0.001$) (Table 2c).

Comparison of Mean Annual Growth Rate Among Exotic American Eels

Back-calculated annual growth rate (G) of the six exotic American eels varied greatly (Figure 2). Growth in the first year was not rapid, as is usually observed in cultured eels due to nutrition (Tzeng, personal observation). Alternatively, if these eels grew slowly in the culture ponds for some reason, their life span in the ponds would not exceed two years because farmers commonly drain the ponds every two years. Because of their older ages at capture, it is obvious that these exotic American eels escaped from the culture ponds very early in life.

Comparison of Growth Rate Among Eel Species and Locations

For each sex, mean annual growth rate (G_a) of exotic American eels from Taiwan was much lower than that of Japanese eels from Taiwan but much higher than eels from Nova Scotia (male: $F = 361.7$, df = 2,53, $P < 0.001$, CA<TA<TJ; female: $F = 330.3$, df = 2,69, $P < 0.001$, CA <

Table 2. Comparison of total length (cm), body weight (g), and age at maturity (yr) of American eels from Taiwan (TA) and Nova Scotia, Canada (CA), and Japanese eels from Taiwan (TJ).

	Canada (American eel)				Taiwan (American eel)				Taiwan (Japanese eel)				Comparison
	n	mean	range	SD	n	mean	range	SD	n	mean	range	SD	
Total length													
Female	26	47.0	37.8–74.0	8.7	4	61.6	61.2–70.0	7.7	42	64.1	49.8–78.5	6.3	CA<TA=TJ
Male	35	35.5	32.6–41.2	1.8	2	42.0	41.5–42.5	0.7	19	55.6	44.1–67.5	7.1	CA<TA<TJ
Weight													
Female	26	211.4	92.6–882.2	179.1	4	450.3	454.6–591.2	153.2	42	452.7	163.6–829.3	169.9	CA<TA=TJ
Male	35	78.9	62.7–115.2	10.0	2	127.3	125.1–129.4	3.0	19	269.4	148.0–461.5	98.8	CA<TA<TJ
Age													
Female	26	17.1	10–29	4.1	4	9.9	8–10	0.9	42	6.9	4–10	1.5	CA>TA>TJ
Male	35	15.4	10.22	3.0	2	8.6	8–9	0.7	19	5.3	4–7	1.5	CA>TA>TJ

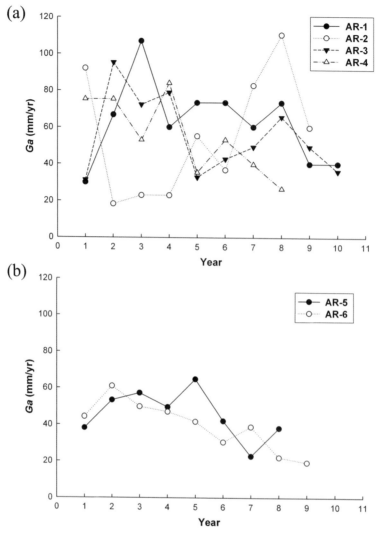

Figure 2. Comparisons of back-calculated annual growth rate for (a) four female and (b) two male exotic American eels in Taiwan.

TA < TJ) and slightly lower than that of eels from the southern United States (Table 3). Although no statistical comparison can be made, the mean G_a values are sufficiently similar that no significant difference likely exists between American eels in Taiwan and those in the southern United States. The Nova Scotia habitat has low pH and low productivity and would be expected to have eels with a lower growth rate than those from a more productive site at that latitude.

Mean annual growth rate of native male (r = –0.94, 95% CI = –1.0 to –0.80, n = 5, $P <$ 0.001, estimated by the bootstrap method) and female (r = –0.69, 95% CI = –0.87 to –0.37, n = 12, P = 0.016) American eels declines significantly with increasing latitude (Oliveira 1999; Jessop, unpublished data). American eels from a wide range of latitudes also showed a better significant negative correlation between G_a and age at maturity for each sex (male: r = –0.95, 95% CI = –1.0 to –0.88, n = 5, $P <$ 0.001; female: r = –0.86, 95% CI = –0.96 to –0.71, n = 12, $P <$ 0.001), while no significant correla-

Table 3. Comparison of latitude, total length (TL), age, and annual growth rates (G_a) by sex for silver American eels (AR) from North America and Taiwan and silver Japanese eels (AJ) from Taiwan

Site	Latitude (°N)	Sex	n	TL (mm)	Age (yr)	G_a (mm·yr^{-1})	Sex	n	TL (mm)	Age (yr)	G_a (mm·yr^{-1})	References
East R., NS (AR)	44.6	F	27	468	17.1	23.8	M	35	354	15.4	19.1	Jessop et al. 2002
Cooper R., SC (AR)	33.2	F	19	563	7.9	64.8						Hansen and Eversole 1984
Charleston Hbr., SC (AR)	32.8	F	38	550	5.8	85.9						Michener and Eversole 1985
Ogeechee R., GA (AR)	32.1	F	7	584	8.6	61.9	M	73	329	5.5	50.4	Facey and Helfman 1987
Altamaha R., GA (AR)	31.4						M	8	387	4.1	81.7	Helfman et al. 1984
Kaoping R., Taiwan (AR)	22.4	F	4	616	9.9	62.2	M	2	420	8.6	48.8	This study
Kaoping R., Taiwan (AJ)	22.4	F	42	628	6.8	92.9	M	19	556	6.3	88.8	This study

tion was found between G_a and TL at the silver stage for either male ($r = 0.32$, $n = 5$, $P = 0.60$) or female ($r = –0.06$, $n = 12$, $P = 0.86$) eels (Jessop, unpublished data).

Sr/Ca Ratios in Otoliths of Exotic American Eels

Otolith Sr/Ca ratios of the six exotic silver American eels increased from the primordium with a peak at the distance 60–100 μm from the primordium, which corresponded to the timing of metamorphosis from leptocephalus to glass eel (Figure 3). Beyond the check associated with metamorphosis, the otolith Sr/Ca ratios decreased rapidly up to the elver check (EC), which is deposited when glass eels enter freshwater in the estuary. Otolith Sr/Ca ratios were greater than 4.0‰ in the early life of five of the six eels. The 4.0‰ Sr/Ca ratio distinguishes between freshwater and seawater habitats (Tzeng et al. 2002, 2003). Sr/Ca ratios increased, exceeding 4.0‰ only at the very edge of the otolith for two eels (AR-1 and AR-3, Figure 3); this was coincident with silvering. However, Sr/Ca ratios at the edge of the otoliths of the other four eels were greater than 4.0‰ for several years (Figure 3). This indicated that these four eels had migrated into and resided in the high-salinity water of the estuary a number of years earlier.

Discussion

In the wild, juvenile eels from northern latitudes grow for a much shorter period of the year than do those from southern latitudes because annual temperatures are lower in the north and above the growth threshold for a shorter period of time. Thus, northern eels are expected to have a lower annual growth rate than more southerly eels. This decreased growth rate may also be reflected in the age of maturity (Vøllestad 1992). Exotic male American eels in Taiwan silvered and migrated to the sea within the range of lengths and growth rates of emigrants in North America. This was consistent with the observation that size of male American eels is not correlated with latitude (Oliveira 1999). As expected, female silver American eels in Taiwan also migrated at sizes more comparable to those in the southern United States, confirming the negative correlations between latitude, length at migration, and growth rate. These results are consistent with Oliveira's (1999) conclusion that the panmictic life cycle of the American eel prevents long-term selection of growth rates in different habitats and that growth rates result from environmental conditions in a habitat. American eels in Taiwan were older at migration and grew much more slowly than did native Japanese eels, suggesting between-species differences in biological characteristics or reduced adaptability to environmental conditions substantially different from those of streams, even in the southern United States.

Sr/Ca ratios at the otolith edges of Japanese eels increased significantly from the yellow to the silver stages, confirming that eels migrate from freshwater to high-salinity waters during silvering (Han et al. 2003). For the six exotic American eels, the Sr/Ca ratio had increased at the otolith edge (<4‰) only very recently for two individuals (AR-1 and AR-3) but was elevated for two to three years for the other four eels (Figure 3). If the rise of Sr/Ca ratios at the otolith edges coincided with silvering, then the spawning migration of these exotic American eels must have been interrupted, causing them to remain in the estuary.

Silver eels are generally thought not to feed because the digestive tract resorbs (Sinha and Jones 1975; Pankhurst and Sorensen 1984; Han et al. 2003). However, Beulleus et al. (1997) observed that cultured male eels may continue to eat and grow in the silver stage but not feed well. Dollerup and Graver (1985) fed male silver eels in which they had repeatedly induced testes matura-

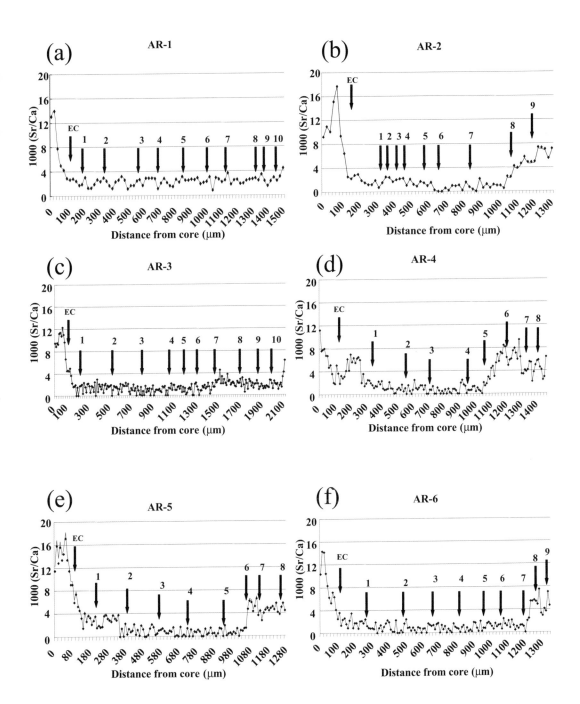

Figure 3. Otolith Sr/Ca ratio analysis for the six exotic American eels from (a) AR-1 to (f) AR-6, respectively. EC indicates the elver check; arrows and numbers (1–10) indicate annuli.

tion with hCG to stimulate sperm development. They found that food intake gradually increased and that the eels grew both in size and weight and their atrophied alimentary tracts regenerated. Thus, silver eels might continue growing, but at a slower rate, if their natural spawning emigration was interrupted. When compared with growth in freshwater, the growth rate of exotic American eels AR-2, 4, and 6 decreased after the fish entered high-salinity water (presumably in the silver stage) (Figure 2). By contrast, Jessop et al. (2004) found that American eel growth was usually higher in estuarine waters than in freshwater. Furthermore, if increased Sr/Ca ratios at the otolith edges represented the silvering stage of the exotic American eels, true mean age and total length at maturity would decrease and mean annual growth rate would increase, becoming more similar to that of American eels in the southern USA (Table 2). We believe that exotic American eels AR-2, 4, 5, and 6 had been in the silver stage for more than one year.

In Japan, exotic European eels have been found in Shinjiko Lake, Mikawa Bay (Zhang et al. 1999), and the Uono River (Aoyama et al. 2000). A migrating silver-phase European eel has also been captured in the East China Sea (Aoyama et al. 2000), indicating that spawning migration of introduced eels might be possible. Since the life cycle and larval transport routes of American eels and Japanese eels are, in general, quite similar (i.e., North Equatorial Current and Kuroshio Current in the north Pacific for Japanese eels; North Equatorial Current and Gulf Stream in the North Atlantic for American eels) (Cheng and Tzeng 1996; Wang and Tzeng 1998, 2000), interspecific hybridization could occur (Han et al. 2002). However, the silver exotic American eels found in the estuary of the Kaoping River in Taiwan seemed to encounter some difficulty orienting properly to a potential spawning site. Thus, the threat of hybridization by exotic American eels with Japanese eels seems unlikely. Further study is needed to assess the ecological importance of in-stream and migratory behaviors of exotic anguillid eels.

Acknowledgments

This study was financially supported by the National Science Council, Taiwan (Grant No. NSC-89-2313-B002-077). The authors are grateful to G.H. Cheng for otolith preparation and data processing and to David Cairns and two anonymous reviewers for helpful comments on an early version of the manuscript.

References

Aoyama, J., S. Watanabe, T. Miyai, S. Sasai, and M. Nishida. 2000. The European eel, *Anguilla anguilla* (L.), in Japanese waters Dana 12:1–5.

Beulleus, K., E. H. Eding, P. Gilson, F. Ollevier, J. Komen, and C. J. J. Richter. 1997. Gonadal differentiation, intersexuality and sex ratios of European eel (*Anguilla Anguilla* L.) maintained in captivity. Aquaculture, 153:135–150.

Campana, S. E. 1999. Chemistry and composition of fish otoliths: pathways, mechanism and applications. Marine Ecology Progress Series 188:263–297.

Castle, P. H. J., and G. R. Williamson. 1974. On the validity of the freshwater eel species *Anguilla ancestralis* Ege from Celebes. Copeia 1974:569–570.

Cheng, P. W., and W. N. Tzeng. 1996. Timing of metamorphosis and estuarine arrival across the dispersal range of the Japanese eel *Anguilla japonica*. Marine Ecology Progress Series 131:87–96.

Dollerup, J., and C. M. Graver. 1985. Repeated induction of testicular maturation and spermiation, alternating with periods of feeding and growth in silver eels, *Anguilla anguilla* (L.). Dana 4:19–39.

Ege, V. 1939. A revision of the genus *Anguilla* Shaw, a systematic, phylogenetic and geographical study. Dana Report 16:1–256.

Facey, D. E., and G. S. Helfman. 1987. Reproductive migrations of American eels in Georgia. Proceedings of the Annual Conference of the Southeastern Association of Fish and Wildlife Agencies 39:132–138.

Francis, R. I. C. C. 1990. Back-calculation of fish length: a critical review. Journal of Fish Biology 36:883–902.

Han, Y. S., C. W. Chang, J. T. He, and W. N. Tzeng. 2001.

Validation of the occurrence of short-finned eel *Anguilla bicolor pacifica* in the natural waters of Taiwan. Acta Zoologica Taiwanica 12:9–19.

Han, Y. S., I. C. Liao, Y. S. Huang, J. T. He, C. W. Chang, and W. N. Tzeng. 2003. Synchronous changes of morphology and gonadal development of silvering Japanese eel *Anguilla japonica*. Aquaculture 219:783–796.

Han, Y. S., C. H. Yu, H. T. Yu, C. W. Chang, I. C. Liao, and W. N. Tzeng. 2002. The exotic American eel in Taiwan: Ecological implications. Journal of Fish Biology 60:1608–1612.

Hansen, R. A., and A. G. Eversole. 1984. Age, growth, and sex ratio of American eel in brackish-water portions of a South Carolina river. Transactions of the American Fisheries Society 113:744–749.

Helfman, G. S., E. L. Bozeman, and E. B. Brothers. 1984. Size, age, and sex of American eels in a Georgia River. Transactions of the American Fisheries Society 113:132–141.

Jessop, B. M., J. C. Shiao, Y. Iizuka, and W. N. Tzeng. 2002. Migratory behaviour and habitat use by American eels *Anguilla rostrata* as revealed by otolith microchemistry. Marine Ecology Progress Series 233:217–229.

Jessop, B. M., J. C. Shiao, Y. Iizuka, and W. N. Tzeng. 2004. Variation in the annual growth, by sex and migration history, of silver American eels *Anguilla rostrata*. Marine Ecology Progress Series 272:231–244.

Li, L.S. 1997. Eel aquaculture. Page 84 *in* K. S. Chang, editor. Aquaculture. Chien-Cheng Publishing Company, Kaohsiung, Taiwan.

Michener, W. K., and A. G. Eversole. 1985. Age, growth, and sex ratio of American eels in Charleston Harbor, South Carolina. 1983 Proceedings of the Annual Conference Southeastern Association of Fish and Wildlife Agencies 37:422–431.

Oliveira, K. 1999. Life history characteristics and strategies of the American eel, *Anguilla rostrata*. Canadian Journal of Fisheries and Aquatic Sciences 56:795–802.

Pankhurst, N. W., and P. W. Sorensen. 1984. Degeneration of the alimentary tract in sexually maturing European *Anguilla anguilla* (L.) and American eels *Anguilla rostrata* (Le Sueur). Canadian Journal of Zoology 62:1143–1149.

Sinha, V. R. P., and J. W. Jones, 1975. The European freshwater eel. Liverpool University Press, Liverpool, UK.

Tesch, F. W. 1977. The eel: biology and management of anguillid eels. Chapman and Hall, London.

Tzeng, W. N. 1982. Newly record of the elver, *Anguilla celebesensis* Kaup, from Taiwan. Bioscience 19:57–66.

Tzeng, W. N. 1996a. Short- and long- term fluctuations in catches of elvers of the Japanese eel, *Anguilla japonica*, in Taiwan. Pages 85–89 *in* D. A. Hancock, D.C. Smith, A. Grant, and J. B. Beumer, editors. Developing and sustaining world fisheries resources: the state of science and management. 2nd World Fisheries Congres, Australia.

Tzeng, W. N. 1996b. Effects of salinity and ontogenetic movements on strontium:calcium ratios in the otoliths of Japanese eel *Anguilla japonica* Temminck and Schlegel. Journal of Experimental Marine Biology and Ecology 199:111–122.

Tzeng, W. N., P. W. Cheng, and F. Y. Lin. 1995. Relative abundance, sex ratio and population structure of the Japanese eel *Anguilla japonica* in the Tanshui River system of northern Taiwan. Journal of Fish Biology 46:183–201.

Tzeng, W. N., Y. Iizuka, J. C. Shiao, Y. Yamada, and H. P. Oka. 2003. Identification and growth rates comparison of divergent migratory contingents of Japanese eel (*Anguilla japonica*). Aquaculture 216:77–86.

Tzeng, W. N., K. P. Severin, and H. Wickström. 1997. Use of otolith microchemistry to investigate the environmental history of European eel *Anguilla anguilla*. Marine Ecology Progress Series 149:73–81.

Tzeng, W. N., J. C. Shiao, and Y. Iizuka. 2002. Use of otolith Sr:Ca ratios to study the riverine migratory behaviors of Japanese eel *Anguilla japonica*. Marine Ecology Progress Series 245:213–221.

Tzeng, W. N. and O. Tabeta. 1983. First record of the short-finned eel *Anguilla bicolor pacifica* elvers from Taiwan. Bulletin of the Japanese Society of Scientific Fisheries 49:27–32.

Tzeng, W. N., H. F. Wu, and H. Wickström. 1994. Scanning electron microscopic analysis of annulus microstructure in otolith of European eel *Anguilla anguilla*. Journal of Fish Biology 45:479–492.

Vøllestad, L. A. 1992. Geographic variation in age and length at metamorphosis of maturing European eel: environmental effects and phenotypic plasticity. Journal of Animal Ecology 61:41–48.

Wang, C. H., and W. N. Tzeng. 1998. Interpretation of geographic variation in size of American eel, *Anguilla rostrata* (Le Sueur), elvers on the Atlantic coast of North America by their life history and otolith ageing. Marine Ecology Progress Series 168:35–43.

Wang, C. H., and W. N. Tzeng. 2000. The timing of metamorphosis and growth rates of American and European eel leptocephali: A mechanism of larval segregative migration. Fisheries Research 46:191–205.

Zhang, H., N. Mikawa, Y. Yamada, N. Horie, A. Okamura, T. Utoh, S. Tanaka, and T. Motonobu. 1999. Foreign eel species in the natural waters of Japan detected by polymerase chain reaction of mitochondrial cytochrome b region. Fisheries Science 65:684–686.

Does Stocking of Danish Lowland Streams with Elvers Increase European Eel Populations?

MICHAEL I. PEDERSEN
Danish Institute for Fisheries Research, DTU, Department of Inland Fisheries
Vejlsøvej 39, DK-8600 Silkeborg, Denmark

Abstract.—To counteract low elver recruitment to the Danish coast, a stocking program has been under development since the late 1980s. Glass eels imported from southern Europe are cultured to 2–5 g and stocked throughout the country in fresh and brackish water. To assess the value of these stockings, selected streams were stocked with eels weighing 3 and 9 g. Poststock evaluations by electrofishing were done 3–63 d after stocking in one system and up to four years later in another system. Instantaneous daily disappearance rate, including emigration and natural mortality, was high (D = 0.006–0.153) in both river systems. The reasons may include low water temperatures combined with a habitat offering too little shelter for the stocked eels.

Introduction

The Danish eel fishery has been decreasing continuously since the 1960s as a result of decreasing recruitment of young eels to the Baltic Sea beginning in the 1940s (Hagström and Wickström 1990). A notable decrease throughout the distribution area has been observed since the end of the 1970s (Dekker 2002).

A stocking program was initiated in 1987 with the purpose of increasing fish yield. Glass eels used for stocking were imported from southern Europe, cultured in commercial eel farms in Denmark, and stocked throughout Danish waters by recreational fishermen. Most fresh- and brackish-water habitats are considered suitable for stocking eels. Streams, in particular, are important growth areas (Rasmussen and Therkildsen 1979), and the natural capacity of streams to produce eels is considered to be underutilized.

Studies concerning stocking methods and population dynamics of stocked eels in running water have been conducted (Bisgaard and Pedersen 1991; Berg and Jørgensen 1994). These studies ran for 12 and 3 months, respectively, but did not evaluate the long-term effects of stocking. The present study was undertaken in two different river systems, carried out over two months and four years. The objective was to assess eel stocking in small streams, considering dispersion, disappearance, mortality, emigration, and growth.

Methods

Study Sites

Eels were stocked in two river systems. Madum Å is a small lowland stream (56°15'N, 8°20'E) with a total length of 25.6 km and a catchment area of 90 km². The stream flow

---

[1] E-mail: mip@dfu.min.dk

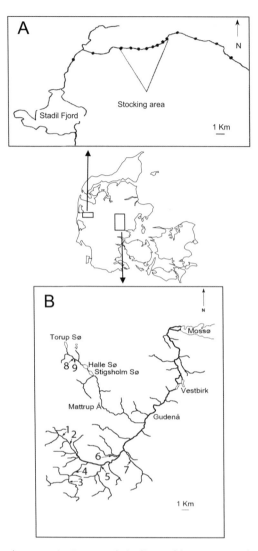

Figure 1. Location of study areas in Denmark indicated by rectangular inserts. A) Map of River Madum Å. • Single sites of 50-m sections electrofished. B) Map of upper part of River Gudenå. Numbers denote experimental sites.

into the brackish Stadil Fjord through extensively farmed agricultural land (Figure 1). Only the lower and upper parts of the stream are regulated by canalisation, and the water is moderately polluted by nutrients and ochre (Jakob Bisgaard, County of Ringkøbing, personal communication). Water depth in the study area varied between 0.2 and 0.7 m and river width between 2.5 and 5.9 m. In the years from 1992 to 1996 the stream was stocked annually in September with 13,000 elvers. Determined by electrofishing (Bohlin et al. 1989) these stockings and naturally emigrating eels produced a density of 0.09 eels $\times$ m^{-2} in 1999.

The other river system was River Gudenå (55°52'N, 9°33'E), a large lowland stream 170 km long with a catchment area of 2,600 km^2. The river system is strongly influenced by human activities, including canalization, nutrient loading from agriculture, and hydroelectric power damming and development. Nine small tributaries in the upper part of the river with water depth 0.1–0.7 m and stream width from 1.5 to 4 m were selected as study areas.

The River Gudenå was stocked with 2.1 million elvers weighing 0.3–1.1 g in 1987, 1988 and 1992 (Berg and Jørgensen 1994). Therefore, in all the experimental streams in River Gudenå, a small population of eels was present (0.03 eels × m^{-2}).

Stocking and Tagging Procedures

Glass eels that were stocked were imported from France during the previous winter and cultured in heated water (25°C), at a commercial eel farm. At this temperature, glass eels reach a size of 3 g and 9 g after 3 and 6 months, respectively. From July 1998 to September 2001, five batches of 3-g eels and six batches of 9-g eels (Table 1) were batch-marked with coded wire tags (Thomassen et al. 2000). After 2–7 d of recovery, tag retention was routinely checked by a tunnel detector. Tag loss 2–7 d after tagging was 3% and 1% in the different batches of 3-g and 9-g eels, respectively.

Tag loss was recorded and the eels were transported in moist polyethylene boxes to the experimental streams.

In Madum Å, the 3-g eels were stocked in July 1998 and the large eels three months later, in September 1998; both sizes were stocked in the same stretch of the stream. The eels were scatter-stocked from a sailing canoe moving slowly downstream. The stocking area of the stream had a length of 5.475 m and stocking density for each size was calculated at 0.44 eels × m^{-2}.

In the tributaries of River Gudenå, tagged eels were stocked from July 2001 to September 2002. Workers wading in the stream scattered eels over 150–200 m stretches. Stocking densities were 1.5–3.6 eels × m^{-2} (Table 1).

Poststocking Assessments

Poststocking assessment was done by stream electrofishing (220 V, continuous DC). In Madum Å, 14 sections 50 m in length were electrofished from 1999 to 2002. Eight sections were inside the stocking area, two were downstream, and four were upstream. In the tributaries of River Gudenå, poststocking assessment was made between 3 and 63 d after stocking. Sections 25 m in length were electrofished at intervals of 50–100 m up and down the stream, beginning about 500 m downstream from the stocking area, and electrofishing was performed until no stocked eels were recorded in one or two sections.

Captured eels in each section were anesthetized, measured (0.5 cm), checked for tags by an R-8000 tunnel detector (Northwest Marine Technology, Inc.), and released in the same section.

Poststocking numbers of eels were estimated by using the removal method. Each section was electrofished two or three times in succession. The number of tagged eels in the stream was subsequently calculated according to Bohlin et al. (1989). In Madum Å, where both size groups were present in the same stretches of river, the 3-g and 9-g eels were separated by size, using 15 cm as the separation criterion.

Instantaneous disappearance rate (D) was calculated as $D = -\ln(N_t/N_o)/t$, where N_o is the number stocked, N_t is poststock number; and t is the number of days between stocking and poststocking surveys.

Results

Poststocking Densities

In Madum Å, the first poststocking survey was done in May 1999, 234 d after the 9-g eels were stocked and 318 d after the 3-g eels were stocked. During that time, the number of stocked eels decreased by 85.5%. The

Table 1. Stocking and recapture data for coded wire tagged eels released in small tributaries to River Gudenå and River Madum Å. Length, weight, number stocked, and stocking density of tagged eels are given for each stream. Post-stocking assessment determined by electrofishing and number of recaptured eels are provided. Rate of disappearance, both daily and at 100 days, are given.

Site	Stream width (m)	Stocking date	Stocked eels Length (cm ± SE)	Weight (g)	Number	Density (eels·m^{-2})	Post-stocking assessment Days after stocking	No. tagged recaptured eels (mean ± 0.95 CI)	Disappearance rate Instantaneous Daily100 days (mean ± 0.95 CL)	Actual %
Madum Å	2-6	July 1998	13.6 ± 1.2	3.4	6,500	0.44	318	830 ± 288	0.0065 ± 0.0009	48
Madum Å	2-6	Sep 1998	17.8 ± 1.9	9.5	6,500	0.44	234	1,056 ± 367	0.0078 ± 0.0013	54
Gudenå (1)	3.0	Sep 2001	18.5 ± 0.9	9.4	1,000	3.6	21	141 ± 72	0.0933 ± 0.0196	100
Gudenå (2)	4.0	Sep 2001	18.5 ± 0.9	9.4	2,040	1.9	24	455 ± 513	0.0625 ± 0.0315	100
Gudenå (3)	2.7	July 2001	12.6 ± 1.0	2.6	1,000	1.5	38	230 ± 128	0.0387 ± 0.0116	098
Gudenå (4)	3.9	Sep 2001	18.5 ± 0.9	9.4	1,068	1.6	3	675 ± 374	0.1529 ± 0.1470	100
Gudenå (5)	1.5	July 2001	13.0 ± 0.8	2.7	500	2.3	44	2 ± 3	0.1255 ± 0.0208	100
Gudenå (6)	1.8	Sep 2001	18.5 ± 0.9	9.4	500	2.3	10	108 ± 84	0.1532 ± 0.0575	100
Gudenå (7)	2.3	July 2001	13.0 ± 0.8	2.7	500	1.7	43	71 ± 144	0.0454 ± 0.0258	099
Gudenå (8)	2.5	July 2002	12.6 ± 1.1	2.8	1,053	2.0	63	71 ± 31	0.0428 ± 0.0058	099
Gudenå (9)	2.5	Sep 2002	18.5 ± 1.3	9.4	1,033	2.3	21	209 ± 82	0.0761 ± 0.0158	100

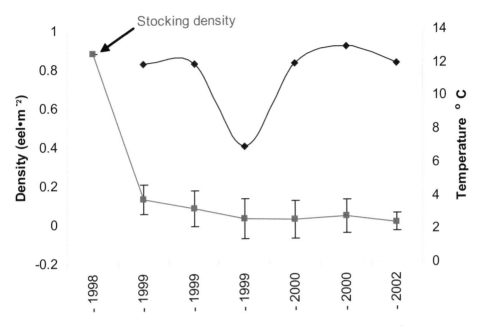

Figure 2. Temporal change in density of stocked elvers in River Madum Å, both size groups pooled, indicated by closed squares and 95% confidence limits. Water temperature indicated by closed diamonds.

decrease was of the same order of magnitude for both 3-g and 9-g eels (Table 1). Numbers have continued to decrease each year, and in May 2002 only 0.4% of the stocked fish were left in the study area (Figure 2).

In tributaries of River Gudenå, densities of stocked fish decreased quickly. Instantaneous disappearance rate on a daily basis ($D \times d^{-1}$) was between 0.039 and 0.153, suggesting that in six of the nine streams, the stocked fish disappeared within 100 d (Table 1).

Instantaneous Disappearance and Stocking Density

There was a weak linear relationship (linear regression, $P = 0.058$; $r^2 = 0.344$), between disappearance (D) and stocking density when eel size was not taken into consideration, suggesting that disappearance, emigration and mortality, or both increased with stocking density (Figure 3). However, when the analyses were separated by weight group, neither the 3-g nor the 9-g eels showed a significant relationship ($P = 0.098$; $r^2 = 0.654$ and $P = 0.389$; $r^2 = 0.189$, respectively), although the 3-g eels showed a slightly positive trend.

Migration

In Madum Å, stocked fish were found 1.0 and 3.5 km upstream from the stocking sites at densities of up to 0.08 eels $\times$ m^{-2} during the study period. No tagged eels were recorded in sections further upstream (5.0 and 7.5 km) and downstream (2.8 and 7.0 km).

In the tributaries of River Gudenå, the fish spread both upstream and downstream (Figure 4). The greatest downstream distance recorded was 250 m and the greatest upstream distance was 600 m.

Growth and Size Distribution

In tributaries of River Gudenå, poststocking length increment was not observed.

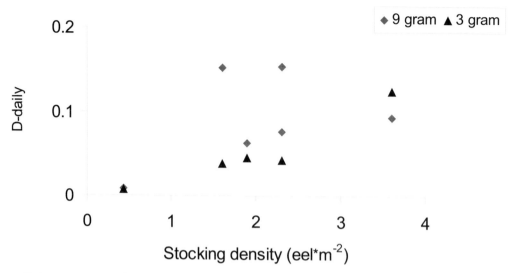

Figure 3. Instantaneous disappearance of stocked elvers from selected streams 1-4 m wide.

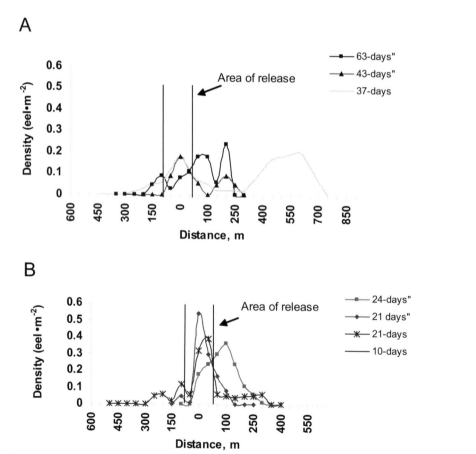

Figure 4. Dispersion of elvers stocked at two different sizes in tributaries of River Gudenå: (A) 3-g eels and (B) 9-g eels. Number of days at each site is the time between stocking and post-stocking survey. Direction of water flow is indicated by horizontal arrow.

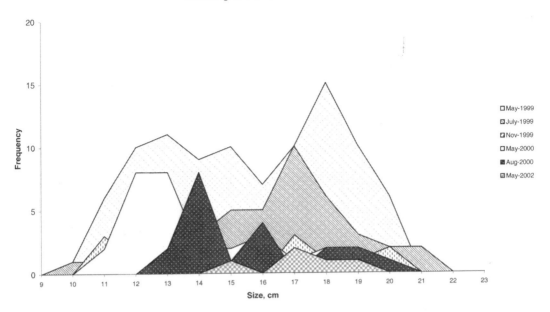

Figure 5. Size distribution of stocked eels in post-stocking survey in River Madum Å recaptured from May 1999 to May 2002.

In Madum Å, tagged eels bigger than 22 cm were never observed (Figure 5) during the study period, suggesting that growth was very limited.

Discussion

Thomassen et al. (2000) tested the use of coded wire tags on eels. They found that retention rates after 28 d were 96.9% for small (3 g) and 99.3% for large (10 g) eels and that the greatest loss (61%) occurred within the first 2 h after marking. Survival of tagged specimens was 100%. Coded wire tags seem to be an appropriate way of tagging eels of this size.

In Madum Å an 85.5% decrease in numbers was found after 9–12 months, and after four years, only 0.4% of the stocked eels were left in the study area. The reduction in numbers is similar to results of Bisgaard and Pedersen (1991), who found a reduction of 84% after one year.

In the tributaries of River Gudenå, the rate of disappearance estimated over 100 d, including mortality and migration, was very high—from 98 to 100% (Table 1). Berg and Jørgensen (1994) found that only 66–92% had disappeared after 100 d. Because natural mortality is a function of size (Ursin 1967), it is not likely that the bigger eels (3 and 9 g) used in this study suffered higher initial mortality than that found by Berg and Jørgensen (1994), who used glass eels or elvers weighing 0.3–1.1 g. Assuming that bigger eels have a lower rate of mortality compared with smaller eels, emigration rather than mortality may explain why eels disappeared from the stocking areas. Upstream migration speed of elvers has been estimated at 0.64 km × day^{-2} (White and Knights 1997). At that speed, stocked eels may leave the stocking areas in River Gudenå in just one day.

The relation of stocking density and poststocking dispersion (Figure 3) suggests that a low stocking rate (<1 eel × m^{-2}) results in the lowest dispersal or disappearance. Therefore, carrying capacity of the streams is important. The carrying capacity of a stream habitat depends upon the availability of both food and shelter. Eels hide in soft bottom substrate, between the roots of trees, and in crevices. Substrates in the study areas consist mostly of sand or gravel. Such habitats possibly lack places to hide compared with habitats with soft bottom and emergent macrophytes, which can be found in the lower and deeper parts of the stocked water systems. These areas are difficult to survey by electrofishing because of increasing water depth, so long-term effects of stocking will have to be assessed by gear that catches large, old eels (e.g., fyke nets and eel traps).

Eels have been shown to grow 2–5 cm a year in Danish streams (Rasmussen and Therkildsen 1979; Bisgaard and Pedersen 1991). In this study, no growth or very little growth occurred. Food availability is not likely a limiting factor, and local landowners and anglers claim that 10–20 years ago, there was a significant eel population in Madum Å. Further, in ongoing stocking experiments in brackish water (Pedersen, unpublished data), eels of the same batches that were stocked in Madum Å have been recaptured at lengths between 35 and 45 cm 2–4 years after stocking, suggesting that the eels stocked in these experiments were of good quality and that the brackish fjord is a better growth habitat.

One obvious difference between these habitats is that the small streams are relatively cold, up to 13°C (Figure 2), whereas shallow brackish habitats may be very close to the optimum temperature for growth (25°C). It therefore seems that the streams may provide a relatively unfavorable habitat. Possibly they are too cold for significant growth and offer little shelter. Therefore, stocking of these streams seems to be of little value, whereas the deeper parts of river systems, including lakes and brackish fjords, seem to offer a better return for stocking effort.

Acknowledgments

I thank my colleagues for valuable help in the field and the anonymous reviewers and the editor for valuable comments on the manuscript. The project was funded by the Danish Rod and License Fund.

References

Berg, S., and J. Jørgensen. 1994. Stocking experiments with 0+ eels *Anguilla anguilla* (L.) in Danish streams: post stocking movements, densities and mortality. Pages in I. G. Cowx. Rehabilitation of freshwater fisheries. Fishing News Books. University of Hull, UK.

Bisgaard, J., and M. I. Pedersen. 1991. Mortality and growth of wild and introduced cultured eels *Anguilla anguilla* (L.) in a Danish stream, with special reference to a new tagging technique. DANA 9:57–69.

Bohlin, T. S., T. Hamrin, G. Heggberget, G. Rasmussen, and S. J. Saltveit. 1989. Electrofishing—theory and practice with special emphasis on salmonids. Hydrobiologia 173:9–43.

Dekker, W., editor. 2002. Monitoring of glass eel recruitment. Netherlands Institute of Fisheries Research report C007/02-WD, IJmuiden, The Netherlands.

Hagström, O., and H. Wickström. 1990. Immigration of young eels to the Skagarak-Kattegat area 1900 to 1989. Internationale Revue der gesamten Hydrobiologie 75:707–716.

Rasmussen, G., and B. Therkildsen. 1979. Food, growth and production of *Anguilla anguilla* (L.) in a Small Danish Stream. Rapport et Proces-Verbaux des Reunions Conseil International pour l'Exploration de la Mer 174:32–40.

Thomassen, S., M. I. Pedersen, and G. Holdensgaard. 2000. Tagging the European eel *Anguilla anguilla* (L.) with coded wire tags. Aquaculture 185:67–61.

Ursin, E. 1967. A mathematical model of some aspects of fish growth, respiration and mortality. Fisheries Research Board of Canada 24:2355–2391.

White, E. M., and B. Knights. 1997. Dynamics of upstream migration of the European eel *Anguilla anguilla* (L.), in the Rivers Severn and Avon, England, with special reference to the effects of man-made barriers. Fisheries Management and Ecology 4:311–324.

Differential Production and Condition Indices of Premigrant Eels in Two Small Atlantic Coastal Catchments of France

Anthony Acou[1]
*Équipe Recherche et Technologie (ERT) 52, Campus de Beaulieu, Bat. 25, 1er étage
Université de Rennes1, 35042, Rennes cedex, France*

Gaelle Gabriel
*Laboratoire de Biologie et de l'Environnement Marin, Université de la Rochelle
Avenue Michel Crépeau, 17042, La Rochelle cedex 9, France*

Pascal Laffaille
*Fish Pass, Bureau Expert Gestion Piscicole
8 allée de Guerlédan, ZA Parc rocade sud 35135, Chantepie, France.*

Eric Feunteun
*Laboratoire de Biologie et de l'Environnement Marin, Université de la Rochelle
Avenue Michel Crépeau, 17042, La Rochelle cedex 9, France*

Abstract.—This paper assesses potential production of premigrant European eels *Anguilla anguilla* based on analysis of sedentary eel populations in two small river systems in western France that are in close proximity. Abundance and biological characteristics were evaluated from electrofishing surveys conducted in three years in September and October, before the catadromous migration of silver eels. Mean density and biomass density of the eel population differed greatly between the systems (39 ± 6 ind.100 m^{-2} [individual per 100 m^{2}] and $1,352 \pm 171$ g.100 m^{-2} in the Frémur River and 3 ± 0.32 ind.100 m^{-2} and 385 ± 42 g.100 m^{-2} in the Oir River). Premigrants were dominated by males in the Frémur (85.8%) and by females in the Oir (79.0%). Estimated premigrant biomass density was 4.5-fold higher in the Frémur (254.5 g.100 m^{-2}/year) than in the Oir (56.0 g.100 m^{-2}/year). Mean Fulton's K condition factor was significantly higher for both sexes in the Oir (0.20 ± 0.004 and 0.20 ± 0.003 for males and females, respectively) than in the Frémur (0.17 ± 0.002 and 0.17 ± 0.004, respectively). The large differences in densities and biological characteristics of eels from neighboring catchments suggest that huge variability of both quantity and quality of silver eel production can be expected at the scale of the European stock.

---

[1]Corresponding author: anthony.acou@univ-rennes1.fr

Introduction

Anguillid eels support important commercial and recreational fisheries (McDowall 1990; Tesch 2003). According to Moriarty and Dekker (1997), 25,000 people earn income from the European eel *Anguilla anguilla*, whose fishery has a direct commercial value of 180 million Euro, plus 380 million Euro added value. However, since the 1980s, the European eel stock has declined substantially throughout its distribution range. The latter includes all accessible continental and coastal hydrosystems that link with the Baltic and North seas, as well as the Atlantic and Mediterranean coasts between Iceland and Morocco (Moriarty and Dekker 1997). The International Council for the Exploration of the Sea (ICES; 1998) has recommended that all means should be taken to restore the depleted stock at all biological stages. In particular, it recommended increased escapement for glass eels, yellow eels, and silver eels and standard international escapement objectives (ICES 1998).

It is now generally agreed that despite uncertainties on the form of the stock-recruit relationship (i.e., the relationship between silver eel escapement from continental waters and subsequent glass eel recruitment back to continental waters), the best way to measure the effect of restoration efforts is to assess production, population structure (size, sex ratio, and age), and breeding potential of silver eels (Feunteun 2002).

In Europe, few quantitative data are available on the size of silver eel runs. Investigations in large water bodies typically use mark–recapture techniques (e.g., the Baltic Sea, Moriarty 1996; the Loire River, Boury et al., poster presented at the American Fisheries Society Annual Meeting 2003). In small river systems, exhaustive surveys have been conducted using wolf traps in a small number of rivers in northern Europe (e.g., the Frémur, Feunteun et al. 2000). However, silver eel escapement is unknown in most European water systems and a more efficient approach is needed to provide silver eel run estimates. In small coastal catchments, surveys are commonly conducted to characterize the status of the sedentary fraction of the eel stocks. Among sedentary eels, a proportion undergoes silvering metamorphosis before they start their downstream migration. Most premigrant eels achieve their silvering in late summer and then wait in the catchment until migration is triggered by environmental factors such as floods (Acou et al. 2000). By enumerating these premigrant eels, it is possible to estimate potential production of silver eels for a water course (Feunteun et al. 2000).

Robinet and Feunteun (2002) hypothesized that the probability that silver eels reach the spawning grounds and reproduce successfully varies among continental growing sites. A pan-European methodology to estimate the overall breeding potential of silver eels according to relevant criteria (fat composition, contamination by chemicals, parasitic load, etc.) is not yet ready for use because of the complexity in implementing such an approach. Use of silver eel condition indices may constitute a first step in this direction. Fulton's K condition factor has been demonstrated to indicate energy reserves of Atlantic salmon *Salmo salar* (Sutton et al. 2000), *Coregonus artedi* (Pangle and Sutton 2005), and *Gadus morhua* (Lambert and Dutil 1997; Grant and Brown 1999). Considering the importance of energy reserves during both transoceanic migration and reproduction of European eels (Boëtius and Boëtius 1980; Robinet and Feunteun 2002), we hypothesize that Fulton's K may represent a good index of silver eel breeding potential.

This paper estimates production of premigrant silver eels based on analysis of sedentary eel populations. To achieve this goal, we compared population characteristics of eel sub-populations in two coastal river systems of western France that vary substantially in

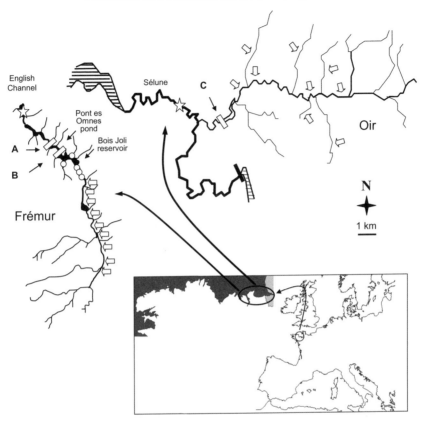

Figure 1. Location and characteristics of the Frémur and Oir catchments. Open arrows represent batches of two or three river sections sampled by electrofishing. Circles on the Frémur represent the locations of fyke-net fishing. Bars indicate the location of major dams. In the Frémur: A, Pont es Omnes dam (4.5 km from the sea) equipped with an eel-pass (designed to pass elvers) and a silver eel trap; B, Bois Joli dam (6 km from the sea) equipped with an eel-lift. In the Oir: C, Cerisel Mill (10 km from the sea). Stars represent tidal limits.

the degree of human development. In order to assess the quality of silver eels produced in each catchment, we focused on sex ratio, mean weight, and Fulton's K condition factor in premigrant eels as indicators of reproduction potential in the two systems.

Methods

Study Sites

Catchment areas of the Frémur and Oir rivers are typical of the numerous river systems in western France. The Frémur is a small river of northern Britanny, which discharges into the English Channel next to Saint Malo (Figure 1). Catchment area is approximately 60 km², and overall river and stream length is 46 km, with 17 km of main stream. Slope varies between 0.1% and 2%, with a mean of 0.6%. Tidal limit is at the Roche Good mill (Figure 1). The watershed contains two dams (Pont es Omnes and Bois Joli, Figure 1), which were impassable until the recent construction of fish lifts (Feunteun et al. 1998). The larger, at Bois Joli, is 14 m high and creates a 3×10^6 m³ reservoir for drinking water. An eel lift for upstream migration was built in 1996. Impoundments formed by the two dams reduce velocity and increase depth, thereby creating aquatic communities dominated by lentic water species (bream *Abramis brama*, roach *Rutilus rutilus*, rudd *Scardinius erythrophtalmus*, tench *Tinca tinca*, northern pike *Esox lucius*, zander *Sander lucioperca*). Wetted area above the Pont es Omnes dam totals 59.9 ha, including 5.3 ha of running waters and 54.6 ha of still waters above the two dams (Figure 1). Six minor works, including pipes under roads, water-flow gauging devices, and bridges, impose temporary obstacles to eel migration, depending on water level (Feunteun et al. 1998). Overall, the Frémur provides a wide range of habitats from high-velocity streams of the trout zone to lentic waters of the bream zone in downstream areas.

The Oir, a small river of southern Normandy, is a tributary of the Sélune that flows into Mont Saint-Michel-Bay (Figure 1). The centre of the Oir catchment is about 65 km east of the centre of the Frémur catchment. The Oir drains a 87-km^2 catchment, and overall length of the system is 120 km, including 25 km of main stem. Mean slope is 1.1%. Total wetted area upstream from Cerisel Mill (Figure 1), including the main stream and tributaries, is 22.9 ha. The Oir is obstructed by only one weir. The Oir is cool and not eutrophic and is one of the best rivers for brown trout *Salmo trutta* and Atlantic salmon in France.

Sedentary Stock Assessment

Sampling was conducted in the low-water-level period (September in the Frémur and October in the Oir), after the beginning of metamorphosis but before the migration of silver eels (Fontaine 1994). Sampling took place in both rivers in 2000, 2001, and 2002. Electrofishing was conducted with a Dream Electronic electrofisher set at DC 300 V and 3 A.

Frémur Sampling

Electrofishing was conducted in 30-m-long river sections delimited by 3-mm-mesh stop nets. A total of 29 river sections were sampled each year (Figure 1). These sections were located between 8.5 and 17 km from the sea. Mean width was 2.5 ± SD 0.5 m (range 0.7–4 m), and mean depth was 0.5 ± 0.1 m (range 0.15–1 m). These river sections covered about 2.3% of the overall stream length upstream of the Pont es Omnes dam (Figure 1). In Pont es Omnes pond and Bois Joli reservoir, eels were sampled with unbaited fyke nets with 6-mm mesh. Four sites were sampled with fyke nets in September 2000, three in September 2001, and two in September 2002.

Oir Sampling

A total of 32, 27, and 24 river sections that ranged between 100 and 1,000 m long were electrofished on the main stream and tributaries in October 2000, 2001, and 2002, respectively. These sections in the main stream were between 11.5 and 19.0 km from the sea. Sampling sections represented on average 8.0% of stream length upstream of Cerisel Mill (Figure 1). Mean width was 2.9 ± SD 1 m (range 0.6–4.5 m), and mean depth was 0.35 ± 0.14 m (range 0.05–0.47 m).

Migratory Potential Characteristics

Eels were anesthetized with 2-phenoxyethanol, measured (TL to the nearest mm) and weighed (W_t to the nearest g). Eels were allowed to recover in cool, well-oxygenated water for about 15 min before being returned to the water. No glass eels were found in either river. In this paper, elvers refers to pigmented eels less than 180 mm long. Most of these would be in their first year in continental waters. Silver eels were identified by three criteria (Feunteun et al. 2000): color of the back and belly, presence of a well-defined lateral line, and Ocular index (OI) greater than 6.5 according to Pankhurst's (1982) silvering threshold value. Ocular index is the relation between TL and mean size of the two eyes, calculated as follows (Pankhurst 1982): OI = $25\pi/8$ TL $\{(A+B)^2_R+(A+B)^2_L\}$, where TL is total length, A and B are, respectively, the horizontal and vertical eye diameters, and R and L are right and left eyes. If only two of the criteria (most often the lateral line and the OI value) were met, the eel was designated as yellow/silver. Silver and yellow/silver eels are collectively referred to as premigrants. If only one (generally the OI value) or none occurred, the eel was recorded as yellow (Feunteun et al. 2000).

Sex was assigned by macroscopic observation of gonads, using the criteria described by Colombo et al. (1984), on subsamples of 75 and 35 silver eels caught in the Frémur and Oir catchments, respectively. In the Frémur, silver eels identified as male by this method ranged from 300 to 434 mm ($N = 44$; mean TL = 366 ± SE 4 mm), and silver eels identified as female ranged from 414 to 677 mm ($N = 31$; mean TL = 528 ± 10 mm). In the Oir, male silvers ranged between 334 and 437 mm ($N = 13$; mean TL = 373 ± 9 mm) and female silver eels ranged between 429 mm and 611 mm ($N = 22$; mean TL = 524 ± 11 mm). In both rivers, all silver eels greater than 440 mm were females, as has been shown in other studies (Rossi and Colombo 1979; Tesch 2003). In order to increase the number of sexed eels, all sampled premigrant eels (yellow/silver and silver eels) were classed as female if their length was greater than 440 mm and male if their length was less than or equal to 440 mm. All premigrant eels were assumed to be sexually differentiated. Sex ratio was expressed as proportion of females or males among premigrant eels. Fulton's K condition factor was calculated as $K = 100 \times W_t/TL^3$ with W_t in g and TL in cm (Cone 1989).

Analysis

Premigrant characteristics.—In a previous study, Feunteun et al. (2000) observed no significant differences in length distribution between premigrant eels sampled in the Frémur catchment in September (electrofishing and fyke nets) and migrant eels captured the following season in the downstream trap at Pont es Omnes (Figure 1). This suggests that the sampling plan used in the Frémur provides reliable information about the silver eel population at the scale of the river system. In the present study, fyke-net results were not used for population estimates but were pooled with electrofishing results to describe the biological characteristics (W_t and K) of premigrant eels. Prior to statistical analysis and to respect normality of distribution, the data were $log(x + 1)$ transformed. Factorial ANOVAs (with river (Frémur and Oir) and Year (2000, 2001, and 2002) as factors) were performed. Posthoc Tukey tests were used when Anovas were significant. χ^2 were used to test sex ratios and migratory potential proportions between years in each catchment. Length, weight, and K data presented are means ± SE.

Abundance Estimates

In both systems, total number and weight of fish in sections were assessed by the depletion method.

Frémur.—In all river sections, fish were removed after electrofishing passes. Most (92%) sessions consisted of two passes; the remainder had three passes. Total estimated eel numbers in each river section were calculated by the weighted maximum likelihood model of Carle and Strub (1978). Catchability was very high (on average 70% of the stand-

Oir.—Fishing sessions consisted of a single removal (C_1) or two-pass sessions (C_1 and C_2) termed "single" and "depletion" fishings, respectively. To estimate total number of eels in the Oir catchment, the model of Carle & Strub (1978) was used in 22 depletion sections. On average, 72% of the standing stock was caught at the first removal, suggesting similar catchabilities between the Oir and the Frémur. A linear regression was used to predict abundance estimated by Carle and Strub (1978) (C_{est}) from C_1 counts. The coefficient of determination (r^2) was tested by ANOVA. Slope and intercept of the linear regression were tested using a *t*-test. Independence between the residuals of the model and C_1 and normality of the residual distribution were tested using Pearson's correlation coefficient (*r*) and one-sample Kolmogorov Smirnov nonparametric test with Lillefor's option, respectively. The resulting relation was then used to assess total number of eels in both single and depletion sections according to C_1 removal.

In both systems, eel density and biomass density (expressed as ind.100 m^{-2} [individual per 100 m^2] and g.100 m^{-2}) for each river section was calculated as total number and weight of estimated eels divided by area of the stream section. Eel density and biomass density are presented as means ± SE.

Stock assessment.—Stock for each catchment was estimated by multiplying mean density and biomass density by total wetted area. In the Oir, which has no ponds, total wetted area was 22.9 ha. In the Frémur, most (91.15%) wetted area is ponds and reservoirs where no measurement of population densities are available. Extrapolation of stream densities to the overall surface of pond/reservoir habitats would lead to biased estimates, since this method would ignore eel microhabitat selection (Broad et al. 2001). In a study on spatial organization of eels in the Frémur, Laffaille et al. (2003) found that large eels tend to be in intermediate-to-high depths with intermediate abundance of vegetation. In Pont es Omnes pond and Bois Joli reservoir, only a narrow shoreline strip (ca. 2.5 m wide) provides such habitats for both small and large eels. Jellyman and Chisnall (1999) for *A. australis* and Schulze et al. (2004) for *A. anguilla* confirmed that eels are mainly confined to shorelines because of the availability of cover (e.g., rocks or macrophytes) and presence of food. The 2.5-m shoreline strip of Pont es Omnes pond and Bois Joli reservoir amounted to 2.1 ha. Thus, total wetted area used for stock-assessment calculations in the Frémur was 7.4 ha (2.1 ha for pond/reservoir habitat and 5.3 ha for running portions).

Feunteun et al. (2000) extrapolated from density estimates to the whole stream surface and analyzed mark–recapture records of PIT-tagged silver eels to assess eel population size in the Frémur catchment. Size of the silver eel stock in the basin was calculated from size of the total silver eel run (trap data) and the fraction of the tagged population recaptured in the run (recapture), using the Lincoln-Petersen method. The two methods produced similar estimates of the numbers of silver eels (3000 silver eels on average in 1996 and 1997), suggesting that both approaches are reliable (Feunteun et al. 2000).

Results

Population structure

Frémur.—Eels captured by electrofishing and fyke netting ranged in length from 56 to 774 mm (Figure 2). Modal length of young eels ranged from 160 to 180 mm between 2000 and 2002. Proportions of elvers (eels < 180 mm) were equivalent in 2000 and 2002 (26.0% and 27.7% of total catch, respectively) but were sig-

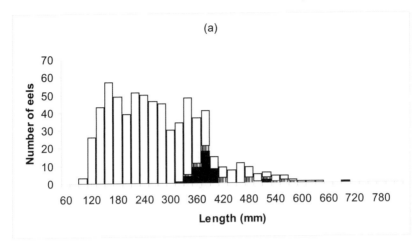
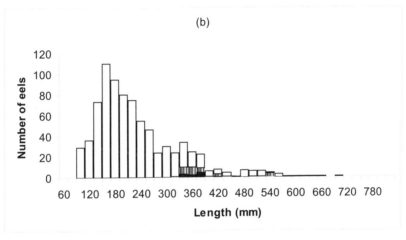
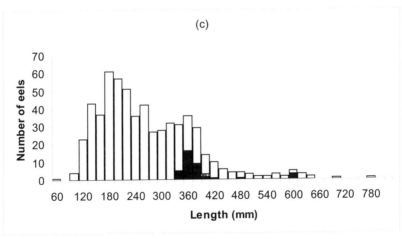

Figure 2. Length histogram of eels sampled by electrofishing and by fyke net in the Frémur catchment in September (a) 2000, (b) 2001 and (c) 2002. Open bars, yellow eels ($N = 614$ in 2000, $N = 770$ in 2001 and $N = 562$ in 2002); solid bars, silver eels ($N = 43$ in 2000, $N = 11$ in 2001 and $N = 37$ in 2002); vertically hatched bars, yellow/silver eels ($N = 9$ in 2000, $N = 30$ in 2001 and $N = 1$ in 2002).

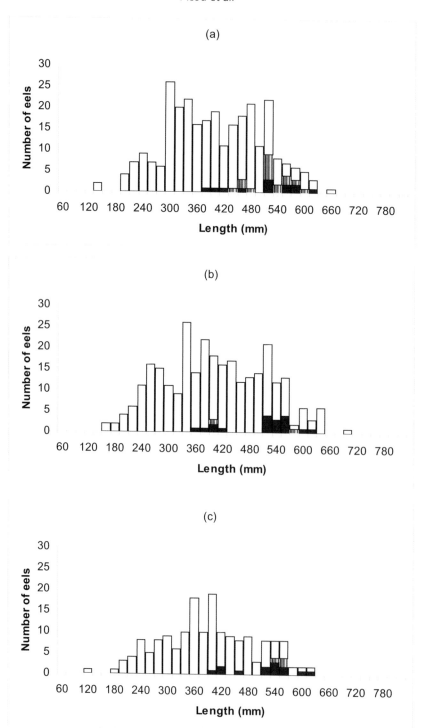

Figure 3. Length histogram of eels sampled by electrofishing in the Oir catchment in October (a) 2000, (b) 2001 and (c) 2002. Open bars, yellow eels ($N = 256$ in 2000, $N = 272$ in 2001 and $N = 155$ in 2002); solid bars, silver eels ($N = 12$ in 2000, $N = 8$ in 2001 and $N = 13$ in 2002); vertically hatched bars, yellow/silver eels ($N = 16$ in 2000, $N = 2$ in 2001 and $N = 3$ in 2002).

Table 1. ANOVA results for the effect of independent variables (year, river, and year × river) on weight and K of male and female premigrant eels (only significant interactions are shown).

	Effect	Sum of squares	df	Mean square	F	P
Male premigrants						
Weight						
	River	18621.46	1	18621.46	46.16	0.00
	Year	2273.80	2	1136.90	2.81	0.06
	Error	50420.50	125	403.36		
K						
	River	0.76	1	0.76	11.92	0.00
	Year	0.10	2	0.05	0.81	0.45
	Error	8.00	125	0.06		
Female premigrants						
Weight						
	River	31320.47	1	31320.47	4.39	0.04
	Year	9544.36	2	4772.18	0.67	0.51
	Error	477489.02	67	7126.70		
K						
	River	1.15	1	1.15	20.99	0.00
	Year	0.11	2	0.05	0.98	0.38
	Error	3.66	67	0.05		

nificantly higher in 2001, with 42.0% of the total catch ($\chi^2 = 3215.72$, df = 2, $p < 0.001$). For all years combined, 85.1% of premigrant eels belonged to the 300-to-440-mm size-class and were assumed to be males. Proportions of males among premigrants were 80.3% in 2000, 87.5% in 2001, and 89.5% in 2002, 85.8% for all years pooled.

Oir.—Eels captured by electrofishing ranged between 117 mm and 682 mm (Figure 3). Length structures of each biological stage (yellow, yellow/silver, and silver) were not statistically different among years (Kolmogorov-Smirnov test, $p > 0.1$), suggesting a steady population over time. Proportion of young eels less than 180 mm represented only 1.1% ($N = 8$) of captures in all years. Premigrant population structure was dominated by females (i.e., eels > 440 mm) in all years (85.7% in 2000, 70.0% in 2001, 81.2% in 2002, 79.0% for all years pooled).

Premigrant characteristics.—The Mean weight of premigrant males was 83 ± SE 2.0 g (range 41–167) in the Frémur and 120 ± 5.5 g (range 79–156) in the Oir. Mean K of premigrant males was 0.172 ± 0.002 (range 0.095–0.231) in the Frémur and 0.197 ± 0.003 (range 0.170–0.217) in the Oir. Mean weight of premigrant females was 256 ± 18.0 g (range 161–541) in the Frémur and 290 ± 11.6 g (range 156–547) in the Oir. Mean K of premigrant females was 0.168 ± 0.004 (range 0.136–0.204) in the Frémur and 0.196 ± 0.003 (range 0.141–0.247) in the Oir. For both sexes, eels were significantly heavier in the Oir than in the Frémur (Table 1; Figure 4). Similarly, Fulton's K condition factor was significantly higher in the Oir than in the Frémur for both sexes (Table 1; Figure 5).

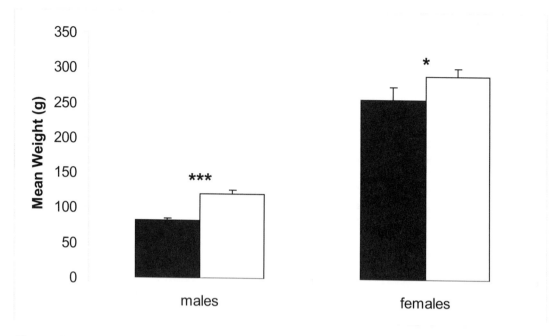

Figure 4. Mean weight (± SE) of potential migrants (yellow/silver and silver eels) for both sexes by river. Solid bars, eels caught in the Frémur R.; open bars, eels caught in the Oir R. Significance of Tukey's posthoc comparison test is shown as * = $P < 0.05$, *** = $P < 0.001$.

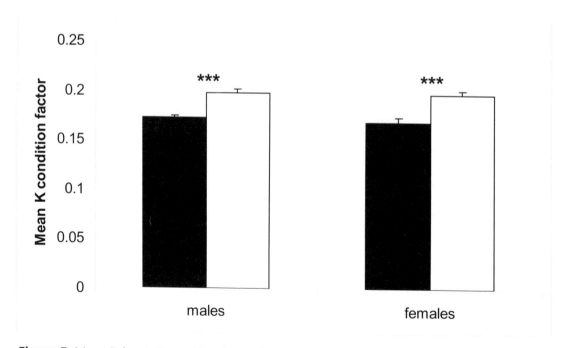

Figure 5. Mean Fulton's K condition factor (± SE) of premigrant (yellow/silver and silver) eels for both sexes by river. Solid bars, eels caught in the Frémur R.; open bars, eels caught in the Oir R. Significance of Tukey's posthoc comparison test is shown as * = $P < 0.05$, *** = $P < 0.001$.

Abundance

Frémur.—Total mean density and biomass density for all stages during the three study years were high, with 39 ± SE 6 ind.100 m^{-2} and 1,353 ± 171 g.100 m^{-2}, respectively (Table 2). Proportion of silver eels was similar in 2000 (5.9%) and 2002 (5.8%) but was significantly lower in 2001 (1.3%) (ANOVA: factor = Year, df = 2, $F = 8.77$, $p < 0.001$). The proportion of yellow/silver eels varied between 0.1% in 2002 and 3.2% in 2001. Thus, yellow/silver eels and silver eels constituted a migratory potential of 8.3% in 2000, 4.5% in 2001, and 5.9% in 2002. Mean biomass density of the population decreased from 1,752 ± SE 400 g.100 m^{-2} in 2000 to 1,126 ± 238 g.100 m^{-2} in 2001 and 1,180 ± 203 g.100 m^{-2} in 2002. Premigrant biomass density dropped significantly from 420 g.100 m^{-2} in 2000 to 172 ± 9 g.100 m^{-2} in 2001 and 2002 (Table 2).

Oir.—A linear regression between C_{est} and C_1 was performed in the Oir catchment ($C_{est} = 1.17 ± 0.13 × C_1 + 1.1 ± 0.52$, $r^2 = 0.80$, $F = 79.9$, $P < 0.001$) with significant slope and intercept (t-Test, $P < 0.05$). No significant correlation between residuals and C_1 was observed ($r = 0.0$, $P = 1$). Abundances of the first removal were log-transformed, since residual distribution did not meet the normality assumption (Kolmogorov-Smirnov test, $d = 0.31$, $P < 0.05$). Estimated mean total density and biomass density were approximately 13- and fourfold lower than in the Frémur, amounting to 3 ± SE 0.32 ind.100 m^{-2} and 385 ± 42 g.100 m^{-2}, respectively (Table 3). During the study period, proportion of silver eels varied from 3.1% of the whole stock in 2000 to 8.2% in 2002, but this variability was not statistically significant (ANOVA, df = 2, $F = 1.65$, $P = 0.19$). Yellow/silver proportions declined significantly from 3.0% in 2000 to 0.1% in 2001 of the overall resident eels (ANOVA, df = 2, $F = 3.85$, $P < 0.05$). Therefore, the proportion of premigrant eels amounted to 6.2% in 2000, 5.4% in 2001, and 8.7% in 2002. Premigrant eel biomass density was stable in time with 48 g.100 m^{-2} in 2000, 51 g.100 m^{-2} in 2001, and 69 g.100 m^{-2} in 2002 (ANOVA, df = 2, $F = 0.15$, $P = 0.86$).

Premigrant Estimates

The population of premigrant eels in the Frémur was estimated to be 2,475 eels (315 kg) in 2000, 1,500 (124 kg) in 2001, and 1,448 (134 kg) in 2002 (Table 2). For the Oir, the premigrant population was estimated as 412 eels (110 kg) in 2000, 412 (117 kg) in 2001, and 595 (159 kg) in 2002 (Table 3). Thus, estimated premigrant populations in the Frémur were approximately fourfold higher than those of the Oir in each year. Estimated Frémur premigrant eel biomass was approximately 1.5-fold higher than that of the Oir during the study period.

However, because of the contrast in sex ratio between rivers, the number of female premigrants was greater in the Oir than in the Frémur (mean population 378 ± SE 57 in the Oir and 286 ± SE 103 in the Frémur) (Table 4). Moreover, because of the larger size of the females in the Oir, the biomass of female premigrants was substantially greater in the Oir (103 ± SE 14 kg/year) than in the Frémur (31 ± 15 kg/year) (Table 4).

Discussion

Numerous studies based on life history traits (population structure, growth pattern, age at silvering) emphasize that the watershed is the relevant ecological unit to assess silver eel biomass (e.g., Feunteun et al. 2000; Acou et al. 2003). The present investigation of silver eel production in two small Atlantic catchments supports this conclusion.

In the Frémur, estimated densities were

Table 2. Characteristics of the sedentary fraction of the eel population from 2000 to 2002 estimated by electrofishing in the Frémur River. Stock is the population size in the whole catchment in numbers and in kilograms, estimated as the product of mean density and area of streams + a 2.5 m wide strip on the perimeter of impoundments. N is the number of sampled stations.

	All stage	Yellow eels	Pre-migrant eels		
			Yellow/silver eels	Silver eels	Total
2000 (N = 29)					
Density (ind.100 m^{-2})					
Mean	39.71	36.41	0.96	2.34	3.30
SE	9.19	8.69	0.28	0.68	0.73
Stock (no.)	29783	27309	716	1758	2475
Biomass (g.100 m^{-2})					
Mean	1751.82	1332.08	155.37	264.37	419.74
SE	402.49	325.84	59.93	95.97	118.37
Stock (kg)	1314	999	117	198	315
2001 (N = 29)					
Density (ind.100 m^{-2})					
Mean	44.54	42.55	1.41	0.59	2.00
SE	13.43	13.08	0.45	0.29	0.65
Stock (no.)	33407	31910	1058	439	1500
Biomass (g.100 m^{-2})					
Mean	1125.84	960.52	118.53	46.78	165.31
SE	238.00	202.60	40.15	23.58	53.27
Stock (kg)	844	720	89	35	124
2002 (N = 29)					
Density (ind.100 m^{-2})					
Mean	32.75	30.82	0.04	1.89	1.93
SE	7.75	7.42	0.04	0.67	0.70
Stock (no.)	24566	23118	31	1417	1448
Biomass (g.100m^{-2})					
Mean	1179.96	1001.44	4.71	173.82	178.53
SE	203.86	158.28	4.71	58.39	60.55
Stock (kg)	885	751	4	130	134

Table 3. Characteristics of the sedentary fraction of the eel population from 2000 to 2002 estimated by electrofishing in the Oir. Stock is the population size in the whole catchment in numbers and in kilograms, estimated as the product of mean density and area of streams. N is the number of sampled stations.

	All stage	Yellow eels	Premigrant eels		
			Yellow/silver eels	Silver eels	Total
2000 (N = 32)					
Density (ind.100 m-2)					
Mean	2.89	2.71	0.09	0.09	0.18
SE	0.44	0.45	0.03	0.05	0.06
Stock (no.)	6610	6206	200	205	412
Biomass (g.100 m-2)					
Mean	342.72	294.80	24.28	23.63	47.91
SE	45.16	42.76	10.13	12.99	16.96
Stock (kg)	785	675	56	54	110
2001 (N = 27)					
Density (ind.100 m-2)					
Mean	3.35	3.17	0.00	0.17	0.18
SE	0.51	0.51	0.00	0.06	0.06
Stock (no.)	7671	7270	11	397	412
Biomass (g.100 m-2)					
Mean	455.37	404.43	1.19	49.75	50.94
SE	83.47	84.26	1.01	21.79	21.89
Stock (kg)	1043	926	3	114	117
2002 (N = 24)					
Density (ind.100 m-2)					
Mean	2.97	2.70	0.02	0.24	0.26
SE	0.17	0.73	0.01	0.09	0.10
Stock (no.)	6793	6190	44	559	595
Biomass (g.100 m-2)					
Mean	356.59	287.34	5.85	63.40	69.25
SE	95.50	87.49	3.78	22.59	23.85
Stock (kg)	817	658	13	145	159

Table 4. Estimated production of male and female pre-migrant (yellow/silver and silver) eels in number (no.) and biomass (kg) in the Frémur and Oir catchments.

	Frémur				Oir			
	2000	2001	2002	Mean ± SE	2000	2001	2002	Mean ± SE
Male pre-migrants								
Production (no.)	1987	1281	1296	1521 ± 233	51	124	111	95 ± 23
Production (kg)	253	106	120	160 ± 47	14	35	30	26 ± 6
Female pre-migrants								
Production (no.)	488	219	152	286 ± 103	361	288	484	378 ± 57
Production (kg)	62	18	14	31 ± 15	96	82	129	103 ± 14

$39 \pm SE\ 6$ ind.100 m^{-2} and $1{,}352 \pm 171$ g.100 m^{-2}. These values are very high compared with other west European catchments (Moriarty and Dekker 1997; Feunteun et al. 1998). For example, Carrs et al. (1999) reported that 71% of density estimates at 1,462 sites in English rivers and streams were less than 5 ind.100 m^{-2}. Vollestad and Jonsson (1988) estimated eel density at 1.16 ind.100 m^{-2} in the Imsa River (Norway), based on the total estimated population size in the catchment divided by the total area of water (including the deeper parts of lakes). Some of the highest density estimates (50–1300 ind.100 m^{-2}) were observed in Danish streams (Rasmussen 1983), including mostly elvers (<150 mm). In Frémur samples, proportions of elvers (<180 mm) varied between 26% and 42% during the study period, suggesting interannual variability of recruitment, which was also observed in an eel-pass survey (Figure 1; Acou, unpublished data). However, we suggest that the shortness of the Frémur, its good location for glass eels arrivals, and the restoration of upstream migration by means of the eel lifts could explain this high abundance (see Feunteun et al. 2000). Moreover, fishing pressure was quite low (no commercial fishery), and anglers focused mainly on cyprinids, esocids, and percids. Lastly, we did not observe predation mortalities, since piscivorous birds (including cormorants and ardeids) were scarce in the study area.

In the Oir River, elvers (eels <180 mm) represented only 1.1% of the total catch during the sampling period. It seems that colonization of the Oir by young recruits is low. Distance from the sea is the most important structuring parameter for abundance and mean size of European eels (Ibbotson et al. 2002). In the present study, distances of electrofishing sampling sections from the sea did not differ greatly between the Frémur (8.5–17 km) and the Oir catchments (11.5–19 km). It seems unlikely that the small difference in distance from the sea (3 km) could explain the large difference in elver proportions in the Frémur (40.0%) and the Oir (1.1%). Configuration of the Oir River could explain part of this variability. The Oir is a small tributary of the main river (Sélune) and flows into the Sélune 8 km from the sea. The Oir discharge was 10-fold lower than that of the Sélune ($1258 \pm SD\ 364$ l/s and 12213 ± 3898 l/s, respectively; INRA, unpublished data) between March and July 1999. Water-flow attraction is crucial for the orientation of glass eels and elvers during their freshwater migration (Legault 1994). We suggest that eel recruitment in the Sélune is higher than in the Oir, as confirmed by sampling in the Sélune (A. Acou, unpublished data). The Frémur, unlike the Oir, recruits all freshwater-seeking eels in its estuary. Thus, global densities (in number and biomass) observed in the Oir were approximately 13- and fourfold weaker (3.07 ± SE 0.32 ind.100 m^{-2} and 385 ± 42 g.100 m^{-2}, respectively) than in the Frémur.

Premigrant fractions are dominated by males (85.8%) in the Frémur and by females (79.0%) in the Oir. Female dominance is commonly found in headwater streams where densities are low (Parsons et al. 1977). Helfman et al. (1987) proposed that female eels have an extended larval period and dominate in northern latitudes due to differential larval distribution. The high variation in sex ratio between the neighboring Frémur and Oir catchments does not support the hypothesis that latitude is a determining factor of sex ratio. Instead, our results are consistent with Krueger and Oliveira's (1999) view that density influences eel sex ratios, with high densities promoting the production of males. However, other factors, such as trophic composition of the aquatic ecosystem, may also influence sex determination.

For both sexes, potential migrants in the Oir had significantly higher mean weight and condition factor than those of the Frémur. Lipid, protein, and energy content in fish are positively related to body condition (Lambert and Dutil 1997; Grant and Brown 1999; Sutton et al. 2000; Pangle and Sutton 2005). Fish with a lower condition index may have encountered poor feeding conditions or parasitic infections (Lambert and Dutil 1997; Yaragina and Marshall 2000). Kangur and Kangur (1998) found that eels in the shallow, eutrophic Lake Vortsjarv in Estonia showed a strong linear relationship ($r = 0.81$, $P < 0.0001$) between condition factor and biomass of invertebrates (i.e., *Chironomus plumosus*), the main trophic resource of the lake. Nutrition condition could vary between the Frémur and the Oir according to (1) food availability, (2) food quality, (3) turnover of food, and (4) intra- and interspecific competition. The high eel density in the Frémur may lead to intensified intraspecific competition in this river. Moreover, because of eutrophication, strong cyanotoxin blooms (especially Microcystin-LR) are regularly observed in the Pont es Omnes pond and Bois Joli reservoir in late summer (L. Brient, University of Rennes, personal communication). We recently analyzed levels of Microcystin-LR in fresh liver of 30 migrant silver eels caught in winter at the Pont es Omnes downstream trap (Figure 1; Acou, unpublished data). Results showed that 50% of them are contaminated with a mean toxin level of 28.1 ± SD 22.4 ng/g. Microcystin-LR has been found to induce severe liver damage and growth inhibition in fish (Rahberg et al. 1991; Kent et al. 1994; Tencalla et al. 1994). In the Oir, eel densities are low and cyanobacteria blooms are not observed. Hence differences in feeding opportunities, as mediated by intraspecific competition and cyanotoxin exposure, may contribute to the differences between the two systems in mean weight and condition factor. Further comparative studies between the rivers are needed to clarify these effects.

At the silver stage, the eel stops feeding and must have large lipid reserves to sustain gonad development during the long migration back to the Sargasso Sea (Boëtius and Boëtius 1980). Based on condition factors, it appears that the probability of reaching the spawning grounds in the Sargasso Sea is higher for silver eels reared in the Oir catchment than in the Frémur catchment.

Premigrant biomass densities in the Frémur and Oir are at the upper and median ranges, respectively, of silver eel biomass densities in European standing waters. For example, in the Imsa River (Norway), a mean silver eel biomass density of 22.7 g.100 m^{-2} was reported between 1975 and 1987 (Vollestad and Jonsson 1988). In salt or brackish Italian lagoons, silver eel biomass density varied between 65 g.100 m^{-2} and 190 g.100 m^{-2} (Rossi 1979; Rossi and Cannas 1984). In our study, estimated premigrant biomass density was 4.5-fold higher in the Frémur (254.5 g.100 m^{-2}) than in the Oir (56 g.100 m^{-2}). However, female premigrant biomass densities were equivalent in the two systems (43 g.100 m^{-2} and 45 g.100 m^{-2}, respectively).

We realize that our results constitute an approximation of silver eel production and that further validation is needed to generalize our methods for small catchments. Schulze et al. (2004) found that eels in a pond concentrated in shallow waters near the shoreline, although some were in deeper water farther from shore. In the Frémur, because density estimates were not available for the impoundments, we assumed that eels in this habitat were limited to a 2.5-m-wide peripheral strip, with density similar to that measured by electrofishing in streams. Under this assumption, eels would be absent from 95% of the Frémur's wetted area. If this assumption is incorrect, our estimates of eel density would nevertheless be roughly valid for running water. Failure of the assumption would have greater consequences on estimates of total stock. If impoundment waters farther than 2.5 m from shore contain eels, even at low densities, the total stock could be much larger than the one estimated in the present study (Table 4). Mean yearly estimated production of premigrant eels in the Frémur River (1,521 ± 233 premigrant males and 286 ± 103 premigrant females; Table 4) may therefore constitute an underestimation of total production.

Our estimates of silver eel production assume a one-to-one relation between premigrant (yellow/silver and silver) eels and escapement of silver eels in the subsequent fall. However, the time required for an eel to complete its silvering process remains unclear (Cottrill et al. 2002). Failure of this assumption could lead to biased estimates of production. To clarify this point, we have begun a study using PIT tags to assess recapture rates of externally identified yellow/silver and silver eels.

To our knowledge, this study is the first to associate quantitative estimates of the number of premigrant eels that will undergo a catadromous migration with data on the quality of migration candidates (i.e., body condition). Even if our method needs further validation, we showed that silver eel production and mean Fulton's *K* condition factor vary between two small river systems (wetted areas < 60 ha) that are in close proximity. European eel stocks exist in small and fragmented subpopulations (Dekker 2000). If rivers that are only 65 km apart show this degree of variability, we can expect a very high level of variation in production ha^{-1} and quality of silver eels across the species' range. Contribution of silver eels by water system is the main component of the current conservation strategy. However, we believe that the question of quality of animals among river systems, which is presumed to influence reproductive success on the spawning grounds, is also a key issue that must be urgently pursued for European eel conservation.

Acknowledgments

We acknowledge the Institut National de Recherche en Agronomie (INRA) of Rennes and the Conseil Supérieur de la Pêche (CSP) of Basse Normandie and their staffs for assistance during the field study in the Oir. We are grateful to Fréderic Marchand and Richard Delanoë for their help. This study was funded by the Fédération de Pêche et de Protection des Milieux Aquatiques d'Ille et Vilaine, the contrat de plan Poissons Migrateurs, and various regional and local councils.

References

Acou, A., E. Feunteun, P. Laffaille, and A. Legault. 2000. Catadromous migration dynamics of European eel (*Anguilla anguilla*, L.) in a dammed catchment. Verhandlungen internationale Verein der Limnologie 27:1–4.

Acou, A., F. Lefebvre, P. Contournet, G. Poizat, J. Panfili and A.-J. Crivelli. 2003. Silvering of female eels (*Anguilla anguilla*) in two sub-populations of the Rhône Delta. Bulletin Français de Pêche et de la Pisciculture 368:55–68.

Boëtius, I., and J. Boëtius. 1980. Experimental maturation of female silver eels, *Anguilla anguilla*. Estimates of fecundity and energy reserves for migration and spawning. Dana 1:1–28.

Broad, T. L., C. R. Townsend, G. P.Closs, and D. J. Jellyman. 2001. Microhabitat use by longfin eels in New Zealand streams with contrasting riparian vegetation. Journal of Fish Biology 59:1385–1400.

Carle, F. L., and M. R. Strub. 1978. A new method for estimating population size from removal data. Biometrics 34:621–630.

Carss, D. N., D. A. Elston, K.C. Nelson, and H. Kruuk. 1999. Spatial and temporal trends in unexploited yellow eel stocks in two shallow lakes and associated streams. Journal of Fish Biology 55:636–654.

Colombo, G., G. Grandi, and R. Rossi. 1984. Gonad differentiation and body growth in *Anguilla anguilla*, L. Journal of Fish Biology 24:215–228.

Cone, R. S. 1989. The need to reconsider the use of condition indices in fishery science. Transactions of American Fishery Society 118:510–514.

Cottrill, R. A., R. S. McKinley, and G. Van Der Kraak. 2002. An examination of utilizing external measures to identify sexually maturing female American eels, *Anguilla rostrata*, in the St. Lawrence River. Environmental Biology of Fishes 65:271–287.

Dekker, W. 2000. The fractal geometry of the European eel stock. ICES Journal of Marine Science 57:109–121.

Feunteun, E. 2002. Restoration and management of the European eel: an impossible bargain? Ecological Engineering 18:575–591.

Feunteun, E., A. Acou, J. Guilloüet, P. Laffaille, and A. Legault. 1998. Spatial distribution of an eel population (*Anguilla anguilla* L.) in a small coastal catchment of Northern Brittany (France). Consequences of hydraulic works. Bulletin Français de Pêche et de la Pisciculture 349:129–139.

Feunteun, E., A. Acou, P. Laffaille, and A. Legault. 2000. European eel (*Anguilla anguilla*): prediction of spawner escapement from continental population parameters. Canadian Journal of Fisheries and Aquatic Sciences 57:1627–1635.

Fontaine, Y. A. 1994. L'argenture de l'anguille: métamorphose, anticipation, adaptation. Bulletin Français de Pêche et de la Pisciculture 335:171–185.

Grant, S. A., and J. A. Brown. 1999. Variation in condition of coastal Newfoundland 0-group Atlantic cod (*Gadus morhua*): field and laboratory studies using simple condition indices. Marine Biology 133:611–620.

Helfman, G. S., D. E. Facey, L. S. Hales, and E. L. Bozeman. 1987. Reproductive ecology of the American eel. Pages 42–56 in Dadswell, M. J., R. J. Klauda, C. M. Moffitt, R. L. Saunders, R. A. Rulifson, and J. E. Cooper. Common strategies of anadromous and catadromous fishes. American Fisheries Society, Symposium 1, Bethesda, Maryland.

Ibbotson, A., J. Smith, P. Scarlett, and M. Aprahamian. 2002. Colonisation of freshwater habitats by the European eel *Anguilla anguilla*. Freshwater Biology 47:1696–1706.

ICES 1998. European eel. Extract of the report of the advisory committee on fishery management, No. 11. ICES, Copenhagen, Denmark.

Jellyman, D. J., and B. L. Chisnall. 1999. Habitat preferences of shortfinned eels (*Anguilla australis*), in two New Zealand lowland lakes. New Zealand Journal of Marine and Freshwater Research 33:233–248.

Kangur, A., and K. Kangur. 1998. Relationship between the population dynamics of Chironomidae and the condition factor of European eel, *Anguilla anguilla* (L.) in Lake Võrtsjärv. Limnologica 28:103–107.

Kent, M. L., R. J. Andersen, C. F. B. Holmes, T. McCready, and D. E. Williams. 1994. Evidence that microcystin LR is the cause of netpen liver disease of Atlantic salmon (*Salmo salar*). International Symposium on Aquatic Animal Health: Program and Abstracts. University of California, School of Veterinary Medicine, Davis, Los Angeles.

Krueger, W. H., and K. Oliveira. 1999. Evidence for environmental sex determination in the American eel, *Anguilla rostrata*. Environmental Biology of Fishes 55:381–389.

Laffaille, P., E. Feunteun, A. Baisez, T. Robinet, A. Acou, A. Legault, and S. Lek. 2003. Spatial organisation of European eel (*Anguilla anguilla* L.) in a small catchment. Ecology of Freshwater Fishes 12:254–264.

Lambert, P., E. Feunteun, and C. Rigaud. 1994. Eel study in freshwater marshes. First analysis of catch probability observed during electric fishing operations. Bulletin Français de Pêche et de la Pisciculture 335:111–122.

Lambert, Y., and J. D. Dutil. 1997. Can simple condition indices be used to monitor and quantity seasonal changes in the energy reserves of Atlantic cod (*Gadus morhua*)? Canadian Journal of Fisheries and Aquatic Sciences 54(Supplement 1):104–112.

Legault, A. 1994. Etude préliminaire du recrutement fluvial de l'anguille. Bulletin Français de Pêche et de la Pisciculture 335:33–41.

McDowall, R. M. 1990. New Zealand freshwater fishes and fisheries—the angler's eldorado. Reviews in Aquatic Sciences 2:281–341.

Moriarty, C. 1996. The European eel fishery in 1993 and in 1994. Fisheries Bulletin 14:1–52.

Moriarty, C., and W. Dekker, editors. 1997. Management of European eel fisheries. Irish Fisheries Bulletin no. 15.

Pangle, K. L., and T. M. Sutton. 2005. Temporal changes in the relationship between condition indices and proximate composition of juvenile *Coregonus artedi*. Journal of Fish Biology 66:1060–1072.

Pankhurst, N. W. 1982. Changes in the skin-scale complex with sexual maturation in the European eel, *Anguilla anguilla* (L.). Journal of Fish Biology 21:549–561.

Parsons, J., K. U. Vickers, and Y. Warden. 1977. Relationship between elver recruitment and changes in the sex ratio of silver eels *Anguilla anguilla* L. migrating from Lough Neagh, Northern Ireland. Journal of Fish Biology 10:211–229.

Rahberg, C. M. I., G. Bylund, and J. E. Erikson. 1991. Histopathological effects of microcystin LR, a cyclic peptide toxin from the cyanobacterium (blue-green alga) *Microcystis aeruginosa* on common carp (*Cyprinus carpio* L.). Aquatic Toxicology 20:131–146.

Rasmussen, G. 1983. Recent investigations on the population dynamics of eels (*Anguilla anguilla* L.) in some Danish streams. Proceedings from the 3rd British Freshwater fish Conference 3:71–77, University of Liverpool, Liverpool, UK.

Robinet, T., and E. Feunteun. 2002. Sublethal effects of exposure to chemical compounds: a cause for the decline in Atlantic eels? Ecotoxicology 11:265–277.

Rossi, R. 1979. An estimate of the production of the eel population in the Valli of Comacchio (Po Delta) during 1974–1976. Bolletino di Zoologia 46:217–223.

Rossi, R., and A. Cannas. 1984. Eel fishing management in hypersaline lagoon of southern Sardinia. Fisheries Research 2:285–298.

Rossi, R., and G. Colombo. 1979. Some observations on age, sex, growth of silver eels (*Anguilla anguilla* L.) in north Adriatic Lagoons. Rapports et Procès-verbaux du Conseil International de l'Exploration de la Mer 174:64–69.

Schulze, T., U. Kahl, R. J. Radke, and J. Benndorf. 2004. Consumption, abundance and habitat use of *Anguilla anguilla* in a mesotrophic reservoir. Journal of Fish Biology 65:1543–1562.

Sutton, S. G., T. P. Bult, and R. L. Haedrich. 2000. Relationships among fat weight, body weight, water weight, and condition factors in wild Atlantic salmon parr. Transactions of the American Fisheries Society 130:1–17.

Tencalla, F. G., D. R. Dietrich, and C. Schlatter. 1994. Toxicity of *Microcystis aeruginosa* peptide toxin to yearling rainbow trout (*Oncorhynchus mykiss*). Aquatic Toxicology 30:215–224.

Tesch, F. W. 2003. The eel, 5th edition. Blackwell Scientific Publications, Oxford, UK.

Vollestad, L. A., and B. Jonsson. 1988. A 13-year study of population dynamics and growth of the European eel (*Anguilla anguilla*) in a Norwegian river: evidence for density dependant mortality, and development of a model for predicting yield. Journal of Animal Ecology 57:983–997.

Yaragina, N. A., and C. T. Marshall. 2000. Trophic influences on interannual and seasonal variation in the liver condition index of northeast Arctic cod (*Gadus morhua*). ICES Journal of Marine Science 57:42–55.

The Metazoan Parasites of Eels in Ireland: Zoogeographical, Ecological and Fishery Management Perspectives

T. KIERAN MCCARTHY[1], KAREN CREED, OISIN NAUGHTON, PAULA CULLEN,
AND LORRAINE COPLEY

Department of Zoology, National University of Ireland
University Road, Galway, Ireland

Abstract.—A new checklist of 36 metazoan parasites recorded in European eels *Anguilla anguilla* in Ireland is presented and reviewed. Some of these parasite taxa are eel specialists but most utilize a range of fish hosts. Many were accidentally brought to Ireland during fish introductions. Changing distributions of preferred intermediate hosts have affected some parasite species. Commercial transport of eels has been implicated in the introduction and spread of several potentially pathogenic parasites, including the Asian nematode *Anguillicola crassus*. The current status of this and two *Pseudodactylogyrus* species, similarly introduced to Ireland, is discussed. Analysis of parasite assemblages of Irish eel populations indicates that individual host characteristics, such as size and diet, are important at the infra-community level. Likewise, variation in biotic and abiotic features of ecosystems is reflected in composition and structure of eel parasite component communities. Environmental changes, such as eutrophication and species introductions, were found to affect eel parasite assemblages. Better regulation of fish introductions and translocations is needed to protect the ecological integrity of Ireland's freshwater systems and to avoid economic damage by nonindigenous parasites. Restrictions on live eel transport and on eel stocking programs may be necessary to protect recreational fisheries and the Irish aquaculture industry.

Introduction

The European eel *Anguilla anguilla*, whose overall distribution was recently reviewed by Dekker (2003), is one of the relatively small number of indigenous fish species that inhabit Ireland's inland waters (Moriarty and Fitzmaurice 2000). In addition to being widely distributed in Irish lakes and rivers, it also occurs in mixohaline and marine littoral habitats round the island (Healy 2003). The well-documented decline of the species in recent years (ICES 2002) has been less extreme in Ireland than in most other parts of its European range. This is generally attributed to the fact that, due to its geographical location, the island has relatively high natural juvenile eel recruitment and because the commercial exploitation of eel stocks, other than in the intensively managed Lough Neagh fishery, is generally low (Moriarty 1988; Callaghan and McCarthy 1992; McCarthy et al. 1999).

Parasites, apart from any economic considerations, are of considerable interest from biogeographical and ecological per-

---
[1]Corresponding author: tk.mccarthy@nuigalway.ie

spectives. Their adaptive morphology and frequently complex life cycles, together with the increasingly recognized contribution that parasites make to biodiversity of aquatic ecosystems, has attracted the attention of many ecologists and fishery biologists (Dogiel et al. 1961; Price 1980; Esch et al. 1990). Likewise, knowledge of parasite distributions, and host-specificities, can be used to address evolutionary questions about their hosts (Marcogliese and Cone 1993). Parasites can provide indirect evidence on the migrations and trophic interactions of their hosts. Also, as is increasingly recognized, they can be used to provide information on anthropogenic impacts on the physical and chemical environments of their hosts (Lafferty 1997), as well as on the changes occurring in regional biotas due to introduction of nonindigenous species of hosts and pathogens (Kennedy 1994).

It is widely believed that parasites are disseminated and introduced into new localities by host movements, including natural and anthropochore dispersal (Kennedy 1993). Available data on fish parasites in Ireland and knowledge of their host-specificities suggests that fish introductions played an important role in the dispersal of many helminth and crustacean parasites (Holland and Kennedy 1997). Over half the freshwater fish species in Ireland are known to have been introduced by man and analyses of apparent discontinuities in parasite distributions of two acanthocephalans, *Pomphorhynchus laevis* and *Acanthocephalus anguillae*, were linked to the introduction of Cyprinidae by Kennedy et al. (1989).

In this paper we present a summary, and new species checklist, of the currently available information on metazoan parasites of eels in Ireland; we review the biogeographical and ecological factors that affect the composition of eel parasite communities in Irish aquatic habitats; and we discuss fishery management issues arising from the increased rate at which nonindigenous eel parasites are being introduced to Ireland.

Study Area

The northwestern European location of the island of Ireland and the influence of the North Atlantic Drift (Gulf Stream) contribute greatly to its mild, moist, temperate climate. Mean annual rainfall levels, which vary from about 750 mm in the eastern lowlands to 1,200 mm in western uplands, and the island's "saucer-shaped" topography are reflected in the variety of inland water-bodies that provide freshwater habitats for its fish. Mean annual air temperatures range from 9.5°C in the northeast to 10.5°C in the extreme south-east of the island, and summer lake water temperatures rarely exceed 20°C. Recent reviews of Irish freshwater habitats, with respect to water quality and fish ecology respectively, were given by Stapleton et al. (2000) and McCarthy and Cullen (2002). Information on environmental conditions in Irish estuaries and coastal zones was also given by Stapleton et al. (2000). A recent review of Irish wetlands by Otte (2003) includes details of coastal lagoons and other habitats of importance to eels. Details of sampling localities and places referred to in this paper are summarized cartographically in Figure 1.

Materials and Methods

Data on the distribution and infection parameters of metazoan parasites of eels from a series of Irish localities (Figure 1) were used to compile a national checklist of eel parasites; to describe geographical distributions of eel parasites in Ireland; and to analyze aspects of the ecology of eel parasite assemblages. Protocols adopted in earlier studies on Irish fish parasites (Conneely and McCarthy 1984) were employed subsequently

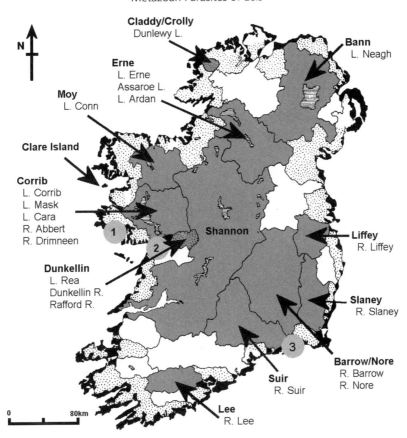

Figure 1. Map of Irish river catchment areas. Three estuarine/marine sites are also highlighted. 1) seashore at Carna, 2) Carnaroo Bay and 3) Cheekpoint on the Waterford Estuary. Catchment area is indicated by stippling. Solid black indicates direct drainage to the sea or small stream systems. Stippled areas indicate catchments of 100–500 km² and unstippled areas indicate catchments >500 km².

in a series of published (Conneely and McCarthy 1986; McCarthy and Rita 1991; Callaghan and McCarthy 1996; Copley and McCarthy 2001, 2005) and unpublished studies on parasites of eels in Ireland, from which the parasite community data for the present paper were obtained. A total of 1,067 individual eels were quantitatively examined for all metazoan parasites and much larger samples were examined specifically for nonindigenous taxa. Thus, data are available from widely distributed Irish localities (Figure 1) that include riverine, lacustrine, estuarine and marine littoral habitats. Parasitological terms recommended and defined by Margolis et al. (1982) and by Esch et al. (1990) have been adopted. TWINSPAN cluster analysis was undertaken on 28 eel parasite data sets from Irish localities, using the Community Analysis Programme (CAP) produced by Pisces Conservation Ltd., UK.

Results

A checklist of the metazoan parasites recorded in eels in Ireland recognizes 36 operational taxonomic units, mostly species (Table 1). The checklist is based on previously published observations as well as to the results (to mid 2003) of ongoing surveys of eel parasites

Table 1. Checklist of Irish eel parasites. A "?" indicates that the status is unknown or not clearly defined.

Group	Species	Authority	Introduced / Native	Eel habitat	Parasite infection location	Specialist eel parasites
Monogenea	Pseudodactylogyrus anguillae	Yin & Sproston 1948	Introduced	Freshwater	Gill	Specialist
	Pseudodactylogyrus bini	Kikuchi 1929	Introduced	Freshwater	Gill	Specialist
Digenea	Helicometra fasciata	Rudolphi 1819	Native	Marine	Intestine	
	Podocotyle atomon	Rudolphi 1802	Native	Marine	Intestine	
	Crepidostomum farionis	Muller 1784	Native	Freshwater	Intestine	
	Crepidostomum metoecus	Braun 1900	Native	Freshwater	Intestine	
	Sphaerostoma bramae	Muller 1776	Introduced ?	Freshwater	Intestine	
	Deropristis inflata	Molin 1859	Native	Marine	Intestine	Specialist ?
	Phyllodistomum sp.		Native	Freshwater	Urether	
	Lecithochirium rufoviride	Rudolphi 1819	Native	Marine	Intestine	
	Lecithochirium furcolabiatum	Jones 1933	Native	Marine	Intestine	
	Diplostomum chromatophorum	Brown 1931	Native	Freshwater	Eye	
	Diplostomum gasterostei	Williams 1966	Native	Freshwater	Eye	
	Diplostomum paraspathaceum	Shigin 1965	Native	Freshwater	Eye	
	Diplostomum pseudobaeri	Razmashkin & Andrynk 1978	Native	Freshwater	Eye	
	Diplostomum spathaceum	Rudolphi 1819	Native	Freshwater	Eye	
Cestoda	Bothriocephalus claviceps	Goeze 1782	Native	Freshwater	Intestine	Specialist
	Proteocephalus macrocephalus	Creplin 1825	Native	Freshwater	Intestine	Specialist
Nematoda	Camallanus lacustris	Zoega 1776	Introduced ?	Freshwater	Intestine	
	Capillaria sp.		?	Freshwater	Intestine	
	Cucullanus truttae	Fabricius 1794	Introduced ?	Freshwater	Intestine	
	Anguillicola crassus	Kuwahar, Nimi & Itagaki 1974	Introduced	Freshwater/Estuarine	Swimbladder	Specialist
	Paraquimperia tenerrima	Linstow 1878	Native	Freshwater	Intestine	
	Raphidascaris acus	Bloch 1779	Introduced ?	Freshwater	Intestine	
	Rhabdochona sp.		?	Freshwater	Intestine	
	Encysted larvae spp. Indet.		?	?	Body cavity	
Acanthocephala	Acanthocephalus anguillae	Muller 1780	Introduced	Freshwater	Intestine	
	Acanthocephalus clavula	Dujardin 1845	Native	Freshwater	Intestine	
	Acanthocephalus lucii	Muller 1780	Introduced	Freshwater	Intestine	
	Echinorhynchus gadi	Zoega 1776	Native	Marine	Intestine	
	Pomphorhynchus laevis	Muller 1776	Introduced	Freshwater	Intestine	
Hirudinea	Piscicola geometra	L.	Native	Freshwater	External	
	Hemiclepsis marginata	Muller 1844	Native	Freshwater	External	
Mollusca	Anodonta cygnea	L.	Native	Freshwater	Gill	
Crustacea	Argulus foliaceus	L.	Native ?	Freshwater	External	
	Ergasilus gibbus	von Nordmann 1832	Native	Freshwater	External	Specialist

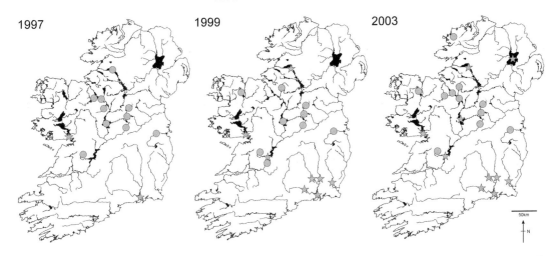

Figure 2. Maps showing the results of surveys of eels carried out to assess the spread of *Anguillicola crassus* in 1997, 1999 and 2003. *A. crassus* was present at sites marked with a star, and absent at sites marked with a circle.

throughout Ireland. In addition to the taxonomic checklist, Table 1 also provides information on the presumed biogeographic status of species in Ireland; the types of aquatic habitat in which they occur; the locations, on or in eels, they parasitize; and the identity of taxa regarded as specialist parasites of eels. Most (78%) of the taxa listed were recorded in eels captured in freshwater habitats, as opposed to estuarine/marine areas of which, so far, only a smaller number (17%) are characteristic. Some eels sampled in estuarine/marine localities had substantial numbers of freshwater parasites, but these are presumed to have been acquired prior to migration by the host eel into the marine capture locality. Most (81%) of the parasites recorded on or in Irish eels can be regarded as generalists, or in some cases accidental parasites, though six or seven are generally recognized as specialist parasites of eel (Table 1).

The first record of the nonindigenous swim bladder nematode *Anguillicola crassus* in Ireland, (McCarthy et al. 1999), was from eels captured in 1997 in the Waterford estuary in southeast Ireland. This discovery prompted a parasitological survey of the northeastern River Erne system (Evans and Mathews 1999; Evans et al. 2001a) and led to a series of investigations on eel parasites throughout the island in an attempt to track the dispersal patterns of *A. crassus* and other introduced eel parasites. The rapid spread of the nematode to the principal exploited eel fisheries in Ireland is shown in Figure 2. The parasite is now known to occur in the major southeastern Irish rivers (Barrow, Nore, Suir and Slaney Rivers), as well as in the central River Shannon system, the western Lough Corrib system, the northwestern River Erne catchment and in the major Lough Neagh fishery in Northern Ireland.

Some results of a recent survey of gill parasites of Irish eels (authors' unpublished data), captured at a variety of localities throughout the island, are summarized in Figure 3. The known distributions of two nonindigenous monogenetic flukes, *Pseudodactylogyrus anguillae* and *P. bini*, both eel specialists, are illustrated in Figure 3a. Both species are now widely distributed in Ireland. The copepod *Ergasilus gibbus*, an eel specialist, which has generally only been recorded from brackish water habitats in Britain and

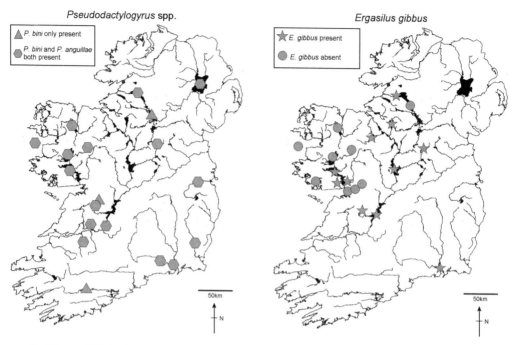

Figure 3. Maps of Irish river systems showing the results of surveys for (a) *Pseudodactylogyrus* species and for (b) the presence or absence of *Ergasilus gibbus*.

mainland Europe, has been found to occur regularly well inland in Ireland. For example, it has been found (Figure 3b) in lakes in the Shannon, Corrib and Erne River basins, as well as in estuarine eels from the southeastern Waterford area (Figure 3b).

Purcell and McCarthy (unpublished data) interpreted variation in eel parasite community composition as a function of population structure and diet of their host community, as inferred from two eel samples from Lough Derg, the largest River Shannon lake (Table 2). The samples were obtained respectively from the littoral and sublittoral zones of the lake, and they differed in respect of eel sizes and diets. The composition of their parasite assemblages reflected these differences (Table 2).

Larger eels from deeper habitats had greater parasite burdens and greater diversity in their parasite communities. Likewise, reflecting increased piscivory, the larger eels were more likely to have parasites such as *Camallanus lacustris* that they had acquired through ingestion of perch fry. Abundances of certain parasites (e.g., *Ergasilus gibbus*) were similarly linked to body size. In the case of the encysted metacercarial flukes, *Diplostomum spathaceum*, higher abundance in the deep water eel sample may also be due to progressive accumulation of these long-lived parasites by the older eels.

A dendrogram (Figure 4) based on TWINSPAN cluster analysis of parasite assemblage composition in 28 samples of Irish eels grouped localities in a manner that reflected the types of habitats from which the eels were obtained. Riverine sites and marine sites are both represented by discrete sample clusters. Among lake samples, dendrogram results corresponded to lake trophic status, as inferred from water quality data that included chlorophyll-a and total phosphorus concentrations and Secchi disk measures of water clarity (data from Stapleton et al. 2000 and various unpublished sources).

Table 2. Mean abundances of parasites of eels in two Lough Derg samples with differing trophic ecology.

Site	Littoral	Deep
No. eels	71	147
Mean eel length (cm)	27	49
Important prey species	*Asellus aquaticus*	*Asellus aquaticus* *Perca fluviatilis*
Diplostomum spathaceum	1.65	9.40
Ergasilus gibbus	0.05	3.00
Acanthocephalus clavula	–	6.8
A. lucii	7.3	3.87
A. anguillae	0.05	0.90
Bothriocephalus claviceps	–	0.65
Paraquimperia tenerrima	5.15	0.27
Raphidascaris acus	–	0.10
Sphaerostoma bramae	0.01	3.30
Proteocephalus macrocephalus	0.02	0.09
Camallanus lacustris	0.75	19.50
Crepidostomum metoecus	0.13	1.49
Capillaria sp.	–	0.05

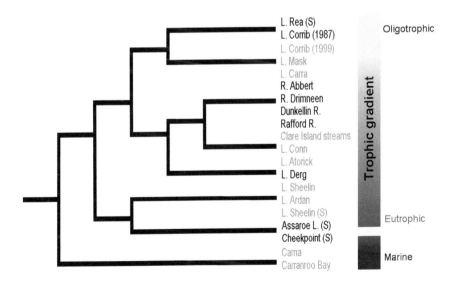

Figure 4. Results of a TWINSPAN analysis on the abundances of eel parasites recorded from 20 different surveys. (S) at three locations indicates that the eels surveyed were silver; all other samples were of yellow eels. Alternation of dark and light fonts indicates the groups of locations which correspond to each TWINSPAN limb.

Discussion

The European eel is an important indigenous component of the species-poor insular freshwater fish fauna of Ireland. It has a history of exploitation dating from over five thousand years ago to the present. Eels are currently commercially fished only during the yellow and silver eel life history stages, though elvers were once used as a food item in some southern localities. The euryhaline eel is widely distributed in Irish lakes and rivers and, as observed by Callaghan and McCarthy (1992) in the Dunkellin River, it can occur in very high densities in coastal rivers and lower reaches of larger rivers. Healy (2003) recorded eels in 32 of the 38 coastal lagoons she studied and the species has also been found at many estuarine and marine littoral sites. However, though the biology of the eel has been well researched in Irish inland waters, relatively little is known about its ecology or parasitology in marine and mixohaline waters.

The list of metazoan parasites presented in Table 1 includes a total of 36 taxa, indicating that the parasitofauna of eels is in not an impoverished, insular, one. Earlier studies in western Ireland, such as those of Conneely and McCarthy (1986) who recorded 13 species of parasites in eels from the Corrib catchment and Callaghan and McCarthy (1996), who recorded 15 species from the small Dunkellin River system, dealt exclusively with eels sampled in freshwater. These and some other records of Irish eel parasites (Kane 1966; Kennedy 1966; Kennedy 1974; Kennedy 1992; Kennedy and Moriarty 1987; Purcell and McCarthy 1995; McCloughlin and Irwin 1991) were included in the recent checklists of Irish freshwater fish parasites compiled by Holland and Kennedy (1997). They listed 20 helminth and crustacean eel parasites for Ireland and noted that the same number was recorded in British eels. These, together with other published observations (Evans et al. 2001b; Evans and Matthews 2000) and the results presented above, suggest that eel parasite assemblages in Ireland are comparable to those in Britain. They may also be comparable to those of nearby continental European countries. In Denmark, for example, Koie (1988a, 1988b) recorded 41 metazoan parasites in eels. The present checklist may include some species that improved taxonomy would show were invalid and this is especially likely among the strigeid eye-flukes. The relatively high number included (Table 1) in the Irish checklist reflects the publication by McCloughlin and Irwin (1991) of records, based on use of a Russian key provided originally by Shigin (1986). These records should be validated by use of modern molecular taxonomic methods and investigations on adult flukes. It is also likely that additional studies will add further helminths to the list, and it is expected that these will mostly be species of nematodes and Digenea with marine life cycles, as comparatively few marine or estuarine Irish eels have yet been examined for parasites. However, the absence of some eel parasites, such as the specialist nematode *Spinitectus inermis* or the generalist cestode *Trianophorus nodulosus,* may reflect biogeographical barriers and incomplete postglacial recolonization of the island. Such effects can be seen in many free-living components of the Irish biota (McCarthy 1986). However, it seems that *S. inermis,* though listed as a freshwater specialist by Kennedy (1992), is more prevalent in estuarine eel populations. If this is the case, then its discovery in Ireland can be anticipated. In the case of another specialist parasite of European eels *Daniconema anguillae,* found in Danish eels (Koie 1988a, 1988b), the situation is less clear-cut and suggests that further research on nematode parasites of Irish eels is needed. The widespread occurrence (Figure 3) of the copepod *Ergasilus gibbus* in Irish inland waters is of interest, as studies on this species elsewhere in Europe suggest it occurs more typically on eels in coastal, brackish water, habitats (Conneely and McCarthy 1986).

Information on parasites of eels elsewhere in Europe suggests that faunal species richness in Ireland may be underecorded at present and that records of up to eight more metazoan species can probably be anticipated. This is particularly true for estuarine and marine eels in Ireland which have only been studied to a minor degree so far. Thus, the total number of such parasites infecting Irish eels may be up to 44, over half the total number listed for European eel throughout its entire range (Reimer 1999). Irish eels are likely to be infected with a greater number of other types of pathogens than is suggested by present records and these would also serve to highlight the diversity of parasites affecting this host. Only limited studies have been undertaken on the Protozoa and microbial pathogens of eels in Ireland, though at least three species of the former have been recorded. The leech-transmitted blood parasite *Trypanosoma granulosum*, observed in western Irish eels, was investigated by Zintl et al. (1997); *Myxidium* sp. have been regularly noted on gills of Irish eels; and external *Ichthyopthirius multifiliis* infections have been noted periodically in eels retained by fishermen and in ascending elvers obstructed by low-flow or artificial obstacles. Likewise, occasional observations have been made on fungal, *Saprolegnia* sp., infections (authors' unpublished data) in eels retained by fishermen and occasional viral/bacterial infections have been noted in Irish eels (J. McArdle, Marine Institute, personal communication).

The species richness of the eel parasite fauna in Ireland (Table 1) is comparable to those recorded in Denmark by Koie (1988a,b), and in Britain by Kennedy (1990) and others. Eel parasite species richness is high in comparison with most other well studied fish hosts in Ireland. In this regard it is interesting to note that the eel is a well-established indigenous species in Ireland. Conneely and McCarthy (1986) pointed out that the native brown trout *Salmo trutta* had a higher number of metazoan parasites than other species investigated in western Ireland. Likewise, indigenous arctic char *Salvelinus alpinus* populations harbor relatively diverse parasite assemblages (Conneely and McCarthy 1984; Doherty and McCarthy 2000) and this historical biogeographical dimension seems to be a general feature of Irish fish parasite assemblages (Holland and Kennedy 1997). However, other ecological factors are also important determinants of the diversity of parasites infecting Irish eels. The well-known migratory and euryhaline aspects of European eel biology are obviously important in this regard. As a consequence of the range of aquatic habitats used by eels in Ireland, eels have a greater probability of being infected by localized or habitat-specific parasites. Likewise, they are exposed to potential exchanges of parasites from virtually all the other fish species occurring in inshore or freshwater habitats in Ireland and such interactions are known to contribute significantly to the composition of fish parasite communities (Leong and Holmes 1981). The ontogenetic trophic niche shifts in the life history of eels, which are linked to body-size and prey availability, involve a progressive change from planktivory to piscivory, and are recognized as contributing to the relative species richness of eel parasite communities (Conneely and McCarthy 1988; Kennedy 1990).

Differences in species composition and parasite abundances in two samples of eels (Table 2), obtained from littoral and sub-littoral areas of Lough Derg in the River Shannon, illustrate the effects of variation in feeding habits of eels of differing sites and habitats. The data on three acanthocephalan species (*Acanthocephalus clavula, A. lucii* and *A. anguillae*) reflect the importance of the aquatic isopod *Asellus* in eel diets in the Shannon lakes. A high level of multiple acanthocephalan species infections in Irish eels has been noted previously (Kennedy and Moriarty 1987; Kennedy 1992; Callaghan and McCarthy 1996). This phenomenon is partly attributable to the fact that though *Asellus aquaticus*, intermediate host to *A. lucii* and *A. anguillae*, is progressively competitively displacing *Asellus meridianus*, intermediate host of *A. clavula*, both isopod species still co-exist in the larger Irish lakes (McCarthy 1986). Another frequently noted feature of Irish eel parasite assemblages is the higher abundance of certain parasites in larger eels (Conneely and McCarthy 1986; Callaghan and McCarthy 1996). In the case of the data presented in Table 2, this effect can be illustrated by the very high abundance of *Camallanus lacustris* in sub-littorally sampled Lough Derg eels. This nematode, which is very prevalent in the Eurasian perch *Perca fluviatilis* population, occurs regularly as a secondary infection in larger eels that feed extensively on perch fry. The infection (Table 2) of larger Lough Derg eels by the tapeworm *Bothriocephalus claviceps* also probably involved ingestion of juvenile fish that had recently ingested copepods infected with *B. claviceps* larvae. Conneely and McCarthy (1986) commented previously on this phenomenon. Subsequently, Kennedy et al. (1992) argued that heavy infections of eels with cestodes provided indirect evidence of planktivory. However, the almost total absence of direct observations of plankton in diets of larger eels in Irish and other European studies on eel feeding habits is difficult to ignore. This is especially so when, as in the present investigations, fry of Cyprinidae and perch, with their stomachs full of recently ingested zooplankton, are regularly observed in stomach contents of larger sized eels.

Variation in eel parasite assemblages can potentially yield information on the feeding habits and local movements of eels. Conneely and McCarthy (1986) noted riverine parasites in lake dwelling eels and lacustrine parasites in river eels, and concluded that these were indicative of movements by individual eels between lake and river habitats in the western Irish Corrib catchment area. Similarly, ongoing studies of marine and mixohaline eel populations in western Ireland (authors' unpublished data) show that eels captured in such habitats are infected by freshwater parasites. It is hoped that further analyses of the parasite assemblages of such eel populations, combined with microprobe analyses of their otolith Sr/Ca ratios (Tsukamoto and Arai 2001) and tracking of tagged individuals, will provide a better understanding of the local migratory activities of European eels.

Parasite assemblages of fishes and other aquatic hosts appear to generally reflect the community structure and ecosystem processes of their habitats. Thus, as initially revealed by the pioneering studies of Wisniewski (1958) in Polish lakes, eutrophic lakes are characterized by parasite faunas in which allogenic species (which use piscivorous birds as definitive hosts) predominate (Esch et al. 1990). The results presented in Figure 4 suggest that variation in eel parasite communities from a series of Irish aquatic habitats reflects the prevailing environmental conditions, particularly trophic status. Various studies (Reimer 1995; Lafferty 1997) indicate the potential effects of environmental change on parasite assemblages. Thus, in addition to its potential use as a "sentinel species" in biomonitoring of pollution, eels may provide indirect parasitological evidence of a variety of anthropogenic impacts on their habitats.

The extent to which species introductions and host translocations have impacted the aquatic parasite fauna of Ireland is evident in the composition of the parasite assemblages of Irish eels. The steady colonization (Figures 2 and 3) of Irish eel populations by nonindigenous parasites, including the Asian swim bladder nematode *A. crassus* and two gill-inhabiting *Pseudodactylogyrus* species in the past decades is of concern to fishery managers. The importance of commercial transport of eels in dispersal of *A. crassus* has been recognized previously in Britain and elsewhere in Europe (Kennedy and Fitch 1990). The initial record (McCarthy et al. 1999) of *A. crassus*, in was from a site close to the Rosslare ferry port used by continental eel dealers, which suggests that the introduction of this nematode involved anthropochore dispersal via eel transport vehicles. The pattern in which it has spread subsequently to Ireland's major commercially exploited eel stocks (Figure 2) in the rivers Shannon, Erne, Corrib, and to Ireland's premier eel fishery on Lough Neagh, mirrors the routes taken by eel dealers transporting live eels. The dispersal of *A. crassus* within different river systems has been variable. It appears to have spread more rapidly through the River Erne catchment (Evans and Mathews 1999; Evan et al. 2001a) than in the Shannon system (Figure 2), where eel fishing is more regulated and fishermen are assigned individual fishing zones. The biogeographical status of the two *Pseudodactylogyrus* species now present in Ireland has been discussed by Kennedy (1993, 1994) who, unlike most European fish parasitologists, does not consider them likely to be introduced species. However, in Ireland the sequential recording of *P. anguillae, P. bini* and *A. crassus* in well researched eel populations such as those in the western Irish River Corrib catchment (Conneely and McCarthy 1984, 1986; McCarthy and Rita 1991; and new records in Figures 2 and 3) strongly suggest that at least in Ireland all three of these helminths are nonindigenous. Furthermore, the transport of live eels for commercial purposes seems also to have been important in the widespread dispersal of the *Pseudodactlyogyrus* species. However, perhaps because of their direct life cycles, these gill-flukes appear to have dispersed more rapidly to unexploited Irish eel populations and more remote locations. The spread of *A. crassus* and the *Pseudodactylogyrus* species to Ireland from continental Europe where they are all now widespread illustrates the ease with which aquatic pathogens can be distributed by human agency. The potential risks to Ireland's economically important recreational fisheries and developing aquaculture industry that could arise if live transport of eels continues to take place in a relatively unregulated manner is now more widely recognized and this may lead to stricter control measures. Furthermore, as stocking with infected eels has been shown to be important in the spread of *A. crassus* in other European countries such as Belgium (Belpaire et al. 1989; Audenaert et al. 2003), proposals to enhance productivity of Irish eel fisheries by means of inter-river system elver stocking will also have to be critically reviewed.

Acknowledgments

Financial support for this study was provided (to T. K. McCarthy) by the Higher Education Authority, Dublin (PRTLI-C3 Marine Science Research Programme: Project MSR1.5) and, from 1992 to 2003, by ESB (Electricity Supply Board), Dublin.

References

Audenaert, V., T. Huyse, G. Guemans, C. Belpaire, and F. A. M. Volkaert. 2003. Spatio-temporal dynamics of the parasitic nematode *Anguillicola crassus* in Flanders, Belgium. Diseases of Aquatic Organisms 56:223–233.

Belpaire, C., D. De Charleroy, K. Thomas, P. Van Damme, and F. Ollevier. 1989. Effects of eel restocking on the distribution of the swimbladder nematode *Anguillicola crassus* in Flanders, Belgium. Journal of Applied Ichthyology 5:151–153.

Callaghan, R. M., and T. K. Mc Carthy. 1992. Variations in population structure and growth rate of eels in the Dunkellin river system, western Ireland. Irish Fisheries Investigations Series A 36:61–69.

Callaghan, R. M., and T. K. Mc Carthy. 1996. Metazoan parasite assemblages of eels in the Dunkellin catchment, western Ireland. Archives of Polish Fisheries 4:147–174.

Conneely, J. J., and T. K. Mc Carthy. 1984. The metazoan parasites of freshwater fishes in the Corrib catchment area, Ireland. Journal of Fish Biology 24:363–375.

Conneely, J. J., and T. K. Mc Carthy. 1986. Ecological factors influencing the composition of the parasite fauna of the European eel, *Anguilla anguilla* (L), in Ireland Journal of Fish Biology 28:207–219.

Conneely, J. J., and T. K. Mc Carthy. 1988. The metazoan parasites of trout (*Salmo trutta*) in western Ireland. Polish Archives of Hydrobiology 35:443–460.

Copley, L., and T. K. Mc Carthy. 2001. The first record of the monogenean gill fluke *Pseudodactylogyrus bini* (Kikuchi 1929) in Ireland, with observations on other ectoparasites of River Erne eels. Irish Naturalists' Journal 26:405–413.

Copley, L., and T. K. Mc Carthy. 2005. Some observations on endoparasites of eels, *Anguilla anguilla* (L), from two lakes in the River Erne catchment. Irish Naturalists' Journal 28:31–34.

Dekker, W. 2003. On the distribution of the European eel (*Anguilla anguilla*) and its fisheries. Canadian Journal of Fisheries and Aquatic Sciences 60:787–799.

Dogiel, V. A., G. K. Petrushevski, and Y. I. Polyanski. 1961. Parasitology of fishes. Oliver and Boyd, Edinburgh.

Doherty, D., and T. K. Mc Carthy. 2000. The metazoan parasites, diets and general biology of arctic char *Salvelinus alpinus* in two Irish lakes. Verhandlungen der Internationalen Vereinigung fur Theoretische und Angewandte Limnologie 27:1056–1061.

Esch, G. W., A. W. Shostak, D. J. Marcogliese, and T. M. Goater. 1990. Patterns and processes in helminth parasite communities: an overview. Pages 1–19 in G.W. Esch, A. Bush, and J. Aho, editors. Parasite communities: patterns and processes. Chapman and Hall, London.

Evans, D. W., and M. A. Matthews. 1999. *Anguillicola crassus* (Nematoda, Dracunculoidea); first documented record of this swim bladder parasite in eels in Ireland. Journal of Fish Biology 55:665–668.

Evans, D. W., and M. A. Matthews. 2000. First record of *Argulus foliaceus* on the European eel in the British Isles. Journal of Fish Biology 57:529–530.

Evans, D. W., M. A. Matthews, and C. A. Mc Clintock. 2001a. The spread of the eel swimbladder nematode *Anguillicola crassus* through the Erne system, Ireland. Journal of Fish Biology 59:166–168.

Evans, D. W., M. A. Matthews, and C. A. Mc Clintock. 2001b. First record of *Pomphorhynchus laevis* (Acanthocephala) in fishes from Northern Ireland. Journal of Fish Biology 59:166–168.

Healy, B. 2003. Coastal lagoons. Pages 51–78 in M. Otte, editor. Wetlands of Ireland: distribution, ecology, uses and economic value. University College Dublin Press, Dublin.

Holland, C. V., and C. R. Kennedy. 1997. A checklist of parasitic helminth and crustacean species recorded in freshwater fish from Ireland. Biology and Environment: Proceedings of the Royal Irish Academy 97B:225–243.

International Council for the Exploration of the Seas (ICES). 2002. Report of the ICES/ EIFAC Working Group on Eels. ICES CM2002/ACFM:03.

Kane, M. B. 1966. Parasites of Irish freshwater fishes. Scientific Proceedings of the Royal Dublin Society 18B:205–220.

Kennedy, C. R. 1966. The helminth parasites of some Irish freshwater fish. Irish Naturalists' Journal 15:196–199.

Kennedy, C. R. 1974. A checklist of British and Irish freshwater fish parasites with notes on their distribution. Journal of Fish Biology 6:613–644.

Kennedy, C.R. 1990. Helminth communities in freshwater fish: structured communities or stochastic assemblages. Pages 131–156 in G. W. Esch, A. Bush and J. Aho, editors. Parasite communities: patterns and processes. Chapman and Hall, London.

Kennedy, C. R. 1992. Field evidence of interactions between acanthocephalans *Acanthocephalus anguillae* and *Acanthocephalus lucii* in eels. Ecological Parasitology 1:122–134.

Kennedy, C. R. 1993. Introductions, spread and colonization of new localities by fish helminth and crustacean parasites in the British Isles: a perspective and appraisal. Journal of Fish Biology 43:287–301.

Kennedy, C. R. 1994. The ecology of introductions. Pages 189–208 in A.W. Pike and J.W. Lewis, editors. Parasitic diseases of fish. Samara Publishing, Cardigan, UK.

Kennedy, C. R., R. M. Bates, and A. F. Brown. 1989. Discontinuous distributions of the fish acanthocephalan *Pomhorhynchus laevis* and *Avanthocephalus anguillae* in Britain and Ireland. Journal of Fish Biology 34:607–619.

Kennedy, C. R., and D. J. Fitch. 1990. Colonization, larval survival and epidemiology of the nematode *Anguillicola crassus*, parasitic in eel, *Anguilla anguilla*, in Britain Journal of Fish Biology 36:117–131.

Kennedy, C. R., and C. Moriarty. 1987. Co-existence of congeneric species of Acathocephala: *Acanthocephalus lucii* and *A. anguillae* in eels *Anguilla anguilla* in Ireland. Parasitology 95:301–310.

Kennedy, C. R., P. Nie, J. Kaspers, and J. Paulise. 1992. Are eels planktonic feeders? evidence from parasite communities. Journal of Fish Biology 41:567–580.

Koie, M. 1988a. Parasites in European eel *Anguilla anguilla* (L.) from Danish freshwater, brackish and marine localities. Ophelia 29:93–118.

Koie, M. 1988b. Parasites in eels *Angulla anguilla* (L.) from eutrophic Lake Esrum, Denmark. Acta Parastitologica Polonica 33:89–100.

Lafferty, K. D. 1997. Environmental parasitology: what can parasites tell us about human impacts on the environment. Parasitology Today 13:251–255.

Leong, T. S., and J. C. Holmes. 1981. Communities of metazoan parasites in open water fishes of Cold Lake, Alberta. Journal of Fish Biology 18:693–713.

Marcogliese, D., and D. K. Cone. 1993. What metazoan parasites of eels tell us about evolution of American and European eels. Evolution 47:1632–1635.

Margolis, L., G. W. Esch, J.C. Holmes, A.M. Kuris, and G. A. Schad. 1982. The use of ecological terms in parasitology (Report of an *ad hoc* committee of the American Society of Parasitologists). Journal of Parasitology 68:131–133.

McCarthy, T. K. 1986. Biogeographical aspects of Ireland's invertebrate fauna. Occasional Publication of the Irish Biogeographical Society 1:67–81.

McCarthy, T. K., and P. Cullen. 2002. Ireland's changing freshwater habitats: anthropogenic impacts, fishery management problems and ecohydrological perspectives. Ecohydrology and Hydrobiology 2:143–148.

McCarthy, T. K., P. Cullen, and W. O'Connor. 1999. The biology and management of River Shannon eel populations. Fisheries Bulletin (Dublin) 17:9–20.

McCarthy, T. K., and S. D. Rita. 1991. The occurrence of the monogenean *Pseudodactylogyrus anguillae* (Yin and Sproston) on migrating silver eels in western Ireland. Irish Naturalists' Journal 23:473–477.

McCloughlin, T. J. J., and S. W. B. Irwin. 1991. The occurrence of eyeflukes in fish from the Erne catchment area. Irish Naturalists' Journal 23:409–414.

Moriarty, C. 1988. The eel in Ireland. Went Memorial Lecture, 1987. Royal Dublin Society Occasional Papers in Science and Technology No. 4.

Moriarty, C., and P. Fitzmaurice. 2000. Origin and diversity of freshwater fishes in Ireland. Verhandlungen der Internationalen Vereinigung fur Theoretische und Angewandte Limnologie 27:128–130.

Otte, M. 2003. Wetlands of Ireland: distribution, ecology, uses and economic value. University College Dublin Press, Dublin.

Price, P. W. 1980. Evolutionary biology of parasites. Princeton University Press, Princeton, New Jersey.

Purcell, P., and T. K. McCarthy. 1995. Metazoan parasite assemblages of yellow eels (*Anguilla anguilla* L.) in Lough Derg. Abstracts of the Fifth Environmental Researcher's Colloquium, University College Cork, 13–15 January.

Reimer, L. W. 1995. Parasites, especially of piscine hosts, as indicators of eutrophication. Applied Parasitology 36:124–135.

Reimer, L. W. 1999. Krankheiten, parasiten und schadinungen. Pages 301–322 *in* F. W. Tesch, editor. Der Aal Paraey Buchverlag and Blackwell Scientific Publications Wissenschafts-verlag, Berlin.

Shigin, A. A. 1986. Trematode fauna of the USSR. *Diplostomum metacercariae*. Izdatel'stvo "Nauka". Moscow. (Original in Russian; English translation provided by J. Chubb, Liverpool University)

Stapleton, L., M. Lehane, and P. Toner. 2000. Ireland's environment: a millennium report. Environmental Protection Agency, Dublin.

Tsukamoto, K., and T. Arai. 2001. Faculative catadromy of the eel *Anguilla japonica* between freshwater and seawater habitats. Marine Ecology Progress Series 220:265–276.

Wisniewski, W. L. 1958. Characterization of the parasitofauna of an eutrophic lake. Acta Parastitologica Polonica 6:1–64.

Zintl, A., R. R. Poole, H. P. Voorheis, and C. Holland. 1997. Naturally occurring *Trypanosoma granulosum* infections in the European eel, *Anguilla anguilla* from the west coast of Ireland. Journal of Fish Diseases 20:333–341.

Part III

Status and Dynamics

Long-Term Trends in Size and Abundance of Juvenile American Eels Ascending the Upper St. Lawrence River

Lucian A. Marcogliese[1]

30 Salem Road, R. R. 1, Ameliasburgh, Ontario K0K 1A0 Canada

John M. Casselman

*Ontario Ministry of Natural Resources, Applied Research and Development Branch
Glenora Fisheries Station, R. R. 4, Picton, Ontario K0K 2T0 Canada*

Abstract.—The eel ladder at the Moses-Saunders Dam at Cornwall, Ontario, provides the longest recruitment index of migrating juvenile American eels *Anguilla rostrata* in the species' range, spanning 30 years from 1974 to 2003. Historically, mean size of eels ascending the ladder during the peak midsummer migration period was significantly smaller than mean size of eels in the total annual run. From the 1970s to 2000s, mean size during peak migration increased significantly ($P < 0.0001$), a 1.4- and 2.6-fold increase in length and weight, respectively. In 1988, length surpassed a transitional size of 400 mm and has remained above this level since 1993. A new index of passage of small eels (<400 mm) during peak migration was developed to better indicate young eel recruitment. From 1975–1983, the new index indicated a high percentage (61.2–93.8%) of small eels, but a decline started in the mid-1980s, and in 1988, for the first time fell below 50% of peak passage (46.6%). To date, the declining trend of small eel passage continues (1989–2002, $\bar{x} = 31.4 \pm 12.7$–95% CI). Not only has the number of eels ascending the ladder decreased significantly during peak migration (>3 orders of magnitude, 1982–2001), but there has been a coincident significant increase in the size of eels. Recruitment of small, young eels has essentially ceased.

Introduction

Juvenile American eels *Anguilla rostrata* migrate through the St. Lawrence River to Lake Ontario, where they remain until they become maturing silver or "silvering" eels, at which time they migrate back to the ocean and spawn. The Moses-Saunders Power Dam, Cornwall, Ontario, and the St. Lawrence Seaway were constructed between 1954 and 1958 (Eckersley 1982). Construction of the power dam and seaway did not completely block movement of American eels (hereafter referred to as eels) to Lake Ontario but likely reduced their numbers (Kolenosky and Hendry 1982), since large congregations of eels could be seen at the base of the dam each year (Liew 1982).

In August 1974, a prototype eel ladder designed by the Ontario Ministry of Natural Resources (OMNR) was installed at the Moses-Saunders Dam (Reid 1981) to facilitate the upward passage of eels migrating to the

---
[1] Corresponding author: marcogliese@sympatico.ca

upper St. Lawrence River and Lake Ontario and to alleviate problems associated with eels clogging pump intakes (Whitfield and Kolenosky 1978; Eckersley 1982).

Since 1974, the Research and Assessment Branches of OMNR have intensively monitored eels at the Moses-Saunders Power Dam, providing the longest index of migrant recruiting eels across their range. The methodology used to count eels ascending the ladder varied with technological advances, eel density, and available resources (Casselman et al. 1997a). Duration of ladder operation varied among years (60–148 d), but the ladder was always functional during peak migration (Casselman et al. 1997a). Standardization of ladder data to the 31-d peak migration period provided an index of recruitment that could be compared among years (Casselman et al. 1997a; Marcogliese et al. 1997).

The number of eels ascending the ladder has shown dramatic declines over the course of the index (Casselman et al. 1997a; Marcogliese et al. 1997). Eel passage peaked in 1982 and 1983, with more than one million eels ascending the ladder annually (>26,000/d during peak migration). After 1986, eel passage declined steadily and significantly (Casselman et al. 1997a). By 2002, only 55 eels/d ascended the ladder during peak migration, a 500-fold decrease from 1982.

Since 1975, extensive biological data on eels have been collected, but size data have not been fully analyzed and reported (Casselman 2003; McGrath et al. 2003). Casselman (2003) reported that both length and age of eels ascending the ladder have increased with time, but age interpretations and validation are not complete. The overall purpose of this research, therefore, was to analyze the size of eels ascending the ladder to provide better precision and understanding of recruitment dynamics. The specific objectives were to (1) document and examine the size of eels ascending the ladder from 1975 to 2002, (2) compare the size of eels between those ascending the ladder during annual passage and those ascending during the 31-d peak migration period, (3) examine the relationship between number and size of eels ascending the ladder, and (4) develop an index of small eel recruitment during the 31-d peak migration period. Historically, there are no distinct size classes of eels ascending the ladder; the typical length distribution is unimodal and normally distributed, albeit with a few outliers (Shapiro-Wilk normality tests). Preliminary age interpretations indicated a range in age from 2 to 15+ years (Liew 1982). Thus, the ladder index needed to be refined by reducing the age bias. An index of small eels would better and more directly indicate initial recruitment from the Sargasso Sea because, on average, small eels are younger and more homogeneous in age (Liew 1982; Casselman 2003).

Methods

From 1974 to 2003, extensive data sets have been compiled on eels ascending the ladder at the Moses-Saunders Power Dam, Cornwall, Ontario (Figure 1). Between 1975 and 1978, over 36,000 eels collected at the exit chute of the ladder were tagged and released at various locations above and below the dam to study eel movement, mortality, and ladder efficiency (Liew 1975, 1977, 1978, 1979, unpublished reports). In addition, biological data were collected to help understand age-length relationships, growth, and movements. This work has continued to date. Over the 30-year period, size data were collected by several OMNR districts and independent contractors. The sampling protocol was incompletely recorded as data sources included "gray" documents, annual reports, logbooks, and compilation sheets. From the mid-1970s to the early 1980s, most eels were anesthetized, tagged, and released as part of the tagging program. Some eels were retained for their calcified structures (Liew 1975, 1977, 1978, 1979, unpublished reports). More re-

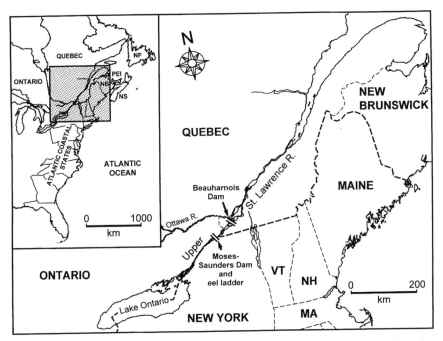

Figure 1. Map showing sites in the migration route for American eels ascending the upper St. Lawrence River and Lake Ontario.

cently (1990s, 2000s), eels were collected, frozen, thawed, and measured, except in the late 1990s, when eels were fitted with PIT tags and released (McGrath et al. 2003). Length was measured to the nearest millimeter, but weight measurements varied from the nearest gram to the nearest 0.01 g.

Size of Eels

Total length of 8,881 eels that ascended the ladder was measured; 8,670 of these were also weighed. Initially, to understand changes in eel size, we calculated mean length and weight of eels by decade and identified homogeneous groups by Kruskal-Wallis nonparametric analysis of variance (ANOVA) and pairwise comparison of means, with α at 0.05. This analysis was conducted for both annual passage, which included all eels at all times of the year, and for the 31-d peak migration period.

Historically, the majority of eels ascending the ladder did so during the 31-d peak migration period (Casselman et al. 1997a). We compared size of eels between annual and peak passage on a yearly basis. Because of much higher passage rates, a disproportionate number of eels were measured in the 1970s compared with more recent years. Thus, for both annual passage and the 31-d peak migration period, we used annual mean size to calculate overall mean size and 95% confidence limits (CL) of eels from 1975 to 2002, to test statistically between annual passage and peak migration (paired t-test), and to analyze trends over time (unweighted least squares linear regression). Within years, mean size was tested statistically between annual passage and the 31-d peak migration period (two sample t-test—α 0.05).

Defining the Size of a Small, Juvenile Eel

To determine if the dramatic decline in recruitment to the upper St. Lawrence River and Lake Ontario was related to the size of eels ascending the ladder, we employed two methods to define the size of a small juvenile eel. Casselman (2003) and McGrath et al. (2003) reported that length of eels ascending the ladder had increased with time. Thus, we compared length of eels in the 1970s, the start of the ladder index when passage rate was high, to size in the 2000s, when passage rate was very low. We calculated the mean and 95% CL for both periods. The midpoint between the upper and lower confidence limits for the two distributions was calculated (Seelbach and Whelan 1988; Marcogliese and Casselman 1998). The second method involved calculating the cusum of mean length from 1975 to 2002. Cusum is the cumulative sum of the residuals minus the mean of the residuals, which indicates temporal trends. A transitional period was identified, and the annual mean length of eels during that period was calculated. The average of the two methods was calculated and termed the separation criterion, which was used to distinguish smaller and larger eels that ascended the ladder. Annual mean length of eels prior to and after the transitional period was calculated to define the average size of small and large eels ascending the ladder.

Abundance of Small, Juvenile Eels Ascending the Ladder

From 1975–2002, using the separation criterion, the percent of small juvenile eels ascending the ladder during the 31-d peak migration period was calculated from length data. The percent of small eels before, during, and after the transitional period, when eel size changed, was tested statistically (ANOVA = α 0.05). In addition, we regressed percent of small eels by year to identify significant trends (unweighted least squares linear regression). Over the 30-year period of the eel ladder, there were some missing data. In 1996, the ladder was operational, but passage and size data were not collected (Casselman et al. 1997a). There were six additional years (1979, 1980, 1992, 1994, 1995, and 1997) during which length data within the 31-d peak migration period were not available or too few samples were measured. For these 6 years, the percent of small eels was estimated using the aforementioned regression equation. Percent of small eels during peak migration was converted to numbers by applying percentages to counts during the 31-d peak migration period. The resulting values provided a new index of small juvenile eel recruitment to the upper St. Lawrence River and Lake Ontario.

Relationship Between Number and Size of Eels

To obtain a descriptive relation between eel length and numbers, we analyzed the relationship between length and $\log_{(10)}$ numbers of eels ascending the ladder during the 31-d peak migration period (unweighted least squares linear regression).

All statistical tests were performed with Statistix (Anonymous 1996).

Results

Size of Eels Over Time

Mean size of eels ascending the ladder during annual passage increased significantly across decades ($P < 0.007$), and the coefficient of variation continually decreased (Table 1). Only mean length and weight in the 1990s and 2000s were not significantly different from each other. During the 31-d peak migration period, mean size of eels followed a similar increasing trend. From the 1970s to 2000s, mean size was significantly larger with each successive decade (1970s, 331 ± 4 mm—95% CI, 55.0 ± 2.4 g; 2000s, 458 ± 8

Table 1. Mean size of American eels ascending the ladder at Moses-Saunders Power Dam, by decade. Kruskal-Wallis nonparametric Analysis of Variance was used to test and compare means for statistical differences ($\alpha = 0.05$). C.I.=confidence interval; CV=coefficient of variation.

Size	Decade	Annually[a]				31 Day Peak Migration[b]			
		N	Mean	C.I.	CV	N	Mean	C.I.	CV
length (mm)	1970s	3,930	341[1]	2.7	25.6	1,308	331[1]	4.2	24.9
	1980s	3,291	380[2]	2.8	21.3	1,162	356[2]	4.2	20.6
	1990s	1,019	457[3]	4.8	17.0	167	417[3]	10.6	16.6
	2000s	641	460[3]	5.9	16.4	321	458[4]	8.4	16.7
weight (g)	1970s	3,930	59.8[1]	1.5	81.1	1,308	55.0[1]	2.4	79.9
	1980s	3,291	84.4[2]	2.2	76.3	1,162	67.9[2]	2.7	69.6
	1990s	1,019	138.0[3]	4.9	58.2	167	104.2[3]	7.9	49.7
	2000s	430	142.9[3]	7.2	52.9	195	141.8[4]	10.3	51.2

[a] Length ($P = 0.0068$) and weight ($P = 0.0059$) significantly different among decades.
[b] Length ($P = 0.0018$) and weight ($P = 0.0012$) significantly different among decades.
[1, 2, 3] Homogeneous groups in which the means were not significantly different.

mm, 141.8 ± 10.3 g; $P < 0.002$), and the coefficient of variation decreased (Table 1).

From 1975–2002, annual mean length and weight of eels ascending the ladder showed significant increasing trends for both annual passage and during peak migration ($P < 0.0001$) (Figure 2 and 3). Mean length increased from approximately 350–450 mm, while weight increased from approximately 70–140 g. Highly significant differences were recorded for both length ($P = 0.0002$, $N = 21$) and weight ($P = 0.0004$, $N = 21$) (paired t-tests) between annual passage and peak migration (Figure 2 and 3).

While mean size of eels increased from 1975 to 2002, within-year differences between annual and peak passage decreased (Table 2). In most years up to the midpoint of the series, mean length and weight were significantly smaller during peak migration than during annual passage. These trends started to change in the mid-1980s (Table 2). In 1988, mean length during peak migration surpassed 400 mm for the first time (401 ± 13 mm, 96.9 ± 9.4 g—95% CI), and in 1989, weight surpassed 100 g (458 ± 24 mm, 151.8 ± 23.3 g). Except for 1999, size has remained above these levels since 1993 and there have been no significant differences in mean size of eels between annual and peak passage. Mean length and weight have shown an increasing trend throughout the years.

Defining the Size of a Small Juvenile Eel

Overall mean length of eels in the 1970s (341 ± 3 mm—95% CI) was significantly smaller than in the 2000s (460 ± 6 mm) (Table 1). The midpoint between the upper 95% CL from the 1970s and the lower 95% CL from the 2000s was 399 mm (Figure 4A). Cusum analysis indicated the transitional period from small to large eels occurred in 1984–1988, a five-year period when cusum values changed minimally (Figure 4B). Annual mean length during the transitional period was 401 ± 13 mm. The average length of these two methods was 400 mm. Thus, we defined the separation criterion between smaller and larger eels ascending the ladder as under 400 mm. In addition, cusum analy-

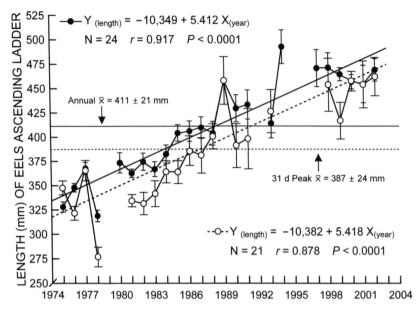

Figure 2. Relation of mean length of eels that ascended the ladder at Moses-Saunders Power Dam and year, 1975 to 2002, during annual passage (closed circles, solid regression line) and during the 31 d peak migration period (open circles, dashed regression line). Vertical bars are 95% confidence limits. Overall mean length and 95% confidence intervals (C. I.) are indicated.

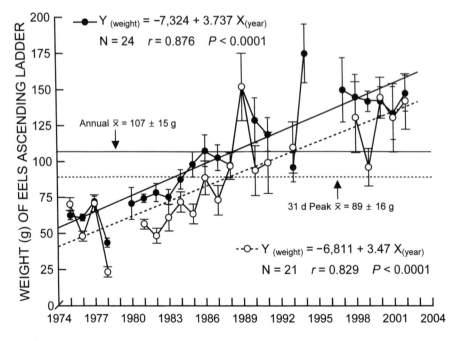

Figure 3. Relation of mean weight of eels that ascended the ladder at Moses-Saunders Power Dam and year, 1975 to 2002, during annual passage (closed circles, solid regression line) and during the 31 d peak migration period (open circles, dashed regression line). Vertical bars are 95% confidence limits. Overall mean length and 95% Confidence Intervals (CI) are indicated.

Table 2. Annual mean length and weight of eels ascending the ladder at Moses-Saunders Power Dam compared to mean size during the 31 day peak migration period. Two sample t-test was used to determine if means were significantly different. * = $P < 0.05$; ** = $P < 0.01$.

Year	N	Length (mm) Annual	Length (mm) Peak	P	Weight (g) Annual	Weight (g) Peak	P
1975	926	330	348	0.0003**	63	70	0.0107*
1976	1,202	348	322	0.0000**	61	48	0.0000**
1977	863	368	366	0.7186	72	71	0.7128
1978	939	319	277	0.0000**	44	23	0.0000**
1979							
1980	138	374			60		
1981	1,209	363	335	0.0000**	74	56	0.0000**
1982	375	375	332	0.0000**	78	48	0.0000**
1983	350	367	342	0.0010**	75	61	0.0073**
1984	250	383	364	0.0143*	88	72	0.0017**
1985	350	404	364	0.0000**	98	64	0.0000**
1986	275	406	386	0.0344*	108	89	0.0201*
1987	225	410	381	0.0082**	103	73	0.0001**
1988	84	404	401	0.7342	98	97	0.9297
1989	35		458			152	
1990	134	430	391	0.0085**	129	94	0.0034**
1991	71	434	398	0.0288*	119	99	0.1040
1992							
1993	77	414	427	0.3934	96	110	0.1703
1994	65	493			175		
1995							
1996							
1997	67	471			150		
1998	109	472	454	0.2845	145	131	0.4063
1999	496	465	417	0.0000**	142	96	0.0000**
2000	437[a]	457	458	0.9253	142	144	0.7799
2001	52	455	454	0.9794	134	130	0.8327
2002	152	469	462	0.5315	148	142	0.6211

[a] Weight calculated on a subsample of 226.

sis helped define the mean size of small and large eels ascending the ladder. From 1975 to 1983, prior to the transitional period, cusum values steadily decreased, indicating mean length of eels was less (355 ± 18 mm) than the overall mean (411 ± 21 mm). After the transitional period, cusum values steadily increased (1989–2002), indicating larger eels (456 ± 14 mm) than the overall mean.

Abundance of Small, Juvenile Eels Ascending the Ladder

Prior to transition, percent of small eels during peak migration was very high ($\bar{x} = 79.4 ± 6.9$ -95% CI), compared with the transitional period ($\bar{x} = 60.8 ± 13.9\%$) and the period after transition ($\bar{x} = 33.3 ± 7.8\%$) (differences were highly significant, $P < 0.0001$). In 1986,

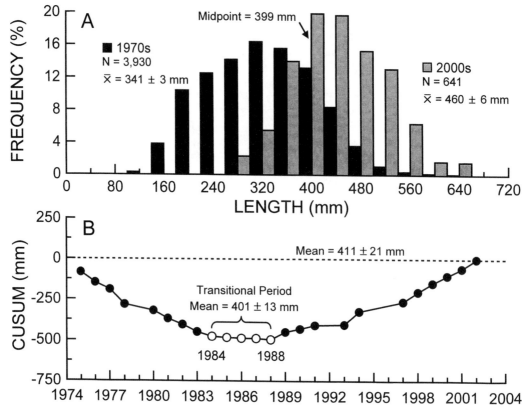

Figure 4. A – Length frequency distribution of eels that ascended the ladder at the Moses-Saunders Power Dam in the 1970s and 2000s. The boundary (399 mm) used to define a smaller, juvenile eel is the midpoint between the upper 95% confidence limit of the 1970s and the lower 95% confidence limit of the 2000s. **B** – Cusum analysis of mean length by year, 1975 to 2002. Transitional period between smaller and larger eels is indicated, 1984 to 1988 ($\bar{x}$ length = 401 mm). Average of **A** and **B** is taken as the separation criterion (<400 mm). Sample size (*N*), means, and 95% CI are indicated.

percent of small eels dropped to 55.2%, and by 1988, the percent of small eels fell below 50% for the first time (46.6%). Since 1993, small eels have accounted for fewer than 34% of all eels during peak passage, and by 2002, they represented only 18% (Table 3).

From 1975 to 2002, there was a highly significant declining trend in the annual percent of small eels under 400 mm ascending the ladder during peak migration ($P < 0.0001$, $R^2 = 0.750$, $N = 21$).

Regression equation:

<400 mm $_{(peak\ period\ \%)}$ = 5218.4 – 2.598$x_{(year)}$

By applying the percent of small eels to the 31-d peak migration index, a new index of small juvenile recruitment was developed (Table 3; Figure 5). In 1982 and 1983, the peak years of the ladder index, 86% and 78%, respectively, of all eels ascending the ladder during peak migration were under 400 mm in length. This calculates to 23,531 and 20,718 small eels per day, respectively. Most recently, from 1998 to 2002, the number of small eels ascending the ladder per day ranged from 4 to 13 (18–33%).

Table 3. Index of small eels (<400 mm) ascending the ladder per day at Moses-Saunders Power Dam during the 31-d peak migration period. Percent (%) of small eels measured in subsamples was applied to total number per day to calculate Index (N) and calculate the regression of percent by year. CI = confidence interval.

Year	Index (N)	% of Total	% Predicted by Regression		
			Regression	95% CI	Residual
1975	10,932	75.9	88.1	11.0	−12.2
1976	8,633	83.3	85.5	10.4	−2.2
1977	12,248	61.2	82.9	9.8	−21.7
1978	15,428	93.8	80.3	9.3	13.5
1979[a]	14,754		77.7		
1980[a]	6,798		75.1		
1981	11,547	83.7	72.5	7.7	11.2
1982	23,531	85.7	69.9	7.3	15.7
1983	20,718	78.4	67.3	6.9	11.1
1984	10,716	71.2	64.7	6.6	6.5
1985	13,513	73.0	62.1	6.3	10.9
1986	2,970	55.2	59.5	6.1	−4.3
1987	5,380	58.0	56.9	6.0	1.1
1988	2,536	46.6	54.3	6.0	−7.7
1989	991	17.1	51.7	6.0	−34.6
1990	1,957	63.2	49.1	6.2	14.1
1991	668	54.5	46.5	6.4	8.0
1992[a]	122		43.9		
1993	69	29.6	41.3	7.0	−11.7
1994[a]	1,939		38.7		
1995[a]	243		36.1		
1996[b]			33.5		
1997[a]	45		30.9		
1998	13	22.2	28.3	9.4	−6.1
1999	9	33.3	25.7	10.0	7.6
2000	11	24.2	23.1	10.6	1.1
2001	4	20.0	20.5	11.2	−0.5
2002	10	18.3	17.9	11.9	0.4

[a] Regression used to calculate index.
[b] No data collected.

Relationship Between Number and Size of Eels

Between 1975 and 2002, there was a highly significant relationship ($R^2 = 0.636$, $P < 0.0001$, $N = 21$) between length and $\log_{(10)}$ number of eels ascending the ladder per day during peak migration. As the number of eels dramatically declined from the 1970s to 2000s, the length of eels significantly increased.

Regression relationship:

$$\text{Length}_{(peakperiod)} = 511.89 - 37.28 \times \log \text{Ladder}_{(number)}$$

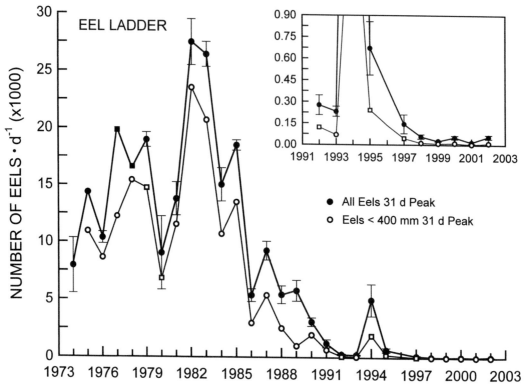

Figure 5. Number of eels/d (closed circles) and number of small eels/d (<400 mm—open circles) that ascended the ladder at the Moses-Saunders Power Dam, Cornwall, Ontario, during the 31-d peak migration period, 1974 to 2002. The 95% confidence limits are indicated. Daily counts were not available for 1977 and 1978 (closed square), so peak migration was estimated (Casselman et al. 1997a). For years in which size data were not available, number of small eels/d (open squares) were calculated using the regression of percent small by year (Table 3).

Discussion

Dramatic declines in numbers of eels ascending the ladder at the Moses-Saunders Power Dam, Cornwall, Ontario, coincided with a significant increase in length and weight ($P < 0.0001$), indicating a loss of smaller juveniles. While eel numbers decreased by more than 3 orders of magnitude (1982–2001), mean length and weight during annual passage increased by 35% and 139%, respectively, from the 1970s to the 2000s. During the 31-d peak migration period, increases of 38% (length) and 158% (weight) were recorded (Table 1). With each successive decade, the variability in size decreased (CV), thus fewer small eels were seen ascending the ladder.

From 1975 to 2002, eels were significantly smaller during peak migration than during annual passage (length—$P = 0.0002$, weight—$P = 0.0004$). Thus, small eels migrated up the upper St. Lawrence River to Lake Ontario during the peak migration period more often than at other times of the year. This may be related to seasonal trends in water temperature (Liew 1982), with the greatest activity by small eels occurring during the warmest period. Although mean size was significantly smaller during peak migration compared with annual passage, both showed significant increasing trends over time (Figure 2 and 3). Examination of annual changes, however, indicated that as size increased, significant differences between peak migration and annual passage decreased, further indicating the loss of the smallest eels (Table 2).

Classifying small, juvenile eels provided an additional tool to examine and understand recruitment dynamics. The average of two methods was used to develop a separation criterion (<400 mm) for smaller and larger eels that ascend the ladder. From 1975 to 2002, the percent of eels classified as small during peak migration declined significantly over time ($P < 0.0001$). When eel passage was high, percent of small eels ascending the ladder was very high, and vice versa.

Continued refinement of the ladder index improves our understanding of recruitment dynamics. The ladder index of annual passage provided an estimate of total eel recruitment to the upper St. Lawrence River and Lake Ontario stock. Standardization of this index increased precision by providing an estimate of mean daily recruitment to the stock during the 31-d peak migration period (Casselman et al. 1997a; Marcogliese et al. 1997). The new index of small eels during peak migration is a further refinement because it removes some of the age bias. Small eels are of similar age and younger (Liew 1982; Casselman 2003), thus providing an index more indicative of early recruitment.

The small juvenile recruitment index confirmed that small eels constituted the majority of eels in the 31-d period of peak migration (Figure 5). The loss of small eels has not only caused the dramatic decline in numbers but is now shifting the seasonal distribution of eels ascending the ladder. Historically, at the start of migration (usually late May to early June) larger eels ascended the ladder first, followed in July and August by very large numbers of smaller eels during the peak period. Often a very small pulse of larger eels ascended the ladder in late September and early October. McGrath et al. (2003) reported this fall pulse post 1996, however, it is common throughout most of the annual ladder index. Historically, the fall pulse was minute in comparison to the midsummer peak period and was often difficult to detect. For example, in 1982, the summer mode represented 84.1% of total passage (27,489/d), while the fall pulse represented only 1.9% of total passage (1,026/d). Recently, the midsummer mode of small eels has declined so dramatically that the small pulse of larger eels in the fall has become more prominent and may soon become the peak run. In 2002, the midsummer mode represented 64.3% of total passage, while the fall mode represented 20.5%. At first glance, it appears that the fall pulse is increasing, but numbers of eel/d confirm that both the summer peak (55.2/d) and the fall pulse (13.7/d) have virtually collapsed. The significant decline of small recruits from more than 20,000/d during peak migration (1980s), to <15/d most recently (Table 3; Figure 5) forewarns of the complete collapse of the upper St. Lawrence River and Lake Ontario stock.

Several hypotheses might explain the dramatic decrease in numbers and the subsequent loss of small eels. These include changes to growth rate, ladder efficiency, count reliability, and migration barriers.

Preliminary analysis of size-at-age data indicates that growth rate of eels has not increased and thus does not explain the loss of small recruits ascending the ladder (Casselman et al. 1997a; Marcogliese et al. 1997). If growth rate had increased, one would expect to see high densities or pulses of larger eels but of similar age, as in the past. In 1975, mean age of eels was 6 years and the modal age was 5 years (Liew 1976, unpublished report). From 1975 to 1978, eels smaller than 400 mm ranged in age from 2 to 8 years, and eels between 400 and 475 mm were 8–11 years (Liew 1982). More recently, Casselman (2003) reported that eels from the 1990s were larger and older (493 ± 17 mm, 11.9 ± 1.1 year—95% CI) than eels from the 1970s and 1980s (363 ± 15 mm, 5.6 ±

0.1 year). These results are very similar to size-at-age results reported by Liew (1982). Thus, the loss of small eels cannot be explained by increased growth rate.

We believe the eel ladder and index continue to function reliably. The ladder is located in ice-sluice 1, which was selected because it was unused and because large numbers of eels congregated there in the 1970s, attracted by relatively low current velocity (Ontario Hydro and OMNR 1986). Since 1981, there have been no major modifications or design changes to the ladder that would affect the number or size of eels that ascend it. From 1974 to1981, OMNR conducted extensive tests on the prototype wooden ladder, and modifications were made that maximized eel movement and efficiency and reduced operating problems and cost. Studies encompassed aspects such as slope of the trough; water depth, velocity, and discharge; vegetation type; shape of entrance chute; number of resting boxes; and shade (Eckersley 1982). By the late 1970s, Liew (1982) reported the efficiency of the ladder was very high, as eels ascended the ladder almost immediately upon reaching the dam. Knowledge gained during the experimentation period was incorporated into the permanent aluminum ladder, which was installed in 1980–1981 (Eckersley 1982) and is still operational today.

Methods used to count eels have varied from indirect estimates to direct counts. Casselman et al. (1997a) provide a more detailed description of eel-ladder operations and counting methodologies. For indirect counting methods, protocols were revised through the years to increase accuracy of the estimate, and direct verification of numbers was conducted (Vladykov et al. 1975, unpublished; Liew 1975, 1977, unpublished report; Martel 1979, 1987; Schraeder 1980, unpublished report; Mack 1983, unpublished report). For a 10-year period, an electronic eel counter provided direct counts that were validated with manual counts. Occasionally, however, direct counts were affected by pump failures, maintenance and repairs, or problems installing the electronic counter, which mainly occurred during the start of the operating season (Gauthier 1988, unpublished; Mack 1983, unpublished report; Aubry 1989, 1990, unpublished reports; Kentell 1993, 1994, unpublished). Standardization of the ladder index to the 31-d peak migration period eliminated the influence of start-up and most operational problems on the index (Casselman et al. 1997a).

Barriers to upstream migration cannot explain the dramatic decline in numbers or the increased size of eels ascending the ladder and the reduction of small eels. Barriers to migration are in the form of temporary traps used during studies, as well as permanent dams, canals, and locks.

Eel traps fished at the base of the Moses-Saunders Dam did not intercept small eels before they could reach the ladder. From 1997 to 2001, the New York Power Authority (NYPA) conducted eel-passage studies at the dam. Eel traps were fished along the base of the dam and in and around ice-sluices close to the ladder. The traps consisted of an elevated trough with water flow at the entrance, with a net at the exit chute. Currents created by these traps were designed to simulate potential passage upstream, similar to the eel ladder. Length data indicated that small eels were not being intercepted by these traps (= 449–473 mm, N = 11,807) (Milieu 1999, 2003). Eels caught in these traps were similar in size to eels ascending the ladder (Figure, 2, Table 2), which also verifies that the ladder had not inadvertently become selective toward larger eels.

Permanent barriers to upstream migration have not been constructed on the St. Lawrence River since the 1960s, and existing dams, canals, and locks did not selectively barricade small eels. It was generally thought that the construction of the St. Lawrence Seaway reduced the number of eels reaching the upper St. Lawrence River and Lake Ontario (Kolenosky and Hendry 1982). Prior to installation of ladders, eels must have used canals and locks to bypass the dams. This was not an efficient passage system, because thousands of eels of varied size congregated at the base of the Moses-Saunders Dam each year before the ladder was installed (Liew 1982).

Verdon and Desrochers (2003) reported a significant correlation between the Moses-Saunders annual-passage index and lock usage below Beauharnois Dam the previous year. On that basis, they suggested that decreased lock usage below Beauharnois Dam, Quebec, 80 km downstream from Moses-Saunders (Figure 1) may have reduced upstream migration and affected eel counts at Moses-Saunders Dam. Tagging studies, however, indicated that most PIT-tagged eels that were released by the Beauharnois Dam did not pass both dams in less than three migrating seasons (Verdon and Desrochers 2003). Thus, while lock usage plays a role in upstream eel migration, a decrease in use the previous year most likely does not significantly affect eel counts at the Moses-Saunders eel ladder. Verdon and Desrochers (2003) acknowledge that reduction in lock usage alone cannot account for the very large reduction in eel counts at Moses-Saunders Dam. If decreased lock usage had a significant impact on counts, it suggests that small eels are selectively blocked. This did not occur, however, as large congregations of small eels were not accumulating below the Beauharnois Dam. Between 1994 and 2001, to facilitate migration, eels were trapped below Beauharnois and transported upstream (approximately 5,000–25,000/year). Length data for five years between 1994 and 1999 indicated that mean size of trapped and transported eels was large, ranging from 440 to 484 mm ($N = 36,773$) (Milieu 1999; Verdon and Desrochers 2003).

To further aid in upstream eel migration, two eel ladders have recently been installed at the Beauharnois Dam. In 2002, the first ladder was operational and annual passage was 10,503 eels. In 2003, the second ladder was installed and operational. Total annual passage of the two ladders in 2003 was 30,149 eels. PIT-tagging studies indicate that it is too early to determine the effects of eel ladders at Beauharnois on eel ladder counts at Moses-Saunders (Verdon and Desrochers 2003). To date, however, the transport of eels upstream between 1994 and 2001 has not made a noticeable difference in eel counts at Moses-Saunders (Figure 5). Thus, the annual passage of 10,000 and 30,000 eels in 2002 and 2003 by ladders at Beauharnois Dam will likely have little impact either. To put this into perspective, the most recent substantial pulse of eels ascending the ladder at Moses-Saunders Dam occurred in 1994. In that year, the ladder passed 4,998 eels/d during the 31 d peak migration period and total passage exceeded 163,000 eels. Presently, all indications suggest extremely low densities of the smallest and youngest eels.

Eel ladder indices are a valuable management tool. The 31 d peak migration index is a consistent predictor of eel movement up the upper St. Lawrence River into Lake Ontario. It is highly correlated with commercial electrofishing and harvest in the upper St. Lawrence River and Lake Ontario, and index trawling in the Bay of Quinte (Casselman et al. 1997b). These indices have shown the same declines in eel abundance, which has fallen to such a low level that a viable commercial fishery no longer exists.

The new index of small eels is an important subcomponent of the 31-d peak migration period. It indicates changes in abundance of younger eels (<400 mm), which may be a first signal of changes in recruitment from the Sargasso Sea, and changes in abundance of older eels that have been in the St. Lawrence River system for a number of years (>400 mm). For example, data for 2003 indicated a decrease in the number of eels ascending the ladder (40 ± 10 / d—95% CI) compared to 2002 (55 ± 14 / d). From 2002–2003, the index of small eels ascending the ladder was almost identical, decreasing from 10 to 9 eels/d, while the remainder of the decrease was attributed to larger eels. This indicates that not only are small recruits decreasing, but now larger eels may be decreasing at a more dramatic rate. To maintain this level of analysis, we need to maintain these ladder indices and look for small eels as a first signal of recruitment success and failure. In addition, to further understand recruitment dynamics, we need more detailed data regarding age of eels ascending the ladder.

Acknowledgments

We thank the many field technicians who worked for the Ontario Ministry of Natural Resources (formerly the Department of Lands and Forests) collecting and maintaining massive amounts of data over the past 30 years. We are especially indebted to Mike Eckersley, who was for many years the keeper of the historical data. We thank Kevin McGrath and the New York Power Authority, who provided some of the more recent size data. Compilation and acquisition of data and reports that cover an extensive time period is difficult. We thank the people who aided in the acquisition process. We thank Yves de Lafontaine, Roy Stein, and Thomas Pratt, who provided constructive reviews of the manuscript. Finally, we thank Environment Canada for providing the initial funds for this research through the Ecological Monitoring and Assessment Network (EMAN).

References

Anonymous. 1996. Statistix: users' manual, version 1.0 for Windows. Analytical Software, St. Paul, Minnesota.

Casselman, J. M. 2003. Dynamics of resources of the American eel, *Anguilla rostrata*: declining abundance in the 1990s. Pages 255–274 *in* K. Aida, K. Tsukamoto and K. Yamauchi, editors. Eel biology. Springer-Verlag, Tokyo.

Casselman, J. M., L. A. Marcogliese, and P. V. Hodson. 1997a. Recruitment index for the upper St. Lawrence River and Lake Ontario eel stock: a re-examination of eel passage at the R. H. Saunders Hydroelectric Generating Station at Cornwall, Ontario, 1974–1995. Pages 161–169 *in* R. H. Peterson, editor. The American eel in eastern Canada: stock status and management strategies. Canadian Technical Report of Fisheries and Aquatic Sciences no. 2196.

Casselman, J. M., L. A. Marcogliese, T. J. Stewart, and P. V. Hodson. 1997b. Status of the upper St. Lawrence River and Lake Ontario eel stock–1996. Pages 106–120 *in* R. H. Peterson, editor. The American eel in eastern Canada: stock status and management strategies. Canadian Technical Report of Fisheries and Aquatic Sciences no. 2196.

Eckersley, M. J. 1982. Operation of the eel ladder at the Moses-Saunders Generating Station, Cornwall 1974–1979. Pages 4–7 *in* K. H. Loftus, editor. Proceedings of the 1980 North American Eel Conference. Ontario Fisheries Technical Report Series No. 4.

Kolenosky, D. P., and M. J. Hendry. 1982. The Canadian Lake Ontario fishery for American eel (*Anguilla rostrata*). Pages 8–16 *in* K. H. Loftus, editor. Proceedings of the 1980 North American Eel Conference. Ontario Fisheries Technical Report Series No. 4.

Liew, P. K. L. 1982. Impact of the eel ladder on the upstream migrating eel (*Anguilla rostrata*) population in the St. Lawrence River at Cornwall: 1974–1978. Pages 17–22 *in* K. H. Loftus, editor. Proceedings of the 1980 North American Eel Conference. Ontario Fisheries Technical Report Series No. 4.

Marcogliese, L. A., and J. M. Casselman. 1998. Scale methods of discriminating between Great Lakes stocks of wild and hatchery rainbow trout, *Oncorhynchus mykiss*, and a measure of natural recruitment in Lake Ontario North American Journal of Fisheries Management 18:253–268.

Marcogliese, L. A., J. M. Casselman, and P. V. Hodson. 1997. Dramatic declines in recruitment of American eel (*Anguilla rostrata*) entering Lake Ontario–long-term trends, causes and effects. Manuscript report. Ontario Ministry of Natural Resources, Picton.

Martel, R. G. 1987. Operation of the R. H. Saunders Generating station eel ladder, 1982 to 1986. Ontario Ministry of Natural Resources, Cornwall District.

McGrath, K. J., D. Desrochers, C. Fleury, and J. W. Dembeck, IV. 2003. Studies of upstream migrant American eels at the Moses-Saunders Power Dam on the St. Lawrence River near Massena, New York. Pages 153–166 *in* D. A. Dixon, editor. Biology, management, and protection of catadromous eels. American Fisheries Society, Symposium 33, Bethesda, Maryland.

Milieu, Inc. 1999. 1999 upstream and PIT tag detection studies. Preliminary report to New York Power Authority. Milieu Inc, Laprairie, Quebec.

Milieu, Inc. 2003. Investigation of release locations for upstream migrating American eel at the Robert Moses Power Dam. Report to New York Power Authority. Milieu Inc., Laprairie, Quebec.

Ontario Hydro and Ontario Ministry of Natural Resources. 1986. Robert H. Saunders-St. Lawrence Generating Station. Pamphlet. Ontario Hydro, Cornwall, Ontario.

Reid, D. A. 1981. Design of a replacement eel ladder at the R. H. Saunders Generating Station, Cornwall, Ontario. Presented at the 22nd annual meeting of The Canadian Society of Environmental Biologists, Montreal. Underwood McLellan, Rexdale, Ontario.

Seelbach, P. W., and G. E. Whelan. 1988. Identification and contribution of wild and hatchery steelhead stocks in Lake Michigan tributaries. Transactions of the American Fisheries Society 117:444–451.

Verdon, R., and D. Desrochers. 2003. Upstream migratory movements of American eel *Anguilla rostrata* between the Beauharnois and Moses-Saunders Power Dams on the St. Lawrence River. Pages 139–151 *in* D. A. Dixon, editor. Biology, management, and protection of catadromous eels. American Fisheries Society, Symposium 33, Bethesda, Maryland.

Whitfield, R. E., and D. P. Kolenosky. 1978. Prototype eel ladder in the St. Lawrence River. Progressive Fish-Culturist 40:152–154.

Decline of the American Eel in the St. Lawrence River: Effects of Local Hydroclimatic Conditions on CPUE Indices

YVES DE LAFONTAINE[1]

*Centre Saint-Laurent, Environnement Canada
105 McGill Street, Montréal, Québec H2Y 2E7, Canada*

MICHEL LAGACÉ

Parc Aquarium du Québec, 1675 des Hôtels, Ste-Foy, Québec G1W 4S3, Canada

FERNAND GINGRAS

138 rue du Pont, Saint-Nicolas, Québec G7A 2T2, Canada

DENIS LABONTÉ, FRANÇOIS MARCHAND, AND EDITH LACROIX

*Centre Saint-Laurent, Environnement Canada
105 McGill Street, Montréal, Québec H2Y 2E7, Canada*

Abstract.—Changes in abundance, seasonal occurrence, and mean size of American eels *Anguilla rostrata* in the lower St. Lawrence River during the past 50 years were examined. Catch per unit effort indices were calculated from daily catch records of eels captured in an experimental trap fishery and from the personal logbooks of a knowledgeable fisher. These two indices indicated a significant declining trend in eel catch rate by more than 50% since the early 1970s. Interannual fluctuations in catch rate were not related to variability in water level or water temperature. The timing of eel occurrence varied significantly between years and was inversely correlated to water level in August and September. It is hypothesized that eel movement is strongly determined by climatic/hydrological conditions in the previous summer. The average weight of eels has increased by 30% over the past eight years. The decline in catch rate and the increase in mean size of migratory silver eels in recent years are interpreted as the most significant symptoms of low recruitment levels and the precursor signal that the eel fishery in the lower St. Lawrence River may not be sustainable in the near future.

Introduction

Fishing for American eels *Anguilla rostrata* during their seaward migration is one of the main traditional activities of people living along the St. Lawrence River in the province of Québec (Canada) since the early days of colonization (Montpetit 1897; Casselman 2003). During the 20th century, eel fishing developed into an important and very lucrative fishery in the river, as well as in other areas along the Atlantic coast of North America. Catches and number of fishers gradually

[1] Corresponding author: Yves.DeLafontaine@ec.gc.ca

increased during that time (Robitaille et al. 2003). Eel landings in Québec, officially recorded since 1920, peaked at just over 1,000 t per year between 1933 and 1935 during the Great Depression. At the end of the Second World War, annual landings dropped below 250 t but climbed again in the late 1950s and remained relatively stable, between 300 and 600 t (mean = 445), during the 1960s and 1970s.

Signs of a decline were first noted during the 1980s (Castonguay et al. 1994a), and landings have continued to decrease, dropping below 300 t in 1992 and below 200 t since 1999. Consequently, there has been a gradual reduction of the number of fishers and fishing effort in the lower reaches of the St. Lawrence River since the 1950s. Although eel fishing depended largely on socio-economic pressure in the past, the very recent decline represents an unprecedented and historical minimum in Québec landings. Declines in American eels were also reported in other rivers along the east coast of North America during the late 1980s and early 1990s, reinforcing the signal first observed in the St. Lawrence River (Richkus and Whalen 2000). Because only female eels occur in the Great Lakes–St. Lawrence River system, this unprecedented decline in catches raises concern about conservation of the species.

The causes of the recent decline remain unclear and highly speculative. Castonguay et al. (1994b) hypothesized that in addition to habitat loss and pollution, changes in oceanic larval transport contributed to recruitment failures, which have exacerbated the decline in eel catches in recent years. An analysis of long-term variations in eel landings in the Great Lakes–St. Lawrence River system led Robitaille et al. (2003) to identify recruitment overfishing as the principal cause of decline. Precise estimates of eel abundance for the St. Lawrence River are nonetheless lacking, and the rate of the population decline over past decades has remained largely unquantified.

The various fishing gears used in the different fishing areas and changes in fishing effort among areas over time have hindered development and validation of a catch-per-unit-effort (CPUE) index for estimating eel abundance in Québec. The lack of adequate CPUE estimates and the decline in landings, concomitant with the reduced number of fishers, render the analysis of the declining patterns difficult (Robitaille et al. 2003). In the absence of eel population estimates, Castonguay et al. (1994b) used the number of eels captured at the Saint-Nicolas experimental weir fishery operated by the Parc Aquarium du Québec, near Québec City, as the only abundance index of the St. Lawrence River migratory eel. Annual eel catches recorded since 1971 at this site indicated a slight decline from 1987 to 1992. The validity of this data series for long-term monitoring and assessment of eel status remains untested, however.

The effects of various environmental factors, principally water level, moonlight, temperature, and turbidity, on seaward migratory behaviour of eels are relatively well documented (Lowe 1952; Vollestad et al. 1986; Vollestad et al. 1994; Parker and McCleave 1997; Cairns and Hooley 2003). Rivers are usually dynamic systems that vary substantially from year to year in response to climatic fluctuations that could, theoretically, make eel abundance estimates more variable. Surprisingly, however, the influence of hydrological and environmental conditions on eel catches has been largely ignored or was presumed to be negligible in previous analyses of annual fluctuations in eel fisheries. Annual discharge and water levels of the St. Lawrence River are characterized by long-term cyclic changes showing positive autocorrelation with 26-year lags (Hudon 1997). The influence of this long-term variation on the eel decline has not been investigated. The lack of adequate time series for abundance and other population characteristics of eels largely impeded the testing of hypotheses on the causes of decline and on the potential link between environmental conditions and the seaward migratory behaviour and abundance of eels in the river.

This study examines long-term variations in abundance and individual size of American eels in the lower St. Lawrence River by comparing daily catches of eels recorded at the Saint-Nicolas experimental weir fishery with those of commercial fishing gear. Our first objective was to use CPUE indices derived from both experimental and commercial fisheries data to quantify the level of variability and the rate of change in abundance and size of eels between 1944 and 2002. A second objective was to test the effect of hydrological variability on total catches and migratory patterns of eels in the lower river to determine whether this factor significantly influenced the decline. Finally, we assessed the appropriateness of the Saint-Nicolas experimental weir fishery for long-term monitoring of eel status in the river.

Methods

Study Area

The St. Lawrence River is the main outflow of the Laurentian Great Lakes and extends over 500 km from the downstream end of Lake Ontario to the St. Lawrence Estuary (Environment Canada 1996). At its downstream end, between Trois-Rivières and Québec City, the river comes under the progressive influence of semidiurnal tides, which generate high daily water-level variability (tidal range up to 4.5 m at Québec City) and current reversal, but its water remains entirely fresh (Godin 1979; El-Sabh and Silverberg 1990). Daily discharge at the outflow (Québec City) varies between 8,500 and 24,000 $m^3 \cdot s^{-1}$ throughout the year, with an annual mean of 12,600 m^3/s (Bouchard and Morin 2000). Water level and flow have been regulated since 1960 by hydropower dams in the upper river. The fluvial sector near Québec City (Figure 1) has always been an important fishing site for the American eel (Robitaille and Tremblay 1994), mainly because the river constricts there to a width of <1 km. The area is somewhat comparable to a counting fence through which all eels from the river basin must pass during their seaward migration, thus offering an excellent opportunity for eel monitoring.

Experimental Weir Fishery Data

We compiled the number of eels captured at the Saint-Nicolas experimental weir fishery since 1971. Data on daily catches have been compiled since 1975, whereas only total annual catch data are available for 1971–1974. The fishery is located on the south shore of the river (46°44.49'N; 71°17.75'W), approximately 500 m upstream from the Québec City bridge (Figure 1). The gear is set each year to provide live specimens of fish to the Parc Aquarium du Québec, and its location and operation have remained unchanged since 1971.

The eel weir consists of a box trap at the end of a 95-m leader line running perpendicular to the shoreline. The leader line is made of a 1½-inch mesh net attached to vertical posts equally spaced and held in place by cables and ropes. The height of the vertical net attached at the bottom is adjusted to reach the surface at high tide (4.3 m maximum). The box trap is a closed square wooden frame covered by a 1½-inch wire-mesh net and has one opening at its junction with the leader line, permitting fish to enter the trap. A liner made of ¾-inch wire-mesh net is set between the 0-m and 1-m marks along the inside side walls of the box trap. Wing nets made of netting similar to the leader line are attached to each of the two corners of the trap facing the shore and extend 10 m from

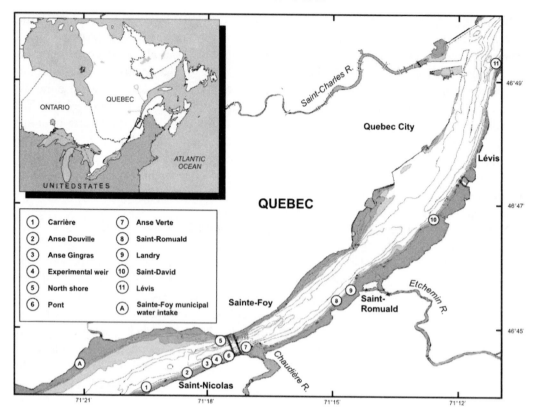

Figure 1. Map of the St. Lawrence River near Québec City and location of eel-fishing weirs referred to in this study.

the trap. The box trap is positioned directly on the bottom just below the daily low-tide line to ensure that the bottom of the trap remains in the water.

Between 15 May and 31 October each year, the trap was visited twice daily at every low tide, and the number of individuals of every fish species captured was recorded. Daily eel catch was obtained by adding up the number of fish captured during the two visits; total annual catch corresponded to the addition of all daily catches over the entire fishery operation. Eels from three to five daily catches each week were individually measured for total length (±1 mm) and total body weight (±1 g) in the sampling years 1994, 1995, 1999, 2000, and 2002, following the protocol of de Lafontaine et al. (2001).

Commercial Weir Fisheries Data

Daily records of eels captured in commercial weirs for 29 years between 1944 and 1998 were compiled from the personal logbooks of Fernand Gingras, who fished for eels in the Québec City area. Data were obtained from 10 different weir sites between Saint-Nicolas and Lévis, separated by a distance of ~15 km (Figure 1). The number of weirs deployed in any year ranged from one to four, yielding a total of 81 weir-catch data sets. Design of the commercial weirs was similar to the Saint-Nicolas experimental weir, but without the smaller mesh size used for the inside liner of the box trap. Each weir was adapted to its specific location by adjusting the length and height of the leader line, depending on the width and slope of the shore. Since these fixed gears were not modified and were set at the same location year after year, they were assumed to represent a relatively constant and standard effort over space and time. Although the fishing season usually started in July or August, catch data for each weir were recorded from 1 September until early November, when fishing normally ceased.

In 56 of the 81 weir data sets, daily catches were recorded as the sum of the number of eels captured during the two daily weir visits. In the remaining cases, only weekly records or the cumulative catch expressed in both terms of total number and total biomass of eels captured were available. The annual CPUE index thus corresponded to the total number of eels captured after 1 September each year. From 1977–1983, only the total annual biomass of eels was recorded for the Saint-Romuald site; total annual catch at that site was therefore estimated from the relationship between annual total biomass and annual total catch at other locations during the same time. Personal logbooks were not available for 1947–1963, 1971–1976, and 1984. Catches for 1970 were excluded from the analysis because a ban on eel consumption due to mercury contamination halted commercial fishing activities early in the season.

Mean individual weight (nearest g) of eels in commercial weirs was estimated by dividing the total biomass by the total number of eels captured in a specific weir during a given fishing year. These estimates and those from the experimental weir were used to examine variation in eel size.

Historical Commercial Landings Data

Annual landings of eels and total number of eel fishers along the St. Lawrence River were provided by the Ministère de la Faune et des Parcs du Québec (FAPAQ) for 1920–1992 and by the Ministère de l'Agriculture, des Pêcheries et de l'Alimentation du Québec for 1993–2002.

Data from 1941 were missing. Fishing conditions were unusual in 1970, 1971, and 1985 because of mercury and mirex contamination, so those years were excluded from the data set (see Robitaille et Tremblay 1994).

Environmental Data

Data on water level and flow in the St. Lawrence River since 1944 were supplied by the Canadian Hydrological Service, Environment Canada. Daily water flow ($m^3 \cdot s^{-1}$) at the outflow at Québec City was estimated using an algorithm computing the sum of daily discharge measured at the Beauharnois hydropower dam (upstream from Montreal) and that of the various tributaries emptying into the river between Beauharnois and Québec City (Bouchard and Morin 2000). This estimation is necessary because the reversing tidal currents make it difficult to measure daily water flow at Québec City. Daily water level was measured at Jetty No.1 in the Port of Montreal, because this gauging station is unaffected by tides. Measured daily water level at Jetty No.1 and calculated daily water flow at Québec City were strongly correlated during the ice-free period (Pearson correlation coefficients [r] varied between 0.91 and 0.96 for each month between April and November), indicating that instantaneous water level is a good surrogate for discharge in the river. Actual measurements of water level were thus used in our analysis.

Since May 1977, daily water temperature (°C) has been recorded at the John Labatt Brewery water intake, located upstream from the Lachine Rapids at Montreal in the main channel of the river. Temperature was initially monitored with a mercury thermometer, and an electronic thermometer has been used in recent years. This data series was validated against daily water temperature recorded since 1986 at the municipal drinking water intake on the north shore at Sainte-Foy, 4.4 km upstream from the Saint-

Nicolas experimental weir fishery (Figure 1). The temperature at Montreal was generally 1°C warmer than that measured at Sainte-Foy, but temporal fluctuations were virtually identical at the two stations, indicating a similar temperature signal. The longer data series from the Montreal station was therefore used in our analysis. Monthly averages of both hydrological and temperature data were calculated for each year of data.

Data Analysis

Total catch was taken as an index of catch per unit effort (CPUE) for each weir in each year. Because catch records from commercial weirs started on 1 September, daily catches from the experimental weir fishery were divided into summer (15 May to 31 August) and fall (1 September to 31 October), providing two seasonal CPUE indices for each year. This allowed the experimental weir fall CPUE and the commercial CPUE to be compared for the same fishing season. To minimize the effect of potential spatial variability (due to the various weir locations) in trend analysis, standardized CPUE (SCPUE) was calculated by dividing the annual CPUE by the average CPUE for the entire time series of records for each weir.

Annual trends in environmental variables and eel abundance (CPUE, SCPUE) were first assessed by visual inspection of the data and by performing Pearson correlation analysis between each parameter and year. Whenever applicable, linear regression or second-order polynomial regression models between CPUE and year were fitted and annual residuals were calculated to remove any long-term trend in CPUE indices. Long-term variability in commercial-weir CPUE was tested by comparing mean CPUE of all weirs over five-year intervals (1975–1979, 1980–1984, and so on) by means of analysis of variance (ANOVA) and nonparametric Kruskall-Wallis test. Between-sites comparison of the pattern of temporal variability in eel abundance was tested by Spearman correlation analysis using the differences in SCPUE between two consecutive years for each weir. Significant correlation coefficients between two weirs would indicate a similar pattern of interannual variability in catches at these two sites.

The relationship between mean monthly values of water level, water flow and water temperature between May and October was tested by Pearson correlation analysis in adjusting the probability level by the Dunn-Sidak method to correct for multiple comparisons (Sokal and Rohlf 1995). Given the expected correlation between water level and temperature, the relative influence of these two variables on the interannual fluctuations in eel abundance (either CPUE or residual values) was tested by stepwise multiple regression analysis, using the monthly means of hydrological variables and water temperature from May to November as independent variables.

For each weir and each year of data, we plotted the cumulative frequency of daily eel abundance as a function of time and determined the dates when 10%, 50% and 90% of the cumulative annual catch was recorded. The median date of capture (i.e., 50% of total catch) was used as an index of the seasonal timing of eel occurrence. This index is often assumed to represent the migratory timing of migrating species (Leggett and Whitney 1972; Robards and Quinn 2002). Duration of the eel migration in each year was estimated by calculating the number of days between the dates at which 10% and 90% of total catch was captured. Stepwise multiple regression analysis was performed to detect significant interactions between environmental variables and eel migratory timing and duration. Synchronism in daily catches at the various fishing sites was assessed by a Kolmogorov-Smirnov (K-S) two-sample test on the time series of daily catches from paired sites for each year. The D-statistic from the K-S test was used as an index of similarity in catch patterns between pairs of weirs and was correlated with geographic distance between the two weirs and environmental variables to determine whether synchronism in eel catches was affected by these factors.

Within-year and year-to-year variation in mean length and weight of eels captured at the Saint-Nicolas experimental weir between 1994 and 2002 was tested by two-way factorial ANOVA. We also used a Kolmogorov-Smirnov two-sample test to test for interannual difference in size-frequency distribution. The parameters of the eel weight-length relationship were estimated by fitting a power function model (W = a · L^b) using the NLIN regression procedure in SAS. Model residuals were computed and tested by one-way ANOVA (year effect) to assess differences between years in the length-weight relationship. All statistical analyses were performed with the SAS system package for Windows.

Results

Experimental Weir Fishery

The total number of eels caught at the Saint-Nicolas experimental weir between 1971 and 2002 declined significantly (Figure 2a). After reaching a peak of 597 in 1972, catches continuously declined through the 1980s to a minimum of 187 in 1989. This corresponded to a three-fold difference in 17 years. Catches remained low in the early 1990s but have fluctuated more widely since 1998, with catches in 1999, 2001 and 2002 as high as those observed prior to 1980. Because of the high catches observed in recent years, the long-term variation in eel captures was better predicted by a second-order polynomial relationship (CPUE = 594.67 − 32.43 year + 0.78 year^2; r^2 = 0.64, P < 0.0001, n = 32; where year is number of years since 1970) than by a simple linear model (r^2 = 0.32, P < 0.001).

Hydrological conditions of the St. Lawrence River have changed considerably since 1965 (Figures 2b–d). A rapid shift from a low to a high hydrological regime occurred between 1965 and 1972, followed by a general declining trend toward low hydrological conditions in recent years, particularly in 1995, 1999, and 2001. Mean summertime water level (July–September) has declined by ~35%, peaking at 7.55 m in 1974 and reaching a minimum of 5.40 m in 1965 and 2001 (Figure 2b). Year-to-year fluctuations were more pronounced during the 1990s. Variation in mean river flow at Quebec City during the summer months has also varied by 30% since 1965 (Figure 2c) and was strongly correlated with water level (r = 0.977, P < 0.0001, n = 37). Mean monthly values of level and flow between May and November were also strongly correlated, with coefficients being highest (r varying from 0.93 to 0.97, P < 0.01, n = 37) for values of the corresponding month. Concomitant with the gradual decline in water level and flow, there has been a significant positive trend in mean summertime water temperature of 1.5 °C between 1977 and 2002 (r = 0.61, P = 0.0009) (Figure 2 d). Mean monthly water temperatures between May and November were negatively correlated with monthly water level and flow, indicating that low-water years were often associated with warmer water temperatures. Highest correlation coefficients (r varying between −0.565 and −0.730, P < 0.05, n = 25) were between mean water level of a particular month and mean water temperature of the previous month.

Results of the stepwise multiple regression analysis showed that total annual eel catch was not significantly related to variations in river flow, water level, or water temperature (P > 0.10) (Table 1). Similar results were obtained with residuals of the CPUE-versus-year relationship.

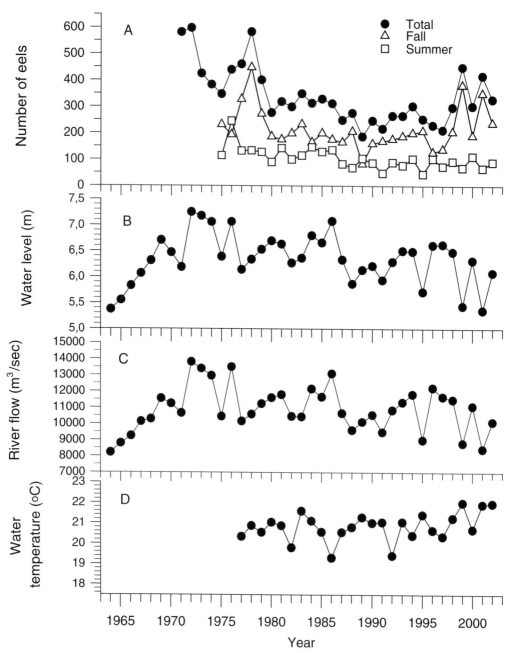

Figure 2. Year-to-year variation in (A) total eel catch (May 15–October 31), (B) water level, (C) river flow, and (D) water temperature during the summer months (July 1–September 30) between 1965 and 2002.

Table 1. Results of stepwise multiple regression analysis to test the effect of environmental variables on various eel CPUEs at the experimental weir fishery

Dependent variable	Environmental variable selected	Partial R^2	F-value	p-value	Model R^2
Annual CPUE	No variable selected				
Annual CPUE residuals	No variable selected				
Summer CPUE	(+) Mean level in July–August	0.428	17.99	0.0003	0.561
	(−) Year	0.132	6.94	0.015	
Summer CPUE residuals	(+) Mean level in July	0.258	8.34	0.008	0.258
Fall CPUE	(−) Mean level in July–August	0.236	7.44	0.012	0.236
Fall CPUE residuals	(−) Mean level in July–August	0.240	7.57	0.011	0.240
Fall/Total catch ratio	(−) Mean level in July–September	0.547	28.96	<0.0001	0.547

Summer (15 May–31 August) and fall (1 September–31 October) eel CPUEs have exhibited different patterns of interannual variation in abundance since 1975 (Figure 2a) and were not significantly correlated with each other ($r = 0.02$, $P = 0.9$, $n = 28$). Summer catches were characterized by a significant gradual decline over time ($r = -0.61$, $P = 0.0005$, $n = 28$), but fall catches did not exhibit any long-term monotonic trend ($r = -0.11$, $P = 0.58$, $n = 28$). Results of a stepwise regression analysis indicated that summer catches were *positively* related with mean water level in July and August, whereas fall catches were *negatively*, but less strongly, related with the same variable (Table 1). Models run with the CPUE residuals yielded similar results for both summer and fall catches. In all cases, mean water level during summer was always preferably selected over water temperature, the latter being not significant ($P > 0.1$). Fall catch contributed between 44.1% and 84.7% of the total catch each year. The ratio of fall catch to total catch was negatively related to mean water level during summer (July–September) ($r^2 = 0.547$, $P < 0.0001$, $n = 28$) (Table 1).

Commercial Weirs

CPUEs for commercial weirs varied considerably among years and among sites, suggesting a relatively high degree of spatial variability in eel captures in the Québec City section of the St. Lawrence River (Figure 3a). Total catch of commercial weirs was generally higher than that of experimental weirs. The highest annual CPUE was recorded at Saint-David, where 6,761 eels were landed in the fall of 1965. At that site, a maximum of 603 fish were trapped during a single fishing night, exceeding the total catch reported for an entire fishing season at the experimental weir. Overall, catches at Anse Douville and Saint-Romuald were higher than at other sites. Mean CPUE during the 1975–1979 interval was significantly higher than those reported before 1970 or during the 1980s and 1990s ($n = 7$, ANOVA F-value = 4.9, $P = 0.003$; Kruskall-Wallis test = 15.7, $P = 0.015$).

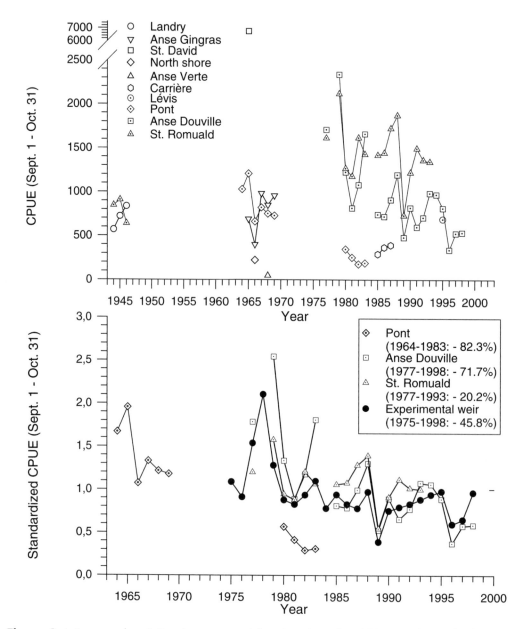

Figure 3. Interannual variation in commercial weir eel catches (CPUE and standardized CPUE, SCPUE) for fall (September 1–October 31) between 1944 and 2002. Percentages of decline in catch rate are indicated for four fishing sites.

SCPUE values calculated for three weir sites with sufficiently long data series (>10 years) clearly showed a long-term declining trend in abundance at each location (Figure 3b). SCPUE at the "Pont" site indicated a major reduction of 82.3% in abundance between 1964 and 1983 (20 years). Catches declined by 71.7% at Anse Douville between 1977 and 1998 and by 20.2% at Saint-Romuald over a slightly shorter time interval (1977–1993). The decline in eels captured at the experimental weir over the same period (1971–1998) was 45.8%. Negative correlation coefficients between SCPUE and year were significant ($P < 0.05$) in all cases except for Saint-Romuald. Years of high and low catches occurred simultaneously at all sites, and patterns of interannual variability in SCPUE at Anse Douville, Saint-Romuald, and the experimental weir were strongly correlated to each other (Spearman rank correlation, $P < 0.05$), revealing strong parallelism in year-to-year variability in catches between sites.

Commercial CPUEs or SCPUEs were not correlated with water level or water temperature for all sites with more than 10 years of records (Pont, Anse Douville, Saint-Romuald). Residual SCPUE values correlated against year calculated to filter out the interannual declining trend were not related to hydrological variables or water temperature.

Short-Term Variability in Abundance

Daily eel catches in any year were characterized by large, rapid fluctuations over time (Figure 4 a, b). The pattern of these daily changes was relatively similar between sites, however. No significant difference was found between daily catch patterns for any pair of sites ($n = 86$ paired comparisons using the Kolmogorov-Smirnov test). Paired comparisons of daily catches were also performed after lagging one of the two series (usually the downstream site) by up to three days to verify the existence of a delay in short-term fluctuations between sites. In all cases, similarity in the pattern of daily abundance between two sites showed no more than a one-day lag, indicating that the short-term variability in daily catches was essentially in phase among stations. Maximum deviation (the D-value from the K-S test), which corresponded to the statistical difference in daily catches at two sites (without any lag), was independent of the geographical distance separating two sites (Figure 4c).

Timing of Eel Occurrence

Between 1975 and 2002, the median date of eel capture at the experimental weir for the entire season (15 May–31 October) varied between 26 August and 5 October, with the exception of a very early date of 16 August in 1989. Presumably this was due to the very low fall catches. This corresponded to a 40-d difference in the median date of capture between years. Results from a stepwise regression model using monthly averages of both water level and temperature as independent variables showed that the mean water level in late summer (August–September) was again preferably selected (over water temperature) to explain the interannual variability in the median date of capture at the experimental trap. The best predictive model (Figure 5) was:

Median date = 361.76–15.73 Mean water level in August–September ($r^2 = 0.656$, $P < 0.0001$, $n = 27$)

On average, 90% of the eel captures at the experimental weir occurred during a period of 102 d ($n = 28$, SD = 11.1; range = 81–119 d). The duration of eel occurrence was positively related to water level in June and water temperature in October (duration = –54.07 + 17.06 water level in June + 3.08 temperature in October, $r^2 = 0.665$, $P < 0.001$, $n = 25$).

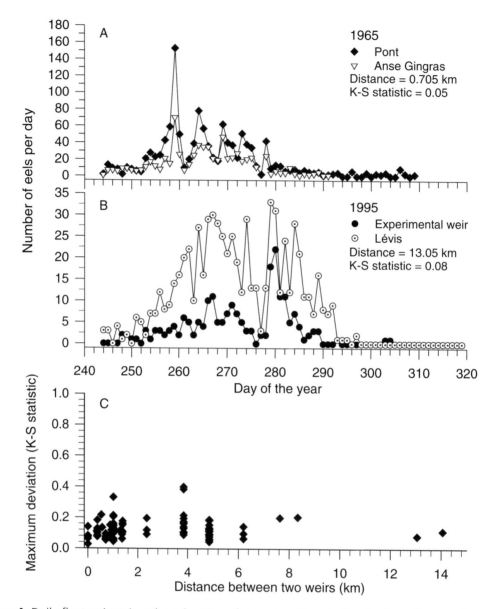

Figure 4. Daily fluctuations in eel catch at two fishing locations in the Québec City area for two different years (A, B), and the D-value of the K-S statistical test comparing daily catch distributions at two weirs as a function of the geographical distance separating the two fishing locations (C).

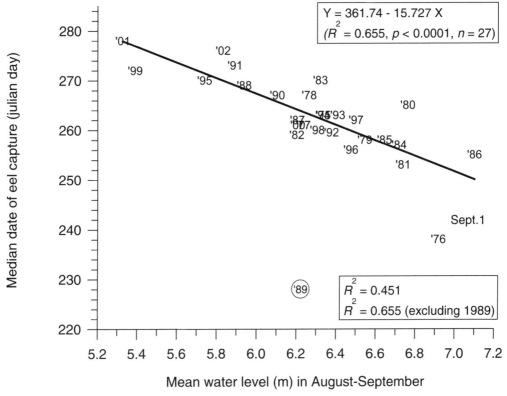

Figure 5. Median date of eel capture at the Saint-Nicolas experimental weir as a function of mean water level in August and September in the St. Lawrence River between 1975 and 2002, plotted as year of capture.

In any year, the median date of eel capture in fall (1 September–31 October) among weir locations usually varied by fewer than three days. The median date of the fall catch was not significantly correlated with year ($P > 0.05$), indicating no long-term change in the migration period between 1944 and 2002. It was inversely (and weakly) correlated with water level in October (Spearman $r_s = -0.347$, $P = 0.047$, $n = 33$). Results of the stepwise regression analysis using the shorter time series between 1978 and 2002, for which temperature data were available, showed that mean water temperature in late summer (August–September) explained 46.9% of the variance in the median date of eel catch in the fall (median date of fall catches = 210.06 + 2.935 mean water temperature in August–September, $r^2 = 0.469$, $P < 0.001$, $n = 25$). Water level was not selected ($P > 0.05$) by the regression model.

Size Variation

Size distribution of eels captured at the experimental weir revealed a significant decrease in the proportion of small (and younger) individuals between 1994 and 2002 (Figure 6). Results of paired comparisons (the K-S test) indicated that size frequency distribution was not statistically different between 1994 and 1995 but differed significantly from that in 1999 and 2000 and, more importantly, from that in 2002, a year that was characterized by the largest modal size of eels during this period. Eel size increased

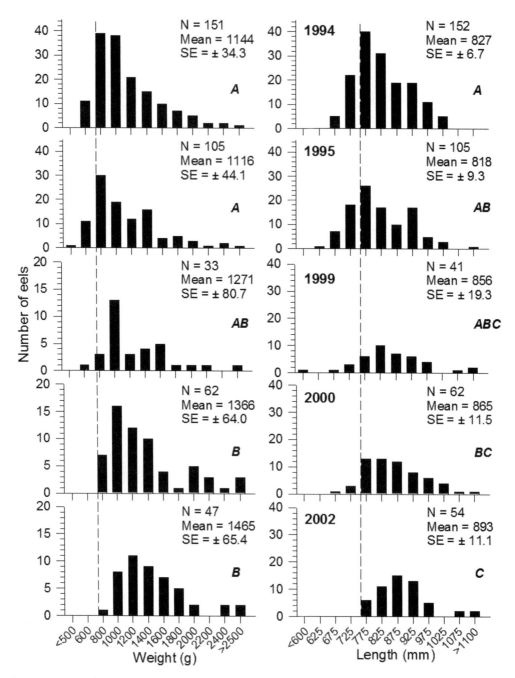

Figure 6. Size-frequency distribution of length and weight of American eels captured at the experimental weir (September 1–October 31) for five years between 1994 and 2002. Years with similar letters indicate that distributions were not statistically different ($P < 0.05$). Note that the Y-axis differs among graphs.

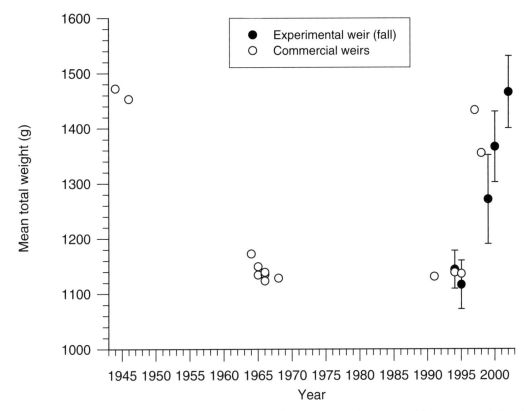

Figure 7. Interannual variation in mean weight of American eels captured by commercial weirs and by the experimental weir fishery between 1944 and 2002. Bars indicate standard errors around the mean.

between May and October every year. Results of the two-way ANOVA confirmed that the size of eels varied between years ($F = 11.74$, $P < 0.0001$, df = 4) and between seasons (summer < fall) ($F = 5.37$, $P = 0.021$, df = 1). The interactive term (year X season) was not significant ($P > 0.05$), implying that the increasing trend in average size of eels over the years was significant for both summer and fall catches. The length-weight relationship for eels at the experimental weir between 1994 and 2002 was computed as:

Weight (g) = 6.314×10^{-7} Length (mm)$^{3.1701}$ ($r^2 = 0.88$, $P < 0.0001$, $n = 568$)

Results of ANOVA on model residuals did not reveal any significant change in weight-length relationship between years.

The recent increase in the mean weight of eels was also noted in commercial weirs during the 1990s (Figure 7). Heavier eels were apparently also landed during the mid-1940s (mean weight = 1,450 g and 1,475 g in 1944 and 1946, respectively), while the mean weight of eels ranged between 1,130 and 1,180 g during the 1960s and the early 1990s.

Discussion

CPUE indices from both the experimental trap and individual commercial weirs confirmed that population size of American eels in the lower St. Lawrence River has declined continually since the mid-1970s (Figures 2 and 3). The relatively high catches observed at the experimental weir in 1999 and 2001 were quite different, but information obtained from the three remaining local fishers in the Québec City area confirmed that the eel catch rate in those two years was indeed greater than in the years immediately before and after (Bernard Côté, fisher at St-Romuald, personal communication). The fact that these high catches were reported in years of unusually low water regime (1999 and 2001; Figure 2) suggests some hydrological effect on eel catches.

Our analysis indicated, however, that the long-term trend in eel catch rate was not related to variations in water level or water temperature of the river. This suggests that the long-term decline in numbers was not the result of variable spatial distribution and accessibility to fishing gear in response to long-term changes in hydrological or thermal conditions during the year of capture. These results imply that annual CPUE indices estimated from total eel catch at individual weir sites were not statistically biased by interannual environmental variability and may therefore represent valid surrogates of the eel population size in the lower St. Lawrence River. The reasons for the higher catches between 1999 and 2001 remain unknown but could be related to the closure of the Richelieu River eel fishery in 1998 (Verdon et al. 2003). Presumably, part of this unfished component might have become available and contributed to the eel catches of the Québec City sector, because fishing effort between the Richelieu River and Québec City is relatively small.

Yet hydrological factors did have an effect on short-term variability in eel catches in the lower St. Lawrence River. The finding that summer and fall catches at the experimental trap were significantly related, but in the opposite direction, to water level during late summer (Figure 2a) can be explained by the effect of hydrography on migratory behaviour of eels. The influence of floods on seaward migratory activity of the European eel *Anguilla anguilla* has been well described by Lowe (1952), who first demonstrated that eel catches (indicative of eel movement) in small Irish rivers tended to peak on days following a rapid increase in water level during the fall.

The exact mechanism linking water-level changes and downstream movement of eels remains unknown, though evidence indicates that external stimulus (such as current, moonlight or temperature) associated with flood (Lowe 1952) or endogenous rhythms (Cairns and Hooley 2003) are important drivers. Vollestad et al. (1986) demonstrated that the start of the annual migration of European eels in River Imsa, a small river (discharge = 2–10 $m^3 \cdot s^{-1}$) in Norway, started earlier in years with high discharge in the fall. These authors subsequently showed in a tagging experiment that eel movement was directly affected by water discharge (Vollestad et al. 1994). Our results, showing an inverse relationship between water level (which is strongly correlated to water discharge in the St. Lawrence River, see Materials and Methods) and the median date of capture of American eels in the St. Lawrence River, a large river with very high but relatively stable discharge (~7000 $m^3 \cdot s^{-1}$) during summer, were virtually identical to those obtained in a much smaller and more variable river system by Vollestad et al. (1986). The median date of eel occurrence was earlier during years of high water level (and flow) in late summer (August–September), which therefore resulted in a higher proportion of eels being captured before September in the experimental trap. Inversely, years of very low water level delayed the migration activity, resulting in a proportionally higher number of eels captured after September 1.

Vollestad et al. (1986) indicated that the start of European eel migration (usually in September) was also positively related to water temperature during the two months (July and August) before migration activity. Similar results were obtained in the St. Lawrence River, where the median date of eel occurrence was also positively correlated with summer water temperature. The duration of the annual eel run was positively related to water level in summer and to water temperature in October. This may result from the combination of two processes controlling the start and the end of the silver eel migration. As indicated above, the migration process would start earlier in years of high water level, while the eel run would stop later during years of warmer water conditions in the fall. Low temperature is known to decrease migration activity of eels (Tesch 2003), and results from Vollestad et al. (1986) indicated that European silver eels stopped migrating at temperatures below 4°C. Results of the partial regression analysis revealed that the movement of American eel in the lower St. Lawrence River was more driven by hydrology than by water temperature. This supports conclusions by Vollestad et al. (1986) that water temperature was important for the start of the migration but that water discharge was the key environmental variable determining migration speed of European silver eels in rivers.

The above results led us to hypothesize that the migratory behaviours of both American and European eels are controlled by similar factors associated with water flow and discharge in small and large rivers. Given the expected link between water temperature and hydrological variables in riverine systems (as found here for the St. Lawrence River), it might be difficult to rely on empirical statistical evidence for distinguishing the relative contributions and roles of temperature, discharge, and water level as factors stimulating and controlling yearly eel migration in rivers. For example, our results showed that the median date of occurrence was equally related to water level and water temperature in August and September, depending on the length of the time series analyzed.

As Tesch (2003) pointed out, it may be hard to imagine how water level per se can have a direct influence on eel migratory behaviour, which could be more affected by water current and flow. As explained above (see Materials and Methods), water level and water flow are very strongly linked in the St. Lawrence River, so water level represents the best proxy variable for water discharge, the latter being not directly measured in the Québec City area of the river. The most important finding here is that climatic/hydrological conditions during August and September strongly affect migration activity and distribution of eels in the lower part of the river. Discharge in the river has been regulated since 1960, resulting in a large reduction in the amplitude of seasonal variation in water flow and level. Since 1970, mean water level (and flow) has dropped by nearly 30%, with a major reduction in the amplitude of fall flooding. This change in hydrological regime likely has had a direct effect on eels by delaying their seaward movement, as demonstrated by the later median date of capture in the lower St. Lawrence River (Figure 5). Since both temperature and water level are also strongly dependent on climatic conditions, future climatic changes are expected to affect the annual seaward run of silver eels. By modifying time of passage and duration of eel occurrence in the lower river, climatic changes resulting in warmer water and lower discharge will delay the silver eel run and will also indirectly alter local eel fishing activity.

From an evolutionary perspective, the impact of later migration on eels is unknown. A delay in seaward migration as a result of either water level or temperature, or both, mediated by large-scale environmental (water level regulation) and climatic changes as has been observed over past decades in the St. Lawrence River Basin, might subsequently affect gonadal development, arrival of adult eels at the breeding site, time of spawning, and larval hatching success in the ocean. Comeau et al. (2002) hypothesized that changes in the timing of seasonal migrations of Atlantic cod *Gadus morhua* between 1986 and 1999 resulted from physiological changes in fish size due to a widespread cooling in near-bottom water temperature in the Gulf of St. Lawrence, which, in turn, affected energy reserves for migration and reproduction. Our results do not provide any supporting evidence that variation in eel size (Figure 7) would explain the 40-d variation observed in migration timing during the past three decades (Figure 5). We thus conclude that the observed variability in downstream movement of eels in the St. Lawrence River was not related to physiological changes in eel size but was mainly determined by climatic/hydrological conditions during summer.

SCPUE at individual weir locations indicated that eel catch rate dropped between 46% and 82% in 20 years. SCPUEs in the 1970s were also significantly higher than those observed in the mid-1940s and mid-1960s and would correspond to a peak in American eel abundance during the second half of the 20th century. This long-term variation in individual weir CPUE was somewhat analogous to that of eel landings in Québec, which have been characterized by two peaks, one in the 1930s and the other in the 1970s, each being followed by periods of low catches in the 1940s and 1990s (Robitaille et al. 2003). The recent decline in eel abundance since 1985 represented a continent-wide phenomenon in eastern North America (Richkus and Whalen 2000; Casselman 2003). Although Richkus and Whalen (2000) did not report the rate of change in eel CPUE for various fishing districts, inspection of their data clearly showed that the decline in CPUE between 1985 and the late 1990s was often greater than 50%, as was calculated here for the St. Lawrence River. These authors did warn about the necessity of comparing abundance trends over a longer timeframe, because the observed decline could simply result from unusually high recruitment in the 1970s. Significantly higher eel abundance was also reported in rivers of the mid-Atlantic region of United States during the mid-1970s (Geer 2003). Higher CPUEs for the St. Lawrence River over the same time were therefore consistent with the hypothesis that the abundance of American eels peaked across a large part of its distribution range during the 1970s (Casselman 2003).

The similarity in abundance trends between our CPUE indices from the St. Lawrence River and those reported in other regions across the entire distribution range would thus imply that the long-term variation in the abundance of American eels from the St. Lawrence River did not result from factors exclusively affecting the eel population of the Great Lakes–St. Lawrence River system. Robitaille et al. (2003) argued that the international demand for eels led to increased fishing effort on all developmental stages of eels throughout their range and concluded that recruitment overfishing was largely responsible for the recent decline in eel catches. The number of registered eel fishers in the lower St. Lawrence River (i.e., the fluvial estuary between Lake St-Pierre and Ile d'Orléans) did, however, drop from 49 to 30 between 1985 and 2002. Despite this major (40%) reduction in fishing effort, the average tonnage of eels landed per active fisher also declined dramatically (by 50%), ranging from 2.8 t to 1.4 t per year per registered fisher. This implies that recruitment overfishing by local fishing is not a major explanation for the recent decline of eels in the lower river.

Even though absolute CPUE values varied between sites, a high degree of parallelism in standardized catch rates was found between the experimental weir site and other commercial fishing sites in the Québec City area. This relatively similar pattern in year-to-year abundance fluctuations between sites was largely explained by the short-term synchrony in daily catches at the various weirs. We believe that the Saint-Nicolas experimental weir fishery is representative and is thus an important tool for eel monitoring and assessment in the lower St. Lawrence River.

The somewhat cyclic CPUE pattern, characterized by periods of low and high values since 1944, would indicate that long-term variation in eel recruitment is driven by large-scale factors affecting the entire distribution range of the species in North America, as originally suggested by Castonguay et al. (1994a, 1994b). The catastrophic decline in the numbers of eels migrating upstream to Lake Ontario at the Cornwall ladder since 1986 (Casselman et al. 1997) has been advocated as evidence for a major recruitment failure of the eel population. On average, the American eel spends 8–12 years in Lake Ontario before returning to the sea (Casselman 1987). Our results revealed that fall CPUEs in 1996 and 1997, both at the experimental trap and in commercial weirs, were the lowest observed since 1975 and 1944, respectively (Figures 2 and 3). The 10-year lag between years of these lowest fall CPUEs and the first major decline in upstream migrants at Cornwall in 1986 strongly supports the hypothesis that recruitment failure is largely responsible for the major decline in eel catches in the St. Lawrence River during the late 1990s.

Although it is recognized that recruitment has been dramatically low since the mid-1980s, the monotonic decline in summer eel catches, which dropped by more than 50% between 1975 and 2002 at the experimental weir (Figure 2), indicates that the number of eel recruits in the Great Lakes–St. Lawrence River has declined continuously since the mid-1970s. Eels captured during the summer months were significantly smaller (and younger) than those making up the fall catch and consisted of a variable proportion of yellow eels each year. Catch rates of yellow eels in Chesapeake Bay also dropped by 50% between 1979 and 1999 (Geer 2003). The similarity in the rate of change between these two regions over approximately the same time period is rather striking despite the regional differences in fishing effort and activities and provides further evidence to support the recruitment failure hypothesis.

Similarly, the dramatic decline in European eel abundance since the late 1980s has been associated with a major recruitment failure caused by long-term climatic changes, but not with fishing mortality (Knights 2003). The apparent synchronism in eel population changes in both North America and Europe provides additional support for the hypothesis that animal population dynamics may be spatially synchronized by large-scale climate, as recently observed for terrestrial animals (Post and Forchhammer 2002).

Data from commercial weirs indicated that the eels captured in 1944 and 1946 were larger than those captured between 1965 and 1995 (Figure 7) and were apparently very similar to the estimated mean size (1,480 g) of emigrating eels during prehistoric Iroquoian fishing activities in the St. Lawrence River (Casselman 2003). Data gathered by Robitaille et al. (1988) from various fisheries biologists and technicians in Québec, revealed that eels from the St. Lawrence River in the 1970s and 1980s weighed approximately 15% less than those captured in the 1940s and 1950s. This variation in average size was apparently not related to changes in gear selectivity. Our results on the average weight of eels captured in commercial weirs from the same location over a period of 50 years (Figure 7) were consistent with that information and reflect major changes in population dynamics over time.

The recent increase in average size of eels observed at the experimental trap and in commercial catches was mainly due to the virtual absence of smaller (and correspondingly younger) individuals (Figures 6 and 7), as indicated by a corresponding decrease in the proportion of young recruits in the catch. Data collected in the early 1970s by Larouche et al. (1974) showed that the age distribution of eels in the St. Lawrence fluvial estuary ranged from 10 to 25 years, with a mean age of 16.8 years. The average weight of commercially exploited eels in the lower part of the river did not vary much between 1965 and 1995 (Figure 7), suggesting that age structure of the eel catch probably remained the same during that period. The significant increase in individual weight by nearly 30% since 1995 clearly indicated a major shift in the age structure of migratory silver eels, which consisted mainly of older individuals in recent years. Alternatively, it could be hypothesized that the weight increase is due to a recent change in individual growth rate. Although data on weight at age are unavailable to verify this possibility, this alternative hypothesis seems untenable because the maximum size of eels has remained unchanged since 1995. Considering that the status of the eel stock is traditionally assessed in terms of the total weight of landings, one can foresee the risk of underestimating the rate of change in population abundance due to a concomitant increase in individual fish size. In light of the above results, it is strongly advocated that eel sampling and monitoring in the St. Lawrence River (as well as in other rivers) include measurements of individual fish size. In this regard, the maintenance of the Saint-Nicolas weir fishery is recommended for long-term monitoring of eel status.

A similar inverse relationship between individual size and population size in eels has also been recently documented for the Richelieu River at the outflow of Lake Champlain (Verdon et al. 2003). Annual eel catch in the Richelieu River collapsed from a high of 72.9 t in 1981 to a low of 4.7 t in 1997, forcing the closure of that fishery in 1998. Between 1987 and 1997, average eel weight increased by 50% (from 1.5 kg to 2.2 kg).

The absence of similar data on temporal trends in both abundance and individual size of eels for other rivers in North America precluded further analysis of this inverse relationship over a broader regional context. The gradual drop in summer eel catches since 1975 (Figure 2) and the corresponding substantial increase in the average size of individual eels between 1994 and 2002 (Figure 6) led us to conclude that eel recruitment in the St. Lawrence River has been severely impaired since the mid 1970s and has largely contributed to the present low abundance of the Great Lakes–St. Lawrence River eel population. Data for 2003 indicate that average weight of eels captured at the experimental weir has continued to increase, reaching 1.52 kg, a value not seen since 1944 (Figure 7). Given that eel fisheries are entirely based on immature fish, the increase in individual fish size and the decrease in overall abundance should be interpreted as another significant symptom of low recruitment levels and the signal of the imminent loss of this unique resource from the St. Lawrence River ecosystem.

Acknowledgments

Our sincere and warmest thanks are expressed to John Casselman, Queen's University, for his advice and general support for this study and for his generous invitation to participate to the Eel Symposium held in Québec City in August 2003. We also wish to acknowledge the financial support of the Parc Aquarium du Québec, which has been able to maintain the operation of the experimental weir fishery since 1971 despite numerous budget cuts and other administrative constraints throughout the years. We express our gratitude to Bernard Côté, a local eel fisher, for his continuous help and his information on recent eel catches and size measurements. We are also grateful to the numerous summer students and technicians for their generous help and continuous interest during the fieldwork at the experimental weir fishery between 1994 and 2002. We thank Tom Pratt and an anonymous reviewer for their critical and constructive reviews of the manuscript. This study was partially funded by the Environmental Conservation Branch of Environment Canada–Quebec Region and by the International Joint Commission as part of the International Lake Ontario–St. Lawrence River Study Board.

References

Bouchard, A., and J. Morin. 2000. Reconstitution des débits du fleuve Saint-Laurent entre 1932 et 1998. Environnement Canada, Service Météorologique du Canada, Monitoring et technologies. Rapport technique RT- 101:1–73.

Cairns, D. K., and P. J. D. Hooley. 2003. Lunar cycles of American eels in tidal waters of the southern Gulf of St. Lawrence, Canada. American Fisheries Society Symposium 33:265–274.

Casselman, J. M. 2003. Dynamics of resources of the American eel, *Anguilla rostrata*: declining abundance in the1990s. Pages 255–274 *in* K. Aida, K. Tsukamoto, K. Yamauchi, editors, Eel Biology, Springer-Verlag, Tokyo.

Casselman, J. M. 1987. Determination of age and growth. Pages 209–242 *in* A. H. Weatherly and H. S. Gill editors, The Biology of Fish Growth. Academic Press, London.

Casselman, J. M., L. A. Marcogliese, and P. V. Hodson. 1997. Recruitment index for the upper St. Lawrence River and Lake Ontario eel stock: a re-examination of eel passage at the R. H. Saunders hydroelectric generating station at Cornwall, Ontario, 1974–1995. Pages 161–169 *in* R. H. Peterson editors The American eel in eastern Canada: stock status and management strategies. Proc. Eel Workshop, Jan. 13–14, 1997, Quebec City, QC. Can. Tech. Rep. Fish. Aquat. Sci. No. 2196:1–174.

Castonguay, M., P. V. Hodson, C. M. Couillard, M. J. Eckersley, J.-D. Dutil, and G. Verrault. 1994a. Why is recruitment of the American eel, Anguilla rostrata, declining in the St Lawrence River and Gulf? Canadian Journal of Fisheries and Aquatic Sciences 51:479–488.

Castonguay, M., P. V. Hodson, C. Moriarty, K. F. Drinkwater, and B. M. Jessop. 1994b. Is there a role of ocean environment in American and European eel decline? Fisheries Oceanography 3:197–203.

Comeau, L. A., S. E. Campana, and G. A. Chouinard. 2002. Timing of Atlantic cod (*Gadus morhua* L.) seasonal migrations in the southern Gulf of St. Lawrence: interannual variability and proximate control. International Journal of Marine Science 59:333–351.

de Lafontaine, Y., K. Turgeon, A. Kemp, C. Ménard, D. Labonté, P. Dubé, and M. Parent. 2001. Protocoles de mesure, d'étiquetage et de conservation des poissons à des fins de suivi environnemental et d'analyse chimique. Environnement Canada, Région du Québec, Direction de la Conservation, centre Saint-Laurent, Montréal, Rapport Scientifique et Technique, ST- 211:1–105.

El-Sabh, M. I., and N. Silverberg. 1990. Oceanography of a large-scale estuarine system, The St. Lawrence, Coastal and Estuarine Studies editor. Springer-Verlag, New York.

Environment Canada. 1996. State of the environment report on the St. Lawrence River. Volume 1: The St. Lawrence Ecosystem. Environment Canada-Quebec Region, Environmental Conservation. Montreal, Canada, Editions Multimonde.

Geer, P. J. 2003. Distribution, relative abundance, and habitat use of American eel *Anguilla rostrata* in the Virginia portion of Chesapeake Bay. American Fisheries Society Symposium 33:101–116.

Godin, G. 1979. La marée dans le golfe et l'estuaire du Saint-Laurent. Naturaliste Canadien 106:105–121.

Hudon, C. 1997. Impact of water level fluctuations on St. Lawrence River aquatic vegetation. Canadian Journal of Fisheries and Aquatic Sciences 54:2853–2865.

Knights, B. 2003. A review of the possible impacts of long-term oceanic and climate changes and fishing mortality on recruitment of anguillid eels of the northern hemisphere. The Science for the Total Environment 310:237–244.

Larouche, M., G. Beaulieu, and J. Bergeron. 1974. Quelques données sur la croissance de l'anguille d'Americanérique (*Anguilla rostrata*) de l'estuaire du Saint-Laurent. Ministère de l'Industrie et du Commerce. Direction générale des Pêches maritimes, Direction de la recherche, Quebec, Canada. Rapport annuel 1973.

Leggett, W. C., and R. R. Whitney. 1972. Water temperature and the migrations of American shad. Fish. Bull 70:659–670.

Lowe, R. H. 1952. The influence of light and other factors on the seaward migration of the silver eel (*Anguilla anguilla* L.). Journal of Animal Ecology 21:275–309.

Montpetit, A.-N. 1897. Les poissons d'eau douce du Canada. Beauchemin, C-O. & fils. Montreal.

Parker, S. J., and J. D. McCleave. 1997. Selective tidal

stream transport by American eels during homing movements and estuarine migration. J. mar. biol. Ass. UK 77:871–889.

Post, E., and M. C. Forchhammer. 2002. Synchronization of animal population dynamics by large-scale climate. Nature (London) 420:168–170.

Richkus, W. A., and K. Whalen. 2000. Evidence for a decline in the abudance of the American eel, *Anguilla rostrata* (LeSueur), in North America since the early 1980s Dana 12:83–97.

Robards, M. D., and T. P. Quinn. 2002. The migratory timing of adult summer-run steelhead in the Columbia River over six decades of environmental change. Transactions of the American Fisheries Society 131:523–536.

Robitaille, J. A., P. Bérubé, S. Tremblay, and G. Verreault. 2003. Eel fishing in the Great Lakes/St. Lawrence River system during the 20th century: signs of overfishing. American Fisheries Society Symposium 33:253–262.

Robitaille, J. A., and S. Tremblay. 1994. Problématique de l'anguille d'Americanérique (*Anguilla rostrata*) dans le réseau du Saint-Laurent. Ministère de l'Environnement et de la Faune, Direction de la Faune et des Habitats, Rapport technique.

Robitaille, J. A., Y. Vigneault, G. Schooner, C. Pomerleau, and Y. Mailhot. 1988. Modifications physiques de l'habitat du poisson dans le Saint-Laurent de 1945 à 1984 et effets sur les pêches commerciales. Pêches et Océans Canada, Québec, Rapport technique canadien des sciences halieutiques et aquatiques 1608:1–45.

Sokal, R. R., and F. J. Rohlf. 1995. Biometry: the principles and practice of statistics in biological research. 3rd edition. Freeman, San Francisco.

Tesch, F.-W. 2003. The eel, 5th edition. Blackwell Scientific Publications. Oxford.

Verdon, R., D. Desrochers, and P. Dumont. 2003. Recruitment of American eels in the Richelieu River and Lake Champlain: Provision of upstream passage as a regional-scale solution to a large-scale problem. American Fisheries Society Symposium 33:125–138.

Vollestad, L. A., B. Jonsson, N.-A. Hvidsten, and T. F. Naesje. 1994. Experimental test of environmental factors influencing the seaward migration of European silver eels. Canadian Journal of Fisheries and Aquatic Sciences 45:641–651.

Vollestad, L. A., B. Jonsson, N.-A. Hvidsten, T. F. Naesje, O. Haraldstad, and J. Ruud-Hansen. 1986. Environmental factors regulating the seaward migration of European silver eels (*Anguilla anguilla*). Canadian Journal of Fisheries and Aquatic Sciences 43:1909–1916.

The American Eel Fishery in Delaware: Recent Landings Trends and Characteristics of the Exploited Eel Population

JOHN H. CLARK[1]

Delaware Divison of Fish and Wildlife
Post Office Box 330, Little Creek, Delaware 19961, USA

Abstract.—American eels *Anguilla rostrata* were fourth in landings and third in value in the Delaware commercial finfish fisheries from 1999 to 2002. Landings and effort dropped while catch per unit effort (CPUE) varied during the period. Bait eel landings decreased more than food eel landings. The number of licensed eelers in Delaware dropped from 121 in 1997 to 77 in 2002. American eels collected from the commercial fishery ranged in length from 216 to 838 mm (mean 427 ± 133 SD), in weight from 13.6 to 820 g (mean 205 ± 205 SD), and in age from 2 to 12 years (mean 5 ± 2 SD). The length–weight relationship was $W = 0.00000065 \times L^{3.18}$. Von Bertalanffy length-at-age parameters calculated from the sampled eels were $L_\infty = 547$, $k = 0.43$, and $t_0 = 0.38$. Linearized catch curve analysis indicated an instantaneous disappearance rate of 0.59. The estimate of natural mortality (M) was 0.25, giving a fishing mortality (F) of 0.34. Yield-per-recruit analysis suggested that overfishing may be occurring in Delaware's commercial American eel fishery.

Introduction

The American eel *Anguilla rostrata* has supported a valuable commercial fishery in Delaware since colonial times (Raasch 1997). Despite its importance and longevity, Delaware collected little information about this fishery until adoption of the interstate fishery management plan for American eel (Atlantic States Marine Fisheries Commission 2000). Delaware instituted mandatory landings reporting in 1999 in anticipation of the plan's passage. Landings prior to 1999 were estimated from a limited survey of eelers, and the accuracy of these estimates cannot be verified. American eels were fourth in landed weight and third in value among commercially caught finfish from 1999 to 2002 (Whitmore and Cole 2003). Delaware was among the top states in eel landings during the same period, accounting for 10–15% of the U.S. total each year (National Marine Fisheries Service, Fisheries Statistics and Economics Division, personal communication).

The American eel fishery remains Delaware's least regulated commercial fishery despite the recent reporting requirements (State of Delaware 1999). The fishery has open access but requires a separate license from other commercial fisheries. Anyone planning to hold or sell more than 25 eels per day or fish more than two eel pots must purchase an eel license. Legal gear includes eel pots, fyke nets, seines, and minnow traps, but nearly all commercial effort is conducted with eel pots. There are no limits on the number of pots fished by an eeler, and there is no mesh size

[1] E-mail: john.clark@state.de.us

requirement for eel pots. Commercial effort is restricted to tidal waters and all eels kept must be at least 153 mm long.

An investigation of Delaware's commercial eel fishery began in 2000 after passage of the ASMFC American eel management plan. This work focused on trends in commercial landings, effort, and catch per unit effort (CPUE), and length, weight, age, and growth of commercial samples. Declines in American eel populations (Casselman 2003) have prompted concerns about the sustainability of eel fisheries. A recent yield-per-recruit analysis of estuarine American eel populations in Maryland suggested that these populations were overfished (Weeder and Uphoff 2003). The Delaware eel fishery is similar to that of Maryland, thus a similar analysis was conducted for Delaware eel populations.

Methods

Beginning in 1999, licensed Delaware eelers were required to keep logbooks detailing days fished, number of pots fished per day, and weight and type of eels landed. Eelers were asked to classify landed eels as bait if they were sold for bait and yellow if they were sold for food. Since bait eels are at the yellow eel stage, eels sold for food will be referred to hereafter as food eels. Most bait eels were under 350 mm and smaller than food eels, although the sizes of the two groups overlapped. CPUE was calculated as kg caught per pot-day

Two commercial eelers agreed to allow Delaware Division of Fish and Wildlife (DDFW) staff to collect on-board samples of American eels during their fishing trips. Attempts to enlist more cooperators were unsuccessful, but the Delaware eel fishery was close to homogenous in gear, bait used, and fishing strategy. The two cooperators were typical of Delaware licensed eelers in that they used rectangular pots of 1.27-by-1.27-cm mesh with one entrance and one throat. Pots were baited with half a female horseshoe crab *Limulus polyphemus* cut longitudinally. Pots were typically fished in an area until catch per pot started to drop; pots were then moved to another area, and so on. Pots were often returned to previously fished areas after the fished area had gone unfished for as little as a month. The two cooperators provided good coverage of the Delaware estuary since they fished their pots in Delaware River, Delaware Bay, and several tidal tributaries of the river and bay. All pots were fished in oligohaline (0.5–5 ppt) to polyhaline (>8 ppt) tidal water. Eels collected during the on-board sampling trips were measured for total length to the nearest mm and weighed to the nearest 0.1 g. Otoliths were removed for aging.

Glass eels were captured in a 0.8-mm mesh fyke net with a 1.23-by-1.23-m mouth at the Millsboro Pond Spillway on Indian River during January through April from 2000 through 2002 (Clark 2002).

Otoliths were glued to glass slides with clear adhesive and then polished with fine-grit sandpaper (Secor et al. 1992) but were not stained. The mounted otoliths were examined with a dissecting microscope, and annuli were counted by two readers. The first and subsequent annuli were determined using the method described by Weeder and Uphoff (2003), thus eels were considered to be age 0 in the year of their arrival in continental waters.

Lengths, weights, and ages were used to characterize length-weight and length-age relationships, as well as size and age distributions by year of American eels captured in the commercial fishery.

Pooled length and age data from the commercial fishery and from glass eel sampling were used to fit a von Bertalanffy length-at-age curve using Fishery Analyses and Simulation Tools (FAST) (Slipke and Maceina 2000).

Continental-phase American eels may be lost to a population by natural mortality, by fishing mortality, or by departure for the spawning ground. These factors sum to disappearance rate. A linearized catch curve (Sparre and Venema 1992) was used to estimate disappearance rate by regression of the natural log of the mean number of eels caught by age for 2000 through 2002 (SAS Institute 1990). The catch curve was fitted to the first age considered fully recruited to the fishery, which was modal age plus one year (Sparre and Venema 1992) through the oldest age with a mean catch greater than one. The data also were used to calculate 95% confidence intervals for the disappearance-rate estimate. Natural mortality was estimated by the same method used for commercially caught Maryland eels (Weeder and Uphoff 2003), $3/T_{max}$, where T_{max} is the maximum age (Anthony 1982). Departure for the spawning ground was considered to be a small or negligible part of the disappearance rate. Hence fishing mortality (F) was estimated by subtracting M from disappearance rate.

A Thompson-Bell Yield Per Recruit (Y/R) analysis (Gabriel et al. 1989) was used to estimate Y/R and to calculate the F-based biological reference points $F_{0.1}$ and F_{max} to compare with current F. $F_{0.1}$ is the point at which the slope of the Y/R curve is 0.1 (10%) of the initial slope and is considered the optimal yield per recruit, while F_{max} is the maximum yield per recruit (Quinn and Deriso 1999). In addition to mean weight by age, this analysis requires the proportion recruited to the fishery by age and the proportion of F and M occurring before spawning. The proportion of eels recruited to the fishery by age (partial recruitment vectors) estimated for eels captured in Maryland during 1999 (Weeder and Uphoff 2003) was used in the Y/R analysis. The proportion of F and M that occurred prior to spawning was set to one because eels leave Delaware to spawn and then die.

Results

American eels were caught by commercial eelers in Delaware River, Delaware, Indian River, and Rehoboth Bays and in most tidal tributaries of the river and bays. Commercial landings in Delaware were 36% lower in 2002 than in 1999 (Table 1). The decrease in landings corresponded with decreasing effort. Decreasing effort was due in large part to declining numbers of eelers, since the number of eel licenses issued by Delaware decreased from a high of 121 in 1997 to 77 in 2002. Mean CPUE increased from 0.65 kg/pot-day in 1999–0.96 kg/pot-day in 2001 but fell to 0.66 kg/pot-day in 2002. Food eels made up the bulk of the catch in all years. The bait eel share of the total catch dropped from 37% in 1999 to 21% in 2002.

On-board sampling with commercial cooperators was conducted on three trips in 2000 and on four trips in each of 2001 and 2002. All trips were taken between June and October. Eighty-two American eels were taken in 2000, 149 in 2001, and 123 in 2002.

The mean length of sampled eels increased each year (Table 2), and eels longer than 400 mm made up a larger proportion of the catch in 2002 than in either previous year (Figure 1). The length–weight relationship for all sampled eels was $W = 0.00000065 \times L^{3.18}$ ($n = 328$, Adjusted $r^2 = 0.97$, $p < 0.001$).

Sampled eels ranged in age from 2 to 12, but 51% were either 4 or 5 years old (Figure 2). Samples from 2002 had a smaller proportion of young eels (age 3 or less) than the previous two years. Only 17 of the 267 sampled eels were older than age 7.

Although the sampled eels showed great variation in length at age (Figure 3), mean length of the sampled eels increased with age from ages 2 through 8. Mean length of eels older than 8 was less than the mean length of eels aged 8.

Mean length of glass eels collected in 2000–2002 was 57 mm (Clark 2002), and their mean age was estimated to be 0.65

Table 1. Commercial landings and CPUE (kg per pot-day) of American eels in Delaware, 1999–2002.

Year	Number of eel licenses	Pot-days	Bait	Eels landed (kg) Food	Total	CPUE
1999	113	97,030	23,544	40,034	63,578	0.65
2000	100	73,815	15,691	38,416	54,107	0.73
2001	90	57,172	12,882	42,237	55,118	0.96
2002	77	61,339	8,359	32,184	40,543	0.66

Table 2. Mean length and weight of sampled American eels caught in Delaware tidal waters, 2000–2002

Year	n	Total length (mm) Mean	SD	Weight (g) Mean	SD
2000	82	411	148	179	193
2001	149	417	130	197	206
2002	123	449	124	238	208
All combined	354	427	133	205	205

years based on a published glass eel aging study (Wang and Tzeng 2000).

Length at age was calculated for ages represented by two or more eels. Mean annual size increments between ages for sampled eels during ages 2 through 10 was 32 mm (±63 mm SD). The Von Bertalanffy model that fit the data best for glass eels through age-10 eels (Figure 3) had a k of 0.43, a t_0 of 0.38, and an asymptotic length (L_∞) of 547 mm. The asymptotic length was shorter than the largest eel (838 mm) but similar to the mean length (545 mm) of the oldest four ages used in the model.

The catch curve regression for American eels age 5 through 9 (Figure 4) had good fit ($p < 0.0007$, Adjusted $r^2 = 0.98$), and disappearance rate was estimated to be 0.59 with 95% confidence intervals of 0.46–0.71. The M estimate was 0.25 using the maximum age of 12 from the sampled eels. The resulting estimate of F was 0.34.

Current F (0.34) was greater than $F_{0.1}$ (0.25) but less than F_{max} (0.50) on the Y/R curve (Figure 5), which implied that the resource was being fished beyond the optimal level although not necessarily overfished (Quinn and Deriso 1999).

Discussion

Commercial eel landings and effort in Delaware decreased during the four years after logbook-based data collection began in 1999. CPUE did not decrease during the period. Declining effort due to declining prices rather than a lack of eels was the probable cause for the drop in landings.

The decrease in effort was reflected in the number of licensed eelers in Delaware during the past decade. The number of eelers licensed in Delaware rose during the early 1990s through 1997 due to the glass eel fishery and to a high shore price for bait and food eels ($4.40–$6.60/kg). The subsequent drop in licenses issued was a consequence of the

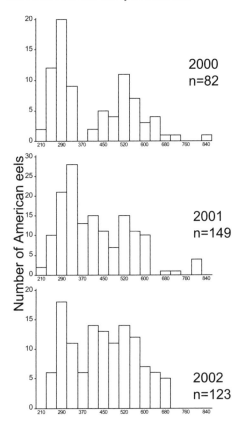

Figure 1. Length frequency of American eels sampled from commercial catches in Delaware, 2000–2002.

glass eel fishery closure in 1996 and a large drop in the price paid for bait and food eels. Several former eel licensees told the author they would not fish for eels again until prices recovered. In addition to low prices for eels, many eelers noted that the cost of bait had almost doubled during the past five years due to management-plan-imposed restrictions on Delaware's horseshoe crab fishery (ASMFC 1998).

The mean length of commercially caught American eels in Delaware during 2000 through 2002 (427 mm) was greater than that of American eels commercially caught in several Maryland tidal rivers in 1998 (300 310 mm) (Weeder 1998). The smaller size of Maryland eels may have been due to smaller mesh used in Maryland eel pots, more intense exploitation, or a combination of the two. Delaware has no mesh size requirement for eel pots, but the cooperators all used 1.27 × 1.27 cm; Maryland requires eel pots of mesh smaller than 1.27 × 1.27 cm to have a 10.2-by-10.2-cm escape panel of 1.27-by 1.27-cm mesh. Weeder (1998) reported that eel pots with mesh smaller than 1.27-by-1.27 cm with no escape panel were still widely used despite the mesh regulation. High fishing mortality was thought to be responsible for a decrease in mean length at age for commercially caught eels in Maryland tidal rivers (Weeder and Uphoff 2003).

The length–weight relationship derived from commercially caught Delaware eels indicated that Delaware American eels returned a weight (mean difference <10%) for a given

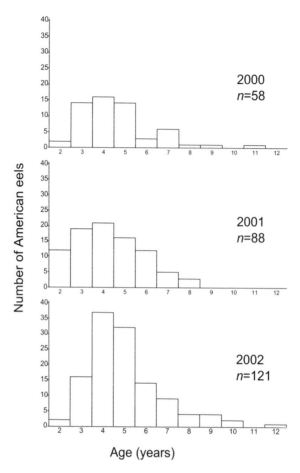

Figure 2. Age distribution of American eels sampled from commercial catches in Delaware, 2000–2002.

length similar to those from South Carolina (Hansen and Eversole 1984), the New York Bight (Wilk et al. 1978), and Lake Ontario (Hurley 1972).

The age distribution of commercially caught eels in Delaware resembled that of exploited estuarine populations in South Carolina's Cooper River (Hansen and Eversole 1984) and Georgia's Altamaha River (Helfman et al. 1984) in that 4- and 5-year-old eels made up over 50% of the catch and the maximum age was 12 or less.

Mean length at age for estuarine eels leveled off at 580 mm and age-7 in South Carolina (Hansen and Eversole 1984), 493 mm and age-7 in Virginia (Owens and Geer 2003), and 590 mm and age-8 in Delaware. Because mean length at age increased slowly or not at all beyond this age, the von Bertalanffy equation fit the Delaware data better than a linear equation, and the asymptotic length estimate (547 mm) seemed a fair approximation of maximum length. The von Bertalanffy curve, calculated from mean length at age, does not necessarily indicate the growth pattern of individual eels because American eel growth was found to be linear in studies conducted in both estuarine (Weeder and Uphoff 2003) and freshwater habitats (Oliveira and McCleave 2000).

The lack of increase in length at age after age 8 and the relatively short asymptotic

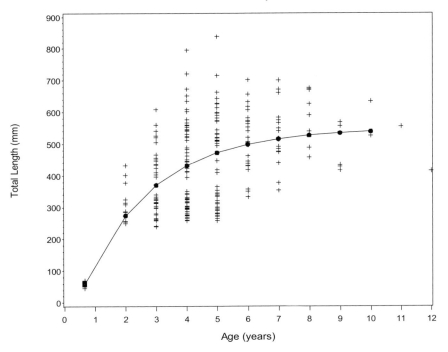

Figure 3. Actual lengths (+) and the von Bertalanffy predicted lengths (●) at age for commercially-caught American eels (N=267) and a sample of glass eels caught in 2000–2002 (N=100). The von Bertalanffy parameters are L_∞ = 547, k = 0.43 and t_0 = 0.38 (r^2=0.95, p<0.0001).

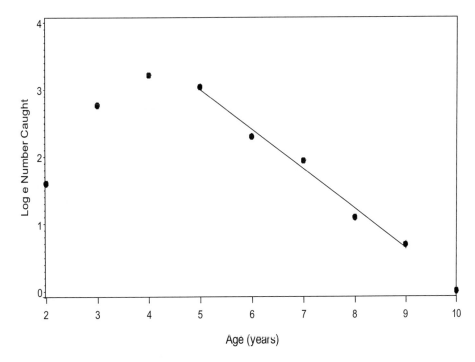

Figure 4. Catch curve of natural log American eels caught versus age. Regression fitted to ages 5 through 9 was: Log_n (American eels) = 5.95–0.59 x (age).

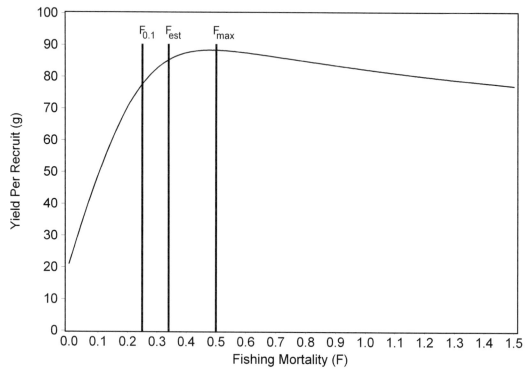

Figure 5. Yield per recruit versus fishing mortality for commercially-caught American eels in Delaware. F_{est} was the estimated fishing mortality. F_{max} was the maximum yield and $F_{0.1}$ was 10% of maximum slope of the yield per recruit curve.

length of the Delaware estuarine eels may have been an artifact caused by high fishing mortality, spawning emigration, and pooling eels of both sexes. High fishing mortality would crop off the fastest-growing eels so that older eels remaining in the population would be skewed to slow growers. The growth of estuarine eels in Maryland was fit best by a linear model for those caught in 1981, but by 1999 increased fishing pressure so reduced length at age for those older than age 4 that a von Bertalanffy model provided the best fit (Weeder and Uphoff 2003). The mean length at age of older eels could also be skewed toward slow growers if the spawning emigration of Delaware estuarine eels was linked to a critical length, since the fastest growers would leave to spawn at younger ages. Finally, the aged eels were not sexed, so the lengths at each age may have included fast-growing females and slower-growing males. Males were found to grow much slower than females in a Rhode Island tidal river (Oliveira 1999).

Conversely, American eels in Delaware may have a relatively short asymptotic length because they mature at a smaller size than in other systems. Emigrating female silver eels captured in a nontidal portion of Indian River in southern Delaware that was closed to commercial fishing had a mean length of 571 mm during fall emigration (Barber 2004). Although these eels were much older (mean age 12) than the estuarine eels in this study (mean age 5), their mean length at emigration was similar to the calculated asymptotic length of estuarine eels despite there being no fishing pressure to crop off large eels. Barber (2004) also sexed 101 commercially caught estuarine eels captured in 2002 and found them to be almost exclusively female, thus a preponderance of small male eels was not likely responsible for the relatively short asymptotic length of the estuarine eels.

The Delaware commercial and silver eel samples were all taken from sites close to the ocean (<100 river km), and this may have been a factor in the relatively small size at maturity. American eel density in several Virginia rivers decreased as distance from the ocean increased, but the decrease was greatest for small eels (<375 mm) (Smogor et al. 1995). American eels taken from the Shenandoah River in Virginia at sites from 350 to 570 river km from the mouth of the Potomac River had a mean length of 733 mm, but American eels taken from Potomac River tributaries at sites from 20 to 270 river km (rkm) from the river mouth had a mean length of 226 mm (Goodwin and Angermeier 2003). The two Virginia studies did not address size at emigration, but the results suggested that estuaries in this region, such as those in Delaware, might contain a high abundance of relatively small eels.

The catch curve used to estimate Z had good linear fit, which suggested that the low number of older eels in the commercial catch was not primarily due to emigration. An age-based emigration effect would have been suspected if the number of eels in the older age groups (>age 7) decreased sufficiently to cause the right-hand end of the catch curve to bend downward rather than to follow a straight path. The catch curve could have failed to detect emigration despite emigration having a significant effect on availability of eels to the commercial fishery if emigration is based more on length than on age. The population decrease due to emigration would then be spread across several age groups and may even have followed the pattern seen in the catch curve.

The M estimate for Delaware was identical to the estimate of 0.25 for commercially exploited estuarine American eel populations in Maryland (Weeder and Uphoff 2003), both being based on the maximum age of sampled eels. These M values may have been overestimates if fishing pressure reduced the maximum age. Estimation of M from field data are complicated by the fact that eels that disappear from a natural population may have emigrated to the spawning ground. A disappearance rate of 0.26 for American eels from an unfished estuary in Prince Edward Island, Canada, was calculated by comparing actual and simulated age distributions (ICES 2001). The disappearance rate for an unfished European eel $A.$ $anguilla$ population in Sweden was 0.23 and was derived from a catch curve containing seven years of age data by assuming M plus emigration was equal to Z (Svedang 1999). The similarity of these disappearance estimates for unfished systems to Delaware and Maryland estimates of M lends credence to the M estimate used in this paper.

The estimate of F (0.34) was in the range of those estimated in previous studies. Reported mean F of exploited estuarine American eel populations ranged from 0.27 in Maryland (Weeder and Uphoff 2003) to 0.50 in Prince Edward Island (ICES 2001). Mean F of exploited European eel populations in Sweden was 0.31, with a range of 0.16–0.42 (Svedang 1999).

The Y/R analyses of Delaware American eels resulted in F exceeding the calculated $F_{0.1}$, which suggested that overfishing could be occurring (King 1995). The Y/R analysis must be considered exploratory in that it used a small dataset and rested on several unverified assumptions, notably that American eels exhibited von Bertalanffy growth rather than linear growth, that the catch curve adequately described Z, and that M was constant. These factors constrain the reliability of estimates of F for Delaware eels. Maryland Y/R analyses of estuarine American eels captured in 1981, which had a large age range and linear growth, and those captured in 1999, which had a truncated age range and asymptotic growth, demonstrated the sensitivity of this technique to changes in growth characteristics (Weeder and Uphoff 2003). $F_{0.1}$ and F_{max} calculated from Y/R analysis using the 1999 weight-at-age data were greater than the 1999 estimated F; however, $F_{0.1}$ and F_{max} calculated from a Y/R analysis using the 1981 weight at age were less than the 1999 estimated F, suggesting overfishing was severe (Weeder and Uphoff 2003). This implies that the $F_{0.1}$ and F_{max} calculated from the Delaware Y/R analysis may be too high if fishing pressure caused the Delaware estuarine eels to undergo a similar reduction in weight at age to those in Maryland. The $F_{0.1}$ and F_{max} estimates would thus be masking the extent of overfishing.

In addition to the Y/R results, Weeder and Uphoff (2003) presented evidence for growth overfishing in Maryland by comparing age and growth data for 1981 and 1999. The eels sampled in 1999 had a truncated age structure and length range compared with those sampled in 1981, indicating that fishing pressure was removing eels before they could reach a size that would optimize yield. Landings in the European eel fishery on Sweden's west coast were fairly steady during 1993 through 1997, but growth overfishing was occurring, since the catch was dominated by small eels (Svedang 1999). Growth overfishing was taking place in Maryland and Sweden at fishing mortality rates similar to that estimated for Delaware.

The American eel fishery in Delaware may be overfished, but CPUE remained high enough during 1999 through 2002 to keep eeling profitable. The Delaware eel fishery might have realized greater yield per recruit if fishing effort had been reduced, but prices were higher for the smaller bait eels than for the larger food eels, so improved yield per recruit would not necessarily have increased economic returns. This investigation indicates that close monitoring of Delaware's commercial American eel fishery must continue to ensure that effective management actions can be taken to preserve this important resource.

Acknowledgments

Bradley Egolf and Jordan Zimmerman assisted in collection of the eels and processed all of the eels. Desmond Kahn provided valuable assistance with data analysis. Edward Farrall and Michael Stansky were ideal cooperators and provided both eels and their knowledge of the fishery. This work was funded in part by Federal Aid in Sportfish Restoration Grant F-47-R.

References

Anthony, V. 1982. The calculation of $F_{0.1}$: a plea for standardization. Northwest Atlantic Fisheries Organization, Serial Document SCR 82/VI/64, Halifax, Nova Scotia, Canada.

ASMFC (Atlantic States Marine Fisheries Commission). 1998. Interstate fishery management plan for horseshoe crab. ASMFC, Fishery management report no. 32, Washington, D.C.

ASMFC (Atlantic States Marine Fisheries Commission). 2000. Interstate fishery management plan for American eel. ASMFC, Fishery management report no. 36, Washington, D.C.

Barber, R. E. 2004. Sex ratio of silver American eels (*Anguilla rostrata*) migrating out of two southern Delaware streams. Master's thesis. University of Delaware, Newark.

Casselman, J. M. 2003. Dynamics of resources of the American eel, *Anguilla rostrata*: declining abundance in the 1990s. Pages 255–274 in K. Aida, K. Tsukamoto, and K. Yamauchi, editors. Eel biology, Springer-Verlag, Tokyo.

Clark, J. H. 2002. Annual report: diadromous species research-American eel. Project F-47-R-12. Delaware Division of Fish and Wildlife, Dover.

Gabriel, W. L., M. P. Sissenwine, and W. J. Overholtz. 1989. Analysis of spawning stock biomass per recruit: an example for Georges Bank haddock. North American Journal of Fisheries Management 9:383–391.

Goodwin, K. R., and P. L. Angermeier. 2003. Demographic characteristics of American eel in the Potomac River Drainage, Virginia. Transactions of the American Fisheries Society 132:524–535.

Hansen, R. A., and A. G. Eversole. 1984. Age, growth,

and sex ratio of American eels in brackish-water portions of a South Carolina river. Transactions of the American Fisheries Society 113:744–749.

Helfman, G. S., E. L. Bozeman, and E. B. Brothers. 1984. Size, age, and sex of American eels in a Georgia river. Transactions of the American Fisheries Society 113:132–141.

Hurley, D. A. 1972. The American eel (*Anguilla rostrata*) in eastern Lake Ontario. Journal of the Fisheries Research Board of Canada 29:535–543.

ICES (International Council for the Exploration of the Sea). 2001. Report of the EIFAC/ICES working group on eels. ICES CM 2001/ACFM:03.

King, M. 1995. Fisheries biology, assessment and management. Fishing News Books, Oxford, England.

Oliveira, K. 1999. Life history characteristics and strategies of the American eel, *Anguilla rostrata*. Canadian Journal of Fisheries and Aquatic Sciences 56:795–802.

Oliveira, K., and J. D. McCleave. 2000. Variation in population and life history traits of the American eel, *Anguilla rostrata*, in four rivers in Maine. Environmental Biology of Fishes 59:141–151.

Owens, S. J., and P. J. Geer. 2003. Size and age of American eels collected from tributaries of the Virginia portion of Chesapeake Bay. Pages 117–124 *in* D. A. Dixon, editor. Biology, management and protection of catadromous eels. American Fisheries Society, Symposium 33, Bethesda, Maryland.

Quinn, T. J., and R. B. Deriso. 1999. Quantitative fish dynamics. Oxford University Press, New York.

Raasch, M. S. 1997. Delaware's freshwater and brackish-water fishes: a popular account, 3rd edition. Delaware Nature Society, Hockessin.

SAS Institute. 1990. SAS/STAT user's guide, version 6, 4th edition, volume 2. SAS Institute, Cary, North Carolina.

Secor, D. H., J. M. Dean, and E. H. Laban. 1992. Otolith removal and preparation for microstructural examination. Pages 19–57 *in* D. K. Stevenson and S. E. Campana, editors. Otolith microstructure examination and analysis. Canadian Special Publication of Fisheries and Aquatic Sciences no. 117.

Slipke, J. W., and M. J. Maceina. 2000. Fishery analyses and simulation tools (FAST). American Fisheries Society, Bethesda, Maryland.

Smogor, R. A., P. L. Angermeier, and C. K. Gaylord. 1995. Distribution and abundance of American eels in Virginia streams: tests of null hypotheses across spatial scales. Transactions of the American Fisheries Society 124:789–803.

Sparre, P. and S. C. Venema. 1992. Introduction to tropical fish stock assessment. Food and Agriculture Organization of the United Nations, Fisheries Technical Paper 360/1.

State of Delaware. 1999. Delaware Code, Title 7, Part 1, Chapter 18: Eel fishing. Available: www.delcode.state.de.us/title7/c018/index.htm. (September 2005).

Svedang, H. 1999. Vital population statistics of the exploited eel stock on the Swedish west coast. Fisheries Research 40:251–265.

Wang, C. H., and W. N. Tzeng. 2000. The timing of metamorphosis and growth rates of American and European eel leptocephali: a mechanism of larval segregative migration. Fisheries Research 46:191–205.

Weeder, J. A. 1998. Completion report-Maryland eel population study project 3-ACA-026. Maryland Department of Natural Resources Fisheries Service, Annapolis.

Weeder, J. A., and J. H. Uphoff. 2003. Effect of changes in growth and eel pot mesh size on American eel yield per recruit estimates in upper Chesapeake Bay. Pages 169–176 *in* D. A. Dixon, editor. Biology, management and protection of catadromous eels. American Fisheries Society, Symposium 33, Bethesda, Maryland.

Whitmore, W. H. and R. W. Cole. 2003. Commercial fishing in Delaware 2002. Delaware Division of Fish and Wildlife, Dover, Delaware.

Wilk, S. J., W. W. Morse, and D. E. Ralph, 1978. Length-weight relationships of fishes collected in the New York Bight. Bulletin of the New Jersey Academy of Science 23(2):58–64.

Long-Term Changes in Recruitment, Population Dynamics, and Status of the European Eel in Two English River Systems

ANTHONY BARK[1], BETH WILLIAMS, AND BRIAN KNIGHTS

Department of Geography, King's College London, Strand, London WC2R 2LS, UK.

Abstract.—Long-term changes in eel stock status are examined in two catchments in England. The River Severn supports the UK's major glass eel fishery. The Rivers Piddle and Frome and Poole Harbour form a linked river/tidal lagoon system supporting yellow and silver eel fisheries. Eel population density and structure in lower Severn tributaries appear unchanged since the early 1980s, as does eel distribution in the upper catchment. It is concluded that, despite a decline in glass eel numbers and increased fishing pressure in the 1990s, recruitment continues to be sufficient to fill local carrying capacity. In contrast, in the Piddle and Frome, population density has declined sharply since the 1970s, and there has been a major change in sex ratios from male to female domination. Although currently high, female silver eel escapement is likely to decline sharply over the next few years from the Piddle and possibly the Frome. It is postulated that the productive tidal lagoon acts as a sink for declining glass eel recruits so that fewer elvers and yellow eels are entering the rivers. Fishing pressure on harbor stocks is unquantified but potentially high. Management options and priorities for the two catchments are discussed.

Introduction

Recruitment and stock levels of the European eel *Anguilla anguilla* appear to have been high and relatively stable during the 1950s, 1960s, and 1970s but are generally perceived to have declined steadily from the early 1980s to the present. Data relating to glass eel recruitment from a range of European countries have been compiled by the ICES/EIFAC Working Group on Eel (ICES 2003) and suggest that the decline may approach 99% (Dekker 2003). International Council for the Exploration of the Sea (ICES 1999) has stated that "the European eel stock is outside safe biological limits and the current fishery is not sustainable." The underlying cause of the decline in recruitment and stock levels is unclear but may involve inter alia: habitat loss due to man-made immigration barriers (White and Knights 1997); overexploitation of glass, yellow, and silver eels (Moriarty and Dekker 1997); accumulation of xenobiotic lipophilic organic compounds such as PCBs in body fat (Robinet and Feunteun, paper presented at the American Fisheries Society Annual Meeting, 2003); infection by the swim bladder nematode *Anguillicola crassus* introduced to Europe in the 1970s (Kennedy and Fitch 1990; Bruslé 1994; Ashworth and Blanc 1997); or oceanic factors

---

[1]Corresponding author: tony.bark@kcl.ac.uk

associated with the North Atlantic Oscillation Index affecting the development of leptocephali and their migration to the European continental shelf (Knights 2003). A review of the possible causes of recruitment decline is given in Knights et al. (2009, this volume).

Great Britain lies within the central third of the distribution range of *A. anguilla* and has an extensive Atlantic coastline. It might therefore be expected that the impact of declining glass eel recruitment on yellow eel populations would be less severe in the United Kingdom than in more distant parts of the species' range, such as the Mediterranean, Baltic, or northern Scandinavia. However, only scattered information is available on the current and historic status of eel stocks in Great Britain, and long-term monitoring data are lacking. The general paucity of quantitative data on eels reflects a traditional lack of interest in managing the species, which is of low commercial and culinary importance in Britain and is of minimal sport-fishing interest.

Knights et al. (2001) reviewed available fisheries survey data for England and Wales and found no evidence of a significant decline in river eel stocks or in commercial yellow and silver eel catches between the late 1970s and 1997. Although catches may have declined subsequently, this could reflect declining effort because of poor market prices rather than a shortage of catchable eels (Knights et al. 2009). There are no fisheries-independent time series relating to glass eel recruitment in mainland Britain, and commercial fisheries data (catch returns and UK Customs and Excise import and export records) are the only means of assessing trends. These catch-related data suggest that declines in glass eel recruitment from the 1970s to the 1990s have been less severe than in many parts of Europe, falling by some 75–90% but appearing to stabilize in the late 1990s.

The study described here uses detailed eel surveys of British river systems for which there are verifiable historic data to quantify temporal changes in eel stock status. It was considered that, ideally, historic datasets should have the following attributes.

• Data should relate to west, south, and east coast rivers (i.e., a range of positions relative to the main Atlantic migration pathways of glass eels) and should include both exploited and nonexploited catchments.

• Historic surveys should be quantitative, have employed reproducible methodology, and be of sufficient scale to provide a basis for meaningful statistical comparison.

• Historic data should include information on population density, length frequency, length–weight relationship, population age structure, and growth rate.

• Data should relate to the 1970s or early 1980s, or both, so as to bridge the period of maximum glass eel recruitment and subsequent decline.

• Original data should be available, rather than edited or abridged data from published reports or papers.

Although a variety of data sets met some of these requirements (reviewed by Knights et al. 2001), only two historic data sets could be located that largely met all the criteria. These related to the River Severn on the Atlantic coast of Britain and the Piddle/Frome system, which discharges to the English Channel (Figure 1).

Study Sites and Historic Data

River Severn

The River Severn rises in the Welsh mountains and runs for 350 km before feeding into the Bristol Channel, a large funnel-shaped inlet in southwest Britain. The Severn Estuary supports the UK's largest glass eel fishery.

Aprahamian (1986, 1988) surveyed 109 sites spanning the River Severn catchment in 1983/84, recording eel distribution, abun-

Figure 1. Map showing the location of the Rivers Severn, Piddle, and Frome and Poole Harbour.

dance, age, and growth. Surveys employed electrofishing with population estimates based on catch depletion using two, three, or four fishing sweeps of typically 100-m lengths of channel. Age of eels from each sample site was determined, enabling a comparison of growth rates in different parts of the catchment. The complete raw data set, including individual lengths and weights, was available for analysis.

Rivers Piddle and Frome

The Piddle and the Frome form a linked system, both entering the western end of Poole Harbour 2 km downstream of the tidal limit. Both rivers are productive chalk streams and are similar in character. Poole Harbour, with its restricted connection to the sea, forms a large, predominantly saline coastal lagoon (38 km^2 at high water spring tide) that becomes brackish at its western end. A large part of this area is composed of intertidal areas and mud flats. Poole Harbour supports a commercial yellow eel fyke-net fishery. Yellow eels are not exploited on either of the rivers. However, a fixed silver eel trap on the River Piddle about 2 km upstream of the tidal limit is fished each autumn, and a silver eel trap on the River Frome is used on three or four occasions in some years.

We located six data sets that relate to the Rivers Piddle and Frome, spanning 1963–1992 (Table 1). Most sampling was by electrofishing. Raw data sets were not available.

Methods

In order to assess current eel stock status in the study catchments, a resurvey program was undertaken. This was designed to provide the optimum match to the original surveys in site location and survey timing and, where practical, to survey methodology. A further objective was that resurveys should be of sufficient scale to allow meaningful comparison between historic and contemporary data.

Survey sites of approximately 100 m of stream were electrofished, typically using three upstream fishing sweeps to enable triple catch depletion population estimates. In a few instances, where erratic catch depletions were obtained, four sweeps were used. The electrofisher used 50 Hz pulsed direct current to a hand-held anode, with the eels being caught in 3-mm-mesh-size hand nets. To draw eels from their burrows and hideaways and to achieve an acceptable capture efficiency, it was necessary to use higher current and voltage settings and to proceed more slowly along the channel than would normally be employed for other finfish. On completion of each fishing run, the eel catch was anesthetized with benzocaine (approximately 0.5 mL of a 50 g · L^{-1} solution of benzocaine in acetone per liter of water in the sedation tank). All eels were individually measured to the nearest millimeter and weighed to the nearest gram. A subsample of eels across the size range was taken for age determination and in some cases (see below) for macroscopic sex determination.

For the River Severn, it was possible to match sites, survey methodology, and timing relatively precisely. In 1998, 24 of the original 109 Severn sites were resurveyed, all 24 sites being on tributaries in the lower part of the catchment. The lower Severn is delineated by Upper Lode Weir at Tewkesbury, which is the upper limit of tidal influence. Sixteen of the 24 sites, plus one additional site, were resurveyed in 1999. Fourteen sites were resurveyed in 2002. The River Piddle was resurveyed in 1999 and 2003. The River Frome was resurveyed in 1999 and 2000, as shown in Table 1.

Migrating silver eels were sampled from the commercial traps on the Piddle and Frome during autumn 1999, 2000, and 2002 to determine size and age distribution and sex ratios of emigrants. Samples were taken throughout the silver eel fishing season to avoid bias arising from the tendency of males to migrate early and females later.

The Friedman test was used to compare density and biomass data between years (data were not expected to be normally distributed). For comparisons of overall length frequencies across years, one-way analysis of variance (ANOVA) was applied (n values were very large and lengths were assumed to be normally distributed). For comparisons of sex ratio and the proportional contribution of length classes between years, the chi-squared test was used. Values for P are quoted to three decimal places (but when $P = 0.000$ it is expressed as $P \leq 0.0005$ for clarity).

Results

River Severn

Figure 2 shows mean eel population (number 100 m^{-2}) and biomass (g 100 m^{-2}) density for those River Severn sites common to all survey years (1983, 1998, 1999, 2002, and 2003). Although there is variation in population density and biomass between individual years, (Friedman: $P = 0.018$), there is no indication of a significant downward trend in yellow eel stocks. Figure 3 shows cumulative length-frequency plots for all eels captured in 1983, 1998, 1999, and 2002. The plot lines for 1998 and 1999 lie significantly to the right of the 1983 line (ANOVA: $P \leq 0.0005$), indicating a reduction in the proportion of small eels in the population. The 2002 plot line, although closer to that for 1983, is also significantly different (ANOVA: $P = 0.001$). Figure 3 also shows cumulative length frequency for the same sites and years for eels greater than 120 mm. This effectively excludes eels less than 2–3 years old, based

Table 1. Historic study sites and data with comparable re-survey dates and sites for the Rivers Piddle and Frome, Dorset, UK.

Researcher/ organization	River	Year	Surveyed area/site	Historic Surveys								Re-surveys	
				Survey method	Eel life stage	Population estimate method	Density	Biomass	Eels Aged	Length Frequency plots	Sex Determined	Year	Surveyed area/site
Morrice et al. (undated)	Piddle	1976/77	13.7 km in 21 contiguous sections	Electro-fishing >250 mm	Yellow/ silver	Mark recapture	Yes	Yes	Yes	84	No	1999 & 2003	11 sites over the original 13.7 km
Morrice et al. (undated)	Piddle	1976/77	Tidal limit	Funnel net	Silver	-	No	No	Yes	279	Size based n=1629	1999, 2000 & 2002	Fixed rack 2 km upstream of tidal limit
Mann & Blackburn (1991)	Frome - Tadnoll Brook	Intermittently 1973–1984	2km stretch of stream	Electro-fishing	Yellow/ silver	Catch depletion	Yes	Yes	Yes	588	Gonad examination, n=1126	1999 & 2000	8 sites within original 2 km survey stretch
Mann & Blackburn (1991)	Frome – Mill Stream	Pooled data 1963–1984	1 site	Electro-fishing	Yellow/ silver	-	No	No	Yes	No	No		
Ibbotson et al. (1994)	Frome – Mill Stream	Monthly June 1991–Feb. 1992	5 sites	Electro-fishing	Yellow/ silver	Catch depletion	Yes	Yes	No	No	No	}1999	One of the original sites
National Rivers Authority (1990)	Frome & Piddle	August 1990	6 sites	Electro-fishing	Yellow/ silver	Catch depletion	Yes	Yes	Yes	No	No	1999	6 original sites

on age-length relationships determined for River Severn eels in 1999. The closeness of the match of the four length-frequency lines in Figure 3 suggests that variable recruitment to the Severn tributaries, as implied by Figure 2, has had minimal effect on postjuvenile population structure.

The 1983–1984 data set also includes 66 sites in the upper Severn catchment. Routine UK Environment Agency electrofishing surveys of the upper Severn undertaken through the 1990s cover all the same tributaries. These latter surveys were aimed primarily at salmonids and are therefore unlikely to yield reliable density and biomass measures for eels (Knights et al. 2001). However, since the agency data cover more than 250 upper-catchment sites, they provide an excellent picture of eel distribution if used on a presence/absence basis. GIS mapping showed that all tributaries with eels present in 1983/84 had eels in the late 1990s. The two data sets (1983/84 and 1990s) provide no indication of diminishing upper-catchment distribution. A reduction of distribution range within a large catchment would indicate a declining eel stock.

Rivers Piddle and Frome

Figure 4 shows temporal trends in density and biomass in the rivers Piddle and Frome. Since there were differences in the way the various data sets were collected, the extent to which the data are statistically comparable is uncertain, and caution is required in data interpretation. Statistical analysis has therefore been limited to comparison of the 1999 and 2003 Piddle data.

The two main surveys, in the lower Piddle and the Tadnoll Brook (River Frome), suggest a major drop in population density from the 1970s to 1999, with estimated densities falling by 60% in the lower Piddle and by 74% in the Tadnoll Brook. Biomass also appears to have declined in both rivers. However, the decline in biomass is less marked than in density, approximately 43% for the Piddle and 29% for the Tadnoll Brook. In

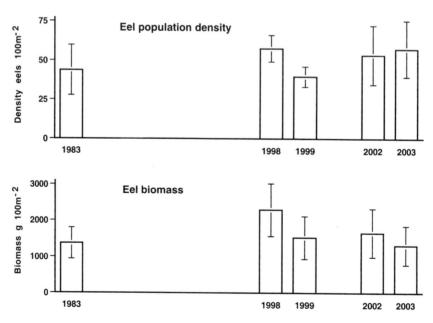

Figure 2. Eel population density and biomass density in tributaries of the Lower Severn, with 95% confidence intervals.

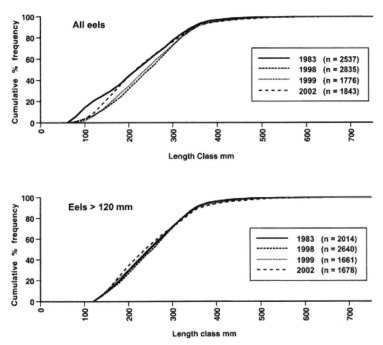

Figure 3. Cumulative percentage length frequency distribution of eels in tributaries of the Lower Severn. Upper panel, all length classes. Lower panel, >120 mm eels only.

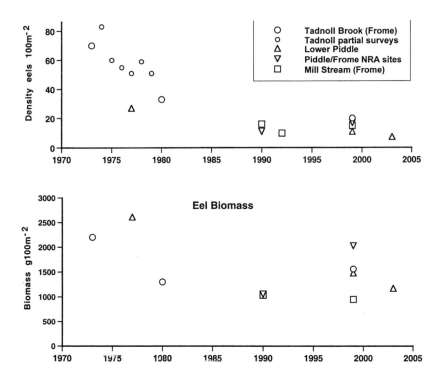

Figure 4. Temporal trends in eel population density and biomass density in the Rivers Piddle and Frome. See Table 1 for sources and types of data.

the River Piddle, density declined further between 1999 and 2003 (Freidman, $P = 0.035$), but biomass did not decline significantly (Freidman: $P = 0.132$). In the River Piddle, the overall decline in population density and biomass from the late 1970s to the present is approximately 72% and 60%, respectively.

Figure 5 shows changes in length-frequency distribution for the various temporal comparisons within the River Frome system. In each case, there is a significant shift to larger eel sizes (chi squared: main river $P = 0.007$, Mill Stream $P \leq 0.0005$, Tadnoll Brook $P \leq 0.0005$). Figure 6 shows the proportion of eels larger than 450 mm, which are assumed to be female, in the portion of the population over 250-mm in the two river systems. (The 250-mm minimum size was used because only data for >250-mm eels are available for the 1976–1977 River Piddle survey.)

Figure 7 illustrates temporal changes in population density of four size classes of eels in the River Piddle: smaller than 250 mm (recent recruits), 250–350 mm (immature males and females), 350–450 mm (maturing males and immature females), larger than 450 mm eels (maturing females). The change in the relative proportion of the dif-

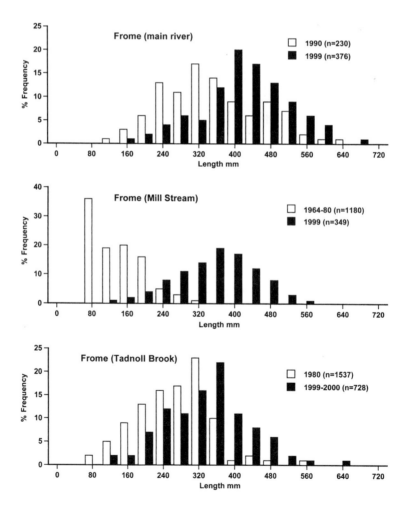

Figure 5. Temporal changes in percent length frequency distributions for eels in the River Frome. See Table 1 for data sources.

European Eel Changes in Two English River Systems 249

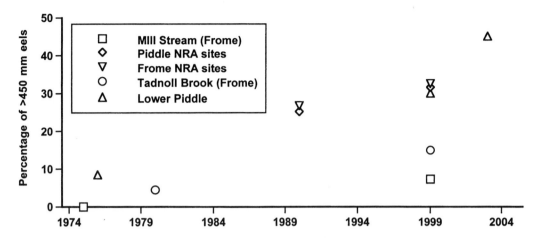

Figure 6. Temporal trends in the percentage of large female eels in the non-juvenile (>250 mm) populations of the Rivers Piddle and Frome. Data sources are given in Table 1. All eels greater than 450 mm are assumed to be female. The historic Mill Stream (River Frome) data relates to eels sampled between 1963 and 1986, therefore the median year of 1975 is used.

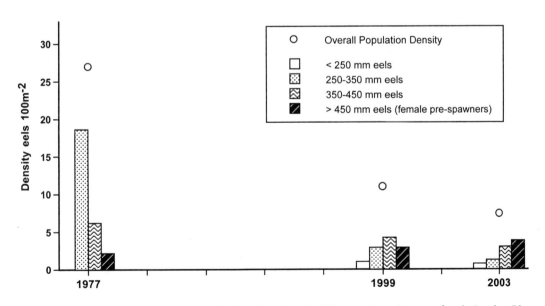

Figure 7. Temporal changes in population density of different size classes of eels in the River Piddle. The 1977 data set relates only to eels >250mm.

ferent size classes is highly significant (chi squared: $P \leq 0.0005$,). Furthermore, although there appears to have been a major decline in population density of the smaller size classes of eels, the current population density of eels larger than 450 mm (female prespawners) appears to be almost double that of 1977.

Sex-ratio data for the Tadnoll Brook in 1982–1983, based on gonad examination of a sample of 1,126 eels greater than 250 mm is given in Mann and Blackburn (1991). Therefore a new sample of 246 eels greater than 250 mm was collected from the Tadnoll Brook in 2000 for sex determination. In the Tadnoll Brook, the male:female ratio was 3.7:1 in 1982–1983 and 0.43:1 in 2000 (chi squared: $P \leq 0.0005$). Small samples of silver eels were also obtained from the fixed trap on the main River Frome (downstream of the Tadnoll Brook tributary) in 1999, 2002, and 2003. These yielded a male:female sex ratio of 0.64:1 ($n = 365$)

The current sex ratio in the River Piddle was determined from silver eels caught in the fixed trap in 1999, 2000, and 2002. This allowed a direct comparison with the sex ratio in 1976–1977, which was also determined from migrating silver eel catches. Gonad examination of all silver eels between approximately 420 and 480 mm in length showed that 450 mm could be used as a male/female cut-off length with negligible error. Based on a total sample of 1,629 silver eels, the 1976–1977 male–female ratio was 2.75:1. However, in 1999–2002, based on a total sample of 1,051 silver eels, the male:female ratio had changed to 0.08:1. Gonad examination of yellow eels in the 250-to-450-mm size range (potential males of sexable size) captured during the 2002 electrofishing confirmed the paucity of males in the population. Historic and current length-frequency plots for River Piddle silver eels, which illustrate the significant change in sex ratios (Friedman: $P \leq 0.0005$), are shown in Figure 8.

Discussion and Conclusions

River Severn

This study shows that, based on site-by-site comparison of tributaries of the lower Severn, there appears to have been no significant change in eel population density or biomass since 1983/84. Although length-frequency analysis indicates fewer very small eels in the population, exclusion of eels under 120 mm from the data set shows population structure to be effectively identical. The use of 3-mm mesh nets and assiduous attention to the capture of small eels during the later surveys implies that observed declines in the number/proportion of small eels are not simply artifacts of fishing effort.

It is necessary to consider the potential impact of the River Severn glass eel fishery, the only large-scale glass eel fishery in the UK. Commercial catch data for the Severn (and elsewhere in the UK) are based on catch returns from individual fishermen to the local licensing office as total seasonal catch with no requirement for information on fishing effort. Customs and Excise import and export files provide data on eels in the form of tonnage and price per kg. Neither data set is likely to be accurate or complete. However, by using both data sets, Knights (2001) was able to elucidate the underlying trends. Glass eel catches were probably in the order of 50 metric tons (mt) per annum (principally from the Severn/Bristol Channel but some from other parts of the UK) in the late 1970s but had dropped to some 10–20 mt by the late 1990s. Due to a rapidly escalating market price for glass eels in the second half of the 1990s, fishing effort, as indicated by license sales, more than doubled. Thus it would appear that the Severn glass eel fishery was taking an increasing proportion of a declining glass eel run during the latter period. Thus the constancy of eel stock status in the Severn has been maintained against a backdrop of

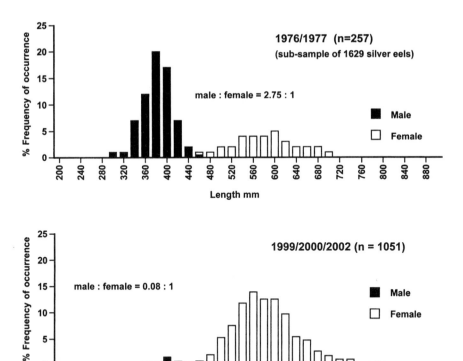

Figure 8. Percentage frequency of occurrence of male and female silver eels from the River Piddle in 1976/1977 and 1999/2000/2003.

declining glass eel recruitment to the tidal river and increased fishing pressure.

Glass eels entering the freshwater river and tributaries in the second half of the 1990s (typically 120–220 mm by 2002) numerically dominated the catch during the 2002 electrofishing surveys. If low recruitment and increased fishing effort during the later 1990s had negatively affected river eel stocks, then this should have been apparent in both the population density and population structure data for 2002. It is therefore concluded that, to date, and despite a major decline in glass eel numbers, recruitment to the Severn system is still sufficient to meet the local carrying capacity. This undoubtedly stems from the proximity of the Bristol Channel and Severn Estuary to one of the main glass eel migration routes from the Atlantic and to the favorable tidal regime (15-m vertical range and long horizontal excursion), which facilitates selective tidal transport up the estuary.

The Severn glass eel fishery is prosecuted with hand-held dip nets operated from the bank. Despite large numbers of licensed netsmen, it remains a relatively low-intensity fishery. Thus, despite the precautionary approach, there appears to be little justification for imposing additional restrictions on the fishery beyond the recently implemented policy of nonexpansion. The Severn glass eel fishery contrasts sharply with those on some French estuaries on the Bay of Biscay, where high numbers of powered craft fitted with large nets are potentially capable of taking a major proportion of the glass eel stock. However, even with this fishing pressure, significant recruitment still occurs (e.g., by way of the pass recently fitted to the Arzal Dam on the Vilaine, France) (Feunteun et al. 2003).

Rivers Piddle and Frome

The "no detectable change" status of the Severn eel stock is in marked contrast to the Rivers Piddle and Frome, where major changes to eel stocks are apparent during the past 25 years. In both of these rivers, declining recruitment appears to have led to a substantial fall in population density, resulting in an aging population of larger individuals. The most striking feature is the change in sex ratios. A historically heavily male-dominated population in the River Piddle (male:female 2.75:1 in 1976–1977) has given rise to an overwhelmingly female-dominated population (male:female 0.08:1 in 1999–2003). Gonad examination of yellow eels has confirmed that the current predominance of female silver eels reflects an underlying change in sex ratios and is not simply a function of an aging population. A comparable, although less extreme, change has occurred in the Tadnoll Brook, a tributary of the River Frome (male:female 3.7:1 in 1983–1984 and 0.43:1 in 1999–2000). It has long been recognized (see Knights et al. 2001 for examples) that high population densities (the typical lower-catchment situation) give rise to male-dominated populations, while low population densities (the typical upper catchment situation) give populations dominated by large females. That eel sex ratios changed in the Piddle and Frome in response to declining recruitment is therefore in line with expectations. However, the extent of the observed change is particularly dramatic.

It is necessary to consider the Piddle and Frome in the context of Poole Harbour, the large coastal lagoon into which the rivers drain. The surface area of the harbor is approximately 38 km^2, whereas that of accessible freshwater habitat (river channel and off-channel still waters) is less than 5% of this. The harbor is therefore the dominant part of the catchment. Local anecdotal reports suggest that relatively large numbers of elvers used to ascend both rivers. However, by 1999, there were very few small eels in the electrofishing catches from either river, suggesting that, if they did so at all, eels tended to migrate upriver at several years of age. It has therefore been hypothesized (Knights et al. 2001) that low glass eel recruitment during the 1990s was insufficient to exceed the carrying capacity of Poole Harbour. Being a typical estuary and therefore relatively productive (McLusky and Elliot 2004) and warm (mean water temperatures: January 6°C and July 19°C), the harbor may act as a sink for available recruits. If population pressure acts as a major trigger for upstream migration, that trigger has been removed. Based on the Piddle survey data for 2003, there has now been a substantial decline in the numbers of medium-sized eels (350–450 mm), implying that the sink effect of the harbor has intensified and that even older eels are entering the rivers in decreasing numbers. The relative importance of coastal, estuarine, and freshwater habitats to catadromous eels and movements between these habitats is discussed by Knights et al. (2009).

The foregoing hypothesis presupposes that population densities have declined in the harbor. There has been an active fyke-net fishery in Poole Harbour for many years, but as is typical for eel fisheries, this has been largely unregulated until recently, and there are no official catch returns prior to the 1990s. However, the development and decline of the fishery has been well documented by a former harbor eel fishermen (Castle 1998, unpublished report). Catches during the late 1960s to early 1970s were about 30 metric tons per year, or nearly 8 kg ha^{-1} (this Figure accords well with estimates by Morrice (1989)), but may have fallen to about 1.3 kg ha^{-1} by the late 1990s, a decline of 80–85%. It has also been claimed Castle 1998, unpublished report) that the average size of eels caught in Poole Harbour has declined, implicating size overfishing, but there are no quantitative data to support this.

Although less than it was 30 years ago, fishing pressure in Poole Harbour is still intense, with up to 100 fyke-net ends laid nightly throughout the summer. Yields now are clearly well below the 10+ kg ha^{-1} that might be expected from a relatively warm and productive coastal lagoon (Tesch 2003; Moriarty and Dekker 1997). Although unsupported by reliable quantitative data, the inference is that the eel population of Poole Harbour is below, possibly well below, carrying capacity, due to a combination of reduced recruitment and continued fishing pressure. This is a plausible explanation for the apparent lack of impetus for upriver migration that clearly now prevails in the rivers Piddle and Frome. However, it is important to recognize that the interplay of factors governing upstream migration is likely to be complex and that the relative importance of potential migrational cues may vary. For example, there is some experimental evidence to suggest that the tendency either to settle in coastal or estuarine environments or to migrate to freshwater may be, at least in part, innate, with distinct saltwater- and freshwater-preferring glass eel contingents (Tosi et al. 1990; Édeline and Élie 2004).

But does the data presented here demonstrate a major decline in eel stock status in the Piddle and Frome since the late 1970s? In part, the answer depends on viewpoint. It could be argued that from a species perspective (and possibly a fishery perspective), optimum benefit accrues from maximum escapement of large, fecund females. Based on sex ratios and on actual river densities of eels larger than 450 mm (i.e,. females due to silver within several years), the number of female silver escapees may now be twice that of the 1970s. In contrast, the number of male silvers currently produced is very low, perhaps 5% of the 1970s level. The situation for the River Frome appears to follow a similar pattern. Thus on the basis of current female spawner escapement, the two river stocks appear to be performing well. However, the overall length-frequency distribution for the Piddle in 2003 (Figure 7) shows a major shortfall of medium-sized eels. This implies that the current high output of female silvers will probably fall sharply in the next few years. The Frome eel population structure has changed less dramatically but appears to be heading in the same direction.

Even the most pessimistic prognosis for future silver eel escapement from the two rivers may be of relatively limited consequence within the overall context of the Frome/Piddle/Poole Harbour complex, given the harbor's far greater eel production potential. As has been the case in the rivers, declining population densities in Poole Harbour are likely to be offset by an increasing proportion of females in the harbor stock. A small sample of 42 eels from Poole Harbour collected by the Environment Agency in 1996 suggested that the proportion of female eels in the population was already relatively high (catch not sexed but 30% >450 mm). However, a tendency to produce fewer, but larger, female eels imposes its own risks. If it is to survive to silver emigration stage, a large female must avoid capture by an intensive fyke-net fishery for many more years than a small male.

Management Considerations

In March 2001, the UK Environment Agency published its first National Eel Management Strategy (Environment Agency 2001). This establishes generalized objectives for eel management, and initially, glass eel licenses were capped to prevent further expansion of the glass eel fishery. Additional targets and actions will be implemented as the strategy develops. However, any UK actions will be influenced by European Union initiatives. In October 2003, the European Union (EU Commission 2003) published proposals for a European Eel Management Plan. If taken forward, this will set pan-European targets, as befits a panmictic (or near-panmictic) stock but will recognize that local actions will need to be based at the catchment level.

In the case of the Severn, the evidence presented here indicates that limiting the glass eel fishery to its current level, or even its former 1990s peak level, would be an adequate management strategy. There is no scientific case for additional restrictions to the fishery.

The Piddle/Frome/Poole Harbour system presents a very different picture. There is quantitative evidence that river eel stocks are undergoing, or are about to undergo, a major decline and more anecdotal evidence that harbor stocks may also be depleted. Since this river/coastal lagoon system is potentially a major contributor to overall eel stocks along the south coast of England, it should be viewed as a local priority in any stock-recovery plan.

One of the most effective potential actions for the Piddle/Frome/Poole Harbour system would be to stop or severely limit the yellow eel fishery in Poole Harbour. This would allow more harbor eels to reach maturity and maximize silver eel escapement, irrespective of the level of glass eel recruitment. Potentially, this could also boost recruitment to the rivers, with higher harbor densities of larger eels promoting upriver migration. However, management initiatives that affect all stakeholders equitably are politically more acceptable. Thus any restrictions on the harbor fishery would ideally be matched by a corresponding restriction on the albeit limited silver eel fishery on the rivers.

Based on current results, there is a clear management case at the river-basin level for application of the precautionary approach and the imposition of blanket fishing restrictions across the Piddle/Frome/Poole system. But given the lack of firm data on stock status in Poole Harbour, which undoubtedly supports the core of the local eel population, it could be suggested that such a restriction would be hard to justify. Equally, the do-nothing option of continuing an essentially unregulated fishery means accepting the risk, albeit unquantifiable, of an accelerating decline in silver eel escapement, which may also be deemed unacceptable. However, on a national scale (England and Wales only), yellow and silver eel fisheries (about 1,640 fyke net (ends) licenses and 12 licensed silver eel racks and traps in 2003) currently harvest some 46 mt annually. Although local fisheries such as the Piddle/Poole Harbour system may have a local impact, the national commercial eel fishery in Britain almost certainly has minimal impact on numbers of silver eels leaving UK waters. It is therefore proposed that a detailed assessment of eel stock status in Poole Harbour should be an immediate priority. This would delay potential management intervention for a year or two, but delays of this magnitude, even if fisheries impacts are shown to be locally severe, are unlikely to be of major national consequence. If backed by a scientifically justified case, a management plan is likely to be accepted more readily and will thus ultimately be of greater benefit to the species.

Acknowledgments

The authors thank all of the riparian land owners for access to the sampling sites. We are also grateful Jim Adami and Tony Medley for the silver eel samples from the River Piddle and River Frome eel traps. We thank Miran Aprahamian for access to the raw data for the 1983–1984 eel surveys of the River Severn. Hannah Mossman, Anthony Wu, Holly Edwards, Becky Wilson, and Joseph Downing assisted with the electrofishing surveys. Peter Milligan advised on data analysis. The 1998–1999 studies were funded jointly by the UK Environment Agency and the UK Ministry of Agriculture Fisheries and Food (MAFF) and formed a part of EA R&D Project W2–028 (MAFF R&D Project SF0307). Additional sampling in 2002 and 2003 was funded by the UK Department for Environment, Food and Rural Affairs (DEFRA) under Project No. SF0236.

The views expressed in this paper are those of the authors alone and may not reflect those of the funding bodies.

References

Aprahamian, M. W. 1986. Eel (*Anguilla anguilla* L.) production in the river Severn, England. Polskie Archiwum Hydrobiologii 33:373–389.

Aprahamian, M. W. 1988. Age structure of eel, *Anguilla anguilla* (L.). populations in the River Severn, England and River Dee, Wales. Aquaculture and Fisheries Management 19:365–376.

Ashworth, S. T., and C. Blanc. 1997. *Anguillicola crassus*, a recently introduced aggressive coloniser of European eel stocks. Bulletin Français de la Pêche et de la Pisciculture 344/345:335–342.

Bruslé, J. 1994. L'anguille Européenne, *Anguilla anguilla*, un poisson sensible aux stress environmenteaux et vulnérable à diverse atteintes pathogènes. Bulletin Français de la Pêche et de la Pisciculture 335:237–260.

Dekker, W. 2003. Eels in crisis. ICES Newsletter 40:10–11.

Édeline, É., and P. Élie. 2004. Is salinity choice related to growth in juvenile eel *Anguilla anguilla*? Cybium 28 (Supplement 1):77–82.

Environment Agency 2001. The national eel management strategy. Environment Agency, Bristol, UK.

EU Commission 2003. Development of a community action plan for the management of the European Eel. Commission of the European Communities, Brussels.

Feunteun, E., P. Laffaille, T. Robinet, C. Briand, A. Baisez, J.-M. Olivier, and A. Acou. 2003. A review of upstream migration and movements in inland waters by anguillid eels: towards a general theory. Pages 191–213 *in* K. Aida, K. Tsukamoto and K Yamauchi, editors. Eel biology. Springer Verlag, Tokyo.

Ibbotson, A., P. Armitage, W. Beaumont, M. Ladle, and S. Welton. 1994. Spatial and temporal distribution of fish in a lowland stream. Fisheries Management and Ecology 5:143–156.

ICES (International Council for the Exploration of the Sea) 1999. ICES cooperative research report N° 229, Report of the ICES Advisory Committee on Fisheries Management 1998: 393–405, Copenhagen.

ICES (International Council for the Exploration of the Sea). 2003. Report of the ICES/EIFAC Working Group on Eels. ICES CM 2003/ACFM:06, Copenhagen.

Kennedy, C. V., and D. J. Fitch. 1990. Colonisation, larval survival and epidemiology of the nematode *Anguillicola crassus*, parasitic in the eel, *Anguilla anguilla*, in Britain. Journal of Fish Biology 36:117–131.

Knights, B. 2001. Economic evaluation of eel and elver fisheries in England and Wales. Environment Agency Technical Report No. W2–039/TR/2. Environment Agency, Bristol, UK.

Knights, B. 2003. A review of the possible impacts of long-term oceanic and climate changes and fishing mortality on recruitment of anguillid eels of the Northern Hemisphere. The Science of the Total Environment 310:237–244.

Knights, B., A. Bark, M. Ball, F. Williams, E. Winter, and S. Dunn. 2001. Eel and elver stocks in England and Wales—status and management options. R & D Technical Report W248, Environment Agency, Bristol, UK.

Knights, B., A. Bark, and B. Williams. 2009. Management of European eel populations in England and in Wales: a critical review and pragmatic considerations. Pages 367–380 *in* J. M. Casselman and D. K. Cairns, editors. Eels at the edge: science, status, and conservation concerns. American Fisheries Society, Symposium 58, Bethesda, Maryland.

Mann, R. H. K., and J. H. Blackburn. 1991. The biology of the eel *Anguilla anguilla* L. in an English chalk stream and interactions with juvenile trout *Salmo trutta* L. and *Salmo salar* L. Hydrobiologia 218:65–76.

McLusky, D. S., and M. Elliott, editors. 2004. The estuarine ecosystem: ecology, threats and management. Oxford University Press, Oxford, UK.

Moriarty, C., and W. Dekker, editors. 1997. Management of the European eel. Fisheries Bulletin no 15, Dublin.

Morrice, C. P. 1989. Eel fisheries in the United Kingdom. MAFF Internal Report No 18. MAFF, Lowestoft, UK.

Morrice, C. P., B. R, Buckley, and B. Stott. Uundated. The yellow and silver eel (*Anguilla anguilla* L.) populations of a chalk stream in southern England. Internal draft report, MAFF, Lowestoft, England.

National Rivers Authority 1990. A survey of eel stocks in the River Frome and River Piddle. Internal report, National Rivers Authority, Wessex Region, UK.

Tesch, F. W. 2003. The eel, 3rd edition, edited by J. E. Thorpe. Blackwell Scientific Publications, Oxford, UK.

Tosi, L., A. Spampanato, C. Sola, and P. Tongiorgi. 1990. Relation of water odour, salinity and temperature to ascent of glass eels, Anguilla anguilla (L.): a laboratory study. Journal of Fish Biology 36:327–340.

White, E. M., and B. Knights. 1997. Dynamics of upstream migration of the European eel, *Anguilla anguilla* L., with special reference to the effects of man-made barriers. Fisheries Management and Ecology 4:311–324.

Abundance Trends of Glass Eels between 1978 and 1999 from Fisheries Data in the Gironde Basin, France

Laurent Beaulaton[1],* and Gérard Castelnaud
*CEMAGREF, unité Ecosystèmes estuariens et poissons migrateurs amphihalins
50 avenue de Verdun, Cestas Cedex 33612 France*

Abstract.—The glass eel is fished in the Gironde Basin, France, with large push nets, scoop nets, and the recently introduced small push net. This study uses fishery data to generate fisheries and abundance indicators for glass eels. Total catch, total effort, and catch per unit effort (CPUE) were calculated for the period 1978–1999 by classical statistical methods and by general linear models (GLM). Use of GLM enabled the correction of sampling variation and offered better trend estimation than classical CPUE. During the study period, the principal source of glass eel landings shifted from the scoop net fishery in the tidal river to the large push net fishery in the estuary. General linear model-based CPUEs for large push nets and for scoop nets showed that glass eel abundance declined by a factor of two to three at the beginning of the 1980s. Since 1985, abundance has stabilized at a low level and shows no sign of recovering. The abundance trend of glass eels in the Gironde Basin confirms the decline in glass eel populations observed elsewhere in Europe.

Introduction

The European eel *Anguilla anguilla* is an important cultural and economic resource. Eel fisheries are particularly intense in the rivers and lagoons of France, where all continental stages (glass, yellow, and silver) are targeted. Eel fisheries have the highest volume and cash value of any amphihaline species in France. Harvest in 1997, all developmental stages combined, was calculated at 700 t with a market price of 65 million euros (Castelnaud 2000). High prices paid for glass eels in recent years (>100 euro/kg) have further bolstered the species' economic value. For these reasons, the eel is much sought after.

Eel recruitment has been declining in Europe since about 1980 (Lobon-Cervia 1999; Dekker et al. 2003; ICES 2005). Recruitment indicators include fishery-dependent data (mostly glass eel landings) and fishery-independent data. Catch per unit effort (CPUE) is generally a better indicator of abundance than harvest data (Gascuel et al. 1995; but see Briand et al. 2003). However, CPUE series for glass eels are rare. The Gironde Basin in western France is the only European location where three different metiers are used to fish glass eels and where data that enable calculation of CPUE are recorded. Using data from CEMAGREF's GIRPECH database (Castelnaud et al. 2001), we estimated fisheries indicators over the period 1978–1999 for professional and non-professional fishermen by classical methods and by general linear models (GLM). We

[1]Corresponding author: laurent.beaulaton@onema.fr
*Current address: Office National de l'Eau et des Milieux Aquatiques, Direction Scientifique et Technique, Immeuble Le Péricentre, 16, avenue Louison Bobet, 94132 Fontenay-sous-Bois Cedex, France

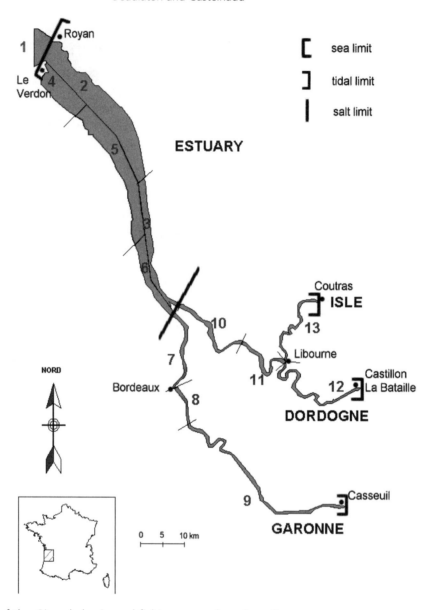

Figure 1. map of the Gironde basin and fishing zones (numbered).

then compared the ability of these two approaches to indicate trends in glass eel recruitment reliably.

Description of Glass Eel Fishing

Study Area

The Gironde Basin (Figure 1), as described by Castelnaud et al. (2001), is the lower part of the Garonne Basin, including the tidal part of the Dordogne and Garonne rivers and their common estuary. The basin stretches about 160 km inland from the Atlantic Ocean and is divided into 13 fishing zones, grouped into three compartments: the Estuary, made up of zones 2–6 (73 km); the Garonne, zones 7–9 (85 km); and the Dordogne, zones 10–13 (75 km). The Garonne and the Dordogne (which includes the lower Isle River) compartments are freshwater but tidal.

Glass Eel Fishing

Glass eels are targeted in the study area by professional fishermen who are officially permitted to sell their catch, and by nonprofessional fishermen (recreational anglers and poachers), who lack authorization to sell. In the tidal river compartments (zones 7–13), professional and nonprofessional fishermen use scoop nets, and beginning January 1996, professionals use small push nets. In the estuary (zones 2–6), professionals use large push nets.

Fishing with Scoop Nets

The scoop net, called *tamis* in France, is the traditional device used for glass eel fishing. It is a large round or oval landing net that is deployed from a boat close to the river's edge by professional fishermen or on shore by nonprofessionals. Fishing typically starts at the beginning of the flood tide and finishes two hours after the beginning of the ebb tide. This fishery is carried out exclusively at night, using a lamp and by making slow movements with the net against the current to catch the eels (Rochard 1992; Girardin et al. 2004).

For professional fishermen, the maximum size permitted is 1.2 m diameter and 1.3 m deep. Maximum diameter and depth are 0.5 m for nonprofessionals. Mesh size varies but is usually 1.5 mm (Girardin et al. 2004). Fishing is allowed in the tidal river compartments from 15 November to 15 April for professionals and from 1 December to 15 April for nonprofessionals. The fishery is closed between 1800 hours on Saturdays and 0600 hours on Mondays.

Fishing with Large Push Nets

This method, called *pibalour* in France, consists of pushing two nets with rigid rectangular frames against the current. The frames are placed either at the front or at the sides of a boat. Regulations limit the number of frames to two, the surface area of nets to 7 m^2, boats to 10 gross registered metric tons, and engine power to 60 hp. There is no regulation on mesh size, and the fishermen use a mesh size of 2–4 mm at the opening of the net and 1–2 mm at the end (Rochard 1992). Fishing takes place mainly during flood tide. This technique is permitted in the estuary from 15 November to 31 March. In March, the fishery is closed between 1800 hours on Saturdays and 0600 hours on Mondays.

Fishing with Small Push Nets

This fishing technique, called *drossage* in France, is similar to the large push net. Two circular nets, 1.2 m in diameter, are mounted on the sides of the boat. The net must not be more than 1.3 m deep. Boats must be under 8 m in length, with maximum engine power of 100 hp but throttled back to 60 hp. The season runs from 15 November to 15 April and is closed between 1800 hours on Saturdays and 0600 hours on Mondays. The small push net fishery is permitted only in the tidal river compartments. It was first authorized in January 1996.

Monitoring the Fishery

Since 1977, CEMAGREF has monitored the glass eel fishery through a sample of cooperating professional fishermen (see Castelnaud et al. 2001). Composition of the sample fluctuates from one season to the next. We set up the "GIRPECH" database in 1994 to compile and verify historic fisheries data and as a repository for new data (Castelnaud et al. 2001). Catch data were collected yearly by visiting each fisherman individually. Data were recorded at the best precision available (by tide or by day) but sometimes the fishermen give us only aggregated data by 2-week periods, by month, or by season. The fishing zone was identified and data were classified into two levels of quality according to data reliability and whether effort data were included. Quality 1 represents data of the better quality. We recorded total number of active fishermen for each zone and each métier from information coming from administrative agencies, fishermen's organizations, and cooperating fishermen. This data gave us nominal effort and were used to scale up from our sample to the whole population. Cooperating fishermen represented 13% and 5%, respectively, of the whole population of large push net and scoop net fishermen in the 1980s and 22% and 20% in the 1990s. For small push nets, our sample represented 28% of the whole population of small push net fishermen.

The glass eel fishing season, which usually runs from November to April, will be referred to by the year of the second part of the season (e.g., the season from November 1998 to April 1999 is termed the 1999 season).

Analysis

Classical Method

As in Castelnaud et al. (2001), the classical theory of stratified sampling (Cochran 1977) was used to calculate total seasonal catch and effort for each métier. Mean catch and mean effective effort per zone (or group of zones) and per métier were calculated for each season using data of both quality levels from our sample of cooperating fishermen. Total catch and total effective effort were calculated for each zone (group of zones) and each métier by multiplying mean catch and effective effort by the nominal effort (total number of active fishermen) per zone and métier. Summed total catch and total effort per zone (group of zones) gave total catch and effort for the entire Gironde Basin, for each métier, and for the whole population of fishermen. All of these calculations were accompanied by the calculation of 95% confidence intervals. Catches are reported in metric tons, and the unit of effort is one day's fishing. The three métiers are treated separately in both classical and GLM (see below) analyses because there is no equivalence among units of effort. The stratification into "zone" was not used for a given season unless zone means differed (empty intersection of confidence intervals for the zones). Not all zone stratifications were investigated, since these data have been analyzed elsewhere (Girardin et al. 2004). We thus determined that:

For the large push net métier, only zone 3 had significant differences in catch and effort compared with other estuary zones; and

For the scoop net and the small push net métier, Garonne and the Dordogne compartment had significant differences in catch and effort.

Following Castelnaud et al. (1994), we assumed that nonprofessionals in the tidal river compartments had similar scoop net mean catches and mean efforts as professionals. Thus we used professional mean catches and effort and total number of active nonprofessionals to estimate total catches and effort of nonprofessionals.

We assumed that the system under study met the requirements of homogeneity and independence needed to consider that CPUE is proportional to abundance (Beverton and Holt 1957; Gulland 1969; Ricker 1975; Kleiber and Perrin 1991).

To calculate seasonal CPUEs for the three métiers, no other stratification was applied. We simply used a mean of the CPUE per cooperating fisherman, using only data of quality 1. The CPUE for a fisherman is defined as total catch divided by total effort for the season. We did not estimate CPUE for nonprofessional fishermen because we had no direct data from this category.

GLM method

Presentation of the Model

To maximize proportionality between CPUE and abundance, we used a GLM to correct distortions of catch and effort data from our nonrandom sample of cooperating fishermen.

The use of GLMs is common in fisheries science (examples in Castelnaud et al. 2001). The GLM procedure in SAS software (SAS 2000) was used to carry out this analysis.

GLMs are a generalization of traditional linear models and account for variation in observations (here, CPUE) by the addition of effects (McCullagh and Nelder 1989). We used a logarithmic transformation to give positive predicted values and to stabilize the variance (Legendre and Legendre 1979; Castelnaud et al. 2001). Before taking the logarithm, we added 1 to the CPUE (Dekker 1998; Castelnaud et al. 2001) to avoid the problem of zero catches, which would give nil CPUEs for which the logarithm could not be calculated. The constant of 1 was chosen so that only the positive part of the logarithmic function was used. We tested the normality of residuals (an assumption of the GLM procedure) with a Kolmogorov-Smirnov test using the capability procedure in SAS.

Presentation of the Effects

We tested different effects, as well as combinations of these effects. For brevity, we present only the model that was selected on the basis of biological and statistical significance. Other tested models gave similar results.

Tested effects were:

Season—for estimating interseasonal changes in abundance;

Tide month—for estimating within-season changes in abundance, based on the tidal calendar. See details below;

Tide—for estimation of changes in abundance within the tidal cycle. See details below;

Fisherman—to account for variation in fishing skill among fishermen;

Season × tide month interaction – to represent variation in seasonality.

The selected model is expressed as:

ln (CPUE + 1) = season + tide month + tide + fisherman + season × tide month + error

Detail of the Tide Month Effect

The French Marine Hydrographic and Oceanographic Service predicts tidal coefficients, which are the differences in height between high tide and low tide, on an arbitrary scale from 20 to 120. High coefficients correspond to a spring tide (mean 95) and low ones to a neap tide (mean 45). The tide-month effect was added to analyze intraseasonal changes. A tide half-month is the interval between two minimum tide coefficients (i.e., between two neap tides). A tide month is a succession of two tide half-months (Figure 2).

We used tidal rather than calendar months because glass eel movements are tidally influenced (Lowe 1950; Martin 1995; Jessop 2003). One tide month thus includes all the phases of the tide (spring tide, neap tide, etc.).

The number of days in a tide month varies between 27 and 30 (mean 28.5). Tide month 1 began with the first neap tide in October and ended before the official opening of the fishing season on 15 November. This ensured that the entire fishing season was covered. Since there were only 13 catch data points in tide month 1 during the study years, we did

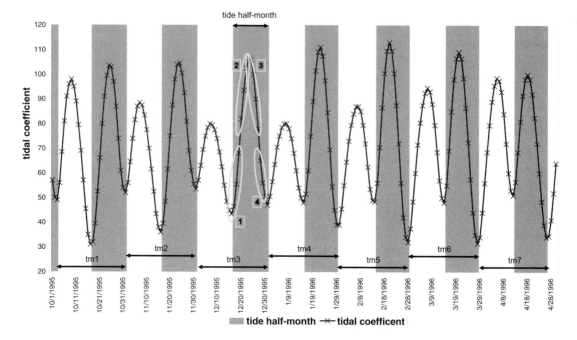

Figure 2. The 1996 glass eel fishing season, divided into tide half-months according to tide coefficients. One gray bar and one white bar form a tide month ("tm x": tide month x). The ovals group days by tide phase (see details of the tide effect in the text).

Table 1. Earliest, mean, and latest dates of the beginning of tide months.

	Date of beginning of tide month						
	1	2	3	4	5	6	7	End of 7
Earliest	2/10	28/10	23/11	27/12	23/01	25/02	25/03	22/04
Mean	5/10	3/11	3/12	2/01	1/02	2/03	31/03	27/04
Latest	12/10	10/11	11/12	10/01	9/02	10/03	8/04	30/04

not use data from this tide month.

Note that this type of division does not follow the civil calendar (Table 1). For example, the closing of the large push net fishing season (31 March) comes either at the end of tide month 6 or at the beginning of tide month 7, depending on the season.

Detail of the Tide Effect

The tide effect is based on a breakdown of a tide half-month into four parts (Figure 2).

1. First half of rising coefficients.
2. Second half of rising coefficients.
3. First half of falling coefficients.
4. Second half of falling coefficients.

Data Used

Only quality 1 data with effort specification per day or per tide (see Methods) were used in analyses. Since small push nets came into use only recently, GLM was applied only to the large push net and scoop net metiers. Catch per unit effort was calculated per day or per tide, per cooperating fisherman and per zone.

Relevance of the Model

The model was evaluated as follows:
The adjusted coefficient of determination indicated the strength of the model;
Fisher tests indicated the significance of the model and its effects; and
Kolmogorov-Smirnov tests evaluated the normality of residuals.

Estimating CPUE Per Season and Per Tide Month

Once we had evaluated the different effects, it was possible to calculate mean CPUE per season by adding the effects of a given season and the arithmetical means of the other effects. In the same way, to calculate mean CPUE per tide month, we added the effect of a given tide month to the arithmetical means of the other effects. The lsmeans procedure in SAS was used to carry out this function (SAS 2000).

Comparison of the Two Methods

In theory, all metiers in the fishery should give the same assessment of the abundance of stocks (Chadwick and O'Boyle 1990). In order to test this hypothesis, we regressed the large push net CPUE against the scoop net CPUE, as estimated using the classical method and by GLM. We used the SAS reg procedure (SAS 2000). The regression was expressed as large push net = a × scoop net + b, where the constant b was kept only if it was significant at the 5% level (student test). We used a student test to judge the significance of the model, and the coefficient of determination (R^2) was computed.

Using the same approach, we regressed CPUE calculated using the classical method against CPUE based on GLM for each métier to examine the effect of calculation method on the CPUE series.

Results

Classical Method: Estimate of Catch, Effort, and CPUE

Total catch by professionals using large push nets fluctuated between 14 and 50 mt from 1978 to 1999 (Table 2; Figure 3). Two effort phases were evident. From 1978–1988, about 40 nominal fishermen exerted about 2,500 effective days of effort annually; from 1989 to 1999, about 70 nominal fishermen exerted about 5,000 d annually (Table 3). The increase in effort corresponded with a sudden increase in the price of glass eels. CPUE fell by half between 1978 and 1984 (mean 15.5 kg/d) and between 1985 and 1999 (mean 7.7 kg/d). Since 1985, CPUEs have more or less stabilized around 6–7 kg/d.

For professionals using scoop nets, effort decreased at least 90% and catch decreased at least 99% between 1978 and 1981 and between 1996 and 1999 (Tables 2 and 3). For CPUE, there was a major drop between 1981 and 1982, followed by relative stability (1978–1981: 20.7 kg/d; 1982–1999: 4.7 kg/d). Scoop net catches prior to 1996 are similar to summed professional catches by small push nets and by scoop nets after 1996. Moreover, scoop net catches have dropped considerably since 1996. Thus the introduction of small push nets does not seem to have produced an overall increase in glass eel harvest in the tidal river compartments.

Total catches by all fishermen were high at the beginning of the study period, with a mean of 289.1 mt between 1978 and 1981 and a peak of 430 mt in 1980 (Table 2).

Table 2. Total catches (metric tons) and CPUE (kg/boat/day, by classic and GLM methods) by professional (PRO) and non-professional (non-PRO) fishermen in the Gironde basin between 1978 and 1999. x = stratification into zones was used for this season (see Methods).

Season	Large push net - PRO			Scoop net					Small push net		Total
	Landings	CPUE			PRO			Non-PRO	PRO		landings
	(t)	Classical	GLM	Landings	CPUE			Landings	Landings	CPUE	(t)
				(t)	Classical	GLM		(t)	(t)	Classical	
1978	26.7	12.8	10.3	83.3	16.5	6.8		107.8			217.8
1979	28.0	14.0	10.0	89.7	15.5	6.6		116.2			234.0
1980	45.8	25.4	17.8	167.3	27.1	9.0		217.1			430.2
1981	45.5	14.9	9.5	78.3 x	23.5	7.2		150.6			274.4
1982	49.6	10.9	8.4	36.6	6.3	4.6		36.5			122.8
1983	49.5	12.7	9.0	25.8	5.2	4.6		26.9			102.2
1984	30.5	17.6	9.6	26.0	5.5	5.4		26.0			82.6
1985	16.3	8.1	5.4	11.7	3.6	2.0		11.8			39.8
1986	26.3	8.8	5.6	13.6	5.4	6.1		14.4			54.3
1987	31.9	13.5	4.3	25.0	8.0	3.4		28.6			85.5
1988	25.4	9.3	4.7	6.7	4.6	3.1		6.7			38.9
1989	37.5	7.1	4.3	15.6 x	7.4	2.6		17.3			70.5
1990	28.6	5.6	3.7	8.6	3.0	1.2		9.0			46.2
1991	36.0	8.5	4.4	9.6 x	4.6	0.9		14.5			60.0
1992	17.0	4.5	2.6	8.0	4.3	1.7		12.8			37.8
1993	29.6 x	8.9	4.9	11.6	5.4	3.2		21.7			62.9
1994	34.6 x	9.2	5.3	6.5	4.2	2.3		12.4			53.5
1995	47.5	7.9	4.4	9.6	3.7	2.5		18.9			75.9
1996	21.4 x	4.7	3.4	1.5	2.3	1.6		4.2	2.2	1.8	29.4
1997	33.0 x	6.3	3.4	3.6	7.3	2.3		6.4	7.9 x	3.3	50.9
1998	14.1 x	3.8	2.7	0.4	0.7	1.2		1.0	1.7	1.4	17.2
1999	40.6	8.9	4.0	0.8	1.7	1.6		2.7	7.5 x	2.2	51.6

Catches halved after 1982 and then dropped below 100 t in 1984, with a mean for 1984–1999 of 53.6 t. Nonprofessionals made an important contribution to total catches, particularly in the 1980s. Catches by large push nets (professionals only) were fairly stable compared with the scoop net metiers.

For all metiers and categories of fishermen, confidence intervals are relatively wide until the end of the 1980s and narrower in the 1990s. This is due to the small number of cooperating fishermen during the first-decade period and high variability among fishermen.

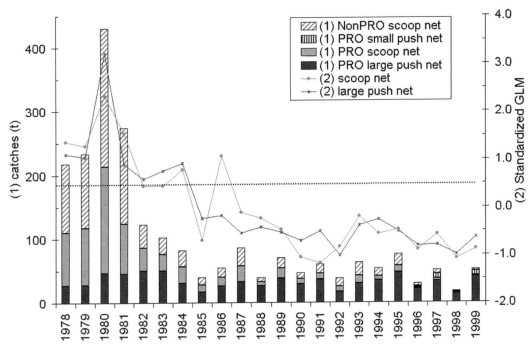

Figure 3. Total catches for the three metiers and standardized CPUE (from GLM) for the large push net and the scoop net métiers.

GLM Method: Estimate of the CPUE

Indicators of the appropriateness of the GLM model for large push nets and for scoop nets are presented in Table 4. The GLM has few degrees of freedom (1% for the large push net métier and 4% for the scoop net métier), thus being parsimonious (for a definition of parsimony, see Johnson and Omland 2004). The coefficients of determination (R^2 and adjusted R^2) for both métiers are about 45%. The model and the various effects are all highly significant, with P-values < 0.0001. However, the residuals are not normal.

For both métiers, we observed high CPUEs at the beginning of the study period (1978–1984 mean. 10.6 kg/d for the large push net métier and 6.3 kg/d for the scoop net metier; Table 2 and Figure 3). Since 1985, CPUEs have decreased by factors of 2–3 and have fluctuated around a low level (1985–1999 mean: 4.2 kg/d for the large push net metier and 2.4 kg/d for the scoop net metier). The scoop net CPUE calculated by GLM showed a peak in 1986 that did not appear in the scoop net CPUE calculated by the classical method or in the large push net CPUEs. The GLM method requires more accurate data than the classical method; as a consequence, the data from only one fisherman, who appears to be particularly efficient, was used in 1986. Thus this peak probably corresponds to a sampling problem rather than a true peak in CPUE. Also, we note peaks in classical CPUEs in 1987 for the large push net and the scoop net metiers, but none in GLM-based CPUEs (Table 2). One particularly efficient large push net fisherman was added to the sample in this season. If we recalculate CPUE for 1987 by the classical method with this fisherman excluded, the peak disappears and the curve looks much like that obtained by GLM. For the scoop net métier, if we consider only the two fishermen (whose performance was only average) common to seasons 1986,

Table 3. Estimated nominal (number of active fishermen) and effective (number of days) fishing effort on glass eels by professional (PRO) and non-professional (non-PRO) fishermen in the Gironde basin between 1978 and 1999. x = stratification into zones was used for this season (see Methods).

Season	Large push net - PRO		Scoop net			Small push net - PRO		Total
			PRO		Non-PRO			
	Nominal fishermen	Effective days	Nominal fishermen	Effective days	Nominal fishermen	Nominal fishermen	Effective days	nominal fishermen
1978	41	1558	285	5919	369			695
1979	41	2132	285	5680	369			695
1980	41	3116	285	6918	370			696
1981	41	2798	285	6477	370			696
1982	41	3311	265	6161	264			570
1983	40	3760	226	6683	235			501
1984	40	2960	194	4882	194			428
1985	40	1710	192	3328	194			426
1986	40	2467	189	2961	200			429
1987	40	2280	157	3585	180			377
1988	40	2538	160	1728	160			360
1989	65	5128	122	2760	127			314
1990	66	5102	117	3089	123			306
1991	67	4909	93	3298	135			295
1992	66	4563	85	2696	135			286
1993	64	4296	76	2275	142			282
1994	64	4518	76	2064	144			284
1995	73	5783	72	2750	142			287
1996	66	4838 x	48	853	130	42	1293	286
1997	75	6122	64	818	116	65	3058 x	320
1998	76	5238	44	537	104	58	1255	282
1999	74	4688 x	25	450	87	74	3399	260

Table 4. GLM model parameters for large push net and scoop net CPUE

	Degrees of freedom		R^2	R^2 adjusted	Significance (F test)		Normality of residuals
	Model	total			Model	Effects	Kolmogorov-Smirnov test
Large push net	145	14783	45.3%	44.8%	<0.0001	all <0.0001	<0.01
Scoop net	138	3237	45.5%	43.1%	<0.0001	all <0.0001	<0.01

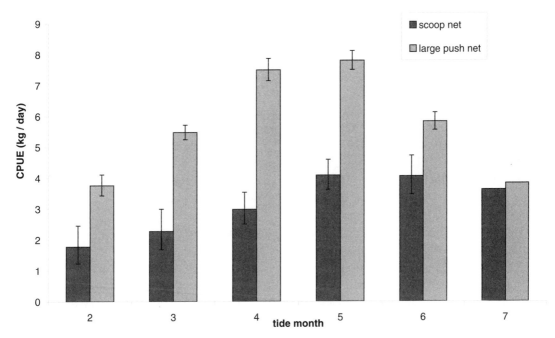

Figure 4. CPUE per tide month for the large push net and scoop net métier. Vertical bars represent confidence intervals.

1987, and 1988, then the 1987 season does not present a peak either.

Catch per unit effort per tide month for the large push net and the scoop net métiers followed a Gaussian curve (Figure 4). Large push net CPUE peaked in mid-season (period 4/5, end January/beginning February). Scoop net CPUE peaked near the end of the season (period 5/6 or end February/beginning March).

The GLM for both large push nets and scoop nets indicated that CPUE was strongest during Phase 3 (first half of falling coefficient; see Methods), followed by Phases 2 and 4. CPUE was lowest in Phase 1. The variation of predicted CPUE due to tide effect is less important than the variation due to other effects.

Comparison of the Classical Method and the GLM method

Regression analysis revealed significant relations between scoop net and large push net CPUEs using both methods (Table 5 and Figure 5). The R^2 for the GLM CPUEs (81%

Table 5. Characteristics of regressions relating large push net CPUE to scoop net CPUE using classical and GLM methods.

	Equation for the model	Significance (P>F)	R^2	Adjusted R^2	P Y-intercept
method	Large push net = 0.5605 x sccop net + 5.9305	<0.0001	60.85%	58.90%	<0.0001
GLM	Large push net = 1.4029 x sccop net + 1.1704	<0.0001	80.52%	79.55%	0.0908
GLM	Large push net = 1.6361 x sccop net	<0.0001	94.61%	94.35%	/

with y-intercept) was stronger than the R^2 for the classical CPUEs (61% with y-intercept). Moreover, the presence of a y-intercept in the classical regression indicates a bias in the relation between CPUEs of both métiers calculated using by this method. The CPUEs for the two métiers thus seem to demonstrate the same trend, which reflects abundance.

The fact that there is a stronger and unbiased relationship between scoop net CPUE and large push net CPUE with GLM suggests that the GLM method is more efficient at indicating glass eel abundance trends.

Regression analysis revealed significant relations between CPUE calculated using the classical method and GLM for both métiers (Table 6 and Figure 6). The R^2 for large push net CPUEs (86% with y-intercept) was stronger than the R^2 for the scoop net CPUEs (72% with y-intercept). Moreover, the presence of a y-intercept in the scoop net CPUE regression indicates a bias in the relation between CPUEs of both methods calculated for this metier. The relation between CPUEs calculated using both methods appears to be stronger for large push nets than for scoop nets.

Discussion

All estimates were made with data supplied by a nonrandom sample of cooperating fishermen, whose composition varied among seasons. Major variations in catch and effort can be observed among fishermen. Consequently the estimate depends to a great extent on the sample of cooperating fishermen, which has to be representative, and on the quality of their data, which must be accurate. We note that for stratification by zone, CEMAGREF attempted to recruit during each season and for each zone the maximum number of fishermen disposed to cooperate and to report data of good quality.

Classical Method

Catch and effort estimates highlight a major shift in the Gironde fishery. In the early 1980s, the scoop net fishery in the tidal river compartment was the main source of landings. As the scoop net fishery rapidly decreased, the large push net fishery in the estuary became the principal fishery. This change was mainly due to a drastic decrease in the number of scoop net fishermen and their landings (decrease >90%) in the tidal river compartment while the number of large push nets doubled and their landings in the estuary remained stable.

Catch and effort indicators allow us to place CPUEs (calculated from samples) in their contexts (entire fisheries) and prevent misinterpretation of CPUE due, for example, to a short-term change in effort. We found a decrease in abundance, given the relative uni-

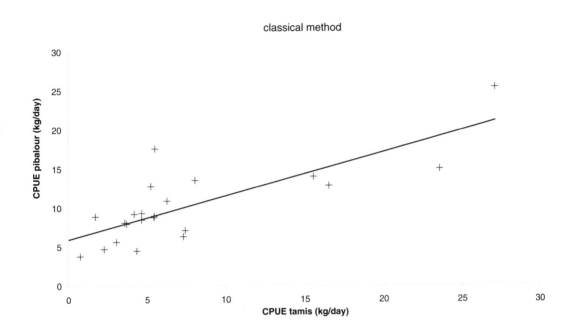

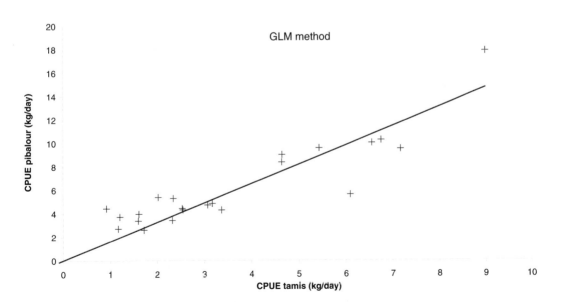

Figure 5. Regression between the scoop net CPUE and large push net CPUE calculated using the classical method (top) and GLM method (bottom)

Table 6. Characteristics of regressions relating CPUE using classical method to CPUE using GLM for large push net and scoop net.

Metier	Equation for the model	Significance (P>F)	R^2	Adjusted R^2	P Y-intercept
large push net	GLM = 0.6735 x class. − 0.5796	<0.0001	86%	85%	0.4072
large push net	GLM = 0.6270 x class.	<0.0001	97%	96%	/
scoop net	GLM = 0.2842 x class. − 1.4898	<0.0001	72%	71%	0.0013

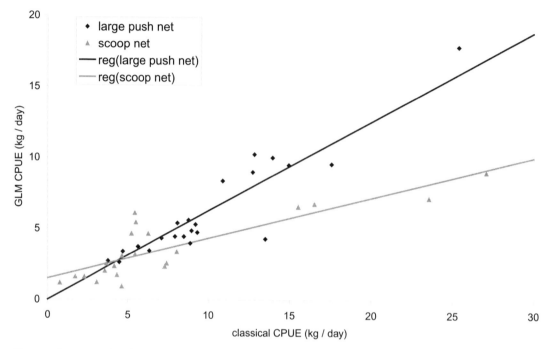

Figure 6. Regression between CPUE calculated using the classical method and CPUE calculated using GLM method for large push net and the scoop net.

formity of large push net catches, while effort increased, and a similar marked drop in scoop net catches while effort decreased, but more slowly than catch. The fisheries indicators of the different métiers thus lead us to conclude a drop in glass eel abundance over the past 20 years.

The introduction of the small push net métier in the tidal river compartments in 1996 did not enable professional fishermen to increase their CPUE or even to maintain their total landings (scoop net + small push net) in the tidal river compartment. The same observation was made on the Adour Basin after the introduction of small push nets there in 1995 (Prouzet et al. 2000).

Rough estimates of catch and effective effort by nonprofessionals show that this category had a high level of fishing pressure at least during the 1980s. The marked decrease in their catches after 1995 is associated with the emergence of the small push net métier. According to fishermen, small push nets tend to disperse the glass eels, making them less accessible to scoop nets. This mainly affects nonprofessional scoop net fishermen because professional scoop net fishermen didn't fish in these zones before the introduction of the small push net. Another explanation may come from the way nonprofessional catches are estimated with the mean catches of professionals with the scoop net métier. In fact, more and more professional fishermen are abandoning scoop nets in favor of small push nets. Those who fish with scoop nets often do so as a complement to the small push net métier and not as an entirely separate métier, as was the case before 1996.

GLM Method

The adjusted coefficients of determination (around 45%) remain acceptable, since they fall within the limits stated by Goni et al. (1999). Compared with reports they quote, our study contains a relatively large quantity of data, especially for the large push net metier (>14,000 data points).

The model respects Sparre's "good" model criteria (1985, in Brêthes 1990). Indeed, it was suitable for both major metiers because it is relatively simple, the parameters are easy to interpret, and it uses already existing data.

The residuals in the GLM model are not normal, mainly because of extreme values. However, linear models are fairly robust in the face of deviations from the normality assumption (SAS 2000), especially when the residuals reveal an absence of plurimodality (Castelnaud et al. 2001). Moreover, the model and effects are highly significant.

Our main reason for using the GLM method was to correct for fluctuations in the sample of cooperating fishermen, a difficulty also encountered in an earlier study on migration of spawning allice shad *Alosa alosa* (Castelnaud et al. 2001) The GLM approach is relatively efficient for this exercise. For example, the peak in 1987, caused by data from one fisherman, disappears with the GLM

method. General linear models also have limitations. It requires catch per day or per tide, to permit analysis of tide effects. In the 1986 season, only a single scoop net fisherman provided data that met this criterion. If, in 1986, this single fisherman had had larger catches than his average for other seasons, he would have artificially swelled the CPUE for that season. The fisherman effect assigns a constant productivity to each fisherman from one season to another, which, in reality, is inexact. Variations exist for all the cooperating fishermen and for all seasons (acquired experience, new equipment, etc.), but when the sample size is large, these epiphenomena are averaged out.

A relaxation of data-acceptance criteria would permit the use of a larger amount of data. If the tide effect was set aside and the tide month effect was replaced by calendar month, then landings and effort by calendar month, which are recorded, could be used at the expense of a less detailed analysis of factors influencing CPUE.

Gascuel et al. (1995) showed that in the case of symmetrical or asymmetrical intra-seasonal CPUE curves, and in contrast to plateau curves, which represent an equilibrium between catch and the arrival of the glass eels, the use of CPUE as an abundance index is valid. The curves showing the tide month effect (Figure 4) are symmetrical for the large push net metier and asymmetrical for the scoop net metier. This supports the validity of glass eel CPUE in the Gironde as an abundance index.

Comparison of the Classical Method and the GLM Method

There is a strong linear relationship between CPUE for the two major métiers. The relation is better and more unbiased with the GLM-based CPUE than with the classical CPUE, which demonstrates the advantage of the GLM approach. Fishing with large push nets does not therefore appear to distort to any great extent the glass eel abundance signal that is transmitted to the scoop net fishery upstream. Two perhaps complementary hypotheses can be put forward: first, large push net effort is relatively constant throughout and between seasons; and second, this type of fishing takes too few glass eels to modify the glass eel abundance signal.

The relation between CPUE calculated by the classical method and the GLM method is better and less biased for large push nets than for scoop nets. This indicates that GLM makes fewer corrections for large push net data than for scoop net data. Our sample of fishermen using large push nets thus seems to be less subject to fluctuation than those using scoop nets.

We conclude that the most reliable and meaningful abundance series in the Gironde Basin is the large push net CPUE calculated using GLM.

Glass Eel Abundance Trends in the Gironde Basin

The glass eel abundance trend in the Gironde Basin reported herein corresponds to the decline in eel populations observed elsewhere in France (Guerault and Desaunay 1989; Castelnaud et al. 1994; Prouzet et al. 2000) and across Europe (ICES 2003; Dekker 1998, 2000; Dekker et al. 2003). All note a sharp drop at the beginning of the 1980s. The particular feature of our study is that the trend is confirmed by two métiers in the same river basin.

Conclusion

We demonstrate that estimates of catch, effort, and CPUE for two métiers (large push net, scoop net) converged to indicate a major drop in glass eel abundance. Catches with large push nets remained relatively stable while effort doubled and, in the same period, catches and effort with scoop nets decreased considerably. This induced a major shift from a scoop net-dominated fishery to a large push net-dominated fishery.

The GLM models were clearly suited to calculating CPUE: they enabled us to correct sampling variations and produced estimates that agreed with classical CPUEs. Abundance decreased two- to threefold between 1980 and 1985 in both métiers and then fluctuated with no consistent trend until 1999. The GLM approach requires catch data with effort recorded per day or per tide and in sufficient quantities to permit inclusion of effects such as tides.

This study confirms that, after a considerable drop in the 1980s, glass eel abundance is now in a period of stagnation at a low level, with no signs of an upturn. The eel population needs a global restoration plan as stated by the EIFAC/ICES working group on eels. Since the glass eel fishery contributes to eel mortality, our findings imply that current regulations should be strictly applied (i.e., illegal fishing should be suppressed) while new restrictions are necessary for all categories of fishermen (e.g., season, size of gear, closed zones).

Acknowledgments

We thank Pierre Dumont and Guy Verreault for their support and Yves Le Gat, Eric Rochard, Paul Gonthier, and Patrick Lambert for their help and advice.

References

Beverton, R. J. H., and S. J. Holt. 1957. On the dynamics of exploited fish populations. Her Majesty's Stationery Office, London.

Brêthes, J. C. 1990. Le processsus d'évaluation des stocks. Pages 17–30 *in* J. C. Brêthes, and R. N. O'Boyle, editors. Méthodes d'évaluation des stocks halieutiques. Centre International d'Exploitation des Océans, Québec.

Briand, C., D. Fatin, G. Fontenelle, and E. Feunteun. 2003. Estuarine and fluvial recruitment of European glass eel in an Atlantic exploited estuary. Fisheries Management and Ecology 10:377–384.

Castelnaud, G. 2000. Localisation de la pêche, effectifs de pêcheurs et production des espèces amphihalines dans les fleuves français. Bulletin Français de la Pêche et de la Pisciculture 357/358:439–460.

Castelnaud, G., D. Guerault, Y. Desaunay, and P. Élie. 1994. Production et abondance de la civelle en France au début des années 90. Bulletin Français de la Pêche et de la Pisciculture 335:263–287.

Castelnaud, G., E. Rochard, and Y. Le Gat. 2001. Analyse de la tendance de l'abondance de l'alose *Alosa alosa* en Gironde à partir de l'estimation d'indicateurs halieutiques sur la période 1977–1998. Bulletin Français de la Pêche et de la Pisciculture 362/363:989–1015.

Chadwick, M., and R. N. O'Boyle. 1990. L'analyse des données de capture et d'effort. Pages 77–101 *in* J. C. Brêthes and R. N. O'Boyle, editors. Méthodes d'évaluation des stocks halieutiques. Centre International d'Exploitation des Océans, Québec.

Cochran, W. G. 1977. Sampling techniques, 3rd edition, Wiley, New York.

Dekker, W. 1998. Long-term trends in the glass eels immigrating at Den Oever, the Netherlands. Bulletin Français de la Pêche et de la Pisciculture 349:199–214.

Dekker, W. 2000. The fractal geometry of the European eel stock. ICES Journal of Marine Science 57:109–121.

Dekker, W., J. M. Casselman, D. K. Cairns, K. Tsukamoto, D. J. Jellyman, and H. Lickers. 2003. Worldwide decline of eel resources necessitates immediate action. Fisheries 28(12):28–30.

Gascuel, D., E. Feunteun, and G. Fontenelle. 1995. Seasonal dynamics of estuarine migration in glass eels (*Anguilla anguilla*). Aquatic Living Resources 8:123–133.

Girardin, M., G. Castelnaud, and L. Beaulaton. 2004. Surveillance halieutique de l'estuaire de la Gironde - suivi des captures 2002 - étude de la faune circulante 2003. Rapport pour EDF CNPE du Blayais, étude n°91, CEMAGREF groupement de Bordeaux, Cestas, France.

Goni, R., F. Alvarez, and S. Adlerstein. 1999. Application of generalized linear modeling to catch rate analysis of Western Mediterranean fisheries: the Castellon trawl fleet as a case study. Fisheries Research 42:291–302.

Guerault, D., and Y. Desaunay. 1989. Evolution de l'abondance de la civelle (*Anguilla anguilla*) dans les estuaires de la Loire et de la Vilaine (France) 1977–1988. Pages 1–8 and annexes in EIFAC Working Party on Eel, 1989, Porto, Portugal.

Gulland, J. A. 1969. Manuel d'évaluation des stocks d'animaux aquatiques. Première partie—analyse des populations. FAO, Manuel FAO de science halieutique no 4, Rome.

ICES (International Council for the Exploration of the Sea). 2003. Report of the ICES/EIFAC Working Group on Eels. ICES CM 2003/ACFM:06, Copenhagen.

ICES. 2005. Report of the ICES/EIFAC Working Group on Eels. ICES CM 2005/I:01, Copenhagen.

Jessop, B. M. 2003. Annual variability in the effects of water temperature, discharge, and tidal stage on the migration of American eel elvers from estuary to river. Pages 3–16 *in* D. A. Dixon, editor. Biology, management, and protection of catadromous eels. American Fisheries Society, Symposium 33, Bethesda, Maryland.

Johnson, J. B., and K. S. Omland. 2004. Model selection in ecology and evolution. Trends in Ecology and Evolution 19:101–108.

Kleiber, P., and C. Perrin. 1991. Catch-per-effort and stock status in the U.S. North Pacific albacore fishery: reappraisal of both. Fishery Bulletin 89:379–385.

Legendre, L., and P. Legendre. 1979. Ecologie numérique: Tome 1: le traitement multiple des données écologiques. Masson, Collection d'écologie no 12, Paris.

Lobon-Cervia, J. 1999. The decline of eel *Anguilla anguilla* (L.) in a river catchment of northern Spain 1986–1997. Further evidence for a critical status of eel in Iberian waters. Archiv Fur Hydrobiologie 144:245–253.

Lowe, R. H. 1950. Factors influencing the runs of elvers in the river Bann, Northern Ireland. Journal du Conseil International pour l'Exploration de la Mer 17:299–315.

Martin, M. H. 1995. The effects of temperature, river flow, and tidal cycles on the onset of glass eel and elver migration into fresh water in the American eel. Journal of Fish Biology 46:891–902.

McCullagh, P., and J. A. Nelder. 1989. Generalized linear models. Chapman and Hall, London.

Prouzet, P., F. Sanchez, M. N. De Casamajor, N. Bru, and R. Drouilhet. 2000. Impact de la pratique du tamis poussé en zone maritime de l'Adour sur l'abondance des civelles et sur leur pêche. IFREMER, St-Pée sur Nivelle, France.

Ricker, W. E. 1975. Computation and interpretation of

biological statistics of fish populations. Fisheries Research Board of Canada Bulletin, no. 191.

Rochard, E. 1992. Mise au point d'une méthode de suivi de l'abondance des amphihalins dans le système fluvio-estuarien de la Gironde, application à l'étude écobiologique de l'esturgeon *Acipenser sturio*. Thèse de doctorat, Université de Rennes, France.

SAS. 2000. SAS OnlineDoc, Version 8. SAS Institute Inc.

Part IV

Movement, Migration, and Barriers

Three-Dimensional Movement of Silver-Phase American Eels in the Forebay of a Small Hydroelectric Facility

LEAH BROWN[1,*], ALEX HARO AND THEODORE CASTRO-SANTOS

S. O. Conte Anadromous Fish Research Center, Biological Resources Discipline
U.S. Geological Survey, One Migratory Way, Turners Falls, Massachusetts 01376, USA

Abstract.—Declines in the population of the American eel, *Anguilla rostrata*, along the northwestern Atlantic have stimulated resource managers to consider the impact of hydroelectric facilities on silver-phase eels as they migrate downstream to the sea. During the fall of 2002, we investigated the movement of migrant eels passing downstream of a small hydroelectric facility on the Connecticut River (Massachusetts). We used three-dimensional acoustic telemetry to monitor fine-scale movement of telemetered silver eels in the forebay (the first 100 m of area directly upstream of the dam). Eel movements were tracked approximately every three seconds, and individual swimming pathways were reconstructed to compare the three-dimensional results with biotelemetry methods previously used at this site; conventional telemetry systems included radio, PIT, and acoustic telemetry. We found that three-dimensional acoustic telemetry provided the necessary fine-scale resolution to characterize dominant movement patterns and locations of passage. Eels were detected at all depths throughout the forebay; however, they spent the greatest proportion of their time near the bottom, with occasional vertical movements to the surface. Eels exhibited a range of movements interpreted to be downstream searching behavior, including altered vertical and horizontal positions at or near the trash racks and various looping movements directly upstream of the trash racks and throughout the entire forebay. A substantial number of these eels (28%) were detected re-entering the acoustic array on multiple dates before passing the station. The majority (89%) were detected passing downstream of the dam through the turbines.

Introduction

Downstream migration of freshwater eels can be restricted by hydroelectric facilities (Haro et al. 2000b; Richkus and Whalen 2000; EPRI 2001; Dixon 2003). As migrant eels travel downstream and encounter hydroelectric facilities, they may experience migration delays within the impoundments created by dams, be impinged on intake screens or trash racks, or be exposed to direct turbine mortality or turbine-induced injuries (Berg 1986; Adams and Schwevers 1997; Haro et al. 2000a; EPRI 2001; Haro et al. 2003; Richkus and Dixon 2003). Turbine mortality at each hydroelectric facility can be extremely variable, depending on runner type, size, speed, number of blades, blade spacing and thickness, and size of the fish (Berg 1986; Boubée et al. 2001; EPRI 2001; Larinier and Travade 2002).

---

[1] Corresponding author: lbrown@htisonar.com
*Current address: Hydroacoustic Technology, Inc. 715 NE Northlake Way, Seattle, Washington 98105 USA

Turbine mortality of downstream migrant eels has frequently been estimated to be more than 25% and turbine-induced injuries may be even higher, yet few studies have investigated the behavior of reproductively mature silver-phase eels as they approach, encounter, and pass downstream of hydroelectric facilities (Haro et al. 2000b; Boubée et al. 2001; EPRI 2001; McCleave 2001; Behrmann-Godel and Eckmann 2003; Dixon 2003; Durif et al. 2003; Watene et al. 2003).

Initial biotelemetry studies of silver-phase eels have focused on general migratory behavior and patterns of downstream movement in freshwater and estuarine habitats. These studies have shown that initial downstream movements occur at night and are typically associated with heavy precipitation and high-flow events (summarized by Tesch 1977 and Haro 2003). More recent studies investigated movements and passage of silver-phase eels at or near hydroelectric facilities where eels frequently displayed movements interpreted to be searching behaviors within a project forebay, the impounded area directly upstream of the dam (Haro et al. 2000a; Behrmann-Godel and Eckmann 2003; Durif et al. 2003; Watene et al. 2003).

In 1996 and 1997, conventional biotelemetry studies (radio, PIT, and acoustic) were conducted at Cabot Station, a small hydroelectric facility on the main stem of the Connecticut River (Haro et al. 2000a). Downstream movement of silver-phase eels occurred primarily at night, and some of the eels appeared to spend varying amounts of time in search of a downstream-passage route in the forebay rather than passing directly through trash racks. Eels traveling downstream were observed at a variety of depths, including the surface, and were detected quickly altering their swimming depth. Migrant eels were recorded entering the forebay up to 15 times before passing, and the majority of migrant eels were believed to have passed downstream through the turbines. However, the limited radio and acoustic (primarily one-dimensional) telemetry methodologies could not adequately describe the behavior of eels with high spatial resolution or provide exact locations and depths at which eels passed through the trash racks.

To improve downstream passage, a better understanding of the behavior of migrant eels as they encounter hydroelectric dams and their movement around such obstacles is required. The primary objective of this study was to use three-dimensional (3D) acoustic telemetry to build on the foundation of telemetry data collected by Haro et al. (2000a) at Cabot Station and to further characterize downstream movements of adult silver-phase eels with higher spatial and temporal resolution. Secondary objectives included establishing the number of occurrences detected within the forebay for each telemetered eel, as well as a more specific location of passage through the trash racks; determining the portion of detections by depth of migrant eels throughout the entire forebay and directly upstream from the turbine intakes and trash rack structures; and reviewing operating conditions at the time of passage.

Methods

Study Site

The experiment was conducted in the forebay of Cabot Station from 4 October to 21 November 2002 (Massachusetts, Connecticut River, river kilometer (rkm) 198; Figure 1). Cabot Station is outfitted with six vertical Francis turbine runners; total generation capacity during the study (when units 1, 2, 5, and 6 were operating at maximum generation capacity) was 38.2 megawatts per hour (MW), and average flow was 262 $m^3 \cdot s^{-1}$. Two recently replaced runners, units 1 and 2, which are located at the south end of the powerhouse, were operated up to 10.3 MW per unit throughout the study (Figure 2). Units 3 and 4, located in

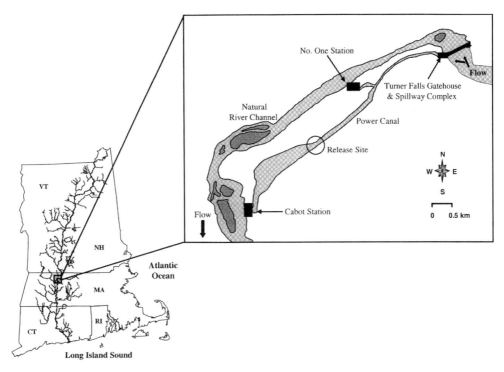

Figure 1. Study site showing the location of Cabot Station hydroelectric facility and power canal (between the Turners Falls Gatehouse and Cabot Station), Connecticut River, Massachusetts (rkm 198).

the middle of the powerhouse, were not operating during the study period because the runners were being replaced, identical to those at units 1 and 2 in 2001. The remaining two units, 5 and 6, which are located on the north end of the powerhouse, were operated up to 8.8 MW per unit throughout the study. The turbines were not operated in a specified pattern; unit generation (on/off) was highly variable.

The forebay is approximately 10 m deep. At the powerhouse, water flows through the trash racks, a series of bar racks spaced 3.2 cm apart from the surface to 3.5 m deep. At depths more than 3.5 m, the bar spacing of the trash racks is 10.2 cm. Approach velocities at the trash racks ranged from 0.3 (minimum generation capacity) to 1.2 $m^3 \cdot s^{-1}$ (maximum generation capacity; Haro et al. 2000a).

Although Cabot Station does not have downstream-passage structures built specifically to reduce turbine entrainment of silver-phase eels, a surface bypass is located in the forebay for passage of juvenile Atlantic salmon *Salmo salar* in the spring and juvenile American shad *Alosa sapidissima* in the fall. The surface bypass is located adjacent to turbine unit 1 at the south end of the powerhouse and is positioned to attract downstream migrants primarily within a meter of the surface (Figure 2). A 1,000-W mercury-vapor light used to enhance passage of juvenile shad illuminates the bypass entrance and a considerable area of the forebay intake area; walkways are also illuminated at night. During the fall of 2002, the bypass was operated from 1 September to 15 November at 2–3% of the facility's maximum flow and was typically between 6 and 8 $m^3 \cdot s^{-1}$. Historically, only a few eels have been collected at this surface bypass sampler each season (Haro et al. 2000a).

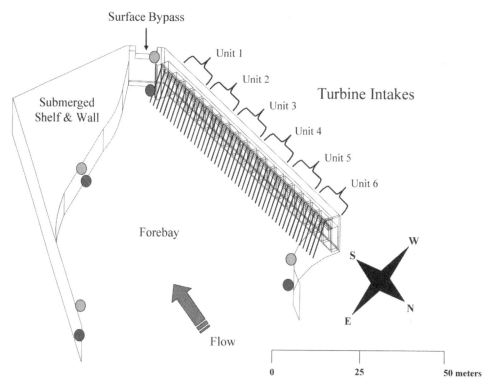

Figure 2. Cabot Station forebay with hydrophone locations (light gray circles = surface hydrophones, dark gray circles = bottom hydrophones), the trash rack structure positioned at 17-degree slope (vertical lines), and turbine unit intakes. Total depth is 10 m, with a level bottom. Units 3 and 4 were not operational during the time of the study.

Telemetry

The primary spatial telemetry system used at Cabot Station during the fall of 2002 was a Hydroacoustic Technology, Inc. (HTI) model 290 Acoustic Telemetry Receiver. This system is designed to calculate the 3D position of a tagged fish based on the difference in arrival times of tag signals at multiple hydrophones strategically positioned in a forebay. The hydrophone array was positioned to detect movements of telemetered eels within 100 m upstream of the powerhouse. Eight 300 kHz hydrophones were deployed throughout the forebay: four were mounted approximately 1 m below the surface and four approximately 1 m from the bottom of the canal (Figure 2). We used HTI model 795F tags (8 mm diameter by 18 mm length, weight 2.1 g, 300 kHz, 2.9–3.1 s ping rate); each tag was programmed to emit a unique frequency. To verify system precision and accuracy, test tags were deployed at known positions within the forebay.

In addition to acoustic telemetry, we tagged fish with conventional coded radio tags (Lotek model MCFT-3D; 10 mm in diameter by 29 mm in length, weight 3.7 g, 148.5 MHz, 5 s burst rate). Radio-tagged eels were monitored in the forebay and tailrace of Cabot Station with 4- and 9-element yagi antennas and Lotek SRX-400 data-logging receivers. We also implanted a passive integrated transponder (PIT) tag into each eel (Texas Instruments TIRFID system; 3 mm in diameter by 32 mm in length, weight 0.8 g, 134.2 kHz). To detect migrant eels passing at the surface bypass, a PIT detection antenna and a data-logging receiver were installed in the bypass entrance (Castro-Santos et al. 1996). All telemetry systems logged data continuously for the duration of the study; data were downloaded every several days, and receiver clocks were synchronized (nearest s) to Eastern Standard Time. We terminated data logging nearly two weeks after the last detection (13 November) and after water temperature fell below 5°C. Water temperature was recorded hourly with a LI-COR LI-1000 data logger and a thermocouple sensor placed in the power canal.

Fish Capture, Tagging, Release, and Monitoring

Twenty silver-phase American eels were collected at the Hadley Station downstream bypass sampler in Holyoke, Massachusetts (rkm 140). These downstream migrants were large, more than 500 mm total length, and presumably mostly female, based on size (Krueger and Oliveira 1997). Collections were made between 18:30 and 23:00 h, and fish were transported to the U.S. Geological Survey, S.O. Conte Anadromous Fish Research Center throughout October 2002. Eels were typically held 24 h for observation before tagging; transmitters were surgically implanted using methods similar to those of Baras and Jeandrain (1998).

Each eel was anesthetized in a 10% clove oil and ethanol stock solution added to a 10-l ambient river-water bath. Eels were typically held in the anesthesia bath for 10–15 min before tagging. Once the eels were heavily sedated, total length (TL) and eye diameter (horizontal and vertical) were measured to the nearest 0.1 mm. Eye indices, a metric for estimating yellow-phase metamorphosis to the migratory silver phase, were calculated from horizontal and vertical eye-diameter measurements using methodology from (Pankhurst 1982). The eye index (I) was calculated using the equation:

$$I = ([(v + h)^2/4]\pi * 100)/TL$$

where v is vertical diameter of the eye, h is horizontal diameter of the eye, and TL is total body length of the individual eel. Silver-phase American eels typically have an eye index between 6.0 and 13.5, with a bronze coloration along the lateral line that separates the dark, silver back from the white belly (Pankhurst 1982). Eels were tagged if this criterion was met.

After characteristics were recorded, eels were placed in a surgical trough, an additional supply of anesthetic solution was circulated through the gills, and transmitters were surgically implanted in the abdomen. The incision was closed with two to three sutures, and tissue adhesive (Vetbond by 3M) was administered to aid in closing of the incision. The duration of surgical implantation of transmitters did not exceed five minutes. Upon completion of the surgery, each eel spent a minimum of 30 min in an initial recovery tank before being transferred to a large (1,000 l) acclimation tank supplied with ambient river water for an additional 48-h observation period to allow eels to recover from surgery and to verify tag functionality.

Eels were released into the power canal approximately 1.5 km upstream of Cabot Station. Movements of eels in the canal and downstream of Cabot Station were monitored with an additional portable radio-telemetry receiver and yagi antenna. Eels were determined to have passed downstream of Cabot Station when the final 3D detection was positioned at the trash racks or the bypass, confirmed when radio-telemetry detections ceased throughout the stretch of the power canal and within the forebay. Downstream passage was also confirmed by the initial radio-telemetry detections logged in the tailrace downstream of Cabot Station.

Data Analysis

The 3D acoustic telemetry data were compiled and organized into a database. Records were filtered with HTI software (*AcousticTag* and *MarkTags*) to remove erroneous signals received during data collection (HTI 2000). Poorly recorded signals are typically caused by either noise interference (commonly associated with operation of hydroelectric dams and high-voltage environments) or a secondary, reflection of the acoustic tag signal (multipath echo). Additionally, we removed any invalid depth records from the dataset that were a result of poor signal selection (i.e., multipath echo included in the calculation of 3D positions created detections at depths >10 m; maximum forebay depth). All detections were plotted in 3D, and eel tracks were reviewed for trends in downstream movements as they encountered the facility (Figure 3 and 4).

We classified each eel occurrence in the forebay as the time from when the eel first entered the acoustic array until the time of passage or movement back upstream outside the acoustic array. Detections separated by less than 15 min were considered a single occurrence. For each of the telemetered eels, median duration of occurrence in the forebay was calculated to the nearest minute, and total residence time within the power canal (referred to as canal residence time) was calculated to the nearest h, beginning with the time of release to the time of exit at Cabot Station. Acoustic, radio, and PIT tag telemetry data were compared to determine final locations of downstream passage (i.e., upstream of forebay, through the surface bypass, or through the turbines).

All detections were combined and analyzed using the chi-square test to determine the proportion of time spent in the upper (0–3.3 m), middle (3.4–6.6 m), and bottom (6.7–10.0 m) portions of the water column in the forebay. To illustrate the distribution of detections by depth, the total number of detections were combined and analyzed at 1-m depth intervals. Because of annual sediment accumulation along the floor of the forebay and the unevenness of depth during monitoring, we combined the two meters closest to the bottom of the power canal. Forebay detections were further analyzed by grouping the proportion of detections within 10 m of the trash racks into three horizontal zones (similar to the classifications defined by Haro et al. 2000a); units 1 and 2 (south), units 3 and 4 (center), and units 5 and 6 (north). Proportion of detections within each zone at each of three depth categories (lower, middle, and upper) were arcsine transformed. To allow for comparisons with Haro et al. (2000a), we conducted separate chi-square analyses of horizontal and vertical distributions.

Results

Calibration tests indicated that 95% of all detections were within 0.26 m horizontally and 0.93 m vertically of the true positions. Our confidence level decreased slightly when the tag was suspended in the water column for prolonged periods; standard error increased in the third dimension (depth) to 1.07 m. We were unable to determine a single source of the increased error but believe it was caused by several factors, including the innate error in the system due to the geometry of the hydrophone array, conservative 3D parameters used during the generation of position(s), and unknown hydraulic conditions that may have altered the test tag position during calibration tests. Acoustic noise did not seem to influence the quality of received signals, but ambient electrical noise intermittently decreased signal detection quality. Recorded tracks of eels were generally continuous, although pings from transmitters were occasionally not detected when tags were in the margins of the forebay.

Eels were collected from the Connecticut River (Hadley Station Bypass Sampler, 140-

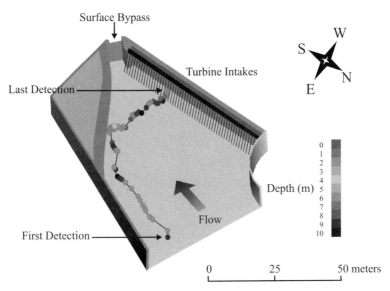

Figure 3. Three-dimensional track of Eel ID 9 in the forebay of Cabot Station (26 October 2002). The depth of each detected position is displayed in gray scale (see legend). This eel spent 8.0 min in the forebay during this occurrence before it passed at 20:02 through unit 2. At the time of passage, Cabot Station was generating at 6.3 MW, which is less than 17% total station capacity, and only unit 2 was operating. The total flow was 112.8 m^3·s^{-1} at the time of passage.

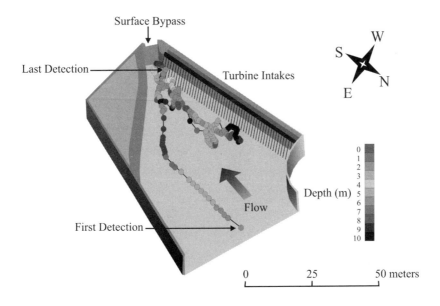

Figure 4. Three dimensional track of Eel ID 10 in the forebay of Cabot Station (23 October 2002). The depth of each detected position is displayed in gray scale (see legend). This eel spent 18.1 min in the forebay during this occurrence before it passed at 18:02 through unit 1. At the time of passage, Cabot Station was generating at 37.5 MW, which is approximately 98% full generation capacity, and turbine units 1, 2, 5, and 6 were operating. The total flow was 315.2 m^3·s^{-1} at the time of passage.

Table 1. Summary of forebay occurrence data of telemetered eels detected in the forebay at Cabot Station. Median duration of occurrence(s) is measured in min. Depth distributions were calculated based on per cent of total time each eel spent in each of the three depth intervals (0–3.3 m, 3.4–6.6 m, 6.7–10.0 m), summed over all occurrences. Horizontal location distributions were calculated as a per cent of the total time each eel spent in one of the three horizontal locations (south, units 1 and 2; center, units 3 and 4; north, units 5 and 6) to a distance of 10 m upstream of the trash racks. Downstream passage routes were assigned based on last detection and are indicated by B for surface bypass, N for northern turbine units (units 5 and 6), and S for southern turbine units (units 1 and 2). Eels 6 and 11 were not detected in the forebay.

Eel ID	Number of Occurrences	Median (Range) Duration of Occurrence(s)	Passage Route	Distribution of Detections by Depth (%)			Distribution of Detections by Location (%)		
				0 – 3.3 m	3.4 – 6.6 m	6.7 – 10 m	North	Center	South
1	3	14.1 (2.9 - 15.8)	B	9.1	31.5	59.4	11.1	32.0	57.0
2	1	6.4	B	39.7	46.6	13.8	0.0	0.0	100.0
3	3	9.6 (4.1 - 14.3)	N	12.6	25.5	61.9	28.0	31.8	40.2
4	3	10.6 (3.0 - 14.7)	N	3.3	41.9	54.7	21.8	16.5	61.7
5	4	17.1 (5.9 - 33.7)	S	10.6	26.2	63.2	6.0	11.1	82.9
6	0	---	---	---	---	---	---	---	---
7	1	3.6	S	15.2	39.4	45.5	0.0	0.0	100.0
8	1	1.4	S	27.3	45.5	27.3	0.0	28.6	71.4
9	2	19.9 (10.9 - 28.8)	S	18.6	30.9	50.5	22.3	8.2	69.5
10	1	8.0	S	1.8	38.2	60.0	0.0	0.0	100.0
11	0	---	---	---	---	---	---	---	---
12	1	17.5	S	10.9	36.8	52.2	22.9	12.4	64.8
13	1	8.6	S	11.7	25.5	62.8	2.4	10.7	86.9
14	1	8.8	S	19.2	35.8	45.0	0.0	0.0	100.0
15	1	1.9	S	26.3	47.4	26.3	0.0	11.1	88.9
16	1	1.7	N	11.4	60.0	28.6	100.0	0.0	0.0
17	1	10.9	N	18.6	18.6	62.8	100.0	0.0	0.0
18	2	75.6 (35.0 - 116.2)	N	6.2	14.9	78.9	41.0	30.1	28.9
19	1	2.4	N	3.3	41.9	54.7	100.0	0.0	0.0
20	1	1.8	S	4.2	29.2	66.7	0.0	0.0	100.0
Median	1	8.6		11.6	36.3	54.7	8.6	9.5	70.5

rkm) between 27 September and 13 October 2002. A total of 20 silver eels were collected, tagged, released, and monitored in the forebay of Cabot Station. Mean TL was 707.5 mm and mean eye index was 7.74 mm. Eels were released between 13:00 and 16:00 h on 4 October (Eel ID 1–4), 13 October (Eel ID 5), 18 October (Eel ID 6–10), 23 October (Eel ID 11–15), and 1 November (Eel ID 16–20). Water temperatures ranged from 19.7°C (4 October) to 7.0°C (13 November) between the first day of release and the last detected downstream movement in the forebay.

Of the 20 telemetered eels released into the canal, 18 (90%) entered the forebay acoustic array at least once (Table 1). All eels detected in the forebay eventually passed downstream of Cabot Station by using either the turbines or surface bypass as a final passage route. Most of the detections occurred at twilight or at night; 15 out of the 18 eels (83%) that entered the forebay and passed downstream of the station did so between 18:00 and 22:00 h. Eight of the 18 (44%) eels moved downstream into the forebay within the first 24 h following release. Most eels were detected entering the forebay where the dominant flow existed, primarily in the center of the power canal or slightly to the east of the true center. Mean depth of eels entering the forebay was 6.06 m, but eels were detected entering the forebay throughout the entire water column (0.38 m to 9.85 m). Twenty-eight per cent of eels (5 out of 18) were detected re-entering the acoustic array on multiple dates, from one to four times, before passing the station.

Duration of each occurrence in the forebay was variable. Median duration was 11 min, ranging from 1.4 min to 2.8 h. Eel transit times, or total time from release to first forebay detection, were also variable; median transit time was 4.7 h but ranged from 1.0 h to 294.1 h. Median canal residence time was 49 h but ranged from 1.1 h to 294.1 h (12.3 d). Nearly all eels (16 out of 18) used the turbines as a final route of passage; four were detected at or near the entrance of the surface bypass, but only two were confirmed to have passed at that location. The 3D acoustic telemetry indicated that the remaining two eels that were recorded at the entrance of the surface bypass continued to search for a downstream passage route and ultimately passed through the turbines. All passage events were confirmed with the use of radio and PIT telemetry. Of the eels that passed downstream through the turbines, 12 out of 16 (75%) were detected using the southern turbine intakes of units 1 and 2 as a final route of passage. Example tracks of telemetered eels that passed downstream via turbines are illustrated in Figure 3 and 4.

Throughout the forebay, the distributions of detection by depth were highly variable; however, eels spent significantly more time near the bottom (chi-square; $P < 0.001$). While some eels were detected at or near the surface, more than two-thirds of the detections were within the deepest third of the forebay (6.7–10.0 m). The highest percentage of detections occurred near the bottom (Figure 5). Eels also spent significantly more time within the first 10 m directly upstream of units 1 and 2 compared with the other units (chi-square; $P < 0.001$; Figure 6).

The majority of downstream passage events occurred through the turbines; turbine passage was identified under two broad behavioral tendencies. First, eels were detected passing directly through the trash racks and into one of the four turbine units upon their first encounter. Seven eels out of the 16 that passed downstream via the trash racks passed the station through the turbines immediately after contact with the trash racks. Second, the remaining nine eels were recorded passing through the trash racks after one or more combinations of searching behaviors and then passing downstream of Cabot Station through the turbines. At least 50% of these fish undertook vertical searching movements when they encountered the trash racks, swimming up

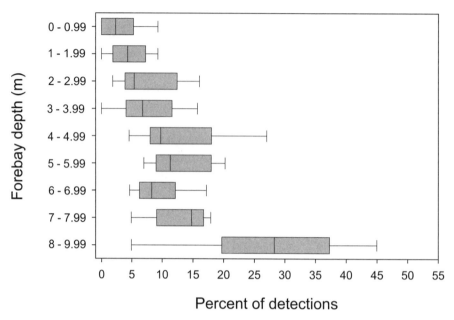

Figure 5. Proportion of time spent by telemetered eels within the entire forebay by depth (1-m intervals). Data were generated from individually standardized track data of 18 eels. Central vertical bar = median; shaded bar = 75th percentile; whisker = 90th percentile.

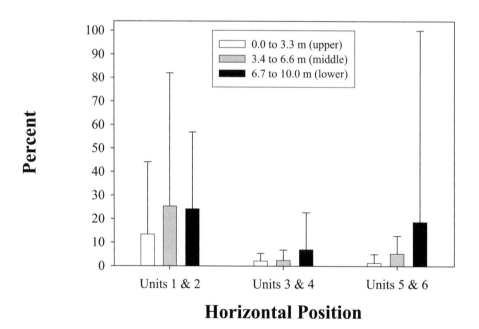

Figure 6. Proportion of time spent by telemetered eels directly upstream of the trash racks (within 10 m) by depth (3 depth intervals) and horizontal position (unit numbers). Data were generated from individually standardized track data of 18 eels. Bar = median; whisker = 90th percentile.

and down in the water column of the forebay. After approaching the trash racks, 10 out of 16 eels also swam horizontally along the trash racks. In addition, 10 out of 16 (63%) exhibited circling movements directly in front of the trash racks and larger circling movements encompassing the entire forebay. Circling movements were often associated with either vertical and/or horizontal searching behavior along the trash racks. Both patterns of pre-passage movement at the trash racks (direct passage versus searching before passage) occurred under both low (<256 $m^3 \cdot s^{-1}$) and high (>256 $m^3 \cdot s^{-1}$) flow conditions.

Discussion

Protection of downstream-migrant fishes at hydroelectric intakes requires that fish be attracted, guided, or physically diverted to safe passage routes. Three-dimensional acoustic telemetry provided a more comprehensive measure of position and eel movements than has been previously possible with conventional telemetry methods. Error in positioning of fish was relatively low; thus, we are confident that our 3D eel movements represent true behaviors in the forebay. The behaviors that were detected as telemetered eels approached and encountered Cabot Station were variable, yet the results of this study supported the findings of Haro et al. (2000a).

Eels moved very little during the day; downstream movements to the forebay occurred primarily within several hours after sunset. Although eels spent a significant amount of time at or near the bottom of the forebay, they were detected swimming near the surface occasionally and were observed rapidly altering their depth of swimming. Some telemetered fish were reluctant to pass either through the racks or into the bypass on their first forebay encounter and did not pass the station for several days, even after several occurrences within the forebay. This trend was observed by Haro et al. (2000a), who reported that some eels attempted to pass Cabot Station up to 15 times.

Similar delays have been noted for other anguillids, particularly European eels *Anguilla anguilla* at a hydroelectric dam in Germany (Behrmann-Godel and Eckmann 2003) and New Zealand longfin *A. dieffenbachia* and shortfin *A. australis* eels at hydroelectric dams in New Zealand (Boubée et al. 2001; Watene et al. 2003). Behrmann-Godel and Eckmann (2003) observed similar circling of European eels within the forebay of a hydroelectric facility. While our sample size is limited ($n = 18$), our results support previous biotelemetry studies conducted on the downstream migration of four silver-phase anguillid species and suggest that behavioral movements at or near hydroelectric facilities may be relatively consistent across taxa.

Only two eels used the surface bypass as a route of downstream passage. Although the surface bypass at Cabot Station is equipped with a uniform acceleration weir-entrance structure, it passes under 3% of the total maximum flow of the project. The extensive lighting at the powerhouse at night, in particular the supplemental illumination in the surface bypass, may have prevented eels from using this route for downstream passage. Although eels have been observed passing through the surface bypass, they have also been video-recorded entering the bypass, reversing direction, and swimming upstream to re-enter the forebay (Haro et al. 2000a; video recording by Haro, unpublished data). The combination of low relative flow, surface orientation, and high illumination may contribute to the ineffectiveness of the bypass for eels.

Eels either passed immediately upon entry into the forebay or were delayed; delay was characterized by searching behaviors and, in some cases, repeated occurrences. The presence of trash racks and the hydraulic conditions at or near the trash racks may be one of the primary reasons silver eels, even those that are large enough, do not always pass quickly though the bar racks and ultimately may slightly alter their downstream-passage behavior. Both patterns of prepassage movement, direct passage during initial encounter of trash racks versus searching before passage, occurred under both low and high flow conditions, which suggests that the behaviors are not driven exclusively by hydraulics.

When close to the trash racks, eels were observed rapidly diving to the deepest portions of the forebay. This is consistent with sounding behavior speculated to occur when eels first come into contact with trash racks or other novel structures (Haro et al. 2000a). In the case of downstream migrant anguillids, responses to hydraulics and topography of forebay environments are complex, but our findings provide some insights into generalized behaviors. As silver eels approach an intake from a head pond or impoundment, they may initially follow dominant flow and drift or swim downstream at mid or upper depths, as they have been shown to do in natural, open-river systems (Tesch 1994; Parker and McCleave 1997). We found that the presence of Cabot Station, and perhaps the illumination associated with the station, may have altered the swimming depth of some migrant eels to deeper locations than those previously reported of migrant eels in natural, unobstructed waterways.

Upon encountering trash racks or other similar structures that obstruct or interrupt downstream migration or flow characteristics, the initial response of eels is to either pass directly through the turbines or sound, reverse direction, and swim laterally or upstream, or a combination of these behaviors. The use of 3D telemetry aided in detecting and characterizing these fine-scale movements and behavioral trends. We found that some eels swam upstream rapidly after initial contact with the trash racks. Within the area 10 m upstream of the trash racks, eels also spent the greatest proportion of time near units 1 and 2, where two-thirds of the eels passed downstream of Cabot Station. This behavior was frequently observed when greater flow passed through these units, which were the primary units operating during the study period and the units where the highest flows and approach velocities occurred. These results suggest that silver eels are attracted to dominant flow fields and support the limited literature of downstream passage of silver eels (Vøllestad et al. 1986; Boubée et al. 2001, 2003; Haro et al. 2003).

The majority of eels passed through the trash racks, likely because of the dominant flow at the trash racks versus the surface bypass. The final locations of downstream passage were detected throughout the entire water column; however, the majority (two-thirds) were detected in the lower portion of the trash racks (3.5–10.0 m deep) probably because of the increase in spacing (10.2 cm) in this region. Nearly half of the eels (7 out of 16) that were last detected passing through the trash racks were subsequently detected moving back upstream through the racks. While it is possible that high approach velocities may have ultimately made it more difficult for some eels to swim back upstream or avoid being entrained through the trash racks, it is apparent that over half the eels that passed downstream of Cabot Station were not passively entrained into the turbine units. Similar behavior of American and European silver-phase eels has been observed with video in response to angled bar racks in laboratory flumes (Adams and Schwevers 1997; Amaral et al. 2003). Downstream migrant fishes and various larval fishes can be easily entrained into turbine units at small-scale hydroelectric facilities (Nestler et al. 1992; Travnichek et al. 1993; Mathur et al. 2000); this does not appear to be typical for all silver-phase eels. More than half of the eels (9 out of 16) did not pass through the trash racks during their initial encounter but first searched for a downstream passage route and then voluntarily passed through the turbines at Cabot Station.

Management Implications

Behaviors of migrant eels in hydroelectric forebays are unlike those of traditional downstream migrant species such as juvenile salmonids and anadromous clupeids, which remain near the surface and can be attracted and guided by directional flow fields and lighting at a bypass entrance (Haro et al. 2000a). While the passage of downstream migrant eels appears to be influenced heavily by directional flow fields, eels are not surface oriented and often are repelled by light. We found that the majority of eels at Cabot Station were delayed during their downstream migration; many of these eels made multiple attempts to pass downstream of this station. Our results also indicate that while eels spend a significant amount of time near the bottom of the power canal, they can alter their position frequently, particularly at or near the trash racks.

Establishing safer downstream passage alternatives for eels is challenging because they appear to be attracted to the dominant flow field, which usually is associated with the turbines unless the turbine units are not generating and a modified downstream passage facility exists or can be built that handles a large enough volume of water to attract downstream migrants before they encounter the turbine intakes. Our results indicate that eels exhibiting searching behaviors within a forebay may have a higher probability of encountering a submerged or bottom bypass entrance than a conventional surface bypass entrance. Recent studies conducted by Durif et al. (2003) illustrate that significantly more European eels will pass a hydroelectric project by means of a submerged bypass than through a traditional surface-oriented bypass.

Although eels appear able to detect and avoid trash rack structures and other obstructions, they can also pass voluntarily through bar racks, limiting opportunities to guide eels to a bypass under these conditions. Development of structures or altered project operations to protect downstream migrant anguillids from entrainment and subsequent turbine mortality are at a very preliminary stage. Behavioral barriers and guidance devices have also been shown to have limited effectiveness for eels (i.e., angled bar racks and louvers, light, sound, water jets and air bubbles, and electrical fields: see Dixon 2003; EPRI 2001; Richkus and Dixon 2003). As an alternative, operational shutdowns may be effective in decreasing overall mortality of silver eels at some small hydroelectric facilities in Maine (Haro et al. 2003). Shutting down hydroelectric facilities in combination with peak environmental conditions during downstream migration of eels (heavy rain, increased flow, perhaps four to six hours after sunset) could reduce the risk of turbine-related injuries and mortality. However, under most circumstances, electricity demands may make this alternative unfeasible. Future efforts to develop effective bypasses or guidance structures should consider these behaviors to improve safer downstream passage of migrant silver eels.

Acknowledgments

The U.S. Fish and Wildlife Service (Region 5: Engineering and Environmental Services) and the U.S. Geological Survey, Biological Resource Discipline, S.O. Conte Anadromous Fish Research Center, funded this study. We thank Northeast Utilities Company for access to the site and assistance with installations by Cabot Station personnel. Additional thanks to Steve Walk and Phil Rocahsa, who assisted with system installation, and John Noreika, who further assisted with graphics. Many thanks to Tim Sullivan, Jamie Pearlstein, and our many other volunteers who provided assistance during the fall of 2002 with eel collection, tagging, and release. We greatly appreciate the invaluable technical support provided by Ken Cash, U.S. Geological Survey, Columbia River Research Center, Cook, Washington, and Mark Timko, Hydroacoustic Technologies, Inc., Seattle, Washington. Additional thanks to two anonymous reviewers for their constructive comments on the manuscript. This study was conducted in partial fulfillment of a Master of Science degree by L. Brown at the University of Massachusetts Amherst.

References

Adams, B., and D. U. Schwevers. 1997. Behavioral surveys of eels (*Anguilla anguilla*) migrating downstream under laboratory conditions. Institute of Applied Ecology, Neustader Weg 25, 36320 Kirtorf-Wahlen, Germany.

Amaral, S. V., F. C. Winchell, B. J. McMahon, and D. A. Dixon. 2003. Evaluation of angled bar racks and louvers for guiding silver phase American eels. Pages 367–376 in D. A. Dixon, editor. Biology, management, and protection of catadromous eels. American Fisheries Society Syposium 33, Bethesda, Maryland.

Baras, E., and D. Jeandrain. 1998. Evaluation of surgery procedures for tagging eel *Anguilla anguilla* (L.) with biotelemetry transmitters. Hydrobiologia 371/ 372:107–111.

Behrmann-Godel, J., and R. Eckmann. 2003. A preliminary telemetry study of the migration of silver European eel (*Anguilla anguilla* L.) in the River Mosel, Germany. Ecology of Freshwater Fish 12:196–202.

Berg, R. 1986. Fish passage through Kaplan turbines at a power plant on the River Neckar and subsequent eel injuries. Vie et Milieu 36:307–310.

Boubée, J. A., C. P. Mitchell, B. L. Chisnall, D. W. West, E. J. Bowman, and A. Haro. 2001. Factors regulating the downstream migration of mature eels (*Anguilla* spp.) at Aniwhenua Dam, Bay of Plenty, New Zealand. New Zealand Journal of Marine and Freshwater Research 35:121–134.

Boubée, J. A., B. L. Chisnall, E. Watene, E. Williams, D. Roper and A. Haro. 2003. Enhancement and management of eel fisheries affected by hydroelectric dams in New Zealand. Pages 357–365 in D. A. Dixon, editor. Biology, management, and protection of catadromous eels. American Fisheries Society, Syposium 33, Bethesda, Maryland.

Castro-Santos, T., A. Haro, and S. Walk. 1996. A passive integrated transponder (PIT) tag system for monitoring fishways. Fisheries Research 28(3):253–261.

Dixon, D. A. 2003. Biology, management, and protection of catadromous eels. American Fisheries Society, Symposium 33, Bethesda, Maryland.

Durif, C., P. Elie, C. Gosset, J. Rives, and F. Travade. 2003. Behavioral study of downstream migrating eels by radio-telemetry at a small hydroelectric power plant. Pages 343–356 in D. A. Dixon, editor. Biology, management, and protection of catadromous eels. American Fisheries Society, Symposium 33, Bethesda, Maryland.

EPRI (Electric Power Research Institute). 2001. Review and documentation of research and technologies on passage and protection of downstream migrating catadromous eels at hydroelectric facilities. EPRI Report Number 1000730. Palo Alto, California.

Haro, A. 2003. Downstream migration of silver-phase anguillid eels. Pages 215–222 in K. Aida, K. Tsukamoto, and K. Yamauchi, editors. Eel Biology. Springer, Tokyo.

Haro, A., T. Castro-Santos, and J. Boubée. 2000a. Behavior and passage of silver-phase American eels, *Anguilla rostrata* (LeSueur), at a small hydroelectric facility. Dana 12:33–42.

Haro, A., T. Castro-Santos, K. Whalen, G. Wippelhauser, and L. McLaughlin. 2003. Simulated effects of hydroelectric project regulation on mortality of American eels. Pages 357–365 in D. A. Dixon, editor. Biology, management, and protection of catadromous eels. American Fisheries Society, Syposium 33, Bethesda, Maryland.

Haro, A., W. Richkus, K. Whalen, A. Hoar, W.-D. Busch, S. Lary, T. Brush, and D. Dixon. 2000b. Population Decline of the American Eel: Implications for Research and Management. Fisheries 25(9):7–16.

HTI (Hydroacoustic Technology, Inc.). 2000. Model 290 Acoustic Tag System Manual. HTI. Seattle.

Krueger, W. H., and K. Oliveira. 1997. Sex, size, and gonad morphology of silver American eels. Copeia 1997(2):415–420.

Larinier, M., and F. Travade. 2002. Downstream Migration: Problems and Facilities. Bulletin Francais De La Peche Et De La Pisciculture 364 Supplement:181–208.

McCleave, J. D. 2001. Simulation of the impact of dams and fishing weirs on reproductive potential of silver-phase American eels in the Kennebec River Basin, Maine. North American Journal of Fisheries Management 21:592–605.

Mathur, D., P. G. Heisey, J. P. Skalski, and D. R. Kenney. 2000. Salmonid smolt survival relative to turbine efficiency and entrainment depths in hydroelectric power generation. Journal of the American Water Resources Association 36(4):737–747.

Nestler, J. M., G. R. Ploskey, J. Pickens, J. Menezes, and C. Schilt. 1992. Responses of blueback herring to high frequency sound and implications for reducing entrainment at hydropower. North American Journal of Fisheries Management 12:667–683.

Pankhurst, N. W. 1982. Relation of visual changes to the onset of sexual-maturation in the European eel *Anguilla anguilla* (L). Journal of Fish Biology 21:127–140.

Parker, S. J., and J. D. McCleave. 1997. Selective tidal stream transport by American eels during homing movements and estuarine migration. Journal of the Marine Biological Association of the United Kingdom 77:871–889.

Richkus, W.A., and D.A. Dixon. 2003. Review of research and technologies on passage and protection of downstream migrating catadromous eels at hydroelectric facilities. Pages 357–365 *in* D. A. Dixon, editor. Biology, management, and protection of catadromous eels. American Fisheries Society, Syposium 33, Bethesda, Maryland.

Richkus, W., and K. Whalen. 2000. Evidence for a decline in the abundance of the American eel, *Anguilla rostrata* (LeSueur), in North America since the early 1980s. Dana 12:83–97.

Tesch, F.-W. 1977. The eel. Chapman and Hall, London.

Tesch, F.-W. 1994. Tracking of silver eels in the Rivers Weser and Elbe. Fischökologie 7:47–59.

Travnichek, V. H., A. V. Zale, and W. L. Fisher. 1993. Entrainment of ichthyoplankton by a warm water hydroelectric facility. Transactions of the American Fisheries Society 122(5):709–716.

Vøllestad, L. A., B. Jonsson, N. A. Hvidsten, T. F. Næsje, Ø. Haraldstad, and J. Ruud-Hansen. 1986. Environmental factors regulating seaward migration of European silver eels (*Anguilla anguilla*). Canadian Journal of Fisheries and Aquatic Sciences 43:1909–1916.

Watene, E. M., J. A. Boubée, and A. Haro. 2003. Downstream movement of mature eels in a hydroelectric reservoir in New Zealand. Pages 295–306 *in* D. A. Dixon, editor. Biology, management, and protection of catadromous eels. American Fisheries Society, Symposium 33, Bethesda, Maryland.

Determining Exit Locations for Eel Ladders at Hydroelectric Power Dams on the St. Lawrence River

KEVIN J. MCGRATH[1]

New York Power Authority, 123 Main Street, White Plains, New York, 10601, USA

RICHARD VERDON

Hydro-Québec, 75 boul. Rene-Levesque ouest, Montreal, Québec H2Z 1A4, Canada

DENIS DESROCHERS AND CAROLE FLEURY

Milieu, Inc., 1435 Chemin de Saint-Jean, LaPrairie, Québec J5R 2L8, Canada

SCOTT AULT

Kleinschmidt Associates, 2 East Main Street, Strasburg, Pennsylvania, 17579, USA

JOHN SKALSKI

University of Washington, 1325 Fourth Avenue, Seattle, Washington, 98101, USA

Abstract.—Additional upstream eel *Anguilla rostrata* passage is planned at the Moses-Saunders Power Dam, Massena, New York, and has recently been implemented at the Beauharnois Power Dam, Montreal, Quebec, on the St. Lawrence River. Mark–recapture studies were conducted to determine the distance upstream of the dams that eel ladder exits should be located to minimize turbine entrainment. In 2001, 9,822 fin-clipped eels were released in equal proportions at 0 m, 90 m, and 1,600 m upstream on the west side of the Beauharnois Power Dam. Return rates to the tailwater were 4.5%, 5.0%, and 3.2%, respectively. In 2002, 16,697 fin-clipped eels were released at the same distances on the east side of the dam. Return rates were 12.0%, 4.2% and 1.1%, respectively. In 2001, 4,400 PIT-tagged eels were released at six locations upstream of the Moses-Saunders Power Dam. Eels released further than 270 m upstream of the dam exhibited a return rate of less than 7%, while those released closer than 270 m had a substantially higher return rate, approximately 50%. Even though the dams are very similar in size and hydraulic capacity, return rates of eels released close to the two dams were substantially different, approximately 50% for the Moses-Saunders Power Dam versus 4.5% (west side) and 12.0% (east side) for the Beauharnois Power Dam. These studies indicate that the siting of an eel ladder exit to minimize entrainment is specific to each dam.

---

[1] Corresponding author: mcgrath.k@nypa.gov

Introduction

The American eel *Anguilla rostrata* is a catadromous panmictic species that spawns in the Sargasso Sea (sea) (Schmidt 1923; Wirth and Bernatchez 2003). The leptocephali larvae drift with the ocean currents, and as they approach the east coast of North America, they metamorphose into glass eels (Tesch 2003; McCleave 1993). Elvers, which are pigmented glass eels, migrate upstream into estuaries, rivers, ponds, and lakes (Dutil et al. 1989; Haro and Krueger 1991). In the St. Lawrence River (river), elvers develop into juvenile yellow eels that continue their migration up the river and into Lake Ontario for 3–12 years (Liew 1982; Casselman 2003). They reside in the river or in Lake Ontario and migrate back to the sea (approximate age 17–25) as maturing yellow or silver eels (Hurley 1972; McGrath et al. 2003a; Tremblay 2004).

To reach the upper part of the St. Lawrence River and Lake Ontario, upstream migrating eels must pass two major hydroelectric dams—the Beauharnois Power Dam and the Moses-Saunders Power Dam. Construction of the Beauharnois Power Dam was begun in the late 1920s and was completed in 1961, while construction of the Moses-SaundersPower Dam began in 1954 and was completed in 1958. Eel ladders were recently (2002 west side and 2003 east side) installed at Beauharnois Power Dam. No passage existed at the dam prior to that, but eels were thought to pass upstream via the adjacent navigation locks. No passage existed at the Moses-Saunders Power Dam between 1958 and 1974 other than through the nearby navigation locks. In 1974, Ontario Power Generation and the Ontario Ministry of Natural Resources installed an eel ladder on the north side of the Moses-Saunders Power Dam (Lannin and Liew 1979; Eckersley 1982). The New York Power Authority plans to install a new ladder on the south side of the Moses-Saunders Power Dam in 2006.

Several authors have described design criteria for eel ladders (Legault et al. 1990; Legault 1992; Boubée 1995; Clay 1995; Porcher 2002; Solomon and Beach 2004). Design criteria largely focus on entrance location, slope, and climbing substrate, and there is little specific guidance for locating the exit of the ladder. Clay (1995) provided general guidance, stating that the exit should be as far upstream as possible to avoid entrainment and return of eels to the tailwater. Solomon and Beach (2004) noted that the exit should be located to avoid entrainment into the downstream flow and that a refuge should be provided for eels at the discharge point. However, there is little cited data on the extent of eel entrainment and little specific guidance on how far upstream to locate the exit for a ladder or on optimum conditions at the release location.

An early study on an experimental eel ladder at Beauharnois Power Dam documented, but did not quantify, entrainment of eels that had exited the ladder (Desrochers 1996). More extensive studies at the Moses-Saunders Power Dam demonstrated that approximately 50% of the eels exiting an existing ladder were being entrained (McGrath et al. 2003b; Milieu 2004). Entrainment can result in turbine mortality or can require eels to re-ascend the ladder to reach upstream habitat. Therefore, both Hydro-Québec and the New York Power Authority had a strong interest in minimizing entrainment at the new ladders at Beauharnois Power Dam and at the planned ladder on the south side of the Moses-Saunders Power Dam.

The purpose of the current studies was to determine the extent of return to the tailwaters by upstream migrating eels that were released at various distances upstream of the dams. This information was used in the design of new and planned ladders.

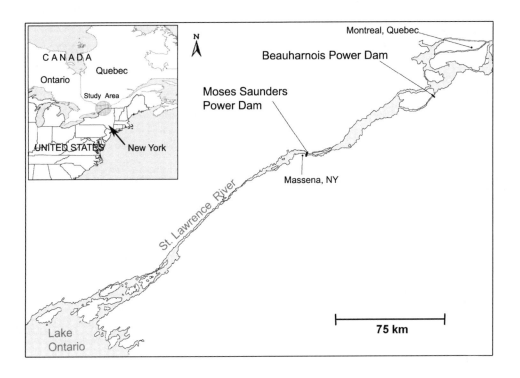

Figure 1. Study area.

Study Area

Studies were conducted at the Beauharnois Power Dam, which is approximately 900 km upstream from the Gulf of St. Lawrence, and at the Moses-Saunders Power Dam, which is an additional 80 km upstream (Figure 1).

The Beauharnois Power Dam is owned by Hydro-Québec. It is about 900 m wide, has a head of 24 m, and comprises 36 generating units (26 Francis units and 10 fixed-blade propeller units) with two auxiliary units on the east side. Installed capacity of Beauharnois Power Dam is 1,657 MW. Provisional space was left for an additional unit (Unit No. 37) on the west side of the dam, but it was never installed. The forebay consists of a 24.5-km-long man-made canal where approximately 85% of the total river flow is diverted to the dam. The average river flow at the dam is 6,620 m^3/s, and maximum flow is 8,200 m^3/s. Two debris sluices, one at each end of the dam, were part of the original installation but have not been used in recent years. Each is 61.5 m long and 1.2 m wide and links the forebay to the tailwater. An eel ladder was installed in each of the sluices—on the west side in 2002 and on the east side in 2003 (Figure 2). The entrance of the west ladder was installed in turbine bay 37 adjacent to the debris sluice, since large numbers of eels were observed in that area. This turbine bay is a 21-m-diameter circular area connected to the tailwater.

The Moses-Saunders Power Dam, which is jointly owned by the New York Power Authority and Ontario Power Generation, is 1 km wide, has a head of 25 m, and contains 32 fixed-blade propeller turbines. Generating capacity is approximately 1,800 MW. Under most operating conditions, all flow in the river passes through Moses-Saunders Power Dam. Average annual discharge at this location is

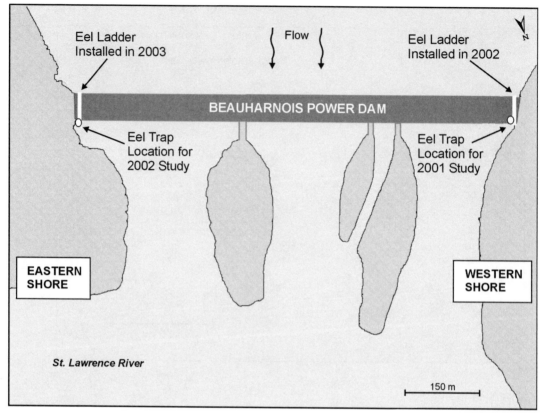

Figure 2. Location of eel traps and eel ladder at the Beauharnois Power Dam in 2001 and 2002.

7,394 m³/s (NYPA 1996). The dam has six ice sluices located in pairs—two at the northern end, two in the middle, and two at the southern end (Figure 3). The ice sluices were intended to pass ice in the winter but have never been used. The ice sluices are approximately 20 m wide, open into the tailwater, and provide a calm backwater area. The original eel ladder is located at the northern end of the dam in ice sluice 1 (Figure 3). The planned eel ladder will be installed in ice sluice 5.

Methods

Study Design

Eels were captured in traps in the tailwater of the dams, fin-clipped or tagged with Passive Integrated Transponder (PIT) tags, released in the forebays at increasing distances upstream of the dams, and recaptured in the tailwater. The extent of their return to the tailwater from each upstream release location was determined on the basis of recapture rates. Studies were carried out in 2001 (Beauharnois Power Dam west side and Moses-Saunders Power Dam) and 2002 (Beauharnois Power Dam east side).

All traps used at Beauharnois Power Dam and Moses-Saunders Power Dam were inclined-ramp traps with a climbing substrate of staggered vertical pipes (McGrath et al. 2003b). A low conveyance flow is provided down the ramp, and a plunging/splashing attraction flow is provided at the base. It is thought that these traps collect almost entirely upstream-migrating eels rather than resident eels because 1) upstream migrating eels are thought to respond to the flow from the trap and the plunging/splashing attractant flow at

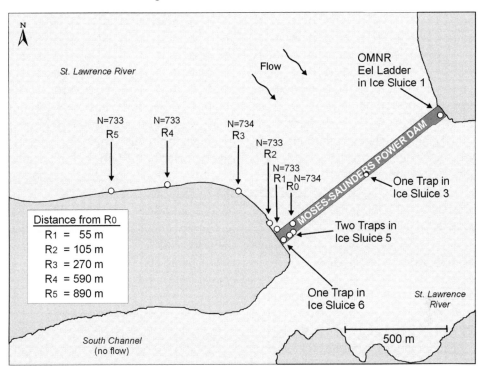

Figure 3. Location of the eel ladder, eel traps and release sites at the Moses-Saunders Power Dam in 2001.

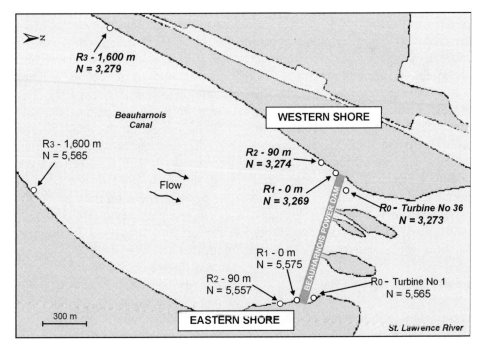

Figure 4. Location of release sites and number of eels released per site at the Beauharnois Power Dam in 2001 and 2002. Bold type is western shore study in 2001, while regular type is eastern shore study in 2002.

the base of the trap (Lannin and Liew 1979; Solomon and Beach 2004); 2) eels collected in the traps show distinct seasonal patterns more characteristic of migrating eels (Milieu 2004); 3) eels must climb "out" of the water onto the inclined ramp—this climbing behavior is associated with migrating eels (Solomon and Beach 2004); and 4) habitat conditions in the tailwater at the hydroelectric dams are thought to be unfavorable for resident eels; given resident eels' small home range (LaBar and Facey 1983; Laffaille et al. 2005), it is unlikely that they would encounter the traps.

Beauharnois Power Dam, West Side

Between 21 June and 14 September 2001, 13,095 migrating yellow eels (average size 421 mm, SD 105 mm) were collected in a trap set in the tailwater on the west side of the dam. The trap was checked every day, and eels were split into four equal size lots, anesthetized, and marked by fin clipping. Each lot received a different mark corresponding to each release site.

After recovery from anesthesia, eels were released along the western shoreline late in the afternoon, generally between 1700 hours and 1800 hours, at three upstream locations (R_1 to R_3) and at a control location, R_0 (Figure 4). The three upstream locations, R_1 to R_3, were 0, 90, and 1,600 m, respectively, from the dam. The control location (R_0) was located in the tailwater in the discharge flow from turbine Unit No. 36 near the west shore (Figure 4). Tailwater traps were operated continuously from 21 June to 14 September, and recaptures were counted daily.

Beauharnois Power Dam, East Side

To assess whether return rates were similar on both sides of the Beauharnois Power Dam, the experiment was repeated on the east side in 2002. Between 6 July and 9 September, 22,262 eels were collected in a trap set in the tailwater along the east shore (average size 388 mm, SD 88 mm). Eels were treated the same as in 2001 and were released along the eastern shoreline at three upstream locations (R_1 to R_3) and at a control location, R_0 (Figure 4). The three upstream locations, R_1 to R_3, were 0, 90, and 1,600 m, respectively, upstream from the dam. The control location (R_0) was in the tailwater in the discharge flow from turbine Unit No. 1, near the eastern shore. Tailwater traps were operated continuously from 6 July to 9 September, and recaptures were counted daily. Details concerning the traps and seasonal data are described in Desrochers (2002) and Bernard and Desrochers (2002).

Moses-Saunders Power Dam

In 2003, 3,564 eels were collected in ice sluices 3 (one trap), 5 (two traps), and 6 (one trap) (Figure 3), PIT-tagged and released in equal lots at five upstream locations and a control location. Eels were tagged during two periods, 25 June to 9 August and 18 September to 15 October, which corresponded with expected peaks in upstream eel migration (McGrath et al. 2003b; Milieu 2004). Tagging was limited to these two periods to control costs. It was reasoned that this would have no impact on the study results, since both the summer and fall migration peaks were covered. In case there were differences in returns to the tailwater between these two periods, the sampling period to collect tagged specimens extended well beyond the recapture time expected for tagged specimens that had returned to the tailwater. Collection for recaptures in the tailwater traps was continuous from 25 June to 1 November and at the eel ladder in ice sluice 1 from 25 June to 2 November. All tagged eels were measured to the nearest mm total length (average size 472 mm, SD 79). Details on the traps, PIT-tagging techniques, and typical annual migration patterns are presented in McGrath et al. (2003b) and Milieu (2003, 2004).

Mark–recapture studies with PIT tags were also conducted at the Moses-Saunders Power Dam in 1997, 1999, and 2000, resulting in a pool (approximately 10,000) of tagged eels in the tailwater area. Some of these previously tagged eels were recaptured during this study. These eels (854) were handled identically to the newly tagged eels and released in equal lots at the five upstream locations and the control location. The recaptured eels and newly tagged eels were tracked separately to determine, and if necessary isolate, any differences in recapture rates between the two groups. This also allowed us to assess whether the immediate effects and stresses from handling and tagging eels with PIT tags (eels tagged in 2001) had an effect on the behavior of the eels.

Both groups of eels, those tagged in 2001 and those tagged in previous years, were separately split into six equal size lots and released after dusk at each of the five upstream locations (R_1 to R_5) and a control location, R_0 (Figure 3). Eels were released after dusk because previous studies at Moses-Saunders Power Dam demonstrated a strong tendency for upstream movement to begin at dusk and continue into the night (Milieu 2004). It was reasoned that releasing shortly after dusk would more closely match natural movement patterns and would provide some protection from potential predators. The five upstream locations, R_1 to R_5, were 55, 105, 270, 590, and 890 m, respectively, upstream from the control release location R_0. The R_0 group was released through a pipe induction system directly into the intake of turbine Unit No. 31 (Figure 3). The current velocity at this control release location was approximately 1 m·s^{-1}, and the end of the induction system was located to ensure complete passage of the R_0 group through Unit No. 31 and into the tailwater.

Analytical Methods

The extent of return to the tailwater from particular release sites was expressed as the return rate (Ricker 1958; Burnham et al. 1987). The return rate was estimated by comparing the recapture rate of eels released at the upstream release sites R_n to the recapture rate of eels released at the control release site R_0 (directly in the turbine intake for Moses-Saunders Power Dam and in the tailwater for Beauharnois Power Dam). The recapture rate is the simple proportion of tagged or marked eels that were released upstream of the dams, then recaptured in the traps or at the eel ladder in the tailwater. The recapture rate incorporates factors such as collection efficiency of the gear, turbine mortality (for Moses-Saunders Power Dam only), natural mortality, and upstream migration potential. The recapture rate from R_0 is a reference value. By comparing the recapture rates from the upstream locations to the control reference rate, the other factors cancel each other and the rate of return from each location is isolated. For the two studies conducted at Beauharnois Power Dam, the control eels were released directly into the tailwater and not into the turbine intakes, thus recapture rates from the control release locations (R_0) do not include the turbine mortality rate. The potential implications, an underestimate of return rates, are addressed in the discussion.

The statistical model for experiments at both dams assumes that all the eels released have the same probability of being recaptured in the traps in the tailwater and at Moses-Saunders Power Dam at the existing ladder. For the Moses-Saunders Power Dam study, it was further assumed that all of the eels released in the turbine intake passed through to the tailwater.

The estimator of return rate $\hat{B}(d)$ at each upstream release location (R_1 to R_5) is:

Table 1. Return rates of eels tagged and released along the west shore of the Beauharnois Power Dam forebay in 2001.

Release Location	Number Released	Number Recaptured	Recapture Rate $\hat{\theta}_n$	Return Rate $\hat{B}(d)$	Confidence Interval 95%
R_0	3,273	975	29.8%	n/a	n/a
R_1	3,269	44	1.3%	4.5%	±1.3%
R_2	3,274	49	1.5%	5.0%	±1.4%
R_3	3,279	31	0.9%	3.2%	±1.1%

$$\hat{B}(d) = \frac{x_n N_0}{N_n y_0}$$

where

N_0 = number of eels released at R_0,

N_n = number of eels released at R_n,

y_0 = number of eels recaptured from release location R_0, and

x_n = number of eels recaptured from release location R_n.

or

$$\hat{B}(d) = \frac{\hat{\theta}_n}{\hat{\theta}_0}$$

where

$\hat{\theta}_n$ = observed recapture rate of eels released at R_n

$\hat{\theta}_0$ = observed recapture rate of eels released at R_0

The half-width of a $(1-\alpha)$ 100% confidence interval of the estimate of return rate has the expected value:

$$\varepsilon = Z_{1-\frac{\alpha}{2}} \sqrt{\hat{B}(d)^2 \left[\frac{1-\hat{B}(d)\hat{\theta}_0}{N_n \hat{B}(d)\hat{\theta}_0} + \frac{1-\hat{\theta}_0}{N_0 \hat{\theta}_0} \right]}.$$

where

$\hat{\theta}$ = estimated probability for control eels to be recaptured and

Z = 1.960 for a 95% confidence interval

The probability of an eel being recaptured was determined using the following formula:

$$\hat{\theta}_0 = \frac{y_0}{N_0}$$

Results

Beauharnois Power Dam, West Side

About 3,270 eels were released at each of the four release sites on the west side of Beauharnois Power Dam in 2001 (Table 1 and Figure 4). A total of 975 controls were recaptured, representing a recapture rate of 29.8%. Recapture rates for R_1 (1.3%), R_2 (1.5%), and R_3 (0.9%) were not statistically different (chi-square, $P < 0.05$). Return rates were calculated as 4.5% (R_1), 5.0% (R_2), and 3.2% (R_3) (Figure 5).

Table 2. Return rates of eels tagged and released along the east shore of the Beauharnois Power Dam forebay in 2002.

Release Location	Number Released	Number Recaptured	Recapture Rate $\hat{\theta}_n$	Return Rate $\hat{B}(d)$	Confidence Interval 95%
R_0	5,565	1,612	29.0%	n/a	n/a
R_1	5,575	194	3.5%	12.0%	±1.7%
R_2	5,557	67	1.2%	4.2%	±1.0%
R_3	5,565	17	0.3%	1.1%	±0.5%

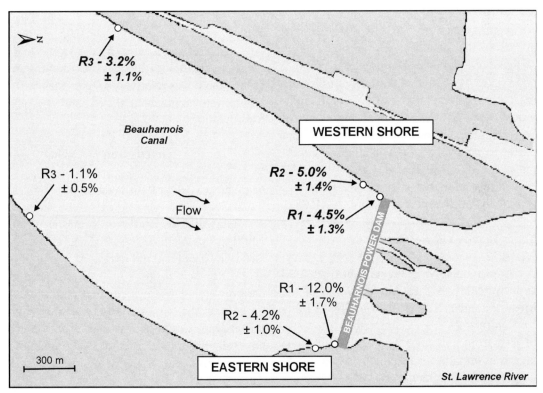

Figure 5. Return rates of eels tagged and released upstream of the Beauharnois Power Dam in 2001 and 2002. Bold type is western shore study in 2001, while regular type is eastern shore study in 2002.

Table 3. Return rates of eels tagged and released upstream of the Moses-Saunders Power Dam in 2001.

Release Location	Number Released	Number Recaptured	Recapture Rate $\hat{\theta}_n$	Return Rate $\hat{B}(d)$	Confidence Interval 95%
R_0	734	120	16.3%	n/a	n/a
R_1	733	61	8.3%	50.9%	±14.8%
R_2	733	62	8.5%	51.7%	±15.0%
R_3	734	8	1.1%	6.7%	±4.7%
R_4	733	7	1.0%	5.8%	±4.4%
R_5	733	4	0.5%	3.3%	±3.3%

Beauharnois Power Dam, East Side

Approximately 5,570 eels were released at each of the four locations on the east side of Beauharnois Power Dam in 2002 (Table 2 and Figure 4). A total of 1,612 controls were recaptured, corresponding to 29% of the individuals released at this site. Recapture rates of eels released at R_1 to R_3 were 3.5%, 1.2%, and 0.3%, respectively, corresponding to return rates of 12.0%, 4.2%, and 1.1% (Figure 5). The difference between recapture rates was significantly different (chi-square, $P < 0.05$).

Moses-Saunders Power Dam

Approximately 733 eels were released at each of the six locations upstream of the Moses-Saunders Power Dam in 2001 (Table 3). Return rates were estimated on the basis of data from eels tagged in 2001 and those tagged in previous years, since no significant difference (chi-square, $P > 0.05$) was found between recapture rates for eels from both groups.

A total of 120 of the 734 controls were recaptured in the traps or detected at the ladder (Table 3), representing a recapture rate of 16.3%. The recapture rates for R_1 to R_5 were 8.3%, 8.5%, 1.1%, 1.0%, and 0.5%, respectively. There was a significant difference between recapture rates at R_1 and R_2 and those at R_3, R_4 and R_5 (chi-square, $P < 0.05$). Return rates ranged from 3.3% to 51.7% from the R_5 to the R_1 release locations (Table 3 and Figure 6), and there was relatively greater variability around the estimates at R_3, R_4, and R_5 compared with R_1 and R_2.

Discussion

Beauharnois Power Dam, West Side

Eels released at three locations up to 1,600 m upstream of the dam had a low return rate (<5%) and did not show any significant difference in probability of recapture in the tailwater. This suggests that entrainment for eels on the west side of the Beauharnois Power Dam would be low even if they were released close to the dam. A comparable study carried out at the same site in 1995 showed similar findings, with only 1.3% of the eels released near the dam recaptured in the tailwater (Desrochers 1996). Water velocity at the release site closest to the dam is low because the nearest turbine intake is more than 25 m away. Surface velocity between the release site and the turbine intake varies between 0.04 m·s⁻¹ and 0.34 m·s⁻¹, and at 5 m depth, it varies between 0.04 and 0.52 m·s^{-1}. According to Knights and White (1998), yellow European eels *Anguilla anguilla* under 100 mm are able to swim against currents of 1.5–2.0 m·s^{-1}. Solomon and Beach (2004) note that the burst speed of European eels in the 400-to-600-mm length range is between 1.25 and 1.35 m·s^{-1}. Therefore, given the relatively large size (average 421 mm) of the migrating eels at Beauharnois Dam and the similarity between European and American eels, it seems likely that individuals could easily avoid entrainment if released close to the dam.

The control release location (R_0) at Beauharnois Power Dam was in the tailwater of turbine Unit No. 36 and not through the turbine; therefore, return rates for release sites R_1, R_2, and R_3 are underestimated since the recapture rate from the control release location does not include any turbine mortality. Turbine mortality rates at Beauharnois are not available for juvenile eels, but for adults (mean size 885 mm), mortality was estimated to be 24% for the fixed blade propeller turbine units and 16% for the Francis turbine units (Desrochers 1995). Turbine mortality rates for eels and other fish such as salmon smolts have been shown to be a function of length, with shorter specimens experiencing less mortality (Larinier and Dartiguelongue 1989; Skalski et al. 2002). Thus one would expect that the shorter juvenile eels (mean length 421 mm) at Beauharnois would have a lower mortality rate than the tested adults. For example, if one were to assume that turbine mortality rate was 10%, then the return rate would be increased by less than 1.5%.

Beauharnois Power Dam, East Side

Unlike the west side, the return rate on the east side of Beauharnois Power Dam decreased with increasing distance from the dam, from 12.0% at R_1 to 1.1% at R_3. Additionally, the return rate from R_1 on the east side (12.0%) was considerably higher than from R_1 on the west side (4.5%).

It is unlikely that this difference in return rates was due to differences in substrate types at the release locations. Both sides of the dam are very similar, with vertical concrete walls near the dam extending upstream of the dam for approximately 90 m. The remainder of the shoreline, extending several kilometers further upstream, is large riprap. However, there are two differences that may have contributed. First, the average size of eels released in the 2002 study on the east side (389 mm) was less than that of eels released in the 2001 study on the west side (421 mm). Although the smaller eels should have been able to swim against the currents in the area, they might have had a slightly reduced swimming capability that could have made them slightly more susceptible to entrainment. Secondly, there is a long-noted pattern of substantially larger quantities of surface debris accumulating on the east side of the forebay of the dam than on the west side. This is mostly due to differences in flow patterns as the water approaches the dam, but wind may also contribute. Differences in flow velocity and direction were not measured in this study, but the observed flow-pattern differences could contribute to the differences in eel return rates.

Moses-Saunders Power Dam

There was a substantial difference in the extent of returns to the tailwater of eels released at different locations upstream of the Moses-Saunders Power Dam. There were two obvious groupings: those closest to the dam (R_1 and R_2) and those farther upstream (R_3, R_4, and R_5) (Figure 6). Those closest to the dam had a return rate of approximately 50%, while the sites farther upstream had return rates of less than 7%. The reason for these differences, apart from distance from the dam, is not readily apparent but is likely related to conditions at the release locations. Unsatisfactory con-

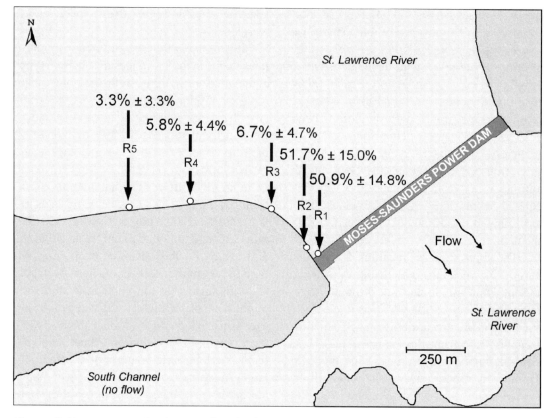

Figure 6. Return rates of eels tagged and released upstream of the Moses-Saunders Power Dam in 2001.

ditions at the release locations, such as poor bottom substrate, inadequate cover, predators, high current velocity, turbulence, eddies, and counter currents, could have resulted in increased movement and exploration. These, in turn, could have led to entrainment. All the release locations were in relatively low-velocity areas, and except for release location R_1, which was adjacent to a concrete wall, all had good bottom substrate (large riprap). Evidently the locations nearest the dam required that the eels move and explore, making them susceptible to entrainment.

An ancillary finding from this study is that the short-term effects and stress from handling and inserting PIT tags into juvenile eels are minimal, given the lack of difference between eels tagged in 2001 and those tagged in the previous years.

Comparison between Moses-Saunders Power Dam and Beauharnois Power Dam

We noted two patterns when we compared return rates from Beauharnois Dam with those at Moses-Saunders Power Dam (Table 4). First, the return rates of eels released 1,600 m upstream of Beauharnois Power Dam (3.2% (west) and 1.1% (east) were low, as were return rates of eels released at the Moses-Saunders Power Dam at more than 270 m upstream (6.7% or less). These roughly comparable rates may represent a base level of migrating eels that exhibit a broad exploratory-like behavior that makes them more vulnerable to entrainment. Similar wandering, or exploratory, behavior has been observed in adult salmon on the Columbia River, where some of the salmon fall back,

Table 4. Comparison of return rates at the Moses-Saunders Power Dam and the Beauharnois Power Dam.

Release Location	Return Rates (%)		
	Moses-Saunders Power Dam	Beauharnois Power Dam	
	South End	East Side	West Side
Close to Dam	50.9	12.0	4.5
~100 m	51.7	4.2	5.0
~300 m	6.7	n/a	n/a
>900 m	3.3	1.1	3.2

largely over spillways at the dams, even after migrating considerable distances upstream (NMFS 2000; Reischel and Bjornn 2003). The second pattern observed is that the return rates of eels released immediately upstream of the dams (R_1) were substantially different at the three locations (4.5% Beauharnois Power Dam west, 12.0% Beauharnois Pwer Dam east, and 50.9% Moses-Saunders Power Dam) even though scale and hydraulic capacity of the hydroelectric projects are very similar. This suggests that the propensity of eels to return to the tailwaters likely depends upon site-specific local conditions at the release locations, such as current velocity, direction of flow, presence of eddies, and availability of sheltering substrate.

Comparison to Other Sites

Reischel and Bjornn (2003) noted that the fallback rates (analogous to our recapture rates) for upstream migrating adult salmon exiting two fish ladders at the Bonneville Dam on the Columbia River were substantially different. They attributed this difference to the location of the ladder exits and their proximity to the shoreline and the spillways. However, in a study conducted at the Safe Harbor Dam on the Susquehanna River, no significant differences were noted in entrainment rates for upstream migrating adult American shad that were released at six locations upstream of the dam (Normandeau 1995). Approximately 60 radio-tagged shad were released at each location—three along the upstream face of the dam and three along a skimmer wall that extended ~45 m upstream of the dam. The entrainment rates, 30% to 44%, were not significantly different, and no apparent pattern relative to distance from the dam was observed.

Very few authors have studied similar movements of upstream migrating juvenile eels at dams. Verdon et al. (2003) studied return rates of yellow eels after ladder passage at the Chambly Dam, a concrete weir on the Richelieu River, Quebec. They found that only 0.6% of the eels released immediately upstream from the dam returned downstream. They concluded that eels were likely not entrained in the water flowing over the dam because the water velocity at the release location was low and the eels stayed close to the bottom substrate, out of the main flow. For European eels, White and Knights (1997) showed that a high proportion of juvenile eels released upstream of dams on the Avon River in England had dropped downstream before resuming migration. Recapture rates of 11.1% and

6.0% were observed downstream from Mill and Stanshard Pit dams, respectively. In this case, young migrating eels, mostly 0+ elvers and 1+ juveniles, might be expected to exhibit reduced swimming capabilities, which may have made them more susceptible to fallback.

Conclusions

Clay (1995), in a general discussion on fishway exits, points out that the exits should be designed to avoid having "fish leave the fishway in an area where they might be readily swept back downstream over the spillway, or through turbines, or into an intake… The fishway exit should therefore be removed some distance from the spillway…" Specific to eel ladders, Clay (1995) notes that "the exit must be carefully located as far as possible upstream to prevent young eels from being swept back over the dam or through the turbines." Knights and White (1998) suggest extending the exit of a ladder or eel passage device into quieter water near rough or weedy bottom that would provide shelter and cover to help eels escape. Solomon and Beach (2004) recommend that to avoid entrainment, eels should not be released directly into the downstream flow and that a refuge should be provided for eels at the release location.

The current studies in part support these recommendations but also clearly demonstrate that the locations for eel ladder exits, to minimize fallback and return to the tailwater at hydroelectric dams, are site-specific. For example, at Moses-Saunders Power Dam, eels need to be released at least 300 m upstream of the dam to substantially reduce their return to the tailwater, while at Beauharnois Power Dam, the results differed, depending upon which side of the dam the eels were released. At the west side of the dam, there would be little return to the tailwater of eels released close to the dam, while on the east side of the dam, eels had to be released at least 90 m upstream to minimize return to the tailwater. Additionally, our studies suggest that a small proportion of eels may still return downstream, depending upon local conditions, the migratory propensity of some of the eels, or the continual active exploratory behavior of juvenile eels.

Acknowledgments

We would like to thank the New York Power Authority and Hydro-Québec for support and funding, Daniel Parker of the New York Power Authority and André Bourbonnais and Del Potts of Ontario Power Generation (OPG) for substantial logistical support, and Tom Tatham of the New York Power Authority for sound scientific guidance. Special thanks to Alastair Mathers from the Ontario Ministry of Natural Resources (OMNR) for access to the OMNR/OPG eel ladder and their data. Finally we thank two anonymous reviewers whose comments greatly improved the paper.

References

Bernard, P., and D. Desrochers. 2002. Étude de la migration des anguilles (*Anguilla rostrata*) du Saint-Laurent et passe migratoire à anguille au barrage de Chambly–2002. b Milieu, Inc., for unité Environnement, division Production, Hydro-Québec, Montréal.

Boubée, J. A. T. 1995. Gravel-lined upstream fish passes. Construction guide. NIWA Consultancy report DOC003 prepared for New Zealand Department of Conservation.

Burnham, K. P., D. R. Anderson, G. C. White, C. Brownie, and K. H. Pollock, editors. 1987. Design and analysis of methods for fish survival experiments based on release-recapture. American Fisheries Society, Monograph 5, Bethesda, Maryland.

Casselman, J. M. 2003. Dynamics of resources of the American eel, Anguilla rostrata: declining abundance in the 1990s. Pages 255–274 *in* K. Aida, K. Tsukamoto, K. Yamauchi, editors. Eel biology. Springer-Verlag, Tokyo.

Clay, C. H. 1995. Design of fishways and other fish facilities, 2nd edition. CRC Press Boca Raton, Florida.

Desrochers, D. 1995. Suivi de la migration de l'anguille d'Americanérique (*Anguilla rostrata*) au complexe Beauharnois, 1994. Milieu Inc. pour le service

Milieu naturel, vice-présidence Environnement et Collectivité, Hydro-Québec, Montreal.

Desrochers, D. 1996. Étude de faisabilité d'une passe migratoire à anguilles (*Anguilla rostrata*) à la Centrale de Beauharnois. Milieu Inc. pour le service Milieu naturel, vice-présidence Environnement et Collectivité, Hydro-Québec, Montreal.

Desrochers, D. 2002. Migration de l'anguille (*Anguilla rostrata*) de la région de Montréal–2001. Milieu Inc.pour Hydraulique et Environnement, Groupe Production, Hydro-Québec, Montreal.

Dutil, J.-D., M. Michaud, and A. Giroux. 1989. Seasonal and diel patterns of stream invasion by American eels (*Anguilla rostrata*) in the northern Gulf of St. Lawrence. Canadian Journal of Zoology 67:182–188.

Eckersley, M. 1982. Operation of the eel ladder at the Moses-Saunders Dam, Cornwall 1974–1979, Pages 4–7 *in* K. H. Loftus, editor. Proceedings of the 1980 North American Eel Conference. Ontario Fisheries Technical Report Series No. 4.

Haro, A. J., and W. H. Krueger. 1991. Pigmentation, otolith rings, and upstream migration of juvenile American eels, *Anguilla rostrata*, in a coastal Rhode Island stream. Canadian Journal of Zoology 69:812–814.

Hurley, D. A. 1972. The American eel (*Anguilla rostrata*) in eastern Lake Ontario. Journal of Fisheries Research Board of Canada 29:535–543.

Knights, B., and E. M. White. 1998. Enhancing immigration and recruitment of eels: the use of passes and associated trapping systems. Fisheries Management and Ecology 5:459–471.

LaBar, G. W., and D. E. Facey. 1983. Local movement and inshore population sizes of American eels in Lake Champlain, Vermont. Transactions of the American Fisheries Society 112:111–116.

Laffaille, P., A. Acou, and J. Guillouet. 2005. The yellow European eel (*Anguilla anguilla* L.) may adopt a sedentary lifestyle in inland freshwaters. Ecology of Freshwater Fish 14(2):191.

Lannin, W. R., and P. Liew. 1979. The eel ladder. Ontario Fish and Wildlife Review 18(1):19–22.

Larinier, M., and J. Dartiguelongue. 1989. La circulation des poissons migrateurs: le transit à travers les turbines des installations hydroélectriques. Bulletin Français de la Pêche et de la Pisciculture 312–313:1–93.

Legault, A. 1992. Étude de quelques facteurs de sélectivité de passes à anguilles. Bulletin Français de la Pêche et de la Pisciculture 325:83–91.

Legault, A., G. Fontenelle, D. Gascuel, and C. Rigaud. 1990. Les passes à anguilles en Europe. Int. Revue ges. Hydrobioly 75:843–844.

Liew, P. K. L. 1982. Impact of the eel ladder on the upstream migrating eel (*Anguilla rostrata*) population in the St. Lawrence River at Cornwall: 1974–1978. Pages 17–22 *in* K. H. Loftus, editor, Proceedings of the 1980 North American Eel conference. Ontario Fisheries Technical Report Series No 4.

McCleave, J. D. 1993. Physical and behavioural controls on the oceanic distribution and migration of leptocephali. Journal of Fish Biology 43(Supplement A):243–273.

McGrath, K., J. Bernier, S. Ault, J.-D. Dutil, and K. Reid. 2003a. Differentiating downstream migrating American eels *Anguilla rostrata* from resident eels in the St. Lawrence River. Pages 315–328 *in* D. A. Dixon editors. Biology, management and protection of catadromous eels. American Fisheries Society, Symposium 33, Bethesda, Maryland.

McGrath, K., D. Desrochers, C. Fleury, and J. Dembeck. 2003b. Studies of upstream migrant American eels at the Moses-Saunders Power Dam on the St. Lawrence River near Massena, NY. Pages 153–168 *in* D. A. Dixon editors. Biology, management and protection of catadromous eels. American Fisheries Society, Symposium 33, Bethesda, Maryland.

Milieu. 2003. 1999 Investigation of abundance, distribution, movement patterns and biological characteristics of upstream migrating American eel at the Moses-Saunders Power Dam and at the Long Sault Dam. New York Power Authority, White Plains, New York.

Milieu. 2004. Installation and operation of PIT-tag detection systems in 2001 at the OMNR eel ladder located at the Moses-Saunders Power Dam. New York Power Authority, White Plains, New York.

NMFS (National Marine Fisheries Service). 2000. Passage of juvenile and adult salmonids past Columbia and Snake River dams. White Paper. Northwest Fisheries Science Center, Seattle.

NYPA (New York Power Authority). 1996. St. Lawrence-F.D.R. Power Project FERC No. 2000. Initial consultation package for relicensing. NYPA, White Plains, New York.

Normandeau Associates. 1995. Report on distribution of telemetered American shad in the tailwaters, spillage areas, and forebays of the Holtwood, Safe Harbor and York Haven Hydroelectric Projects, Susquehanna River, Pennsylvania. Prepared for Pennsylvania Power and Light Company, Safe Harbor Water Power Corporation and Metropolitan Edison Company by Normandeau Associates, Muddy Run, Pennsylvania.

Porcher, J. P. 2002. Fishways for eels. Bulletin Français de la Pêche et de la Pisciculture 364 (supplement):147–155.

Reischel, T., and T. C. Bjornn. 2003. Influence of fishway placement on fallback of adult salmon at the Bonneville Dam on the Columbia River. North American Journal of Fisheries Management 23:1215–1224.

Ricker, W. E. 1958. Handbook of computations of biological statistics of fish populations. Fisheries Research Board of Canada Bulletin No. 119.

Schmidt, J. 1923. The breeding places of the eel. Philosophical Transactions of the Royal Society of London B, Biological Sciences 211:179–208.

Skalski, J. R., D. Mathur, and P. G. Heisey. 2002. Effects of turbine operating efficiency on smolt passage survival. North American Journal of Fisheries Management 22:1193–1200.

Solomon, D. J., and M. H. Beach. 2004. Fish pass design for eel and elver (*Anguilla anguilla*). R&D Technical Report W2-070/TR1 ISBN 184432267X. Environment Agency, United Kingdom.

Tesch, F.-W. 2003. The eel, 3rd edition. Blackwell Scientific Publications Ltd., Oxford, UK.

Tremblay, V. 2004. Strategie de reproduction de l'anguille d'Amerique (*Anguilla rostrata*) chez cinq sous-populations dans le bassin hydrographique du Fleuve Saint-Laurent. Master's thesis. Univerisity of Québec at Rimouski, Québec, Canada.

Verdon, R., D. Desrochers, and P. Dumont. 2003. Recruitment of American Eels in the Richelieu River and Lake Champlain: provision of upstream passage as a regional-scale solution to a large-scale problem. Pages 125–138 *in* D.A. Dixon editors. Biology, management and protection of catadromous eels. American Fisheries Society, Symposium 33, Bethesda, Maryland.

White, E. M., and B. Knights. 1997. Dynamics of upstream migration of the European eel, *Anguilla anguilla* (L.), in the Rivers Severn and Avon, England, with special reference to the effects of man-made barriers Fisheries Management and Ecology 4:311–324.

Wirth, T., and L. Bernatchez. 2003. Decline of North Atlantic eels: a fatal synergy? Proceedings Royal Society of London Series B 270:681–688.

Seasonal Movements of Large Yellow American Eels Downstream of a Hydroelectric Dam, Shenandoah River, West Virginia

STEPHEN D. HAMMOND AND STUART A. WELSH[1]

U.S. Geological Survey, West Virginia Cooperative Fish and Wildlife Research Unit
P. O. Box 6125, Morgantown, West Virginia 26506 USA

Abstract.—Yellow-phase American eels *Anguilla rostrata* migrate upstream extensively in Atlantic coastal river systems. However, few studies have focused on movements of large yellow American eels near dams in upper watersheds of Atlantic coastal rivers. We examined relationships between environmental variables (stream flow, water temperature, and lunar phase) and movements of radio-tagged yellow American eels (518–810 mm TL) near Millville hydroelectric dam in the lower Shenandoah River drainage of the upper watershed of the Potomac River system, West Virginia. Movements of yellow American eels differed seasonally. Water temperature and stream flow were associated with upstream migration during spring. Downstream movements during fall coincided with decreasing water temperatures and darker nights near the new moon. Eels overwintered in thermal refuge areas near tributary mouths. Localized irregular upstream and downstream movements during summer occurred near dusk and dawn and possibly reflected crepuscular foraging. Our study in the Potomac River drainage suggests the need for upstream eel passage at hydroelectric facilities when spring water temperatures exceed 15°C.

Introduction

Upstream migration is an important part of the yellow life stage of American eels *Anguilla rostrata* (ASMFC 2000). Dams undoubtedly delay upstream migration and may have contributed to the apparent population decline of American eels (Richkus and Whalen 2000; Haro et al. 2000); however, populations persist upstream of dams in upper watersheds of Atlantic coastal rivers (Menhinick 1991; Jenkins and Burkhead 1993; Goodwin and Angermeier 2003). Fish ladders installed through cooperative efforts between natural-resource agencies and operators of hydroelectric facilities have assisted upstream passage in some Atlantic coastal rivers, but movements of yellow eels near dams with or without fish ladders are not fully understood (EPRI 1999). A better understanding and evaluation of eel behavior in tailwaters and downstream of dams and of environmental cues for upstream migration are needed to manage and protect yellow American eels.

Data are available on movements of American eels in large rivers (Levesque and Whitworth 1987; Oliveira 1997; Verdon and Desrochers 2003; McGrath et al. 2003), streams (Gunning and Shoop 1962), lakes (Hurley 1972; LaBar and Facey 1983; La-

[1] Corresponding author: swelsh@mail.wvu.edu

mothe et al. 2000), and estuaries (Helfman et al. 1983; Bozeman et al. 1985; Ford and Mercer 1986; Dutil et al. 1989; Barbin et al. 1998). Eel movements vary seasonally (Richkus and Dixon 2003) and are possibly triggered by environmental cues such as water temperature (McGrath et al. 2003; Verdon et al. 2003), precipitation (Tesch 1977; Winn et al. 1975), flow (Euston et al. 1998), and lunar phase (Lowe 1952; Winn et al. 1975; Cairns and Hooley 2003). Movements may be associated with specific environmental thresholds: water temperatures between 10 and 16°C stimulate upstream movements during spring (Smith and Saunders 1955; Groom 1975; Sorensen and Bianchini 1986; Jessop 2003). Fluctuations or sudden changes in water temperature or stream flow may also elicit eel movements (Durif et al. 2003; Verdon et al. 2003). Most studies of American eel movements have focused on small juveniles within or near estuaries (Sorensen and Bianchini 1986; Haro and Krueger 1987; Dutil et al. 1989) or on larger eels (>300 mm TL) in lower sections of coastal watersheds (Jessop 1987; Dutil et al. 1988). However, little information exists on seasonal movements of relatively large (>500 mm TL) yellow eels in upper watersheds or on seasonal movements of yellow eels near dams. Information on eel movements is needed to improve our understanding of eel behavior in the upper reaches of rivers and to assist operational management of hydroelectric facilities in relation to eel passage.

The primary objective of this study was to examine potential environmental cues, such as stream flow, water temperature, and lunar phase, associated with upstream and downstream seasonal movements of eels near the Millville hydroelectric dam in the lower Shenandoah River drainage, an upper watershed of the Potomac River system, West Virginia. Secondary objectives were to estimate average seasonal distances of eels from Millville Dam and to examine crepuscular and nocturnal movements of yellow eels within the tailwater of the dam during summer.

Methods

The study was conducted in a 9-km section (average width 150 m) of the lower Shenandoah River downstream of Millville Dam (Figure 1). The 5-m high Millville Dam diverts water to a canal for power production. The substrate of the 700-m tailwater section is predominantly slanted bedrock with some areas of small boulders, large cobble, and gravel. During low stream flows, exposed bedrock creates pocket pools and braided channels in several areas of the tailwater and in the lower kilometer of the study area. The middle section of the study area contains pool and run habitats with unexposed bedrock, boulder, cobble, and gravel substrates. A road parallels the upper 4-km section of the study area, whereas a footpath provides access to the lower 5-km section. Millville Dam regulates flow within downstream reaches of the Shenandoah River during low to moderate flows, but not during high flows. Millville Dam undoubtedly delays upstream fish movement, but American eels occur in upper reaches of the Shenandoah River (Jenkins and Burkhead 1993); hence the dam is not a complete barrier to upstream passage of eels.

To obtain data on seasonal and nocturnal movements, 20 yellow American eels were captured with a backpack electrofisher from the tailwater of Millville Dam. We anesthetized eels with clove oil (Anderson et al. 1997) and surgically implanted radio transmitters (Lotek MBFT-5, 11 mm × 43 mm, 366-d life) into the abdominal cavity (Ross and Kleiner 1982). Radio tags were implanted in 13 eels (range 518–810 mm) between 8 and 23 September 2001 and in seven eels (range 599–781 mm) between 11 and 27 June 2002. Radio-tagged eels recovered in a live cage for several hours postsurgery and were released near the collection area between the seventh and tenth

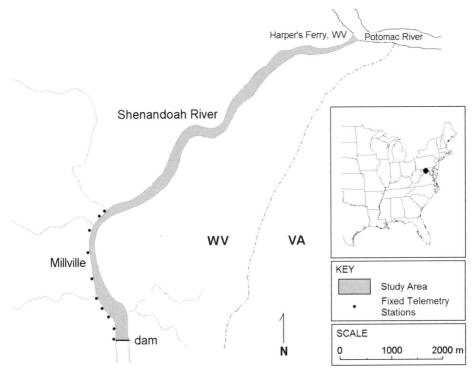

Figure 1. Study area and fixed telemetry stations within a 9 km section of the lower Shenandoah River, West Virginia, from Millville Dam to the mouth of the Shenandoah River.

downstream telemetry stations (see Figure 1). Radio-tagged eels were tracked manually with a Lotek SRX_400 receiver and Yagi antenna and locations were triangulated by using compass bearings and DeLorme 3-D TopoQuads mapping software. Error of triangulated locations was less than 5 m based on electrofishing recaptures of radio-tagged eels. We measured straight-line distances (i.e., minimum distances) between consecutive relocation coordinates of each individual eel. In cases where river sinuosity prevented straight-line distances, we measured the within-river minimum distance between relocations.

Seasonal Movements

For analysis of seasonal movements, we tracked eels during daylight hours from 10 fixed stations within a 3.4-km section of shoreline below the dam (Figure 1). When radio-tagged eels were not located within the 3.4-km section of shoreline below the dam, then we tracked eels within the lower study area. Tracking dates were generally within one-to-two-week intervals from 14 June 2001–28 May 2003, but because of severe weather conditions, several intervals between 15 and 33 d occurred during winter months. Minimum distances during each time interval between relocations were expressed as $m \cdot d^{-1}$. We used PROC MIXED (SAS 1990) to model covariance associated with repeated measures on individual eels (within seasons) and analyzed upstream and downstream movements separately. Given unequal time intervals between relocations, we used the spatial power structure (a generalization of the autoregressive first-order covariance structure for equally spaced data) to address within-subject covariance (Littell et al. 1996). Relocation times between eels were temporally aligned to account for missing values (Littell et al. 1996). Mixed models included season as a fixed effect, where seasons were partitioned into spring (16 March–15 June), summer (16 June–15 September), fall (16 September–15 December), and winter (16 December–15 March). Using the spatial power structure of covariance, least-square means in PROC MIXED (Littell et al. 1996) estimated means of upstream and downstream movements by season.

Seasonal movements were modeled with seven covariates derived from water temperature, stream flow, and lunar phase. Temperature loggers recorded daily water temperatures within the study area from the main channel of the Shenandoah River and one small tributary. River flows (cubic meters per second, cms) were obtained from the U.S. Geological Survey gauge at Millville Dam (http://waterdata.usgs.gov). We used the visible fraction of the moon's surface to quantify lunar illumination, where fractions range from new moon (0.00), first and last quarter (0.50), and full moon (1.00; http://aa.usno.navy.mil/data/docs/MoonFraction.html). For each time interval between relocations, covariates were determined as maximum values of lunar illumination, stream flow, and water temperature and mean values of stream flow and water temperature. Covariates of maximum values were used to model the importance of extreme conditions, whereas those of mean values were used to represent general conditions within relocation intervals. Covariates derived from differences in mean water temperatures and stream flows between consecutive relocation intervals were used to model fluctuations or sudden changes within short time periods.

Given all potential combinations and interactions among season and covariates, many models could be fit to the data; however, we selected 24 models based on published literature of fish movement. Because of the limits of our effective sample size, we avoided models with more than 10 estimable parameters (Burnham and Anderson 2002). The 24 biologically reasonable candidate models (selected before analysis and representing multiple hypotheses, Chamberlin 1965) were ranked by the second-order adjustment to Akaike's information criterion (AICc). This information-theoretic approach, where AICc estimates Kullback-Leibler distance, selects the best model (or suite of competing models) through a parsimonious trade-off among bias, variance, and the number of estimable model parameters and avoids the use of arbitrary significance (alpha) levels for inference from observational data (Burnham and Anderson 2002).

Distance from Dam

We calculated distances between coordinates of eel relocations and Millville Dam to determine seasonal locations of eels relative to the dam. Using the spatial power structure to model within-subject covariance, least-square means in PROC MIXED (Littell et al. 1996) estimated mean distances from the dam by season. The mixed model included season as a fixed effect, with repeated measures taken on radio-tagged eels within each season. This method accounted for missing values and unequal time intervals between locations.

Crepuscular and Nocturnal Movements

We estimated crepuscular and nocturnal movements of eight eels (518–781 mm TL) within the 700-m tailwater of Millville Dam during six nights (25–26, 29–30, and 30–31 July 2002 and 1–2, 6–7, and 8–9 August 2002). Movements (m/h) were estimated for four 2-h time periods (2100–2300, 2300–0100, 0100–0300, and 0300–0500 hours) on each night. Lunar illumination (as described above), stream flow, and water temperature were recorded for each 2-h relocation interval, but water temperature and stream flow were not used as environmental covariates, since there was little variation among nights. To address covariance, we fit the full model (date × time) with unstructured, compound symmetry and first-order autoregressive covariance models using PROC MIXED (Littell et al. 1996) and selected the best model based on the lowest AICc value. Using the best covariate model, a set of five candidate models was fit to the nocturnal movement data and represented alternative hypotheses of eel movements associated with dusk (2100–2300 hours), dawn (0300–0500 hours), dusk and dawn combined, and lunar illumination. For statistical inference, we used AICc to select the best model or models supported by the data.

Results

Sixteen of the 20 radio-tagged American eels were located and positioned 673 times during the 617-d study period (8 September 2001–23 May 2003), with only one location recorded for each tagged eel on each tracking day. Not all tagged eels were relocated on each tracking day, and four eels were not relocated after release. To reduce bias from tag-induced movements, we eliminated the first 30 d of relocation data. Thirteen of the 16 eels were relocated during intervals near the full 366-d tag life, but three eels were not relocated after shorter time periods (263, 237, and 47 d; Table 1).

Seasonal Movements

Movements differed among seasons and among individual eels, with highest rates of upstream movement during spring and highest rates of downstream movement during fall (Table 1). Models without a seasonal effect were unsupported by the data (Table 2). For analysis of upstream movements, AICc selected season × maximum flow as the best model, but two additive models (with temperature fluctuation and/or flow fluctuation) and two interaction models (with average flow and flow fluctuation) were close competitors (Table 2). Based on the five competing "best" models, our data supported an association of higher flows and increasing temperatures with upstream movements during spring. During spring, upstream movements (mean = 33.8 m·d^{-1}, SE = 4.1) exceeded downstream movements (mean = 11.0 m·d^{-1}, SE = 2.5) and co-occurred with water temperatures above 15°C and increased stream flows. Models with a lunar illumination covariate received little weight for the analysis of upstream movements (Table 2).

Lunar illumination was associated with downstream movements, where the two best models (supported by lowest AICc values) were season × lunar illumination and season + lunar illumination + average water temperature (Table 2). These models emphasized the importance of low lunar light (darker nights) and decreasing water temperatures on downstream movements during fall (mean = 18.4 m·d^{-1}, SE = 2.9). During fall, the longest downstream movements (>50 m) within relocation intervals occurred within a narrow range of mean water temperatures (11.0–11.6°C).

Upstream movements of eight individuals (range 32–363 m) during a 7-d relocation interval (2–9 November 2001) influenced the relatively high mean rate of upstream movement during fall (mean = 12.4 m·d^{-1}, SE = 5.3). These large upstream movements from 2 November 2001–9 November 2001 occurred on a waning full moon, with flow (mean = 12.2 cms, maximum = 12.7 cms) and water temperature (mean = 9.1°C, maximum = 9.3°C) relatively unchanged from the previous time interval.

Movements during summer exceeded those of winter but were less than upstream movements in spring and downstream movements during fall. During summer, localized movements occurred within mean water temperatures of 24.1–29.9°C, where eels wan-

Table 1. Mean rates of movement of individual eels summarized by season and direction. Days at large represents the number of days between the release date and the date of last location. SE = standard error. a = Eel not relocated, b = Standard error not estimated when fewer than 3 relocations, c = No upstream movements observed, d = Eel not found during consecutive relocation intervals, e = No downstream movements observed.

Eel tag number	Eel TL(mm)	Release date	Date of last location	Days at large	Movement direction	Winter mean (SE)	Spring mean (SE)	Summer mean (SE)	Fall mean (SE)
150500	601	23 Sep 01	27 Sep 02	369	down	5.4 (2.9)	28.2 (24.7)	6.1 (1.2)	20.2 (16.4)
					up	1.8 (0.4)	51.3 (22)	9.4 (3)	18.8 (13.6)
150520	738	9 Sep 01	23 Aug 02	348	down	11.8 (8.3)	10.3 (3.9)	6.2 (1.7)	17.1 (4.5)
					up	2.8 (0.9)	59.4 (42.1)	6.5 (0.9)	26.4 (9.6)
150600	682	23 Sep 01	18 Sep 02	360	down	a	26.3 (21.5)	16.6 (7.7)	8.5 (b)
					up	a	27.1 (14.1)	20.4 (7.9)	c
150660	518	23 Sep 01	18 Sep 02	360	down	d	4.6 (b)	18.4 (12.2)	d
					up	d	39.6 (26.5)	6.5 (2.8)	d
150760	781	11 Jun 02	23 May 03	346	down	1.8 (0.5)	4.4 (3.5)	6.0 (1.3)	3.4 (b)
					up	0.9 (0.2)	7.8 (3.9)	0.6 (b)	4.5 (2.7)
150780	704	9 Sep 01	23 Aug 02	348	down	2.4 (b)	8.0 (b)	6.7 (2.1)	d
					up	c	51.2 (38)	17.5 (7.3)	d
150800	528	23 Sep 01	16 Aug 02	327	down	1.6 (b)	15.3 (7.6)	6.8 (2.2)	42.9 (31.3)
					up	1.1 (0.1)	42.3 (31.7)	14.2 (0.7)	23.7 (b)
151520	525	23 Sep 01	16 Aug 02	327	down	2.5 (0.4)	7.0 (3.1)	9.6 (3.3)	e
					up	0.5 (0.3)	28.9 (20.8)	13.9 (7)	7.5 (2.2)
151530	670	8 Sep 01	29 May 02	263	down	2 (0.3)	2.5 (1.6)	a	20.4 (b)
					up	2.8 (1.6)	8.6 (2.5)	a	11.4 (6.8)
151540	612	27 Jun 02	23 May 03	330	down	3.1 (0.9)	20.1 (18.9)	e	6.5 (3.6)
					up	7.2 (3.7)	5.1 (3.1)	2.5 (1.1)	11.3 (5)
151550	596	22 Sep 01	23 Aug 02	335	down	1.9 (0.5)	e	13.0 (4.7)	49.7 (b)
					up	c	47.4 (31.1)	16.6 (5.1)	13.8 (4.8)

Table 1. Continued

Eel tag number	Eel TL(mm)	Release date	Date of last location	Days at large	Movement direction	Winter mean (SE)	Spring mean (SE)	Summer mean (SE)	Fall mean (SE)
151570	540	22 Sep 01	18 Sep 02	361	down	6.4 (2.6)	e	25.1 (5.8)	32.9 (13.6)
					up	1.1 (0.4)	38.6 (26.5)	9.3 (3)	29.5 (3.3)
151590	599	25 Jun 02	17 Feb 03	237	down	1.6 (0.7)	a	26.9 (23.2)	3.0 (0.7)
					up	1.9 (0.2)	a	6.6 (3.4)	8.1 (6.4)
					up	1.1 (0.4)	38.6 (26.5)	9.3 (3)	29.5 (3.3)
151590	599	25 Jun 02	17 Feb 03	237	down	1.6 (0.7)	a	26.9 (23.2)	3.0 (0.7)
					up	1.9 (0.2)	a	6.6 (3.4)	8.1 (6.4)
					up	2.2 (0.2)	13.2 (5.8)	1.7 (b)	2.7 (1.1)
151720	708	12 Jun 02	23 May 03	345	down	3.6 (b)	7.8 (3.2)	10.9 (2.4)	3.5 (0.5)
					up	2 (0.2)	14.3 (5)	5.4 (2.6)	2.1 (0.1)

Table 2. Selection statistics for 24 alternative models from separate analyses of upstream and downstream movements; second order adjustment of Akaike's Information Criterion (AICc), distance from lowest AICc (Δi), and Akaike weights (wi). Bold weights represent competing models within each analysis; statistics between upstream and downstream analyses are not comparable. Model Variables include season (movements partitioned by spring, summer, fall, and winter), and six covariates determined from each relocation interval: maximum and mean stream flow, maximum and mean water temperature, maximum lunar illumination, and fluctuations of stream flow and water temperature.

Model	Upstream movements			Downstream movements		
	AICc	Δi	wi	AICc	Δi	wi
Season × Lunar Illumination	570.6	10.0	0.00	408.9	0.0	**0.43**
Season + Mean Flow + Lunar Illumination	567.5	6.9	0.01	412.5	3.6	0.07
Season + Maximum Flow + Lunar Illumination	568.1	7.5	0.01	412.1	3.2	0.09
Season + Mean Temperature + Lunar Illumination	566.0	5.4	0.02	410.2	1.3	**0.23**
Season + Lunar Illumination	566.5	5.9	0.01	410.8	1.9	**0.17**
Season x Mean Flow	561.6	1.0	**0.17**	423.9	15.0	0.00
Season + Mean Flow	568.9	8.3	0.00	422.4	13.5	0.00
Season x Maximum Flow	560.6	0.0	**0.27**	423.6	14.7	0.00
Season + Maximum Flow	569.1	8.5	0.00	422.0	13.1	0.00
Season x Mean Temperature	571.6	11.0	0.00	417.1	8.2	0.01
Season + Mean Temperature	567.4	6.8	0.01	422.7	13.8	0.00
Season + Mean Temperature + Mean Flow	569.5	8.9	0.00	422.7	13.8	0.00
Season x Flow Fluctuation	563.5	2.9	0.06	426.2	17.3	0.00
Season + Flow Fluctuation	564.8	4.2	0.03	422.7	13.8	0.00
Season x Temperature Fluctuation	565.4	4.8	0.02	426.8	17.9	0.00
Season + Temperature Fluctuation	561.5	0.9	**0.17**	423.7	14.8	0.00
Season + Temperature Fluctuation + Flow Fluctuation	561.4	0.8	**0.18**	423.8	14.9	0.00
Season	567.1	6.5	0.01	422.0	13.1	0.00
Lunar Illumination	597.0	36.4	0.00	428.1	19.2	0.00
Mean Flow	601.0	40.4	0.00	441.7	32.8	0.00
Maximum Flow	602.1	41.5	0.00	440.8	31.9	0.00
Mean Temperature	597.9	37.3	0.00	439.0	30.1	0.00
Flow Fluctuation	597.2	36.6	0.00	441.5	32.6	0.00
Temperature Fluctuation	599.4	38.8	0.00	444.8	35.9	0.00

Table 3. Selection statistics for 5 alternative models of nocturnal movements during six summer nights; second order adjustment of Akaike's Information Criterion (AICc), distance from lowest AICc (Δi), and Akaike weights (wi). Movements (m/hr) were estimated within four 2-hour time periods (2100–2300, 2300–0100, 0100–0300, and 0300–0500 hours), where models represent movements associated with dusk (2100–2300 hours), dawn (0300–0500 hours), dusk and dawn, and lunar illumination.

| | Nocturnal movements | | |
Model	AICc	Δi	wi
Dusk/dawn	371.9	0.0	0.54
Dawn	373.1	1.2	0.29
Lunar Illumination	375.7	3.8	0.08
Dusk	375.8	3.9	0.08
Date	379.2	7.3	0.01

dered upstream (mean = 10.5 m·d^{-1}, SE = 4.1) and downstream (mean = 11.5 m·d^{-1}, SE = 1.7). Winter movements were lowest of all seasons (upstream, mean = 2.1 m·d^{-1}, SE = 6.6; downstream, mean = 3.5 m·d^{-1}, SE = 2.4) and were observed within a main-stem water temperature range of 0.8–9.4°C. Most of the tagged eels overwintered in thermal refuge areas near tributary mouths. Winter temperatures at one tributary mouth averaged 7.2°C, whereas main channel temperatures averaged 3.7°C.

Crepuscular and Nocturnal Movements

The compound symmetry covariance model was supported by the data, based on lowest AICc, and was used to estimate means of crepuscular and nocturnal movements. Eels moved irregularly upstream and downstream from 2100 to 0500 hours on six summer nights, with an overall mean movement estimate of 10.2 m/h (SE = 0.48). Data supported the combined dusk and dawn model (Table 3), where movements were greatest during dusk (2100–2300 hours, mean = 10.1 m/h, SE = 0.75) and dawn (0300–0500 hours, mean = 11.4 m/h, SE = 0.75), and slightly less from 2300 to 0100 hours (mean = 9.7 m/h, SE = 0.75) and 0100–0300 hours (mean = 9.6 m/h, SE = 0.75). Despite a wide range of lunar illumination during the six nights (0.0–0.97), data did not support an association between movements and lunar illumination (Table 3). Water temperature and stream flow were not modeled as covariates in the analysis of crepuscular and nocturnal movements, given low variation in water temperature (range 26.4–30.4°C) and stream flow (range 11.8–18.7 cms) among the six summer nights, with less variation among time intervals during each night.

Seasonal Distances from the Dam

Proximity of eels to the Millville Dam corroborated seasonal movements. Eels were farthest from the dam during fall (mean = 1347 m, SE = 287) and winter (mean = 1954 m, SE = 307) and closest during spring (mean = 1014 m, SE = 293) and summer (mean = 831 m, SE = 295; Figure 2). Radio-tagged eels were closest to the dam (mean = 615 m, SE = 102) when water temperatures exceeded 15°C during late spring (26 April–10 June). During early fall (18 September–25 October), eels were also relatively close to the dam (mean = 1200 m, SE = 220) when water temperatures exceeded 12°C. Large differences in mean distances from the dam

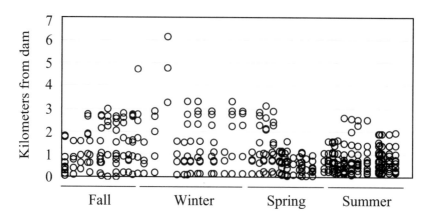

Figure 2. Seasonal distance of radio-tagged American eels from Millville Dam (all relocations plotted for each eel).

between early fall and winter (1,200 versus 1,954 m) and winter and late spring (1,954 versus 615 m) confirmed downstream movements during fall and upstream movements during spring.

Discussion

Our data suggest an association between upstream migration of large (range 518–810 mm TL) yellow American eels and two abiotic variables, water temperature and stream flow, during spring. Given relatively warm spring rains, stream flow and water temperature increase concurrently during spring and may synergistically influence upstream migration. In our study, sudden changes in stream flow and water temperature influenced upstream migration of large yellow eels during spring. In the lower Shenandoah River, water temperature of 15°C stimulated upstream migration and falls within the range of temperature cues, 10–16°C, from eel studies summarized by EPRI (1999). Upstream migration during spring was expected, given similar findings by Sorensen and Bianchini (1986), Haro and Krueger (1988), and Jessop (2003). Studies of eel movements, however, have largely focused on elvers or small yellow eels in lower sections of coastal rivers, and less information is available on movements in upper sections of rivers.

The general pattern of downstream movements of large yellow eels during fall (with some periods of upstream movement) probably reflects downstream and upstream searches for overwintering areas. Downstream movements during fall occurred on darker nights (near new moons) and during decreasing water temperatures, with the greatest movements during relocation intervals at mean water temperatures of 11.0–11.6°C. Although nocturnal movements of eels are well documented (Lowe 1952; Tecsh 1977; Dutil et al. 1988), contrasted results exist for movements associated with lunar phase (see review by Cairns and Hooley 2003). Our data support an association between low levels of lunar illumination and downstream movements of yellow eels during fall. Upstream movements during fall may represent upstream migration instead of searches for suitable winter habitats, where retreat to overwintering areas below the dam possibly occurred after unsuccessful attempts to migrate upstream. A period of upstream migration occurs during fall on the St. Lawrence River (Dutil et al. 1989; McGrath et al. 2003). Smaller yellow eels move upstream during late summer in the lower Shenandoah River. An eel ladder installed at Millville Dam on 31 July 2003 passed 408 eels (mean = 304 mm TL, range 197–510 mm TL) from 22 August 2003–17 September 2003.

Eel locations determined at 1-to-2-week intervals did not indicate directional upstream or downstream migration during summer but supported erratic wandering movements in both upstream and downstream directions. Movement data from night tracking at 2-h intervals also supported localized movements. Eels may establish small home ranges during summer (Gunning and Shoop 1962; Ford and Mercer 1986; Bozeman et al. 1985) and remained within relatively short sections in the lower Shenandoah River during summer. We did not estimate home range sizes from summer movement data, given that the dam biased upstream movement. In our study, crepuscular and nocturnal wanderings during summer probably reflect active foraging, because yellow eels feed primarily at night (Sorensen et al. 1986). Although food availability may influence movements (Helfman 1986), large foraging areas were unlikely in our study area, given large populations of crayfish and cyprinids. Crayfish were common diet items of eels in the Shenandoah River, based on crayfish parts excreted during surgical implantation of radio tags.

Yellow American eels become torpid at water temperatures below 10°C (Walsh et al. 1983); hence, we expected no movements during winter seasons of our study, when water temperatures ranged from 0.8 to 9.4°C. Nyman (1972) and Barila and Stauffer (1980) reported reduced feeding of eels at water temperatures below 14°C, whereas Renaud and Moon (1980) reported that feeding ceased and activity of eels was reduced below 8°C. Euston et al. (1998), however, reported downstream movements of silver eels at water temperatures as low as 6°C. In our study, most individuals moved less than 5 m a day between relocations during winter. Estimates of small upstream (mean = 2.1 m·d^{-1}) and downstream (mean = 3.5 m·d^{-1}) movements during winter probably represent errors in triangulation of relocation coordinates.

Movement data, however, did not support downstream displacement of torpid eels during larger fluctuations in stream flow. Between 1–18 December 2001 (mean = 5.1°C), relatively long downstream movements (11 and 20 m) of two individuals (540 and 728 mm TL, respectively) possibly represent displacement, given that maximum stream flow increased from 15 to 22 cms during that time. Tagged yellow eels did not "silver" during the study period (with the possible exception of an 810-mm eel). Eels moving downstream during fall and winter were not emigrating, because eels (except the 810-mm individual) were relocated within the study area during the following spring and summer. The 810-mm eel was relocated during the first fall season only; our inability to relocate this individual during later efforts has several explanations, including emigration and tag malfunction. Longer mean distances from the dam during winter months possibly reflect the location and use of thermal refugia near tributary mouths. Silver European eels used areas of elevated water temperatures near thermal power plants during winter (Nyman 1975), and other riverine fishes use thermal refuge areas during winter (Raibley et al. 1997; Knights et al. 1995; Gent et al. 1995).

Management Implications

Movement of yellow American eels differed among seasons in the lower Shenandoah River, mainly upstream movements in spring, downstream movement during fall, irregular upstream and downstream movement during summer, and minimal movement during winter. Oliveira (1997), citing Bianchini et al. (1982), hypothesized that yellow eels likely move considerable distances between periods when there appears to be little measured movement. Our data are consistent with this punctuated-movement hypothesis, where upstream movements occur during spring followed by localized movements during summer and relatively little movement during winter. Our data are inconclusive concerning upstream migration of large yellow eels during fall. Movement data from the lower Shenandoah River likely represent behavior of large yellow eels within upper watersheds of other Atlantic coastal streams. From a management perspective, however, we restrict inference to movements of large yellow eels near dams.

Water temperature was important to overall seasonal eel movements, particularly as an environmental cue to upstream movement in spring, combined with increased stream flows. For large yellow eels, our data support spring as the critical period for provision of upstream passage at hydroelectric dams. Data did not support other seasons (fall, winter, and summer) as important for upstream passage of large yellow eels (with the possible exception of fall). Water temperature, combined with darker nights near the new moon, stimulated downstream movement during fall. We believe that downstream movement during fall and more distant locations from the dam during winter reflect use of specific habitat and thermal refuge areas. Although direction of fall movements was generally downstream, a short period of upstream movements also occurred during fall. Possibly eels settled for thermal refuge areas downstream of the dam after unsuccessful attempts of upstream migration. We did not find evidence of upstream migration of large yellow eels during summer, where data from 1-to-2-week intervals and nocturnal data within 2-h time intervals supported localized upstream and downstream movements.

Data from this study provide natural-resource managers with a better understanding of the behavior of large yellow American eels in upper watersheds of Atlantic coastal rivers. Additionally, the data are relevant to the operational management of hydroelectric facilities in relation to eel passage. More studies on relations between eel movements and dams in upper watersheds are needed, however, to better understand seasonal upstream and downstream movements of small and large yellow-phase American eels. Also, given the recent concern to provide eel ladders and upstream passage around dams, further research is needed to better understand downstream passage of emigrant silver American eels.

Acknowledgments

We thank Terry Euston, Ben Lenz, Lara Hedrick, Jessica Smith, and Dave Wellman for their assistance with fieldwork and data collection and Kerry Bledsoe, Douglas Dixon, Barbara Douglas, Larry Earnest, Terry Euston, Gary Harbaugh, Alex Hoar, Charles Simons, and Julie Weeder for their contributions to the project, as well as two anonymous reviewers of the manuscript.

Funding was provided through EPRI (Electric Power Research Institute) of Palo Alto, California; Allegheny Energy; and West Virginia Division of Natural Resources. Reference to trade names does not imply government endorsement of commercial products.

References

Anderson, W. G., R. S. McKinley, and M. Colavecchia. 1997. The use of clove oil as an anesthetic for rainbow trout and its effects on swimming performance. North American Journal of Fisheries Management 17:301–307.

ASMFC (Atlantic States Marine Fisheries Commission). 2000. Interstate fishery management plan for American eel. Fishery Management Report 36, Washington, D.C.

Barbin, G. P., S. J. Parker, and J. D. McCleave. 1998. Olfactory clues play a critical role in the estuarine migration of silver-phase American eels. Environmental Biology of Fishes 53:283–291.

Barila, T. Y., and J. R. Stauffer, Jr. 1980. Temperature

behavioral responses of the American eel, *Anguilla rostrata* (LeSueur), from Maryland. Hydrobiologia 74:49–51.

Bianchini, M., P. W. Sorensen, and H. E. Winn. 1982. Stima dell'abbondanza e shemi di movimento a breve raggio della anguilla Americana, *Anguilla rostrata* (LeSueur) (Pisces, Apodes), nel Narrow River, Rhode Island, USA. Naturalista Siciliano (Supplement 4) 6:269–277.

Bozeman, E. L., G. S. Helfman, and T. Richardson. 1985. Population size and home range of American eels in a Georgia tidal creek. Transactions of the American Fisheries Society 114:821–825.

Burnham, K. P., and D. R. Anderson. 2002. Model selection and multimodel inference: a practical information-theoretic approach, 2nd edition. Springer, New York, New York.

Cairns, D. K., and P. J. D. Hooley. 2003. Lunar cycles of American eels in tidal waters of the southern Gulf of the St. Lawrence, Canada. Pages 265–274 *in* D. A. Dixon, editor. Biology, management, and protection of catadromous eels. American Fisheries Society, Symposium 33, Bethesda, Maryland.

Chamberlin, T. C. 1965 (1890). The method of multiple working hypotheses. Science 148:754–759. (Reprint of 1890 paper in Science).

Durif, C., P. Elie, C. Gosset, J. Rives, and F. Travade. 2003. Behavioral study of downstream migrating eels by radio-telemetry at a small hydroelectric power plant. Pages 343–356 *in* D. A. Dixon, editor. Biology, management, and protection of catadromous eels. American Fisheries Society, Symposium 33, Bethesda, Maryland.

Dutil, J.-D., A. Giroux, A. Kemp, G. LaVoie, and J.-P. Dallaire. 1988. Tidal influence on movements and on daily cycle of activity of American eels. Transactions of the American Fisheries Society 117:488–494.

Dutil, J.-D., M. Michaud, and A. Giroux. 1989. Seasonal and diel patterns of stream invasion by American eels (*Anguilla rostrata*) in the northern Gulf of St. Lawrence. Canadian Journal of Zoology 67:182–188.

EPRI (Electric Power Research Institute). 1999. American eel (*Anguilla rostrata*) scoping study: a literature and data review of life history, stock status, population dynamics, and hydroelectric impacts. EPRI, Palo Alto, California: TR-111873.

Euston, E. T., D. D. Royer, and C. L. Simons. 1998. American eels and hydro plants: clues to eel passage. Hydro Review (August):94–103.

Ford, T. E., and E. Mercer. 1986. Density, size distribution and home range of American eels, *Anguilla rostrata*, in a Massachusetts Salt Marsh Environmental Biology of Fishes 17:309–314.

Gent, R., J. Pitlo, Jr., and T. Boland. 1995. Largemouth bass response to habitat and water quality rehabilitation in a backwater of the upper Mississippi River. North American Journal of Fisheries Management 15:784–793.

Goodwin, K. R., and P. L. Angermeier. 2003. Demographic characteristics of the American eel in the Potomac River drainage, Virginia. Transactions of the American Fisheries Society 132:524–535.

Groom, W. 1975. Elver observations in New Brunswick's Bay of Fundy region. Resource Development Branch, N.B. Department of Fisheries, Fredericton, New Brunswick, Canada.

Gunning, G. E., and C. R. Shoop. 1962. Restricted movements of the American eel, *Anguilla rostrata* (LeSueur), in freshwater streams, with comments on growth rate. Tulane Studies in Zoology 9:265–272.

Haro, A. J., and W. H. Krueger. 1987. Pigmentation, otolith rings, and upstream migration of juvenile American eels (*Anguilla rostrata*) in a coastal Rhode Island stream. Canadian Journal of Zoology 69:812–814.

Haro, A. J., and W. H. Krueger. 1988. Pigmentation, size and migration of elvers (*Anguilla rostrata* (LeSueur)) in a coastal Rhode Island stream. Canadian Journal of Zoology 66:2528–2533.

Haro, A., W. Richkus, K. Whalen, A. Hoar, W-D. Busch, S. Lary, T. Brush, and D. Dixon. 2000. Population decline of the American eel: implications for research and management. Fisheries 25(9):7–16.

Helfman, G. S. 1986. Diel distribution and activity of American eels (*Anguilla rostrata*) in a cave-spring. Canadian Journal of Fisheries and Aquatic Sciences 43:1595–1605.

Helfman, G. S., D. L. Stoneburner, E. L. Bozeman, P. A. Christian, and A. Whalen. 1983. Ultrasonic telemetry of American eel movements in a tidal creek. Transactions of the American Fisheries Society 112:105–110.

Hurley, D. A. 1972. The American eel (*Anguilla rostrata*) in eastern Lake Ontario. Journal of the Fisheries Research Board of Canada 29:535–543.

Jenkins, R. E., and N. M. Burkhead. 1993. Freshwater fishes of Virginia. American Fisheries Society, Bethesda, Maryland.

Jessop, B. M. 1987. Migrating American eels in Nova Scotia. Transactions of the American Fisheries Society 116:161–170.

Jessop, B. M. 2003. Annual variability in the effects of water temperature, discharge, and tidal stage on the migration of American eel elvers from estuary to river. Pages 3–16 *in* D. A. Dixon, editor. Biology, management, and protection of catadromous eels. American Fisheries Society, Symposium 33, Bethesda, Maryland.

Knights, B. C., D. L. Johnson, and M. H. Sandheinrich. 1995. Responses of bluegills and black crappie to dissolved oxygen, temperature, and current in backwater lakes of the Upper Mississippi River during winter. North American Journal of Fisheries Management 15:390–399.

LaBar, G. W., and D. E. Facey. 1983. Local movements and inshore population sizes of American eels in Lake Champlain, Vermont. Transactions of the American Fisheries Society 112:111–116.

Lamothe, P. J., M. Gallagher, D. P. Chivers, and J. M. Moring. 2000. Homing and movement of yellow-phase American eels in freshwater ponds. Environmental Biology of Fishes 58:393–399.

Levesque, J. R., and W. R. Whitworth. 1987. Age class distribution and size of American eel (*Anguilla rostrata*) in the Shatucket/Thames River, Connecticut. Journal of Freshwater Ecology 4(1):17–22.

Littell, R. C., G. A. Miliken, W. W. Stroup, and R. D. Wolfinger. 1996. SAS system for mixed models. SAS Institute, Cary, North Carolina.

Lowe, R. H. 1952. The influence of light and other factors on the seaward migration of the silver eel, *Anguilla anguilla* L. Journal of Animal Ecology 21:275–309.

McGrath, K. J., D. Desrochers, C. Fleury, and J. W. Dembeck, IV. 2003. Studies of upstream migrant American eels at the Moses-Saunders Power Dam on the St. Lawrence River near Massena, New York. Pages 153–166 *in* D. A. Dixon, editor. Biology, management, and protection of catadromous eels. American Fisheries Society, Symposium 33, Bethesda, Maryland.

Menhinick, E. F. 1991. The freshwater fishes of North Carolina. North Carolina Wildlife Resources Commission, Raleigh, North Carolina.

Nyman, L. 1972. Some effects of temperature on eel (Anguilla) behavior. Report, Institute of Freshwater Research 52:90–102, Drottningholm, Sweden.

Nyman, L. 1975. Behaviour of fish influenced by hot-water effluents as observed by ultrasonic tracking. Report, Institute of Freshwater Research 54:63–74, Drottningholm.

Oliveira, K. 1997. Movements and growth rates of yellow-phase American eels in the Annaquatucket River, Rhode Island. Transactions of the American Fisheries Society 126:638–646.

Raibley, P. T., K. S. Irons, T. M. O'Hara, K. D. Blodgett, and R. E. Sparks. 1997. Winter habitat used by largemouth bass in the Illinois River, a large river-floodplain ecosystem. North American Journal of Fisheries Management 17:401–412.

Renaud, J. M., and T. W. Moon. 1980. Characterization of gluconeogenesis in hepatocytes isolated from the American eel, *Anguilla rostrata* LeSueur. Journal of Comparative Physiology B 135:115–125.

Richkus, W., and K. Whalen. 2000. Evidence for a decline in abundance of American eel, *Anguilla rostrata* (LeSueur), in North America since the early 1980s. Dana 12:83–97.

Richkus, W. A., and D. A. Dixon. 2003. Review of research and technologies on passage and protection of downstream migrating catadromous eels at hydroelectric facilities. Pages 377–388 *in* D. A. Dixon, editor. Biology, management, and protection of catadromous eels. American Fisheries Society, Symposium 33, Bethesda, Maryland.

Ross, M. J., and C. F. Kleiner. 1982. Shielded-needle technique for surgically implanting radio-frequency transmitters in fish. Progressive Fish Culturist 44:41–43.

SAS (Statistical Analysis System). 1990. SAS/STAT user's guide, version 6, 4th edition. SAS Institute, Cary, North Carolina.

Smith, M. W., and J. W. Saunders. 1955. The American eel in certain fresh waters of the Maritime Provinces of Canada. Journal of the Fisheries Research Board of Canada 12:238–269.

Sorensen, P. W., and M. L. Bianchini. 1986. Environmental correlates of the freshwater migration of elvers of the American eel in a Rhode Island brook. Transactions of the American Fisheries Society 115:258–268.

Sorensen, P. W., M. L. Bianchini, and H. E. Winn. 1986. Diel foraging activity of American eels, *Anguilla rostrata* (LeSueur), in a Rhode Island estuary. Fishery Bulletin 84:746–747.

Tesch, F.-W. 1977. The eel. Chapman and Hall Ltd., London.

Verdon, R., and D. Desrochers. 2003. Upstream migratory movements of American eel *Anguilla rostrata* between the Beauharnois and Moses-Saunders power dams on the St. Lawrence River. Pages 139–152 *in* D. A. Dixon, editor. Biology, management, and protection of catadromous eels. American Fisheries Society, Symposium 33, Bethesda, Maryland.

Verdon, R., D. Desrochers, and P. Dumont. 2003. Recruitment of American eels in the Richelieu River and Lake Champlain: provision of upstream passage as a regional-scale solution to a large-scale problem. Pages 125–138 *in* D.A. Dixon, editor. Biology, management, and protection of catadromous eels. American Fisheries Society, Symposium 33, Bethesda, Maryland.

Walsh, P. J., G. D. Foster, and T. W. Moon. 1983. The effects of temperature on metabolism of the American eel *Anguilla rostrata* (LeSueur): compensation in the summer and torpor in the winter. Physiological Zoology 56:532–540.

Winn, H. E., W. A. Richkus, and L. K. Winn. 1975. Sexual dimorphism and natural movements of the American eel (*Anguilla rostrata*) in Rhode Island streams and estuaries. Helgoländer Wissenschaftliche Meeresuntersuchungen 27:156–166.

Part V

Stock Assessment and Management

Eel Population Modeling and Its Application to Conservation Management

GIULIO A. DE LEO

Dipartimento di Scienze Ambientali, Università degli Studi di Parma
Parco Area delle Scienze 33A, I-4300 Parma, Italy

PACO MELIÀ[1] AND MARINO GATTO

Dipartimento di Elettronica a Informazione, Politecnio di Milano
via Ponzio, 34/5, I-20133, Milano, Italy

ALAIN J. CRIVELLI

Station Biologique de la Tour du Valat
Le Sambuc, F-13200, Arles, France

Abstract.—We critically review population dynamics models developed for *Anguilla* spp. eels. Despite the (quasi) panmictic nature of temperate eel species, most modeling effort has focused on subpopulations within specific brackish or inland water bodies. Models have been developed along three major lines: cohort approaches, input-output models that directly relate juvenile recruit abundance to migrating mature eels, and stage- or size-structured population models, or both, some of which explicitly account for the observed variability of eel life traits. More recently, attempts have been made to extend demographic analyses to the oceanic phase of the eel life cycle. We discuss eel population models in terms of mathematical complexity and usability, amount and quality of data required for calibration, realism in the description of life cycle and demographic parameters, potential for analyzing different fisheries management strategies, and inclusion of environmental and interindividual stochasticity and uncertainty in parameter estimation. While site-specific analyses are needed to understand eel life history in the continental phase, the generalized decline of eel recruitment requires a global assessment of metapopulation viability under different hypotheses and scenarios. Given the high number of unknowns and untested hypotheses, we emphasize the need to explicitly model uncertainty in parameter estimation and environmental and interindividual stochasticity (e.g., by using bootstrap techniques and Monte Carlo simulations). There is an urgent need for population models that can be used for conservation-based eel management in broad geographic areas where few data are available.

---

[1] Corresponding author: paco.melia@elet.polimi.it

Introduction

Eel stocks are seriously threatened throughout the northern hemisphere. Recruitment of the European eel *Anguilla anguilla* has declined considerably since the late 1970s (Gascuel 1987; Moriarty 1990; Moriarty and Dekker 1997; Girardin et al. 2002; EIFAC/ICES 2003). American *A. rostrata* and Japanese *A. japonica* eels have also experienced recruitment drops in recent decades (Dutil et al. 1989; Castonguay et al. 1994a; Ringuet et al. 2002). In the southern hemisphere, the recruitment of New Zealand longfin eels *A. dieffenbachii* is declining (Hoyle and Jellyman 2002). The causes of this widespread decline are still poorly understood. Possible causes include changes in ocean circulation (Castonguay et al. 1994b; Knights 2003) and the impact of viral infections and the swim bladder parasite *Anguillicola crassus* (Peters and Hartmann 1986; Lefebvre et al. 2002). Habitat disruption, chemical contamination, and overfishing of developmental stages from glass to silver eels are also potential causes of eel decline (Castonguay et al. 1994b; EIFAC/ICES 2003).

Since temperate eel species have long been considered as panmictic (although for the European eel it may not be completely so (Wirth and Bernatchez 2001)), eel recruitment to fishing sites has been assumed for practical purposes as being independent of the adult stock that came from that location. There is now concern that adult spawning stocks no longer produce sufficient recruits to sustain the global population. Eels are vulnerable to recruitment overfishing because of their long prespawning period. Because of their extended life cycle, the effects of overharvesting may become apparent only after a long period (Hoyle and Jellyman 2002).

Since recruitment has been viewed as independent of local stocks, scientific attention has largely focused on optimizing fishing to maximize yield or economic return (De Leo and Gatto 2001). It is now clear that more attention should be paid to the development of sustainable management strategies at a global level and active conservation policies for maintaining the genus *Anguilla*.

Population models can aid this objective by identifying critical components of eel life history, their responses to different environmental forces, and the key variables that affect the viability of eel species. Realistic and well-tuned demographic models also provide tools to better understand the consequences of various management policies on eel conservation.

Due to the lack of information about the oceanic portion of eel life history, most demographic models have dealt exclusively with the continental phase. Although eels may occupy fresh, brackish, or salt waters during their continental period, most models deal only with eels in fresh or brackish waters. However, models that embrace residency in coastal salt water and migrations through open oceanic waters are of crucial importance. Only recently have attempts been made to model the full life cycle of *Anguilla*, including the oceanic phase. Such models sacrifice some complexity in the continental phase while making a number of untestable or not yet tested assumptions on survival, reproductive ability, timing of reproduction, and migration success of mature eels and larvae in the oceanic phase.

This paper summarizes the history and recent advances of eel population modeling and outlines contributions by modeling to a better understanding of eel biology and conservation. We also point out the fundamental features of eel modeling that, in our opinion, are most likely to provide useful insights in the future.

Eel Life History

Eels are amphihaline, catadromous fishes whose biological cycle is well known in the continental phase, while the oceanic phase remains surrounded by much mystery. All *Anguilla* species reproduce in oceanic waters, although actual eel spawning grounds are imprecisely known. Eel larvae, carried by currents toward the continental shelf, develop into small, transparent glass eels. They continue their migration toward continental waters (fresh, brackish, or coastal salt water), where they metamorphose to the elver stage, a small pigmented eel.

The number of elvers entering fresh or brackish water bodies depends on recruitment from the spawning grounds to local nearshore waters and on the proportion of arriving elvers that remain in salt water. This proportion is likely to be influenced by local factors, including wind intensity and direction, freshwater discharge, tidal fluctuations, water pollution, fishing pressure, and obstacles such as dams and sluice gates that regulate water exchange with the sea. As a consequence, effective recruitment to inland waters can vary greatly from year to year, as shown in Figure 1 for the Imsa River (Norway) and the Vaccarès lagoon (France).

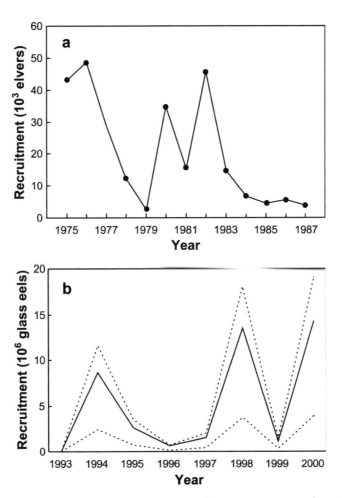

Figure 1. a: Elver recruitment to the Imsa River (Norway) between 1975 and 1987 (from Vøllestad and Jonsson 1988). b: Number of glass eels entering the Vaccarès lagoon (Southern France) between 1993 and 2000, as estimated by Greco et al. (2003). Solid line: expected value; dotted lines: 95% confidence intervals.

After reaching continental settlement areas, elvers gradually become yellow eels. Some yellow eels remain within small home ranges, while others move among habitats, often crossing boundaries between fresh, brackish, and salt waters (Tsukamoto and Arai 2001; Jessop et al. 2002). Finally, yellow eels metamorphose to silver eels, which return to the spawning area, where they mate and die. The fraction of mature eels that survive migration and spawn successfully is unknown, although some estimates have been provided (Reid 2001; Knights 2003; Dekker 2008, this volume) on the basis of untested conjectures. The effect of fishing pressure, water pollution, dams, and habitat loss on the number of eels escaping to the spawning area can vary greatly among sites. The ability of silver eels to reach the spawning area may also be impaired by the effect of *Anguillicola crassus* on body condition (Lefebvre et al. 2003, 2004). As Dekker (2000a, 2008) argued for the European eel, a comprehensive, analytical assessment of the continental stock may not be feasible because it is distributed over a myriad of very small, local sub-stocks. For this reason, the size of the European eel stock can only be guessed on the basis of inductive arguments.

Conservation strategies must be developed at a global level because of the panmictic (or quasi-panmictic) nature of these species. In fact, sound management efforts at a local scale may be useless if the global reproductive potential is threatened by overfishing and human-driven habitat modifications or if complete recruitment failure occurs because of climate change. The panmictic nature of eel species has been thoroughly discussed in a number of papers. Some tropical eels may have multiple spawning sites (Miller et al. 2008, this volume), but for European and American eels, the panmictic hypothesis has not been definitively rejected (Lintas et al. 1998; Daemen et al. 2001; Wirth and Bernatchez 2003; but see also the controversial paper by Wirth and Bernatchez 2001). Hence some form of temporal or spatial segregation might occur for these species (Maes and Volckaert 2002). The possibility that a weakening of the Gulf Stream, caused by global climate change, might reduce the migration success of leptocephali (Knights 2003) poses new threats to eel viability. Thus the debate on panmixia and on identification of spawning areas is not only an interesting life history evolution problem but also an important conservation issue (Wirth and Bernatchez 2003).

A further element characterizing the eel life cycle is delayed sexual differentiation. Sex determination is believed to be environmentally based (Sola et al. 1980; Wiberg 1983), with population density and possibly food availability playing key roles (Colombo and Rossi 1978; Vøllestad and Jonsson 1986). Sex ratios may vary greatly not only among sites but also within the same site over a relatively short time (De Leo and Gatto 1996). Since females grow much larger than males, the factors that influence sex ratio are an important issue in eel modeling and management.

Modeling Eel Population Dynamics

This section reviews major models of eel life history. The main features of these models are summarized in Table 1.

Cohort Models

The first attempts to describe eel demography by mathematical modeling were based on an adaptation of classical population theory (Beverton and Holt 1957) to eels. Sparre (1979), using data from the German Bight, proposed an age-structured model, modified to account for metamorphosis and emigration of silver eels. Rossi (1979) built a static life table of the eel stock in the Valli di Comacchio lagoons (northeast Italy), which he used to estimate natural and fishing mortality and to compare production and yield. He con-

Table 1. Major features of anguillid eel population dynamics models.

Reference	Model Type	Main Purpose	Inputs	Outputs	Major limitations
Gatto & Rossi 1979, Gatto et al. 1982	Cohort model	Predict yield under different fishing regimes	Length distribution of catches	Natural and fishing mortality	Assumes constant recruitment and stable age and size distribution
Vøllestad & Jonsson 1988	Input-output model	Test density dependence of natural mortality, predict yield per recruit	Glass and silver eel numbers, length, sex, maturity and age	Total mortality rate as a function of density, growth rate by age class, yield per recruit	Not flexible, recruitment and escapement must be fully known
De Leo & Gatto 1995, 1996, 2001	Stochastic length and age-structured demographic model	Estimate vital rates, perform bioeconomic analysis of fishery	Length, sex, maturity and age of yellow and silver eels, silver eel numbers	Vital rates, population size and structure, economic benefit as a function of fishing effort	Assumes constant recruitment and stable age and size distribution
Greco et al. 2003	Stochastic length and age-structured demographic model	Estimate vital rates and recruitment variability	Length, sex, maturity and age of yellow and silver eels, catch per unit effort	Vital rates, population size and structure, recruitment size	No density dependence of survival
Dekker 1996, 2000c	VPA-like	Test the impact of modifying fishing effort on spawner output	Length, sex and maturity structure of catches, growth rate, natural mortality	Fishing mortality by length class	No body growth model, natural mortality and terminal fishing mortality imposed *a priori*
Dekker 2000b	VPA-like global model	Assess the European eel stock, estimate fishing pressure	Total catches by region, growth rate, natural mortality	Fishing mortality by length class, stock size	No calibration, parameters are taken from the literature

Table 1. Continued.

Reference	Model Type	Main Purpose	Inputs	Outputs	Major limitations
Francis & Jellyman 1999, Hoyle & Jellyman 2002	Stochastic length-structured demographic model	Predict yield and spawner output per recruit as a function of fishing effort	Harvest length frequencies, length at maturity, natural mortality	Growth and maturation rates, yield and spawner output per recruit	Assumes constant fishing mortality, no density dependence
ICES 2003	Stochastic length-structured demographic model	Estimate yield and spawning output per recruit and mortality rates	Length and age structure, fecundity, mortality	Yield and spawner output per recruit	No rigorous calibration, no density dependence
Lambert et al. 2005	Spatially distributed demographic model	Investigate the spatial structure of eel populations	Demographic model structure and parameters, watershed topology and diffusion parameters	Spatial distribution and structure	Purely theoretical, no calibration on real data
Reid 2001	Multistage stock-recruitment model	Identify the major causes of eel decline, identify research priorities	Natural and fishing mortality, fecundity, inter-stage transition probability	Sensitivity analysis on model parameters	No calibration, no management applications

cluded that the local stock was underexploited but noticed a drop in yields compared with four decades earlier, which he attributed to deterioration of the water system. Gatto and Rossi (1979), using data from the same population, developed a simple dynamic model to estimate the stock and its size distribution, which was then used to assess the profitability of different management strategies (Gatto et al. 1982). These early models provided preliminary insights into eel demography and some aspects of fishery management. However, they neglected key features such as the role of body size and density dependence as regulating factors of the eel's life cycle. Also, they assumed constant recruitment and stable age distributions, which are biologically unrealistic.

Vøllestad and Jonsson's Input–Output Model

Vøllestad and Jonsson (1988), using a long-term data series from the Imsa River (SW Norway), developed an input-output model to predict total biomass and age distribution of silver eels from annual recruitment data. The mortality rate (assumed to be constant with age) was inversely correlated with the number of recruiting elvers, thus giving the first evidence for density dependence in eel mortality.

Vøllestad and Jonsson's (1988) approach provides a powerful tool to predict yields in sites where elver recruitment and silver eel migration can be monitored and where the impact of commercial harvest is also reliably known. However, recruitment and silver eel out-migration cannot be readily measured in most eel fishing areas. The input-output approach may also be difficult to apply where harvest effort varies.

Size and Age-Structured Models

The model developed by De Leo and Gatto (1995) was based on data from the Valli di Comacchio lagoons, Italy. It overcame some major drawbacks of earlier models by including a multiple classification of individuals by age and size. In organisms characterized by strong interindivdual variability, like *Anguilla* eels (Panfili et al. 1994), size may more strongly influence vital parameters (such as survivorship, fecundity, and sexual maturity) than age. Hence population-dynamics models should explicitly recognize size (Caswell 1989). De Leo and Gatto (1995) modeled silvering as a sigmoidal function of body size and sex, whereas mortality was linked to age through a Weibull function (Figure 2). The model accounted for interindividual life history variability by means of a stochastic formulation. This represented a major improvement, as accounting for variability in the life cycle provides fundamental information about the variation of eel harvests and the risk of stock decline.

The weakest element of this approach was that the authors were obliged to assume time invariance of recruitment because no recruitment indices were available. In fact, eel recruitment to fresh and brackish water bodies is highly variable. De Leo and Gatto (1996) applied the model to three data sets from the same sites, though from different time periods (mid-1970s versus late 1980s). Assuming stable age and size distributions for each period, the model indicated declining recruitment. The demographic analysis also revealed the dependence of some important parameters upon density, with prereproductive survival and mean body size at silvering increasing as eel density decreased and sex ratio shifting toward female dominance at low eel densities.

In a further work, De Leo and Gatto (2001) applied their model to a stochastic bioeconomic analysis of eel fishing (Figure 3). The aim was to optimize the economic return from eel fishing at Comacchio by exploring the effects of catching a certain fraction of prereproductive eels and testing whether

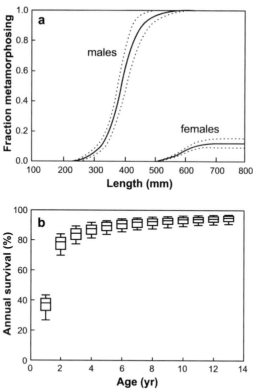

Figure 2. a: Metamorphosis curves from yellow to silver eel as a function of body size for female and male eels at Comacchio (Northern Italy): expected value (solid line) ± SE (dotted lines). b: Age-specific survival estimates (boxes: median and interquartile range; whiskers: 90% confidence intervals). Both graphs have been obtained from the bootstrap distribution of model parameters (from De Leo and Gatto 2001).

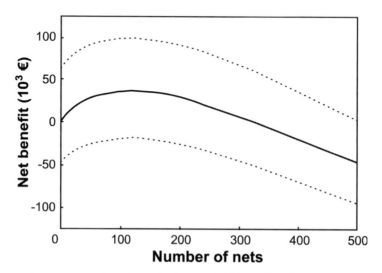

Figure 3. Economic return as a function of yellow eel fishing effort (number of nets used) at Comacchio (Northern Italy), as estimated by De Leo and Gatto (2001). Solid line: mean annual net economic return (averaged over 500 Monte Carlo simulations); dotted lines: 90% confidence intervals.

the declining recruitment from the sea could be effectively supplemented by elver restocking.

More recently, Greco et al. (2003), on the basis of a 7-year data series from the Vaccarès lagoon (southern France), used a modified version of De Leo and Gatto's (1995) model, which relaxed the hypotheses of constant recruitment and stable age and size distributions. This study revealed huge inter-annual recruitment fluctuations (Figure 1b), possibly because of the regulation of water inflow from the sea into the lagoon by sluice gates.

Dekker (1996) proposed a length-structured Markov chain matrix model to assess yellow eel fisheries in Lake IJsselmeer (the Netherlands) and extended this approach (Dekker 2000c) to account for silvering and escapement. Using length data from commercial catches, he calculated mortality coefficients for each length class, and assuming natural mortality, silvering, and escapement rates to be constant, he derived fishing mortalities. He argued that ceasing yellow eel exploitation in Lake IJsselmeer would lead to a many-fold increase in the adult eel population. He concluded that current uncontrolled exploitation levels in the major eel fisheries have negative consequences on the entire stock of European eel spawners.

Francis and Jellyman (1999) used information about the dynamics of the shortfin eel *A. australis* in New Zealand to construct a demographic model with the aim of detecting changes in exploitation rates of commercial fisheries from changes in length distributions. Hoyle and Jellyman (2002) adapted this approach to estimate the effect of different fishing policies on the reproductive success and yield of the whole community of New Zealand eels (shortfin eel and New Zealand longfin eel). Eel length was described as a linear function of age (as documented for New Zealand eels by Jellyman 1997). The model incorporated interindividual variability in growth by modeling 20 growth-rate classes, with growth rates being distributed as a Gaussian random variable. The maturation process was described as in De Leo and Gatto (1995); namely, the silvering rate was assumed to depend upon body size. Natural and fishing mortality rates were assumed to be constant, while fecundity was an allometric function of body size. Since total stock biomass or a suitable abundance index was not known, the authors adopted a per-recruit approach (i.e., they investigated the effect of management alternatives on relative spawning per recruit and relative yield per recruit, where the term "relative" refers to the unexploited population). They concluded that current levels of fishing may seriously affect the sustainability of New Zealand longfin eel fisheries. A major problem of Hoyle and Jellyman's (2002) model is the assumption that the selectivity of the fishing gears is flat with reference to eel body size. This can substantially alter the simulated population structure. Furthermore, density-dependent effects were not taken into account.

A life-table model with stochastic growth for the American eel population of the Gulf of St. Lawrence, Canada, has been developed (EIFAC/ICES 2003). The aim was to assess the impact of fishing on spawning per recruit. Growth was described by a von Bertalanffy curve with the asymptotic mean length distributed as a Gaussian random variable. The size of newly recruited elvers was also assumed to have a Gaussian distribution. Natural mortality and fecundity were expressed as allometric functions of body weight. A constant proportion of eels were assumed to mature and emigrate after attaining a threshold length. A size-independent fishing mortality rate was also assumed to affect survival of eels longer than a certain threshold. Using length data from commercial and research fisheries, mortality and emigration rates were manually tuned until simulated length frequencies resembled field data. A major problem reported by the authors was the difficulty in distinguishing between emigration and natural mortality. Also, density dependence was not considered. Monte Carlo simulations were used to evaluate the reduction in egg deposition due to fishing. This reduction was estimated at about 80%, well above the limits recommended by ICES (2001).

Analysis of Spatially Distributed Virtual Populations

Lambert (2005) set up a matrix model for the continental phase of a virtual eel population in a linear homogeneous watershed. Recruitment was described by shaping the seasonal arrival pattern of glass eels with a beta function. The duration of the sexually undifferentiated phase was distributed as a lognormal random variable, and sexual differentiation was assumed to be density-dependent (with the fraction of males being a logistic function of the percentage saturation of carrying capacity). Silvering rate was also assumed to be a lognormal random variable. Eel movements among compartments within the watershed were modeled as a diffusion process with a movement rate depending upon inter-compartmental density gradients and decreasing with age. Natural mortality was linked to age by means of a Weibull function (as in De Leo and Gatto 1995), but density dependence was also taken into account because the Weibull scale parameter was a function of compartment saturation. Using a pattern-oriented approach (Grimm et al. 1996), different parameter sets were then chosen that were compatible with identifiable patterns of natural data. The aim of the work was chiefly theoretical; namely, to point out some invariant features of eel stock structure within a watershed. The results allowed the authors to conclude that eel management should particularly focus on the downstream part of a river basin, where most sexual determination takes place and where eel density is maximum, especially when recruitment is low.

Global Models

Dekker (2000b) tried a first assessment of the entire European eel stock by setting up a simplified model in what he termed a Procrustean approach (Procrustes was a character from Greek mythology who stretched, or chopped, his guests to make them fit an iron bed). The model used the dynamic-pool model of Beverton and Holt (1957), assuming constant recruitment and stable age distribution. Natural mortality was assumed to be constant, while fishing mortality was estimated by virtual population analysis (VPA; Gulland 1965) on the basis of actual silver eel catches and the assumption of 30% silver eels escaping the fisheries. He identified two major areas characterized by different demographic balances: the Biscay area (Atlantic coasts of Portugal, Spain and France and also the Bristol Channel area of the United Kingdom), where large influxes of glass eels are intensively fished, and the remaining European coasts, where fishing is balanced by eel restocking (from within the same country or from the Biscay area). Fishing mortality of glass eels in the Biscay area was estimated as 99.99966%. The cumulative fishing mortality imposed on the whole European recruitment was estimated at about 96%.

Reid (2001) proposed a multistage stock–recruitment metapopulation model (Mousalli and Hilborn 1986) to describe the life cycle of the entire American eel population. This approach was used to explore uncertainty in vital rates and in the causes of mortality and to assess potential mitigative measures to halt the decline of American eels under different reproductive hypotheses (full panmixia, partial panmixia with time or space segregation or both, no panmixia). He considered six substocks, for which different life histories and anthropogenic influences were assumed, with panmictic reproduction. No size dependence was assumed for vital parameters; but a simple Beverton–Holt density-dependence function was assumed to drive the transition from each age-class to the following. Egg production and recruitment were also considered as density-dependent. Each parameter was assigned a range of values based on available literature. Using Bayesian analysis (Taylor et al. 2000; Wade 2000), the model was run a number of times after fixing a priori some parameter values and assigning random values to others (with values extracted from a uniform distribution in the parameter range). The author finally performed a ranking of the parameters by analyzing the correlation with selected model outcomes (silver eel and egg production). Model results suggested that the most important factors affecting the American eel stock may be environmental changes at the oceanic level, habitat modification and the cumulative effect of fishing and other anthropogenic causes.

Choosing and Tuning the Appropriate Model

The variety of models described in the previous section is not a surprise. In fact, a single *right* model does not exist. Instead, one should try to determine the best model for a certain goal and a certain situation. The choice of the model depends upon a number of circumstances. In particular, when deciding the most appropriate model structure and complexity, one should keep in mind (1) what questions we want to answer or which scenarios we want to analyze, (2) what—and how many—data are available for model calibration, (3) what resources are available for developing the model, and (4) what level of accuracy the model needs to attain to achieve its purposes.

Purely theoretical models may have strong conceptual value and help point out crucial aspects of the problem but be unable to provide operational guidelines to fisheries managers. Eye-tuned models, such as those proposed by EIFAC/ICES (2003) and Reid (2001), can provide quick preliminary answers to important questions, although they are unsuitable for providing precise quantitative management advice.

Population dynamics models developed for management purposes should explicitly consider environmental and interindivdual stochasticity as well as uncertainty in parameter estimation, because these factors can dramatically affect the outcome of viability analyses (Hilborn and Ludwig 1993). Fortunately, demographic uncertainty can easily be included in models (Mangel 1985; Walters 1986; Hilborn 1987) to produce estimates, not just of mean demographic dynamics, but also of its variability. Nonparametric techniques, such as Monte Carlo simulations, are flexible and robust tools for evaluating the probability of persistence and the projected range of population abundance under different management scenarios (Figures 3 and 4). Figure 3 shows economic return as a function of fishing effort on yellow eels at Comacchio as estimated by De Leo and Gatto (2001). The Monte Carlo analysis indicates that even though the expected economic return is positive, it is not significantly different from zero. Figure 4 shows the body growth curve estimated by Greco et al. (2003) for undifferentiated eels in the Camargue lagoons. Again, by using a stochastic model, one cannot only describe the average process but can also estimate the uncertainty associated with it.

The Monte Carlo approach is used extensively in population viability analysis (PVA, Boyce 1992; Possingham et al. 1993; Beissinger and Westphal 1998). Population viability analysis has traditionally been used to assess the extinction risk of terrestrial species but has recently also been applied to aquatic environments (e.g., Morita and Yokota 2002; Burkhart and Slooten 2003). In eel population dynamics, a PVA-like approach has been implemented in the form of Monte Carlo simulations by De Leo and Gatto (1995, 1996, 2001) and EIFAC/ICES (2003).

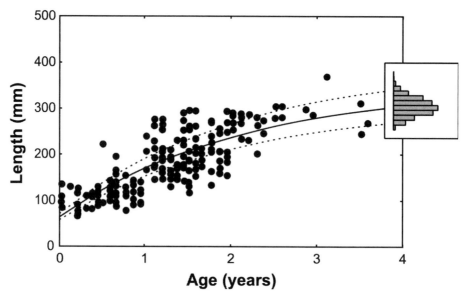

Figure 4. Von Bertalanffy growth curve of undifferentiated eels in the Vaccarès lagoon (Southern France) as obtained by stochastic simulation (Greco et al. 2003). Dots: observed age-length data; solid line: mean value; dotted lines: 95% confidence intervals. The histogram in the box shows the simulated length structure of a cohort aged 4 years.

The outcome of stochastic analyses can be strongly affected by specific assumptions about model parameters and structure (White et al. 2002; Lande et al. 2003). The problem of parameter estimation and model structure can be exacerbated by the lack of reliable data. This is particularly true in conservation biology of rare species, where field data needed to estimate vital rates are often lacking. In the case of eels, the problem is compounded by incomplete knowledge of critical ecological features. As a consequence, stochastic analyses in viability studies must often be performed on the basis of a priori assumptions or even best-guess trials on the expected value and variance of otherwise unknown demographic parameters (Ferson et al. 1989; Mangel and Switzer 1998).

In fact, there is often a trade-off between the complexity of a model and its robustness. Highly complex models are frequently deemed to be the only suitable way to describe multi-faceted ecological problems. Eel population dynamics certainly pose one of these problems, given the complexity of the eel life cycle and the breadth of anthropogenic factors affecting eel survival and reproductive potential. However, the use of a complex model forces the user to overparameterize it with respect to available data and to formulate a number of a priori assumptions on the magnitude of unknown parameters and the shape of their probability distributions (Bearlin et al. 1999). The best compromise between good descriptive power and model robustness is often provided by models of intermediate complexity.

In any case, a rigorous calibration procedure, which includes estimation of noise and parameter variances, is mandatory when developing a model that is not conditioned by subjective opinions. Calibration techniques, such as those described in De Leo and Gatto (1995) or Greco et al. (2003), provide reliable methodologies for generating robust models. Parameter estimation, especially when the available data set is small, can be greatly improved by making use of nonparametric methods, such as the bootstrap (Efron 1979). When possible, model performance should also be tested on a data set different from that used for calibration. Sensitivity analyses for uncertain parameters and model structure are also needed to identify the most critical knowledge gaps (Lindenmayer et al. 2003; Todd et al. 2004).

Dealing with Parameter Uncertainty

Nonparametric computer-intensive statistics provide a useful tool for calibration because they measure the uncertainty associated with parameter estimates, by reproducing the empirical variability observed in the samples. The bootstrap, which mimics the sampling process by randomly resampling from the original data set (Efron 1979) is the most widespread computer-intensive technique and is increasingly applied in ecological studies. A major advantage of nonparametric methods is that they provide *a posteriori* probability distributions for parameter estimates without requiring a priori assumptions on their statistical properties.

We illustrate this procedure by applying it to the calibration of a growth curve. Let us have n eels for which length-at-age data have been measured. The simplest implementation of the bootstrap consists of inserting the original data set of n animals into an urn and randomly extracting the same number of eels with replacement. Replacement means that each eel is to be reinserted into the urn before another is extracted; thus any eel of the original set may be represented more than once in a bootstrap replicate or may not be present at all. This resampling scheme, which assumes an equal probability of selection of every eel in the catch, is not valid for stratified samples (Efron and Tibshirani 1986). In such cases, resampling must be suitably adapted to the original sampling scheme (Pelletier and Gros 1991; De Leo and Gatto 1995; Greco et al. 2003).

The new synthetic data set—the so-called bootstrap replicate—is then used to calibrate the model (in this case, it might be the classical von Bertalanffy curve), obtaining a set of parameters—the so-called pseudovalues. The procedure is then replicated m times, each time providing a new parameter set. Each parameter set will differ more or less from the previous, depending on the results of the random extraction. By repeating the procedure many times ($m = 1,000$ provides sufficiently accurate results in most cases), one obtains an empirical probability distribution of each parameter from which the desired statistics (mean, variance, estimate bias, confidence intervals) can be derived. As an example, Figure 5 shows the bootstrapped empirical distribution of von Bertalanffy's parameters (asymptotic length $L\infty$ and Brody coefficient k) for the eel stock of the Camargue lagoons (as obtained by Greco et al. 2003). It is remarkable that the two parameters have a negative and nonlinear relation: this feature should be taken into account in a Monte Carlo simulation of the eel population. A further example of how the bootstrap can be used in eel demography to quantify parameter uncertainty is provided by Figure 6, which shows the empirical distribution of eel recruitment at Comacchio in 1989 as reported by De Leo and Gatto (2001).

The estimate of the generic parameter θ is then calculated as the mean of the pseudovalues:

$$\theta_B = \frac{1}{m} \sum_{i=1}^{m} \theta_i^*,$$

where θ_i^* is the value (pseudovalue) of the generic parameter θ estimated from the i-th bootstrap replicate ($i = 1...m$). In the case of the von Bertalanffy growth curve, this means that the asymptotic body length $L\infty$ (or the Brody coefficient k) can be estimated simply as the mean of the m values (pseudovalues) of $L\infty$ obtained at each iteration. Confidence intervals or confidence regions can be ob-

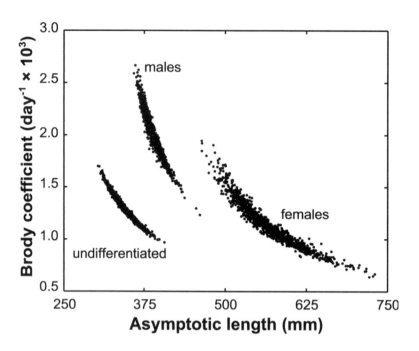

Figure 5. Bootstrap distribution of body growth parameters for undifferentiated, female and male eels at Vaccarès (Southern France) from 1993 to 2000 data (Greco et al. 2003).

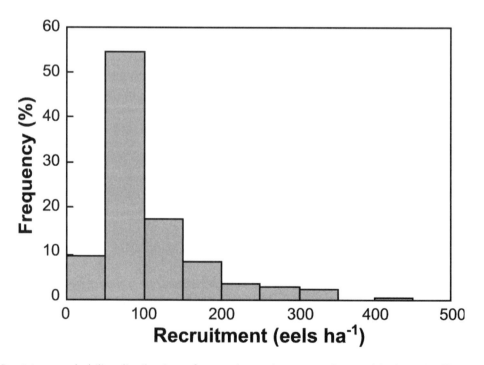

Figure 6. Bootstrap probability distribution of natural recruitment at Comacchio in 1989 (from De Leo and Gatto 2001).

tained directly from the distribution of the pseudovalues. It suffices to determine the interval that contains a given proportion (typically 95%) of the pseudovalues.

There might be a problem of estimation bias. A bias-corrected estimate for the parameter θ is provided by

$$\theta_{B, b.c.} = 2 \cdot \theta_0 - \theta_B$$

(Efron 1982), where θ_0 is the value of the parameter obtained using the original data set (i.e., the eels that were actually caught and measured). To assign a confidence interval to parameter estimates, one can use the bias-corrected percentile method proposed by Efron (1982).

Use of the bootstrap also facilitates comparison of vital rate estimates from different populations or from the same population in different periods. Bootstrap parameter distributions can be compared by means of a randomization test (Edgington 1987). For example, to test the hypothesis that the expected value of a parameter estimated from a given data set is significantly greater (smaller) than the expected value of the same parameter from another data set, one can use the method proposed by Manly (1997): (1) a value θ_i^* is randomly selected from the bootstrap distribution of the parameter obtained using the first data set; (2) a second value $\theta_{2,j}^* (i \neq j)$ is randomly selected from the other bootstrap distribution; (3) the difference between θ_i^* and $\theta_{2,j}^*$ is computed; (4) the procedure is repeated a large number of times (e.g., 10,000); (5) the significance level p is finally computed as the fraction of times the difference

$$\theta_{1,i}^* - \theta_{2,j}^*$$

is strictly negative (positive). For instance, a randomization test allowed De Leo and Gatto (1996) to reveal that the expected value of recruitment abundance in the mid-1970s at Comacchio was significantly larger than that attained at the end of the 1980s.

Conclusions

The study of eel population dynamics is more than 30 years old. Significant progress has been made since the first attempts of the 1970s to describe eel demography by mathematical modeling. The continental phase of the eel biological cycle is now fairly well known. Some key factors regulating the life cycle of this catadromous fish have been identified (e.g., the role of body size as a trigger for sexual differentiation and maturation, the dependence of survival and sex determination upon eel density). However, other important factors are still unknown. Further research is also needed to uncloak the mystery that surrounds the oceanic phase of eel life and to fully understand the impact of fisheries and habitat disruption on eel survival. Nevertheless, incomplete knowledge of these phenomena is not a valid reason for failing to implement conservation measures for the maintenance of this natural resource (ICES 1997). There is now an urgent need to develop guidelines for the sustainable management of eel fisheries even in conditions of uncertainty.

Attempts to simulate the life cycle of continental-phase eel stocks, though not rigorously calibrated on data, have proven useful in improving understanding of factors in the eel decline and in sketching preliminary hypotheses on the long-term demographic fate of eels under different management strategies. Conservation-based management of eels will be greatly enhanced by the availability of suitable models of eel demography. Models should explicitly consider the following: (1) eel growth is characterized by high interindividual variability; (2) important events in the eel life cycle, such as sexual differentiation, metamorphosis to silver eel, fecundity, and catchability, are related to body size rather than to age; (3) density dependence is important in regulating survival and sexual differentiation; (4) eel recruitment is highly variable; (5) the panmictic (or quasipanmictic) population structure means that dependencies between the abundance of the parental stock and recruitment of juveniles can be observed only at a global scale; (6) uncertainty in parameter estimation can be quantified by making use of nonparametric methods such as bootstrapping; (7) intrinsic uncertainty of eel demography and environmental stochasticity can be dealt with by Monte Carlo techniques; and (8) a thorough calibration and validation process is indispensable to fine-tune models to available data and to assess their predictive power.

Because of eel declines, efforts are urgently needed to elaborate effective management guidelines. We need reliable demographic data and sound models. Advances in eel demography will be based on population models that are rigorously calibrated and validated against available data. Given the substantial geographical variability in eel demographic parameters and anthropogenic pressures, it is unlikely that a single population model can provide reliable demographic estimates across ranges and species. On the other hand, decision makers in management agencies require simple and cost-effective tools to analyze the potential consequences of different conservation strategies. We believe that a suite of easy-to-use computer models of eel demography could be developed that would simulate population dynamics and predict consequences of a range of management options. The examination of extant eel dynamics models in this review may help define the nature of generic eel models that will be suitable for widespread use in conservation and management.

Acknowledgments

The authors thank Kenneth Oliveira and Leif Vøllestad for their very useful suggestions which helped improve on an early draft of the manuscript. The work was supported by Istituto di Ingegneria Biomedica (Consiglio Nazionale delle Ricerche, Italy), Direzione Generale per la Pesca e l'Acquacoltura (Ministero delle Politiche Agricole e Forestali, Italy), and Fondation Sansouire (Tour du Valat, France).

References

Bearlin, A. R., M. A. Burgman, and H. M. Regan. 1999. A stochastic model for seagrass (*Zostera muelleri*) in Port Phillip Bay, Victoria, Australia. Ecological Modelling 118(2–3):131–148.

Beissinger, S. R., and M. I. Westphal. 1998. On the use of demographic models of population viability in endangered species management. Journal of Wildlife Management 62:821–841.

Beverton, R. J. H., and S. J. Holt. 1957. On the dynamics of exploited fish populations. Fisheries Investigations Series II, XIX, Ministry of Agriculture, Fishing and Food, London.

Boyce, M. S. 1992. Population viability analysis. Annual Review of Ecology and Systematics 23:481–506.

Burkhart, S. M., and E. Slooten. 2003. Population viability analysis for Hector's dolphin (*Cephalorhynchus hectori*): a stochastic population model for local populations. New Zealand Journal of Marine and Freshwater Research 37:553–566.

Castonguay, M., P. V. Hodson, C. M. Couillars, M. J. Eckersley, J.-D. Dutil, and G. Verreault. 1994a. Why is recruitment of the American eel *Anguilla rostrata* declining in the St. Lawrence River and Gulf? Canadian Journal of Fisheries and Aquatic Sciences 51:479–488.

Castonguay, M., P. Hodson, C. Moriarty, K. Drinkwater, and B. Jessop. 1994b. Is there a role of ocean environment in American and European eel decline? Fisheries Oceanography 3:197–203.

Caswell, H. 1989. Matrix population models. Sinauer Associates Inc., Sunderland, Massachusetts.

Colombo, G., and R. Rossi. 1978. Environmental influences of growth and sex ratio in different eel populations (*Anguilla anguilla* L.) of Adriatic coasts. Pages 313–320 *in* D. S. McLuskey and A. J. Berry, editors. Physiology and behaviour of marine organisms. Pergamon, Oxford, England.

Daemen, E., T. Cross, F. Ollevier, and F. A. M. Volckaert. 2001. Analysis of the genetic structure of European eel (*Anguilla anguilla*) using microsatellite DNA and mtDNA markers. Marine Biology 139:755–764.

Dekker, W. 1996. A length structured matrix population model, used as fish stock assessment tool. Pages 245–259 in I. G. Cowx, editor. Stock Assessment in Inland Fisheries. Fishing News Books, Oxford, England.

Dekker, W. 2000a. The fractal geometry of the European eel stock. ICES Journal of Marine Science 57:109–121.

Dekker, W. 2000b. A Procrustean assessment of the European eel stock. ICES Journal of Marine Science 57:938–947.

Dekker, W. 2000c. Impact of yellow eel exploitation on spawner production in Lake IJsselmeer, the Netherlands. Dana 12:17–32.

Dekker, W. 2009. A conceptual management framework for the restoration of the declining European eel. Pages 3–19 in J. M. Casselman and D. K. Cairns, editors. Eels at the edge: science, status, and conservation concerns. American Fisheries Society, Symposium 58, Bethesda, Maryland.

De Leo, G. A., and M. Gatto. 1995. A size and age-structured model of the European eel (*Anguilla anguilla* L.). Canadian Journal of Fisheries and Aquatic Sciences 52:1351–1367.

De Leo, G. A., and M. Gatto. 1996. Trends in vital rates of the European eel: evidence for density dependence? Ecological Applications 6:1281–1294.

De Leo, G. A., and M. Gatto. 2001. A stochastic bioeconomic analysis of silver eel fisheries. Ecological Applications 11:281–294.

Dutil, J. D., M. Michaud, and A. Giroux. 1989. Seasonal and diel patterns of stream invasion by American eels (*Anguilla rostrata*) in the northern Gulf of St. Lawrence (Canada). Canadian Journal of Zoology 67:182–188.

Edgington, E. S. 1987. Randomization tests, 2nd edition. Marcel Dekker, New York.

Efron, B. 1979. Bootstrap methods: another look at the jackknife. Annals of Statistics 7:1–26.

Efron, B. 1982. The jackknife, the bootstrap and other resampling plans. CMBS-NSF Regional Conference Series in Applied Mathematics 38. Society for Industrial and Applied Mathematics, Philadelphia.

Efron, B., and R. Tibshirani. 1986. Bootstrap methods for standard errors, confidence intervals and other measures of statistical accuracy. Statistical Science 1:54–77.

EIFAC/ICES (FAO European Inland Fisheries Advisory Commission; International Council for the Exploration of the Sea). 2003. Report of the thirteenth session of the joint EIFAC/ICES Working Group of Eels. Copenhagen, Denmark, 28–31 August 2001. EIFAC Occasional Paper No. 36. FAO, Rome

Ferson, S., L. R. Ginzburg, and A. Silvers. 1989. Extreme event risk analysis for age-structured populations. Ecological Modelling 47:175–187.

Francis, R. I. C. C., and D. J. Jellyman. 1999. Are mean size data adequate to monitor freshwater eel fisheries? Marine and Freshwater Research 50:355–366.

Gascuel, D. 1987. La civelle d'anguille dans l'estuaire de la Sèvre Niortaise: biologie, écologie, exploitation, volume 4/1, 4/2. Département Halieutique, École Nationale Supérieure Agronomique, Rennes, France.

Gatto, M., E. Laniado, and R. Rossi. 1982. The management of eels in the Valli di Comacchio lagoon. Pages 303–307 in Proceedings of the International Symposium on coastal lagoons, SCOR/IABO/UNESCO, Bordeaux, France, 8–14 September 1981. Oceanologica Acta 5:303–307.

Gatto, M., and R. Rossi. 1979. A method for estimating mortalities and abundances of the Valli di Comacchio eels. Memorie dell'Istituto Italiano di Idrobiologia Supplement 37:107–114.

Girardin, M., G. Castelnaud, and L. Beaulaton. 2002. Surveillance halieutique de l'estuaire de la Gironde—Suivi des captures 2000—Étude de la faune circulante 2001. Étude Cemagref Bordeaux no 74, Cestas, France.

Greco, S., P. Melià, G. A. De Leo, and M. Gatto. 2003. A size and age-structured demographic model of the eel (*Anguilla anguilla*) population of the Vaccarès lagoon. Internal Report 2003.47, Dipartimento di Elettronica e Informazione, Politecnico di Milano, Milano, Italy.

Grimm, V., K. Frank, F. Jeltsch, R. Brandl, J. Uchmanski, and C. Wissel. 1996. Pattern-oriented modelling in population ecology. Science of the Total Environment 183:151–166.

Gulland, J. A. 1965. Estimation of mortality rates. Annex to Arctic Fisheries Working Group Report (meeting in Hamburg, January 1965). ICES CM 1965, Doc. No. 3.

Hilborn, R. 1987. Living with uncertainty in resource based systems. North American Journal of Fisheries Management 7:1–5.

Hilborn, R., and D. Ludwig. 1993. The limits of applied ecological research. Ecological Applications 3:550–552.

Hoyle, S. D., and D. J. Jellyman. 2002. Longfin eels need reserves: modelling the effects of commercial harvest on stocks of New Zealand eels. Marine and Freshwater Research 53:887–895.

ICES. 1997. Report of the Study Group on the precautionary approach to fisheries management. ICES 1997/Assess 7.

ICES. 2001. Report of the EIFAC/ICES Working Group on eels. Advisory Committee on Fisheries Management, ICES CM 2001/ACFM:03, Copenhagen.

Jellyman, D. J. 1997. Variability in growth rates of freshwater eels *Anguilla* spp. in New Zealand. Ecology of Freshwater Fish 6:108–115.

Jessop, B. M., J.-C. Shiao, Y. Iizuka, and W.-N. Tzeng. 2002. Migratory behaviour and habitat use by American eels *Anguilla rostrata* as revealed by otolith microchemistry. Marine Ecology Progress Series 233:217–229.

Knights, B. 2003. A review of the possible impacts of long-term oceanic and climate changes and fishing mortality on recruitment of anguillid eels of the Northern Hemisphere. Science of the Total Environment 310:237–244.

Lambert, P. 2005. Exploration multiscalaire des paradigmes de la dynamique de la population d'anguilles européennes à l'aide d'outils de simulation. Doctoral dissertation, Université Bordeaux, France.

Lande, R., S. Engen, and B.-E. Sæther. 2003. Stochastic population dynamics in ecology and conservation. Oxford University Press, Oxford.

Lefebvre, F., A. Acou, G. Poizat, and A. J. Crivelli. 2003. Anguillicolosis among silver eels: a 2-year survey in 4 habitats from Camargue (Rhône delta, South of France) Bulletin Français de Pêche et de Pisciculture 368:97–108.

Lefebvre, F., P. Contournet, and A. J. Crivelli. 2002. The health state of the eel swimbladder as a measure of parasite pressure by *Anguillicola crassus*. Parasitology 124:457–463.

Lefebvre, F., B. Mounaix, G. Poizat, and A. J. Crivelli. 2004. Impacts of the swimbladder nematode *Anguillicola crassus* on *Anguilla anguilla*: variations in liver and spleen masses. Journal of Fish Biology 64:435–447.

Lindenmayer, D. B., H. P. Possingham, R. C. Lacy, M. A. McCarthy, and M. L. Pope. 2003. How accurate are population models? Lessons from landscape-scale tests in a fragmented system. Ecology Letters 6:41–47.

Lintas, C., J. Hirano, and S. Archer. 1998. Genetic variation of the European eel (*Anguilla anguilla*). Molecular Marine Biology and Biotechnology 7:263–269.

Maes, G. E., and F. A. M. Volckaert. 2002. Clinal genetic variation and isolation by distance in the European eel *Anguilla anguilla* (L.). Biological Journal of the Linnean Society 77:509–521.

Mangel, M. 1985. Decision and control in uncertain resource systems. Academic Press, New York.

Mangel, M., and P. V. Switzer. 1998. A model at the level of the foraging trip for the indirect effects of krill (*Euphausia superba*) fisheries on krill predators. Ecological Modelling 105:235–256.

Manly, B. F. J. 1997. Randomization, bootstrap and Monte Carlo methods in biology, 2nd edition. Chapman and Hall, London.

Miller, M. J., J. Aoyama, and K. Tsukamoto. 2008. New perspectives on the early life history of tropical anguillid eels: implications for resource management. Pages 103–116 *in* J. M. Casselman and D. K. Cairns, editors. Eels at the edge: science, status, and conservation concerns. American Fisheries Society, Symposium 58, Bethesda, Maryland.

Moriarty, C. 1990. European catches of elver of 1928–1988. Internationale Revue der Gesamten Hydrobiologie 75:701–706.

Moriarty, C., and W. Dekker. 1997. Management of the European eel. Fisheries Bulletin (Dublin) 15.

Morita, K., and A. Yokota. 2002. Population viability of stream-resident salmonids after habitat fragmentation: a case study with white-spotted charr (*Salvelinus leucomaenis*) by an individual based model. Ecological Modelling 155:85–94.

Mousalli, E., and R. Hilborn. 1986. Optimal stock size and harvest rate in multistage life history models. Canadian Journal of Fisheries and Aquatic Sciences 43:135–141.

Panfili, J., M.-C. Ximénès, and A. J. Crivelli. 1994. Sources of variation in growth of the European eel (*Anguilla anguilla*) estimated from otoliths. Canadian Journal of Fisheries and Aquatic Sciences 51:506–515.

Pelletier, D., and P. Gros. 1991. Assessing the impact of sampling error on model-based management advice: comparison of equilibrium yield per recruit variance estimators. Canadian Journal of Fisheries and Aquatic Sciences 48:2129–2139.

Peters, G., and F. Hartmann. 1986. *Anguillicola*, a parasitic nematode of the swim bladder spreading among eel populations in Europe. Diseases of Aquatic Organisms 1:229–230.

Possingham, H. P., D. W. Lindenmayer, and T. W. Norton. 1993. The role of PVA in endangered species management. Pacific Conservation Biology 1:39–45.

Reid, K. B. 2001. The decline of American eel (*Anguilla rostrata*) in the Lake Ontario/St. Lawrence River ecosystem: a modeling approach to identification of data gaps and research priorities. Lake Ontario Committee, Great Lakes Fishery Commission, Ann Arbor, Michigan.

Ringuet, S., F. Muto, and C. Raymakers. 2002. Eels. Their harvest and trade in Europe and Asia. TRAFFIC Bulletin 19(2):2–27.

Rossi, R. 1979. An estimate of the production of the eel population in the Valli of Comacchio (Po Delta) during 1974–1976. Bollettino di Zoologia 46:217–223.

Sola, L., G. Gentili, and S. Cataudella. 1980. Eel chromosomes: cytotaxonomical interrelationships and sex chromosomes. Copeia 1980:911–913.

Sparre, P. 1979. Some necessary adjustments for using the common methods in eel assessment. Pages 41–44 in F. Thurow, editor. Eel research and management. Rapports et Procès-Verbaux des Réunions du Conseil International pour l'Exploitation de la Mer 174.

Taylor, B. L., P. R. Wade, D. P. De Master, and J. Barlow. 2000. Incorporating uncertainty into management models for marine mammals. Conservation Biology 14:1243–1252.

Todd, C. R., S. J. Nichol, and J. D. Koehn. 2004. Density-dependence in population models for the conservation management of trout cod, *Maccullochella macquariensis*. Ecological Modelling 171:359–380.

Tsukamoto, K., and T. Arai. 2001. Facultative catadromy of the eel *Anguilla japonica* between fresh water and seawater habitats. Marine Ecology Progress Series 220:265–276.

Vøllestad, L. A., and B. Jonsson. 1986. Life-history characteristics of the European eel *Anguilla anguilla* in the Imsa River, Norway. Transactions of the American Fisheries Society 115:864–871.

Vøllestad, L. A., and B. Jonsson. 1988. A 13-year study of the population dynamics of the European eel *Anguilla anguilla* in a Norwegian river: evidence for density-dependent mortality, and development of a model for predicting yield. Journal of Animal Ecology 57:983–997.

Wade, P. R. 2000. Bayesian methods in conservation biology. Conservation Biology 14:1308–1316.

Walters, C. 1986. Adaptive management of renewable resources. Macmillan, New York.

White, G. C, A. B. Franklin, and T. M. Shenk. 2002. Estimating parameters of PVA models from data on marked animals. Pages 169–190 in S. R. Beissinger and D. R. McCullough, editors. Population viability analysis. University of Chicago Press, Chicago.

Wiberg, U. H. 1983. Sex determination in the European eel (*Anguilla anguilla* L.). Cytogenetics and Cell Genetics 36:589–598.

Wirth, T., and L. Bernatchez. 2001. Genetic evidence against panmixia in the European eel. Nature (London) 409:1037–1040.

Wirth, T., and L. Bernatchez. 2003. Decline of North Atlantic eels: a fatal synergy? Proceedings of the Royal Society of London Series B-Biological Sciences 270:681–688.

Are American Eel Harvests in Maryland's Chesapeake Bay Sustainable?

JULIE A. WEEDER[1,*] AND JAMES H. UPHOFF, JR.
*Maryland Department of Natural Resources, Matapeake Work Center
301 Marine Academy Drive, Stevensville, Maryland 21666, USA*

Abstract.—We investigated yield per recruit and spawner biomass per recruit of American eels *Anguilla rostrata* in five commercially fished estuarine river systems to determine population status, using a modified form of the Thompson-Bell model. We estimated three biological reference points with this model: F_{max}, $F_{0.1}$, and $F_{replacement}$; eels appeared overfished relative to these reference points. Current fishing mortality rates (F) ranged from 0.37 to 1.19, while F_{max} ranged from 0.33 to 0.51, $F_{0.1}$ ranged from 0.24 to 0.35, and $F_{replacement}$ ranged from 0.20 to 0.32. The percentage of maximum spawning potential (%MSP) needed for replacement of the stock was estimated at 33%, but current %MSP varied between 1% and 28%. ICES guidelines recommend that F equal M in data-poor situations, but Fs in Maryland's upper Chesapeake Bay were two to four times larger than M. American eel populations in the Chesapeake Bay region may now depend on recruitment from other areas along the Atlantic coast where fishing mortality is low.

Introduction

American eels *Anguilla rostrata* are native to Maryland's fresh and tidal waters. From spawning in the Sargasso Sea, larvae drift in the Gulf Stream to populate rivers and estuaries from Brazil to Greenland (Helfman et al. 1987). Adults may travel hundreds of miles upstream to reside in freshwater streams, while others remain in estuaries. After 3 to 10 years (males) or 10 to 20 years (females), adults migrate to the Sargasso Sea, where they spawn and die (Helfman et al. 1987). Although eels once constituted a minor local bait fishery in Maryland's tidal waters, a large export market has developed during the past 30 to 40 years to support demand abroad for aquaculture, stocking, and for human food (Foster 1981; Weeder and Uphoff 1999). Maryland is one of a few states where landings have not decreased over the past 10 years (ASMFC 2000). During 1990–2001, landings were about 300,000 lb (ASMFC 2000).

Nearly all eels in Maryland's fishery are harvested by eel pots constructed to Maryland regulatory standards (Weeder and Uphoff 2003). These pots retain eels as small as 31 cm; most harvested eels are less than 50 cm and are not likely to be nearing sexual maturity (Wenner and Musick 1974; Helfman et al. 1987; Weeder and Uphoff 2003). While large eels are in the greatest demand and bring the highest price, all sizes greater than 15 cm (the State of Maryland's declared maximum size

---

[1] Corresponding author: jweeder@verizon.net
[*]Current address: National Marine Fisheries Service, Southeast Regional Office, 263 13th Avenue South, St. Petersburg, Florida 33701 USA

of an elver) can be legally retained and sold. This harvest strategy is potentially risky because it depends on maintaining a sustainable harvest of immature eels.

Fisheries are managed to achieve certain socioeconomic goals while conserving production of the resource (Sissenwine and Shepherd 1987). The goals of management are usually complex, and it is necessary to identify objectives as biological reference points that identify conservation and yield implications of an exploitation strategy. Yield per recruit (YPR) and spawner biomass per recruit (SBR) are equilibrium methods that can be used to develop biological reference points (Hilborn and Walters 1992).

We modified the Thompson-Bell YPR-SBR model (Gabriel et al. 1989) developed for American eels by Weeder and Uphoff (2003) to determine whether harvest was sustainable in five Maryland tidal tributaries during the period 1997 to 2002. Modification of the model was necessary to represent the complete mortality of eels after spawning, because the standard parameterization of the Thompson Bell model was developed for fishes that were repeat spawners.

We used the YPR-SBR approach to place harvest intensity in Maryland in perspective with accepted biological reference points. We treated American eel populations in our tidal rivers as distinct stocks when we applied this model even though their broad distribution from Greenland to northern South America, catadromous life history, and assumed random mating in the Sargasso Sea strongly indicate that eels are panmictic (Haro et al. 2000). The International Council for the Exploration of the Sea (ICES) Working Group on Eels felt that the management of eels would ideally occur on a primary watershed basis and provided examples of an SBR approach for determining biological reference points (ICES 2001). This study was conducted on the premise that eel stocks considered to be functional management units should be self-sustaining, allowing enough escapement to produce the recruitment necessary to sustain the stock.

Two YPR biological reference points, F_{max} and $F_{0.1}$, were estimated. The fishing mortality rate that maximizes YPR is denoted F_{max} and is relevant to short-term yield but ignores the effect of fishing on future generations (Sissenwine and Shepherd 1987). $F_{0.1}$ occurs where the slope of the YPR function is 0.1 (10%) of the initial slope. $F_{0.1}$ is essentially an arbitrary, conservative choice of F (Hilborn and Walters 1992).

We used SBR analysis to determine F at replacement ($F_{replacement}$); $F_{replacement}$ theoretically results in a level of spawner biomass that produces the number of recruits needed to replace their parents when a compensatory relationship is absent (Sissenwine and Shepherd 1987). SBR analysis characterizes reproductive potential of a stock in terms of spawner biomass produced by a year-class over its lifetime under equilibrium conditions (Goodyear 1993).

Management based on SBR links a harvest strategy to robustness of the stock to recruitment overfishing based on a measured or assumed stock-recruitment relationship. SBR separates conservation objectives from harvest objectives and is not prejudiced by the nature of a harvest strategy implied by YPR analyses (Goodyear 1993).

Methods

Sample Collection

We collected eels in four tidal tributaries of Maryland's Chesapeake Bay (the Severn, Nanticoke, Wye, and Wicomico Rivers) and one tributary of its coastal bays (Assawoman Bay) (Figure 1). Fish were measured to the nearest millimeter and weighed to the nearest gram. Random dips of several hundred kg of eels were purchased from commercial fishers during spring, early summer,

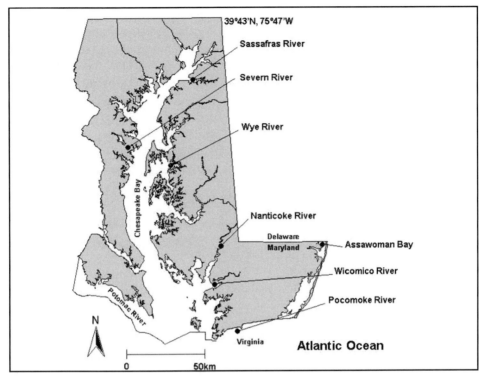

Figure 1. American eel sampling locations in Maryland, 1998–2002.

and fall. Purchased eels were combined over several days in live boxes to minimize day-to-day variation in size. Large eels were uncommon in our random samples, so we sometimes purchased nonrandom samples of large eels. These selected samples were kept and coded separately and were not included in size analyses but were used to develop age-length keys.

Sexual Maturity

We determined sex of eels captured in 2000 and 2001 to identify females (Weeder and Hammond 2008, this volume) and estimated maturity of these females using a modified form of the histological criteria described in Columbo et al. (1984) and Beullens et al. (1997). We used the absence of any visible nucleoli as stage 1. If some cells had nucleoli, we called it stage 1.5. If most cells had nucleoli, we called it stage 2. Some oocytes in stage 2 also had a few lipid vesicles present. Stage 2.5 oocytes had numerous lipid vesicles, but they were mostly in the periphery of the cytoplasm. Stage 3 had abundant lipid vesicles filling the cytoplasm. We assumed that eels in stages 2.5 and 3 were imminent spawners based on the advanced development of their gonads. We calculated binomial confidence intervals around the proportion sexually mature (category 2.5 or greater) for each age. Those ages with confidence intervals that were significantly different from 0 (no age-1 eels were considered mature) were considered precise enough to be useable in predicting maturity at age. We estimated the female maturity schedule at age using linear regression for ages with sufficient precision and assumed 0.99 of 12-year-old eels were mature. The latter assumption left open the possibility of a few mature females older than 12. Maturity of males was not estimated because sample sizes were small and males are not typically considered in SBR modeling.

Age Determination

We determined the age of eels from their otoliths. We ground and polished one or both sagittal otoliths (Secor et al. 1996) and counted the number of opaque and translucent zones. We assumed that translucent zones formed during the winter months when growth was slow and that opaque zones formed during periods of faster growth in summer months (Vladykov 1967; Gray and Andrews 1971). One year in freshwater (freshwater age) equaled one opaque zone and one translucent zone. An eel was considered to be age one in the year of arrival in continental waters (freshwater age = 1).

Two biologists read each otolith in a double-blind design. If ages for an otolith did not agree, it was read independently again at least one day later. If readings still did not agree, the readers discussed the specimen. If the correct age of the eel was still unclear, it was excluded from age analysis. We used established criteria to detect supernumerary zones (after Deelder 1997; Berg 1985; Oliveira 1996) and excluded from analysis any otoliths with suspected supernumerary zones.

Growth

Growth was analyzed as a linear function of age, consistent with studies of American and European eels (Frost 1945; Hansen and Eversole 1984). Growth rates were determined for the Wye, Wicomico, Severn and Nanticoke rivers and for Assawoman Bay. Sex was not considered as a variable in growth rates because the number of eels sexed was small and sex was impossible to predict for eels less than 40 cm. We looked for differences in growth among years from the same river, using analysis of covariance (ANCOVA) to test for differences in slopes of the length at age. Only ages common to each year were considered, and years that were not significantly different were pooled. We also used the Bonferroni t-test to compare the mean size of eels at each age among different rivers. This method controls experiment-wide error by adjusting alpha for the total number of tests. The length-weight relationship for each system was described using the allometric equation: $W = \alpha L \beta$, where W = weight (g), L = length (mm) and α and β were model parameters.

Mortality

Total mortality, Z, and its standard error were calculated for each system using a catch curve based on numbers at age derived from an age-length key (Ricker 1975; Allen 1997). Eels collected over multiple years from the same river were combined to calculate Z; pooling may ameliorate the effect of variable recruitment on the catch curves (Ricker 1975). Natural mortality rate (M) was estimated as $3/T_{max}$ (Anthony 1982), where T_{max} was the oldest age observed during our sampling (12). The annual instantaneous fishing mortality rate equaled $Z–M$ (Ricker 1975).

Yield and Spawner Biomass per Recruit

We calculated YPR and SBR using the procedures of Gabriel et al. (1989). However, we modified the Thompson-Bell model and its inputs to reflect four assumptions about American eel maturity, migration, and natural mortality. We assumed that (1) eels within a system did not migrate to another system; (2) migration was a direct function of maturity; (3) eels migrated in the same year that they matured; and (4) migration to spawn was followed by complete mortality. The Thompson-Bell model determined the number (N_{ts}) and weight (W_{ts}) at spawning at age t as

$$N_{ts} = N_t \, e^{-((c \cdot pt \cdot F) + d \cdot M)} \dots \dots \dots \dots \dots (1)$$
$$W_{ts} = fr_{ts} \cdot N_{ts} \cdot Wi_{ts} \dots \dots \dots \dots \dots (2)$$

The model required age-specific individual weights (Wi_{ts}) and partial recruitment (p_t), $_M$, estimates of the fraction of F and M occurring prior to spawning (abbreviated as c and d, respectively) and a maturity schedule (fraction mature or fr_{ts}; Gabriel et al. 1989). We estimated partial recruitment for each river as the fraction of eels that were 30 cm or greater at each age, because eel pots do not effectively harvest eels less than 30 cm (Weeder and Uphoff 2003). Fraction of F occurring prior to spawning was $c = 1.0$.

We modified the equation for N_t used by Gabriel et al. (1989) to reflect the total mortality of eels after spawning as

$$N_t = (N_t - 1 \cdot e^{-((pt-1 \cdot F) + M\text{resident})}) - (fr_{t-1s} \cdot N_{t-1s}) \ldots (3)$$

Natural mortality (M) was split into $M_{resident}$ and $M_{migrant}$. $M_{resident}$ was used as an instantaneous rate directly in the calculation of N at age for residents in equation (3), while $M_{migrant}$ is represented by the complete death of those eels that mature, migrate, spawn, and die. $M_{migrant}$ was represented as annualized mortality by subtracting ($fr_{t-1s} \cdot N_{t-1s}$) in equation (3) to eliminate the eels after spawning.

We did not adjust our catch curves for $M_{migrant}$, but we needed to estimate it as an instantaneous rate to determine $M_{resident}$ for our Thompson-Bell model. We regressed ln $((1-R_t) + 1)$ against age, where R_t was the proportion mature at age t; the slope of this regression described the instantaneous annual rate of decrease in the probability of being a resident and the slope equaled $M_{migrant}$. $M_{resident}$ was then derived as

$$M_{resident} = M - M_{migrant} \ldots (4)$$

The estimate of $M_{resident}$ was applied to all ages in the model. Since $M_{resident}$ and $M_{migrant}$ were separated, the fraction of M coefficient (d) only applied to resident eels and they were assumed to be subject to $M_{resident}$ year-round ($d = 1.0$).

We used an arbitrary initial cohort of 100,000 at age 0 and ran the model through age 12. We compared the current values of F to F_{max}, $F_{0.1}$, and $F_{replacement}$. Replacement F was determined from the modified Thompson-Bell model by setting as a target the percent of maximum potential spawner biomass needed for replacement (%$MSP_{replacement}$). The estimate of %$MSP_{replacement}$ was made using the following equation from Mace and Sissenwine (1993):

$$\%MSP_{replacement} = \text{intercept} - (0.51 \cdot (log \text{ Wt-}max)) + (0.38 \cdot (log \text{ Wt}50\%_{mat}) + 3.52) \cdot M \ldots (5)$$

where intercept was derived from the regression of %$MSP_{replacement}$ on maximum average weight of multiple pooled fish species in Mace and Sissenwine (1993). We determined the age at which 50% of eels were mature using our maturity schedule, and used the average weight at that age as Wt50%$_{mat}$ (0.52 kg). We used the average weight of silver eels captured from the Pocomoke River (Figure 1) during fall 2000 and 2001 as Wt$_{max}$ (0.64 kg). The fishing mortality rate that corresponds to %$MSP_{replacement}$ is $F_{replacement}$. If fishing mortality rates exceed $F_{replacement}$, the population suffers from recruitment overfishing (Mace and Sissenwine 1993).

Results

Growth

There were significant differences in length at age of eels from most areas ($P > 0.05$). Assawoman Bay and Wye River eels did not differ significantly in size at any shared age ($P < 0.05$). Nanticoke River eels were, on average, consistently smaller than all others at nearly every age and were smaller than all others at their respective ages of full recruitment to the fishery (Nanticoke River, 31.1 cm at age 3; Assawoman Bay, 46.6 cm at age 3, Severn River, 33.8 cm at age 2, Wye River, 39.7 cm at age 2, and Wicomico River, 32.2 cm at age 2). Based on linear regression parameters (Table 1), growth of eels in different systems, in decreasing order, was as follows: Wye, Wicomico, Assawoman, Severn, and Nanticoke.

Maturity

None of the age 1 eels examined (those which had been in freshwater for one year) were sexually mature ($n = 6$). The proportion of eels mature at age 2 was 0.12 (SD = 0.05, $n = 43$); at age 3, 0.18 (SD = 0.06, $n = 45$); at age 4, 0.32 (SD = 0.09, $n = 25$); and at age 5, 0.36 (SD = 0.10; $n = 22$). Sample sizes for ages 6 to 10 were too few ($n = 1$–4) to calculate relative maturity. The relationship between female maturity and age from ages 2 to 5 was as follows: $R = 0.089t - 0.072$, where R = proportion mature and t = age ($r^2 = 0.997$, $P < 0.01$). We used this equation to predict female maturity over the age range of 1 to 12.

Mortality

Eels were captured in the fishery one year after metamorphosis from elvers to yellow eels (freshwater age = 1). We captured eels as old as age 13 in the Nanticoke, but eels older than 9 were absent in other areas. We selected 12 as the maximum age because it was the oldest age-class represented by more than a single eel; therefore, M equaled 0.25. The slope of the regression of $\ln((1 - R_t) + 1)$ against age ($M_{migrant}$) equaled -0.062 ($r^2 = 0.99$, $P < 0.01$). This functional regression slightly overestimated observed maturity. $M_{resident}$ equaled 0.25 minus 0.06, or 0.19.

Fishing mortality rates were highest in the Wye River (1.19, SE = 0.1) and lowest in the Nanticoke River (0.42, SE = 0.04) (Table 1). All values were significantly different from zero ($P < 0.1$). F for the Nanticoke sample was significantly lower than that for the Wye, Severn, and Wicomico, and Assawoman was significantly lower than Wye.

Yield and Spawner Biomass per Recruit

Yield per recruit grouped into two general regions; three systems had higher potential YPR (maximums between 0.05 and 0.07 kg per recruit, and two had much lower potential (maximum YPR ≈ 0.02 kg per recruit; Figure 2). Estimates of F_{max} and $F_{0.1}$ were much higher in Nanticoke River (0.51 and 0.35, respectively) than in the other four systems ($F_{max} = 0.33$–0.38 and $F_{0.1} = 0.24$–0.27; Table 1). In all cases except the Nanticoke River, F was too high to maximize yield, although YPR was not drastically lower than the maximum possible (Table 1; Figure 2). In the Nanticoke River, $F_{current}$ was less than F_{max} but exceeded $F_{0.1}$. In all other rivers, $F_{current}$ exceeded both YPR reference points by wide margins. In the extreme case, $F_{current}$ (1.19) in the Wye River was 3 times higher than F_{max} (0.35) and over 4 times higher than $F_{0.1}$ (0.25; Table 1).

To ensure replacement of the stock, 33% of the maximum spawning potential (%$MSP_{replacement}$) needed to be retained (Table 1). Such levels required $F_{replacement} = 0.20$–0.32, depending on the river; four of five estimates were between 0.20 and 0.23. $F_{replacement}$ was exceeded by $F_{current}$ by a factor of 3 to 5 in every river but the Nanticoke River (Figure 3; Table 1). In the Nanticoke River, %$MSP_{current}$ was 28%. It ranged from 1% to 5% in the other rivers (Figure 3; Table 1).

Discussion

It appears that overfishing of eels in Maryland may be widespread. Current %MSP fell

Table 1. American eel growth parameters and biological reference point data for each of five tidal systems in Maryland.

Parameter/Statistic	Assawoman Bay	Severn River	Naticoke River	Wye River	Wicomico River
Linear Growth (age-length relationship, units cm·yr^{-1})					
N	274	124	320	320	183
Intercept	30.09	25.23	23.08	24.25	18.00
SE	1.65	1.25	1.27	1.13	1.55
Slope	5.14	4.35	3.69	7.28	7.48
SE	0.46	0.50	0.21	0.46	0.55
Length-weight relationship (allometry equation $W=aL^b$, kg and cm)					
N	691	441	1332	2934	1617
Intercept (a)	0.0000007	0.0000020	0.0000010	0.0000020	0.0000030
Slope (b)	3.14	2.98	3.05	2.59	2.91
Biological Reference Points					
M	0.25	0.25	0.25	0.25	0.25
$F_{current}$	0.64	0.74	0.37	1.19	0.72
F_{max}	0.33	0.38	0.51	0.35	0.34
$F_{0.1}$	0.24	0.27	0.35	0.25	0.25
$F_{replacement}$	0.20	0.22	0.32	0.22	0.23
%MSP$_{replacement}$	33%	33%	33%	33%	33%
%MSP$_{current}$	4%	4%	28%	1%	5%
Years pooled	2001, 2002	2000, 2001	2000, 2001	2000, 2002	1998–2000
Z	0.89	0.99	0.62	1.44	1.1
SE	0.1	0.232	0.043	0.103	0.14
Ages used	3–8	2–7	3–13	2–5	2–5
Ages present	1–9	1–7	1–13	1–5	1–5
P.R. vectors – Proportion > 30 cm					
Age 1	0.86	0.55	0	0.47	0.33
Age 2	0.97	0.9	0.65	0.88	0.72
Age 3	1	0.95	0.68	1	0.84
Age 4	0.99	0.91	0.81	1	1
Age 5	1	1	0.86	1	0.85
Age 6	1	1	0.91	1	1
Age 7	1	1	0.86	1	1
Age 8	1	1	1	1	1
Age 9	1	1	1	1	1
Age 10	1	1	1	1	1
Age 11	1	1	1	1	1
Age 12	1	1	1	1	1

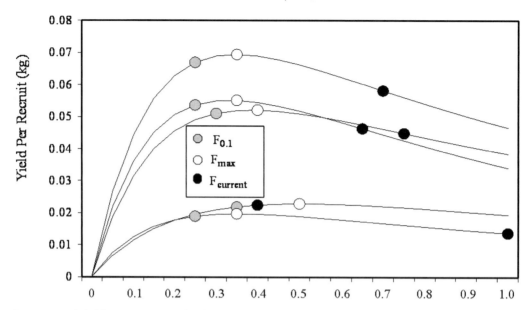

Figure 2. Eel yield per recruit and reference points for five Maryland rivers. The relationships from top to bottom at $F = 0.4$ are for the Wicomico River, Assawoman Bay, Severn River, Nanticoke River, and Wye River.

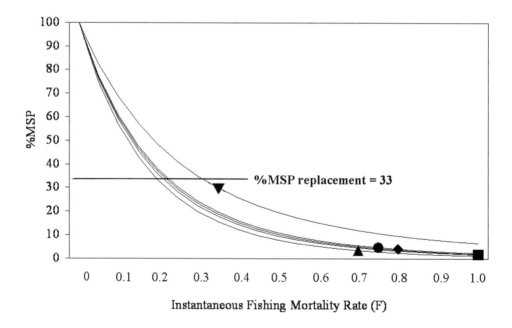

Figure 3. Eel spawner biomass per recruit for five Maryland rivers, with current percent Maximum Spawning Potential (%MSP) for each river and the 33% level for overall replacement. The relationships from top to bottom at $F = 0.4$ are for the Nanticoke River (star), Wicomico River (closed circle), Severn River (closed diamond), Wye River (closed square), and Assawoman Bay (closed triangle).

short, usually far short, of that needed for sustainability in every system we investigated. We considered these systems representative of all tidal rivers in Maryland. We qualify "overfishing," because it is possible that eels have refuge in other lightly exploited areas of the species' broad range that offset the excessive fishing mortality rates occurring locally and allow for suitable spawner biomass in the Sargasso Sea.

Yield per recruit of eels in all rivers we examined was potentially quite variable and was usually below its potential. Weeder and Uphoff (2003) estimated that YPR of Maryland eel populations in 1999 was up to 84% less than that observed in 1981. Our YPR reference points were slightly higher than those in Weeder and Uphoff (2003; F_{max} = 0.19–0.23 and $F_{0.1}$ = 0.14–0.17), indicating that overall M was higher in this version of the Thompson-Bell model. The annualized removal of emigrating eels from the population in this current version was not mathematically equivalent to the constant $M = 0.25$ employed by Weeder and Uphoff (2003). In addition, different rivers were sampled in Weeder and Uphoff (2003) than in this study. It appears that growth, partial recruitment, and F may be specific on a tributary level. These tributary-specific characteristics may complicate stock assessments on a broad regional scale.

Maryland's fishery harvests very small, young eels well before they are able to grow to the size and age required to mature and to maximize yield and value. The same age groups were present in 1981 (up to age 9) that we observed nearly 20 years later, but 5-year-old and older eels were nearly twice as large then (Weeder and Uphoff 2003). Eels that are smaller and become sexually mature at an earlier age are less likely to be caught before emigrating than those that mature later at a larger size (Trippel 1995), but they have reduced reproductive potential (Helfman et al. 1987). If early maturation and associated spawning emigration were occurring, fishing pressure and its influence on growth could be the cause.

The slopes of the linear growth models we employed were positively correlated (r = 0.72) with estimates of Z in the five systems. This correlation suggested that fishing reduced fish density and relieved density-dependent effects, allowing remaining animals access to more food and habitat, resulting in increased growth (Trippel 1995). Differences in habitat quality or system-specific recruitment levels could also lead to differences in growth. Increased growth rates could lead to earlier maturation and emigration of eels. Emigration would influence Z by increasing M, since eels die after spawning. We interpret this as an increase in F, because M was held constant. In this case, increased M would have been an indirect effect of increased F, and SBR was reduced by fishing even though M rose. The correlation of growth and mortality, if real, could introduce bias into our system-specific YPR and SBR estimates because we estimated unfished SBR under the assumption that growth estimates described an unfished population.

We estimated maturity of female eels based on sex-specific data but modeled growth of females with age data, including younger eels of undetermined sex. Sex of some eels smaller than 40 cm could not be determined, either because gonads were not differentiated adequately or because both male and female cells were found (Weeder and Hammond 2009, this volume). We based our sex determination on the differentiation observed at the time gonadal tissue was removed and did not speculate as to the future sex of the specimen. Because Columbo et al. (1984) found that male eels may change sex before the beginning of sexual maturation when eels become silver, we believe that prediction of eel sex when both types of cells were found would be premature.

Helfman et al. (1987) determined that eels in tidal waters have relatively small home ranges; therefore, migration is likely out to sea rather than among tributaries. We could not find evidence in the scientific literature to either support or refute our assumption that eels migrate in the same year they mature. We could not sample freshwater areas where emigration rates may have been different and there were no unfished tidal areas available to us to judge the extent of emigration. However, other researchers have found it to be a minor source of loss to the population each year and have found M and emigration rates similar to ours. Estimates of Z of eels in tidal Hudson River (equivalent to M because a fishery is absent there) ranged from 0.12 to 0.15 (Morrison et al. 2003). At two unexploited sites in Canada, Z equaled 0.25 and 0.28, M equaled 0.19 (Cairns et al. 2000), and instantaneous emigration rates were 0.06–0.09; the latter two rates were similar to our estimates of $M_{resident}$ and $M_{migrant}$, respectively. Our estimates of Z ranged from 0.62 to 1.44 in the four tidal rivers, and when compared to observations from unfished systems, emigration, when compared with fishing, likely accounted for a small part of the loss rate from Maryland's tidal rivers. The ICES Working Group on Eels determined that eel SBR functions were not overly sensitive to hypothetical values of M (0.05–0.40; ICES 2001).

The precautionary approach recommended by the ICES Working Group for Eels indicates that F should not exceed M when inadequate assessment information is available for an assessment (ICES 2000), but our Fs were approximately two to four times higher than M. The use of $F_{replacement}$ as a reference point theoretically results in spawner biomass that produces enough recruits to replace their parents in the absence of compensation (density-independent recruitment; Mace and Sissenwine 1993). An assumption of density-independent compensation will generally result in a conservative assessment of a stock's ability to withstand exploitation (Fogarty et al. 1992). Our estimate of $\%MSP_{replacement}$ (33%) indicated that eels would be sensitive to recruitment overfishing when compared with 91 stocks of the 27 species analyzed by Mace and Sissenwine (1993); about 80% of their estimates of $\%MSP_{replacement}$ were lower than our estimates for the American eel. Assessment of this species over its entire, broad geographic range is currently untenable given data limitations. Until such assessment is possible, applications of existing fisheries models on a lesser geographic scale, such as those described in this paper, provide regional management guidelines which allow for a precautionary approach to American eel management.

Acknowledgments

Steve Hammond and Erik Pertain provided extensive assistance with otolith preparation and aging and data management. John Barnette, Edward Fooks, and Byron Cameron shared socioeconomic information about the eel fishery and provided commercially captured eels over multiple years of the study. We thank the three reviewers who gave constructive comments on an early draft of the manuscript.

References

Allen, M. S. 1997. Effects of variable recruitment on catch-curve analysis for crappie populations. North American Journal of Fisheries Management 17:202–205.

Anthony, V. 1982. The calculation of F0.1: A plea for standardization. Northwest Atlantic Fisheries Organization, Serial Document SCR 82/VI/64, Halifax, Canada.

ASMFC (Atlantic States Marine Fisheries Commission). 2000. Interstate Fishery Management Plan for American Eel (*Anguilla rostrata*):79.

Berg, R. 1985. Age determination of eels, *Anguilla anguilla* (L): comparison of field data with otolith ring patterns. Journal of Fish Biology 26:537–544.

Beullens, K., E. H. Eding, P. Gilson, F. Ollevier, J. Komen, and C. J. J. Richter. 1997. Gonadal differentiation, intersexuality, and sex ratios of European eel (*Anguilla anguilla* L.) maintained in captivity. Aquaculture 153:135–150.

Cairns, D. K., M. C. Lister, and C. D. MachPherson (2000). A preliminary life table for the American eel in the southern Gulf of St. Lawrence, Canada. International Council for the Exploration of the Sea-Working Group on Eels: 1–38.

Columbo, G., G. Grandi, and R. Rossi. 1984. Gonad differentiation and body growth in *Anguilla anguilla* L. Journal of Fish Biology 24:215–228.

Deelder, D. C. L. 1997. Remarks on the age-determination of eels, with length-back calculation. Report of the Joint ICES/EIFAC Symposium on Eel Research and Management (Anguilla spp.), Helsinki, Finland, 9–11 June 1976. EIFAC Technical Paper No. 28.

Fogarty, M. J., A. A. Rosenberg, and M. P. Sissenwine. 1992. Fisheries risk assessment: sources of uncertainty. Environmental Science and Technology 26:440–447.

Foster, J. W. S. 1981. The American eel in Maryland—a situation paper. Maryland Tidewater Administration, Tidal Fisheries Division 21, Annapolis, Maryland.

Frost, W. E. 1945. The age and growth of eels (*Anguilla anguilla*) from the Windermere catchment area: Part I. Journal of Animal Ecology 14:26–36.

Gabriel, W. L., M. P. Sissenwine, and W. J. Overholtz. 1989. Analysis of spawning stock biomass per recruit: an example for Georges Bank haddock. North American Journal of Fisheries Management 9:383–391.

Goodyear, C. P. 1993. Spawning stock biomass per recruit in fisheries management: foundation and current use. Canadian Special Publication of Fisheries and Aquatic Sciences 120:67–81.

Gray, R. W., and C. W. Andrews. 1971. Age and growth of the American eel (*Anguilla rostrata* (LeSueur)) in Newfoundland waters. Canadian Journal of Zoology 49:121–128.

Hansen, R. A., and A. G. Eversole. 1984. Age, growth, and sex ratio of American eels in brackish-water portions of a South Carolina river. Transactions of the American Fisheries Society 113:744–749.

Haro, A., W. Richkus, K. Whalen, A. Hoar, W. D. Busch, S. Lary, T. Brush, and D. Dixon. 2000. Population decline of the American eel: implications for research and management. Fisheries 25:7–16.

Helfman, G. S., D. E. Facey, L. S. Hales, Jr., and E. Bozeman. 1987. Reproductive ecology of the American eel. Pages 42–56 *in* M. J. Dadswell, R. J. Klauda, C. M. Moffitt, R. L. Saunders, R. A. Rulifson, and J. E. Cooper, editors. Common strategies of anadromous and catadromous fishes. American Fisheries Society, Symposium 1, Bethesda, Maryland.

Hilborn, R., and C. J. Walters. 1992. Quantitative fisheries stock assessment: choice, dynamics and uncertainty. Chapman and Hall, New York.

ICES (International Council for the Exploration of the Sea). 2000. Report of the EIFAC/ICES Working Group on Eels. ICES C.M. 2000/ACFM:03, Copenhagen.

ICES (International Council for the Exploration of the Sea). 2001. Report of the EIFAC/ICES Working Group on Eels, 28 August–1 September 2000. ICES CM 2000/ ACFM:03/2001, St. Andrews, New Brunswick, Canada.

Mace, P. M., and M. P. Sissenwine. 1993. How much spawning per recruit is enough? Pages 101–118 *in* S. J. Smith, J. J. Hunt, and D. Rivard, editors. Risk evaluation and biological reference points for fisheries management. Canadian Special Publication of Fisheries and Aquatic Sciences 120.

Morrison, W. E., D. H. Secor, and P. M. Piccoli. 2003. Estuarine habitat use by Hudson River American eels as determined by otolith strontium:calcium ratios. Pages 87–100 *in* D. A. Dixon, editor. Biology, management, and protection of catadromous eels. American Fisheries Society, Symposium 33, Bethesda, Maryland.

Oliveira, K. 1996. Field validation of annular growth rings in the American eel, *Anguilla rostrata*, using tetracycline-marked otoliths. Fisheries Bulletin 94:186–189.

Ricker, W. E. 1975. Computation and interpretation of biological statistics of fish populations. Journal of the Fisheries Research Board of Canada Bulletin, Department of the Environment, Fisheries and Marine Services, Ottawa.

Secor, D. H., J. M. Dean, and E. H. Laban. 1996. Manual for otolith removal and preparation for microstructural examination. Technical Publication No. 1991–01. Electric Power Research Institute and Belle W. Baruch Institute for Marine Biology and Coastal Research, Columbia, South Carolina.

Sissenwine, M. P., and J. G. Shepherd. 1987. An alternative perspective on recruitment overfishing and biological reference points. Canadian Journal of Fisheries and Aquatic Sciences 44:913–918.

Trippel, E. A. 1995. Age at maturity as a stress indicator in fisheries. Bioscience 45(11):759–771.

Vladykov, V. D. 1967. Age determination and age of American eel from New Brunswick waters. Canadian Department of Fisheries and Forestry Progress Report No. 3.

Weeder, J. A. and S. D. Hammond. 2009. Age, growth, mortality, and sex ratio of American eels in Maryland's Chesapeake Bay. Pages 113–128 in J. M. Casselman and D. K. Cairns, editors. Eels at the edge: science, status, and conservation concerns. American Fisheries Society, Symposium 58, Bethesda, Maryland.

Weeder, J. A. and J. H. Uphoff, Jr. 1999. Maryland American Eel Population Study Completion Report No. 34. Maryland Department of Natural Resources, Tidewater Administration, Fisheries Division, Annapolis, Maryland.

Weeder, J. A., and J. H. Uphoff, Jr. 2003. Effect of changes in growth and eel pot mesh size on American eel yield-per-recruit estimates in upper Chesapeake Bay. Pages 167–176 in D. A. Dixon, editor. Biology, management, and protection of catadromous eels. American Fisheries Society, Symposium 33, Bethesda, Maryland.

Wenner, C. A., and J. A. Musick. 1974. Fecundity and gonad observations of the American eel, Anguilla rostrata, migrating from Chesapeake Bay, Virginia. Journal of the Fisheries Research Board Canada 31(8):1387–1390.

Management of American Eels in Lake Ontario and the Upper St. Lawrence River

ALASTAIR MATHERS[1] AND THOMAS J. STEWART

*Ontario Ministry of Natural Resources, Lake Ontario Management Unit
RR#4, Picton, Ontario K0K 2T0 Canada*

Abstract.—The American eel *Anguilla rostrata* is an important component of the aquatic ecosystem of Lake Ontario and the upper St. Lawrence River and historically has been one of the most valuable commercial species in Ontario waters of this system. Between 1984 and 1993, reported annual harvest ranged from 104 to 124 metric tons. Since 1993, eel harvests have declined precipitously in all areas above the Moses-Saunders Power Dam in spite of an increase in price per kg. During 2002, fishers held 85 eel licenses and harvested 12 metric tons (mt) of maturing yellow eel, mostly with hoop nets and trap nets. The numbers of eels migrating into this system in recent years suggests that if fishing effort remains constant, commercial harvests in areas above the dam will be under 3 mt per year between now and 2010. Provincial management programs have imposed license and season restrictions, reduced quotas, and more detailed catch reporting. Sustainable management practices throughout the range of this panmictic species will be required to restore the eel as an abundant species in Lake Ontario and the upper St. Lawrence River.

Introduction

In the province of Ontario, American eels *Anguilla rostrata* occur primarily in Lake Ontario, the upper St. Lawrence River, and the Ottawa River drainage systems. They are rare in Lakes Erie, Huron, and Superior (Scott and Crossman 1998).

This stock has supported a commercial fishery for over a century (Baldwin et al. 1979). From the mid-1980s through the 1990s, reported catches of American eels declined over most of their North American range. Declines have been most dramatic at the northern extremity of the range, and recruitment to the Lake Ontario and the upper St. Lawrence River (LO/SLR) stock has virtually ceased (Casselman 2003). This paper provides information on the LO/SLR commercial fishery and its management from 1996 to 2002, as an update to the report of Stewart et al. (1997).

Methods

Annual harvest statistics, quotas, and licensing data were assembled from annual reports of the Lake Ontario Management Unit of the Ontario Ministry of Natural Resources and from ministry files. Value of harvest was converted to U.S. funds based on exchange rates of the year of harvest. Prior to 1998, fishers reported the weight of fish harvested by species, harvest method and location of capture, and disposition of fish.

[1] Corresponding author: alastair.mathers@mnr.gov.on.ca

Data were recorded for each fishing trip, but the reports were filed on a monthly basis. In 1998, a more rigorous daily catch-reporting system of all species was implemented for all commercial fishers in Ontario. Under this system, reports must be filed for each fishing trip, allowing closer tracking of harvest. Fishing effort is not quantified to a level that would allow calculation of catch per unit effort. Catch reports were summarized for the years 1991–2002 to determine the distribution of harvest by gear for each quota zone (Figure 1).

Eels ascending the ladder at the Moses-Saunders Power Dam at Cornwall have been counted since the ladder was constructed in 1974. These data provide an index of the numbers of eels available to future fisheries in Lake Ontario (Casselman et al. 1997a).

Results and Discussion

Commercial Harvest of Eels in LO/SLR

Commercial fishery statistics for eels in Ontario waters of the LO/SLR are available from 1884 (Baldwin et al. 1979; Casselman 2003). These statistics show that eels are an important component of a multispecies fishery. In the 1960s and 1970s, interest in commercial eel harvest increased coincident with declines in lake whitefish *Coregonus clupeaforis*, cisco *Coregonus artedii*, walleye *Sander vitreus*, white perch *Morone americana*, and other commercially important species (Christie 1973; Hurley 1973). In the 1970s, reported eel harvest increased rapidly in response to new markets, rising prices, and an abundance of eels (Christie et al. 1987; Cas-

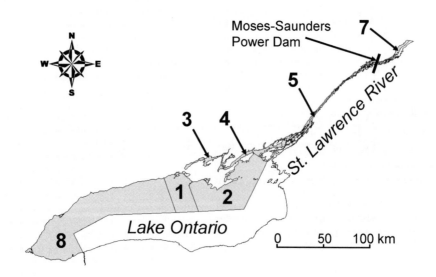

Figure 1. Commercial fish quota zones in Ontario waters of Lake Ontario and the upper St. Lawrence River.

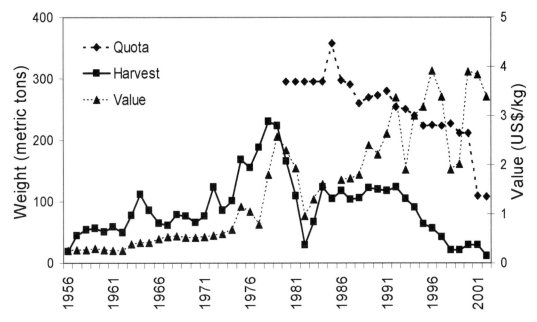

Figure 2. Reported commercial harvest and quota for American eel for Ontario waters of Lake Ontario and the upper St. Lawrence River, 1956–2002. Mean price per kg is also presented.

selman et al. 1997b) (Figure 2). Reported annual harvest peaked at over 200 metric tons in the late 1970s, with a landed value of U.S.$574,000. In 1982/83, European markets for Lake Ontario eels were closed due to contaminant levels, resulting in a dramatic short-term decline in harvest.

Between 1984 and 1993, reported commercial harvest was relatively stable, between 104 and 123 metric tons per year. During that period, price increased from $1.3/kg to over $3/kg, and eels were consistently one of the top three species in value in the LO/SLR commercial fishery. The largest harvest during that period occurred in Lake Ontario proper, followed by the Bay of Quinte (Figure 3).

Between 1993 and 2002, reported annual harvest declined by about 10 metric tons per year, reaching 12 metric tons (mt) in 2002. Annual harvest levels this low have not been recorded since the 1940s, and no decline this dramatic has ever been recorded in the LO/SLR. This decline occurred at a time of rising prices, to almost $4/kg. The decline in harvest was uneven across the LO/SLR area. Harvest in Lake St. Francis (Quota Zone 7 on Figure 1) between 1993 and 2002 remained relatively stable (mean 12 mt per year) (Figure 3). The decline in harvest was greatest in Lake Ontario proper (Figure 3) which includes Quota Zones 1, 2, and 8 (Figure 1).

Licensed gear includes trap nets, hoop nets, eel lines, electrofishing, eel pots, and seine nets. Eel lines (longlines) are a type of gear that is unique to the LO/SLR eel fishery. Eel lines have from 150 to 600 hooks, of 2/0 or 3/0 gauge (Kolenosky and Hendry 1982). The ends of the main line are anchored, but the midsection is suspended in the water column with floats. Hooks may be suspended in the water column and baited with worms, or they may be lowered to the bottom and baited with cut fish.

In 1959–1979, eel lines accounted for 65% of harvest, with hoop nets and trap nets making up the bulk of the remainder (Kole-

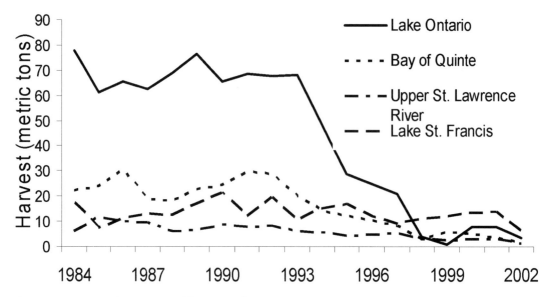

Figure 3. Reported commercial harvest of American eel in Ontario waters of Lake Ontario and the upper St. Lawrence River, 1984–2002. Data for Lake Ontario includes Quota Zones 1, 2, and 8. Data for the Bay of Quinte includes Quota Zones 3 and 4. Data for the upper St. Lawrence River includes Quota Zone 5. Data for Lake St. Francis includes Quota Zone 7.

nosky and Hendry 1982). In 2002, 98% of the harvest was taken in hoop nets and trap nets, with eel lines being the only other gear type reported. Fishers shifted away from eel lines because this gear catches only eels, and as eel abundance declined, the cost of fishing this gear outweighed the returns. Hoop nets and trap nets are set for a variety of species, and in recent years, the markets for live eels have become stronger, making eels caught in entrapment gear more desirable. In 2002, 93% of eels were sold live for a mean price of $3.53/kg, while 7% were sold in the round for a mean price of $2.22/kg.

Seasonal restrictions have been maintained on some types of commercial gears to reduce conflict with angling and pleasure-boat traffic and to limit incidental catch of nontarget species. Eel-line fisheries are open all year, while trap-net and hoop-net fisheries are closed in summer months in the upper Bay of Quinte (Quota Zone 3) and the St. Lawrence River (Quota Zones 5 and 7). The trap-net fishery is open all year in the lower Bay of Quinte (Quota Zone 4) and Lake Ontario proper (Quota Zones 1, 2 and 8).

During much of the 1980s, all eels had to be exported because levels of PCBs and Mirex exceeded Health Canada's recommendations for sales within Canada. By the 1990s, contaminant levels had declined to levels where the sale of eels that weighed less than 1 kg was permitted in domestic markets. By 2002, levels had declined to the point where there were no contaminated-related restrictions on eel sales.

Other Eel Fisheries

Other eel fisheries in Ontario and in the lower Great Lakes are very small relative to the commercial fishery in LO/SLR. Commercial eel fisheries exist in several small lakes adjacent to Lake Ontario and in the Ottawa River; reported harvest totaled approximately 200 kg per year from 1997 to 2002. Eels were fished commercially in New York State waters of Lake Ontario and the upper St. Lawrence River until 1982, when harvest was banned because of concerns over contaminant levels (Lary and Busch 1997). Commercial harvest of eels has occurred in Ontario portions of Lakes Erie and Huron, but these harvests totaled less than 100 kg per year from 1997 to 2002. Surveys of recreational fishers show that eels are not targeted by anglers and are rarely caught by anglers who target other fish species in LO/SLR (approximately 150 kg per year); also few of the eels caught are retained (approximately 10 kg per year). Casselman (2003) reported the historic importance of eel fisheries in the LO/SLR to native peoples. Current use of eels by natives is considered to be small, although quantitative data are lacking.

Management of the Commercial Eel Fishery

The province of Ontario is responsible for the management of American eel fisheries within its waters. Management activities up to 1996 are described by Hurley (1973), Kolenosky and Hendry (1982), and Stewart et al. (1997). Commercial harvest has been managed by use of licensing, quotas, and restrictions on gear, size, and seasons. Ontario's management direction on eels has been as follows.

1. Limit entry by issuing no new commercial eel licenses.

2. Reduce quota for eels when opportunities occur.

3. In cooperation with partners, maintain the upstream eel ladder and associated counter at the Moses-Saunders Power Dam at Cornwall, Ontario.

4. Continue to offer support to programs that further our understanding and management of the American eel population.

No new eel licenses have been issued since 1984. During 2002, 51 fishers held 85 eel licenses in the LO/SLR area; however, eel harvest was reported on only 46 of these licenses. The eel quota for the entire fishery and quota allocated to individual licenses are based on historical eel harvest levels and current abundance of eels. Eel quota was reduced by 103 mt for 2000. This is the largest reduction in quota since quotas were established in 1984 (Figure 2). Quota allocations remain higher than realized harvest but do limit the harvest of a few of the most active fishers.

Future of the Eel Fishery

The eel ladder at the Moses-Saunders Power Dam continues to be an important part of Ontario's eel management program. The facility gives maturing eels access to productive habitat in the LO/SLR and associated watersheds. In addition, migratory activity at the ladder indicates recruitment to the LO/SLR and potential for future commercial fisheries in upstream waters.

Casselman et al. (1997a) found a strong correlation between counts at the Moses-Saunders ladder and reported commercial harvest eight years later. Following this approach, we predicted future potential eel harvests based on ladder counts (Figure 4). Harvest data for 1984–2002 in the area of LO/SLR above the dam were used. Fewer than 60 eels per day were observed at the ladder during the peak migration periods between 1998 and 2002. This represents a 99.8% decline from peak-period migrations in the 1980s. This analysis suggests that, assuming constant fishing effort, commercial harvests in areas above the dam will be less than 3 mt per year between now and 2010. The assumption of constant fishing effort seems unrealistic, and it is likely that fishing effort and harvest levels will fall even lower than the predicted level.

In 2002 and 2003, Hydro-Québec estab-

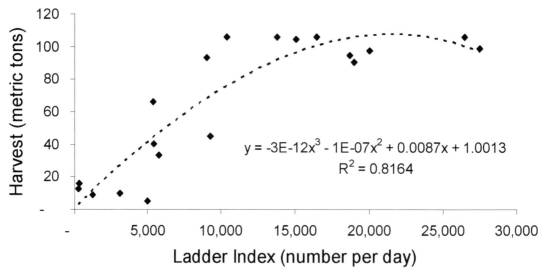

Figure 4. Relationship between reported commercial harvest of eel in areas above the Moses-Saunders Power Dam (total for Quota Zones 1, 2, 3, 4, 5 and 8) in 1984–2002 and the index of eel migrating upstream over the eel ladder. The ladder index data was lagged by eight years following the approach of Casselman et al. (1997a).

lished two new eel ladders at the Beauharnois Dam on the St. Lawrence River downstream of the Moses-Saunders Dam. These ladders may enhance the ability of eels to move upstream to Ontario waters but are unlikely to increase the numbers of eels over the long term.

American eels are widely thought to be a panmictic species (Avise et al. 1986; Wirth and Bernatchez 2003). Wirth and Bernatchez (2003) noted that "panmictic species pose particular problems for conservation because their welfare can be addressed effectively only on a global scale." Scientific syntheses (Castonguay et al. 1994; ICES 2001; Casselman 2003; Casselman and Cairns 2005) continue to highlight the need for continent-scale management approaches.

Management of shared fisheries of the Great Lakes is facilitated by binational Lake Committees established under the Great Lakes Fishery Commission (GLFC; set up in 1954 by a U.S.–Canada convention) and the Joint Strategic Plan for Management of Great Lakes Fisheries (an interagency agreement signed in 1981). The Lake Ontario Committee of the GLFC issued the following position statement on American eels in March 2002.

• American eel are a valuable component of the upper St. Lawrence River/Lake Ontario ecosystem which has contributed to the biological diversity of the system and provided an important commercial fishery in Ontario until the late 1990s.

• The American eel population is in serious decline and recruitment to the upper St. Lawrence River/Lake Ontario has now virtually ceased.

• Without management intervention, extirpation of the American eel in the Great Lakes Basin is likely.

• Management actions within the St. Lawrence River and Lake Ontario should be taken to reduce eel mortality (at all life stages), and encourage safe, effective upstream and downstream migration.

• To prevent extirpation of the American eel from the Great Lakes Basin, and possibly address management issues elsewhere in the eel's range, the actions above should be implemented in conjunction with a management plan to sustain this species throughout its range, coordinated by Canadian and U.S. federal agencies.

In summary, American eels have provided an important fishery in LO/SLR for well over a century. Fisheries managers in Ontario became concerned over the status of the eel fishery as early as 1980. Major declines in the fishery have occurred over the past decade, and predictions based on the level of migration of young eels into LO/SLR suggest the fishery upstream of the Moses-Saunders Power Dam will all but disappear. Actions within Ontario to sustain the fishery in this portion of the eel's range have not been identified to date. The GLFC position statement recognizes the ecological and commercial value of the eel, highlights the gravity of the observed decline, and makes a commitment to pursue continent-scale management planning. Sustainable management practices throughout the range of this panmictic species will be required to prevent extirpation of this important Great Lakes fish species and to restore eels as an abundant species in the LO/SLR.

Postscript

Due to continuing conservation concerns, the province of Ontario closed all commercial eel fisheries within its waters in 2004.

Acknowledgments

This paper is made possible due to the work of the many Ontario Ministry of Natural Resources staff who collected and managed the commercial harvest data. In particular we thank Kelly Sarley for her efforts to provide reliable catch statistics. Thanks to Julie Weeder and John Clark for their helpful comments on an earlier draft of this manuscript.

References

Avise, J. C., G. S. Helfman, N.C. Saunders, and L. S. Hales. 1986. Mitochondrial DNA differentiation in North Atlantic eels: population genetic consequences of an unusual life history pattern. Proceedings of the National Academy of Sciences 83:4350–4354.

Baldwin, N. S., R. W. Saafeld, M. A. Ross, and H. J. Buettner. 1979. Commercial fish production in the Great Lakes 1867–1977. Great Lakes Fisheries Commission Technical Report no. 3.

Casselman, J. M. 2003. Dynamics of resources of the American eel, *Anguilla rostrata*: declining abundance in the 1990s. Pages 255–274 *in* K. Aida, K. Tsukamoto, and K. Yamauchi, editors. Eel biology. Springer-Verlag, Tokyo.

Casselman, J. M., and D. K. Cairns, editors. 2008. Eels at the edge: science, status, and conservation concerns. American Fisheries Society, Symposium 58, Bethesda, Maryland.

Casselman, J. M., L. A. Marcogliese, and P. V. Hodson. 1997a. Recruitment index for the upper St. Lawrence River and Lake Ontario eel stock: a re-examination of eel passage at the R. H. Saunders hydroelectric generating station at Cornwall, Ontario, 1974–1995. Pages 161–169 *in* R. H. Peterson, editor. The American eel in eastern Canada: stock status and management strategies. Canadian Technical Report of Fisheries and Aquatic Sciences No. 2196.

Casselman, J. M., L. A. Marcogliese, T. J. Stewart, and P. V. Hodson. 1997b. Status of upper St. Lawrence River and Lake Ontario eel stock—1996. Pages 106–120 *in* R. H. Peterson, editor. The American eel in eastern Canada: stock status and management strategies. Canadian Technical Report of Fisheries and Aquatic Sciences No. 2196.

Castonguay, M., P. V. Hodson, C.M. Couillard, M.J. Eckersley, J.-D. Dutil, and G. Verrault. 1994. Why is recruitment of the American eel, Anguilla rostrata, declining in the St. Lawrence River and Gulf? Canadian Journal of Fisheries and Aquatic Sciences 51:479–488.

Christie, W. J. 1973. A review of the changes in the fish species composition of Lake Ontario. Great Lakes Fisheries Commission Technical Report no. 23.

Christie, W. J., K. A. Scott, P. G. Sly, and R. H. Strus. 1987. Recent changes in the aquatic food web of eastern Lake Ontario. Canadian Journal of Fisheries and Aquatic Sciences 44(Supplement 2):37–52.

Hurley, D. A. 1973. The commercial fishery for American eel *Anguilla rostrata* (Lesueur) in Lake Ontario. Transactions of the American Fisheries Society 102:369–377.

ICES 2001. Report of the EIFAC/ICES working group on eels. Advisory Committee on Fisheries Management. ICES CM 2001/ACFM:03

Kolenosky, D. P., and M. J. Hendry. 1982. The Canadian Lake Ontario fishery for American eel (*Anguilla rostrata*). Pages 8–16 *in* K. H. Loftus, editor. Proceedings of the 1980 North American eel conference. Ontario Fisheries Technical Report Series no 4.

Lary, S. J., and W. D. N. Busch. 1997. American eel (*Anguilla rostrata*) in Lake Ontario and its tributaries: distribution, abundance, essential habitat, and restoration requirements. Administrative Report 97–01. U.S. Fish and Wildlife Service, Amherst, New York.

Scott W. B., and E. J. Crossman. 1998. Freshwater fishes of Canada. Galt House Publications, Oakville, Ontario.

Stewart, T. J., J. M. Casselman, and L. A. Marcogliese. 1997. Management of the American eel (*Anguilla rostrata*) in Lake Ontario and the upper St. Lawrence River. Pages 54–61 *in* R. H. Peterson, editor. The American eel in eastern Canada: stock status and management strategies. Canadian Technical Report of Fisheries and Aquatic Sciences no. 2196.

Wirth, T., and L. Bernatchez. 2003. Decline of North Atlantic eels: a fatal synergy? Proceedings of the Royal Society of London, Series B. Biological Sciences 270:681–688.

Management of European Eel Populations in England and in Wales: a Critical Review and Pragmatic Considerations

Brian Knights[1],*

School of Biosciences, University of Westminster
115 New Cavendish Street, London W1W 6UW UK

Anthony Bark and Beth Williams

Department of Geography, King's College London
Norfolk Building, Surrey Street, London WC2R 2LS UK

Abstract.—Recruitment and fisheries for the European eel *Anguilla anguilla* have declined in recent decades. We discuss a precautionary-principle approach to stock management that takes into account methodological problems, with particular reference to studies in England and Wales. Pragmatic surrogate Biological Reference Point management targets and compliance assessment are reviewed. Biological Reference Points based on patterns of density, biomass, and mean individual size with distance from tidal limits in relatively pristine rivers are recommended. Distances from the edge of the continental shelf and from spawning areas also need to be taken into account. We make pragmatic suggestions for collation of commercial and fisheries-survey data, setting and monitoring BRP targets and management options to maximize in-river stocks and hence spawner escapement.

Introduction

Fisheries biologists have expressed concern about declines in recruitment and fisheries of the European eel *Anguilla anguilla* over recent decades (Dekker et al. 2003). The American eel *A. rostrata* and Japanese eel *A. japonica* have shown parallel declines (Knights 2003). The International Council for the Exploration of the Sea (ICES) has called for action, and the European Commission and Parliament have proposed stock recovery and Eel Management Plans. National or international initiatives require collation of the best information available on recruitment, stocks, and fisheries to identify parameters for defining precautionary targets. These need to be set and compliance with them enforced to ensure survival of eels through each life stage to maximize spawner escapement and minimize the risk of stock collapse. Although local targets and management initiatives are important, these will have to take into account international dimensions, given the widespread continental distribution of eels (e.g., see Dekker 2009, this volume).

This paper critically reviews information for England and Wales and makes recommendations, in the context of the precautionary principle, for surrogate biological reference point (BRP) management targets and compliance assessment.

---

[1] Corresponding author: PandBKnights@aol.com
*Current address: Department of Geography, King's College London, Norfolk Building, Surrey Street, London WC2R 2LS UK

Causes of Recruitment Declines and Application of the Precautionary Principle

Decadal-scale changes in currents and food supply may have affected survival of leptocephalus larvae during their oceanic migration (Knights 2003). Possible anthropogenic factors include overfishing, habitat loss and degradation, pollution, parasites, and in-river migration barriers (e.g., Dekker 2003; Knights 2003). In the face of such uncertainties, the precautionary approach needs to be applied (Russell and Potter 2003). This states that if there is evidence of threats or irreversible damage to eel stocks, lack of clear scientific information should not be used as a reason for postponing, or failing to take, conservation and management measures. Application of the precautionary approach requires that the best available scientific evidence be used to set management reference points.

Data Collection, Collation, and Analyses

The ICES Working Group on Eels has discussed methods for assessing recruitment, resident stocks, and spawner escapement and has collated information from different countries and proposed management options (e.g., ICES 2004). Studies funded by government agencies in England and Wales provide some of the most complete and countrywide overviews. These form the basis of this paper.

Commercial catch data for glass, yellow, and silver eels can provide useful indications of stocks and changes, although information is often under-reported or incomplete (Knights et al. 2001; Knights 2002). Catch data are also subject to variations in fishing effort in response to international market demands, including competition from eel farms (Knights 2002, 2003; Ringuet et al. 2002). However, analyses of annual import-export and fishing-effort data can provide useful information on recruitment and exploitation for low cost. Fishery licensing systems also help in monitoring exploitation while providing possible means of management control (e.g., limits on numbers, methods, and fishing locations).

Direct assessments of glass eel recruitment were reviewed and recommendations for future monitoring made by Knights et al. (1996, 2001) and Dekker (2002). The timing and extent of glass eel runs vary greatly between years and locations. Also, much of the effective recruitment to freshwater may arise from elvers and yellow eels migrating upstream throughout the year (Naismith and Knights 1988, 1993; White and Knights 1997 a, b; Ibbotson et al. 2002; Feunteun et al. 2003). Silver eel spawner escapement is difficult to measure, and timing and sizes of runs is variable. Furthermore, studies of Sr:Ca ratios in otoliths show that silver eels may have spent part or all of their growth stage in estuarine or coastal waters (Jessop et al. 2002; Tzeng et al. 2003). These findings pose challenges in basing management targets on stock–recruitment models that require direct measurements of recruitment and escapement (ICES 2004).

Efficient and reproducible sampling of yellow eel populations is problematic (Knights et al. 1996). For example, routine multispecies electrofishing surveys can underestimate population densities by as much as 15-fold compared to surveys aimed specifically at sampling eels (Knights et al. 2001; Bark et al. 2009, this volume). Electrofishing samples eels only during daylight when they are hiding in burrows or crevices, thus results may not represent true densities and habitat carrying capacities or overall feeding-habitat preferences (Knights et al. 1996; Knights et al. 2001). Seasonal changes due to migrations can also distort sampling, as illustrated in Figure 1 for the St. Neot River (southwest England). Even larger yellow eels (>35 cm) in upper reaches (>25 km from the tidal limit) show variability, although they might be expected to be relatively sedentary and ter-

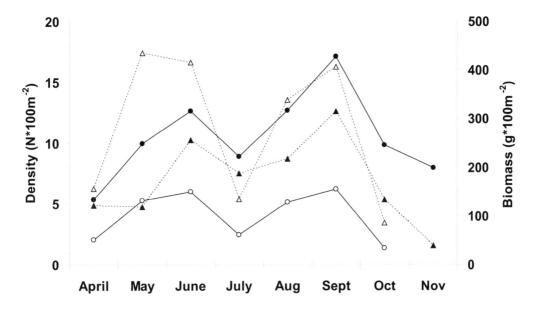

Figure 1. Seasonal changes in mean density (circles and solid lines) and biomass (triangles and dotted lines) of eel populations in the St. Neot River (southwest England), 1977–1980. The graph shows combined data for ten matching upstream sites (u/s) at >25 km from the tidal limit (open symbols) and combined data for six matching downstream sites (d/s) <25 km (closed symbols).

ritorial (Feunteun et al. 2003). Thus, management targets based on population parameters must take into account time of year, as well as survey sites. Similar problems apply to fyke netting and other passive sampling techniques (Knights et al. 1996). These methods also tend to be very size-selective, and estimates of population density can usually be expressed only in relative terms, as catch per unit effort (CPUE).

To help compensate for these drawbacks, all available sources of data should be used, such as scientific studies, fish-counter information, angling tournament records, and power-station intake catches. Ideally, long-term data series should be used from a wide geographical range of habitats of different types. Even if spatiotemporal comparisons are not statistically robust, overviews can be gained and anomalies requiring further attention identified. However, focused spatiotemporal studies need to be conducted for fine-tuning and to produce information for developing models for data-poor situations (e.g., see Bark et al. 2009).

Identification of Parameters for Defining Management Targets

Management targets need to be defined and tested in different eel habitats. Such targets would have biological threshold reference levels (conservation limits) below which stocks should not fall. Considering the uncertainties about eel-stock dynamics and their measurement, the best available information should be used to set management targets above these limits. These can then be used to ensure that appropriate management controls are applied before stocks begin to be negatively affected.

Ideally, conservation limits should ensure production and escapement of sufficient spawning biomass to maintain optimum recruitment. The target generally accepted in Europe is that fishery mortality (or other anthropogenic factors) acting during different life stages should not reduce spawner escapement to less than 40% of that expected in pristine systems. However, there are few catchments, especially in England and Wales, that haven't been impacted by water mills, land drainage, flood regulation, navigation or other human activities, often over many centuries. Thus pristine systems have to be defined as baseline systems that are minimally affected and with eel population data dating from the 1980s, before recruitment showed major declines.

Ideally, models are needed that can link recruitment, impacts of natural and anthropogenic factors on survival through all life stages, and eventual spawner escapement. Models include those based on spawning-stock biomass per recruit; harvest rate; length-, size-, and age-structure; and population dynamics (Sparre 1979; Vøllestad and Jonsson 1988; Naismith and Knights 1990; de Leo and Gatto 1995; Dekker 1996, 2000; Francis and Jellyman 1999; de Leo 2009, this volume). Ideally, limit values should be derived from stock–recruitment relationships, but levels of recruitment and spawner escapement and critical size of the spawning stock are unknown. Thus the status of yellow eel stocks has to be used as a proxy measure of spawner escapement (Dekker 2009. Until robust quantitative models have been developed and validated, simpler ones involving surrogate targets and pragmatic compliance measures will have to be used as discussed below.

Surrogate Targets and Compliance Measures for Riverine Stocks

Patterns of population indices related to environmental characteristics have been proposed as surrogates, such as the BRP model of Knights et al. (2001) and the Reference Condition model (RCM) proposed in ICES (2004). Such models can provide proxy standards for what should be expected in pristine and unexploited waters, based on population indices. Deviations from such patterns would signal the need to assess whether fisheries or other anthropogenic disturbances, such as migration barriers, were to blame. If significant deviations are found, appropriate management measures would need to be instituted.

Population Indices for Setting BRPs

Population indices can be based on optimal levels and catchment distribution patterns of one or more of density, biomass, length-frequency distribution, average individual size, growth rate, age distribution, proportion of silver eels, or sex ratio. At the broad geographical scale, distances of catchments from oceanic migration pathways and the edge of the continental shelf will influence relative levels of recruitment, hence population densities and sex ratios. At the catchment level, key variables are initial levels of recruitment, distance from the tidal limit, habitat productivity, average temperatures and length of the growing season, and availability of substrate for cover during daylight. Unfortunately, relatively little is known about populations in still waters, estuaries, and coastal waters (Jessop et al. 2002; Knights et al. 2001; Oliveira et al. 2001; Tzeng et al. 2003).

Growth Rate and Age-Distribution Indices

A lack of younger age classes in a population could be a sign of overfishing of glass eels or recruitment failure, or both. Conversely, a lack of older eels could signal high fishing mortality of large yellow eels. However, growth rates and size-at-age relationships can be very variable in eels, and problems are compounded by inaccuracies in otolithometry. Inter-seasonal and inter-annual migrations of yellow eels cause further complications, because growth rates of migrants may differ from those of resident eels (Naismith and Knights 1988; White and Knights 1997a; b; Jessop et al. 2002; Tzeng et al. 2003). In addition to the lack of clear predictive precision, the need for large samples and resource costs involved in otolithometry militate against routine use of age structures and growth rates for setting BRPs.

Indices Based on Length-Class Frequencies (LCF) and Sex Ratios

Declines in the proportions of small eels (<20 cm) and increases in those of larger eels in lower river sites can indicate recruitment failures or overfishing of glass eels. Statistically, changes in LCF distributions can be more sensitive indicators of fishing mortality than density or biomass in such habitats (Knights et al. 2001). Overfishing of yellow eels should lead to declines in larger size classes, accompanied by shifts in sex ratios in favor of male eels, as seen in some intensive fisheries (Dekker 1996). However, LCF distributions are often variable in estuaries and in low-density sites in upper reaches of rivers and in still waters. This is because sample sizes are often small and distributions are commonly multi-modal or skewed because of interseasonal and interannual migrations (e.g., see Figure 1).

High variability also affects indices based on relative abundances of size groups representing different life stages (e.g., <15 cm (elvers and small juveniles), 15–30 cm [sexually immature yellow eels], and so on up to female silver eels of >45 cm). Measuring the proportions of males versus females and silver eels in samples can yield useful information, but again, these can be subject to variability. Furthermore, all these approaches require detailed analyses of samples, which are time-consuming and costly. Useful information can, however, be gained from the average length of eels in a site, estimated by dividing biomass by density and then converting weight to length, using appropriate length-weight relationships. For example, Acou et al. (2009, this volume) showed that males would be expected to be dominant at densities more than 40–50 eels·100 m^{-2}, females at densities under 2–4 eels·100 m^{-2}.

Density and Biomass Indices

Electrofishing data are generally the most widely available measures of stock status. Glass eel recruitment failure or overfishing could lead to declines in density and biomass. However, even if density declined relatively quickly, reduced competition would be expected to enhance growth rates and hence maintain biomass. This was demonstrated in modeling studies for the River Loire, France (Feunteun et al. 2000). When recruitment declined, density fell after 2–5 years, but biomasses increased in the short term because of enhanced growth rates at low densities. Biomasses began to decline only after about 2 and 6 years at high and low mortality levels, respectively. Despite these predictions, neither density nor biomass declined significantly in the Loire in comparison with other French rivers (Lambert and Rigaud 1999). The French Bay of Biscay rivers directly face Atlantic migration pathways and thus receive relatively high levels of recruitment and support important glass eel fisheries. Despite high glass eel fishing mortality, the number of survivors appears to have been sufficient to meet local carrying capacities. The same applies to the River Severn in southwest England (Bark et al. 2009).

These findings imply that, ideally, both biomass and density need to be considered in setting BRPs. The impacts of recruitment failure or glass eel overfishing may still not become apparent for many years, but overfishing of yellow eels might be detectable over a shorter time in highly exploited systems where recruitment is relatively poor, for example, as found in the IJsselmeer in the Netherlands (Dekker 2000).

Presence–Absence Data

Mapping of presence–absence data can yield useful information, such as major temporal changes in distribution in catchments. It also helps pinpoint particular bottlenecks. For example, Environment Agency Fisheries Classification System maps for England and Wales show eels present in some upper tributaries of catchments in North Wessex (southwest England) but not in others. Despite major glass eel fisheries being based in the estuaries of these rivers, overall stock levels are high and absences can be clearly related to specific dams and weirs (Knights et al. 2001).

Conclusions Regarding Population Indices

Changes in modal and average size and size-class distributions can provide information about recruitment failures and glass eel fishing mortality in lower river reaches. However, natural variability can be very high, and as discussed above, such data are generally less useful for detecting changes caused by growth overfishing in other river sites. They are likely to indicate growth overfishing only in highly exploited systems where recruitment is poor. Thus density and biomass appear to be the most useful population indices, supplemented if possible by population-structure analyses.

In data-rich situations, temporal trends between surveys can be determined, However, intensive electrofishing surveys have shown that ~20–25 repeat surveys of the same site(s) and at the same time(s) of the year are needed to make robust statistical comparisons (Knights et al. 2001; Bark et al. 2009). In catchments being surveyed for the first time or in data-poor situations, comparisons of density, biomass, and size distributions with distance from the tidal limits can be used to set base targets, as discussed further below.

Habitat Suitability Indices and the Setting of BRPs

Habitat suitability index (HSI) modeling can help clarify the relative importance of various environmental factors on population distributions and other characteristics (e.g., Milner et al. 1993; ICES 2004). In its simplest form, this involves allocating scores to each factor (e.g., from 0 for unsuitable to maintain a viable population to 1 for optimal habitat). A habitat-evaluation procedure is then used to score catchments and compare relationships with reference catchments to validate the parameters of the model and to assess their relative importance.

If enough data are available, an HSI approach can determine statistical relationships between environmental variables and population data. Knights et al. (2001) used this approach for eels in England and Wales, using key habitat parameters derived from literature reviews and those proposed by Schouten (1992, unpublished report) and Klein Bretelier (1996). Eel densities were compared with environmental parameters recorded for the same sites in the (former) National Rivers Authority HABSCORE and Fisheries Classification System (FCS) databases. A total of 361 data sets were analyzed, covering a range of river types, mostly dating from the 1980s when recruitment was still relatively high.

Local habitat preferences of eels were found to be very wide-ranging and, overall, densities were not significantly correlated with altitude, gradient, conductivity, flow, water depth, or substrate and vegetation cover. The only consistently significant relationship was for density (and, to a lesser extent, biomass) to decline logarithmically with distance from the tidal limit. Gradient was not a good overall predictor, probably because eels can easily scale some steeply rising rivers, whereas in others, natural or artificial barriers impede upstream migration. Also, gradients tend to be much lower in the southern and eastern lowlands of England, where the impacts of flood and water-level control structures are greatest. Thus HSI approaches are limited; detailed models derived from one ecosystem can produce good predictions when applied to a similar ecosystem but are restricted in their broader applications. Similar conclusions have been reached in other eel studies (e.g., Growns et al. 1998; Jellyman et al. 2003).

Geographical and Regional BRP Factors

Densities and other population characteristics are strongly dependent on geographical location and regional characteristics of different catchments. Average densities are influenced by the relative magnitude of initial recruitment, which is dependent on migration distance from the Sargasso Sea and from the edge of the continental shelf, where leptocephali detrain from the North Atlantic Drift and commence metamorphosis into glass eels. For example, Figure 2 shows density, biomass, and average length per site with distance from the tidal limits in 11 catchments in the southwest of England compared to nine in the Anglian region on the east coast. The data were collected between the late 1970s and early 1990s, and Figure 2 includes densities of zero for sites where no eels were found. The data show considerable scatter because of natural and sampling variability, but none of the rivers support significant eel fisheries. The southwest rivers are closer to the edge of the continental shelf and thus receive better recruitment than the east coast rivers that discharge into the North Sea. This explains the higher densities in the southwest rivers, smaller mean individual weights, and the predominance of males smaller than 45 cm. Similar patterns are seen in other coastal rivers facing the Atlantic, such as those in Brittany and the Bay of Biscay, France (e.g., Lambert and Rigaud 1999; Feunteun et al. 2003).

In contrast, the east coast rivers of England receive poorer recruitment (Devall 1998), leading to much lower densities, by ~90% on average (Figure 2). Mean biomass was, however, only about 55% of that in southwest England because of the larger average size of eels and predominance of females larger than 45 cm. Densities and biomasses tend to decline more noticeably with distance from tidal limits compared to the southwest rivers. The east coast rivers are productive lowland ones, but they are heavily modified, with tidal sluices, weirs, and other structures forming potentially important migration barriers. Electrofishing is also relatively inefficient in the impounded river reaches. Many recruits may also preferentially inhabit the large shallow estuarine areas associated with these rivers.

These examples show that recruitment and population characteristics are influenced by distance from the edge of the continental shelf (DCS km). Where sufficient data are available for all river reaches, comparisons can be made between mean density, biomass, and body length for a whole catchment and its DCS. Such data for eight individual rivers or regional groupings in England are shown in Figure 3. Data are lacking for Welsh rivers and the salmonid rivers of the northwest and northeast coasts, but there is sufficient for the River Tweed in Scotland. Despite its high latitude, this river supported relatively good eel stocks because of the relatively short DCS of 420 km, with migrants detraining from the North Atlantic Drift to use currents passing around the north of Scotland. Differences in distance from the Sargasso Sea between rivers were minor because of the relatively small latitudinal range between north and south Britain. However, such distances might have to be considered when comparing catchments at more extreme southerly and northerly latitudes.

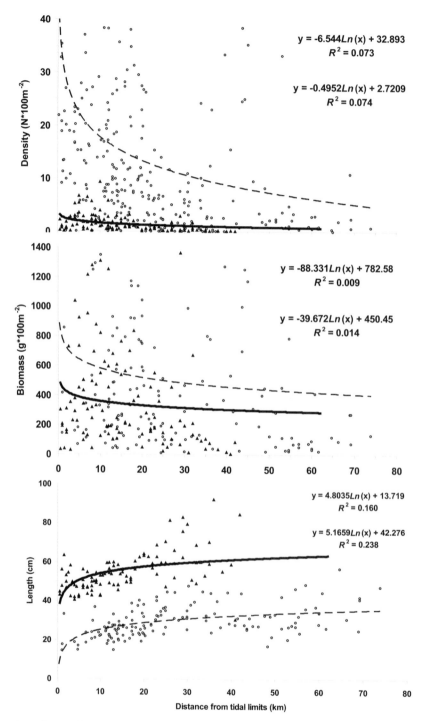

Figure 2. Relationships between density, biomass, and mean individual length per site and distance from the tidal limits during 1989–1990 for eleven rivers in southwest England (open circles and dashed trend lines, 279 sites) and nine east coast rivers (closed triangles and solid trend lines, 104 sites). Seventeen outlier results for density in the southwest rivers have been omitted. In each graph, the uppermost trend line equation refers to southwest England data.

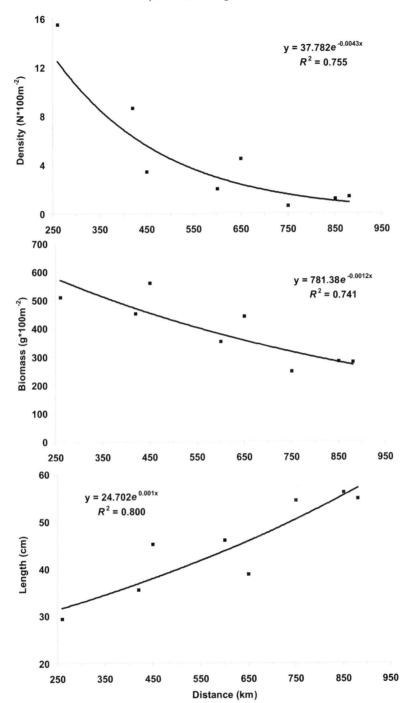

Figure 3. Relationships between average density, biomass, and mean individual weight for various rivers in Britain grouped by region and their approximate distance from the edge of the continental shelf. The sequence with distance is southwest England (9 rivers, 146 sites), River Tweed (northeast Scotland, 30 sites), Wessex (3 rivers, 27 sites), west-central England (5 rivers, 79 sites), south England (4 rivers, 29 sites), Thames (25 sites), Essex (4 rivers, 17 sites), and Anglian region (9 rivers, 106 sites).

Broader international comparisons require the collection of more data, but, for example, the pattern for southwestern rivers in England agrees well with that for French Brittany-Bay of Biscay rivers, which are even closer to the edge of the continental shelf, at 90–100 km (Feunteun et al. 1998, 2003). Similar results might be expected for the Atlantic rivers of the Iberian Peninsula. However, in southwest Portugal, although eels were the second most abundant species after European chub *Leuciscus cephalus*, their distribution and density were principally determined by summer drying up of headwaters at higher altitudes (Magalhães et al. 2002). Conversely, relatively poor recruitment leads to low densities in more distant habitats, such as the IJsselmeer in the Netherlands and the Baltic Sea, at DCS of ~850 km and ~980 km, respectively (Tesch 2003). Similar factors would explain the clines seen in other eel species at higher latitudes in North America (Casselman 2003) and the Far East (Tesch 2003).

The RCM model proposed in ICES (2004) ignored sites with no eels but estimated the exponential change in eel density with river gradient and compared this to the mean pattern of change for a combination of reference rivers from various geographical regions in England. Differences between areas under the curves were assumed to represent shortfalls in spawning stock biomass and spawner escapement, expressed as a percentage. An alternative BRP approach is to utilize density, biomass, and mean length data wherever possible and to make comparisons based on DTL and DCS rather than on gradient. In the absence of truly pristine rivers, baseline rivers need to be selected (i.e., ones of similar geographical positions and types but minimally affected by fisheries, migration barriers, or other human influences). Ideal baseline rivers should also have eel data from the 1970s or 1980s, when recruitment was still relatively high.

Using this BRP approach and comparing datasets for rivers in England and Wales with appropriate reference ones (Figures 2 and 3) has revealed some aberrant relationships and suggested possible causes and management actions (Knights et al. 2001). For example, in some catchments, marked discontinuities in population densities and structures revealed bottlenecks that could be related to specific migration barriers, signaling the need for eel passes. As a broader-scale example, the River Medway in southeastern England discharges into the Thames Estuary and hence into the North Sea at a DCS of ~800 km. Thus recruitment and population status would be expected to be similar to the Anglian reference rivers. However, eels were found in only 26 (41%) of 89 sites surveyed, and density and biomass were only 12.5% and 17.0%, respectively, of the levels predicted from the DCS trend line in Figure 3 (B. Knights, unpublished results). Furthermore, areas under the density and biomass versus DTL curves for the Medway were 10.6% and 15.5%, respectively, of areas for the baseline rivers (Figure 2). Thus it appears that spawner escapement is well below a 40% target, although the average length of eels in the Medway is 60.7 ± 15.6 cm, compared to 54.8 ± 10.1 cm. The most likely reasons for the low stocks are that the Medway is one of the most heavily regulated rivers in England, with barriers to migration posed by tidal sluices and weirs exacerbating the impacts of post1980 recruitment declines. This signals a need to consider eel passes or upstream stocking.

Considering temporal trends, only a few comparisons have suggested that populations in England and Wales have declined since the 1970–1980s, but some of these were found to be due to changes in fisheries-survey techniques over time (Knights et al. 2001). Statistically significant declines have, however, been found in some east coast rivers where migration barriers have probably exacerbated the impacts of declines in recruitment. Continuing surveys are needed to clarify causes and to decide on appropriate management remedies (e.g., the benefits of providing eel passes or stocking). The same applies to the River Piddle on the south coast, where populations have declined since the 1970s (Bark et al. 2009).

No evidence has been found for deleterious impacts of eel fisheries on populations (Naismith and Knights 1990; Knights et al. 2001), even in the River Severn, despite the large glass eel fishery in its estuary (Bark et al. 2009).

Targets, Compliance Measurements, and Management Options

Biological reference point management levels need to be set to help maintain population densities and structures comparable to pristine rivers. However, all rivers in England and Wales (and many throughout Europe and North America) have been modified over centuries, and there is no historical information available on eel stocks. The pragmatic approach discussed above involves selection of reference baseline rivers that are least affected by human intervention and for which information is available on the status of eels before major declines in recruitment occurred. However, natural and sampling variability are often high, and Knights et al. (2001) found that differences of ± 25% in density or biomass were needed to reliably indicate significant changes in a catchment over time or differences from reference rivers.

Compliance Assessment

Examples discussed above show that BRP criteria can be used for detecting noncompliance with BRP management targets set on baseline reference rivers. Tracking of fisheries data are a relatively cost-effective means of gaining broad indications of whether national and international targets are being exceeded. However, rolling programs of well-designed electrofishing surveys in selected indicator rivers (including ones with known eel fisheries) were recommended as the best direct monitoring approach by Knights et al. (2001). More specific one-time-only surveys would be needed if there is any evidence of noncompliance with targets.

Selecting Management Options

If fishing mortality is implicated, exploitation could be controlled by imposing closed seasons. However, because of high natural variability and interseasonal and interannual migrations, these would need to span long periods to be fully effective. Closed-area measures or restrictions on gear numbers, types (including mesh-sizes), and uses may also be beneficial. Silver eel trapping devices, where permitted, should cover no more than 50% of the total width of a channel unless there are other routes for escapement of spawners. Knights et al. (2001) also recommended that licenses should be issued annually to individual fishermen and that these should include relevant conditions (including requirements for annual catch and effort returns).

Proactive management options include the provision of eel passes on barriers and stocking. However, the benefits of these and other management approaches require prior assessment and careful subsequent monitoring (Knights and White 1997, 1998; Pedersen 2009, this volume).

Conclusions

The precautionary principle must be applied to managing eels during their continental life stages to protect spawner escapement from rivers. More research is, however, required on estuarine and coastal populations. Much effort is being devoted to monitoring and quantitative modeling, but the Biological

Reference Point approaches suggested in this paper offer useful pragmatic alternatives.

Acknowledgments

The Environment Agency and the (former) Ministry of Agriculture Fisheries and Food of the United Kingdom jointly funded the studies cited as Knights et al. (2001). The Environment Agency funded the studies cited as Knights (2002). However, the views expressed in this paper are those of the authors alone and may not reflect those of the funding bodies. Thanks are also due to the anonymous reviewers of the manuscript.

References

Acou, A., G. Gabriel, P. Laffaille, and E. Feunteun. 2009. Differential production and condition indices of premigrant eels in two small Atlantic coastal catchments of France. Pages 157–174 in J. M. Casselman and D. K. Cairns, editors. Eels at the edge: science, status, and conservation concerns. American Fisheries Society, Symposium 58, Bethesda, Maryland.

Bark, A., B. Williams, B. Williams, and B. Knights. 2009. Long term changes in recruitment, population dynamics, and status of the European eel in two English river systems. Pages 241–256 in J. M. Casselman and D. K. Cairns, editors. Eels at the edge: science, status, and conservation concerns. American Fisheries Society, Symposium 58, Bethesda, Maryland.

Casselman, J. M. 2003. Dynamics of resources of the American eel, *Anguilla rostrata*: declining abundance in the 1990s. Pages 255–274 in K. Aida, K. Tsukamoto, and K. Yamauchi, editors. Eel biology, Springer-Verlag Tokyo.

Dekker, W. 1996. A length structured matrix population model, used as a fish stock assessment tool. Pages 121–140 in I. G. Cowx, editor. 1996. Stocking and introduction of fish. Fishing News Books/Blackwell Scientific Publications Scientific, Oxford, England.

Dekker, W. 2000. Impact of yellow eel exploitation on spawner production in Lake IJsselmeer, the Netherlands. Dana 12:17–32.

Dekker, W., editor. 2002. Monitoring of glass eel recruitment. Report C007/02-WD. Netherlands Institute of Fisheries Research, Ijmuiden, The Netherlands.

Dekker, W. 2003. Status of the European eel stock and fisheries. Pages 237–254 in K. Aida, K. Tsukamoto, and K. Yamauchi editors. 2003. Eel biology. Springer-Verlag, Tokyo.

Dekker, W. 2009. A conceptual management framework for the restoration of the declining European eel stock. Pages 3–19 in J. M. Casselman and D. K. Cairns, editors. Eels at the edge: science, status, and conservation concerns. American Fisheries Society, Symposium 58, Bethesda, Maryland.

Dekker, W., J. M. Casselman, D. K. Cairns, K. Tsukamoto, D. Jellyman, and H. Lickers. 2003. Worldwide decline of eel resources necessitates immediate action. Quebec Declaration of Concern. Fisheries 28(12):28–30.

De Leo, G. A., and M. Gatto. 1995. A size and age-structured model of the European eel (*Anguilla anguilla* L.). Canadian Journal of Fisheries and Aquatic Sciences 52:1351–1367.

De Leo, G. A., P. Melià, M. Gatto, and A. J. Crivelli. 2009. Eel population modeling and its application to conservation management. Pages 327–345 in J. M. Casselman and D. K. Cairns, editors. Eels at the edge: science, status, and conservation concerns. American Fisheries Society, Symposium 58, Bethesda, Maryland.

Devall, C. A. 1998. Maldon and the tidal Blackwater, volume 1: Heybridge Basin eel industry, 1928–1968. C. E. Devall, Chelmsford, Essex, UK.

Feunteun, E., A. Acou, J. Guillouet, P. Laffaille, and A. Legault. 1998. Spatial distribution of an eel population (*Anguilla anguilla* L.) in a small coastal catchment of northern Brittany (France). Consequences of hydraulic works. Bulletin Français de Peche et Pisciculture 349:129–139.

Feunteun, E., A. Acou, P. Laffaille, and A. Legault. 2000. European eel (*Anguilla anguilla*): prediction of spawner escapement from continental population parameters. Canadian Journal of Fisheries and Aquatic Sciences 57:1627–1635.

Feunteun, E., P. Laffaille, T. Robinet, C. Briand, A. Baisez, J.-M. Olivier, and A. Acou. 2003. A review of upstream migration and movements in inland waters by anguillid eels: towards a general theory. Pages 191–214 in K. Aida, K. Tsukamoto, and K. Yamauchi editors. 2003. Eel biology. Springer-Verlag, Tokyo.

Francis, R. I. C. C., and D. J. Jellyman. 1999. Are mean size data adequate to monitor freshwater eel fisheries? Marine and Freshwater Research 50:355–366.

Growns, I. O., D. A. Pollard, and P. C. Gherke. 1998. Changes in fish assemblages associated with vegetated and degraded banks, upstream of and within nutrient-enriched zones. Fisheries Management and Ecology 5:55–69.

Ibbotson, A., J. Smith, P. Scarlett, and M. Aprahamian. 2002. Colonisation of freshwater habitats by the European eel *Anguilla anguilla*. Freshwater Biology 47:1696–1706.

ICES (International Council for Exploration of the Sea). 2004. Report of the ICES Advisory Committee on Fisheries Management, 2004. C.M. 2004/ACFM:09. International Council for Exploration of the Sea, Copenhagen, Denmark.

Jellyman, D. J., M. L. Bonnett, J. R. E. Sykes, and P. Johnstone. 2003. Contrasting use of daytime habitat by two species of freshwater eel *Anguilla* species in New Zealand rivers. Pages 63–78 *in* D. A. Dixon, editor. Biology, management, and protection of catadromous eels. American Fisheries Society, Symposium 33, Bethesda, Maryland.

Jessop, B. M., J.-C. Shiao, Y. Iizuka, and W.-N. Tzeng. 2002. Migratory behaviour and habitat use by American eels *Anguilla rostrata* as revealed by otolith microchemistry. Marine Ecology Progress Series 233:217–229.

Klein Breteler, J. G. P. 1996. Application of a habitat suitability index model for eel *Anguilla anguilla* in a habitat evaluation procedure for the Netherlands in the 19th and 20th century. EIFAC Working Party on Eels, IJmuiden, The Netherlands. EIFAC/ FAO, Rome..

Knights, B. 2002, Economic evaluation of eel and elver fisheries in England and Wales. Environment Agency Technical Report No. W2–039/TR/2. Environment Agency, Bristol, UK.

Knights, B. 2003. A review of the possible impacts of long-term oceanic and climate changes and fishing mortality on recruitment of anguillid eels of the Northern Hemisphere. The Science of the Total Environment 310:217–244.

Knights, B., A. Bark, M. Ball, F. Williams, E. Winter, and S. Dunn. 2001. Eel and elver stocks in England and Wales–status and management options. EA Research and Development Technical Report W248/MAFF R&D Project SFO307. Environment Agency, Bristol, UK.

Knights, B., and E. M. White. 1997. An appraisal of stocking strategies for the European eel, *Anguilla anguilla* L. Pages 121–150 *in* I. G. Cowx editors. 1997. Stocking and introduction of fish. Fishing News Books/Blackwell Scientific Publications Scientific, Oxford, England.

Knights, B., and E. M. White. 1998. Enhancing immigration and recruitment of eels: the use of passes and associated trapping systems. Fisheries Management and Ecology 4:311–324.

Knights, B., E. White, and I. A. Naismith. 1996. Stock assessment of European eel, *Anguilla anguilla* L. Pages 431–447 *in* I. G. Cowx editors. 1996. Stock assessment in inland fisheries. Fishing News Books/Blackwell Scientific Publications Scientific, Oxford, England.

Lambert, P., and C. Rigaud. 1999. Recherche d'éléments de gestion de la population d'anguilles sur la base des données produites par RHP (Convention d'études CSP-Cemagref No 97 420). Cemagref Departement Gestion des Milieux Aquatiques, Études No. 49, Cemagref, France.

Magalhães, M. F., D. C. Batalha, and M. J. Collares-Pereira. 2002. Gradients in stream fish assemblages across a Mediterranean landscape: contributions of environmental factors and spatial structure. Freshwater Biology 47:1015–1031.

Milner, N. J., R. J. Wyatt, and M. D. Scott. 1993. Variability in the distribution and abundance of stream salmonids and associated use of habitat models. Journal of Fish Biology 43 (Supplement A):103–119.

Naismith, I. A., and B. Knights. 1988. Migrations of elvers and juvenile European eels, *Anguilla anguilla* L., in the River Thames. Journal of Fish Biology 33(Supplement A):161–175.

Naismith, I. A., and B. Knights. 1990. Modelling of unexploited and exploited populations of eels, *Anguilla anguilla* (L.), in the Thames Estuary. Journal of Fish Biology 37:975–986.

Naismith, I. A., and B. Knights. 1993. The distribution, density and growth of European eels, *Anguilla anguilla* L., in the River Thames catchment. Journal of Fish Biology 42:217–226.

Oliveira, K., J. D. McCleave, and G. S. Wippelhauser. 2001. Regional variation and the effect of lake area: river area on sex distribution in American eels. Journal of Fish Biology 58:943–952.

Pedersen, M. I. 2009. Does stocking of Danish lowland streams with elvers increase European eel populations? Pages 149–156 *in* J. M. Casselman and D. K. Cairns, editors. Eels at the edge: science, status, and conservation concerns. American Fisheries Society, Symposium 58, Bethesda, Maryland.

Ringuet, S., F. Muto, and C. Raymakers. 2002. Eels: their harvest and trade in Europe and Asia. Traffic Bulletin 19:80–106.

Russell, I. C., and E. C. E. Potter. 2003. Implications of the precautionary approach for the management of the European eel, *Anguilla anguilla*. Fisheries Management and Ecology 10:395–401.

Sparre, P. 1979. Some necessary adjustments for using the common methods in eel assessment. Pages 41–44 *in* F. Thurow, editors. Eel research and management. Rapports et Procès-Verbaux des Réunions du Conseil International pour l'Exploration de la Mer 174:41–44.

Tesch, F.-W. 2003. The eel, 3rd edition, edited by J. E. Thorpe. Blackwell Scientific Publications, Oxford, England.

Tzeng, W. N., Y. Iizuka, J. C. Shiao, Y. Yamada, and H. Oka. 2003. Identification and growth rate comparisons of divergent migratory contingents of Japanese eel (*Anguilla japonica*). Aquaculture 216:77–86.

Vøllestad, L. A., and B. Jonsson. 1988. A 13-year study of the population dynamics and growth of the European eel *Anguilla anguilla* in a Norwegian river: evidence for density-dependent mortality and development of a model for predicting yield. Journal of Animal Ecology 57:983–997.

White, E. M., and B. Knights. 1997a. Dynamics of upstream migration of the European eel, *Anguilla anguilla* L., with special reference to the effects of man-made barriers. Fisheries Management & Ecology 4:311–324.

White, E. M., and B. Knights. 1997b. Environmental factors affecting the dynamics of upstream migration of the European eel, *Anguilla anguilla* L., in the Rivers Severn and Avon. Journal of Fish Biology 50:1104–1116.

Managing Human Impact on Downstream Migrating European Eel in the River Meuse

MAARTEN C. M. BRUIJS[1] AND R. H. HADDERINGH
KEMA Technical and Operational Services
Utrechtseweg 310, P. O. Box 6800 ET, Arnhem, Netherlands

U. SCHWEVERS AND B. ADAM
Institut für Angewandte Ökologie
Neustädter Weg 25, Kirtorf-Whalen 36320, Germany

U. DUMONT
Ingenieurbüro Floecksmühle
Bachstrasse 62–64, Aachen 52066, Germany

H. V. WINTER
IMARES Institute for Marine Resources and Ecosystem Studies
P. O. Box 68, 1970 AB IJmuiden, Netherlands

Abstract.—To evaluate mortality factors and potential mitigative measures during downstream passage of silver European eel *Anguilla anguilla* in the River Meuse, an integrated study was performed consisting of: 1) telemetric experiments where the descent of 150 transpondered eels was tracked at 14 detection stations; 2) monitoring daily commercial catches; 3) testing a system to predict migration events from activity of captive eels in riverside tanks (the Migromat system); and 4) measuring turbine mortality by netting eels at turbine outlets. Migromat systems installed at two hydropower stations predicted 41 migration events. Most warnings (58.5%) were false positives, but Migromat failed to predict only one migration event. Mortality of eels passing through a turbine at the Linne Hydropower station was 24%. However, part of the downstream migrating population bypassed the turbines by descending over adjacent weirs. Descending eels moved primarily in brief pulses that were associated with increasing discharge and especially during the first half of the night. Thirty-seven percent of transpondered eels released at Ohé en Laak reached the sea. Because both fisheries mortality (estimated at 22–26% by fishing recoveries) and hydropower mortality (estimated at 16–26%) were considerable, a reduction in fisheries harvest and implementation of turbine management by application of the Migromat warning system would substantially increase escapement of silver eels from the River Meuse.

---

[1] Corresponding author: Maarten.Bruijs@kema.com

Introduction

A major decline of worldwide eel (*Anguilla* spp.) populations has been observed (Moriarty and Dekker 1997; Dekker 2004). Although the causes for this decline are unclear, it is recognized that in river systems, successful escapement of silver eels is impaired by fisheries and hydropower stations (Castonguay et al. 1994). However, the extent of these impacts on downstream-migrating silver eel populations is not known. In order to develop effective mitigating measures, there is an urgent need for clearer understanding of how human activities affect downstream-migrating silver eels.

For fisheries, the potential mitigative measure is to curtail or stop silver eel harvest, which would result in an increased number of silver eels reaching the sea. For hydropower stations, varieties of techniques to reduce turbine mortality have been developed or are under investigation, or both, including bypasses and physical and behavioral fish screens (EPRI 2001; DWA 2005; O'Keeffe and Turnpenny 2005). Turbine management is a recent development that combines low cost to the utility with efficient fish protection. For eels, turbine management may be the reduction of approach velocity in front of trash racks and the closure of turbines during peak migration periods (Bruijs et al. 2003; Durif et al. 2003). Turbine closure for longer periods (e.g., the full autumn migration period) entails a substantial loss of electricity production. Closing the turbines for short periods during peak migration is more economically attractive for the electricity utilities. A prerequisite for this is an accurate prediction of silver eel migration events.

In the River Meuse, which flows through France, Belgium, Luxembourg and the Netherlands, silver European eels *Anguilla anguilla* are affected by both commercial fisheries and hydro dams. Fish passage at the Linne power station in the Dutch portion of the river was investigated in 1990–1991 (Hadderingh and Bakker 1998) and in 1999 (Hadderingh and Bruijs 2002). However, cumulative mortality caused by all hydropower stations has not been estimated.

This European Silver Eel Project examined impacts by fisheries and hydropower on the downstream migration of silver eels in the Dutch part of the River Meuse, using 1) telemetry, 2) fisheries statistics, 3) turbine mortality measurements, and 4) evaluation of the Migromat system, which uses activity levels of captive eels to predict migration events (Bruijs et al. 2003; Adam et al. 2004). The telemetry experiments revealed that both fisheries and hydropower impact were considerable (Winter et al. 2005; Winter et al. 2006). The present paper evaluates fishing mortality, turbine mortality, and escapement to the sea of silver eels descending the Meuse and assesses the ability of the Migromat system to increase silver eel escapement by triggering short-term turbine closures.

Study Area and Methods

The River Meuse originates in France, runs through Belgium and Luxembourg, enters the Netherlands at Eijsden, and drains into the North Sea at the Haringvliet (Figure 1). Total length is 935 km, including 300 km in the Dutch section. Total head is 409 m. Most water originates in the Ardennen area of Belgium and France. Because of low soil porosity in the catchment area, rainwater drains rapidly into the river. Hence river level increases quickly after heavy rains, while during dry periods, water input is very limited. Mean discharge at Borgharen, 50 km upstream from Linne, is 250 $m^3 \cdot s^{-1}$, peaking around January and reaching a minimum around July. Mean summer flow is 160 $m^3 \cdot s^{-1}$. The sight depth is inversely proportional to water flow and varies from 20 to 130 cm. Water temperature varies from 2–25°C, with a mean of ~15°C.

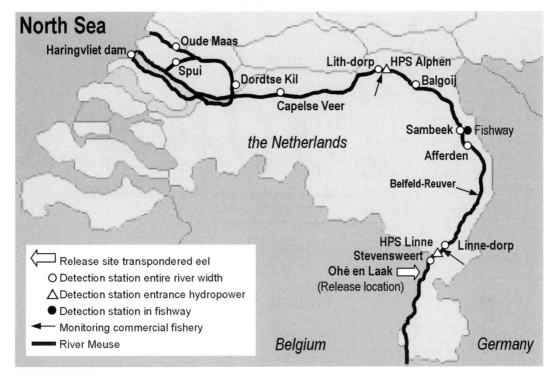

Figure 1. Schematic overview of the telemetry field experiment in the River Meuse in 2002.

Eels are commercially fished in the upstream part of the Dutch section of the River Meuse with stow nets and fyke nets. Fyke netting is most intense in the downstream part. Commercial fisheries were monitored at two locations in 2002 (Belfeld-Reuver and Lith-dorp). In the river stretch from Belfeld to Reuver (3 km), eel catches in four fyke nets were monitored from May to October. On average, these nets are fished at three-day intervals. At Lith-dorp, anchored stow nets were used and inspected daily from May to November. At both locations, the number of silver and yellow eels was recorded.

There are eight hydropower stations on the river's main stem—six in the Belgian section and two in the Dutch section. Silver eel passage and turbine-related injuries were estimated by placing a net directly below one of the four turbine outlets of the Linne hydropower station, the farthest upstream hydropower station in the Dutch part of the river.

Turbine-outlet netting was conducted once every three days in September and October 2002. In total, 17 samplings were performed. Injuries and mortality were established directly on fishing the net. Mortality is defined as direct mortality. Delayed mortality was not investigated; hence the mortality percentages presented are minimum values.

In total, 150 silver eels with a mean length of 74.5 cm (range 64–93 cm) and a mean weight of 897 g (range 588–2086 g) that were captured by fyke nets upstream of Ohé en Laak (Figure 1) in September 2002 were surgically implanted with telemetric tags (Nedap-transponders; Winter et al. 2005; Winter et al. 2006). Downstream migration was monitored by the Nedap Trail telemetry system (Breukelaar et al. 1998; Bij de Vaate and Breukelaar 2001) using 11 fixed detection stations where cables covered the entire river width. Two additional detection stations covered the inlet of the turbines at the two

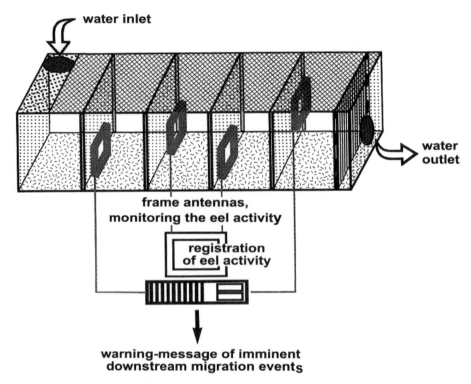

Figure 2. Schematic overview of the Migromat system. Only one of the two tanks is shown.

hydropower locations, and one station was located in the fishway at Sambeek. All outlets to the sea were monitored.

The Migromat system predicts migration events in free-living eels by monitoring activity of eels held in tanks close to the river (Adam 2000). The tanks were stocked with 60 silver eels (mean length 57.8 cm, range 40–93 cm) that had been captured by electrofishing. The system contains two tanks, each with five connected compartments and continuously supplied with river water (Figure 2). Displacements of PIT-tagged eels between the compartments are detected by frame antennae around the openings between compartments. Increases in activity level (i.e., eel passages between compartments) indicate premigratory restlessness and predict migration timing. Migromat systems were installed on the riverbank close to the Linne and Alphen hydropower stations (Figures 1 and 2). Both stations have four horizontal Kaplan turbines with a total capacity of ~10 MW and a maximum head of about 4 m.

Results

Migration of silver eels, as shown by the cumulative passage of eels at each detection station (Figure 3), revealed several distinct peaks, but the main event occurred between 25 and 28 October 2002 during the first increase of river discharge. This migration event started upstream and reached the lower part of the river about three days later. The migration period lasted until January 2003. Based on the telemetry experiment, mortality of transpondered silver eels was 6.7% at Linne and 3.2% at the Alphen power station. These percentages include the number of eels passing over the weir and fishway.

In total, 1,196 eels were captured during 17 turbine passage samplings at the Linne hydro station (Table 1). Only 16 yellow eels

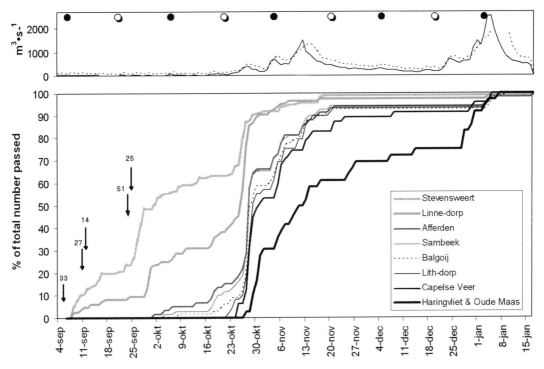

Figure 3. Cumulative percentage of total passages of tagged silver eel per detection station (bottom panel). The arrows indicate the timing and number of eels released at Ohé en Laak. The river discharge at Linne (—) and Alphen (- - -) and lunar phase (o full moon; • new moon) are shown in the top panel.

Table 1. Turbine-related injuries and mortality to eels at the Linne hydropower station, 2 September–22 October 2002.

Eel	Total Number	Not Injured	Total n	Total %	Lethal n	Lethal %	Non-lethal n	Non-lethal %
Silver eel	1180	776	404	34.24	287	24.32	117	9.92
Yellow eel	16	13	3	18.75	0	0.00	3	18.75
Total	1196	789	407	34.03	287	24.00	120	10.03

were caught, which is 1.34% of the total catch. Silver eels had a mean length of 64.7 cm (range 31–95 cm), and most occurred in the 50-to-79-cm length class (Figure 4). Mortality among eels sampled at the turbine outlet of Linne power station was 24%, which includes only the eels passing through the turbine. All were silver eels. However, part of the downstream-migrating population by- passed the turbines by descending over adjacent weirs, so direct turbine mortality as a percentage of the total migrating population would be lower, as shown by the telemetry results. Ten percent of eels sampled at outlets had nonlethal injuries. Mortality rate increased with eel length. Mortality was higher at low flow (30 $m^3 \cdot s^{-1}$) than at high flow (50 $m^3 \cdot s^{-1}$) (Figure 4).

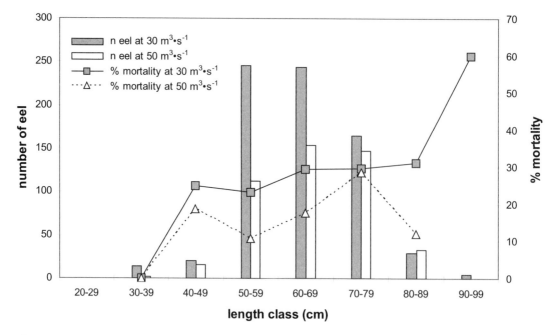

Figure 4. Mortality percentage of eel per length class at discharges of 30 and 50 $m^3 \cdot s^{-1}$ at Linne hydropower station, autumn 2002.

Migromat predicts eel migration from hourly records of activity in the context of normal circadian rhythm. Eels normally show minimum activity at 11:00 and maximum activity around midnight. Daily routine and activity of eels typically change prior to the start of a downstream-migration event. Although occurring mostly during one night, silver eel migration events may last for three subsequent nights. Migromat considers the passage of an animal through two antenna frames within 2 min as an activity point. Eels in the Migromat tanks show marked premigratory restlessness at dusk (around 1800 hours), before the night eels in the river start to migrate (Figure 5), while in nonmigrating periods, activity at dusk is much lower.

On the evenings of 26 and 27 October, Migromat registered sharp increases of activity, with double the intensity of the previous day (Figure 5). Increased downstream passage of tagged eels followed the activity peaks recorded by Migromat (Figure 5).

The Migromat system was in operation for 170 d at Linne and 185 d at Alphen. Migromat predicted 24 migration events at Linne and 17 at Alphen (total 41, Table 2). Transponder data, turbine outlet netting, and reports from commercial fisheries confirmed actual migration events during 10 and 7 (total 17) of the predicted migration events for the two sites, respectively. The rate of false positives, when Migromat predicted migration but migration was not confirmed, was 14/24 (58.3%) in Linne, 10/17 (58.8%) in Alphen, and 24/41 (58.5%) overall. However, this rate of false positives may be an overestimate because transponder and fisheries data may not have detected all migration events. Nonmigration was predicted 146 times at Linne and 168 times at Alphen. Only a single migration (at Linne) was confirmed on a day when Migromat predicted nonmigration (Table 2). The rate of false negatives, when nonmigration was predicted but migration occurred, was 1/146 (0.7%)

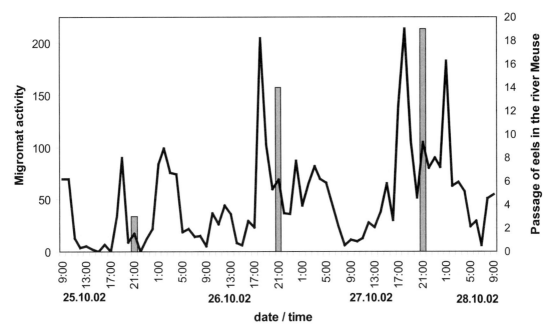

Figure 5. Number of eels passing the Linne hydropower station as determined by the telemetry system (bars) and eel activity index in the Migromat system (line), 25–28 October 2002.

Table 2. Migromat predictions during operating period 29 June 2002–2 January 2003.

	Location					
	Linne		Alphen		Both	
	n	%	n	%	n	%
Number of days migration events were predicted	24	-	17	-	41	-
Number of days migration events were predicted and confirmed	10	41.7	7	41.2	17	41.5
Number of days migration events were predicted but not confirmed	14	58.3	10	58.8	24	58.5
Number of days non-migration was predicted	146	-	168	-	314	-
Number of days non-migration predicted and migration was not confirmed	145	99.3	168	100	313	99.7
Number of days non-migration was predicted but migration was confirmed	1	0.7	0	0.0	1	0.3
Transpondered eels passing during predicted migration events		66		73		69.5
Transpondered eels that died in turbines		6.7		3.2		

for Linne, 0/168 (0.0%) for Alphen, and 1/314 (0.3%) overall.

Migromat migration-event predictions covered 14% and 9% of the investigation periods at Linne and Alphen, respectively. Most (69.5%) passages of transpondered eels through detection stations in front of the two hydro stations occurred during these predicted periods. Thus, if Migromat warnings had been used to trigger turbine shutdowns for the three subsequent nights, and if all eels had readily passed through the weir or fishway, then passage through turbines would have been reduced by 69.5%. However, not all eels migrated in groups during migration peaks; 30.5% were found to pass the two hydro stations individually throughout the overall migration period.

Discussion and Conclusions

Commercial fisheries and hydroturbines cause substantial mortality to migrating silver eels (McCleave 2001; Winter et al. 2006). An integrated study was performed to evaluate mortality factors and potential mitigating measures during downstream passage of silver European eels in the River Meuse.

Recapture rates of transpondered eels by fishermen indicated a fishing mortality of at least 16%, more likely 22–26%. Cumulative mortality due to the two Dutch hydropower stations was at least 9%, more likely 16–26%. In total, 37% of the transpondered eels released at Ohé en Laak reached the North Sea (Winter et al. 2006). This does not incorporate mortality caused by the six hydrostations upstream of the study area. Because fisheries and hydro impacts are considerable and because most downstream-migration movements of silver eels occur in brief pulses, mitigating measures appear both feasible and necessary.

Turbine mortality rate, 24% of the eels passing the turbine, is related to turbine flow. Mortality rates found at 30 and 50 $m^3 \cdot s^{-1}$ are similar to the results of earlier investigations at the Linne station (Hadderingh and Bakker 1998; Hadderingh and Bruijs 2002). At 50 $m^3 \cdot s^{-1}$ flow, mortality rates were highest for eels longer than 70 cm. At 30 $m^3 \cdot s^{-1}$ flow, mortality rate increased gradually with size for eels between 50 and 89 cm. At 50 $m^3 \cdot s^{-1}$ flow, the distance between the turbine blades is larger, resulting in a lower mortality rate for smaller eels. Thus, for hydrostations operating horizontal Kaplan turbines, it is conducive to survival of eels that pass the turbines to keep water flows at 50 $m^3 \cdot s^{-1}$ or higher.

The two hydrostations on the Dutch portion of the Meuse cause mortality to migrating silver eels, but shutting them down during the full autumn migration period would cause a major loss of electricity generation. Exclusion of eels from turbine intakes by means of screens is very costly. This study suggests that the Migromat system might be used to predict migrations of wild eels from the activity levels of captive eels in riverside tanks. Most silver eels were found to migrate at night, an observation made in numerous studies of silver eel migration (Durif et al. 2003). Most (63%) turbine passages occurred during the first five hours of the night (Winter et al. 2006). Migromat predictions could be used to trigger turbine shutdowns in a small fraction of nights during the overall migration period, thereby safeguarding the passage of most migrating eels with a minimum of economic cost.

A major current limitation of Migromat for hydropower operators is the high percentage of false positives (58.5%). False positive warnings would trigger hydro shutdowns that have little conservation benefit. Further work is required to determine if the rate of false positives is over-estimated because of nondetection of some migration events.

Silver eels commonly descend rivers when discharge rises (Euston et al. 1997; Bruijs et al. 2003; Durif et al. 2003), but not all discharge events are accompanied by migration events. No comparative data are available to test the relative success of river discharge versus Migromat as a predictor of eel migration. Even though the timing appeared to be associated with a rise in discharge rather than, for example, moon phase (cf. Lowe 1952), distinguishing various environmental factors in relation to timing of migrations requires study over several years.

In comparison with other European countries, eel fishing pressure in the Netherlands is relatively high (Dekker 2004), while hydropower development is limited. Thus the potential benefits of turbine management as shown in this study are likely to have greater impact elsewhere in the range of the European eel where hydrodams are more common.

The European Water Framework Directive requires undisturbed migration for fish in European river systems, and the European Commission has mandated the preparation of a European eel action plan (EC 2005), which, among other measures, includes the target that management actions must allow an adequate escapement of 40% of the silver eel population from each European river basin. These developments will increase pressure for measures that protect eels and other species during their downstream migrations.

Acknowledgments

This project addresses the activity Energy, Environment and Sustainable Development under the Fifth Framework Program by the European Union. The funders are: ESSENT Energie; NUON Renewable Energy Projects; the Directorate-General of Public Works and Water Management (RWS) (Directorates Oost-Nederland and Limburg); the Dutch Ministry of Economic Affairs (EZ); and the Dutch Ministry of Agriculture, Nature Management and Fisheries (LNV) (Directorates Nature Management and Fisheries).

References

Adam, B. 2000. Migromat®—ein Frühwarnsystem zur Erkennung der Aalabwanderung. Wasser and Boden 52/4:16–19. (In German).

Adam. B., M. C. M. Bruijs, U. Dumont, and H. V. Winter. 2004. Anthropogene Einflüsse auf die Aalabwanderung in der Maas – Ergebnisse eines EG-Forschungsprojekts. Österreichs Fischerei 57:269–277. (In German).

Bij de Vaate, A., and A. W. Breukelaar. 2001. De migratie van zeeforel in Nederland. Rijksinstituut voor Integraal Zoetwaterbeheer and Afvalwaterbehandeling. Report nr 2001.046. Final report. (In Dutch).

Breukelaar, A. W., A. Bij de Vaate, and K. T. W. Focken. 1998. Inland migration study of sea trout (*Salmo trutta*) into the rivers Rhine and Meuse (Netherlands), based on inductive coupling radio telemetry. Hydrobiologia 371/372:29–33.

Bruijs, M. C. M., H. J. G. Polman, G. H. F. M. van Aerssen, R. H. Hadderingh, H. V. Winter, C. Deerenberg, H. M. Jansen, U. Schwevers, B. Adam, U. Dumont, and N. Kessels. 2003. Management of silver eel: human impact on downstream migrating eel in the River Meuse. EU Contract Q5RS-2000–31141. Final Report, KEMA Nederland BV, Arnhem, Netherlands.

Castonguay, M., P. V. Hodson, C. Moriarty, K. F. Drinkwater, and B. M. Jessop. 1994. Is there a role of ocean environment in American and European eel decline? Fisheries Oceanography 3:197–203.

Dekker, W. 2004. Slipping through our hands: population dynamics of the European eel. Doctoral dissertation. University of Amsterdam, Amsterdam, Netherlands.

Durif, C., P. Elie, C. Gosset, J. Rives, and F. Travade. 2003. Behavioral study of downstream migrating eels by radio-telemetry at a small hydroelectric power plant. Pages 343–356 in D.A. Dixon, editor. Biology, management, and protection of catadromous eels. American Fisheries Society, Symposium 33, Bethesda, Maryland.

DWA. 2005. Themen. Fischschutz- und Fischabstiegsanlagen–Bemessung, Gestaltung, Funktionskontrolle. Korrigierte Auflage, Juli 2005. (In German).

EC (European Commission). 2005. Proposal for a council regulation establishing measures for the recovery of the stock of European eel. European Commission, Brussels.

Electric Power Research Institute (EPRI). 2001. Review and documentation of research and technologies on passage and protection of downstream migrating catadromous eels at hydroelectric facilities. Final Report. Prepared for EPRI by Versar, Inc., EPRI Report No. 1000730. Electric Power Research Institute, Palo Alto, California.

Euston, E. T., D. D. Royer, and C. L. Simons. 1997. Relationship of emigration of silver American eels (*Anguilla rostrata*) to environmental variables at a low head hydro station. Proceedings of the International Conference on Hydropower 1997:549–558, American Society of Civil Engineers,

Hadderingh, R. H., and H. D. Bakker. 1998. Fish mortality due to passage through hydroelectric power stations on the Meuse and Vecht rivers. Pages 315–328 *in* M. Jungwirth, S. Schmutz, and S. Weiss, editors. Fish migration and fish bypasses. Fishing News Books, Oxford, UK.

Hadderingh, R. H., and M. C. M. Bruijs. 2002. Hydroelectric power stations and fish migration. Tribune de l'eau 55(619–620/5–6):79–87.

Lowe, R. H. 1952. The influence of light and other factors on the seaward migration of silver eels (*Anguilla anguilla*). Journal of Animal Ecology 21:275–309.

McCleave, J. D. 2001. Simulation of the impact of dams and fishing weirs on reproductive potential of silver-phase American eels in the Kennebec River basin, Maine, USA. North American Journal of Fisheries Management 21:577–590.

Moriarty, C., and W. Dekker. 1997. Management of the European eel. Fisheries Bulletin (Dublin) no. 15.

O'Keeffe N., and A.W.H. Turnpenny. 2005. Screening for intake and outfalls: a best practice guide. Environment Agency, Science Report SC030231.

Winter, H. V., H. M. Jansen, B. Adam, and U. Schwevers. 2005. Behavioural effects of surgically implanting transponders in European eel, *Anguilla anguilla*. Pages 287–295 *in* M.T. Spedicato, G. Marmulla, and G. Lembo, editors. Aquatic telemetry: advances and applications. FAO Special Publications, Rome.

Winter, H. V., H. M. Jansen, and M. C. M. Bruijs. 2006. Assessing the impact of hydropower and fisheries on downstream migrating silver eel, *Anguilla anguilla*, by telemetry in the River Meuse. Ecology of Freshwater Fish 15:221–228.

Management, Research, and Stock Assessment of *Anguillids* in New Zealand

PETER R. TODD[1]

*Ministry of Fisheries
Private Bag 14, Nelson, New Zealand*

Abstract.—The New Zealand eel fishery comprises two species, the shortfin eel *Anguilla australis* and the New Zealand longfin eel *A. dieffenbachii*. A third species, the speckled longfin eel *A. reinhardtii*, is present in small numbers in some areas. Major fisheries in New Zealand are managed under the Quota Management System. Individual transferable quotas are set as a proportion of an annual total allowable commercial catch. The Quota Management System was introduced into the South Island eel fishery on 1 October 2000 and the North Island fishery on 1 October 2004. Freshwater eels have particular significance for customary Maori. Management policies allow for customary take and the granting of commercial access rights on introduction into the Quota Management System. Eel catches have remained relatively constant since the early 1970s. The average annual catch from 1989–1990 to 2001–2002 (fishing year) was 1,313 mt. Catch per unit effort remained constant from 1983 to 1989 and reduced from 1990 to 1999. Statistically significant declines in catch per unit effort for New Zealand longfin eel were found in some areas over the latter period. For management, an annual stock-assessment process provides an update on stock status.

Introduction

The eel fishery in New Zealand is based on the two temperate species of freshwater eels in New Zealand, the shortfin eel *Anguilla australis*, and the New Zealand longfin eel *A. dieffenbachii*. The shortfin eel is also found in Australia, New Caledonia, and some other islands in the southwest Pacific. The spawning ground for this species is thought to be northeast of Samoa (Jellyman 1987). The longfin eel is endemic to New Zealand and offshore islands and is thought to spawn east of Tonga. A third species of freshwater eel, the speckled longfin *A. reinhardtii* has only recently been identified in New Zealand (Jellyman et al.

1996). This latter species has been confirmed as being caught in the commercial eel fishery, but the quantities are thought to be small.

Shortfin and longfin eels occur abundantly throughout New Zealand and have overlapping habitat preferences. Shortfins predominate in lowland lakes and muddy rivers, while longfins prefer stony rivers and penetrate farther inland to high country lakes. Shortfins are abundant in coastal lakes and also in estuarine and marine coastal habitats (McDowall 1990).

Fisheries Management Structure

New Zealand fisheries management is based on property rights. All major fisher-

[1] E-mail: toddp@fish.govt.nz

ies in New Zealand are managed under the Quota Management System (QMS), using individual transferable quotas (ITQs), that was introduced in 1986. Individual transferable quotas exist in perpetuity and are expressed as a proportion of the total allowable commercial catch (TACC). Total allowable commercial catches are a subset of the total allowable catch (TAC) for each fishery after an allowance has been made for noncommercial fishing interests (Maori customary and recreational) and other sources of mortality. A general review of the ITQ system is given by Annala (1996). Total allowable catches and TACCs for the eel fishery were set on the basis of historical commercial catch levels and estimates of customary harvest (North Island and Chatham Islands only), with reductions to allow for sustainable management of the fisheries.

The New Zealand eel fishery is distributed throughout the freshwaters (lakes, rivers, streams, impoundments) and some estuarine and coastal waters across both the North and South Islands, as well as the Chatham Islands.

Customary Maori Eel Fisheries

Maori in New Zealand practiced an indigenous fishery before European settlement. Eels were the most important freshwater fish for early Maori, and prior to European settlement, beginning in about 1840, and up to about the late 19th and early 20th centuries, Maori traditional eel fisheries were well developed. Best (1929), Downes (1918), and McDowall (1990) describe traditional eel fisheries. Maori had extensive knowledge of the time of movements and migrations, methods of trapping, and use of eels as a food resource, and they harvested eels as elvers, feeding eels, and adult emigrants. Schmidt (1925) remarks on the wide variety of capture techniques developed by Maori, including weirs, spears, *hinakis* (eel baskets, Figure 1), and blind channels dug near lake outlets during the autumnal migration of adults (Figure 2). Perhaps the most impressive aspect of traditional eel-fishing techniques used by Maori was the use of weirs to trap adult eels migrating downstream. These weirs demonstrated a high degree of engineering competence developed prior to European colonization. Large upright anchor posts were driven into riverbeds without the aid of conventional European engineering techniques of the time. Downes (1918) describes operational eel weirs in the early 1900s in the Whanganui area (Figure 3). Eel weirs were complex wooden structures with large piles driven into the riverbed and substantial bed logs. *Hinakis*, or catching baskets, were attached to the weirs, and the weirs were placed at an angle across the river to funnel downstream-moving eels into the *hinakis*. The Waikato River and its tributaries were noted for eel weirs, but it is apparent that they were destroyed by floods or were removed to permit navigation by launches and barges, probably about the 1890s. Downes (1918) remarks that eel weirs were common about 1893 in almost every river and stream on the west coast of the North Island, but by 1918 only two were to be found on the Whanganui River and none farther south.

Only a few customary eel fisheries using traditional methods are extant, mostly in areas that have been set aside for exclusive customary access. One of these is at Lake Wairewa in the South Island, where emigrant eels are still harvested by blind channels dug into the shingle bar separating the lakes from the sea (Todd 1978). Contemporary fishing methods such as fyke nets are still used to harvest eels for customary purposes throughout freshwater. Local *iwi* (tribes) or *hapu* harvest eels in areas that were traditionally fished and where specific fishing rights are claimed. Customary fishers prefer eels larger than 700 mm and 1 kg. Commercial fishing has reduced the average size of eels available to customary fishers, particularly in the mainstreams of larger

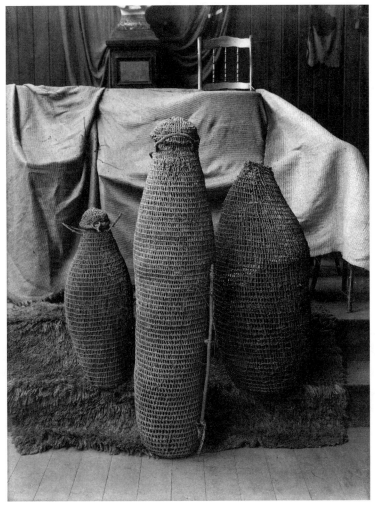

Figure 1. Traditional New Zealand Maori eel fishing methods—hinakis (eel baskets), ca 1910. Photograph courtesy of Alexander Turnbull Library Wellington, New Zealand.

rivers. There is no overall assessment of the extent of past customary take.

Maori still value traditional fisheries and access to eels for customary purposes. Fish stocks managed under the New Zealand QMS require that an allowance be set for customary fisheries purposes before a commercial catch limit is set. Eels remain the most important freshwater fish species for contemporary Maori and are harvested for *hui*, *tangi*, and other customary and *marae* purposes. Estimates of the current customary harvest are limited. For the South Island, most of the customary harvest is taken under the authority of customary permits issued by *kaitiaki* appointed under the customary fisheries regulations. Current catch estimates are approximately 1 mt. For the introduction of the North Island fishery into the QMS, the customary harvest was estimated at 73 mt for shortfins and 46 mt for longfins. The substantial difference in customary harvest between the South and North Island would reflect the substantial difference in the Maori population between the two islands, with fewer Maori living in the South Island.

Figure 2. Traditional New Zealand Maori eel fishing methods—blind channel dug into shingle bar to catch migrating eels, Lake Wairewa, ca 1910. Photograph courtesy of Alexander Turnbull Library Wellington, New Zealand.

In the South Island, Lake Forsyth (Waiwera) and its tributaries have been set aside exclusively for Ngai Tahu customary eel fishing purposes. Other areas, such as the lower Taumutu (Te Waihora), Wainono Lagoon, and the lower Pelorus River, have been set aside as noncommercial areas. In the North Island, commercial fishing has been prohibited from the Taharoa lakes, Whakaki Lagoon, Lake Poukawa, and the Pencarrow lakes (Kohangapiripiri and Kohangatera) and catchments in recognition of the special value of these areas for customary Maori purposes.

The introduction of commercial fisheries into the QMS in 1986 allocated quota to fishing companies and individuals that met the allocation criteria. Part-time fishers, many of whom were Maori, were excluded from the initial allocation. Maori protested against this government action, which eroded their rights as guaranteed by the Treaty of Waitangi signed between the British Crown and some Maori chiefs in 1840. These Maori claims to fishing resources are detailed by Bess (2001). Recognition of the past and present value of fisheries, including eel fisheries, is recognized through legislation providing Maori with commercial access to the fishery and also recognizing customary fisheries. Under the Treaty of Waitangi Settlement Act 1992, Maori were

Figure 3. Traditional New Zealand Maori eel fishing methods—eel pa tuna (eel weir) ca 1910. Photograph courtesy of Alexander Turnbull Library Wellington, New Zealand.

to be granted 20% of all new fish stocks brought into the QMS. Consequently Maori were granted 20% of TACC when each of the South Island, Chatham Island, and North Island fisheries were introduced into the QMS in 2000, 2003, and 2004, respectively. Maori are now the largest quota owners in the New Zealand commercial eel fishery. The settlement of Maori commercial interests in the eel fishery is separate from Maori interest in customary eel fisheries for noncommercial purposes.

Historically freshwater eels did not rate highly in New Zealand's European culture, and many regarded them as a threat to exotic trout species, which were introduced to establish sport fisheries in the late 1800s. In the 1930s and 1940s, eel eradication campaigns were conducted to remove eels from some trout fishery waters in parts of the South Island (Cairns 1942). Bounties were paid for eel tails. During the Second World War, there was some interest in eels as a source of fish oil, but stocks remained relatively unexploited commercially until the early 1960s.

Freshwater eels are an important component of the freshwater ecosystem, and large longfins are the largest fish and predator in New Zealand freshwaters. The longfin eel is one of the largest of all freshwater eel species, the largest reaching around 20 kg in weight and 1.5 m in length. Some large eels have been aged at up to 100 years old. These large eels are piscivorous and feed on a variety of fish species, including other eels and trout.

Commercial Eel Fishery

The current commercial fishery dates from the early 1960s and is centered on the export market to Asia and Europe. Annual catch data are available from 1965 by calendar year. Landings peaked in 1972 at 2,077 t and remained relatively stable from 1983 to 1999, declining from nearly 1,000 t in 2000–621 t in 2005 (Figure 4).

A calendar year effectively includes about half of each natural fishing season, which extends from about October to April or May. Fishing ceases in the winter months, May to September, in the South Island and is substantially reduced in the warmer North Island waters.

Eel catches are more accurately reflected by fishing year, which extends from 1 October to 30 September and over the natural fishing season. Landings since 2000–2001 reduced from just over 1,000 t to 712 t in 2004–2005. The reduction in landings follows progressive introduction of all fisheries into the QMS between 2000 and 2004.

Catch effort landing returns (CELR) provide landings by Quota Management Area (QMA). Prior to the 2000–2001 fishing year, three species codes were used to record species landed: SFE (shortfin), LFE (longfin), and EEU (eels unidentified). A high proportion of eels (46% in 1990–1991) were unidentified between the fishing years 1989–1990 and 1998–1999. Prorating the unidentified catch by the ratio of longfin to shortfin by fishing year provides a history of landings by species (Figure 5); however prorated catches prior to 1999–2000 are influenced by the high proportion of unidentified fish from some eel statistical areas and may not provide an accurate species breakdown. The introduction of new eel catch effort return (ECELR) and eel catch landing return (ECLR) in 2000–2001 improved the species composition information with the deletion of the unidentified category. The species proportion remained relatively constant from the 1995–1996 fishing year until the introduction of the North Island fishery into the QMS in 2004. Shortfins are the dominant species in the fishery, on average constituting 66% of catches between 1995 and 1996 and 2004–2005.

Species proportion of landings varies by geographical area. From analysis of landings made into eel processing factories and estimated catch from CELRs, longfins are the predominant species in most areas of the South Island except for a few discrete locations such as lakes Ellesmere and Brunner and the Waipori Lakes, where shortfins predominate in the landings. Prior to the QMS, in the North Island longfin landings declined relative to shortfin landings over a 13-year period from 1990 to 1991 to 2002 to 2003. Estimated longfin catches declined from about 340 mt to 140 mt over that period, while shortfin landings fluctuated between 360 mt and 600 mt but showed no decline in landings. The eel fishery catches predominantly premigratory feeding eels with the exception of Lake Ellesmere, where significant quantities of seaward-migrating adult eels are taken in February and March.

The New Zealand eel fishery is divided into 11 QMAs, with a TAC, allowances, and TACC set for each (Figure 6). The South Island eel fishery is divided into six QMAs and was introduced into the QMS on 1 October 2000, with longfin and shortfin species combined under fish stocks ANG 11 to ANG 16. Total allowable catches and TACCs were set for species combined. Fishers are required to report catches separately by species. The fishing year for all fisheries extends from 1 October to 30 September except for ANG 13 (Lake Ellesmere), which has a fishing year from 1 February to 30 January (beginning 1 February 2002). The Chatham Island fishery was introduced into the QMS on 1 October 2003 as separate fish stocks longfin and shortfin SFE 17 and LFE 17. The North Island eel fishery was introduced into the QMS

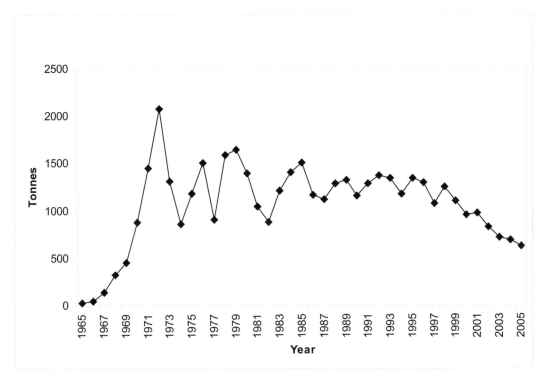

Figure 4. New Zealand commercial eel catches 1965–2005 (tonnes).

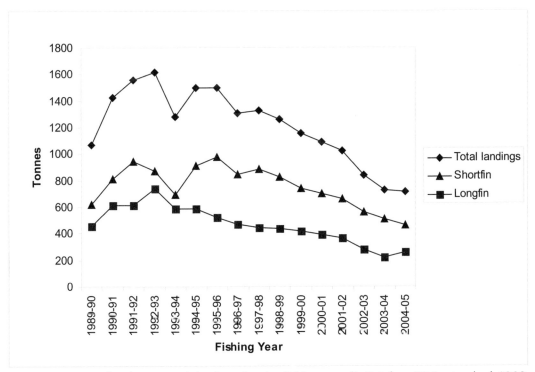

Figure 5. New Zealand commercial eel catches by fishing year (1 October–30 September) 1989–1990 to 2004–2005 (tonnes).

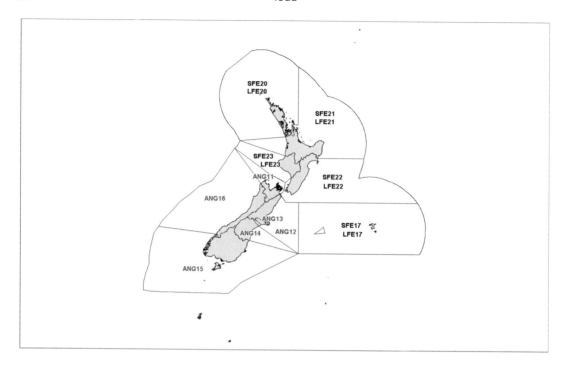

Figure 6. Quota Management Areas for eel fisheries management in New Zealand

Table 1. Total Allowable Commercial Catches (TACCs) and landings (tonnes) for New Zealand eel fisheries for fishing year 2004–2005.

Fish stock North Island	TACC	Reported landings	Fish stock South Island	TACC	Reported landings
SFE 20	149.0	78.48	ANG11	40.0	5.55
LFE 20	47.0	27.42	AGG 12	42.7	4.55
SFE21	163.0	122.95	ANG 13	121.9	121.9
LFE 21	64.0	53.52	ANG 14	35.1	9.0
SFE 22	108.0	80.59	ANG 15	117.7	95.3
LFE 22	41.0	23.86	ANG 16	62.7	44.2
SFE 23	37.0	14.95	Chatham Islands		
LFE 23	41.0	24.52	SFE 17	10.0	1.3
			LFE 17	1.0	0

on 1 October 2004 as separate fish stocks SFE 20–23 and LFE 20–23. Total allowable catches, TACCs, and 2004–2005 reported landings by fish stock for New Zealand eel fisheries are shown in Table 1. All reported landings for the 2004–2005 fishing year were less than the TAC with the exception of ANG 13 (Lake Ellesmere), where the fishery has a large catch of emigrant shortfin eels.

The predominant reason for under catch in the North Island fishery is the recent introduction of the fishery into the QMS. Some fishers sold their quota and left the fishery, and consequently fishing effort reduced. Fishers also report that market forces and economics meant that all available areas were fished. The same reasons apply to the South Island, but the under catch can also be partly attributable to a reduction in stock levels as reflected by the decreases in CPUE.

Virtually all eels are caught by fyke nets, which are usually baited. The eel fishery takes predominantly feeding yellow eels with the exception of lakes Onoke and Ellesmere, where adult migrating silvering eels are targeted during the autumnal migration. Both lakes are coastal with a narrow shingle bar separating the lakes from the sea, and emigrant eels are caught in fyke nets as they congregate near these outlets. Regulations govern size limits and the setting of fyke nets. A national minimum size limit of 220 g applies to the whole of New Zealand. Escape tubes 25 mm diameter are required in fyke nets to allow for escapement of undersized eels. For the South Island, a maximum size limit of 4 kg was introduced to provide some escapement of female longfin eels and in recognition of the needs of customary fishers.

Catch Per Unit Effort

Many of the conventional fisheries sampling and survey techniques for determining relative abundance and population parameters cannot be applied to freshwater eel fisheries because of the nature of their biology and distribution. An exception has been the application of CPUE analysis for freshwater eels in New Zealand.

Jellyman (1994) conducted an unstandardized CPUE analysis for the period 1983–1984 to 1988–1989. The CPUE data showed considerable variation, and few recognizable trends were evident. Various areas showed a wide range in mean annual CPUE, and there was also a wide variation between years for the same areas. Some differences were obvious between regions. For example, the Waikato Basin, an important fishing area, had consistently low CPUE (4.1–4.8 kg per fyke net night), whereas CPUE for the Wairarapa area was relatively high (11.2–22.4 kg per net-night).

Since 1990–1991, an improved catch effort landing return (CELR) form has required fishers to record estimated catch and effort. Despite some initial reservations about the quality of the data, it has been possible to derive standardized CPUE data from 1990–1991 to 1998–1999 (Beentjes and Bull 2002) for the whole New Zealand eel fishery, with updated CPUE for selected areas for the period 1990–1991 to 2000–2001 (Beentjes and Dunn 2003).

Catch per unit effort data are recorded by 21 eel statistical areas (ESAs). Some areas were grouped for analysis. For the period 1990–1991 to 1998–1999, a statistically significant decline in CPUE for shortfin eels was found in only one grouping of ESAs. Total catch of eels from these areas represented 7% of the total estimated landing of shortfins for the nine-year period. A significant decline in CPUE for longfins was found in four of the ESA groupings. The landings from these areas represented 47% of the total estimated landings of longfins over the 9-year period.

Further analyses of CPUE in three ESA groupings that had showed a decline in CPUE for the period 1990–1991 to 1998–1999 were analyzed, using additional catch and effort

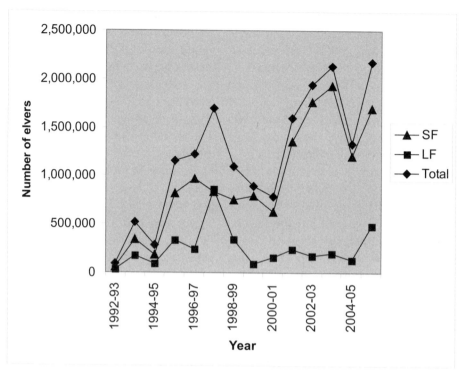

Figure 7. Elver numbers (in 1,000s) at Karapiro Dam (New Zealand), Waikato River by elver season (1 December–30 March) 1992–1993 to 2005–2006.

data for 1999–2000 to 2000–2001 (Beentjes and Dunn 2003). A continued decline in longfin CPUE was observed, indicating that longfin abundance had continued to decline throughout the New Zealand fishery.

Recruitment

Northern hemisphere stocks of *Anguilla* have shown marked declines over recent decades. An indicator of the decline in Europe has been the reduction in catches of glass eels (Dekker 2002). An indicator of the decline in the American eel in Canada has been the reduction in the number of elvers ascending the Moses Saunders Dam on the upper St. Lawrence River (Casselman 2003). There are no fisheries for glass eels in New Zealand, but Jellyman and Sykes (2004) collected data and reviewed the available data for the period 1996–2002. Overall, he found no clear evidence of declines in recruitment of either species over the 7-year sampling period.

Changes in recruitment for longfin eels due to a reduction in population size might not be obvious for many years. The establishment of a long-term data series on either glass eel or elver abundance is required to assess trends in recruitment. Current research on recruitment is aimed at establishing a time series of relative abundance of elvers at key locations in New Zealand where hydro dams restrict upstream passage. The largest monitored runs of elvers are at the Karapiro Dam on the Waikato River. The catch of elvers during 2003–2004 at Karapiro was the highest recorded since accurate record-keeping began in 1995–1996 (excluding 1997–1998). Numbers of longfin elvers appear to have been declining since 1999–2000, and the proportion of longfin as a percentage of total catch has reduced from around 25% to 30% over the period 1995–1996 to 1998–1999 to around 9% to 10% from 2002–2003 to 2004–2005 (Martin et al. 2006). Preliminary results for the 2005–2006 elver season (Jacques Boubee, personal communication) indicate an increase in the percentage of longfins to around 20% of the total catch.

With the lack of long-term time series on recruitment derived from the data sets for glass eels and elvers, a review (Jellyman et al. 2000) of a range of information, including historical observations and some specific catch data on glass eels and elvers, age composition and abundance of juvenile and adult eels, and selective removal of larger female longfins by the commercial fishery, concluded that longfin eels were being overfished and that this has significantly affected recruitment. Several other factors could be responsible for a decline in recruitment, including changes in oceanic conditions affecting spawning, survival and migration of juvenile eels, habitat deterioration in freshwater (loss of habitat, pollution, wetland drainage, hydroelectric dams), and other sources of direct mortality such as the effects of drain clearing and hydroelectric turbines.

Spawning Escapement

The commercial fishery has been selective for larger eels, and in areas that are extensively commercially fished, there are few female longfin eels above the minimum size at emigration. This has raised concern about the escapement of sufficient spawning female longfin eels to maintain recruitment. There is no information on the exact relationship between the stock of emigrating eels and recruitment of glass eels. Given the biology of eels, it would be extremely difficult to establish such a relationship in a manner that would have any predictive power and practical application to management so as to ensure adequate recruitment. Nevertheless an obvious strategy for sustainable management of any freshwater eel fishery would be to ensure adequate spawner escapement. Spawner escapement could be achieved by targeting a reduction of the harvest of larger eels or migrating adult eels or by setting aside reserve areas to maintain an unexploited population to maximize spawner escapement, or both. In New Zealand, very little commercial fishing is targeted at migrating eels. The South Island commercial fishery has an upper size limit of 4 kg. Population modeling (Jellyman et al. 2000) suggests that this upper size limit is unlikely to be effective because many eels are captured before they reach this size. The use of reserve areas will provide some spawner escapement, but the question remains as to what escapement is required.

Based on GIS modeling, Graynoth (2004) estimated that for longfin eels, 5% of habitat throughout New Zealand is in water closed to fishing where there is protected egress to the sea to ensure spawning escapement. A further 10% of longfin habitat is in areas closed to fishing in upstream areas but where the spawning migration could be subject to exploitation in downstream areas. An additional 17% of longfin habitat is in small streams that are rarely or not fished. Therefore, about 30% of longfin habitat in the North Island and 34% in the South Island is either in reserve or in rarely or not fished areas. Biomass estimates of migrant longfin females in reserve and rarely fished or unfished areas suggest that these areas are sufficient to maintain present longfin stocks but insufficient to rebuild stocks. These estimates depend on available longfin eel biomass estimates from different habitats. Data on eel biomass is lacking in several representative habitat types in the North Island. Biomass estimates for longfin migrating female stocks are periodically updated as additional data on longfin biomass in different habitat types becomes available.

Stock Assessment, Research, and Management

The Ministry of Fisheries convenes several working groups to assess the current status of stocks (see Sullivan et al. 2005, unpublished report). A specific working group is convened for freshwater eels. The ministry also purchases research relevant to the decision-making processes to ensure sustainable use of the resource. For most research purchased relevant to management of commercial fisheries, a portion of the cost is recovered from commercial fishers. The ministry plans research through the establishment of separate research planning groups, which cover various fish-stock groupings (deepwater, middle depth, shellfish, inshore finfish, snapper, rock lobsters, and freshwater eels) that represent all stakeholders, fisheries managers, and researchers.

For freshwater eels, the Eel Fishery Assessment Group has identified four main areas of research: monitoring the species, size, and sex composition of major commercial fisheries to establish changes in these parameters, CPUE analysis as an index of relative abundance, monitoring recruitment to establish a time series of data on relative recruitment, and estimating areas closed to fishing to allow for spawner escapement. The Eel Working Group reviews the results from this research and any other sources of relevant information, which are included in the annual review of stock status. This review may lead to management recommendations, including any variation to TACs and TACCs, and any other management measure that may be required for sustainable management of the eel stocks. In the most recent 2005 assessment of the status of eel stocks in New Zealand, the working group recognized that there are no stock assessments or reliable data or time series on which to base specific recommendations on catch levels or other management measures. Given the biology of eels and the difficulty of applying conventional stock-assessment techniques, there is a high risk that current exploitation levels for longfin eels in particular, coupled with past and present anthropogenic impacts, are not sustainable. Based on available information, the working group does not consider that the same risk applies to shortfin eels.

The working group considers that specific management action is required to improve the spawner escapement of longfin eels. It is not possible to recommend specific reductions in TACs, but measures are required to increase spawner escapement of longfin eels to improve recruitment. Measures could include reductions in catch levels, changes to minimum size limit and maximum size limits, area closures to improve spawner escapement, and spatial management to increase yields from stocked areas. An immediate reduction in overall catch levels could be a first step in reducing fishing mortality and improving spawner escapement. Problems are recognized with sustainable use of longfin eels (Jellyman et al. 2000), and some of these problems can be addressed through the Quota Management System, which provides a range of tools to manage the commercial, customary, and recreational fisheries.

The longfin eel has been classified as in "gradual decline" as the result of a review of the threat status of native flora and fauna by the New Zealand Department of Conservation (Molloy et al. 2002). The "gradual decline" classification is the lowest threat ranking and indicates an expected decline of 5% to 30% over the next 10 years and into the future if current threats continue. There is no threat of extinction. Factors leading to the classification were the data suggesting poor recruitment in some years, fishing pressure, loss of habitat, and the implications of a sex-ratio bias in one area of the South Island. The combination of these factors is thought to place the species at risk of decline. The threat ranking can be reassessed when new information is available and the threatened status removed if the longfin population has stabilized or increased. Since the introduction of North Island eels into the QMS, factors contributing to the threat status of longfin eels have been reduced.

However, a difficulty with overall management of eel stocks is the myriad of effects, apart from commercial harvest, that influence sustainability of the resource. It is estimated that since European settlement, about 90% of wetland habitat in New Zealand has been lost. Drainage and flood-control activities, as well as the operation of hydroelectric dams, continue to affect eel habitat and eel stocks. Several authorities are responsible for managing natural resources, including eels, outside of the commercial fishery. The Department of Conservation advocates for fish passage and protection of freshwater habitat. Regional Authorities are responsible through the Resource Management Act 1991 for minimizing the impact of habitat change on freshwater fauna. Successful management of eel stocks to ensure sustainability requires the cooperation of several organizations and the sharing of information.

What is difficult is the integration of the other agencies and water resource users that also affect eel stocks, through habitat loss, drainage clearance, and hydro impacts on fish passage. Effective integration to ensure the sustainability of eel stocks is a challenge for all.

References

Annala, J. H. 1996. New Zealand's ITQ system: have the first eight years been a success or a failure? Reviews in Fish Biology and Fisheries 6:43–62.

Beentjes, M. P., and B. Bull. 2002. CPUE analyses of the commercial freshwater eel fishery. New Zealand Fisheries Assessment Report 2002/18.

Beentjes, M. P., and A. Dunn. 2003. Catch per unit effort (CPUE) analysis of the commercial freshwater eel fishery for selected areas for the period 1990–91 to 2000–01. New Zealand Fisheries Assessment Report 2003/53. Minsitry of Fisheries, Wellington, New Zealand.

Bess, R. 2001. New Zealand's indigenous people and their claims to fisheries resources. Marine Policy 25:23–32.

Best, E. 1929. Fishing methods and devices of the Maori. Dominion Museum Bulletin of New Zealand volume 12.

Cairns, D. 1942. Life history of the two species of fresh-water eel in New Zealand. III. Development of sex. Campaign of eel destruction. New Zealand Journal of Science and Technology 23(4B):173B–178B.

Casselman, J. M. 2003. Dynamics of resources of the American eel, *Anguilla rostrata*: declining abundance in the 1990s. Pages 255–274 *in* K. Aida, K. Tsukamoto, and K. Yamauchi, editors. Eel biology. Springer-Verlag, Tokyo.

Dekker, W. editors 2002. Monitoring of glass eel recruitment. Report C007/02-WD, Netherlands Institute of Fisheries Research, Ijmuiden, The Netherlands.

Downes, T. W. 1918. Notes on eels and eel-weirs (tuna and pa-tuna). Transactions and Proceedings of the New Zealand Institute 50:296–316.

Graynoth, E. 2004. Spawning escapement of female longfin eels. Final Research Report for the Ministry of Fisheries project EEL 2002–03.

Jellyman, D. J. 1987. Review of the marine life history of Australian temperate species of *Anguilla*. Pages 276–258 in M. J. Dadswell, R. J. Klauda, C. M. Moffitt, R. L. Saunders, R. A. Rulifson, and J. E. Cooper, editors. Common strategies of anadromous and catadromous fishes. American Fisheries Society, Symposium 1, Bethesda, Maryland.

Jellyman, D. J. 1994. The fishery for freshwater eels (*Anguilla* spp.) in New Zealand. New Zealand Fisheries Assessment Research Document 94/14.

Jellyman, D. J., B. L. Chisnall, L. H. Dijkstra, and J. A. T. Boubee. 1996. First record of the Australian longfinned eel, *Anguilla reinhardtii*, in New Zealand. New Zealand Journal of Marine and Freshwater Research 47:1037–1340.

Jellyman, D. J., E. Graynoth, R. I. C. C. Francis, B. L. Chisnall, and M. P. Beentjes. 2000. A review of evidence of a decline in abundance of longfinned eels (*Anguilla dieffenbachii*) in New Zealand. Final Research Report for Ministry of Fisheries Research project EEL9801, Wellington, New Zealand.

Jellyman, D. J., and J. R. E. Sykes. 2004. Review of glass eel recruitment, 1996–2002. Final Research Report, Ministry of Fisheries Research Project MOF2002/03F, Ministry of Fisheries, Wellington, New Zealand.

Martin, M., J. Boubee, E. Bowmann, and D. Griffin. 2006. Recruitment of freshwater eels: 2004–2005 and 2005–2006. Draft New Zealand Fisheries Assessment Report. Ministry of Fisheries, Wellington, New Zealand.

McDowall, R. M. (1990). New Zealand Freshwater Fishes. A natural history and guide. Heinemann Read, Auckland, New Zealand.

Molloy, J., B. Bell, M. Clout, P. de Lange, G. Gibbs, D. Given, D. Northon, N. Smith, and T. Stephens. 2002. Classifying species according to threat extinction. A system for New Zealand. Threatened Species Occasional Publication 22. New Zealand Department of Conservation, Wellington, New Zealand.

Schmidt, J. 1925. On the distribution of fresh-water eels (*Anguilla*) throughout the world. II Indo-Pacific region. A bio-geographical investigation. Kongelige Danske Videnskabernes Selskabs Skrifter 10(4):329–382.

Todd, P. R. 1978. Wairewa Maoris stick by old eeling methods. Catch (New Zealand) 5(2):24.

Part VI

Panel: Status, Assessment, and Conservation Concerns

International Eel Symposium Panel Presentations and Discussions

The following is the transcript of the taped presentations and discussions on the theme *STATUS, ASSESSMENT, AND CONSERVATION CONCERNS OF EELS (panelists and audience)*

Facilitator/Moderator:
Michael L. Jones
Department of Fisheries and Wildlife
Michigan State University
East Lansing, MI 48864

Panelists:
Martin Castonguay
Institut Maurice-Lamontagne
850 route de la Mer
Mont-Joli, Quebec G5H 3Z4

Henry Lickers
Director, Department of the Environment
Mohawk Council of Akwesasne
P.O. Box 579
Cornwall, ON K6H 5T3

Gail Wipplehauser
Department of Marine Resources
21 State House Station
Augusta, ME 04333-0021

Willem Dekker
Netherlands Institute for Fisheries Research
P.O. Box 68, 1970 AB IJmuiden
The Netherlands

Roy Stein
Department of Evolution, Ecology, and Organismal Biology
The Ohio State University
1314 Kinnear Road
Columbus, OH 43212-1156

Introduction, John Casselman

When we organized this international symposium, David and I agreed that we didn't want just another eel symposium, but we wanted one that would move the concern about the decline of the species to a new level. We decided to include a panel discussion in the symposium so that people could air their personal observations, comments, and suggestions. We were very fortunate that each person we approached for the panel enthusiastically supported our efforts. We were able to assemble people who can help us start to address this issue, and most importantly, we were able to get Mike Jones as moderator/facilitator. Mike is a professor at Michigan State University and a colleague of mine. We used to work together at the Glenora

Fisheries Station. When Mike left Glenora, we stayed in touch, so I'm really pleased to have Mike here with us. We thank him for agreeing to our request to act as moderator.

Mike Jones:
Thank you, John. The first and most significant distinction that I bring to this meeting is that absolutely everything I know about eels I've learned in the past 48 hours, so I have very little technical to contribute to this. My role is to help moderate and facilitate the discussion that we would like to encourage you in the audience and the panel members to have. I'm going to invite each of the panel members to offer a few very brief remarks, about two to three minutes worth of comment, their perspectives on what we've heard over the past couple of days. Then I'm going to open up the discussion to the floor and invite you to both respond to the panelists' comments and offer your own thoughts. Our objective here, to use John's words from the beginning of the symposium, is to try to take this to the next level. Most of the people in this room are scientists, and as scientists, we could probably spend the next 13 hours talking about all the science that we've talked about in the past couple of days. I'd like to urge you all as we go through this discussion to focus as much as you can on, not so much on the science itself, but on its implications in terms of action. John's desire to take this to the next level I think reflects the whole theme of this symposium about the worldwide decline in fish stocks and particularly our concerns about eels, which we've learned about in the past couple of days. So as you're thinking about what you'd like to say, try to focus your ideas on management. Try to focus your thinking on comparisons. One of the wonderful things about this symposium is the opportunity to hear the perspectives of people working on eels from all over the world, and I think the benefit from comparison will be extremely valuable as well. So those are my guidelines. I will try to ensure that once the panel is finished, everyone gets a chance to speak. But other than that, I'm just here to try to keep track and maybe take some notes on this virtual flip chart they call a computer. I'm going to go down the row and ask the panelists to introduce themselves—their names are also up on the overhead right now—and to offer a few words from their perspective, and then we'll open it up to discussion. So Willem, why don't you start.

Willem Dekker:
I'm Willem Dekker. I'm 47 years old and I do remember fishing in the Netherlands at night using a lamp, that all the big eels were in front of you and you wanted to get rid of them. I remember how it was in the old days. We have one monitoring station this year without any big eels being caught at all. I wanted to introduce my view on the subject. The whole annual meeting is about wild stocks. Well, essentially that's what we have seen in eels, and to my mind, we have to spot the problem. We have to ring the alarm bell that they are declining. We have to find out the causes in order to develop a remedy and to take action, and following that, we have to cross our fingers and hope we were right. Around 1990, we started really noticing the problem, at least here in North America, and we have rung the alarm bell. But we are still in that phase. The word "decline" is the most used word during this symposium. We are only just starting to discuss some of the causes. As a consequence, we are very late in developing remedies, and in my view, it will take at least another 10 years to have that part finished. So for practical purposes, stop developing remedies, stop finding out what is the one and only cause — there isn't one and only cause — and go directly to implementation of management. There is no time to waste. The stocks are going down very fast. The problem at the moment is

whether managers can do anything. To my mind that's the big question, and if we can't solve that question, the eel will be gone before we have solved it. Thank you.

Mike Jones:
Thank you. We'll just move on to the next panelist, Martin Castonguay.

Martin Castonguay:
My name is Martin Castonguay. I work with Fisheries and Oceans Canada, in Mont Joli about 350 kilometers down the river on the south side. My background is with eels, but I have not been very active in eel research over about the past 10 years. But it was kind of John to invite me to this panel, and being the program chair of this American Fisheries Society Annual Meeting, I did not have much chance to attend many of the papers of this symposium, unfortunately. However, I did see the four overview papers, and I also saw a few other papers here and there. From the overview papers, we're seeing catch and recruitment declines all over the range worldwide. This simultaneous decline of Indo-Pacific and Atlantic eels suggests that similar factors are at play. In my mind, it is hard to envisage that an oceanic factor acting at the same time in all oceans in the northern hemisphere as well as the southern hemisphere would be a likely explanation. To me it's not very likely. I think that the primary cause of this decline is anthropogenic rather than oceanic—habitat degradation, habitat loss due to dams, contamination, and fishing. So we know that unfortunately habitat degradation is often irreversible. When a shopping center is built on a marsh, there won't be wetlands anymore. Sure, you can do dam removals—that's been attempted in the United States—but from what I understand, dam removal only concerns obsolete dams. We don't have many obsolete dams around here, because we have very powerful companies that are using dams, and dam removal is not something that will ever be considered on a wide scale. So fixing the habitat is certainly not something that can be thought of in the short term to try to help eel stocks. The fishing factor is the obvious one, the one where we can have the most direct and positive effect. We have to work really hard toward reducing fishing effort to increase escapement of silver eels. We need to reduce fishing effort drastically to increase escapement. I recommend a moratorium on commercial fishing for eels in Canada. I think that should be science's position in Canada. We have a meeting this Friday of a Canadian Eel Working Group, and that's one thing we should talk about, and this is only an American eel discussion at this point. I would further argue that Canada having declared a moratorium would be in a strong position and have the moral high ground to go and see its neighbor to the south and request the same from the U.S. Let's do it differently than we did with the cod. With the cod, we waited until it was too late to act. We've seen what happened there. We had a first moratorium and the stock has hardly recovered at all. Let's not repeat the same mistake with the American eel. So let's put the precautionary principle to good use.

Mike Jones:
Thank you, Martin.

Gail Wipplehauser:
I'm Gail Wipplehauser, I work for the Maine Department of Marine Resources, and there are five of us who manage all the diadromous species in the state, including eels. The American eel problem really didn't come to our attention until about 1995 or 1996 when the fishery got

so big, and that's what really caused a lot of concern in the United States. I think probably one of the best things that ever happened was that the Atlantic States Marine Fisheries Commission developed a management plan for the eel. The good thing is that it allows us to develop some kind of standard for all the states. There are teeth in this management plan, and if states do not abide by the plan, the fisheries can be shut down. So that's one good thing that's happened. Part of that plan required that if states didn't have their fisheries managed, they either had to cap their fisheries or put something in place to hold them steady. Maine really reduced their elver fishery, and they capped their silver eel fishery, and that has been slowly declining because the people in that fishery are aging. So that fishery is slowly declining, and I think our recommendation would be that it just die out and when those people stop fishing, then the fishery is gone. The other good thing about the Atlantic States Marine Fisheries Commission Management Plan was that it required us to start collecting harvest statistics, which a lot of the states didn't collect. We also are collecting effort statistics, and that's been very useful. We instituted the young-of-the-year survey, so every state has to sample at least one site. It was very interesting this past year. Almost all the states saw a decline in the number of glass eels that were coming in. I think there were only two states that didn't see that. So it's a good relative indicator. That was the whole idea of the survey—it was something quick that people could do. It was relatively cheap.

One of the objectives of the management plan is to increase recruitment of young eels and to grow habitat, increase the amount of escapement into the ocean. Because of the way hydro power projects are licensed, essentially every state has to do it on their own. These projects are licensed for 30 to 50 years, and the licensing process takes about 5 to 6 years. So before 1996 there really was no eel passage in any of our hydro power sites. Since then I've been through about 19 new licensing projects. Two dams have been removed. Two more dams will probably be removed. Two non-hydro dams have been removed, and we have about 16 or 17 projects where we're putting in upstream or downstream passage for eels. On some of those we're requiring shutdowns at night for extended periods of time. So all those things will provide better and safer passage of eels upstream and downstream. For the relatively short period of time we've had, I think that we're making some progress. I know a lot of the other states along the East Coast are also paying particular attention to upstream and downstream passage.

Mike Jones:
Thank you, Gail.

Henry Lickers:
My name is Henry Lickers. I'm the director of the Department of the Environment for the Mohawk Council of Akwesasne. The Mohawk Council of Akwesasne lives in a complex jurisdiction. We sit in Quebec, Ontario, and New York State, so we have two federal governments, three state governments, and a number of different municipalities. Then, of course, we have the Mohawk Council of Akwesasne, the tribal council in the United States, and we have the Mohawk Nation Council of Chiefs, which is the traditional council. It has existed, as we say, since time immemorial. We've lived in this area for probably the last 10,000 years, and the archaeology shows that we've utilized the environment in our area and all the components of it for that length of time. We were first. I remember when I was a young biologist, I'd come back from New Zealand where I had done some of my graduate work, and

I came back to Akwesasne and they needed a biologist to look at some work. I can remember one of the old fishermen coming to me in 1978 and saying: "Henry, the eels are disappearing. We're finding that there's nowhere near the numbers there were before. Now what are you going to do about it?" So I went out and took a look at eels and tried to find somebody who would be interested in it and, you know, it was very hard to find anybody. There were a few people who were talking about it, a few people who were interested in it. But it didn't seem to be one of those species that too many people really wanted to look at. They're slimy, they're icky, they aren't the type of things that people would kiss. Although I saw that picture today of that big eel and I thought, Wow, that's a supermodel, that one! So it's a great honor to be here because what I see before me is a whole group of people who are saying that this is important. Eels as a component in the environment are a very important thing, and we cannot let them go. I haven't heard anybody say "No, they're over, they're gone, let them go."

So I'll say to you that there are a number of things that we're worrying about. In 1978 the eel fishermen at Akwesasne said that they would fish no eels anymore and they stopped fishing eels, and there were a number of reasons for that. One was the decrease in the number of eels they saw and also the heavy contaminant loads that were in our area that were doing in those eels. Third was the thousands—yes, thousands—of carcasses that washed up on the shores of our reserve that all had turbine damage on them from going through the turbines at power stations. And our fishermen said we couldn't continue to abuse this fish because it was so necessary to the environment, and so we stopped. And somebody would say, "What was the impact of that?" The impact of that was so great that in 1990 Canada and the United States were required to call in the armies of both countries in order to subdue a problem at Akwesasne. It wasn't only because of the eels, but it was because of the general collapse of the environment in which we lived. We could no longer fish the St. Lawrence River, because in 1978 we could find something like 178 contaminants in fish in our area. Indian Affairs told us that we should start an eel fishery and send all those eels to Europe because they would take a much higher level of contaminants. I can remember saying this to one of my grandmothers, and I thought she was going to hit me. She said, "Henry, if these fish are so contaminated that you won't feed them to your babies, why would you feed them to anybody else!" And that was the end of the discussion as far as the women were concerned at Akwesasne.

But the collapse of the eel and the fishery at Akwesasne also led to a collapse of trading—the fur trade in our area too, because the dams that went in would no longer allow the marshes to be flooded the way they were in the past, and so trapping ended. Now with that, industry came into our area, Reynolds Metals and ALCOA and fluorides inundated our cattle population, and they died. And so you have a group of about 14,000 people who live in the center of the St. Lawrence depending upon an ecology to live by. And in the Dirty Thirties, our people used to ship food out to non-native communities because we knew you needed it. With the collapse of those industries (we call them traditional industries in our community), the non-traditional economics came in. We all know them. They're gambling, drugs, transport of aliens across borders—all of these types of things began to replace those traditions that we had, and in our community some people opposed those. So in 1990 a revolution took place in which part of our community fought the other part of the community for control. The gamblers and what we know as the warriors established themselves as these new—call them non-communal entrepreneurs—who were going to turn our community into a place where all these good things could be had from gambling and all these other things. The problem is, our community said, No, we wouldn't have them. And so we went to war and the people were kicked out of our community and they went to Kahnawake. When they got to Kahnawake, they found they couldn't stay there, so they needed an issue because they knew that they would be arrested the next day because the army was hard on their trails. At that same time there was a small place just north of Montreal that had had a lands claim for 150 years, and that place was called Oka. The next thing you know, Canada had a revolution where you had native people who were branded freedom fighters and the week before had been shooting at their own people at Akwesasne.

So when you ask me what are the impacts of this and how serious is this decline in the eel population, I tell you that if we do not take care of this and we do not do something about it, the impacts on our society will be just as great. Too many of these things have happened in the past. When we look at buffalo, we look at caribou, we look at passenger pigeons, and all the things that we've seen and our people have seen in this society and we watch them disappear, we can't allow it again.

I'm happy to be here when I see people who are as concerned about them as I am. Stopping or banning eel fisheries, I think it would be a small cost now. We're looking at the tail end of this population. I remember my grandfather used to say to me, "Henry, when the buffalo were really great, nobody worried about the site that they came from, but as the numbers got smaller and smaller and smaller, they worried about site. Suddenly you weren't worried about the big herds. We worried about little sites." And today what I'm hearing people here talk about is where is the site that they breed? Not that there is this enormous number of eels that we can look at it as a stock.

The last thing I'll say to you is that eels have an intrinsic value unto themselves and the value that they have to the environment far outweighs anything that we can feed our people, far outweighs the cost of a small fishery that we would depend upon. Yes, we will find other things to eat, and I think that eels should be allowed to live in this world because they truly are a magnificent thing. Thank you.

Mike Jones:
Thank you, Henry.

Roy Stein:
Remind me next time, Henry, to sit on the other side of you.

My name is Roy Stein. I'm on the faculty of Ohio State University. I also happen to be sitting up here as a representative from the Great Lakes Fishery Commission, which is, as some of you may not know, a bi-national organization that's dedicated to sea lamprey control in the Great Lakes, healthy ecosystems, and in the context of this particular symposium, cooperative fishery management. I sit before you as one of those commissioners, actually the one who signed the check from our organization in partial support of this international symposium, and I have to tell you that we got our money's worth. With 56 presentations and 36 posters, I am quite impressed—and being a fish biologist but not an eel biologist—with the quality of the presentations and the tremendous enthusiasm (as exhibited by the previous speaker) by the presenters and the audience alike throughout and the rather serious circumstances in which we now find ourselves with regard to eel populations. Upon this template and in the spirit of the last formal presentation that we had as part of the symposium, I would urge all of you to work cooperatively and to improve the status of eel species around the world. As just one organization, my organization here in North America, we stand ready to assist you and your informal organization in any way we can, be it financial, logistical, or even intellectual. Whatever you decide are your next steps, we at the Great Lakes Fishery Commission will be there to help in any way that you all deem appropriate. Thank you for the opportunity just to say those few words, and as the science discussion progresses, maybe I'll weigh in. Thank you very much.

Mike Jones:
I'd like to thank all the panelists. I think that's a very provocative start to our discussion. At this point, I would invite anybody from the audience to raise their hand. If it's at all possible, try to move to the microphone. And my advice to people who would like to speak, you're welcome to direct your comments to one of the members of the panel or, alternatively, just a general comment. So the floor's open at this point.

Alex Hoar:
My name's Alex Hoar. Thank you very much for your comments. If the decline of the eel is as dire as we've heard and as the multiple speakers have asked to take action, why not ask the biggest fishermen on the river to let the eels go free and have hydroelectric projects shut down at night and let the eels go free and try to see if we can't increase the escapement instead of killing anywhere from 10 to 25% that pass. That would be a lot better than closing down the fisheries because we wouldn't really be closing down the hydroelectric stations. Maybe they could spill enough water to let eels go by and still be generating or shut down completely if that's what it takes. That would stimulate them to figure out how to provide free passage for eels at their facilities. I think it would provide a motivation to move quickly in that direction. We have facilities that shut down now, and it was their option because it was the cheapest and it's working well. There are others that would be more difficult because of their size. There are others that would cause great economic harm. I'm talking about mom-and-pop operations. But still, why not put out a call to let the eels go free? We would have to determine perhaps better indicators for downstream migration. Maybe we could come up with better predictive models. I'll let the experts on eels grapple with that one. A second point. If there are habitats out there now that do not contain eels but may have in the past—I'm talking about large reservoirs—should we be putting eels into them in order to increase the number and increase the escapement that might be possible and just hope that there's some response to that? But I'd be interested in people's feedback on both suggestions.

Mike Jones:
Anyone on the panel like to comment on that?

Willem Dekker:
I arrived late last night and I worked during the night hours to find out how to present essentially my view. We are in the order of magnitude of 1% of what it has been before. If we allow all of

them to survive, I'm rather worried that we will never be able to get the 30% spawning stock we had in the past. We are at this moment, in my view, at a point in time where it might be already simply too late. Essentially what you are saying is I restrict to one point of action. No, don't restrict yourself. Reduce fisheries where possible.

Mike Jones:
Any other comments on that or other comments?

Eric Feunteun:
I'm Eric Feunteun. Well, just to give my thinking about restocking. In France we've been talking about restocking quite a lot, and what we've decided at the national level was to recommend not to develop, not to implement restocking projects that would translocate elvers or glass eels fished in one river to another geographical area because simply we're not sure that we will increase the stock. If we want to do this to manage fisheries, this is okay, but if we say we're restocking from one river to another to sustain the population, we're really far from being sure that it's efficient. So, for the moment we say that we can do this for very short periods, it's never sufficient to restore the population as a whole. That's the French advice and it's very much debated in Europe at the moment.

Mike Jones:
John, you would like to speak to that?

John Casselman:
Yes, I'd like to comment on this because I think the restocking program has many different facets. For example, if you look at the Great Lakes Fishery Commission, whenever we lost lake trout in lakes in the Great Lakes, we tried to control lamprey and then we tried to stock lake trout to rehabilitate. But I very specifically remember Ken Loftus, director of Ontario fisheries, telling me that those lake trout are our miner's canary and we need to keep them in people's faces. And I think if you look at a restocking program, it can do many things. If we stock, we're not necessarily trying to produce eels in order to go back to the Sargasso and spawn. It could well be that they would help people understand that the issue is still there. If you look at Lake Ontario and the upper St. Lawrence River—and I'm sure it's going to be the lower St. Lawrence River shortly—they're virtually gone. When the Onondaga of the St. Lawrence Iroquois speared in the inshore waters in the 1600s, we know there were probably 60 eels per hectare and, in fact, half the fish biomass was eels. Our commercial fisherman went out this year and indexed the middle of the east end of Lake Ontario. This year he caught one eel in 5 hectares. Ten years ago he could get 20 eels per hectare. So they're rapidly disappearing from Lake Ontario. So what are we going to do here? Are we going to allow this habitat to become vacant? We are repeating the decline in Oneida Lake, farther inland, where in the 1900s in the eel weirs, they caught 100 tons of eels each year. In the past 25 years, farther up the watershed, they saw only two eels in that lake. So if we let these eels disappear from Lake Ontario, they're going to disappear from our traditional knowledge and our consciousness, and I don't think that's acceptable. So I think we need to be at least looking at restocking programs, and I would recommend that we consider it in the St. Lawrence River and Lake Ontario.

Mike Jones:
Somebody has a comment on that?

Brian Knights:
I'm Brian Knights. Yes, my question is about recovery time and targets. What are we looking for? Are we trying to get back to abundances in the late 1970s? What do we want to go back to?

Mike Jones:
I'll reiterate the question, since you didn't speak into the microphone. The question, for the record, is what should be the appropriate targets for recovery if we are going to embark on a recovery program for eels. Henry?

Henry Lickers:
First, I'd like to see them there. We have no eels. I want to see them first. Regardless of what we do, I want my people to see them again. Right now we're not seeing any, so I'm not even at the point that says let's propose a target. I just want my children to be able to look and see eels and make sure that they're there. I think that when we start talking about eel targets and what we should be looking at we'll have a lot more things to consider. But we know that probably the biggest environmental impact we have in the world today is not the eels—it's us. Our population is growing like we're a cancer over the surface of the earth. And the longer it keeps going like that, there won't be space for anything else. So we have many big problems that we've got to deal with. I'd really just like to see the eels back. You're talking about one or two. I know that when my fishermen go out and they look, even though they're not fishing for them, they're saying that you don't see them. You don't see them the way you did and again I'd like to be able to just see them back.

Let me put it this way. I really think that what we have to do is start, like you're saying, restocking. Reduce mortalities, reduce fishing. Because what I'm also hearing from everybody is that we're not really sure what's happening in the Sargasso, what's happening in between, what's happening there. But we know that at the end point where we are, there's something dreadful happening, and it's been happening for a long time.

Mike Jones:
I want to make sure we do two things. One is I'd like this audience to think about the genuine desire and sense of urgency for action. What can a learned group like this actually do? I'd like to hear comments on that. I'd also like, before we're finished, to hear a little bit more about the global perspective on this issue and whether the concerns that we're hearing, particularly with regard to Atlantic eels, are issues that are shared. And there needs to be a global perspective from the concern of Pacific eels as well. So I urge commentary on those two subjects. Julie?

Julie Weeder:
I guess throughout this meeting we've been kind of overtaken with frustration. But I think many of us feel that we really have a problem and we really have to do something. It seems to me that we've kind of reached the end of what scientists can do. We have the science, and we've told people about it. We've told the appropriate people about it repeatedly, but nothing

is happening. If anything, of course, we're finding things are even more dire than we thought, even at the last symposium possibly. So I suggest that we take our heads out of the water and move toward a public action, really focus our effort on trying to get more people interested in caring about this population or these species, I should say, because I think that there is a global environmental community and I think that there's global interest in addressing ecological issues. And if we could get this out there as something to galvanize people around, I think maybe we could actually make things happen. You know, it seems to me that what we've been trying to do so far is just not working.

So, one specific idea I had, I think we need some professional help with this kind of thing. We all need to be analyzed anyway, because how could we barely care about eels at all, but we had heard from the Great Lakes Fishery Commission that they would be able to address funding issues in the future, and possibly other agencies would too. I don't know if this is something people do, but why don't we just hire somebody to get the issue out there? Take more of a public relations approach. We have all the evidence to provide to people. If we found somebody who really knew how to galvanize people around the issue, we would be able to provide them with the information they needed and hopefully the funding that is needed to really do something about this. I think once it got out there, if it was something that these major environmental organizations paid attention to, I'm sure we could all agree that there are lots of people who would care about it if it was on their radar. So there's kind of a different approach to what we're trying to do here. We might consider branching out into other ideas.

Mike Jones:
I hear you saying that you're urging this collection of concerned people who care about eels to form something more formal that would become the mechanism that would then foster advocacy, secure resources from perhaps international commissions that ultimately would take the action of not continuing to discuss the science but rather to try and raise the sort of global consciousness of this symbolic creature, things like that.

Julie Weeder:
I certainly don't think this should happen in place of any of the things that we're doing here. And I also would want to avoid being bogged down in forming another organization to address this. You know, we form the organization, then two years later we may have the money for a meeting, then we take another two years to figure out who to talk to. You can obviously see that I'm pretty frustrated about this. It seems to me that everything people have said so far is that we have to do something right now. So, if we can come up with some way that we don't get bogged down in bureaucracy and even take a quick and easy approach to this and drum up support if we can. It doesn't have to be a big organized collective of people who get together. It can just be some people from this meeting. I don't know how to organize it, but just try to get some sources of funding, hire somebody who knows how to do this and get out there.

Mike Jones:
A gimmick. How about if we get a bunch of images of people kissing eels and carry them around as your mantra. Henry.

Henry Lickers:
One of the things that I always stress and has been stressed to me many times is that if you get 25 biologists in a room, they'll think about how to come up with more research funds for themselves. I agree. I think that what you need is to broaden the people who are concerned about it. If you got Claudia Schiffer as one of the people who was going to look at eels, I guarantee you'd have thousands of people talking. If you had 15 lawyers here talking about eels, the direction would be completely different. But what the lawyers would be doing is turning back to you guys and saying, "Well, what data do we have? What are the issues?" And so I think what you need to do is broaden your action, bring more people into it. The sociology of this, for example, at Akwesasne has been immense. As I said, the governments both have spent $1.5 billion policing Akwesasne since 1990. Just think how much money you folks could use if we used that all for eel research. We could hold each eel as it went up the river. But we continuously throw good money after bad. So I look not only to our biology people but I look to the sociologists. I look to the political scientists. I look to all of these other people. What do they believe about eels, and have we asked them? If we haven't asked them, then we're the ones who are at fault.

Mike Jones:
I think that's an appeal to everybody in this room, all of whom probably when you go back to the institutions where you work have contacts who walk those paths, and you should talk to them about this.

Kim Houston:
I'm Kim Houston, with Fisheries and Oceans and Habitat Operation in headquarters. A lot of these things are coming together in my mind. I'm thinking about some of the things that Martin said earlier and then what Julie just said. There might be other mechanisms out there. From my perspective, I'm thinking of habitat managers. We have a mechanism in the Fisheries Act in Canada to conserve and protect fish habitats. We have biologists out in the field who are doing reviews of any kind of proposals but they need to know if there is an issue. They need to know what types of habitat they're supposed to be protecting. We might not be able to restore some of the habitats that have already been lost, but we can protect what we have now. So I think we should probably look for other mechanisms. I was just brought into this whole issue recently from a habitat perspective, just as an offshoot, because people kept saying it's a habitat problem. And the more I become aware of it, the more I see that there are simple things that we, as habitat managers, can do to help this cause. So you might want to go out there and find other groups or organizations who have mechanisms that they can implement. We might not be aware of them, but we should try to find them. I think that this whole idea of getting the message out there is important. With Atlantic salmon, you have a huge lobby group. They're an important species, so they get a lot of money and a lot of resources. Maybe we have to do something like that with eels. We have to get the profile out there.

Mike Jones:
Martin?

Martin Castonguay:
Yes, I'd like to respond to this. I agree that's certainly a valuable way to increase and enhance

habitat, but it's not enough. We need to do more than that. The situation is too urgent to start forming committees and at the pace eel committees are moving, five years from now you'll still be talking about forming the committee. So I think we need more urgent action than this.

Brian Knights:
Brian Knights from the University of Westminster. Interesting that Henry mentioned lawyers and things like that. That immediately made me think that in a court of law, if we went up and said eels are declining because of all these things going on in fresh water, a lawyer would say, "Well, what's happening on the marine side? What's happening in the ocean?" I'm a little concerned that we're getting a bit too fixated on the freshwater area and not recognizing the possibilities of enormous changes out there, whereas, as I said earlier, a 0.1% change in mortality rate in the ocean can lead to an order of magnitude difference in terms of recruitment. I'm not denying that we need to act. Long-term changes roughly coincide with similar fluctuations in the environment over 20-to-25-year cycles. Such factors might substantially affect the relationship between spawning stock and recruitment. Consequently, it's suggested that using a steady state perspective—and this is why I asked my earlier question of what do we go back to, the late 1970s or what, what's our aim—consequently it's suggested that using a steady state perspective for the population dynamics may lead to mismanagement of the stock. Was this northeast Arctic cod? What's it do with eels? If you look in *Fisheries and Oceanography*, there's a paper on sardines. If you look at a paper by Charvez, which is on sardines and anchovies, eels follow the anchovy pattern. Anchovies have been down and sardines have been up. It is now starting to reverse and anchovies are coming up. I do feel that enormous events go on out in the ocean that we've been ignoring recently. People are going to say, "Well, wait a minute. What about the oceanic side? What are you aiming back to? Are you aiming back to the 1970s or the average over the last few centuries?" I'd just like some views on that from the panel.

Mike Jones:
I'm going to invite the other two gentlemen who are waiting patiently in line to comment and then we'll return to the panel.

Don Jellyman:
I'm Don Jellyman from New Zealand. Just to bring a bit of an Indo-Pacific perspective, basically a brief response to Brian. I'm sure you're right, very likely so. I can see in theories, of course, that there's very little we can do about oceanic phases where there are a lot of anthropogenic effects. I'm thinking that Martin touched on that. Is it coincidence that we have declining trends in other species of eels, including our New Zealand longfin?

Just two brief comments on our species. One is the restocking program, which has been partially successful in some catchments. The cynical side of that is the hydro operators have said you've now created a problem for us. Whereas we had no silver eel escapement in these catchments before because we had no recruitment, you put eels in and you've created a problem. Now, there are some positive sides to that as well. The second one is that our fisheries managers are between a rock and a hard place because we have no recruitment databases. So they're saying, "Produce solid evidence that will stand up under litigation that will prove we have a recruitment failure."

We have snippets of information, and at this stage, as I've said, these are not sufficient to invite the precautionary principle. But one trump card that we do have is our own native people, our Maori people, who have a very strong affiliation with eels and also are very politically persuasive. Perhaps for us that's a route that we may be more effective in than just trying a purely scientific one and trying to convince the managers it's enough information to make some tough decisions. Allied to that, we need to learn from the European and American experiences. Our problem could be longer because the generation times of our longfinned eels are measured in 30 or 40 or even 50 years. So if you have a problem, we probably have a bigger one to come.

Mike Jones:
Thank you.

Brian Jessop:
I'm Brian Jessop, and I've been thinking about approaches to addressing how we take action on the perception that stocks have declined severely and I do believe in many cases the actuality of that. But one of the processes that has not yet been mentioned that has been used in the past and will continue to be in reference to stocks and decline is the endangered species process. I think some thought should be given to how one might proceed through that. I know there are established procedures, and I may be incorrect, but I think as far as Canada is concerned, the eel has already gone through the COSEWIC process and has not managed to make the grade. This is a hurdle that this meeting is going to have to jump past in order to make progress on this. Perhaps the earlier assessment was in error and, if so, you're going to have to demonstrate this and a review of the process. I'm sure there are some people here who are closer to the most recent COSEWIC review and could address this better than I can.

Mike Jones:
Thank you. I'm going to continue with the lineup. I just want to appeal to the mood of the group here. It's almost 25 minutes after 3. We officially ended at 20 minutes after 3. I don't get the sense that everybody's clamouring for the doors. There is an AFS business meeting that starts at 3:30 and it would be imprudent for me, especially with Martin here, not to advise you that that is happening, and go if you need to go. But I think we have a captive audience. You want us to continue this discussion for a few more minutes? Willem and Martin had indicated to me they wanted to say something before we continue.

Martin Castonguay:
That's a very good point, Brian. In fact, there are many ways by which in Canada you can have a moratorium, and the COSEWIC listing is one. At this point the latest list I saw, it was not yet in the vulnerable category, but it's the category just below. I saw it on an intermediate list, so it's up for examination, I guess pretty soon. I'm not exactly sure what it means but I could check it out. We have people at the office who are quite well versed in this. But that's certainly a possible route. That's a good comment.

Willem Dekker:
You answered Brian Knights, I will answer Brian. The oceanic phase—first of all, I don't believe in the synchrony of the decline of the stocks. The Japanese eel was at least 10 years

earlier. The proof for the synchrony in both the Atlantic species is rather weak and I can undermine part of your proof.

Brian Knights:
That's okay, I can take it.

Willem Dekker:
That's not the point. The point is, yes, it might be oceanic, but no, it might also be anthropogenic. Where is the burden of proof? The real declaration and the precautionary approach very clearly state, stop all anthropogenic impacts if there is a question about the burden of proof. I'm warning that we are more or less at the last chance. If we don't do anything now, we are back to a situation where you can't go out sampling in the ocean. There aren't any left. You can't go through Lake Ontario to sample eels. There aren't any left. So we have ignored the burden of proof for at least 20 years. This is our last chance.

Mike Jones:
I'm going to invite the last two gentlemen who are standing to comment and then I'm going to ask the panel if they have some final words.

Kevin Reid:
I'm Kevin Reid. As the biologist for the Ontario Commercial Fisheries' Association, I thought it would be wise to say something about this proposal for calling for a moratorium on fishing of eels. I'd be the first to admit that it's possibly a very substantial fishing mortality, particularly of yellow phases. But calling for a moratorium at this point is sort of like saying that the last straw that broke the camel's back was the only straw that broke the camel's back and that if we're dealing with catchments that have commercial fisheries and hydroelectric concerns on the same catchments, to talk about fishing moratoriums without major efforts being made, as Alex pointed out, with respect to upstream passage and downstream passage is just not on as far as I am concerned. I think that it's not fair to the commercial fishers, and both sides have to take responsibility for part of this problem. You know, fisheries have been going on for hundreds of years in Kamaraska and so forth, and it was only after the Seaway and the construction of the Seaway that we started to see many of these effects. It's no coincidence that the only viable commercial fishery in the upper St. Lawrence now for eels is in Lake St. Francis and Lake St. Pierre downstream of the two dams. And finally, with respect to this comment about stocking programs, I think that's not a bad idea inherently, but we have to perform some form of risk assessment or risk analysis before we embark on that. For example, decisions about the source of the stock will be absolutely critical, especially concerning some of the discussions we've had here about geographic stock structure.

Doug Dixon:
Doug Dixon with EPRI. I didn't respond right away to Alex's recommendation until my heart rate came down a little bit. On the east coast of the United States there are about 500 licensed and exempt hydroelectric plants that represent somewhere between 10,000 and 15,000 megawatts of electricity. You shut them all down, Alex, where are you going to get the electricity?

Alex Hoar:
It would only be for a few minutes.

Speaker identity unannounced:
Right now the recommendation I've seen is as long three months if we can get something like the Migromat working. But right now that's 10,000 to 15,000 megawatts of electricity. I don't know if you know what 10,000 to 15,000 megawatts of electricity is. That's about 10 to 15, maybe as many as 20, nuclear power plants...

So you have to replace that electricity if you have a shutdown. You're not building any nuclear power plants, you can't build new generation that fast so the only way you can replace it is burn more coal. If you burn more coal, you have to mine more coal. And you know what's associated with burning of coal—basically, you take the problem from this room and you make it your neighbour's room. Sometimes there just are not simple solutions to problems like that. I joked the other day when I said the New York Eel Authority, referring to the New York Power Authority. You know, this is an organization in the United States that has done more research on eels, for the benefit of eels, than any other organization in the United States and that's even more than the U.S. Fish and Wildlife Service, National Marine Fishery Service, Atlantic States Marine Fisheries Commission. In Canada probably Hydro-Québec has done the same. I think if you looked to work with them and work with others to find solutions, there'd be much more accomplished rather than alienating them by haphazardly throwing out statements like blowing up dams.

So essentially, I think in industry, as I have brought to this issue, there is a concern but shutting down does not necessarily work. And Alex and I have also had this at another time at another meeting. But if you give me $100,000 today, I'll go get you 100,000 eels. I can buy an eel in Chesapeake Bay for $1. You go shut down a plant, a small hydroelectric plant, for three months, that's going to be a lost revenue, between $75,000 and $100,000 that might have protected only 60 eels. Now granted, those are out-migrating female eels very important to the stock, but those 100,000 eels that I could have bought for bait would grow up some day to be big eels. I think relative to a fishery that has a food component, it is exceptionally important and should be maintained or should be carefully considered. But to power companies, when you can use this fish for bait and you can buy it for $1, it's a very difficult message to pass up the power chain to get to them to say that you have to spend $2 to $3 million to build the louvre system to protect 60 eels when I can buy 100,000 for $100,000.

Mike Jones:
The panel is going to revolt against me unless I let them speak.

Henry Lickers:
I'd love to work with a power authority, but they don't want to work with us, and especially on these types of issues where we've been debating with them for a long time. This is using a jurisdiction to say, "Oh yes, we want to work with you," but then using a jurisdiction to separate people who do. My problem with the New York Power Authority is that it continuously hides from us. We've been in this relicensing thing with the New York Power Authority for all this time and have been just trying to discuss issues, but the Mohawk Council of Akwesasne and

the Traditional Council of Akwesasne have been frozen out of that discussion. Instead, what they've said is that they're now working with the St. Regis Tribe as the federally recognized Indian tribe in the United States. If they really want to work with us, then they should work with us all not work with just the individuals they think that they want to work with. So, lots of politics in this issue, and it will continue.

Willem Dekker:
Yes, that's exactly the point I would like to make. I think it was Julie who said there's frustration. Yes, there is. Not because people are arguing, but there's nothing being done. That's the frustration.

Mike Jones:
Two people are waiting to speak and I will invite you to come forward. I'm going to blow the whistle though at 3:45 in deference to the panel members, to myself, to all of you who probably desperately need a personal moment. So, I'll invite these two gentlemen and I'm afraid that that's going to be all the comments that we will have time for from the floor and then I'll let the panel members have the final word.

Speaker identity unannounced:
I don't want to take time from the panel. But I'm a little tired of people blaming the ocean for a problem that's widespread throughout the world. We don't know a lot about what goes on in the ocean, but what we do know is what's going on in fresh water. And I'd like to argue a little bit against some of the comments that have been made today about the perspective between the ocean and the continental habitats. A study that was done by Dieter Busch a few years ago suggested that something in the order of 80% of the eel habitat in North America has either been eliminated or access severely restricted by human activities. And I think that's documented in the report. We have to work on what we have control over. We can work to understand the other issues, but we can take action only on those things for which we have some control. And that's what happens in continental waters. With respect to a fish that reproduces one time in its life I'd like to argue a little bit against what Brian said because mortality at one life stage affects another life stage only dependent on what parameters you put in the model. I've done a little playing around with some of those numbers as well and it doesn't really make very much difference where you put the mortality in because every fish you kill hasn't yet reproduced. So I'd just like to make the suggestion that while we're all urging some kind of action let's not hide any longer behind some supposed ignorance about what happens in the ocean.

Giulio De Leo:
In order to be a little bit provocative, I would say that if we step out of this room and we interview the majority of the people attending this meeting, they probably won't know much about eel dynamics and the collapse. There is a nice poster in the room down there talking about education in schools, kindergartens and so on. They have beautiful stories on tuna fishing, on dolphins, on turtles, on blue whales and so on, but there is nothing about eels. And I'm thinking about Italy at least, the country I come from, the public is actually aware about these fishes. It's not really restricted to a bunch of technicians or scientists working in these areas. So I think we really have to do more about communication. And if I go back to Italy

and I try to talk to the media—well, I'm not a Nobel Prize winner, I'm not Claudia Schiffer, so I won't be able to gather much attention. So in order to try to be a little bit more concrete, I think that we could come out from these panels with the idea to write a short declaration or appeal for eel conservation that I can take, which will be signed by all you distinguished scientists, and I can take it back to Italy, to my own country and send it to non-governmental organizations—I mean like the international wildlife, the IWF or the local one—I can send it to people working in academia and to the public decision makers. In order to try to make people sensitive and with my fellow colleagues from Europe, we can send this piece of paper, this appeal to the European Union and to the general direction of environment in order to make people sensitive. So this is something I think we can do, because we are a group of scientists and this is our job.

Mike Jones:
Thank you, good point. Okay, I'm going to give you the final word, gentlemen at the front, and we're going to go backwards this time, so we'll start with Dr. Stein.

Roy Stein:
I guess just a couple of observations that I made during the conversations this afternoon, and I'll relate it to a species or a set of species that I know a bit more about and that's our Pacific salmon. I would say relative to the people who are concerned that I wish we would move away from the ocean versus continental perspectives. I think there are mortality factors operating in both those areas, and I think we ought to know something about what's going on. And remember that with Pacific salmon, at least in our country—in the States—and in Canada, we really didn't appreciate the role of ocean productivity in influencing those stocks. And don't forget that with Pacific salmon, hatcheries and stocking were not the answer.

Gail Wipplehauser:
Well, I guess I'm going to continue doing what I've been doing, trying to protect eels moving upstream and downstream and trying to reduce fisheries on them and working with other people in other states who contact me for information. I was interested in Alex's idea about sort of having a blanket Prescription 18 for eels that would require shutdown of hydro power plants. I was wondering if there was something that this organization could do. Write a recommendation? Would that be useful? Then I think that would be a good idea.

Speaker identity unannounced:
You can't. Where are you going to replace the lost power? You have to burn more coal.

Gail Wipplehauser:
Well, we could start with replacing all the incandescent lights with power-saving lights. We could start by replacing some of the old refrigerators with new efficient refrigerators.

Speaker identity unannounced:
That's a different type of campaign. But to sit here and say you're going to have Section 18 prescriptions for all power plants—that is not going to work and it's going to alienate the industry that you most want to work with.

Gail Wipplehauser:
I've been working with them. We don't have passage at any of our hydro power plants, and we have some people who have signed agreements who are trying to back out of them. Sorry.

Mike Jones:
I'm going to intervene here. With all respect to the opinions of both of the current speakers, one of the things it's impossible to do in a discussion like this is to reach consensus on contentious issues. What we can do is put these issues on the table, and we can recognize that this is not a simple problem with a simple solution. My sense is that there's nobody in this room who, however frustrated and anxious they are for action, has a sense that there are simple solutions to this problem. I think that's where we have to leave it in the context of this forum. So if I may move to Martin?

Martin Castonguay:
Well, I was going to say I have nothing else to say but I'll say it again. I think the only thing we can do is control fishing. That's all we can do in the short term.

Willem Dekker:
I think there's one other point I would like to make, and that is that we're not sure what's happening in the stock, so we're not sure what to do. That's the point we made today, and I added that to my belief, that means you have to go forward to the phase of action. But the other point is that there are lots of interesting details, interesting data about the eels that have not been analyzed in this framework. I'm convinced that we have to proceed with our research to address the issues that have come forward here as the fundamental uncertainties, and I'm convinced that many of the uncertainties can be solved in a rather short time if we are willing to cooperate to use the information that is around.

Mike Jones:
All right. I feel completely ill equipped to offer the final word on a symposium that I said I knew nothing about to start with. So all I'll say in closing is just that it has been a very interesting experience for me to have participated in this symposium and to be sitting up here at this point. I detect that despite the sort of dire straits that the species, the set of species that you are so, you care so much about are in, I sense a great deal of passion. Some of that passion may reflect itself in contentious or differing views on what the most important questions or what the most important solutions are, but I sense a great deal of passion. I think that you collectively should seize the opportunity as you've talked about here to turn that passion into positive action, into raising the public consciousness about this vitally important issue. So, thank you for your attention, and thank you panellists for your contributions to this. I probably should offer to turn the microphone over to our symposium convenors to give you your marching orders.

John Casselman:
A very special thanks to you, Mike, and to the panel for your participation. There are a couple of comments that David and I would like to make. It is apparent that there is passion here, tremendous passion. We have an issue. The question is, What do we do about it? We feel that we need an action plan, some type of declaration of concern, and we think that

assembling this proceedings and getting this material together is, in fact, an action plan. Also, although I have never heard of it, maybe we could work together on something like the Migratory Birds Convention Act. Why could we not have a Migratory Eels Convention Act? A cooperative agreement among all involved. However, David and I think the initial solution is unilateral action, and we challenge each of you to take on this unilateral action and start to do something about this issue of eel declines. Everyone of us could make a difference. And certainly disagreeing and being in controversy on this issue is not going to solve the problem. Ultimately, we all need to work together. Possibly we could do this by preparing a declaration of concern, as Giulio De Leo has suggested.

Thanks to each of you for contributing and participating. I think that the challenge is clear: we all need to make a difference and move this to the next level. So, in that context I'd like to ask Henry Lickers if he would give us an official closing—a traditional Haudenosaunee closing.

Part VII

Closing

Traditional Haudenosaunee Closing and Blessing

HENRY LICKERS
Director, Department of the Environment
Mohawk Council of Akwesasne
Cornwall, ON K6H 5T3, Canada

I'm very proud to stand in front of you all here. I was thinking about, we were talking about organizations and similar things. Well, I think we've formed our organization already from the faces I see around us. And I think we can call ourselves the Excellent Eels League (EEL) and I think those excellent EELs will go out from here to their homes and talk about these issues and make sure that everyone around you understands and knows your positions and that we will work and see each other again. I was thinking maybe Sean Connery could be the person for us.

We say that whenever we are gathered one of us is chosen to give a greeting and thanksgiving and so now I'm going to ask you and lay a heavy responsibility upon all of you. And the responsibility is this—that you've come a long way to be here and you've left people behind. I know that it is the custom among your people to thank each other for being here. But it is the custom of the Haudenosaunee for you to send back our thank yous. I want you to go back to your communities and tell your spouses that we are very very appreciative of the sacrifice that they have made. We want you to go back to your elders in your communities and say to them of the things that we've talked about here but tell them also that we know that you are active people in your community and that you are needed by them. Tell them that we appreciate that sacrifice. Look to your children, because you have been away from them for a long time and they look for you every day and we know how important they are to you. So, please, go back to them from the assembled people here and tell them just how much we understand that sacrifice that they have made. Tell the men and women in your community that this group of people here appreciates them and they understand how much you are needed in your communities because you wouldn't be here unless you were active and one of the most active people in your communities. So go back to them and tell them that we appreciate this. The Haudenosaunee say go back and look unto the land that you stand upon because out of that land comes the seven generations into the future and those generations are the generations that we're working for. For it is not us that will benefit from the work that we do here today it will be our grandchildren and our great grandchildren. So go back to them also and tell them that the sacrifices that they have made we appreciate them. I ask you to turn your minds to all of the other people upon this world because they also are important to us and their opinions will help us. So I ask you now to bring together your minds and think about the people of this world and can we agree that they are important to us.

I ask you to think about the Mother Earth as she continues to carry out her responsibility to us, giving us all of the things that we need upon this world and if we look to that earth and in the color of those soils we see the color of all of our skins and that as a true mother she takes care of us. I ask you to think about the fishes of this world, that which we've talked about today, but all of the other species of fishes that are in those waters and oceans that surround us for they are carrying out their responsibility to us and to creation and they need no one to describe to them how to do that. And so I ask you to bring together your minds and think about the waters and the fishes of this world and can we agree that they are important to us. I ask you to think about the animals of this world that are beside us, the 4-legged animals and the birds that sing. It never ceases to amaze me that in the morning when I hear the voices of my brothers and sisters, the birds, that it swells my heart and makes my spirit sing. And when I see those animals that live with me, some of them even in our own houses and we call them pets, but we treat them like our brothers and sisters. The animals that live in the far off places, the wildernesses, are also our brothers and sisters and require and need us to be responsible for them. So I ask you now to bring together your minds and think about the animals and the birds of this world and can we agree that they are important to us. I ask you to think about the plants of this world as they continue to support us and all of the rest of creation. The Haudenosaunee hold the three sisters—corn, beans and squash—as important to us but there are many other medicinal plants out there that are fulfilling their responsibility to us and sometimes when we forget how to use those plants, we can look to the animals and they will show us how to use them. And then there are the trees, the forests that surround us, that have provided us with the oxygen in this air. I ask you now to bring together your minds and think about those trees and plants of this world and can we agree that they are important to us. I ask you to think about the four great winds that blow around us. We know that those winds blow cleansing airs to us and keep us.

The Haudenosaunee talk about the grandfathers or the voices of the grandfathers as we listen to the thunder and lightning that comes. And when they come, those grandfathers warn us of things that are happening in our world that we must be ever vigilant of. So when you listen and you hear that thunder make sure you take heed that there is a danger close. I ask you now to bring together your minds and think about the four great winds and the voices of the grandfathers and can we agree that they are important to us. Every day we see our elder brother the sun rise and every day our elder brother the sun fulfills his responsibility to us and every day that sun continues to warm the faces of our children as they play. That we could carry out our responsibilities to creation as regular as the sun does. I ask you now to bring together your minds and think about the sun and can we agree that he is important to us.

At night we see our grandmother the moon as she turns her face to us every 28 days and that 28-day cycle is the cycle of all female things upon this world. And she has great power to move all of the waters of this world even the waters in the first environment, the womb. So I ask you now to bring together your minds and think about the grandmother moon and through her all female things upon this world, and can we agree that she is important to us. In the past the Haudenosaunee said that they could talk to the stars but we have long since forgotten how to do that. But the stars continue to carry out their responsibility to us, guiding us across the surface of this earth and as the Haudenosaunee say, giving us the dew in the morning that we see on the grass. So I ask you now to bring together your minds and think about the stars, and can we agree that they are important to us. There is a sacred world around us in which four great sacred beings that the Haudenosaunee hold dear can help and guide us.

In times of confusion and in times of wonder sometimes we have doubt in our hearts, but if we look deep into our hearts we can see those spirits and understand what they say. So the Haudenosaunee says we must listen deeply to ourselves and deeply to our neighbours that these four great spirits will help us to go to guidance, giving us guidance to peace and harmony upon this world. Also, we know that there have been many great teachers before us. Each of us that sits here today casts back in our minds to the teachers who have taught us our things, but there are teachers beyond those who have come and their voices echo to us down the corridors of time, each of them teaching us how to live upon this world. Each of them bringing us a message of harmony. I also ask you though to listen to the small voices in the community for sometimes from those small voices in your community come great knowledge and great wisdom. That we acknowledge all of the teachers of this world.

And so I come to a place where the Haudenosaunee say that we must never ask anything of the Creator, but for you I'll violate that today and I'll ask only two things. I'll ask that as you travel from this place to the place of your lodgings and your homes and your communities that no impediment is placed in your way and that you arrive there safely. And the second thing I'll ask on your behalf of the Creator is that when you arrive at your home that you see the happy smiling faces of your kin and your community people and that while you've been here no misfortune has befallen them. These are the things I will ask of the Creator. And so now I'll cover this council fire that we may be able to go our own separate ways and I'll untie the knot that bound us together here. But before we do that, I'd like us to bring together one last time our finest thanksgiving and our finest thoughts that we send them to the Creator of all things for the beauty and bounties that have been put around us.

This ended the symposium

Part VIII

Posters—Titles, Authors, and Abstracts

Posters of the International Eel Symposium Titles, Authors, and Abstracts

A number of posters were submitted as part of the symposium. They covered a broad range of topics, as indicated by the titles and abstracts provided here. The authors were introduced, and the senior authors provided a two-minute rapid overview during the presentation. This presentation was in addition to being part of the usual American Fisheries Society poster session.

1.
Spatiotemporal Variations in the Distribution of an Eel (*Anguilla anguilla* L.) Population in a Small Dammed Catchment (the Frémur)

Acou, A. Equipe Muséologie et Biodiversité, UMR 6553, Campus de Beaulieu, Université de Rennes 1, 35042 Rennes cedex, France
Robinet, T. Laboratoire de Biologie et de l'Environnement Marin, Université de la Rochelle, Avenue Michel Crépeau, 17042 La Rochelle cedex, France
Guillouët, J. Fish Pass, Bureau Expert Gestion Piscicole, 8 allée de Guerlédan, ZA Parc rocade sud, 35135 Chantepie, France
Feunteun, E. Laboratoire de Biologie et de l'Environnement Marin, Université de la Rochelle, Avenue Michel Crépeau, 17042 La Rochelle cedex, France (eric.feunteun@univ-lr.fr)

A sub-population of European eels (*Anguilla anguilla*) was sampled along the length of a small coastal catchment during summer for seven consecutive years to determine spatiotemporal variations of population characteristics. Two hypothesis were explored: firstly, do habitat preferences vary among sizes and sex; secondly, are habitat preferences and spatial organization patterns influenced by population parameters (density, size structure, and sex ratio). Thus years, spatial distribution, and habitat characteristics were simultaneously explored using a GLM approach. For each of the four selected length classes (<150, [151–300], [301–450] and >451 mm), variations of abundance were better explained by spatial (distance to the sea and to a dam) and temporal (yearly variations of downstream migration) factors than habitat. Variation in eel size distribution between years was minimal for elvers and yellow eels even though high recruitment variability has been observed since 1996. This suggests that young recruits (i) delayed their upstream migration, and/or (ii) settled in deeper habitats, and/or (iii) had low survival during their migrating stages. Variability of the spatiotemporal distribution patterns was then discussed regarding the development of the river and the saturation of the habitats, suggesting that carrying capacity was reached in the whole river system.

2.
Development and Implementation of Biological Reference Points for the Management of the European Eel (*Anguilla anguilla* (L.))

Bark, A. W. *Department of Life Sciences, Franklin-Wilkins Building, 150 Stamford Street, Waterloo, London, SE1 9NN*
El-Hosaini, H. S. *Department of Life Sciences, Franklin-Wilkins Building, 150 Stamford Street, Waterloo, London, SE1 9NN*
Kirkwood, G. P. *Renewable Resources Assessment Group, Department of Environmental Science & Technology, Imperial College London, Prince Consort Road, London. SW7 2BP*
Knights, B. *Applied Ecology Research Group, University of Westminster, 115 Cavendish Street, London. W1M 8JS.*
Williams, B. *Department of Life Sciences, Franklin-Wilkins Building, 150 Stamford Street, Waterloo, London, SE1 9NN*

The UK Department for Environment, Food, and Rural Affairs is funding a 4-year research project, aiming to establish biological reference points (BRPs) for appropriate management units for the European eel (*Anguilla anguilla*) in England and Wales. The results will inform decision-making, fishery monitoring, management approaches, and harvest strategies around England and Wales, with potential for application elsewhere in Europe and to anguillids in other continents. Principal objectives: i) to develop, program, and test models for population dynamics, stock assessment, and management strategies suitable for application to eel fisheries in key catchments; ii) to research and develop methods for establishing BRPs (as targets and limits) to inform practical and sustainable management of eel stocks and fisheries within appropriate management units; iii) to develop recommendations for appropriate decision structures, management approaches, and harvest strategies within the context of the ICES precautionary approach and the UK National Eel Management Strategy; iv) to specify data requirements and practical monitoring options for assessing compliance of eel stocks with reference points; v) to provide a practical demonstration of the development of BRPs and the application of monitoring approaches in appropriate test catchments.

3.
A Stage-Structured Model to Predict the Effect of Temperature and Salinity on Glass Eel (*Anguilla anguilla*) Pigmentation Development

Briand, C. *Institution Aménagement Vilaine 56130 La Roche Bernard France*
Fatin, D. *Institution Aménagement Vilaine 56130 La Roche Bernard France*
Lambert, P. *Cemagref, Unité Ressources Aquatiques Continentales, F-33612 Cestas Cedex France*

The pigmentation of the European glass eel (*Anguilla anguilla*) was studied experimentally. Samples were kept in net cages in estuarine and fresh waters and in aquaria at controlled temperature. The pigmentation kinetic from stage VB to VIA3 was modelled by gamma cumulative functions. These functions varied with respect to the couple temperature-salinity whose effects were adjusted by beta functions. The model could be used to predict the evolution of pigment stages in the Vilaine estuary and used as a tool to explain the glass eel population dynamic. However, it failed to predict pigmentation in groups collected in other localities in Europe, for example, from the Mediterranean. The consequences are discussed in light of the endocrine control of pigmentation and the possible role of the endocrine state of larvae reaching the continent.

4.
Historic American Eel Habitat in Tributaries of Lake Ontario, Estimation Using GIS and Gap Analysis Methods

Dittman, D. E. Tunison Laboratory of Aquatic Science, US Geological Survey, Cortland NY
McDonald, R. P. Tunison Laboratory of Aquatic Science, US Geological Survey, Cortland NY

The anguillid eel is experiencing a worldwide decline. The challenges that these catadromous species encounter during their complex life cycle include a long gamut of predators, human exploitation, habitat modification, and habitat restrictions during their legendary migrations and 20-to-30-year residence in fresh water. The American eel (*Anguilla rostrata*) was once extremely common in the New York tributaries of Lake Ontario, and this stock was a major contributor to the panmictic population. Eels are currently at low levels of abundance in most Lake Ontario tributaries. We use historic records and New York DEC fisheries database records to document American eel distribution and apparent abundance. These historic records, combined with use of GIS mapping and GAP analysis methods that synthesize available habitat parameters for tributary segments, allow mapping of likely historic eel distributions. The production of these maps incorporates American eel habitat models and presence of natural impassible barriers (major waterfalls). The next step in this research is to use the US Army Corps of Engineers' National Inventory of Dams (2002) to map restrictions on available and suitable eel habitats imposed by human-generated impassible barriers.

5.
Population and Life History Measures of American Eel (*Anguilla rostrata*) in the Lower Niagara River, NY

Dittman, D. E. Tunison Laboratory of Aquatic Science, US Geological Survey, Cortland NY.
Trometer, E. Lower Great Lakes Fishery Resources Office, U.S. Fish and Wildlife Service Amherst, NY

The catadromous species, American eel (Anguilla rostrata), has historically been a key ecological component of the native aquatic community in shallow warm-water habitats of eastern North America. All current population and recruitment indicators point to a continuing sharp population decline in the Lake Ontario–St. Lawrence River (LO–SLR) eel stock. Data covering the current distribution, population characteristics, and ecology of this native species in much of the LO–SLR watershed are limited. Lake Ontario produces eels that have been considered a significant contribution to the production of the entire species. Among the many eel unknowns is information on current local abundance of freshwater resident yellow eels, population dynamics, and habitat utilization. We conducted an evaluation of a resident population of immature American eels in the lower Niagara River, NY. We measured physical habitat parameters to map habitat suitable for eels, catch rates with night and day electrofishing, eel length and weight, and age of a subset of animals. A comparison of these population and life-history data with those of eels from the St. Lawrence estuary, Maine, and the Hudson River serves to increase our knowledge of the range of variability in American eel populations.

6.
Estimation of the Production and Fishery Mortality of Silver Eels by the Loire River System, France

Feunteun, E. P. Laboratoire de Biologie et d'Environnement Marins, Université de La Rochelle, Avenue Enrico Fermi, 17042 La Rochelle Cédex, France.Eric.feunteun@univ-lr.fr
Boury, P. Laboratoire de Biologie et d'Environnement Marins, Université de La Rochelle, Avenue Enrico Fermi, 17042 La Rochelle Cédex
Robinet, T. Laboratoire de Biologie et d'Environnement Marins, Université de La Rochelle, Avenue Enrico Fermi, 17042 La Rochelle Cédex

In order to face the decline of European eels, ACFM has recently recommended to base recovery plans on the enhancement of spawning biomass leaving inland waters. If a range of studies and surveys now enables the assessing of recruitment in river systems of Europe and Northern Africa, few have focused on the estimation of production of silver eels by small river systems but none were performed in large systems. In France, a study has been undertaken on one of the largest western Europe rivers: the Loire. Cooperation with professional fishermen shows that each year approximately 20 tonnes of glass eels and 50,000 female silver eels are caught. The fishery pressure on stocks and escapement of silver eels (maturing spawners) has been assessed by a mark-recapture experiment during a two-year experiment. In 2001, more than 1,500 eels were marked and about 14% were recaptured. It was then possible to determine migration periods and relations with environmental parameters. Population characteristics are estimated in order to assess escapement of silver eels and breeding potential of the river system. These results are presented and discussed to propose a general management plan of the species at the scale of the whole river system.

7.
Seasonal Movements of American Eels in the Lower Shenandoah River, West Virginia

Hammond, S. D. West Virginia Cooperative Fish and Wildlife Research Unit, West Virginia University, 322 Percival Hall, Morgantown, WV 26506
Welsh, S. A. West Virginia Cooperative Fish and Wildlife Research Unit, West Virginia University, 322 Percival Hall, Morgantown, WV 26506

The Atlantic States Marine Fisheries Commission recently listed research needs, including analysis of movements, to address management and conservation issues concerning the apparent population decline of the American eel (*Anguilla rostrata*). We surgically implanted radio tags into 13 yellow eels (518–810 mm TL) during fall 2001 and into seven yellow eels (362–781 mm TL) in 2002. These eels were captured, tagged, and released in the Shenandoah River below Millville Dam, West Virginia. Eels were relocated weekly for 16 months using triangulation techniques. Movements of each eel were measured and tabulated per month and season. Movements in spring were associated with changes in water temperature and stream flow. Very little other movement was observed during the other seasons. Several eels overwintered near mouths of tributaries with warmer water temperatures (~2–3°C warmer) than the main stem.

8.
Age and Growth, by Migratory Contingent, of Silver American Eels from a Nova Scotia River

Jessop, B. M. Department of Fisheries and Oceans, Bedford Institute of Oceanography, P.O. Box 1006, Dartmouth, Nova Scotia, B2Y 4A2, Canada
Shiao, J.-C. Department of Zoology, College of Science, National Taiwan University, Taipei, Taiwan 10617, ROC
Iizuka, Y. Institute of Earth Sciences, Academia Sinica, Nankang, Taipei, Taiwan 11529, ROC
Tzeng, W.-N. Department of Zoology, College of Science, National Taiwan University, Taipei, Taiwan 10617, ROC

Concern exists about declines in river-specific stocks of, and perceived effects on, the larger population of American eels (*Anguilla rostrata*) and the subsequent production of sexually maturing (silver) eels. To test specific hypotheses, better information is needed on the temporal change in life-history characteristics of specific stocks under varying regimes of exploitation. Few studies have examined aspects of annual growth rates for each sex and age and sex composition at migration of unexploited populations of silver American eels. This study will examine age composition and growth rates, for each sex, of silver American eels from an unexploited stock. The environmental history of fishes has been examined by analysis of the temporal pattern of Sr:Ca ratios in their otoliths. Tsukamoto et al. (2002) hypothesized that marine/estuarine residency of *Anguilla* spp. should occur more frequently at high latitudes. We determined that 64% of 64 silver eels examined showed evidence of a history of freshwater-estuarine migration as yellow eels. No comparative data exist from more southerly stocks. We also examine the hypothesis that such a migratory contingent will show differences in annual growth rates reflective of their relative residence times in fresh and estuarine waters.

9.
Effects of Water Temperature Changes on the Endogenous and Exogenous Rhythms of Oxygen Consumption in Glass Eels (*Anguilla japonica*)

Kim, W. S. Marine Environment and Climate Change Laboratory, Korea Ocean Research and Development Institute, Ansan, PO Box 29, Seoul 425-600, Korea waskim@kordi.re.kr;
Yoon, S. J. Marine Environment and Climate Change Laboratory, Korea Ocean Research and Development Institute, Ansan, PO Box 29, Seoul 425-600, Korea
Moon, H. T. Department of Oceanography, Chungnam National University, Taejon 305-764, Korea
Lee, T. W. Department of Oceanography, Chungnam National University, Taejon 305-764, Korea

Oxygen consumption rate of glass eels (*Anguilla japonica*) was measured to determine the effects of water temperature changes on their endogenous and exogenous rhythms. Glass eels were exposed to different water-temperature patterns during simulated 12-, 14-, and 24-h cycles. Oxygen consumption rate of wild glass eels exhibited a clear endogenous circatidal rhythm while kept in constant darkness at 15±0.1°C. However, if the temperature was varied, the glass eels' oxygen consumption rate coincided with the gradually increasing water temperature ((Delta)t = 1°C per 12 or 24 h) in the experimental chamber. This minor variation in water temperature ((Delta)t = 1°C per 12, 14 or 24 h) was significant enough to affect the rhythmicity of the glass eels' oxygen consumption rate. Results indicate that the glass eels' oxygen consumption rate is controlled not only by an endogenous circatidal rhythm but also by exogenous rhythms related to small environmental changes, such as water temperature changes of as little as 1°C. The possible mechanisms underlying these temperature responses are discussed, and the implications of the findings for the eco-physiology and metabolic activity rhythms of glass eels are highlighted.

10.
Early Growth History of *Anguilla japonica* Determined from Otolith Microstructure in Glass Eels

Lee, T. W. Department of Oceanography, Chungnam National University, Taejon 305-764, Korea twlee@cnu.ac.kr

Moon, H. T. Department of Oceanography, Chungnam National University, Taejon 305-764, Korea

Kim, G.-C. Fisheries Oceanography and Zooplankton Ecology Research Lab., School of Earth and Ocean Sciences, University of Victoria, P.O. Box 3055 STN CSC, Victoria, BC, V8W 3P6

Early growth history of eels (*Anguilla japonica*) was determined by examining otolith microstructure of glass eels collected from the three Korean estuaries from January to May in 1998. Mean total length (57.1±2.09 mm, mean±SD) and mean daily growth increments in otoliths of glass eels (188±9.6 d) did not show significant geographic and temporal differences. The discrepancy between the back-calculated spawning times from glass eel otoliths and leptocephalus otoliths indicates that glass eel otoliths may stop growing during their migration over the continental shelf. Glass eel otoliths consist of an inner transluscent zone formed during the leptocephalus stage and an outer opaque zone formed during metamorphosis. Mean age at the onset of metamorphosis was estimated to be 129±7.1 d, and mean duration of the metamorphic stage was estimated to be 45±5.0 d. On average, 15±5.1 growth increments were observed outside the metamorphic zone. We considered that the otoliths stop growing after the glass eels migrate over the continental shelf at temperatures below 13.5°C. Mean total length at the onset of metamorphosis was estimated to be 51.7±3.44 mm using the relationship between total length and otolith radius of leptocephali.

11.
Interpretation of the Dramatic Decrease in Otolith Sr/Ca Ratios and the Difference in Daily Age at Metamorphosis of Two Marine Eels

Ling, Y.-J. Department of Zoology, College of Science, National Taiwan University, Taipei, Taiwan 106, ROC.
Iizuka, Y. Institute of Earth Science, Academia Sinca, Nankang, Taipei, Taiwan 106 ROC
Tzeng, W.-N. Department of Zoology, College of Science, National Taiwan University, Taipei, Taiwan 106, ROC. wnt@ccms.ntu.edu.tw

Japanese eels (*Anguilla japonica*) display a dramatic decrease in otolith Sr/Ca ratios during metamorphosis from the oceanic leaf-like larva (leptocephalus) to the glass eel entering fresh water. Two possible causes exist: the environmental and the physiological. To validate hypotheses about the causes, we selected two marine eels: the pike eel (*Muraenesox cinereus*) and the moray eel (*Gymnothorax reticularis*), which metamorphose without entering fresh water. We then examined daily growth increments in otoliths for the differences between species and inferred the evolutionary meaning of their age at metamorphosis. Sr/Ca ratios in otoliths of both eels decreased sharply at metamorphosis, as it does for the Japanese eel. The decrease in otolith Sr/Ca ratios may result from physiological factors such as ontogenic change, rather than environmental factors such as salinity. The mechanism of the decrease in otolith Sr/Ca ratios during metamorphosis was reviewed. Mean (±SD) age at metamorphosis is 36.7 ± 7.1 days ($n = 22$) for the rock moray eel, which is significantly lower than 66.4 ± 15.9 days for the pike eel ($n = 18$) ($p < 0.01$). Both marine eels metamorphose at a younger age than does the Japanese eel, 115.8 ± 8.1 days (Cheng and Tzeng 1996) ($p < 0.01$). The differences in age at metamorphosis may relate to the distance of the spawning area from the coast, larval dispersal pathway, or reproductive and developmental strategies.

12.
Difference in Salinity Choice and Adaptation Between Temperate Eel (*Anguilla japonica*) and Tropical Eel (*A. marmorata*) Elvers

Shiao, J. C. Institute of Zoology, Academia Sinica, Novnkang, Taipei, Taiwan 115, ROC
Tzeng, W. N. Department of Zoology, College of Science, National Taiwan University, Taipei, Taiwan 106, ROC
Hwang, P. P. Institute of Zoology, Academia Sinica, Novnkang, Taipei, Taiwan 115, ROC

Previous studies have found that *A. japonica* is predominately found in brackish water while *A. marmorata* is overwhelmingly found in fresh water. A compartmentalized tank with water of salinity ranging from 0 to 30 ppt was designed to test salinity choice of *A. japonica* and *A. marmorata* elvers. Initially, elves of the two species, collected from the river mouth, were stocked in the sea-water area (SW, 30 ppt). Most elvers of both species stayed in salinities of 0 to 10 ppt, and few elvers stayed in 20 and 30 ppt, indicating that elvers can adapt to a wide range of salinity but prefer lower salinities. Elvers acclimated in fresh water for two weeks were transferred to 35 ppt sea water and fresh water respectively to understand their response to acute salinity change. All *A. japonica* elvers survived, but the mortality rate of *A. marmorata* elvers increased from 4% at hour 10 to 73% at hour 24 in the fresh water-sea water group. No mortalities occurred in the fresh water-fresh water group. These results indicate that sea-water adaptation capability differed between *A. japonica* and *A. marmorata*, which may relate to their habitat use during the freshwater growth stage.

13.
Catch Decline Rates of Japanese Eel (*Anguilla japonica*), in Relation to Environmental Conditions in Rivers, Japan

Tatsukawa, K. Ocean Research Institute, University of Tokyo, 15-1, Minamidai-1, Nakano, Tokyo 164-8639 Japan
Sakai, T. Ocean Research Institute, University of Tokyo, 15-1, Minamidai-1, Nakano, Tokyo 164-8639 Japan
Matsuda, H. Ocean Research Institute, University of Tokyo, 15-1, Minamidai-1, Nakano, Tokyo 164-8639 Japan

Annual catches of the Japanese eel (*Anguilla japonica*), more than 50 tons since 1965, have been recorded from 11 rivers in Japan. These eel catch curve profiles from 1967 to 1996 were divided in two river groups, ARG and BRG, by multiple regression analysis. The decline rate (Z) of catch during 30 years in ARG was higher than that of BRG. A relationship between Zs and river environmental factors, such as COD, SS, DO, number of colitis germs group, coefficient of river regime, catch of fish, index of habitat limited area by dam construction (IHL), and index of habitat destruction indicated as unit water volume caused by dam (IHD), was examined by multivariate analysis. Both IHL and IHD among these factors produced more powerful effects on Z. The eel stock in ARG might have suffered severely from a dam construction as compared with that in BRG. Stopping a tendency of catch decline and also increasing eel stocks in rivers, rehabilitating and restoring eel habitats to a former state should be a task of great urgency for our country.

14.
Reproductive Strategy Among Five Subpopulations of American Eel in the St. Lawrence Watershed

Tremblay, V. Département de Biologie, Université du Québec à Rimouski, 300, Allée des Ursulines, Rimouski, QC, Canada G5L 3A1, valerie.tremblay@fapaq.gouv.qc.ca

Recruitment of the American eel (*Anguilla rostrata*) is declining in the St. Lawrence watershed, where the sex ratio is unbalanced in favour of females. As a semelparous species, this demographic dominance enhances its implication on the reproductive potential of the species. Thirty specimens of five different subpopulations were collected at sites ranging from 2,845 to 4,288 km from the Sargasso Sea. The sustained hypothesis is that fecundity varies among subpopulations; the subpopulation furthest from the Sargasso Sea is expected to show the lowest fecundity at a specific size and the greatest somatic fat stores, whereas the nearest subpopulation should show the opposite reproductive strategy. The evaluation of individual fecundity (gonadosomatic index, egg counts) and the analysis of morphological (weight, size, otolith aging) and physiological (total lipids) parameters on mature migrating female eels should demonstrate that subpopulation fecundity is correlated negatively to its migration distance. Migration distance should influence the trade-off between reproductive and somatic investments among subpopulations and reproductive fitness. Because of panmixia, no genetic influence is expected to explain the variability in reproductive traits among subpopulations. Migration distance and environmental parameters might determine life acquisition and allocation of resources. Results are discussed in a management perspective.

15.
Genetic Differentiation of Japanese Eel (*Anguilla japonica*) Inferred from GA/GT Microsatellite Loci

Tseng, M. C. *Department of Zoology, College of Science, National Taiwan University, Taipei, Taiwan 106, ROC. aqsunkimo@yahoo.com.tw*
Tzeng, W. N. *Department of Zoology, College of Science, National Taiwan University, Taipei, Taiwan 106, ROC.*
Lee, S. C. *Institute of Zoology, Academia Sinica, Taipei, Taiwan 106 ROC*

Population structure of the Japanese eel (*Anguilla japonica*) was studied using polymorphic microsatellites as genetic markers. Six microsatellite loci (AJMS-1, 2, 3, 5, 6 and 10) were resolved from 371 individuals collected from northeastern Asian countries, including Taiwan, China, Japan, and Korea. The results indicate high genetic polymorphism as represented by high observed heterozygosity (0.60–0.83). Five of six loci in each of the samples showed a departure from Hardy-Weinberg equilibrium ($p < 0.05$). The widely ranging unbiased Nei's genetic distances (0.04–0.17, mean 0.10), support a possible regional substructuring of the population. Genetic differentiation represented by values of Fst and Rst mostly revealed significance among the nine samples investigated. Samples shown on the unrooted Neighbor-joining tree were largely divided into three groups: a low-latitudinal group (Shantou, Tanshui, Fangliao, and Tungkang), a high-latitudinal group (D'cheon-myon, Yalu River, and Hangzhou), and a Japanese group (Mikawa Bay). Lower genetic distances were observed among several temporal samples in Taiwan. The evidence shown by this study refutes the previous assumption of a panmictic population.

16.
Annual Survey of Glass Eel (*Anguilla rostrata*) Recruitment in the Marine District of New York State

Vecchio, V. J. *NY Department of Environmental Conservation, Division of Fish, Wildlife, and Marine Resources, Bureau of Marine Resources, East Setauket, New York, USA*
O'Riordan, H. N. *NY Department of Environmental Conservation, Division of Fish, Wildlife, and Marine Resources, Bureau of Marine Resources, East Setauket, New York, USA*
Saulino, R. *NY Department of Environmental Conservation, Division of Fish, Wildlife, and Marine Resources, Bureau of Marine Resources, East Setauket, New York, USA*
Prussick, C. B. *NY Department of Environmental Conservation, Division of Fish, Wildlife, and Marine Resources, Bureau of Marine Resources, East Setauket, New York, USA*

Beginning in 2000, New York initiated a survey to investigate glass eel recruitment and deployed a glass eel fyke in the tidal portion of the Carman's River, which flows south for

17.7 kilometers into Bellport Bay on Long Island's south shore. The watershed area is 182 square kilometers. The tidal portion of the river is 5.8 kilometers (NYSDEC 1995). The fyke is checked daily between March and April. Catch of glass eels was 13,491 during 2002, 1,877 during 2000, and 353 during 2001. Catch of elvers was 459 during 2002, 316 during 2000, and 157 during 2001. Geometric mean catch of glass eels was significantly higher in 2002 than in the previous two years. Geometric mean catch of elvers was also significantly higher in 2002 than in the two previous years. During 2002, 1,072 glass eels and 291 elvers were measured for length and weight. Glass eels were examined for their pigmentation stage by methods described in Haro and Krueger (1988). Mean length of glass eels was 61.0 millimeters and ranged between 49.7 and 74.4 millimeters. Mean weight of glass eels was 0.175 grams and ranged between 0.082 and 0.358 grams. Of the glass eels examined for pigmentation, 92% were graded stage 2, 3, or 4, with 40% graded stage #3. Mean length of the 291 elvers was 82.8 millimeters and ranged between 62.4 and 149.4 millimeters. Mean weight of elvers was 0.678 grams and ranged between 0.237 and 4.212 grams.

17.
Otolith Marking as a Useful Tool in the Evaluation of Eel Stock Enhancement Programs

Wickström, H. Swedish National Board of Fisheries, Institute of Freshwater Research, SE-178 93 DROTTNINGHOLM, Sweden

Small eels (*Anguilla anguilla*) are difficult to tag. Passive integrated transponders (PIT) have been used to tag eels as small as 10 g, and recently coded wire tags also were successfully employed in a Danish study of eels (> = 2 g) before stocking. The stock enhancement program in Sweden uses mainly elvers imported from the UK, which, after an approved period in quarantine, are stocked in lakes and along the coast of the Baltic Sea. To identify recaptures and evaluate the outcome of stocking schemes, otoliths were marked by bathing elvers of about 1 g in a bath of $SrCl_2$ or alizarin complexone before stocking. In one lake 5,000 alizarin-marked elvers were stocked in 1997. Another lake was stocked yearly from 1999 to 2002 with 17,800 strontium-marked elvers in total. Among those, about 2,900 were also tagged with PIT. Up to and including the first part of 2003, a number of recaptures were made from both lakes. I describe the methods used, during both marking and detection, and provide examples of the appearance of marks, both in reference eels (samples from the marking occasions) and in eels recaptured after some years in the lakes, respectively.

Part IX

Quebec Declaration of Concern

(Reprinted from American Fisheries Society *Fisheries* Magazine)

Worldwide decline of eel resources necessitates immediate action
Québec Declaration of Concern

The steep decline in populations of eels (*Anguilla* spp.) endangers the immediate future of these legendary fish. With less than 1% of major juvenile resources remaining, precautionary action must be taken immediately to sustain the stocks.

Eels are curious animals. Despite decades of scientific research, crucial aspects of their biology remain a mystery. In recent decades, juvenile abundance has declined dramatically (Figure.1): by 99% for the European eel (A. anguilla) and by 80% for the Japanese eel (*A. japonica*). Recruitment of American eel (*A. rostrata*) to Lake Ontario, near the species' northern limit, has virtually ceased. Other eel species also show indications of decline. The causes of the downward trends are yet unclear, in part due to the catadromous life history of these fishes, which has so far made it impossible to observe their spawning adults in the open ocean. Because of this, the annual spawning stocks of eels that successfully complete the long migration to their spawning areas have never been assessed. The lack of access to basic life history information about the oceanic phase of eels makes it especially difficult to monitor and identify the cause of their population declines. This is in distinct contrast with other declining fishes such as anadromous salmon, whose spawning adults can be relatively easily surveyed when they return to freshwater to spawn, and Atlantic cod, which spawn relatively close to continental margins and can be surveyed by standard fishery techniques. In the case of eels, which depend on freshwater and estuarine habitats for their juvenile growth phase, anthropogenic impacts (e.g., pollution, habitat loss and migration barriers, fisheries) are considerable and may well have been instrumental in prompting these declines. Loss of eel resources will represent a loss of biodiversity but will also have considerable impact on socioeconomics of rural areas, where eel fishing still constitutes a cultural tradition. Research is underway to develop a comprehensive and effective restoration plan. This, however, will require time. The urgent concern is that the rate of decline necessitates swifter protective measures. As scientists in eel biology from 18 countries assembled at the International Eel Symposium 2003 organized in conjunction with the 2003 American Fisheries Society Annual Meeting in Québec, Canada, we unanimously agree that we must raise an urgent alarm now. With less than 1% of juvenile resources remaining for major populations, time is running out. Precautionary action (e.g., curtailing exploitation, safeguarding migration routes and wetlands, improving access to lost habitats) can and must be taken immediately by all parties involved and, if necessary, independently of each other. Otherwise, opportunities to protect these species and study their biology and the cause of their decline will fade along with the stocks.

> The International Eel Symposium 2003 at the Québec City AFS Annual Meeting, convened by Casselman and Cairns, focused on worldwide concern about the declining status of anguillid eels, their assessment and management. The symposium resulted in a universal call to action. Since the symposium, the concern is now being widely publicized. The declaration stemming from the symposium is provided here.

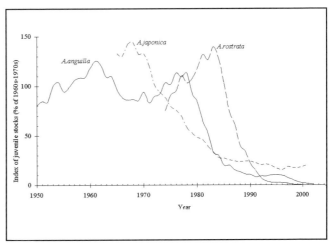

Figure 1. Time trends in juvenile abundance of the major eel stocks of the world. For *Anguilla anguilla*, the average trend of the four longest data series is shown, which trend appears to occur almost continent-wide; for *A.rostrata*, data represent recruitment to Lake Ontario; for *A.japonica*, data represent landings of glass eel in Japan

Prepared Québec City, 14 August 2003. Submitted by the undersigned:

For researchers of European eel:
Willem Dekker
Netherlands Institute for
 Fisheries Research
Animal Sciences Group
Wageningen University and
 Research Centre
P.O. Box 68
1970 AB IJmuiden,
The Netherlands.
tel. +31 255 564 646
willem.dekker@wur.nl

For researchers of American eel:
John M. Casselman and
 David K. Cairns
(convenors of the symposium)
c/o Ontario Ministry of
 Natural Resources
Glenora Fisheries Station
Picton, Ontario K0K 2T0, Canada.
tel. +1 613 476 3287
john.casselman@mnr.gov.on.ca,
CairnsD@dfo-mpo.gc.ca

For researchers of Japanese eel:
Katsumi Tsukamoto
Ocean Research Institute
University of Tokyo
Nakanoku, Tokyo 164-8639, Japan.
ktpc@ori.u-tokyo.ac.jp

For researchers of southern-temperate eels:
Don Jellyman
National Institute of Water and
 Atmospheric Research Ltd.
P.O. Box 8602
Christchurch, New Zealand.
jellyman@niwa.co.nz

For Aboriginal Nations involved with eel:
Henry Lickers
Haudenosaunee
Department of the Environment
Mohawk Council of Akwesasne
Cornwall Island, Ontario K6H 5R5, Canada
hlickers@akwesasne.ca

Background to this correspondence

This letter was prepared as a result of the plenary discussion at the end of the International Eel Symposium. Following a suggestion by Giulio A. De Leo (University of Parma, Italy), we unanimously agreed to bring this immediate concern to light. Signatories to this letter have been selected to represent the scientific communities working on each of the *Anguilla* species, listed in order of magnitude of the resource, with representation by Aboriginal Nations because of their longstanding association with eel. Participants in this discussion were, in alphabetical order by country (affiliation) and name:

ABORIGINAL NATIONS: H. Lickers
BELGIUM: C. Belpaire, G.E. Maes
CANADA: D. Cairns, J. Casselman, M. Castonuay, B. Jessop, M. Jones, L. Marcogliese, K. Reid, V. Tremblay, G. Verreault
DENMARK: M. Pedersen
FRANCE: L. Beaulaton, C. Briand, G. Castelnaud, C. Durif, E. Feunteun, P. Lambert, C. Sechet
GERMANY: U. Dumont
INTERNATIONAL (Great Lakes Fishery Commission): C. Goddard, R. Stein
IRELAND: T. McCarthy
ITALY: G. De Leo
JAPAN: J. Aoyama, M. Miller, K. Tatsukawa, K. Tsukamoto
KOREA: T. W. Lee
MOROCCO: A. Yahyaoui
NETHERLANDS: W. Dekker
NEW ZEALAND: J. Boubee, D. Jellyman, P. Todd
SWEDEN: H. Wickström
TAIWAN ROC: Y. S. Han, S.-C. Lee, M.-C. Tseng, W. N. Tzeng
UNITED KINGDOM: A. Bark, B. Knights, B. Williams
UNITED STATES OF AMERICA: L. Brown, S. Hammond, A. Haro, L. M. Lee, J. McCleave, V. Vecchio, J. Weeder, S. Welsh

Annotated list of selected literature references documenting declines

European eel *Anguilla anguilla*:

Moriarty, C. 1997. The European eel fishery in 1993 and 1994: First report of a working group funded by the European Union Concerted Action AIR A94-1939. Fisheries Bulletin (Dublin) 14: 52 pp.
In 1994-1997, a concerted action was sponsored by the European Commission to compile an overview of existing information on the European eel. In this first report, factual information on eel fisheries throughout Europe was compiled.

Moriarty, C., and Dekker, W. (eds.) 1997. Management of the European Eel. Fisheries. Bulletin (Dublin) 15: 110 pp.
This report, following Moriarty (1997), discusses the status of the European eel stock in the early 1990s, and explores options for restoration of the stock and fisheries.

ICES (International Council for the Exploration of the Sea). 2002. ICES cooperative research report N° 255, Report of the ICES Advisory Committee on Fishery Management, 2002: 940-948.
Upon request by the European Commission, the International Council for the Exploration of the Sea (ICES) has provided scientific advice for sustainable management of the European eel stock. ICES recommends that an international recovery plan be developed for the whole stock on an urgent basis and that exploitation and other anthropogenic mortalities be reduced to as close to zero as possible, until such a plan is agreed upon and implemented. wwwices.dk/products/cooperative.asp

_____ 2003. Report of the ICES/EIFAC Working Group on Eels. ICES C.M. 2002/ACFM:06
Management advice by ICES is based on a lengthy report of the joined ICES/EIFAC working group on eels, which elaborates on the time series, the anthropogenic impacts, and the required management measures. This report is the most recent, in an ongoing process of gathering information and compiling management advice. wwwices.dk/reports/acfm/2002/wgeel/WGEEL02.pdf

Dekker, W. 2003. Status of the European eel stock and fisheries. pages 237-254 *in* K. Aida, K. Tsukamoto, and K. Yamauchi eds., Eel Biology, Springer-Verlag, Tokyo.
This paper provides an overview of existing information on geographical distribution and time-trend in fisheries for the various life stages, discusses causes and consequences of the decline, and considers required research for sustainable management of the European eel stock.

American eel *Anguilla rostrata*:

Castonguay, M., P. V. Hodson, C. M. Couillard, M. J. Eckersley, J-D Dutil, and G. Verreault. 1994. Why is recruitment of the American eel, *Anguilla rostrata*, declining in the St. Lawrence River and Gulf? Canadian Journal of Fisheries and Aquatic Sciences 51:479-488.
Drastic declines in juvenile American eel recruitment to the upper St. Lawrence River-Lake Ontario stock are documented. Potential causes are discussed: there is little evidence that commercial fishing and oceanic changes are the cause. Emphasizes that recruitment declines could be species-wide.

Casselman, J. M., L. A. Marcogliese, T. Stewart, and P. V. Hodson. 1997. Status of the upper St. Lawrence River and Lake Ontario American eel stock—1996. Pages 106-120 *in* R.H. Peterson ed. The American eel in eastern Canada: stock status and management strategies. Proceedings of eel workshop, January 13-14, 1997, Québec City, QC. Canadian Technical Report of Fisheries and Aquatic Sciences 2196.
In an extensive review of the American eel in eastern Canada, stock status and management strategies, long-term catch records, along with

numerous scientific indices, are examined for the once large upper St. Lawrence River-Lake Ontario stock. Declines in the 1990s are unprecedented and correlate with well-documented recruitment declines, which in the past two decades amount to a decrease of three orders of magnitude. Important and valuable commercial fisheries have virtually disappeared.

Richkus, W. A., and K. Whalen. 2000. Evidence for a decline in the abundance of the American eel, *Anguilla rostrata* (LeSueur), in North America since the early 1980s. Dana 12:83-97.

The preponderance of data suggests a continent-wide decline in American eel abundance. There are statistically significant negative trends in Ontario, Québec, Virginia, and New York. There are no statistically significant increasing trends. Possible reasons: ocean conditions, pollution, habitat degradation, recruitment overfishing, growth overfishing, hydroelectric dams.

EIFAC/ICES Working Group on Eels. 2001. Report of the EIFAC/ICES Working Group on Eels, St. Andrews, N.B., 28 August—1 September 2000. Advisory Committee on Fisheries Management, International Council for the Exploration of the Sea, ICES CM 2001/ACFM:03, Copenhagen.

This report reviews American eel abundance trends, impacts caused by fisheries and by dams, assessment and management tools, and conservation needs. Reductions in habitat, declining or neutral abundance trends, severe decline in abundance in northern areas, continuous exploitation, and unknown oceanographic effects support the adoption of the precautionary approach. Efforts should be made to reduce human-induced mortality wherever possible. www.ices.dk/reports/acfm/2000/wgeel/wgeel00.pdf.

Casselman, J. M. 2003. Dynamics of resources of the American eel, *Anguilla rostrata*: declining abundance in the 1990s. Pages 255-274, chapter 18, *in* K. Aida, K. Tsukamoto, K. Yamauchi (eds.) Eel Biology. Springer-Verlag Tokyo.

Reviews dynamics and status of American eel from prehistoric and historic times to the present, emphasizing the past 50 years. Long-term catch and scientific indices are numerous and emphasize unprecedented and dramatic declines, particularly in association with commercial harvest during the past decade throughout the entire species range. Recruitment decreases precipitously and in synchrony with catch and resource declines. Causal factors are reviewed but are inconclusive. Encourages joint management plans and reductions in human-induced mortality.

Japanese eel *Anguilla japonica*:

Tatsukawa, K. 2003. Eel resources in East Asia. pages 293-300 *in* K. Aida, K. Tsukamoto and K. Yamauchi, eds., Eel Biology. Springer-Verlag, Tokyo.

This paper provides an overview of existing information on time-trend in fisheries for the various life stages, and discusses causes of observed declines.

Tzeng, W-N. 1997 Short- and long-term fluctuations in catches of elvers of the Japanese eel *Anguilla japonica* in Taiwan. *In* D. A. Hancok, D.C. Smith, A. Grand and J. P. Beumer, ed. Developing and sustaining world fisheries resources: the state of science and management. 2nd World Fisheries Congress Proceedings, CSIRO publishing, Collingwood, Australia.

This paper provides catch data for the Japanese eel elver in Taiwan, China, Korea and Japan since 1972-1992. The catch revealed an approximately 11-year cycle with a peak in 1979 and a drastic decline in recent years. This corresponds to trends in the American (*A. rostrata*) and European (*A. anguilla*) eels. Overfishing and habitat degradation were probably the main causes of the recent declines.

New Zealand eels *Anguilla australis* and *Anguilla dieffenbachii*:

Glova, G. J., Jellyman, D. J. and Bonnett, M. L. 2001. Spatiotemporal variation in the distribution of eel (*Anguilla* spp.) populations in three New Zealand lowland streams. Ecology of Freshwater Fish 10:147-153.

The density of small longfin eels, *Anguilla dieffenbachii* (<100 mm) in three study streams was consistently lower for three years of study, indicating poor recruitment of this species.

Hoyle, S. D., and D. J. Jellyman, 2002. Longfin eels need reserves: modelling the effects of commercial harvest on stocks of New Zealand eels. Marine and Freshwater Research 53: 887-895.

Results of a conceptual model of spawner per recruit suggests that present level of exploitation of *Anguilla dieffenbachii* might result in severe depletion of the spawning stock and the current management measure of an upper size limit is ineffectual as the probability of capture before achieving this size is high. www.publish.csiro.au/?act=view_file&file_id=MF00020.pdf

McCleave, J. D. and D. J. Jellyman. In press. Male dominance in the longfin eel population of a New Zealand river: probable causes and implications for management. North American Journal of Fisheries Management.

Female *Anguilla dieffenbachii* were virtually absent in an extensive study of eels from a southern New Zealand river, despite dominating this area historically. These changes are attributed to extensive commercial harvest.

Jellyman, D. J., E. Graynoth, R. I. C. C. Francis, B. L. Chisnall, and M. P. Beentjes. 2000. A review of the evidence for a decline in the abundance of longfinned eels (*Anguilla dieffenbachii*) in New Zealand. Final Research Report, Ministry of Fisheries Research Project EEL9802.

This report reviewed available data for evidence of a decline in recruitment of longfin eels, *Anguilla dieffenbachii*—it included information on glass eel and elver catches and species proportions, age composition of both juvenile and adult eels, changes in abundance and size distribution of longfins; computer models were used to simulate the influence of changes in recruitment on size and age composition of populations. The report concluded that longfins are being overfished and this has significantly affected recruitment.

Index

Italicized f and t refer to figures and tables

A

abundance of eels, long-term trends in, 191–204
Acanthocephala, 178t
Acanthocephalus anguillae, 178t, 181t, 183
Acanthocephalus clavula, 181t, 183
Acanthocephalus lucii, 181t, 183
AcousticTag software, 282
adaptive management, 12–13
African longfin eel (*Anguilla mossambica*), 72, 73t
African mottled eel (*Anguilla bengalensis labiata*), 72, 73t
age estimation, 89, 116, 352
age-distribution indices, 372–373
age-structured models, 335–338
Akaike's Information Criterion (AICc), 318–319t
allice shad (*Alosa alosa*), 271
allozyme analysis, 30
Alosa sapidissima (American shad), 279
Altamaha River, 133t
Amakusa Islands, Japan, 29f
American eel (*Anguilla rostrata*), 85–100
    age, 118
    age determination, 89, 116, 352
    in Chesapeake Bay, 113–126
    commercial fishery in Delaware, 229–238
    density, 123–124
    effects of translocation, 129–134
    exotic, 137–146
    fecundity estimation, 88–89
    growth, 118–120, 352, 353–354
    growth comparisons, 116
    growth rates, 132–133
    juvenile, 191–204
    in Lake Ontario/upper St. Lawrence River, 361–367
    length distributions, 117–118, 119f
    mortality, 116, 120, 124–126, 352, 354
    otoliths, 137–146
    phenotypic plasticity, 96–97
    reproduction strategies of, 85–100
    sex determination, 114–117, 120–122
    sex differences, 124
    sex ratio, 124, 133
    sexual maturity, 114–117, 120–122, 351, 354
    size, 118
    size-related fecundity, 91–95
    spawner biomass per recruit, 350, 352–353, 354
    studies of population genetics, 60t
    subpopulation characteristics, 91
    sustainability of harvests, 349–358
    treatment of gonads, 88–89
    yellow-phase, 311–322
    yield per recruit, 350, 352–353, 354
American shad (*Alosa sapidissima*), 279
analysis of variance (ANOVA), 89
Anguilla anguilla. see European eel (*Anguilla anguilla*)
Anguilla australis. see shortfins (*Anguilla australis*)
Anguilla bengalensis bengalensis (Indian mottled eel), 72, 73t
Anguilla bengalensis labiata (African mottled eel), 72, 73t
Anguilla bicolor bicolor (Indian shortfin eel), 73t, 74, 79–80
Anguilla bicolor pacifica (Indonesian shortfin eel), 73t, 74
Anguilla borneensis (Indonesian longfinned eel), 73t, 74
Anguilla celebensis (Indonesian mottled eel), 73t, 74

Anguilla dieffenbanchii. see longfins (*Anguilla dieffenbachii*)
Anguilla interioris (New Guinea eel), 73t, 784
Anguilla japonica. see Japanese eel (*Anguilla japonica*)
Anguilla marmorata (giant mottled eel), 60t, 72, 78f
Anguilla megastoma (Polynesian longfin eel), 73t, 74
Anguilla mossambica (African longfin eel), 72, 73t
Anguilla obscura (Pacific shortfinned eel), 73t, 74
Anguilla reinhardtii (Australian longfinned eel), 73t, 74
Anguillicola crassus, 179, 184–185
Annaquatucket River, 133t
annual growth rates, 139
Appalachian brook crayfish (*Cambarus bartonii*), 130
arctic char (*Salvelinus alpinus*), 183
Asellus aquaticus, 184
Asellus meridianus, 184
Ashley River, 41
Assawoman Bay, 355t, 356f
Atlantic salmon (*Salmo salar*), 86, 158, 279
Australian longfinned eel (*Anguilla reinhardtii*), 73t, 74

B

Beauharnois Dam, Montreal, Quebec, 295–308
    east side, 304–305
    eel ladder, 203
    eel traps, 300
    location of release sites, 299f
    return rates of eels, 302t, 303f, 303t
    west side, 302–305
biological reference point (BRP), 369–379
    compliance assessment, 379
    compliance measures for riverine stocks, 372
    conservation limits, 371
    geographical/regional factors, 375–379
    habitat suitability index, 374–375
    indices, 372–374
    recruitment declines, 370
    surrogate targets, 372
    targets, 371–372
biomass index, 373
black sea bass (*Centropristis striata*), 125
bootstrap replicate, 341
Bothriocephalus claviceps, 181t, 184
bream (*Abramis brama*), 160
Brody coefficient, 341
brook trout (*Salvelinus fontinalis*), 130
brown trout (*Salmo trutta*), 183

C

Cabot Station, Connecticut River, 277–289
    fish tagging and monitoring, 281
    hydrophone locations, 280f
    location of, 279
    surface bypass, 287
    time spent by eels, 286f
    trash tracks, 288
Cagayan River, Philippines, 78f
Camallanus lacustris, 180, 181t, 184
Cambarus bartonii (Appalachian brook crayfish), 130
Capillaria sp., 181t
catch effort landing returns (CELR), 398
catches, decline in, 23–24
catch-per-unit-effort (CPUE), 207–226
    Chesapeake Bay eels, 124
    classical method, 263–264
    effect of hydroclimatic conditions, 207–226
    general linear model, 265–267
    New Zealand eel fisheries, 47–49, 401–402
    seasonal, 260–261
Centropristis striata (black sea bass), 125
Cestoda, 178t
Chesapeake Bay, sustainability of eel harvests in, 349–358
Cimandiri River, 79
cisco (*Coregonus artedii*), 362
cohort models, 332–335
commercial fisheries, 229–238
    catch-per-unit-effort, 215–217
    in Delaware, 229–238
        actual lengths of American eels, 235f
        age distribution of, 234f

commercial landings, 232t
length and weight of American eels, 232t
length frequency of American eels, 233f
yield per recruit vs. fishing mortality, 236f
impact on migrating silver eels, 390–391
in New Zealand, 398–401
St. Lawrence River, 210–211, 215–217
Connecticut River, Massachusetts, 277–289
fish tagging and monitoring, 281
hydrophone locations, 280f
location of, 279
surface bypass, 287
time spent by eels, 286f
trash tracks, 288
conservation limits, 371
Coreginus artedi, 158
Coregonus clupeaforis (whitefish), 362
Crepidostomum metoecus, 181t
crepuscular movements, 314–315, 319
Crustacea, 178t
customary fishery, 45, 394–397
cyanotoxin blooms, 171
cypirinids, 130

D

Dahl-Lea formula, 138–139
Daniconema anguillae, 182
Delaware commercial fisheries, 229–238
actual lengths of American eels, 235f
age distribution of, 234f
commercial landings, 232t
length and weight of American eels, 232t
length frequency of American eels, 233f
yield per recruit vs. fishing mortality, 236f
density, 123–124, 373
Digenea, 178t
Diplostomum spathaceum, 180, 181t
downstream movements, 315–319
drossage, 259

E

East Asia Eel Consortium (EASEC), 30
eel ladder, 191–204, 295–308
eel lines, 363–364
eels
abundance of, 191–204
biological reference point, 369–379
catch-per-unit-effort, 207–226
effects of hydroclimatic conditions, 207–226
in English river systems, 241–254
exotic, 137–146
female American eels, 85–100
genetic differentiation, 59–67
juvenile, 191–204
New Zealand eels, 37–52, 393–405
population genetics of, 60t
population management, 369–379
population modeling, 329–344
premigrant, 157–172
reproduction strategies, 85–100
silvering stages, 103–111
stocking of lowland streams, 149–156
tropical, 71–82
yellow-phase, 311–322
El Niño Southern Oscillation (ENSO), 27–28, 40
electrofishing, 41
elvers, 149–156, 331
English river systems, 241–254
biomass density, 247f
eel population density, 247f, 249f
European eel stock status in, 241–254
Frome, 243, 246–250, 252–253
length distributions of eels, 247f, 248f
Piddle, 243, 246–250, 252–253
Severn, 242–246, 250–252
sex ratios of eels, 251f
environment, effect of, 122–123
Epinephelus niveatus (snowy grouper), 125
Ergasilus gibbus, 179–180, 181t, 182
Esox lucius (northern pike), 160
estuaries, 123
estuarine eels, 28, 29f
European chub (*Leuciscus cephalus*), 378

European eel (*Anguilla anguilla*), 3–18
    biological reference point, 369–379
    causes of decline, 6–7
    continental life stage, 4
    decline in stock, 3–4
    downstream migration of, 383–391
    in English river systems, 241–254
    fishing harvest from continental waters, 5–6
    framework for management process, 7–8
    glass eel fisheries, 14
    habitat loss, 13–14
    landings, 6*t*
    management problems, 9–13
        adaptive management, 12–13
        reference points and proxies, 10–11
        subsidiarity and orchestration, 11–12
        tit-for-tat, 13
    management strategies, 4–6
    metazoan parasites of, 175–185
    population management in England and Wales, 369–379
    recruitment from ocean, 4–5
    silver eel fisheries, 15
    silvering stages of, 103–111
    stock status, 4–5
    stocking with elvers, 149–156
    studies of population genetics, 60*t*
    temporal/spatial scales of management process, 15–17
    temporal/spatial scales of stock dynamics, 8–9
    yellow eel fisheries, 14–15
European Silver Eel Project, 384
exotic American eels, 137–146
    annual growth rates, 138–139, 140–144
    morphological characters, 140*t*
    morphological indices, 140
    otolith Sr/Ca ratios, 144–146
    otoliths, 139
    total length at annulus formation, 138–139
eye index (EI), 108, 109*f*

F

fat content, 86
fecundity
    estimation of, 88–89
    size-related, 91–95
Fishery Analyses and Simulation Tools (FAST), 230
Frémur River, France, premigrant eels in, 157–172

G

Gadus morhua, 158
general linear model (GLM), 261, 271–272
genetic differentiation, 59–67
    DNA extraction, 61–62
    levels of genetic variation, 64*t*
    microsatellite loci, 62
    Nei's genetic distance, 65*f*
    sampling, 61
    sampling localities, 62*f*
    topological tree, 62*f*
genetic distance, 65*f*
giant mottled eel (*Anguilla marmorata*), 72, 78*f*
Gironde Basin, France, 257–272
glass eel fisheries, 14, 77–80
    abundance of, 257–272
    age at metamorphosis, 77–80
    catch-per-unit-effort, 265–267
    in East Asia, 23*f*
    estimate of catch, 262
    Gironde Basin, France, 257–272
    monitoring, 259–260
    push nets, 259
    scoop nets, 259
    species composition, 77
    tide effect, 262
    tide month effect, 261–262
    timing of recruitment, 77
gonadosomatic index (GSI), 88–89, 109*f*
gonads, 88–89
growth rates
    and age distribution, 372–373
    Chesapeake Bay eels, 132–133, 352–354

effect of translocation, 131–132
New Zealand freshwater eels, 43
and stocking, 153–155

H

habitat loss, 49–51
habitat suitability index (HSI), 374–375
hapu, 394
hinakis (catching baskets), 394
Hirudinea, 178t
hoop nets, 363–364
hui, 395
human impacts, 26
Hydroacoustic Technology, Inc., 280
hydroclimatic conditions, effects of, 207–226
hydroelectric facilities, 295–308
    exit locations for eel ladders, 295–308
    impact on migrating silver eels, 390–391
    impact on silver-phase eels, 277–289
    and silver eel fisheries, 15

I

Ichthyopthirius multifiliis, 183
Indian mottled eel (*Anguilla bengalensis bengalensis*), 72, 73t
Indian Ocean, 72
Indian shortfin eel (*Anguilla bicolor bicolor*), 73t, 74, 79–80
individual transferable quotas (ITQs), 394
Indonesian longfinned eel (*Anguilla borneensis*), 73t, 74
Indonesian mottled eel (*Anguilla celebensis*), 73t, 74, 78f
Indonesian Seas, 72
Indonesian shortfin eel (*Anguilla bicolor pacifica*), 73t, 74, 79–80
input-output model, 335
International Council for the Exploration of the Sea (ICES), 103
isolation by distance (IBD), 63
iwi, 394

J

James River, 133t
Japanese eel (*Anguilla japonica*), 21–31
    factors in population fluctuation, 26–30
        oceanographic conditions, 27–28
        population structure, 30
        sea eels, 28–30
        spawning area, 26, 27f
    genetic differentiation of, 59–67
    historical catches, 24f
    international trade of, 23f
    proportions of migratory types, 29f
    resources of, 22–26
        decline in catches, 23–24
        eel industry in East Asia, 22–23
        population estimates, 25–26
        reasons for population decline, 25–26
Java Islands, 72
    juvenile American eels, 191–204
    abundance of, 194, 197–198
    defining size of, 195–197
    number and size, 194, 199
    size of, 193–194
    size over time, 194–195

K

kabayaki (grilled eel), 23–24
kaitiaki, 395
Karapiro Dam, 40–41, 402
Kruskall-Wallis One-Way Analysis of Variance, 89, 193
Kullback-Leibler distance, 314
Kuroshio Current, 27, 77

L

Lake Kohangapiripiri, 395
Lake Kohangatera, 395
Lake Morin, 133t
Lake Ontario, 361–367
    annual growth for American eel, 133t
    commercial fish quota zones, 363f

commercial harvest of eels in, 362–364
future of eel fishery in, 365–367
management of commercial fisheries in, 365
Lake Poukawa, 395
Lake Wairewa, 394–395
length-class frequencies (LCF), 373
leptocephali, 74–77
defined, 71
migration of, 27–28
Leuciscus cephalus (European chub), 378
life history, 329–332
Linne Hydropower station, 383–391
lipid content, 89
Loire River, France, 24*f*
longfins (*Anguilla dieffenbachii*), 37–52
age and growth, 41–42
annual commercial catch in New Zealand, 46*f*
catch-per-unit-effort (CPUE), 47–49
densities of, 42*t*, 43
distribution of, 38–39
escapement of, 44–45
genetic structure, 39
growth rates, 43
habitat loss, 49–51
indicators of status, 51*t*
management practices, 51–52
migration of, 40
recruitment, 39–41
sex ratios, 43–44
spawning, 39
Lower Grey River, 50
lowland streams, stocking of, 149–156
growth and size distribution, 153–155
and instantaneous disappearance, 153
and migration, 153
poststocking assessments, 151
poststocking densities, 151–153
tags, 151
lunar illumination, 315

M

Madagascar Island, 80
Maine rivers, 133*t*
Maori eel fisheries, 394–397
marae, 395

marble eel (*Anguilla marmorata*), 60*t*
MarkTags software, 282
Megalops atlanticus (tarpon), 78
metazoan parasites, 175–185
microsatellite loci, 30, 62
migration
downstream, 383–391
recruitment index, 191–204
and stocking, 153
Migromat system, 386, 388–390
Mikawa Bay, Japan, 29*f*
Millville Dam, 319
Mindanao Current, 27–28, 77
molecular tools, 60*t*
Mollusca, 178*t*
Monogenea, 178*t*
Monte Carlo analysis, 339
Morone americana (white perch), 362
mortality, 116, 124–126, 352, 354, 390
Moses-Saunders annual-passage index, 202
Moses-Saunders Dam, 304–307
eel ladder, 200
eel ladder exits, 295–308
eel traps, 300–301
location of eel ladder, 299*f*
return rates of eels, 304*t*
movements, effect of translocation, 131
%MSP (percentage maximum spawning potential), 353, 358
mtDNA analysis, 30
Myrophis punctatus (speckled worm eel), 78
Myxidium sp., 183

N

Nanticoke River, 123
Naticoke River, 355*t*, 356*f*
natural mortality, 353
Nedap Trail telemetry system, 385
Nei's genetic distance, 65*f*
Nematoda, 178*t*
New Brunswick, 133*t*
New Guinea eel (*Anguilla interioris*), 73*t*, 74
New York Power Authority (NYPA), 202
New Zealand eels, 393–405
age and growth, 41–42
annual commercial catch in New Zealand, 46*f*
catch effort landing returns, 398

catch-per-unit-effort, 401–402
catch-per-unit-effort (CPUE), 47–49
changes in size distribution, 47–49
commercial catches, 399f
commercial fisheries, 398–401
commercial fishery, 45–47
customary fishery, 45, 394–397
densities of, 42t, 43
distribution of, 38–39
escapement of, 44–45
fisheries management structure, 393–394
genetic structure, 39
growth rates, 43
habitat loss, 49–51
impact of commercial fishing on, 37–52
indicators of status, 51t
length frequency, 48f
management practices, 51–52
migration of, 40
quota management areas, 400f
recruitment, 39–41, 402–403
sex ratios, 43–44
silver eel escapement, 44–45
spawning, 39
spawning escapement, 403
stock management, 404–405
total allowable commercial catches, 400t
nocturnal movements, 314–315, 319
North Equatorial Current, 27–28
northern pike (*Esox lucius*), 160

O

Oir River, France, premigrant eels in, 157–172
Ontario Ministry of Natural Resources (OMNR), 191–192
opaque zone, 116
otoliths, 137–146
overfishing, 26

P

Pacific salmon, 86
Pacific shortfinned eel (*Anguilla obscura*), 73t, 74

Pagrus pagrus (red porgy), 125
Pankhurst's eye index, 108, 109f
Paraquimperia tenerrima, 181t
parasites, 175–185
passive integrated transponder (PIT), 298
Pelorus River, 395
Perca fluviatilis, 184
Pinnopolis Dam, 133t
Poigar River, Sulawesi Island, 77, 78f, 79
pollution, 26
polymerase chain reaction (PCR), 62, 63t
Polynesian longfin eel (*Anguilla megastoma*), 73t, 74
Pomphorhynchus laevis, 178t
Poole Harbour, 243
population
    estimates of, 25–26
    reasons for decline in, 25–26
population management, 369–379
    compliance assessment, 379
    compliance measures for riverine stocks, 372
    conservation limits, 371
    geographical/regional factors, 375–379
    habitat suitability index, 374–375
    indices, 372–374
    recruitment declines, 370
    surrogate targets, 372
    targets, 371–372
population modeling, 329–344
    bootstrap distribution, 342f
    choosing models for, 339–341
    cohort models, 332–335
    eel life history, 329–332
    global models, 338–339
    input-output model, 335
    Monte Carlo approach, 339
    parameter uncertainty, 341–344
    size and age-structured models, 335–338
    spatially distributed virtual populations, 338
Poso River, Sulawesi Island, 78f
premigrant eels, 157–172
    abundance estimates, 161–162, 166
    characteristics of sedentary fraction, 168–169t

migratory potential characteristics, 160–161
    population estimates, 166
    population structure, 162–166
presence-absence data, 374
Procrustean approach, 338
Proteocephalus macrocephalus, 181*t*
proxy targets, 15–16
Pseudodactylogyrus anguillae, 179–180
Pseudodactylogyrus bini, 179–180
Pseudodactylogyrus sp., 184–185
pseudovalues, 341
push nets, 259

Q

Québec El Fishermen's Union, 129–134
quota management areas, 230
quota management system (QMS), 394

R

Raphidascaris acus, 181*t*
recapture rates, 301–304
recruitment, 39–41
    areas, 80–81
    causes of decline, 370
    New Zealand eels, 402–403
    timing of, 77
red porgy (*Pagrus pagrus*), 125
reference condition model (RCM), 372
reproduction strategies, 85–100
    age estimation, 89
    fecundity estimation, 88–89
    and migration distance, 97–99
    and phenotypic plasticity, 96–97
    size-related fecundity, 91–95
    statistical analyses, 89–90
    study area, 87
    subpopulation characteristics, 91
    treatment of fresh eels, 87–88
    treatment of gonads, 88–89
Réunion Island, 80
Rhomboplites aurorubens (vermillion snapper), 125
river channelization structures, 26
river eels, 28, 29*f*
River Frome, 243, 246–250, 252–253
River Gudenå, Denmark, 149–156
River Loire, France, 373
River Madum Å, Denmark, 149–156
River Meuse
    downstream migrating eel in, 383–391
    telemetry field experiment in, 385*f*
River Midway, 378
River Piddle, 243, 246–250, 252–253
River Severn, 242–246, 250–252
rivers, channelization of, 49
roach (*Rutilus rutilus*), 160
rudd (*Scardinius erythrophtalmus*), 160

S

sagitall otoliths, 138
Salmo salar (Atlantic salmon), 86, 158, 279
Salmo trutta (brown trout), 183
Salvelinus alpinus (arctic char), 183
Salvelinus fontinalis (brook trout), 130
Sander lucioperca (zander), 160
Sander vitreus (walleye), 362
Sanriku Coast, Japan, 29*f*
Saprolegnia sp., 183
Sargasso Sea, 26
Scardinius erythrophtalmus (rudd), 160
scoop net, 259
sea eels, 28–30
seasonal movements, 311–322, 315–319
Severn River, 355*t*, 356*f*
sex determination, 114–117, 120–122
sex differences, 124
sex ratios, 43–44, 124, 132, 133, 373
sexual maturity, 114–117, 120–122, 351, 354
Shenandoah River, West Virginia, movement of American eels in, 311–322
shortfins (*Anguilla australis*), 37–52
    age and growth, 41–42
    annual commercial catch in New Zealand, 46*f*
    catch-per-unit-effort (CPUE), 47–49
    densities of, 42*t*, 43
    distribution of, 38–39
    escapement of, 44–45
    genetic structure, 39
    growth rates, 43
    habitat loss, 49–51

indicators of status, 51t
length frequency, 48f
management practices, 51–52
migration of, 40
recruitment, 39–41
sex ratios, 43–44
spawning, 39
silver eels
downstream migration of, 277–289, 383–391
exotic, 137–146
impact of hydroelectric facilities, 277–289
migration of, 44–45
otolith Sr/Ca ratios, 144–146
relative spawning per recruit, 46f
reproduction strategies, 85–100
three-dimensional movement, 277–289
silvering index, 105–108
silvering stages, 103–111
classification functions, 108t
data analysis, 105
five stages in, 104
morpho-anatomical parameters, 106t
seasonal variations in, 108–110
silvering index, 105–108
size of eels
defining, 195–197
distribution of, 153–155
long-term trends in, 191–204
and migration distance, 97–99
size-structured models, 335–338
snowy grouper (*Epinephelus niveatus*), 125
Softmap software, 87
Solomon Islands, 72
somatic tissues, 89
spawner biomass per recruit (SBR), 350, 352–354
spawning, 39
spawning area, 26, 27f, 80–81
spawning escapement, 403
speckled longfin (*Anguilla reinhardtii*), 37
speckled worm eel (*Myrophis punctatus*), 78
Sphaerostoma bramae, 181t
Spinitectus inermis, 182
%SPR (percentage spawner production per recruit), 10, 14

St. Lawrence River, 361–367
commercial fish quota zones, 363f
commercial harvest of eels in, 362–364
commercial weir fisheries in, 210–211, 215–217
daily catches, 217
decline of American eels in, 207–226
description of, 209
experimental weir fishery in, 209–210, 213–215
future of eel fishery in, 365–367
management of commercial fisheries in, 365
reproduction strategies of American eels in, 85–100
size and abundance of juvenile American eels, 191–204
size distribution of eels, 219–221
timing of eel occurrence, 217–219
water level and flow, 211–212
St. Lawrence River watershed, 85–100
Statview software, 89
stocking, 149–156
of Danish lowland streams, 149–156
density, 153
effects of, 129–134
growth and size distribution, 153–155
and migration, 153
poststocking assessments, 151
poststocking densities, 151–153
procedures, 151
Sud-ouest River, 133t
supernumary zone, 116
swim bladder parasite (*Anguillicola*), 9
Systat software, 89

T

tags, 281
tamis (scoop net), 259
tangi, 395
tarpon (*Megalops atlanticus*), 78
telemetry, 281, 383–391
tench (*Tinca tinca*), 160
Thompson-Bell model, 352–353
tide month effect, 261–262

Tinca tinca (tench), 160
tit-for-tat, 13
Tomini Bay, 76
Topsail Pond, 133*t*
total allowable catch (TAC), 394, 398
total allowable commercial catch (TACC), 394, 398, 400*t*
total catches, 264*t*
total length at annulus formation, 138–139
translocation
    effects of, 129–134
    and growth, 131–132
    and movements, 131
    and sex ratio, 132
translucent zone, 116
trap nets, 363–364
Treaty of Waitangi, 395
Trianophorus nodulosus, 182
tropical anguillid eels, 71–82
    glass eels, 77–80
    leptocephali, 74–77
    management strategies for, 81–82
    recruitment areas, 80–81
    spawning areas, 80–81
    species and subspecies, 73*t*
    species ranges, 72–74
Trypanosoma granulosum, 183
Tungkang River, Taiwan, 78*f*

U

upstream movements, 315–319

V

vermillion snapper (*Rhomboplites aurorubens*), 125
virtual population analysis, 338
von Bertalanffy growth curve, 340*t*, 341
vs. International Financial Reporting Standards, 79–80

W

Waikato Catchment, 50
Waikato River, 40–41, 394
Wainono Lagoon, 395
walleye (*Sander vitreus*), 362
water temperature, 321
Weibull function, 335
weir fisheries, 209–211
West Mariana Ridge, 26
wetlands, drainage of, 49
Whakaki Lagoon, 395
Whanganui River, 394
white perch (*Morone americana*), 362
whitefish (*Coregonus clupeaforis*), 362
Wicomico River, 355*t*, 356*f*
Wye River, 125, 355*t*, 356*f*

Y

yellow American eels, 311–322
    crepuscular movements, 314–315, 319
    downstream movements, 315–319
    nocturnal movements, 314–315, 319
    seasonal movements, 311–322
    upstream movements, 315–319
yellow eel fisheries, 14–15
yield per recruit (YPR), 350, 352–354

Z

zander (*Sander lucioperca*), 160